WEEDS OF THE NORTHEAST

WEEDS
of the
NORTHEAST

SECOND EDITION
Revised and Expanded to Include the Mid-Atlantic States

Joseph C. Neal
Richard H. Uva
Joseph M. DiTomaso
Antonio DiTommaso

COMSTOCK PUBLISHING ASSOCIATES AN IMPRINT OF

CORNELL UNIVERSITY PRESS | ITHACA AND LONDON

First edition first published 1997 by Cornell University Press. Second edition 2023. First printing, Cornell Paperbacks, 1997

Printed in China

Library of Congress Cataloging-in-Publication Data

Names: Neal, Joseph C. (Joseph Crowell), author. | Uva, Richard H. (Richard Hart), 1969– author. | DiTomaso, Joseph M., author. | DiTommaso, Antonio, author.
Title: Weeds of the Northeast / Joseph C. Neal, Richard H. Uva, Joseph M. DiTomaso, Antonio DiTommaso.
Description: 2nd edition. | Ithaca [New York] : Comstock Publishing Associates, an imprint of Cornell University Press, 2023. | "Revised and expanded to include the mid-Atlantic states." | Includes bibliographical references and index.
Identifiers: LCCN 2021006005 | ISBN 9781501755729 (paperback)
Subjects: LCSH: Weeds—Northeastern States—Identification. | Weeds—Canada, Eastern—Identification. | Weeds—Middle Atlantic States—Identification.
Classification: LCC QK118 .N33 2021 | DDC 581.6/520974—dc23
LC record available at https://lccn.loc.gov/2021006005

CONTENTS

ACKNOWLEDGMENTS

The following individuals and organizations generously contributed their time, resources, and expertise to the development of this book. They gave us information on the status of weed species throughout the Northeast and in various cropping systems, offered tips on how to identify important weeds, reviewed the proposed layout and content of the book, and lent us photographs. We thank them all for their support and advice.

In particular, we thank Andrew F. Senesac, Weed Science Specialist for Cornell Cooperative Extension, Riverhead, New York, for his extensive contributions to the first edition of this book. Joe DiTomaso thanks Sue DiTomaso for her patience during the writing of this book. Joe Neal thanks Graeme Bourdôt and AgResearch NZ for hosting his scholarly leave and facilitating work on this revision. Antonio DiTommaso thanks Scott H. Morris for assisting with species profiles. Thanks also to Julia Dagum and Celine Jennison for their help. Finally, thank you to Claudia Zan and Luca DiTommaso for their patience during this book project. We were also assisted by numerous taxonomists to resolve questions of nomenclature. In particular, Ed Cope at the L. H. Bailey Hortorium at Cornell University assisted extensively in the preparation of the first edition. Alexander Krings, curator of the herbarium at North Carolina State University, gave generously of his time and expertise. Thanks also to Ines Schönberger and the rest of the staff at the Allen Herbarium at Manaaki Whenua—Landcare Research, Lincoln, New Zealand for their welcoming support and access to collections. We thank all of the contributors to the *Flora of North America*, an extensive collection of authoritative species nomenclature and details on which we heavily relied. We also appreciate the numerous suggestions and critical advice from many members of the Northeastern Weed Science Society.

Many colleagues contributed photographs for use in this and the first edition. Each photograph is credited to the owner. Randall Prostak at the University of Massachusetts contributed numerous photographs from his digital weed herbarium; Scott H. Morris from Cornell University also contributed numerous photographs to the second edition; as did Katy Chayka of MinnesotaWildflowers.info. Photos by J. K. Clark and J. O'Brien © 2007 Regents of the University of California were used by permission. We thank Matt Bertone, director of the Plant Disease and Insect Clinic at North Carolina State University, for his generous contribution of seed photos. We appreciate the fine work of USDA staff who made available many seed photographs through the USDA-NRCS PLANTS Database. We also thank the Syngenta Crop Protection AG (formerly, Ciba-Geigy Corporation) for allowing us to reprint many illustrations from their books *Grass Weeds 1* and *2*, *Monocot Weeds 3*, and *Dicot Weeds 1*. Similarly, we are grateful to The Scotts Company for permitting us to use drawings from the *Scotts Guide to the Identification of Grasses*. Bente Starcke King, formerly scientific illustrator at the L. H. Bailey Hortorium at Cornell University, drew illustrations for the book, as did Richard Uva.

We thank the following organizations for financially supporting the development of the first edition: Cornell University College of Agriculture and Life Sciences, Genesee Fingerlakes Nursery and Landscape Association, Golf Course Superintendents Association of New England, Massachusetts Turf and Lawn Grass Association, Inc., Nassau-Suffolk Landscape Gardeners Association, New York State Integrated Pest Management Program, New York State Turfgrass Association, Northeastern Weed Science Society, Pennsylvania Christmas Tree Growers Association, Pennsylvania Foundation for Ornamental Horticulture, and the Virginia Nurserymen's Association.

J. C. N., R. H. U., J. M. D., and A. D.

WEEDS OF THE NORTHEAST

ABOUT THIS BOOK

This second edition of *Weeds of the Northeast* is a practical guide to the identification of common, ecologically, and economically important weeds of the northeastern United States, mid-Atlantic states, upper midwest, and southern Canada. It is also a reference book for those aspects of weed biology and ecology important to weed management. Since first publication of *Weeds of the Northeast* in 1997, many weeds have expanded their range or prevalence in the northeastern United States. For example, waterhemp, Japanese stiltgrass, and garlic mustard were rare in the region in 1996, but they are now widespread. These and many other species of importance have been added to this second edition. Furthermore, species of importance in the mid-Atlantic states and upper Midwest have been added to improve the utility of the book in those regions. Additionally, since the publication of the first edition there have been many changes in plant nomenclature. In this second edition we have followed the naming conventions used in the *Flora of North America*. For genera that had not yet been published in the *Flora of North America*, the most recently published authoritative source was used. Standardized common names of weeds are from the Weed Science Society of America's *Composite List of Weeds*.

Using vegetative as well as floral characteristics for identification, this up-to-date manual describes 540 weed species that infest agronomic and horticultural crops, turfgrass areas, nurseries, gardens, and noncrop areas such as natural areas, landscapes, and roadsides. In compiling the species list, we defined the Northeast and mid-Atlantic states as the region south to North Carolina, north to Maine and southeastern Canada, and west to Wisconsin. The weeds included are terrestrial species that decrease crop yields or quality, reduce the aesthetics or functionality of landscapes and turfgrass areas, impact natural ecosystems, or adversely affect human or animal health. Also included are species with the potential to spread and infest more acreage and crops than they do now, as well as species considered crops in some areas and weeds in others. For example, orchardgrass and timothy are often cut for forage yet are highly competitive weeds in orchards and reduced-tillage areas. Similarly, red maple is a desirable landscape tree, but its seedlings are a constant aggravation in mulched landscape beds.

The book contains several tools for identifying weeds. The main tool for identifying an unknown specimen is the dichotomous key to all the species described in the book. This key, unlike those found in most identification manuals, relies on vegetative characters, for example, leaf arrangement, lobes or toothing on the leaf margin, and presence and placement of hairs, rather than floral characters to separate the species. The vegetative key is designed to narrow the choices to a few possible species. The identity of the specimen can then be confirmed by reading the descriptions of the species and comparing the specimen with the drawings and photographs. Unlike many dichotomous keys, these keys may include species in several sections of the key to compensate for variable vegetative characteristics.

We have organized the species descriptions into four main groups: non-flowering or spore-producing plants, monocots (including grasses and grass-like weeds), herbaceous broadleaf (dicot) weeds, and woody weeds (including species that appear woody). Within each main group, the weeds are presented in alphabetical order by family name, genus, and species. The species descriptions provide a wealth of information in a condensed format: what the weed looks like at various stages of growth, how it propagates and spreads, the crops or management systems in which it is common, its geographic distribution, whether it is toxic to humans or livestock, and more. Accompanying each description are drawings and color photographs of identifying characteristics, seeds, and early and late stages of growth.

To facilitate both easy access to information about a species and easy comparison among species, we have presented the species descriptions in a standardized format, as shown on the facing page. The common names are from the Weed Science Society of America's *Composite List of Weeds*. Scientific names use the nomenclature presented in the current edition of the *Flora of North America* or the most up-to-date authoritative reference available. Key characteristics for identification, dispersal, or management, as well as those of general importance are in boldface type. Following the species descriptions are tables designed to assist in the comparison of similar species and an illustrated glossary.

Although we diligently reviewed the book for accuracy, as with all human endeavors, mistakes can occur. If you notice an error or have important information to add, please write to Joseph C. Neal, Department of Horticultural Science, Box 7609, North Carolina State University, Raleigh, NC 27695-7609.

Format and content of a species description:

Common name (*Scientific name*)
SYNONYMS:

GENERAL DESCRIPTION: A summary of the weed's life cycle, growth habit, size, and special characteristics, including poisonous compounds and effects.

PROPAGATION / PHENOLOGY: How the weed propagates and spreads, when plants emerge, and what climatic or other factors affect germination, growth, and development (when information is available).

SEEDLING: A description of the seedling or of the emerging shoots of perennial weeds.

MATURE PLANT: A description of the vegetative characteristics of mature plants.

ROOTS AND UNDERGROUND STRUCTURES: A description of underground structures, with particular attention to vegetative propagules of perennial weeds.

FLOWERS AND FRUIT: A description of the flowers, fruit, and seeds, as well as the season(s) of occurrence.

POSTSENESCENCE CHARACTERISTICS: A description of the weed in the dormant season and any persistent characteristics of dead or dormant plants that may be useful in identification.

HABITAT: A description of the environs in which the weed is frequently found and of cropping systems, soil types, and management inputs that affect its distribution and spread.

DISTRIBUTION: Information on where the weed occurs in North America and (when available) where it is a serious problem.

SIMILAR SPECIES: Descriptions of species that resemble the weed, whether related to it or not. For each similar species, if there is a full description elsewhere in the book, or if the species is described in a table, the common and scientific name are listed. If there is no full description, the common and scientific name, as well as the authority, are provided in the description of the species it most closely resembles.

HOW TO IDENTIFY A WEED

When trying to identify an unknown weed, use the vegetative key to narrow the choices. When the key or tables have eliminated all but a few species, compare the photographs of your remaining choices and read the descriptions of each of those species before deciding on the weed's identity.

We organized the vegetative key in typical dichotomous fashion, with two choices (same numbers) at each juncture. **Consider both choices before moving on to the next pair of choices.** This key differs from most dichotomous keys in several ways. First, it is based on vegetative characters rather than floral characters. Second, it is designed to narrow your choices—not separate individual species. Third, because we recognize that it is easy to make "wrong turns" in an identification key, many species appear in several different parts of the key, even though technically they do not belong at some of those points. For example, birds-eye pearlwort (*Sagina procumbens*) occurs at three points in the key: with the non-flowering plants, because it is often mistaken for a moss; with the flowering plants that have whorled leaves, because although its leaves are actually opposite, they can appear to be whorled when the axillary buds sprout; and with the flowering plants that have opposite leaves, its correct place. Some plants may have alternate and opposite leaves at different growth stages. These species appear in each relevant part of the key.

It may take some practice to learn how to use the key. We suggest you start with a species you know before trying to identify an unknown one. If your unknown specimen does not fit the descriptions, go back to an earlier point in the key and search for a "wrong turn." If none is apparent, it may be that the weed is not in the book, since we could not include every species you might encounter. If you cannot positively identify your specimen, send a sample to your state or county Cooperative Extension office for identification.

VEGETATIVE KEY TO THE WEEDS

1. Non-flowering: liverworts, mosses, and horsetails (*Equisetum* spp.) . . . . **Part A**
1. Flower and seed producers
    2. Stems **herbaceous**
        3. Grasses and grass-like species: **monocots** (leaves usually parallel-veined and sheathing the stem) . . . .**Part B**
        3. Broadleaf species: **dicots** (leaves usually with branched veins) . . . . **Part C**
    2. Stems **woody**: shrubs, woody vines, trees, brambles, and tree saplings . . . . **Part D**

Part A. Non-flowering plants, including spore producers, mosses, algae, and primitive spore-producing plants

1. Hollow, erect, jointed stems . . . . **horsetail** and **scouringrush** (p. 22)
1. Mat-forming . . . . **liverworts** (p. 18)
    mosses and **algae** (p. 20)
    birdseye pearlwort (a flowering plant often mistaken for a moss) (p. 274)

Part B. Grasses and grass-like species: monocots (leaves usually parallel-veined and sheathing the stem at the base)

1. Leaves relatively broad, often ovate or lanceolate (habit and leaves reminiscent of a dicot) . . . . **dayflowers** (p. 24)
    doveweed (p. 26)
    basketgrass (p. 70)
1. Leaves narrow, often basal (leaves and habit reminiscent of a grass):
    2. Stems 3-angled, sharply triangular in cross section . . . . **sedges** (pp. 28, 30)
        kyllingas (p. 32)
    2. Stems roundish or sometimes flattened:
        3. From a bulb. . . . . **onion** and **garlic** (p. 36)
            star-of-Bethlehem (p. 38)
        3. From fibrous roots, rhizomes, or stolons:
            4. Leaves hollow and round, stem-like . . . . **rushes** (p. 34)
            4. Leaves flat not hollow or round (grasses):
                5. Leaves folded in the bud (see illustrated glossary):
                    6. Short auricles present. . . . . **perennial ryegrass** (p. 68)
                    6. Auricles absent:
                        7. Ligule a fringe of hairs. . . . . **sandburs** (p. 48)
                            bermudagrass (p. 50)
                            bahiagrass (rolled but may appear folded) (p. 86)
                        7. Ligule membranous:
                            8. Blade with a prow (boat) shaped tip . . . .**bluegrasses** (p. 94)
                                rough stalk bluegrass (p. 96)
                            8. Blade tip otherwise. . . . . **bluestems** and **broomsedge** (p. 40)
                                orchardgrass (p. 52)
                                goosegrass (p. 58)
                                perennial ryegrass (p. 68)
                                bahiagrass (p. 86)

5. Leaves rolled in the bud:
    9. Auricles present (long or short) . . . . **quackgrass** (p. 60)
                                                 tall fescue (p. 98)
                                         Italian ryegrass (p. 68)
                                          vernalgrasses (p. 42)
    9. Auricles absent:
        10. Ligule absent. . . . . **rushes** (p. 34)
                               barnyardgrass and **junglerice** (p. 56)
        10. Ligule present (considered present even if very small):
           11. Ligule a fringe of hairs (or appears so):
               12. Mature leaf blades mostly >30 cm long . . . .
                                         cogongrass (p. 66)
                                         fall panicum (p. 80)
                                         common reed (p. 92)
                                         giant reed (p. 92)
                                         shattercane (p. 102)
                                         johnsongrass (p. 104)
               12. Mature leaf blades mostly <30 cm long . . . .
                                         bermudagrass (p. 50)
                                         crowfootgrass (p. 58)
                        stinkgrasses and **lovegrasses** (p. 62)
                                         basketgrass (p. 70)
                                         witchgrass (p. 78)
                                         fall panicum (p. 80)
                                         wild-proso millet (p. 82)
                       thin paspalum, **alexandergrass**,
                                     and **bahiagrass** (p. 86)
                                         foxtails (p. 100)
                                         signalgrass (p. 106)
        11. Ligule membranous:
               13. Upper surface of blade hairy . . . . **bromes** (p. 46)
                                   large crabgrass (p. 54)
                                         velvetgrass (p. 64)
                                     vernalgrasses (p. 42)
                                         tall oatgrass (p. 44)
                                             oat (p. 44)
                                     crowfootgrass (p. 58)
                                         cogongrass (p. 66)
                                         paspalums (p. 86)
                                         knotgrass (p. 84)
                               Texas signalgrass (p. 106)
           13. Upper surface of blade mostly hairless or only hairy near
               the ligule region:
               14. Leaf blades relatively short (most leaf blades on
                   mature plants <15 cm long). . . . .
                             . . . .**smooth** and **southern crabgrass** (p. 54)
                                         ryegrasses (p. 68)
                                   Japanese stiltgrass (p. 70)
                                   wirestem muhly (p. 74)
                                     nimblewill (p. 76)
                             creeping bentgrass (p. 76)
                                     knotgrass (p. 84)
                       colonial bentgrass and **redtop** (p. 96)

14. Leaf blades relatively long (most leaf blades on
mature plants >15 cm long)..............................
.... **oats** and **tall oatgrass** (p. 44)
Japanese brome (p. 46)
southern crabgrass (p. 54)
crowfootgrass (p. 58)
tall fescue (p. 98)
dallisgrass, **vaseygrass**, and **knotgrass** (p. 84)
reed canarygrass (p. 88)
timothy (p. 90)
shattercane (p. 102)
johnsongrass (p. 104)
eulaliagrass or **miscanthus** (p. 72)
thin paspalum and **bahiagrass** (p. 86)

Part C. Broadleaf species: dicots
(leaves usually with branched veins)

1. Lower leaves **opposite or whorled** (2 or more leaves/node), not a
basal rosette:
  2. Lower leaves or all leaves whorled:
    3. Stems square, ridged, or winged ....

opposite   whorled

....**scarlet pimpernel** (leaves opposite
or whorled) (p. 422)
bedstraws (p. 446)
field madder, **piedmont bedstraw** (p. 450)
    3. Stems rounded:
      4. Plants prostrate.................................... **lawn burweed** (p. 216)
pearlworts (leaves opposite, axillary shoots
give appearance of whorled) (p. 274)
knawel (leaves opposite, axillary shoots
give the appearance of whorled (p. 278)
carpetweed (p. 380)
      4. Plants erect ....**corn spurry** (p. 274)
purple loosestrife (leaves may be opposite or whorled) (p. 368)
toadflaxes (leaves mostly alternate,
lower leaves may be opposite, or whorled) (p. 396)
garden loosestrife (p. 356)
garden valerian (p. 466)
  2. Lower leaves opposite:
    5. Stems square (view cut in cross section):
      6. Leaves with spines on the midrib, leaf surfaces wrinkled....................
...........................**common teasel** (stems square or round) (p. 312)
      6. Leaves without spines, not conspicuously wrinkled:
        7. Leaf margins entire or nearly so .... **scarlet pimpernel**
(leaves opposite or in whorls of 3) (p. 422)
little starwort (p. 282)
healall (p. 364)
creeping thyme (p. 364)
        7. Leaf margins regularly toothed or lobed ....
.... **beggarsticks** and **spanishneedles** (p. 162)
ground ivy (p. 358)
henbit and **deadnettles** (p. 360)

field and **jagged chickweed** (p. 272)
thymeleaf speedwell (p. 284)
common chickweed (p. 284)
Virginia buttonweed and **poorjoe** (p. 444)
Paraguayan (pink) purslane (p. 420)
puncturevine (p. 472)
16.   Leaf tips blunt or rounded; not pointed . . . .
. . . . **thymeleaf speedwell** (p. 284)
pennyworts (p. 146)
dichondras (p. 300)
purslane speedwell (p. 402)
common purslane (p. 420)
moneywort (p. 424)
puncturevine (p. 472)
12.   Upper surface of leaf blade hairy or rough (hairs may be small; use lens):
17.   Upper leaves alternate on flowering stems . . . . **speedwells** (p. 402)
slender speedwell (p. 404)
17.   Upper leaves opposite on flowering stems . . . . **eclipta** (p. 180)
lawn burweed (p. 216)
chickweeds (p. 272)
thymeleaf sandwort (p. 284)
poorjoe (p. 444)
Brazilian and **Florida pusley** (p. 448)
germander speedwell (p. 404)
puncturevine (p. 472)

1.   Lower leaves **alternate** (1 leaf/node); or, a **basal rosette** present;
or, plant yellow, "leafless," thread-like, twining stems:
18.   Plant yellow or orange, stems "leafless," thread-like,
and twining . . . . **dodders** (p. 298)
18.   Plant otherwise, leaves alternate or in a basal rosette:
19.   Leaves or stems with spines or prickles:
20.   Spines at the leaf bases or nodes only . . . .

alternate   basal rosette

. . . . spiny amaranth (p. 122)
spiny cocklebur (p. 230)
prickly sida (p. 378)
20.   Spines in other locations:
21.   Fresh foliage exudes a white sap when cut . . . . . **prickly lettuce** (p. 202)
annual sowthistle (p. 220)
perennial sowthistle (p. 218)
spiny sowthistle (p. 220)
21.   Fresh foliage does not exude a white sap when cut. . . . .
. . . . **Russian-thistle** (p. 110)
musk thistle (p. 164)
plumeless thistle (p. 164)
Canada thistle (p. 172)
bull thistle (p. 174)
lawn burweed (spines on fruit only) (p. 216)
Japanese hops (p. 268)
common teasel (p. 312)
mile-a-minute (p. 412)
horsenettle (p. 458)
buffalobur (p. 462)

19. Leaves and stems unarmed:
    22. Leaves compound **OR** leaves simple but cut/lobed >75% of the way to the midvein:
        23. Leaves compound (with distinct leaflets):
            24. Mature leaves with 3 leaflets:
                25. Individual leaflets with a prominent indentation at the tip (heart-shaped) . . . . **woodsorrels** (p. 388)
                25. Individual leaflets rounded or pointed at the tip:
                    26. Leaf margins with many prominent teeth . . . .
. . . . **sweetclovers** (p. 334)
Indian mock-strawberry (p. 438)
wild strawberry (p. 440)
rough cinquefoil (p. 442)
hop clovers (p. 344)
                    26. Leaf margins entire or nearly so:
                        27. Plant a sprawling or ascending vine . . . .
. . . . **kudzu** and **ticktrefoil** (p. 336)
bittersweet nightshade (p. 528)
                        27. Habit otherwise. . . . .
. . . . . . **annual lespedeza** and **Korean clover** (p. 326)
lespedezas (p. 328)
birdsfoot trefoil (p. 330)
black medic (p. 332)
bittersweet nightshade (p. 528)
rabbitfoot clover (p. 342)
clovers (p. 346)
hop clovers (p. 344)
            24. Leaves with more than 3 leaflets:
                28. Leaves pinnately compound (or appearing so):
                    29. Mature leaves dissected (1st order leaflets deeply divided) . . . . **wild chervil** (p. 126)
spotted waterhemlock and **poison-hemlock** (p. 128)
wild celery (p. 130)
wild carrot (p. 132)
hedgeparsleys (p. 138)
tansy ragwort (p. 210)
lawn burweed (p. 216)
common tansy (p. 224)
filarees (p. 352)
yellow fieldcress (p. 258)
chamberbitter and **long-stalked phyllanthus** (often mistaken for pinnately compound) (p. 392)
                    29. Mature leaves not dissected (1st order leaflets <u>not</u> deeply divided):
                        30. Leaflet margins toothed or lobed. . . . .
. . . . **bishop's goutweed** (p. 124)
giant hogweed, **angelica**, and **cow-parsnip** (p. 134)
wild parsnip (p. 136)
hedgeparsleys (p. 138)
greater celandine (p. 390)
common tansy (p. 224)
field yellowcress (p. 256)

30. Leaflet margins entire (not toothed)...............
........................**lawn burweed** (p. 216)
bittercresses (p. 242)
lesser swinecress (p. 248)
cypressvine morningglory (p. 302)
goatsrue (p. 324)
birdsfoot trefoil (p. 330)
sicklepod and **coffeeweed** (p. 338)
hemp sesbania (p. 340)
vetch and **crown vetch** (p. 348)
chamberbitter and **long-stalked phyllanthus** (p. 392)

28. Leaves palmately compound .... **lawn burweed** (p. 216)
birdsfoot trefoil (p. 330)
buttercups (pp. 426, 428, 432)
cinquefoils (p. 442)

23. Leaves simple and cut/lobed greater than 75% of the way to the midvein (without distinct leaflets):

    31. Leaves palmately cut, about as wide as long ....
...............**giant hogweed**, **angelica**, and **cow-parsnip** (p. 134)
Japanese hops (p. 268)
morningglories (p. 302)
geraniums (p. 354)
Venice mallow (p. 372)
musk mallow (p. 372)
bristly mallow (p. 376)
buttercups (pp. 426, 428, 432, 434)
parsley piert (p. 436)
cinquefoils (p. 442)

    31. Leaves pinnately cut, longer than wide:
        32. Leaves dissected (leaflets deeply divided)...................
...............................**common yarrow** (p. 148)
common ragweed and **ragweed parthenium** (p. 150)
mugwort (p. 158)
chamomiles (p. 154)
tansy ragwort (p. 210)
common groundsel (p. 212)
pineapple-weed (p. 206)
dogfennel (p. 184)
bittercresses (p. 242)
yellowcresses and **yellow fieldcress** (pp. 256, 258)

        32. Leaves not dissected (leaflets not further divided):
            33. Leaf blades conspicuously hairy ....
...........................**common ragweed** (p. 150)
mugwort (p. 158)
cornflower (p. 166)
wild radish (p. 254)
mustards (p. 262)
bittersweet nightshade (p. 528)

            33. Leaf blades lacking conspicuous hairs ....
...............................**knapweeds** (p. 168)
chicory (p. 170)
dandelion and **falsedandelion** (p. 226)
yellow rocket (p. 236)

shepherd's-purse (p. 240)
bittercresses (p. 242)
field pepperweed (p. 246)
Virginia pepperweed (p. 252)
yellowcresses (pp. 256, 258)
cutleaf evening-primrose (p. 386)
bittersweet nightshade (p. 528)

22. Leaves simple, entire or cut/lobed less than 75% of the way to the mid-vein:
    34. Ocrea present:
        35. Habit prostrate and mat forming; leaves 1–3 cm long . . . .
          . . . . **prostrate knotweed** (p. 414)
        35. Habit otherwise:
            36. Plant a vine . . . .**wild buckwheat** (p. 406)
                mile-a-minute (p. 412)
            36. Plant not a vine. . . . . . . **Japanese** and **giant knotweed** (p. 408)
                smartweeds and **ladysthumb** (p. 410)
                red sorrel (p. 416)
                docks (p. 418)
    34. Ocrea absent:
        37. Plant a vine or vine-like prostrate stems. . . . .
          . . . . **hedge bindweed** (p. 294)
                field bindweed (p. 296)
                dichondras (p. 300)
                morningglories (p. 302)
            Guadeloupe cucumber and **yellow passionflower** (p. 306)
                wild cucumber and **burcucumber** (p. 308)
                Chinese yam and **air potato** (p. 310)
                bristly mallow (p. 376)
                lesser celandine (p. 430)
                bittersweet nightshade (p. 528)
        37. Plant not vine-like:
            38. Margins of the lower leaves entire or nearly so, leaves unlobed:
                39. Upper leaf surface distinctly hairy
                    (conspicuous hairs): . . . .**hawkweeds** (p. 196)
                    cornflower (p. 166)
                    knapweeds (p. 168)
                    horseweed (p. 176)
                    trampweed (p. 186)
                cudweeds and **pussytoes** (p. 190)
                  British yellowhead (p. 200)
                  hawkweed oxtongue (p. 208)
                  hoary alyssum (p. 238)
                  kochia (seedling) (p. 292)
                clammy groundcherry (p. 456)
                  common mullein (p. 452)
            39. Upper leaf surface not hairy, only sparsely hairy, or hairs
                small and inconspicuous:
                40. Leaf blades linear or narrowly lanceolate (blade
                  >3 times longer than wide):
                    41. Basal rosette present . . . .**asters** (p. 222)
                    horseweed (p. 176)
                    British yellowhead (p. 200)
                    salsifies (p. 228)

perennial pepperweed (p. 250)
wallflower mustard (p. 262)
common evening-primrose (p. 386)
plantains (p. 398)
smooth groundcherry (p. 456)
41.   Basal rosette absent . . . . **dayflowers** (p. 24)
doveweed (p. 26)
winged waterprimrose (p. 108)
asters (p. 222)
sneezeweeds (p. 192)
British yellowhead (p. 200)
salsifies (p. 228)
wormseed mustard (p. 262)
perennial pepperweed (p. 250)
kochia (p. 292)
spurges (p. 318)
toadflaxes (p. 396)
common evening-primrose (p. 386)
40.   Leaf blades rounded or ovate (not lanceolate or linear; blade <3 times longer than wide):
    42.   Lower leaves with dense, white-wooly hairs on the underside; blades large (often about 50 cm long and 40 cm wide) . . . . **common burdock** (p. 156)
    42.   Lower leaves not densely hairy on the underside; blades smaller:
        43.   Basal rosette present . . . . **English daisy** (p. 160)
plantains (p. 400)
lesser celandine (p. 430)
crowfoot buttercup (p. 434)
        43.   Basal rosette absent:
            44.   Plant prostrate or nearly so . . . . **prostrate pigweed** (p. 112)
livid amaranth (p. 112)
slender amaranth (p. 122)
lesser celandine (p. 430)
purslanes (p. 420)
New Zealand bittercress (p. 242)
            44.   Plant erect or ascending:
                45.   Leaves with distinct petioles and netted venation . . . . **tumble pigweed** (p. 110)
pigweeds and **amaranths** (pp. 112, 114, 118, 120, 122)
common pokeweed (p. 394)
smooth groundcherry (p. 456)
bittersweet nightshade (p. 528)
black nightshade (p. 460)
                45.   Leaves lacking distinct petioles; leaf bases form a sheath around the stem; parallel venation (broadleaf-like monocots) . . . .

. . . . **dayflowers**
(actually monocots) (p. 24)
doveweed (p. 26)
chamberbitter or **phyllanthus** (p. 392)

38. Margins of the lower leaves toothed and/or leaves lobed:
    46. Basal rosette or basal leaves present or plant developed from a basal rosette:
        47. Leaf margin with rounded or pointed indentations extending 25–75% of the way to the midvein:
            48. Fresh foliage exudes a milky-white sap when cut (with fresh sample only) . . . . **chicory** (p. 170)
smooth hawksbeard (p. 178)
catsears (p. 198)
dandelion and **false-dandelion** (p. 226)
Asiatic and **tall false hawksbeard** (p. 232)
            48. Fresh foliage does not exude a milky-white sap when cut . . . . **cornflower** (p. 166)
oxeye daisy (p. 204)
horseweed and **fleabanes** (p. 176)
yellow rocket (p. 236)
shepherd's-purse (p. 240)
bittercresses (p. 242)
wild mustard (p. 260)
wild radish (p. 254)
yellowcresses and **yellow fieldcress** (pp. 256, 258)
mustards (p. 262)
moth mullein (p. 452)
cutleaf evening-primrose (p. 386)
        47. Leaf margin with rounded or pointed indentations extending <25% of the way to the midvein:
            49. Erect stems bearing flowers only, no leaves (scapose) . . . . **English daisy** (p. 160)
cornflower (p. 166)
plantains (p. 400)
dandelion (p. 226)
violets (p. 470)
Asiatic hawksbeard (p. 232)
            49. Erect stems leafy:
                50. Leaf blades conspicuously hairy . . . .
. . . . **common burdock** (p. 156)
horseweed and **fleabanes** (p. 176)
American burnweed and **thickhead** (p. 182)
cudweeds (p. 190)
Asiatic and **tall false hawksbeard** (p. 232)
moth mullein (p. 452)
groundcherry (p. 456)
                50. Leaf blades not conspicuously hairy. . . . .
. . . . **American burnweed** and **thickhead** (p. 182)
oxeye daisy (p. 204)
garlic mustard (p. 234)
damesrocket (p. 244)
field pepperweed (p. 246)
Virginia pepperweed (p. 252)
wallflower mustard (p. 262)

common mallow (p. 374)
evening-primroses (p. 386)
false-dandelion (p. 226)
pennycresses (p. 264)
groundcherries (p. 456)
violets (p. 468)

46. Basal rosette absent:
    51. Leaves with rounded or pointed indentations
        extending 25–75% of the way to the midvein.........
        ....**oxeye daisy** (p. 204)

horseweed (p. 176)
common groundsel (p. 212)
musk mallow (p. 372)
common mallow (p. 374)
bristly mallow (p. 376)
cutleaf evening-primrose (p. 386)
apple of Peru, **jimsonweed**, and **large
thornapple** (p. 454)

    51. Leaves with rounded or pointed indentations extend
        <25% of the way to the midvein:
        52. Leaves of the middle portions of the stem with
            prominent petioles:
            53. Upper leaf surface not conspicuously
                hairy......... **common cocklebur** (p. 230)

common lambsquarters and **Mexican tea** (p. 288)
goosefoots (p. 288)
copperleafs (p. 314)
musk mallow (p. 372)
common mallow (p. 374)
bristly mallow (p. 376)
apple of Peru (p. 454)
jimsonweed and **large thornapple** (p. 454)
groundcherry (p. 456)
nightshades (p. 460)
violets and **pansy** (p. 468)

            53. Upper leaf surface conspicuously hairy.....
                ....**rough fleabane** (p. 176)

common sunflower and **Jerusalem
artichoke** (p. 194)
goosefoots (p. 288)
velvetleaf (p. 370)
bristly mallow (p. 376)
prickly sida and **spurred anoda** (p. 378)
mulberryweed (p. 382)
clammy groundcherry (p. 456)
hairy nightshade (p. 460)

        52. Leaves of the middle portions of the stem sessile
            or nearly sessile.............................
            .... **horseweed** and **fleabane** (p. 176)

American burnweed (p. 182)
oxeye daisy (p. 204)
goldenrods (p. 214)
garlic mustard (p. 234)
damesrocket (p. 244)
field pepperweed (p. 246)

Virginia pepperweed (p. 252)
oraches (p. 286)
goosefoots (p. 288)
tropic croton (p. 316)
venuslookingglasses (p. 266)
evening-primroses (p. 386)

Part D. Stem woody: shrubs, woody vines, woody ground covers, trees, brambles, and tree saplings

1. Leaves simple:
    2. Plant a woody groundcover, vine or vine-like:
        3. Leaves alternate:
            4. Stems with spines or prickles . . . .**briars** (p. 526)
            4. Stems lacking spines or prickles:
                5. Stems with tendrils . . . .**wild grapes** (p. 534)
                porcelainberry (p. 530)
                5. Stems lacking tendrils:
                    6. Leaves deeply toothed or lobed . . . . **bittersweet nightshade** (p. 528)
                    ivys (p. 480)
                    6. Leaves toothed or entire, but not deeply lobed or toothed . . . .
                    . . . .**bittersweets** (p. 492)
                    bittersweet nightshade (p. 528)
        3. Leaves opposite . . . . **Japanese honeysuckle** (p. 488)
        periwinkles and **wintercreeper** (p. 478)
    2. Plant a shrub or tree:
        7. Leaves alternate:
            8. Ocrea present . . . .
            . . . . **knotweeds** (herbaceous but often mistaken for woody) (p. 408)
            8. Ocrea absent:
                9. Spines or thorns present:
                    10. Leaf margin toothed . . . .**Callery pear** (p. 518)
                    10. Leaf margin entire:
                        11. Leaves in clusters at nodes . . . .**barberries** (p. 484)
                        11. Leaves not in clusters at nodes, but obviously alternate . . . .
                        . . . .**autumn-**, **thorny-**, and **Russian-olive** (p. 496)
                9. Spines or thorns absent:
                    12. Leaf margin entire:
                        13. Plants a large grass with hollow culms (stems) . . . .
                        . . . . **bamboos** (p. 512)
                        13. Plants not a grass and without hollow stems . . . .
                        . . . . **Scotch broom** (p. 500)
                        glossy buckthorn (p. 516)
                        catalpa (p. 510)
                    12. Leaf margins toothed:
                        14. Cut stems with milky white latex . . . . **white mulberry** (p. 540)
                        14. Cut stems lacking milky white latex:
                            15. Leaves triangular in shape, base of leaf blade perpendicular to petiole . . . .**common cottonwood** (p. 542)
                            15. Leaves lanceolate to ovate, base of leaf blade tapered to petiole:
                                16. Leaves, particularly upper, lanceolate (length >2.5 times width) . . . . **groundsel shrub** (p. 482)
                                black willow (p. 542)

16. Leaves ovate (length <2.5 times width):
    17. Stems winged, leaf margins doubly serrate . . . .
    . . . . **winged elm** (p. 494)
    17. Stems not winged, leaf margins more finely toothed
    . . . . **black cherry** (p. 542)
    common chokecherry (p. 542)
    Callery pear and **serviceberry** (p. 518)
    alderleaf buckthorn (p. 516)

7. Leaves opposite or sub-opposite:
    18. Leaves palmately lobed. . . . . **Norway maple** (p. 536)
    red maple (p. 536)
    18. Leaves not palmately lobed:
      19. Venation pinnate, leaf margins entire. . . . . **privets** (p. 508)
      honeysuckles (p. 490)
      19. Venation usually pinnate, sometimes palmate, leaf margins toothed:
        20. Base of leaf round-lobed. . . . . **princesstree** and **catalpa** (p. 510)
        20. Base of leaf not round-lobed, tapered to petiole. . . . .
    . . . . **burning bush** (p. 494)
    European buckthorn (p. 516)

1. Leaves compound:
  21. Plant a vine:
    22. Leaves alternate:
      23. Prickles present . . . . **brambles** (p. 522)
      23. Prickles absent:
        24. Leaflets 3 per leaf . . . . . . **poison-ivys** and **Atlantic poison-oak** (p. 476)
        three-leaf akebia (p. 504)
        24. Leaflets 5 or more:
          25. Leaflets palmately compound . . . . **Virginia-creeper** (p. 532)
          chocolate vine (p. 504)
          25. Leaflets pinnately compound. . . . . **trumpetcreeper** (p. 486)
          wisterias (p. 502)
    22. Leaves opposite. . . . . **virgin's bower** (p. 514)
  21. Plant a shrub or tree:
    26. Leaflets 5 or fewer. . . . . **Atlantic poison-oak** (p. 476)
    box elder (p. 536)
    ashes (p. 540)
    Scotch broom (p. 500)
    26. Leaflets 6 or more:
      27. Leaflets once pinnately compound:
        28. Plants with spines or thorns . . . . **multiflora rose** (p. 520)
        black locust (p. 538)
        28. Plants lacking spines or thorns:
          29. Leaves opposite. . . . . **ashes** (p. 540)
          29. Leaves alternate:
            30. Leaflets with toothed margins . . . . . . **tree-of-heaven** (p. 524)
            30. Leaflet margins entire . . . . **dwarf sumac** (p. 474)
            poison-sumac (p. 474)
      27. Leaflets twice pinnately compound . . . . **honey locust** (p. 538)
      chinaberry and **devil's walking stick** (p. 506)
      silktree (p. 498)

Liverworts

General Description: **Branching, moss-like**, primitive plants that **grow flat on the ground**.

Reproductive Characteristics: Reproduction occurs **vegetatively and by spores. Small, bud-like branches (gemmae)** are produced in cup-like structures on the surface of the plant. Drops of rain fall into these cups and mechanically detach and disperse the gemmae. This appears to be the more important means of dispersal in nursery and greenhouse crops. Stalked umbrella-like structures contain spore-producing reproductive organs that, at maturity, release the spores.

Mature Plant: Most weedy liverworts are thallose **(lobed or ribbon-like)**. They lack distinct axes, leaves, and stems.

Roots and Underground Structures: Attached to the soil by root-like structures (rhizoids).

Important Species: ***Marchantia polymorpha* L.** is a common weed of container-grown nursery crops and also occurs in irrigated turfgrass and landscapes, and in excessively moist areas. Its tissues are dull green, forked or lobed, and ribbon-like, with prominently sunken midribs. Individuals may grow to 12 cm or more in length. Several plants growing together can form a mat. ***Lunularia cruciata* (L.) Dumort.** has crescent-shaped, cup-like structures (gemmae receptacles), unlike *Marchantia polymorpha,* which has round receptacles. In the northeastern United States, *Lunularia cruciata* is found only in greenhouses.

Postsenescence Characteristics: None of note.

Habitat: Liverworts are weeds in container crops, greenhouses, and irrigated turfgrass. They grow on **excessively moist soil**, as well as on rocks and tree bark. Liverworts require moister conditions than mosses.

Distribution: Several species occur throughout the United States.

Liverwort foliage
with gemmae cup
structures

A. Senesac

Liverwort habit

A. Senesac

Liverwort fruiting
structures

A. Senesac

19

Mosses and Cyanobacteria

GENERAL DESCRIPTION: **Primitive, mat-forming** plants usually found on shady, moist surfaces. **Most mosses are perennial.**

REPRODUCTIVE CHARACTERISTICS: Mats spread **both vegetatively**, crowding out other species, **and by airborne, desiccation-resistant spores.** Capsules containing the spores are produced at the tips of the leafy shoots on leafless stalks. Spores are released and dispersed by air. Those that land on moist surfaces absorb water and germinate to form protonema (minute, branching filaments).

MATURE PLANT: Leaves are small, usually only a few millimeters long, lack petioles, and are often awl-shaped. They are arranged spirally on slender stems. Dense mats or patches of moss plants may hold considerable amounts of water by capillary action.

ROOTS AND UNDERGROUND STRUCTURES: Root-like structures (rhizoids) develop at the base of the leafy stems and absorb water and salts from the soil. True conductive tissue is absent, and many species absorb water through the surfaces of the stems and leaves.

IMPORTANT SPECIES: **Silver thread or silvery bryum (*Bryum argenteum* Hedw.)** grows in **many diverse habitats**—for example, on dry, compact soils, sandy areas, and waste places. It is a common weedy moss in paths, turfgrass, golf greens, between bricks of walks, and in the cracks of sidewalks. Crowded, overlapping leaves at the ends of stems give the stem a smooth, cylindric shape. Mature leaves are white (lack chlorophyll) and give this moss its bright silvery gray appearance. **Haircap moss (*Polytrichum commune* Hedwig)** is taller than silver thread moss. Green stems 5–10 cm tall (occasionally taller) are densely covered with sessile, alternate, overlapping, slender leaves, 6–8+ mm long by 1–2 mm wide; leaf tips are recurved. Vegetative plants resemble very young pine seedlings. Plants reproduce by spores and by rhizomes. The tops of male fruiting stems form a distinctive splash cup for dispersing sperm cells. The species is distributed throughout North America, adapted to diverse habitats, and can be particularly troublesome in cranberry production, reducing yield.

POSTSENESCENCE CHARACTERISTICS: None of note.

HABITAT: Mosses are most **often found in shady, moist sites**, but **many species are adapted to a variety of site conditions.** They are frequently weeds in irrigated turfgrass (particularly golf greens and shady lawns), container-grown crops, greenhouses, and perennial crops such as tree fruit, where the soil is undisturbed.

DISTRIBUTION: Many species occur throughout the United States.

SIMILAR SPECIES: **Birdseye pearlwort (*Sagina procumbens*)** is a mat-forming broadleaf weed found in similar habitats. Its erect flower stalks resemble the leafless stalks subtending the spore-bearing capsules of mosses, but they have small, white flowers or seed capsules. Unlike mosses, birdseye pearlwort has a fibrous root system and alternate leaves. **Cyanobacteria (blue-green algae)** can form in thin golf turf and resemble patches of moss. Digging into a dry patch will reveal a very thin, crusty layer unlike mosses that will have a thicker spongy layer. **Nostoc (presumed to be *Nostoc commune* Vaucher ex Bornet & Flahault)** is a cyanobacterium that has become common in container nurseries throughout the United States and Canada. *Nostoc* forms dark green, gelatinous masses on persistently moist surfaces such as nursery ground cloth, black plastic, or gravel pads. When wet, these mats are slippery, creating safety hazards for workers. Without water, plants dry quickly to a flaky, brown mass that is easily scraped off ground cloth but will return rapidly when irrigation is resumed.

J. Neal

…oss (partially cut out) in golf green

R. Uva

Moss with fruiting capsules

K. Ghantous

…cap moss

J. Neal

Nostoc on ground cloth

J. Neal

Algal crust in golf green

Field horsetail (*Equisetum arvense* L.)

SYNONYMS: common horsetail, horsetail fern, meadow-pine, pine-grass, foxtail-rush, scouring-rush, bottle-brush, horsepipes, snake-grass

GENERAL DESCRIPTION: A primitive, **rhizomatous perennial with 2 stem forms:** an **erect, leafless, cone-bearing stem**, which emerges in early spring, and a later-emerging **vegetative stem** with whorls of leafless branches at the nodes, giving the plant a bottle-brush appearance. Vegetative stems grow erect or prostrate at the base with an ascending tip.

REPRODUCTIVE CHARACTERISTICS: Reproduction is primarily by **creeping rhizomes** that bear tubers. Reproduction by spores is also possible but probably not significant in agricultural systems. At the ends of fertile unbranched stems, cones that are 0.5–3.5 cm long produce thousands of minute spores from mid-April to May. The fertile stems soon wither and die, giving way to the vegetative branched stems. Of primary concern are the rhizomes, which, along with starch-filled tubers, are easily spread by cultivation, in topsoil, and in infested balled-and-burlaped nursery crops.

MATURE PLANT: **In the spring, the fertile stems are whitish, succulent, unbranched, and bear a terminal cone.** They grow to 30 cm or more in height and are approximately 8 mm thick. The fertile stems have dark, toothed sheaths (modified leaves) at the nodes (14–20 mm long). The teeth (5–9 mm long) are attached and form a tube around the stem. Fertile stems wither and desiccate soon after the spores are shed. **Vegetative stems emerge after the fertile stems have withered.** They are **green, hollow, grooved,** and grow **erect** or prostrate at the base with an ascending tip to 10–50 cm or more in height and 1.5–5 mm thick. **Branches grow in whorls from the middle and upper nodes** of the stem and are attached below the toothed sheaths. Branches are 3- or 4-angled, unbranched or sparsely branched. Stems and branches are coated with hard silica deposits. Leaves are small, scale-like, and black-tipped; 8–12 are joined into a sheath or tube around the stem at the nodes.

ROOTS AND UNDERGROUND STRUCTURES: **Extensive rhizome system** can grow to a depth of 1.5 m below the soil surface. Rhizomes are forked, have a dark, felt-like coating, and bear small tubers.

POSTSENESCENCE CHARACTERISTICS: Vegetative stems die at the end of the growing season, turn black, and, by late autumn, are not generally found.

HABITAT: Field horsetail is a common weed of landscapes, orchards, and nursery crops. It grows on many different soils but does particularly well on sandy soils, on neutral or slightly basic soils, and in areas where the water table is high and soil drainage is poor. It is also found in low meadows, pastures, small fruit crops, roadsides, woodlands, and embankments. Field horsetail is **resistant to most herbicides used in agriculture**.

DISTRIBUTION: Found throughout the United States and Canada.

SIMILAR SPECIES: **Scouringrush (*Equisetum hyemale* L.)** is found only in wet areas and can be distinguished by its evergreen stems that lack, or have very few, branches throughout the growing season.

J. Neal

Field horsetail habit

J. Neal

Field horsetail fruiting stalks

J. DiTomaso

Scouringrush fruiting stem

R. Uva

Scouringrush habit

A. DiTommaso

eld horsetail stem

R. Prostak

Field horsetail

Asiatic dayflower (*Commelina communis* L.)

SYNONYM: common dayflower

GENERAL DESCRIPTION: An **annual monocot** that **resembles a dicot**. It initially grows erect but with time takes on a creeping or somewhat ascending habit. Stems are light green, somewhat succulent, branched, and root at the nodes.

PROPAGATION / PHENOLOGY: Propagation is generally **by seeds**. Vegetative reproduction is possible when stems fragment and root at the nodes to form colonies.

SEEDLING: The first leaf blade is oblong to oval with a rounded point; **veins in the leaf are parallel**. Later leaves are lanceolate. Blades are generally wider than those of the grasses.

MATURE PLANT: Stems grow to 50 cm tall and 80 cm long and are swollen at the nodes, appearing jointed. **Stems and leaves are thick and fleshy. Leaves lack petioles and are simple**, lanceolate to lance-ovate, rarely ovate, pointed at the apex and rounded at the base, and often hairy on the upper and lower surfaces. Blades are 3–5 times as long (5–12 cm) as wide (1.5–4 cm) and have **smooth margins and parallel veins. Sheaths at the base of the blade clasp the stem**, forming a 1–2 cm long tube. Hairs are often present at the base of the blade where the sheath opens.

ROOTS AND UNDERGROUND STRUCTURES: Fibrous root system. Where they touch the ground, **stems root at the nodes**.

FLOWERS AND FRUIT: Flowers, produced from July through September in small clusters (cymes) in the leaf axils, are enclosed by a clasping, folded, green, leaf-like bract. Flowers have **2 larger blue petals above and 1 smaller white petal below**. Each flower lasts only a day. The spathe (1.5–3 cm long) has dark green veins, is separated at the base, and is on a long flower stalk (1–7 cm) arising from the leaf axils. Fruit is a 2-celled capsule, usually with 2 seeds per cell. Seeds are 2.5–4.5 mm long, brown, pitted, and flat on one side and rounded on the other.

POSTSENESCENCE CHARACTERISTICS: Foliage and stems are very susceptible to frost and do not persist.

HABITAT: Asiatic dayflower is primarily a weed of landscapes and field and container nurseries, but is found in most cropping systems. Usually found growing on moist, rich soil in shady areas, it does not tolerate cultivation or mowing.

DISTRIBUTION: Originally native to Asia, it has escaped cultivation to become a weed in the eastern half of the United States.

SIMILAR SPECIES: **Spreading dayflower (*Commelina diffusa* Burm. f.)** is an annual with a reclining or creeping growth habit. It is found in turf areas and is most common in the southeastern and south-central United States. Unlike that of Asiatic dayflower, the **reduced flower petal is blue, not white. Erect dayflower (*Commelina erecta* L.)** is usually found on sandy sites and is differentiated by its perennial life cycle and erect growth habit. In addition, erect dayflower's **leaf-like bracts are fused** at the base. **Tropical spiderwort or Benghal dayflower (*Commelina benghalensis* L.)** is a mound-forming, summer annual or perennial (in warmer climates) and a federal noxious weed. The **leaves are broader** than Asiatic dayflower and the plant **spreads by rhizomes**. Underground flowers and seeds are produced at the rhizome nodes.

J. Neal

siatic dayflower habit

J. Neal

Asiatic dayflower seedling

J. Neal

Asiatic dayflower flower

J. Neal

Tropical spiderwort seedling

J. Neal

Tropical spiderwort rhizomes and underground flowers

J. DiTomaso

Asiatic dayflower seeds, 4.3 mm

Doveweed (*Murdannia nudiflora* (L.) Brenan)

Synonyms: *Aneilema nudiflora*, *Commelina nudiflora*, nakedstem dewflower

General Description: A prostrate, **mat-forming**, **summer annual** with **broad, grass-like foliage and thick, succulent stems**. Doveweed is not well controlled by glyphosate and many soil-residual herbicides.

Propagation / Phenology: Reproduces by seeds. **Seeds germinate in late spring** in warm, moist soil and continue through summer. No germination occurred in temperatures below 20°C (68°F) with optimum germination at 28°C (82.5°F). Prostrate **stems will root at the nodes**, thus the plant can propagate vegetatively via stem fragments. Plants flower and fruit continuously from late summer to the first frost.

Seedling: Leaves are 4–12 cm long by 5–12 mm wide, pointed, with **parallel veins; alternate and clasping the stem** with a sheath. When very young, it can easily be confused with a grass. The stems are succulent, trailing, root at the nodes, and often maroon at the base.

Mature Plant: Similar to young plants. Prostrate, rooting at the nodes, typically no more than 20 cm tall and will persist in mowed sites. Established plants will form dense mats.

Roots and Underground Structures: Thick, fleshy roots do not produce adventitious shoots.

Flowers and Fruit: Plants flower from mid-summer to autumn. Flower stalks are erect and loosely branched. Flowers with **3 petals and 3 sepals** bilaterally symmetrical. Petals are **light blue to purplish**; 3 **green sepals are shorter than the petals**. Fruits are oval capsules 2.5–5 mm long; light green turning bluish-black or dark gray at maturity. The style is persistent on the immature fruit. Seeds are pitted, dark brown to gray, 1.4–1.8 mm in length and 1–1.3 mm in width.

Postsenescence Characteristics: Dead plants do not persist.

Habitat: Most problematic in sites with persistent moisture. Historically, doveweed was observed in turf, nursery crops, landscape plantings, and ditch banks; however, occurrences in soybean and cotton fields increased with the adoption of glyphosate-tolerant cropping systems.

Distribution: Primarily a weed of the southeastern and mid-Atlantic states, but persistent populations have been reported in garden or nursery sites as far north as New York.

Similar Species: A similar species, **marsh dayflower (*Murdannia keisak* (Hassk.) Hand.-Maz.)**, is more restricted than doveweed to wetland sites. Sepals of marsh dayflower are about as long as the petals, whereas the sepals of doveweed are shorter than the petals. Also, leaves taper to a sharper point compared to doveweed.

Doveweed, young plant

Doveweed seedling

Doveweed flower

Marsh dayflower flower

Doveweed fruit

1 mm

Doveweed seeds

Yellow nutsedge (*Cyperus esculentus* L.)

SYNONYMS: yellow nut-grass, nut sedge, chufa, northern nut-grass, earth almond

GENERAL DESCRIPTION: A **perennial with 3-angled stems**, **long**, **grass-like leaves**, yellowish-green foliage, and 0.5–2 cm long **tubers** at the ends of **rhizomes**. Flowers are in spikelets at the ends of the stems.

PROPAGATION / PHENOLOGY: **Reproduction is primarily by tubers**, although viable seeds can also be produced. Tubers sprout and seedlings emerge from April until mid-July. **Rhizomes** can also spread the weed. Dormant tubers may remain viable for 10 or more years and are easily spread by cultivation, in topsoil, and with nursery stock.

SEEDLING: Seedlings are not often found. When present, seedlings are **very grass-like** but soon develop the characteristic **3-sided (triangular in cross section) base**.

MATURE PLANT: Leaves are flat and shiny or have parallel veins that form grooves and ridges. **Yellow-green blades are narrow** (3–8 mm wide) **and grass-like**. Leaves are produced at the base of the plant in groups of 3, forming a sheath around the stem. Flowering stems are erect, unbranched, **triangular in cross section**, smooth, yellow-green, and generally solitary.

ROOTS AND UNDERGROUND STRUCTURES: **Rhizomes and tubers are present.** Tubers are 0.5–2 cm long, rounded, ridged or scaled, white at first, turning brown and then black. Tubers are produced at the end of rhizomes beginning in late June and continuing into autumn. A single plant may produce hundreds or several thousand in a season. Most tubers are found in the first 15 cm of the soil. They require a chilling period to break dormancy. After germination, tubers produce a primary basal bulb 1–2 cm beneath the soil surface; the bulb develops fibrous roots, then rhizomes, secondary basal bulbs, and tubers.

FLOWERS AND FRUIT: Individual flowers are inconspicuous, similar to those of grasses, and are organized into yellowish or brownish spikelets, 1–3 cm long, and flattened. They are present from July to September. Spikelets occur at the ends of stems in terminal umbel-like clusters. Bracts below the flower clusters are leaf-like and often longer than the flower cluster. The single seed is enclosed within a 3-angled, yellowish-brown, elliptic fruit (achene). Achenes are 1.5 mm long.

POSTSENESCENCE CHARACTERISTICS: In late summer, foliage may become yellow to reddish-brown owing to a common rust disease. Foliage and the rhizomes die with the first killing frost. Only the tubers overwinter.

HABITAT: Yellow nutsedge is a weed of most agricultural, horticultural, and nursery crops as well as turfgrass and landscapes. It is found growing in many soil types and exposures but is most common on well-drained, sandy soils or damp to wet sites. Infestations often start in wet areas, then spread.

DISTRIBUTION: Found throughout North America.

SIMILAR SPECIES: **Purple nutsedge (*Cyperus rotundus* L.)** has dark green leaves and stems and reddish-brown or purple spikelets, whereas yellow nutsedge has yellow-green leaves and stems and yellowish or brown spikelets. Purple nutsedge develops **tubers along the length of the rhizomes**; yellow nutsedge tubers form only at the tips. Although nutsedge may resemble grasses, grasses do not produce leaves in groups of 3 and do not have tubers or 3-angled stems.

J. Neal

Yellow nutsedge colonial habit

J. Neal

Yellow nutsedge rhizomes and tubers

J. Neal

Nutsedge leaf tips: *left*, yellow; *right*, purple

J. Neal

Nutsedge flower heads: *left*, purple; *right*, yellow

J. O'Brien © 2007 UC Regents

Yellow nutsedge nutlets

29

Rice flatsedge (*Cyperus iria* L.)

SYNONYMS: ricefield flatsedge

GENERAL DESCRIPTION: A **clump-forming, summer annual** sedge with **triangular stems** in cross section. All shoots arise from the base and form a **tufted growth habit**, with **fibrous roots** that are often dark red. Seedheads are open and branched, with light yellow to tan flattened florets. Many species of annual sedges are important in agriculture and horticulture. They vary in size, but all have triangular stems, clumping growth, and lack rhizomes or tubers.

PROPAGATION / PHENOLOGY: Reproduce by **seeds** that germinate from spring through late summer. Rice flatsedge seedlings grow rapidly and can produce seeds within 8 weeks of emergence. Fresh seed germinates rapidly, resulting in **multiple generations per year**. Plants die at first hard frost.

SEEDLING: Young seedlings are grass-like but by the third or fourth leaf stage are distinguished from grasses by a triangular base formed by overlapping leaf sheaths. Seedlings form new sprouts at the base (tillers), thus enlarging the clump.

MATURE PLANT: Clumps to 45 cm in height develop many tillers. Yellow-green leaf blades are grass-like, 15–40 cm long by 3–6 mm wide, arching, glossy above with a prominent midvein. Within 6 to 8 weeks after emergence, plants start forming erect flower stalks.

ROOTS AND UNDERGROUND STRUCTURES: Densely fibrous root system. Some roots near the crown often have a reddish to reddish-brown color. No rhizomes or stolons.

FLOWERS AND FRUIT: Flowers are at the ends of **stiff, erect stalks**, triangular in cross section, in branched umbel-like clusters. Each plant produces **many flowering stalks**. Individual flowers are inconspicuous, similar to those of grasses, yellow to yellow-green. Florets are flattened (compressed), linear to ellipsoid, approximately 1 cm in length (occasionally to 2 cm). Florets turn tan as they age. Seeds (achenes) are mature and begin to shed while florets are still "green," but most seeds are retained until the inflorescence is tan, when they disperse. Achenes are brown and approximately 1.5 mm long.

POSTSENESCENCE CHARACTERISTICS: Plants die with a hard frost and are not persistent.

HABITAT: Most common in consistently moist areas, but the species is highly adaptable. A major weed of rice and not common in arable agronomic cropping systems, except in persistently moist or poorly drained areas. Common in container nurseries and urban landscapes. Shorter-statured species of annual sedges will tolerate mowing and be problematic in turf.

DISTRIBUTION: Introduced from Asia and East Africa and is now distributed throughout the eastern half of the United States, north to Massachusetts. Many other species of annual sedges are present throughout North America.

SIMILAR SPECIES: **Compressed sedge (*Cyperus compressus* L.)** is common in turfgrass, landscapes, and nurseries but is much smaller with distinctly flattened floral spikes. **Fragrant flatsedge (*Cyperus odoratus* L.)** is larger and generally more robust, and florets are in spherical clusters. **Yellow nutsedge (*Cyperus esculentus*)** does not tiller and has rhizomes and tubers. **Toothed flatsedge (*Cyperus dentatus* Torrey)** has similar foliage and seedheads but is a perennial arising from a thickened basal stem that can be rhizomatous. Rice flatsedge is also similar to some clump-forming ***Kyllinga* species**, but annual kyllinga flowers are in tight, rounded clusters.

J. Neal

Rice flatsedge plant

J. Neal

Rice flatsedge seedling

J. Neal

Rice flatsedge inflorescence

J. Derr

Fragrant flatsedge inflorescence

J. Neal

Compressed sedge

J. Neal

Rice flatsedge seeds

False-green kyllinga (*Kyllinga gracillima* Miq.)

SYNONYMS: *Cyperus brevifolioides*, *Kyllinga brevifolia* var. *gracillima*, pasture spikesedge

GENERAL DESCRIPTION: Warm-season, **perennial sedge**, with **glossy, grass-like leaves and creeping rhizomes**. False-green kyllinga is most problematic in turfgrass and ornamental plantings, forming dense mats from a prolific network of rhizomes that crowd out grasses. Native to tropical America.

PROPAGATION / PHENOLOGY: **Reproduction is by seeds and vegetatively from rhizomes.** Plants often produce large quantities of highly viable seed. Under favorable conditions, new plants establish from short rhizome fragments.

SEEDLING: Seedlings are grass-like, with long, slender leaves that taper to a point. Like other sedge species, overlapping leaves come in ranks of 3, resulting in **shoots** being **triangular in cross section**.

MATURE PLANT: Unmowed plants form clumps 10–20 cm tall (rarely taller), but mowed plants form a dense mat. Leaves are usually dark green, glossy, flat, 6–15 (rarely to 30) cm long by 1.5–3.5 mm wide, with a sheathing base fused around the stem. Sprouts from rhizomes are densely spaced. Flower stems are erect and triangular in cross section.

ROOTS AND UNDERGROUND STRUCTURES: Rhizomes are shallow (sometimes considered stolons), 0.5–2 mm diameter, with closely spaced nodes, and are covered with reddish-brown, lanceolate scales 6–13 mm long. During the warm season, rhizomes can grow more than 2.5 cm per day. Plants with short rhizomes and short internodes sometimes appear tufted.

FLOWERS AND FRUIT: Flowering occurs May to November, sometimes earlier in warm locations. Spikelet **heads are dense**, **round to ovoid, 7–12 mm long, with 3–4 leaf-like bracts 4–20 cm long** just below the numerous sessile spikelets. **Longest bracts are usually erect**, appearing as an extension of the stem. Shorter bracts are spreading to slightly reflexed. Spikelets are flat, ovate, 3.5–4.5 mm long, pale green to reddish-brown. Achenes are flattened, 2-sided, elliptic, and 1.5–1.8 mm long.

POSTSENESCENCE CHARACTERISTICS: Foliage turns brown or purplish-brown in late season.

HABITAT: Turf, ditches, landscaped areas, and ornamental plantings. Often in over-watered or poorly drained sites. Established plants tolerate close and frequent mowing, and some shade and drying.

DISTRIBUTION: Most common in upper piedmont and mountains of the southern states but present throughout the mid-Atlantic states and north to New York and Rhode Island.

SIMILAR SPECIES: **Green kyllinga (*Kyllinga brevifolia* Rottb.)** is more common in the coastal plain of the southeastern states, although also north to Pennsylvania and New Jersey. These species can be distinguished only by seed morphology or flower timing. The scale keels of green kyllinga seeds are toothed, and false-green kyllinga are smooth. Green kyllinga flowers during most summer months, whereas false-green kyllinga flowers in late summer until frost. **Tufted kyllinga (*Kyllinga pumila* Michx.)** is a native species that resembles green kyllinga. However, it is a tufted, clump-forming, summer **annual that lacks rhizomes** and, although more widespread, is not as problematic in turf as green or false-green kyllinga. **Yellow (*Cyperus esculentus*) and purple nutsedge (*Cyperus rotundus*)** can occupy a similar habitat as green kyllinga but are distinguished by having small, round or oblong tubers (~0.5–2.5 cm diameter or wider) in rhizomatous chains or at the ends of slender rhizomes. Green kyllinga may resemble some grasses but lacks a ligule or a conspicuous junction between the blade base and sheath.

Green kyllinga habit and rhizome (false-green kyllinga habit is nearly identical)

False-green kyllinga creeping stem

False-green kyllinga inflorescence (and uneven bracts)

Tufted kyllinga

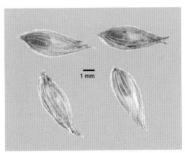

False-green kyllinga seeds

Slender rush (*Juncus tenuis* Willd.)

SYNONYMS: path rush, field rush, slender yard rush, wire-grass, poverty rush

GENERAL DESCRIPTION: A **clump-forming**, grass-like **perennial** (15–60 cm tall), with **narrow, wiry, rounded stems**.

PROPAGATION / PHENOLOGY: Reproduction is both vegetative and **by seeds**.

SEEDLING: Seedlings are very small with slender, **grass-like leaves** only 1 mm wide. **Whitish auricles** (1–3.5 mm long) are present at the junction of the leaf blade and sheath.

MATURE PLANT: **Stems are round, hollow, wiry, and dark green. Leaves are basal and flat, inwardly rolled at the margins to almost rounded** (0.5–2 mm wide). Sheaths cover ⅓–½ the height of the stem and have thin, dry, papery margins with a pair of papery, ligule-like auricles at the junction of the blade and sheath. Ligules are absent.

ROOTS AND UNDERGROUND STRUCTURES: **Fibrous roots** are present at the nodes of **short rhizomes**.

FLOWERS AND FRUIT: Flowers occur from June through August and are produced in clusters (cymes) near the ends of the stems. Two (1–10 cm long) **leaf-like bracts often extend beyond the flower cluster**. Flowers are small, greenish-brown (2.8–5 mm long), with lanceolate sepals and petals (3 each). Fruits are egg-shaped capsules (2.6–4.2 mm long) that split into 3 sections at maturity. Seeds are small (0.5 mm or smaller in length) and orange-brown.

POSTSENESCENCE CHARACTERISTICS: Plant often turns brown at top. Wiry, erect stems may persist throughout the winter.

HABITAT: Slender rush is a weed of turfgrass, landscapes, and nursery crops, especially along paths and in gravel or stone driveways and roads. It also grows in pastures, meadows, and waste places, on both moist and dry sites. It is particularly successful in compacted soils.

DISTRIBUTION: Found throughout the United States and southern Canada.

SIMILAR SPECIES: Rushes can be distinguished from grasses and sedges by their round stems and the presence of sepals and petals. Many other species of rushes can be weedy. **Soft rush (*Juncus effusus* L.)** is also a densely tufted, native perennial (to 1.3 m tall) with short, thick rhizomes. Soft rush can be distinguished from slender rush by its inflorescence. The lower inflorescence bract of soft rush appears as a continuation of the stem, such that the flower clusters appear to project laterally from the stem. In slender rush, the inflorescence bract does not appear as an extension of the stem and, thus, the flower clusters appear to be terminal. Soft rush occurs in wetlands, including those in meadows, pastures, and on rangeland and pasture in nearly all states. Cattle will not graze it, which can increase its dominance in pastures lacking a dry period during the summer.

J. Neal

Slender rush habit

J. DiTomaso

Soft rush habit

R. Uva

Slender rush flower heads

J. DiTomaso

Slender rush seeds, 0.4 mm

Wild garlic (*Allium vineale* L.)

SYNONYMS: field garlic, scallions, wild onion, crow garlic

GENERAL DESCRIPTION: A **bulbous perennial** with grass-like leaves that emerge in the early spring. All plant parts have a **strong scent of garlic or onion** when crushed. The stems are unbranched (30 cm to 1 m high), usually producing a cluster of tiny, aerial bulbs at the top of the stems in place of the flowers, or red-purple, pink, or white to green flowers. In areas under stress from repeated mowing or cultivation, the foliage is more slender and does not produce flower stalks or aerial bulblets.

PROPAGATION / PHENOLOGY: Reproduction is **by aerial bulblets** and **underground bulblets**, but **rarely by seeds**. Plants grow rapidly in early spring to summer, produce flowers in May and June, then senesce.

SEEDLING: Seedlings are **grass-like with hollow, hairless leaves** that are round in cross section.

MATURE PLANT: **Basal leaves arise from the bulb. Leaves are linear**, grooved above, 15–60 cm long by 2–10 mm wide, **smooth, round, and hollow. Foliage has the scent of garlic or onion. Flowering stems are solid**, unbranched, smooth, erect, and leafless above; they become stiff with age.

ROOTS AND UNDERGROUND STRUCTURES: Fibrous roots are attached to the bottom of a rounded to egg-shaped bulb (1–2 cm in diameter). The **bulbs have a papery outer coating** often with distinctive puzzle-like cell architecture. **Bulblets** form at the base of the larger bulbs. Some are soft and germinate in the first autumn; others are hard and remain dormant over the winter, germinating the following spring or 1–5 years later.

FLOWERS AND FRUIT: **Flowers or bulblets are produced in May and June at the top of the stems in globe-shaped umbels** that are surrounded by a single 1-parted papery sheath-like spathe. **Aerial bulblets are often produced** at the top of the stem **in place of flowers** and **develop long, tail-like green leaves.** Flowers, when present, are red-purple or pink, sometimes white or greenish and on long pedicels (0.5–2.5 cm). They do not generally produce seed in the northeastern United States. Fruit is an egg-shaped, 3-parted capsule at the end of the stems above the short bracts (2–3.5 mm long), with 2 seeds per cell. Seeds (3 mm long) are flattened, black, and wrinkled.

POSTSENESCENCE CHARACTERISTICS: Plants die back in the summer, but the leafless stalks, bearing the capsule, may remain.

HABITAT: Wild garlic is a weed of turfgrass, nursery crops, landscapes, winter wheat, and other cereal crops. In wheat, the heads of aerial bulblets easily shatter during harvest, contaminating the flour and giving it a garlicky odor and flavor. When grazed in pastures, wild garlic can impart a garlicky odor and flavor to beef and dairy products. Wild garlic usually grows on rich soils but can tolerate a wide range of soil conditions.

DISTRIBUTION: Found throughout the eastern half of the United States.

SIMILAR SPECIES: **Wild onion (*Allium canadense* L.)** is similar except the leaves **are flat in cross section, not hollow**, and the **bulb has a fibrous, net-veined outer coating**, unlike the thin membranous outer coating of wild garlic. Wild onion has a 3-parted spathe below the flower cluster and does not produce hard dormant bulbs. Its habitats are similar to those of wild garlic.

R. Uva

Wild garlic foliage and bulbs

J.Neal

Wild garlic habit

R. Uva

Wild garlic bulblets

J. DiTomaso

Left, wild onion seeds, 3.0 mm; *right*, wild garlic seeds, 3.1 mm

Star-of-Bethlehem (*Ornithogalum umbellatum* L.)

SYNONYMS: summer snow-flake, star-flower

GENERAL DESCRIPTION: A **bulbous perennial** frequently sold commercially as a spring-flowering ornamental. It has escaped cultivation and can grow as tufts in lawns and landscapes in the early spring. All parts of the plant are **poisonous** if ingested.

PROPAGATION / PHENOLOGY: Reproduction is primarily **by small bulbs (bulblets)** formed around the base of the parent bulb. Bulbs are renewed each year. Seed production is rare but has been reported in North America. Young plants are noticeable in turf in early spring before the first mowing and in late spring in landscape beds.

SEEDLING: **Rare** in North America.

MATURE PLANT: Basal leaves are linear, and flowering stems are up to 30 cm high and leafless (scapes). The **grass-like leaves** (10–30 cm long by 2–6 mm wide) are fleshy and dark green, with a **whitish, grooved midrib**, similar to crocus.

ROOTS AND UNDERGROUND STRUCTURES: Ovate **bulbs** grow in clumps and are subtended by a fibrous root system.

FLOWERS AND FRUIT: **Flowers**, present from April through June, are **bright waxy white** (occasionally bluish) on branched, open clusters (corymbiform racemes) at the end of leafless flower stalks. The 6 petals (tepals) are lanceolate-oblong (1.5–2 cm long) and white above with a distinctive green stripe underneath. Seedpods are present in mid- to late spring. Fruits are 3-lobed, egg-shaped capsules containing several seeds. Seeds are black, somewhat egg-shaped (1.5 mm long), and have a granular surface.

POSTSENESCENCE CHARACTERISTICS: Plants die back to a bulb soon after setting seed in early summer.

HABITAT: Star-of-Bethlehem has escaped cultivation and is a weed of turfgrass and landscapes, often found in and around old flower gardens. It is less common in meadows, along roads, and in waste areas. **Early-season maturation and senescence enable this weed to escape most control measures.**

DISTRIBUTION: Common in the northern United States, the Piedmont region of the southern states, and Canada.

SIMILAR SPECIES: Several bulbous cultivated flowering plants resemble star-of-Bethlehem, but few have escaped to become weedy.

R. Uva

Mature star-of-Bethlehem plants and bulbs

R. Uva

Emerging star-of-Bethlehem shoots

R. Uva

Star-of-Bethlehem flowers

Broomsedge (*Andropogon virginicus* L.)

Synonyms: beard-grass, whiskey grass, broomsedge bluestem, sedge grass

General Description: A **clump-forming perennial grass** with erect, branching, flowering stems (50 cm to 1 m high). Most commonly recognized in the dormant stage as persistent tan clumps of dried leaves and stems.

Propagation / Phenology: Reproduction is **both vegetative and by seeds**. Seedlings emerge in late spring or early summer. Clumps enlarge by **short rhizomes**.

Seedling: Young **leaves are folded in bud**, and the **sheaths are strongly compressed** (flattened). The **ligule is membranous** but fringed **with hairs** on the upper margin. **Hairs** are present at the junction of the blade and sheath.

Mature Plant: Foliage is smooth or sparsely hairy and often has a whitish or bluish cast on the surface. Leaves are folded in the bud, auricles are absent, and the ligule is 1 mm long and membranous, with a fringe of hairs on the upper margin. Stems are slightly flattened, often with long, soft hairs at the uppermost nodes, and branched in the upper part. Blades are folded (keeled) near the base, linear (10–30 cm long by 2–8 mm wide), and sharply pointed at the apex. The upper surface of the blade may be hairy toward the base and along the margins in the region of the ligule. Sheaths are compressed (flattened) and smooth but may be hairy along the margins. The collar is narrow, hairy at the edges, and divided by the midvein.

Roots and Underground Structures: Densely fibrous root system from **short rhizomes**.

Flowers and Fruit: Flowering occurs from July through September. The **conspicuously silky-haired inflorescence** is produced along the upper half of the stem in the sheathed axils of the upper leaves. Spikelets are in racemes in groups of 2–4 (2–4 cm long). Two spikelets are present at each point of attachment, one sessile (fertile) with a long awn (2–4 cm), the other stalked (sterile) and lacking an awn.

Postsenescence Characteristics: **In the fall**, **plants turn reddish-tan** and stems become stiff, **persisting well into winter**. The hairy racemes of the spikelets are easily recognizable when the stiff stems blow in the wind.

Habitat: Broomsedge is a weed of low-maintenance pasture, turfgrass, nursery crops, and other perennial crops. It is usually found in open, sunny locations on low-fertility and drought-prone soils, particularly unmanaged meadows, roadsides, and waste areas.

Distribution: Found in California and throughout the eastern half of the United States, but not common in the northern New England states.

Similar Species: **Little bluestem (*Schizachyrium scoparium* (Michx.) Nash** [syn.: *Andropogon scoparius* Michx.]) is very similar, but its flower clusters (racemes of spikelets) are solitary, whereas those of broomsedge are in groups of 2 or more. **Big bluestem (*Andropogon gerardii* Vitman)** is generally larger than broomsedge (to 2 m in height) and has a longer raceme of stalked spikelets (5–10 cm).

Broomsedge habit (dormant)

J. Neal

Broomsedge
collar region

Juvenile broomsedge

J. Neal

oomsedge fruit

J. Neal

Little bluestem
collar region

J. DiTomaso

Broomsedge seed, 3.5 mm (including lemma)

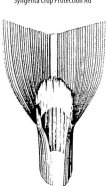

Big bluestem
collar region

J. DiTomaso

Left, little bluestem seed, 8.0 mm (including lemma); *right*, big bluestem seed, 6.5 mm (including lemma)

Sweet vernalgrass (*Anthoxanthum odoratum* L.)

Synonym: spring grass

General Description: Short-lived, tufted, cool-season **perennial** to 0.6 m tall, with **spike-like panicles**. Foliage has a high coumarin content, which gives it the **sweet fragrance** of fresh-mowed hay, especially when cut. Native to Europe. The species has been documented as tolerant of some grass-selective herbicides.

Propagation / Phenology: Reproduction is by seeds, and achenes generally disperse only short distances.

Seedling: Little information is available. Leaves are **rolled in the bud**, auricles are absent, **ligules are membranous, sheath is open and hairy**, and leaves usually have short hairs.

Mature Plant: Vegetative characteristics are similar to seedlings. Ligules are membranous, 1–6 mm long, sometimes slightly ciliate along the top. The sheath is open, sometimes sparsely hairy. Auricles are often present, rounded, to 1 mm long, with a few long hairs. The basal leaves are 10–30 cm long and are often sparse when plants are flowering. Flowering stems are erect to ascending and lack hairs. The nodes are often dark, and the leaves are flat, lack hairs or are only sparsely hairy, 3–6 cm long by 2–7 mm wide, with margins often sparsely ciliate.

Roots and Underground Structures: Roots fibrous, fine, often dense. Some texts state that slender rhizomes may be present, but the authors have not seen evidence of this.

Flowers and Fruit: Plants flower from May to June. Numerous flower stalks each have one **spike-like panicle**, 2–8 cm long by 0.5–1.5 cm wide, apex tapered to a point, and turning **yellowish-brown**. Spikelets are 7–10 mm long, flattened. Florets are 3 with 2 of them awned: the uppermost fertile, 2 mm long, and awnless, the lower 2 each consist of a hairy sterile lemma with a slender awn from the back. The lower sterile lemma has a short straight awn from the middle or upper section of the back. The upper sterile lemma has a slender bent awn from the base of the back and is about equal to or slightly longer than the longest glume.

Habitat: Found on coastal grassland, hay fields, orchards, roadsides, and open disturbed places. Tolerant of low-fertility, drought-prone sites but grows well in more conducive conditions, especially if competition from other species is reduced by the use of selective herbicides.

Distribution: Found throughout the eastern half of the United States and Canada, and in West Coast states.

Similar Species: Vegetatively the plant might be mistaken for many other clump-forming grasses, but the spike-like panicle is distinctive. **Annual vernalgrass (*Anthoxanthum aristatum* Boiss.)** is a less common annual to 0.3 m tall that closely resembles sweet vernalgrass, except that it is smaller in most respects. In addition to being an annual, annual vernalgrass is distinguished by having narrow leaves, 1–2 mm wide, and smaller spikelets, 4–8 mm long. Native to Europe and found in most Northeast and mid-Atlantic states.

Sweet vernalgrass habit

J. Neal

Sweet vernalgrass leaf

J. DiTomaso

Sweet vernalgrass inflorescence

J. Neal

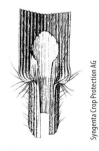

Sweet vernal-grass collar

Syngenta Crop Protection AG

Annual vernalgrass collar

Syngenta Crop Protection AG

5 mm

J. O'Brien © 2007 UC Regents

Sweet vernalgrass seeds and spikelets

Wild oat (*Avena fatua* L.)

Synonyms: wheat oats, oat-grass, flax-grass

General Description: An **annual grass** with stout, **erect stems** to 1 m in height. It can grow solitary or in a tuft.

Propagation / Phenology: Reproduction is **by seeds**. **Cool, moist conditions promote germination**, which occurs primarily in the spring. Tillers are produced 2–4 weeks after emergence. Seeds fall to the ground as they ripen, usually before crop harvest.

Seedling: **Leaves are rolled in the bud. Auricles are absent**, and **ligules are membranous**, large, whitish, and pointed. Leaves may be smooth or hairy. Hairs, when present, are both small and large; larger hairs are sparse.

Mature Plant: Leaves are rolled in the bud, and auricles are absent. Ligules (2–6 mm long) are membranous, rounded, and torn at the top (lacerate). Blades are linear, not keeled (7–40 cm long by 4–18 mm wide), rough to the touch, and taper to a pointed tip. Blades are often hairy near the ligule and on the margins near the base. Sheaths are compressed and vary from smooth to occasionally sparsely hairy. Collars are sparsely hairy at the edges. Stems are smooth and erect.

Roots and Underground Structures: Extensive fibrous root system.

Flowers and Fruit: Flowers from July to September. **Spikelets are in a loose, open, drooping, panicle** (15–40 cm long and up to 20 cm wide). Spikelets are nodding, and the florets (1–3 cm long) have a twisted, angled, dorsal awn (3–4 cm long) that straightens and twists with changes in humidity. A single plant can produce 100–150 seeds.

Postsenescence Characteristics: Flowering stems persist. Long glumes (1–2 cm) will remain on spikelets for an extended period.

Habitat: Wild oat is a weed of agronomic crops, especially spring cereals, as well as of vegetables, nursery crops, and landscapes. Found on heavy clay and clay-loam soils, it prefers cool climates and moist soil and often grows on the lower, moister regions of agricultural fields.

Distribution: Most common in the western United States and in the northern Great Plains of the Midwest. Occasionally a weed as far east as New York.

Similar Species: The bent awns of wild oat can distinguish it from cultivated **oat (*Avena sativa* L.),** which has straight awns or none at all. In addition, the panicles of wild oat are looser and wider than those of oat. **Sterile (or animated) oat (*Avena sterilis* L.)** is a less common, cool-season annual to 1.2 m tall. Sterile oat is distinguished from wild oat by having bent awns mostly 35–90 mm long that are short, hairy, and twisted below the bend. It occurs in eastern Canada, Pennsylvania, New Jersey, and possibly elsewhere. Sterile oat hybridizes with wild and cultivated oats and appears to be the oldest progenitor of a certain line of oats. It can be an aggressive weed of fields and disturbed areas in the Mediterranean region and some other regions with a similar climate. Native to southern Europe. The spikelets of **tall oatgrass (*Arrhenatherum elatius* (L.) J.S. Presl & C. Presl)** can resemble *Avena* spp., but tall oatgrass is a perennial, often with bulbous basal internodes. Though the lemma awns are long (10–17 mm) and bend, those of wild and sterile oat are much longer (>30 mm). Tall oatgrass is native to Europe and is a weed of small grains. It is found in the mid-Atlantic states, as far north as New Jersey and Pennsylvania.

C. Elmore

Wild oat habit

J. DiTomaso

Wild oat seedhead

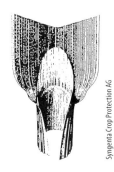

Syngenta Crop Protection AG

Wild oat collar region

J. K. Clark © 2007 UC Regents

Wild oat collar

Syngenta Crop Protection AG

Tall oatgrass

J. O'Brien © 2007 UC Regents

Wild oat seeds and spikelets

45

Downy brome (*Bromus tectorum* L.)

SYNONYMS: downy chess, cheatgrass, downy brome-grass, slender chess, early chess, drooping brome, wall brome

GENERAL DESCRIPTION: A **summer or winter annual**, 10–60 cm in height, that ranges in habit from **clump-forming and erect to spreading**.

PROPAGATION / PHENOLOGY: Reproduction is **by seeds**; seeds germinate in early to mid-spring and in late summer to mid-autumn.

SEEDLING: The first leaf blade is linear (8 cm long by 2 mm wide) and opens perpendicular to the ground. **Leaves are rolled in the bud**, **lack auricles**, and have a **membranous ligule** (1 mm long) that is delicately fringed at the top. **Young leaf blades are twisted and appear to be spiraling upward.** Blades have **soft, short, dense hairs** (<1 mm) on both surfaces. Rounded sheaths have similar hairs and are whitish with a tinge of red at the base.

MATURE PLANT: Leaves and ligule are similar to those of the seedling. **Blades** are flat, **hairy** on both surfaces, and sharply pointed (3–21 cm long by 2–6 mm wide). **Sheaths** are rounded, **hairy**, and have prominent pinkish veins.

ROOTS AND UNDERGROUND STRUCTURES: The **root system is fibrous**. Downy brome does not root at the nodes.

FLOWERS AND FRUIT: Flowers are produced between May and July. The seedhead is a drooping, dense, soft, purplish panicle (4–18 cm long). Spikelets are 3–8 flowered (1–2.5 cm long) with long awns (10–18 mm). Seed is grooved, yellow to reddish-brown, and 6–8 mm long.

POSTSENESCENCE CHARACTERISTICS: The characteristic drooping seedhead may persist.

HABITAT: Found on dry, sandy or gravelly soil in meadows, pastures, and wasteland, downy brome is a weed of turf, nurseries, landscapes, pastures, winter grains, and agricultural crops. It is a major weed of rangeland in the western United States.

DISTRIBUTION: Found throughout the United States, except the Southeast.

SIMILAR SPECIES: **Cheat or chess (*Bromus secalinus* L.)** is smooth or with occasional hairs on the blades and the lower sheaths. The awns of cheat are shorter (3–5 mm long) than those of downy brome. **Japanese brome (*Bromus arvensis* L. [syn.: *Bromus japonicus* Thunb. ex Murr.])** is also a winter annual grass to 0.9 m tall with soft florets and weak, slender awns. It is distinguished from downy brome by the shorter awns on the lemma (5–11 mm), lack of drooping mature flowers, fewer hairs on the foliage, and shorter teeth at the tip of the lemma (≤1 mm). Japanese brome is native to Eurasia and is common throughout the United States. **Common velvetgrass (*Holcus lanatus*)** has a coat of dense hairs on the blades and leaves, but differs from downy brome in that the back of the ligule is hairy in mature plants, sheaths are compressed, and the blades of young plants are not twisted.

Downy brome habit

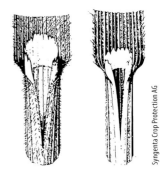

Collar regions: *left*, downy brome; *right*, cheat

Flowering stems: *top*, Japanese brome; *bottom*, downy brome

Downy brome seedling

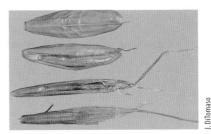

Top, cheat seeds, 7.5 mm (to tip of lemma); *bottom*, downy brome seeds, 10.5 mm (to tip of lemma)

47

Longspine sandbur (*Cenchrus longispinus* (Hack.) Fern.)

SYNONYMS: bear-grass, bur-grass, hedgehog-grass

GENERAL DESCRIPTION: A coarse-textured, light green, clump-forming **summer annual** with prostrate or ascending tillers (20–40 cm tall, occasionally to 80 cm), which root at the lower nodes and terminate with a spike of **spiny burs**.

PROPAGATION / PHENOLOGY: Reproduction is **by seeds**; seedlings emerge in the spring and early summer. The spiny burs are dispersed by sticking to the skin and fur of animals and to shoes and clothing. The dried burs can also float on water.

SEEDLING: **Leaves are folded in the bud. Ligule is a fringe of hairs**, 0.7–1.7 mm long. The **blade is rough**, sometimes sparsely hairy with long hairs at the base near the ligule and collar. The **sheath is smooth** (glabrous) **with finely hairy margins, compressed** (flattened), and often tinged red. The collar is narrow but distinct and lighter in color. Tillers initially ascend but become more prostrate with age and mowing. Lower node of tillers can develop adventitious roots.

MATURE PLANT: **Tillers elongate in radial (or pinwheel) fashion** from the crown. Flowering stalks are coarse and wiry, with swollen nodes. **Vegetative characteristics are similar to those of seedling plants.** Mature leaf blades are light green, 6–18 cm long by 3–8 mm wide, flattened, and sometimes coiled. Leaf sheaths are strongly compressed, and the collar is broad. Lower stems become maroon with age.

ROOTS AND UNDERGROUND STRUCTURES: A fibrous root system from the crown, with adventitious roots developing at the lower nodes of the tillers.

FLOWERS AND FRUIT: Tillers terminate in a spike-like raceme of flowers and **bur-like fruit**. Plants flower over an extended period of time, between July and September (longer if weather permits). Each spike has 6–15 burs (involucre). Each bur is rounded to egg-shaped (globose to ovate), 6–10 mm in diameter, with short hairs.

POSTSENESCENCE CHARACTERISTICS: Late in the season, the lower foliage turns straw-colored, and the stems are reddish to maroon. The entire **plant, including the burs, turns straw-colored after frost**. The wiry stems and spiny burs can persist through the winter. Burs may remain on or near the soil surface through the next summer.

HABITAT: Usually found on sandy soils but can survive in a variety of soil types. A common turfgrass weed in the southeastern United States and occasionally a weed of cultivated crops.

DISTRIBUTION: Longspine sandbur and **field sandbur (*Cenchrus spinifex* Cav.** [syn.: *Cenchrus incertus* M.A. Curtis]) are most common along the coastal Southeast but have been reported as far north as Massachusetts and west to California. Locally a problem in the Midwest, north-central states, and Great Lakes region.

SIMILAR SPECIES: Seedlings may **resemble other species with hairy ligules**, particularly **foxtails (*Setaria* spp.)** and **fall panicum (*Panicum dichotomiflorum*)**. However, foxtails and panicums are rolled in the bud, whereas sandbur is folded. There are **several weedy species of sandbur**. Many are very similar to longspine sandbur and are differentiated primarily by the shape of the burs. **Field sandbur** is also a common summer annual or, in some locations, a short-lived perennial weed. It can be distinguished from longspine sandbur by its burs, which are ovoid (less rounded) and smaller (3–4 mm wide).

Longspine sandbur habit

J. K. Clark © 2007 UC Regents

Syngenta Crop Protection AG

Field sandbur
collar region

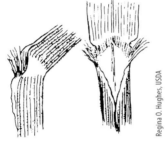

Regina O. Hughes, USDA

Longspine sandbur collar region

J. Neal

Longspine sandbur inflorescence

J. DiTomaso

Longspine sandbur collar and
sheath

J. DiTomaso

Longspine sandbur seed, 9 mm
(including spines)

Bermudagrass (*Cynodon dactylon* (L.) Pers.)

SYNONYMS: *Capriola dactylon,* scutch-grass, dogs-tooth-grass, wire grass, couch grass

GENERAL DESCRIPTION: A **wiry perennial** with **spreading rhizomes and stolons**. The **leaves are gray-green to bluish-green**. Bermudagrass has a spreading, prostrate to ascending habit, forming dense mats when mowed, but it may grow erect (10–30 cm tall) in unmowed areas. In the southern United States and transition zones, bermudagrass is a valuable lawn and pasture grass, but its competitiveness has made it a formidable weed in most crops.

PROPAGATION / PHENOLOGY: Reproduction is **primarily by stolons and rhizomes** and less commonly by seeds.

SEEDLING: **Leaves are rolled in the bud, auricles are absent,** and the **ligule is a row of hairs** (0.5 mm long). **Blades are smooth** on both surfaces, **relatively short and narrow**, with slightly rough margins. **Sheaths are green and smooth. Collars** are narrow, white, **smooth on the youngest seedlings** only, but **hairy on older seedlings.** Shoots emerging from rhizomes are more robust than seedlings. On these shoots, leaves are rolled in the bud for "wild type" common bermudagrass, but turf-type, hybrid bermudagrass varieties often have a folded vernation.

MATURE PLANT: **Ligule is similar to that of seedlings. Leaves** are flat, with **a ring of white hairs in the collar** region. Blades are linear-lanceolate, relatively short (5–16 cm long by 2–5 mm wide), and smooth or with hairs toward the base of the blade. **Margins are slightly rough. Sheaths** are **strongly compressed** and smooth or with a **few hairs** (1–3 mm long) **in the collar** region.

ROOTS AND UNDERGROUND STRUCTURES: Flattened **stolons are abundant**, with shoots arising from the axils of brownish leaf sheaths. **Rhizomes** are hard, scaly, and sharp, forming a dense sod. Roots are present at the nodes of both stolons and rhizomes.

FLOWERS AND FRUIT: Flowers are present in July and August. The **seedhead** consists of **3–7 finger-like spikes** approximately 4 cm long (3–10 cm) **radiating from a central point at the terminal end of the stems.** Flattened spikelets are in 2 rows on one side of the spike. Each spikelet produces 1 seed (1.5 mm long).

POSTSENESCENCE CHARACTERISTICS: Plants become dormant with frost. Straw-colored foliage persists through the winter and into spring.

HABITAT: Bermudagrass is a weed of most crops but is most troublesome in perennial crops, as well as turfgrasses and landscapes. It tolerates a wide range of soil and site conditions, including drought.

DISTRIBUTION: Found throughout the southern United States, north to southern New Jersey and occasionally farther north.

SIMILAR SPECIES: **Nimblewill (*Muhlenbergia schreberi*)** and **wirestem muhly (*Muhlenbergia frondosa*)** have a similar gray-green color, coarse-textured appearance, and habitat. However, they grow more erect and are considerably less competitive than bermudagrass. In addition, they are more cold-tolerant and consequently are found at higher latitudes in the Northeast.

Bermudagrass habit,
showing stolons

J. Neal

Syngenta Crop Protection AG

Bermudagrass
collar region

J. Neal

Bermudagrass stolon

J. Neal

Bermudagrass inflorescence

J. O'Brien © 2007 UC Regents

Bermudagrass seeds, 1.7 mm

Orchardgrass (*Dactylis glomerata* L.)

SYNONYMS: cocksfoot, cock's foot

GENERAL DESCRIPTION: A **clump-forming perennial** that can grow to more than 1 m in height but can tolerate mowing.

PROPAGATION / PHENOLOGY: Reproduction is **by seeds. Crown enlarges by tillering.**

SEEDLING: The first leaf blade opens perpendicular to the ground. **Leaves are folded in the bud, lack auricles, and have a finely toothed membranous ligule** (3–5 mm long). **Blades are long** (7–12 cm long by 1.3–2.3 mm wide), smooth on both surfaces and on the margins, light green, strongly keeled, and folded near the ligule. **Sheaths are flattened and keeled**, smooth, whitish at the base, and loosely appressed to the stems.

MATURE PLANT: **Leaves are similar to those of the seedlings. Ligules are somewhat longer in mature plants** (5–7 mm). **Blades are bluish-green, very long** (7–30 cm long by 3–8 mm wide), and somewhat rough on the surfaces and margins. Blades are strongly keeled and V-shaped in cross section. **Sheaths are strongly compressed** and keeled, and the collar is broad and prominent.

ROOTS AND UNDERGROUND STRUCTURES: Root system is very dense and fibrous. Orchardgrass does not produce rhizomes.

FLOWERS AND FRUIT: Flowers occur from late spring through mid-summer. The **seedhead is a stiff, branched panicle**, 5–20 cm in length. Spikelets are fan-shaped and appear densely crowded and sessile in 1-sided clusters. Awns, if present, may be to 2 mm long.

POSTSENESCENCE CHARACTERISTICS: A perennial grass that remains green year-round.

HABITAT: Orchardgrass is a forage grass but is also a weed of turf, landscapes, nursery crops, and other perennial horticultural crops. It tolerates partial shade to full sunlight and is found in fields, disturbed sites, and roadsides.

DISTRIBUTION: Occurs throughout much of North America, excluding the Florida peninsula.

SIMILAR SPECIES: **Goosegrass (*Eleusine indica*)** has similar folded sheaths; however, orchardgrass has a large membranous ligule, whereas goosegrass has a smaller membranous ligule (≤2 mm) that is cleft in the center. In vegetative stages other large bunch-type grasses may appear similar but can be differentiated from orchardgrass by the distinctive inflorescence.

Orchardgrass
habit

A. Senesac

Orchardgrass
collar region
The Scotts Company

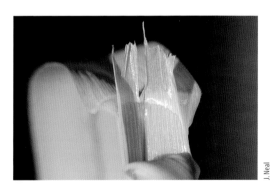

Orchardgrass ligule and collar

J. Neal

Orchardgrass inflorescences

J. Neal

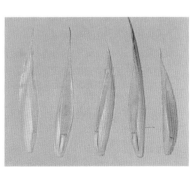

Orchardgrass seeds, 8 mm

J. DiTomaso

53

Large crabgrass (*Digitaria sanguinalis* (L.) Scop.)

SYNONYM: hairy crabgrass

GENERAL DESCRIPTION: A **summer annual** that can grow **prostrate** and spreading **or ascending** to 1 m in height.

PROPAGATION / PHENOLOGY: Reproduction is **by seeds**; seeds germinate from mid-spring through late summer. Vegetative spread can occur by rooting stems, but it is not considered an important means of propagation.

SEEDLING: The first leaf blade is lanceolate to linear, 3–4 times longer than wide, and opens parallel to the ground. Crabgrass seedlings are upright. Leaves are linear with tapered leaf tips, and are about 10 times longer than wide (5–12 cm long by 4–10 mm wide). **Leaves are rolled in the bud**, **lack auricles**, and have a **jagged, membranous ligule. Stiff hairs on the blade and sheath are at a 90° angle to the plant surface.** The collar is broad with long hairs at the margin.

MATURE PLANT: **Leaves and ligule are similar to those of seedlings. Blades** are about 12 times longer than wide (3–20 cm long by 3–14 mm wide) and have **hairs on both surfaces and on the sheath**. More mature plants have **compressed sheaths**. Tillering begins after the 4–5 true-leaf stage (late spring, early summer). Tiller internodes elongate later in the season (mid- to late summer). **Elongated stems root at the nodes.** On maturing plants, older sheaths and leaves may turn dark red or maroon.

ROOTS AND UNDERGROUND STRUCTURES: Roots are fibrous, with adventitious roots arising from the nodes of elongated tillers.

FLOWERS AND FRUIT: Flowers occur in mid- to late summer. The **seedhead commonly consists of 3–5(–13) spikes clustered at the top of stems.** Spikelets are elliptic and in 2 rows along the spike. Each spikelet contains a single shiny, yellow-brown seed (2–3 mm long).

POSTSENESCENCE CHARACTERISTICS: Large crabgrass dies with the first killing frost and appears as brown patches in an otherwise green lawn. It is recognized by long, wire-like "stems" and seedheads that persist well into the winter.

HABITAT: Large crabgrass is a common weed of most agronomic and horticultural crops as well as turf and landscapes. It can tolerate poor, dry conditions but is found in nearly every soil type and crop. It is also common along roads and in waste areas.

DISTRIBUTION: Common throughout the United States and other temperate and tropical regions of the world.

SIMILAR SPECIES: **Smooth crabgrass (*Digitaria ischaemum* Schreb. ex Muhl.)** is similar to large crabgrass but has few hairs on the blade and sheath and is generally smaller. **Southern crabgrass (*Digitaria ciliaris* (Retz.) Koel.)** has hairs on the sheaths but lacks hairs on the blades and is more common in the southeastern than in the northeastern United States. Later in the season, large crabgrass may lack hairs on some leaf blades, which makes it very difficult to distinguish from southern crabgrass. On large crabgrass spikelets, the upper glume is only ⅓ to ½ as long as the spikelet under magnification. In contrast, on southern crabgrass the upper glume will be > ½ as long as the spikelet.

Large crabgrass habit

J. Neal

Large crabgrass seedling

J. Neal

Large crabgrass seedling
(2 tillers)

R. Uva

Spikelets: *left*, large
crabgrass; *right*,
southern crabgrass

Syngenta Crop Protection AG

Smooth crabgrass seedhead

J. DiTomaso

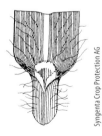

Large crabgrass
collar region

Syngenta Crop Protection AG

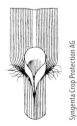

Smooth
crabgrass
collar region

Syngenta Crop Protection AG

Southern
crabgrass
collar
region

Syngenta Crop Protection AG

Left to right: southern crabgrass
seeds, 2.8 mm (with lemma);
smooth crabgrass seeds, 1.9 mm
(with lemma); and large crabgrass
seeds, 2.6 mm (with lemma)

J. DiTomaso

Barnyardgrass (*Echinochloa crus-galli* (L.) Beauv.)

SYNONYMS: watergrass, cockspur grass, panic-grass, summergrass, billion dollargrass

GENERAL DESCRIPTION: A **summer annual** with erect, thick, **clump-forming** stems (1.5 m tall). In turf, plants grow prostrate to produce a mat-like rosette.

PROPAGATION / PHENOLOGY: Reproduction is **by seeds**; seeds germinate in early spring to mid-summer.

SEEDLING: The first leaf blade is linear and opens parallel to the ground. **Leaves are rolled in the bud, lack auricles,** and **have no ligule.** Blades are 7–14 cm long by 3–5 mm wide, smooth on both surfaces, with rough margins. Sheaths are somewhat compressed, tinted maroon toward the base, and usually smooth but occasionally with hairs at the base. The collar is green and smooth.

MATURE PLANT: **Leaves are similar to those of seedlings,** and **ligules are absent.** Blades are 10–20 cm long by 5–20 mm wide, lack hairs, and are smooth to somewhat rough on both surfaces. The **midvein is distinct** and keeled in the basal portions of the leaf. **Sheaths are open, compressed,** and smooth but sometimes have a tuft of short hair at the base. The collar is whitish, broad, and smooth.

ROOTS AND UNDERGROUND STRUCTURES: **Roots are fibrous** and shallow. Tillers often form adventitious roots where they touch the soil.

FLOWERS AND FRUIT: Flowering occurs from July through September. The **seedhead is a coarsely branched green to purplish panicle.** Spikelets are single-seeded, barbed along the nerves, and can have a long terminal awn (2–10 mm). The length of the awns varies among biotypes. The seed is shiny, oval (3–4 mm long), and brownish, with longitudinal ridges.

POSTSENESCENCE CHARACTERISTICS: Plants are killed by the first frost. The large, thick stems and fan shape of tillers remain well into winter.

HABITAT: Barnyardgrass is a very common weed in irrigated crops, including turf, landscape, nursery, and agricultural crops. It is **usually found on moist, rich soils** and is common in cultivated areas, ditches, and waste places.

DISTRIBUTION: Found throughout much of the United States, Canada, and Mexico.

SIMILAR SPECIES: **Junglerice (*Echinochloa colona* (L.) Link)** is a Eurasian summer annual similar to barnyardgrass and occurs in the same type of habitats but is not as common. It is often more prostrate but can also grow erect. Typically junglerice has purplish, transverse bands along the blade, but this is not always the case. In addition, the first inflorescence branches are shorter (1–3 cm) than barnyardgrass (3–7 cm). It is found sporadically through the southeastern, northeastern, and mid-Atlantic states. **Johnsongrass (*Sorghum halepense*)** and **fall panicum (*Panicum dichotomiflorum*)** have coarse-textured foliage and may resemble barnyardgrass in their mature forms, but both johnsongrass and fall panicum have a distinct ligule.

Barnyardgrass habit

Barnyardgrass collar

Junglerice inflorescence

Barnyardgrass inflorescence

Junglerice leaf blade

Left to right: barnyardgrass seeds and junglerice seeds

57

Goosegrass (*Eleusine indica* (L.) Gaertn.)

Synonyms: silver crabgrass, wire-grass, yard-grass, crowfoot-grass, crows foot grass, bullgrass

General Description: A **summer annual** that usually produces a **prostrate, mat-like rosette** with stems radiating from a central point but can grow erect to 60 cm in height. The **flattened leaf sheaths in the rosette** are **whitish to silvery**, hence the common synonym silver crabgrass.

Propagation / Phenology: Reproduction is **by seeds**; seeds germinate in early to midsummer when soil temperatures are above 18°C (65°F). **Goosegrass usually germinates 2–3 weeks later than crabgrass.**

Seedling: The first leaf blade is about 3–5 times longer than wide and opens parallel to the ground. **Leaves are folded in the bud, lack auricles, and have a short, membranous, unevenly toothed ligule (≤1 mm) that is cleft in the center.** Blades are 2–4.5 cm long by 3–5 mm wide, smooth on both surfaces, strongly folded along the midrib, and have distinct individual veins. **Sheaths are smooth, prominently compressed, and light green to white at the base.** The collar is broad and hairless.

Mature Plant: **Leaves are similar to those of seedlings.** The **ligule is membranous** (1–2 mm long) and **cleft in the center. Blades are folded along the midvein** (5–20 cm long by 3–6 mm wide), **smooth** or occasionally sparsely hairy on both surfaces, and have rough margins. The loosely overlapping **sheaths are smooth** to sparsely hairy toward the ligule and **whitish at the base.** The **collar is broad**, white, and sparsely hairy at the edges.

Roots and Underground Structures: The **root system is fibrous.** Goosegrass does not root at the nodes.

Flowers and Fruit: Flowers are produced from June through September. Seedheads mature in late summer through early autumn but persist into winter. **Seedheads consist of 2–6(–10) spikes in clusters at the top of stems. Spikelets are flattened in 2 rows** along the spike and contain 3–6 reddish-brown to black seeds (1–1.8 mm long).

Postsenescence Characteristics: Goosegrass dies after the first hard frost. Characteristic flat tillers radiating from a central point and seedheads persist well into winter.

Habitat: Goosegrass is a common weed of turf, nursery, landscape, and agricultural crops. It is also found in gardens, roadsides, and waste areas on most soil types. **It tolerates close mowing, compacted soils, and drought.**

Distribution: Found throughout the southern United States, extending northward to Massachusetts, North Dakota, Utah, and along the West Coast.

Similar Species: **Crowfootgrass (*Dactyloctenium aegyptium* (L.) Willd.)** is a summer annual with similar growth habit and inflorescence. It has rolled vernation; ligules are membranous, 0.5–1 mm tall with a short fringe of hairs along the top. In contrast, goosegrass has folded vernation and ligules are not hairy on the top. The inflorescence is branched like goosegrass but all branches are from a single point, whereas goosegrass often has an additional branch below the others. Crowfootgrass is more common in the southeastern coastal plains but present in many eastern states. Native to Africa. **Crabgrasses (*Digitaria* spp.)** are similar in overall growth habit, but leaves are rolled in the bud. **Orchardgrass (*Dactylis glomerata*)** is a perennial with strongly compressed sheaths and leaves folded in the bud, but it has a much larger ligule (5–7 mm) than goosegrass.

Goosegrass habit

A. DiTommaso

J. Neal

Goosegrass inflorescence

J. Neal

Crowfootgrass inflorescence

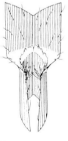

Syngenta Crop Protection AG

Goosegrass
collar region

Syngenta Crop Protection AG

Crowfootgrass
collar region

J. Neal

Goosegrass seedling

J. O'Brien © 2007 UC Regents

Goosegrass spikelet and
seeds, 1.7 mm

Quackgrass (*Elymus repens* (L.) Gould)

Synonyms: *Agropyron repens*, *Elytrigia repens*, quitch grass, couch grass, wheat-grass, shelly-grass, knot-grass, devils-grass, scutch-grass, quick grass

General Description: A **rhizomatous perennial** that generally grows erect (1.2 m high), bending at the nodes. It can tolerate mowing.

Propagation / Phenology: Reproduction is **by seeds and rhizomes**.

Seedling: The first leaf blade is narrow, about 90 times longer than wide, and opens perpendicular to the ground. **Leaves are rolled in the bud; auricles are present** but may be undeveloped and difficult to see on very young seedlings. The **ligule is membranous and very short (0.4 mm long).** Blades are 10–20 cm long by 2–2.5 mm wide, hairy to smooth on the upper surface, and smooth on the lower surface. **Sheaths can also be hairy or smooth.** When present, hairs are short (<0.5 mm); they are most numerous on the lower parts of very young seedlings but are most obvious on the blade and sheath of the first leaf. The collar is whitish and divided by prominent veins.

Mature Plant: **Leaves are rolled in the bud; auricles are narrow, slender, and clasp the stem. The ligule is membranous and very short (<1 mm).** Blades are 4–30 cm long by 3–10 mm wide, flat, hairy to smooth on the upper surface and smooth on the lower surface. **Sheaths are rounded and smooth,** but **those near the base of the plant may have short hairs.** The collar is broad.

Roots and Underground Structures: Fibrous roots arise at the nodes of the **long, sharp-tipped rhizomes**.

Flowers and Fruit: Plants flower in June and July. The **seedhead is a long spike** (5–20 cm). Spikelets are 4–6 seeded and 1–1.5 cm long, arranged in 2 rows along the axis. Awns are usually present and are 0.5–10 mm long.

Postsenescence Characteristics: This perennial grass remains green year-round.

Habitat: Quackgrass is a weed of most agronomic and horticultural crops as well as turf, nurseries, and landscapes. It grows in cultivated fertile soil, areas where reduced tillage is practiced, and waste areas.

Distribution: Found throughout much of the northern United States and Canada, except South Carolina and Florida west to southern Arizona.

Similar Species: **Tall fescue (*Schedonorus arundinaceus*) and the ryegrasses (*Lolium* spp.)** are similar to quackgrass and may have auricles present, but they lack elongated rhizomes and grow in clumps.

Quackgrass habit in corn

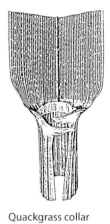

Quackgrass collar region

Quackgrass rhizome

uackgrass inflorescence

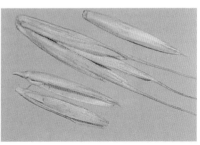

Quackgrass seeds, 9 mm
(including lemma)

Stinkgrass (*Eragrostis cilianensis* (All.) Vign. ex Janch)

Synonyms: *Eragrostis major, Eragrostis megastachya, Poa cilianensis*, candy grass, snakegrass

General Description: Tufted, **summer annual** to 0.6 m tall. At maturity, the plants are dominated by numerous, fairly dense panicles. Plants typically have a strong, **unpleasant, musky scent**. Reportedly poisonous to livestock but plants are typically avoided.

Propagation / Phenology: **Reproduces by an abundant amount of seed.** The extremely small seeds fall near the parent plant and disperse to greater distances by way of water, soil movement, and human activities such as agricultural operations and landscape maintenance. Most seeds germinate in spring shortly after crabgrass emerges.

Seedling: Leaves **rolled in the bud, ligule is a fringe of hairs**, sheath is open and glabrous except for a few long, wispy hairs at the collar. Glands, when present, are minute, slightly raised to wart-like bumps with a pit at the center; easiest to see with 20x magnification.

Mature Plant: Stems often spreading, sometimes branched, slightly flattened to round in cross section, bent at the lower nodes, with a **glandular area just below most nodes. Leaf blades are 10–20 cm long by 2–8 mm wide**, glabrous and sometimes waxy on the underside, and **margins and usually the midvein of lower surface are lined with minute glands, especially near the base.** Sheaths and sometimes lower blades sparsely longhairy. Sheaths usually at least sparsely glandular, with tufts of long hairs at the collar margin. Ciliate ligules 0.4–1 mm long. Auricles lacking.

Roots and Underground Structures: Root systems are fibrous, often shallow.

Flowers and Fruit: Plants flower, often prolifically, in summer through early autumn. Panicles usually slightly open, dense, mostly 5–20 cm long. Spikelets 5–18 mm long, 2.5–3 mm wide, narrowly lanceolate or oblong, flattened, lack awns, and consist of few to many closely overlapping florets. Most spikelet stalks lack glands. Glumes and lemmas keeled and have 1 or more glands. Florets (5)10–45 per spikelet, 2–2.5 mm long. Seeds ovoid to spherical, 0.6 mm long, smooth, orange-brown.

Postsenescence Characteristics: Tufts of tan, desiccated foliage and flowering stems may persist for a short time.

Habitat: Disturbed places, agronomic and vegetable crop fields, orchards, roadsides, pastures, waste places, and urban sites. Often grows in sandy soil.

Distribution: Not very common nor particularly weedy in most areas but reports of naturalized populations are increasing. Found throughout the Northeast, mid-Atlantic states, and southern Canada. Native to Europe.

Similar Species: **Tufted lovegrass (*Eragrostis pectinacea* (Michx.) Nees ex Steud.)** is also a summer annual with open panicles. Unlike stinkgrass, it **lacks glands** and **does not have an unpleasant scent**. In addition, it has much smaller spikelets (5–8 mm long by 1.2–2 mm wide) and fewer florets (5–15) compared to stinkgrass. It is native throughout North America and sometimes weedy. **Lacegrass (*Eragrostis capillaris* (L.) Nees)** is also an annual that lacks glands. It has spikelets even smaller than tufted lovegrass (2–5 mm long by 1–1.3 mm wide) with fewer florets per spikelet (2–5). It is also native to the eastern United States and grows in open, dry, sandy riverbanks, floodplains, and roadsides. Plants may resemble **barnyardgrass (*Echinochloa crus-galli*)**, but barnyardgrass lacks ligules, is more robust, and the spikelets are noticeably larger. *Eragrostis* species may be mistaken for several panicums, with similar inflorescences and ciliate ligules. Unlike *Eragrostis* spp., **fall panicum (*Panicum dichotomiflorum*)** lacks long hairs at the collar, and **witchgrass (*Panicum capillare*)** has densely pubescent sheaths and blades.

J. DiTomaso

Stinkgrass habit

J. DiTomaso

Tufted lovegrass collar and sheath

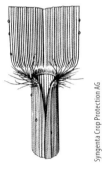

Syngenta Crop Protection AG

Stinkgrass collar region

Syngenta Crop Protection AG

Tufted lovegrass collar region

J. DiTomaso

Stinkgrass inflorescence

J. DiTomaso

Tufted lovegrass inflorescence

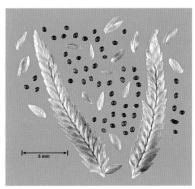

5 mm

J. O'Brien © 2007 UC Regents

Stinkgrass seeds and spikelets

63

Common velvetgrass (*Holcus lanatus* L.)

Synonym: velvet-grass

General Description: A **clump-forming perennial** with **grayish-green**, **velvety foliage.** It may grow prostrate in turf or erect to 1 m tall.

Propagation / Phenology: Reproduction is **by seeds. Clumps enlarge rapidly by aggressive tillering.**

Seedling: The first leaf blade opens perpendicular to the ground. **Leaves are rolled in the bud, lack auricles, and have a membranous ligule (1.5 mm),** which is jagged at the top. **Blades** are 3.5–9 cm long by 1 mm wide and **covered with short hairs** (<0.5 mm long) **on both surfaces. Sheaths are slightly compressed, with short hairs** at a 90° angle to the surface. Hairs are less noticeable as they progress up the plant. The base of the sheath and the collar are white.

Mature Plant: **Leaves are similar to those of seedlings, but the ligule is somewhat larger** (1–4 mm) **and hairy on the back surface. Blades** are 4–20 cm long by 4–10 mm wide, pale green, flat, covered with **dense, soft hairs. Sheaths are also velvety hairy**, pink-nerved, compressed, and slightly keeled, with margins open almost to the base. Collars are hairy and narrow.

Roots and Underground Structures: **Root system is fibrous.**

Flowers and Fruit: Flowers occur from June through August. **Seedheads are soft-hairy, grayish, purple-tinged panicles** (5–15 cm long by 1–8 cm wide) **produced on hairy stems.** At maturity, panicles dry to a light tan color. Spikelets are 2-seeded (4 mm long) with an awn (1–2 mm) on the second floret. The awn becomes curved or hooked when dry.

Postsenescence Characteristics: As older leaves senesce in autumn and winter, portions of the clumps turn yellow, but some leaves remain green.

Habitat: Common velvetgrass is a weed of low-maintenance turf, forage crops, and orchards. It often grows on damp, rich soil in open areas of meadows, fields, and roadsides. In addition to moist, poorly drained, and acidic soils, it can tolerate a wide range of other conditions, including drought.

Distribution: Common on the West Coast and in the eastern United States extending from Virginia to Mississippi, and into Ohio, Indiana, and Illinois. Not as common in the extreme northern states.

Similar Species: The dense coating of velvety soft hairs on the blade and sheath of common velvetgrass easily distinguishes it from most other grasses, except **downy brome (*Bromus tectorum*).** However, mature downy brome is an annual that lacks hairs on the back of the ligule. In addition, leaves of young common velvetgrass are not twisted.

Common velvetgrass habit

J. DiTomaso

J. Neal

Common
velvetgrass
inflorescence

Common velvetgrass
collar region

Syngenta Crop Protection AG

J. DiTomaso

Common velvetgrass hairy stem
and foliage

J. O'Brien © 2007 UC Regents

Common velvetgrass seeds, 2.5 mm
(largest)

65

Cogongrass (*Imperata cylindrica* (L.) Beauv.)

Synonyms: blady grass, Japanese bloodgrass, kunai grass

General Description: A **perennial**, **rhizomatous grass** with nodding stems (0.5–1.5 m in height) that can form dense stands that expand in a circular fashion. Plants produce a distinctive, **fluffy seedhead**. A cultivated variety, 'Red Baron', is used in landscaping. This cultivar has showy, purplish-red leaves and flowers rarely but may revert to green, floriferous "wild type" with age. Cogongrass is **a federal noxious weed**. Many states also regulate the cultivated variety.

Propagation / Phenology: Reproduction is by **wind-dispersed seeds**, from expanding **rhizomes**, and from rhizome fragments. The fluffy seeds are also easily dispersed on mowing equipment. Viable seeds are produced only by cross pollination. Seeds have no dormancy and germinate within a month after ripening.

Seedling: In the habitats commonly invaded by cogongrass, seedlings are inconspicuous. When present, seedlings are rolled in the bud, have a membranous ligule with a ragged top and a fringe of short hairs.

Mature Plant: Has no apparent stem other than the flowering stalk. Leaf blades are basal, 1–3 cm wide and to 200 cm long, and have rough, **finely serrated margins**. Blade tips sharply pointed. Sheaths are hairless to densely hairy. **Ligules membranous** (0.5–1 mm long **with a fringe of hairs**). High silica content gives the leaves a coarse texture. **Blades have a distinctive, off-center, white midrib** (may be inconspicuous on younger leaves). **Upper leaf surfaces are hairy near the base** of the blade; undersides of blades are hairless.

Roots and Underground Structures: A dense and extensive **fibrous root system and thicker rhizomes**. Rhizomes are segmented with short internodes and flaky scales. Produces many **sharp rhizome tips**, which can pierce the roots of other plants. Length varies depending on soil type but can reach up to 1 m in loose soils.

Flowers and Fruit: Flower and seed production varies between populations, and some populations do not flower at all. Flowering generally occurs from early to late spring in warmer climates. The **seedhead** is a large, **cylindrical panicle** (10–20 cm long) of awnless, paired spikelets. Each spikelet has a fringe of white, silky hairs (12 mm long), giving the seedhead a **fluffy appearance**. Seeds are brown, oblong, and 1–1.3 mm long.

Postsenescence characteristics: After frost, dead vegetation is persistent through winter. Dead leaves form dense mats of thatch that suppress other vegetation and may create a fire hazard in areas with burning regimes.

Habitat: A weed of disturbed areas, roadsides, meadows, and pastures. Cogongrass is well adapted to fire and has invaded southeastern pine-oak communities that experience frequent fire events. Cogongrass is shade- and drought-tolerant and can grow in areas of high salinity.

Distribution: Found throughout the southeastern United States with isolated reports of plants as far north as Virginia. New infestations should be reported to appropriate state authorities.

Similar Species: Vegetatively, cogongrass may resemble many robust perennial grasses. Cogongrass generally flowers earlier than similar grasses. **Johnsongrass (*Sorghum halepense*)** has similar leaves but has a central rather than offset midvein. In addition, Johnsongrass has leafy stems, whereas cogongrass leaves are basal. The young inflorescence may resemble that of **foxtails (*Setaria* spp.)**, but the entire inflorescence is denser. Foxtails do not form fluffy seeds.

Cogongrass infestation

N. Loewenstein, Auburn University

Cogongrass immature inflorescence

B. Lassiter

Cogongrass seedhead

B. Lassiter

Cogongrass crown with tillers and rhizomes

B. Lassiter

Cogongrass rhizomes have a sharp tip

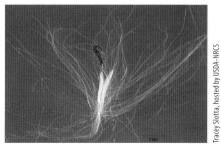

Tracey Slotta, hosted by USDA-NRCS PLANTS Database

Cogongrass seed

Italian ryegrass (*Lolium multiflorum* Lam.)

Synonyms: *Lolium italicum, Lolium perenne* ssp. *multiflorum*, annual ryegrass, Australian rye

General Description: An **erect, clump-forming, winter annual** reaching 1 m in height, but will tolerate close mowing.

Propagation / Phenology: Reproduction is **by seeds**; seeds germinate from early to late spring and late summer into mid-autumn.

Seedling: The first leaf blade is long and narrow, oriented perpendicular with the soil surface. **Leaves are rolled in the bud; auricles are usually present but may be absent on very young seedlings, and the ligule is membranous (2 mm long).** Blades are about 50 times as long as wide (10–14 cm long by 2–3 mm wide), lack hairs, and have prominently raised veins. Sheaths are also smooth and often reddish at the base.

Mature Plant: **Auricles are narrow, long, and claw-like. Blades** are long and tapered (6–20 cm long by 4–10 mm wide), **glossy below and rough above**, with prominent veins and smooth margins. Sheaths are rounded, and the collar is broad.

Roots and Underground Structures: The **root system is fibrous.** Stems do not root at the nodes.

Flowers and Fruit: The **seedhead is a terminal spike** (10–40 cm long). The **spikelets are placed alternately along the flowering stem.** Each spikelet is 1.5–2.5 cm long and consists of 10–20 florets and **long awns (5–8 mm). Spikelets contain only 1 glume**.

Postsenescence Characteristics: Senescence occurs in warm, dry weather, usually after seed maturation. Foliage turns yellow, then straw-colored.

Habitat: Italian ryegrass is a weed of grain, turf, nursery, and other cool-season or perennial crops. It is also found in waste areas and cultivated crops in most soil types.

Distribution: Occurs throughout the United States.

Similar Species: **Perennial ryegrass (*Lolium perenne* L.)** is shorter (30–60 cm tall), has small or malformed auricles, has spikelets with 6–10 florets, and is a **perennial. Awns are often absent or greatly reduced.** Italian ryegrass is more robust in habit than perennial ryegrass. **Quackgrass (*Elymus repens*)** also has awns and a seedhead that can look similar to that of ryegrass. However, quackgrass is a rhizomatous perennial with spikelets subtended by 2 basal bracts (glumes), whereas all species of ryegrass have only 1 basal bract.

Italian ryegrass habit

J. Neal

Italian ryegrass
collar region

Syngenta Crop Protection AG

Perennial ryegrass
collar region

Syngenta Crop Protection AG

Italian ryegrass
inflorescence

J. Neal

Perennial ryegrass inflorescence

J. Neal

Left, Italian ryegrass seeds,
6.5 mm (not including awn);
right, perennial ryegrass seeds
(without awn), 6.0 mm

J. O'Brien © 2007 UC Regents

5 mm

Japanese stiltgrass (*Microstegium vimineum* (Trinius) A. Camus)

SYNONYMS: flexible sasagrass, Nepalese brown top, Mary's grass, bamboograss, and others

GENERAL DESCRIPTION: A **shade-tolerant**, prostrate to erect, sprawling, and freely branched **summer annual** with spreading stems that root at the lower nodes. The **stems are stiff and climb over other vegetation**, reaching >1 m in height but remains prostrate if mowed.

PROPAGATION / PHENOLOGY: Reproduces by seeds. Seeds germinate in early spring, and flowers and seeds from mid-September through October. Japanese stiltgrass can produce large numbers of seeds:16,000–50,000 per square meter. Seeds spread by water, animals, and human activities (hikers' clothing, mowing equipment, and so forth). Germination does not require light.

SEEDLING: Young seedlings easily distinguished from other summer annual grasses by the **very broad, rounded first leaf**. Subsequent leaves are broadly elliptic, wider than most other grasses. Leaves are **rolled in the bud; ligules are short (~0.5 mm), membranous, with hairs on the backside.** Auricles are absent. **Leaf blades are broader than many other grasses**, particularly under shady conditions.

MATURE PLANT: Leaves on older plants are narrowly elliptic, about 8 times longer than wide (3–8 cm long by 5–10 mm wide), sparsely hairy on the upper surface, and hairless or nearly so on the underside. The sheath has a hairy margin and the collar region is hairy, but otherwise lacks hairs. Stems are wiry, smooth, and glossy, often reddish, branching and rooting at the lower nodes. The plants can form dense mats more than 30 cm thick in forests but may climb to more than 1.5 m where objects provide a "ladder."

ROOTS AND UNDERGROUND STRUCTURES: Shallow, fibrous root system. Stems are weakly attached to roots.

FLOWERS AND FRUIT: Flowers in autumn in a branched spike, with 1–3 (rarely 6) branches, each 3–5 cm long. Inconspicuous flowers are also produced within leaf sheaths. Spikelets are in pairs on the rachis, each 4.5–6 mm long and hairy, one sessile and the other on a short pedicel. Only one of the spikelets in each pair is fertile; the fertile one sometimes has a slender awn 4–8 mm long. At least some of those flowers are cleistogamous (self-fertilized before the flower opens). This adaptation requires early removal before seedheads are visible to prevent seed production.

POSTSENESCENCE CHARACTERISTICS: Dead plants leave a tan-colored, straw-like mulch in forest floors. The straw persists through winter and into spring and early summer.

HABITAT: Most common in shady, moist areas including wetlands, woodlands, parks, ditch banks, utility rights-of-way, mulched landscape beds, and low-maintenance turf. Infestations typically begin in disturbed sites but once established can spread to undisturbed areas.

DISTRIBUTION: Native to East Asia. Now widely distributed throughout the eastern United States from northern Georgia to New England.

SIMILAR SPECIES: **Basketgrass (*Arthraxon hispidus* (Thunb.) Makino)** grows in similar habitats throughout most of the mid-Atlantic and Northeast. Basketgrass leaves clasp the stem and have hairy leaf sheaths whereas stiltgrass leaves taper at the base and sheaths are hairless. **Wavyleaf basketgrass (*Oplismenus hirtellus* (L.) P. Beauv. ssp. *undulatifolius* (Ard.) Scholz)** is a stoloniferous perennial. Leaves have wavy undulations and hairs on the sheath, and florets have long awns. Currently only documented in Maryland and Virginia but likely spreading.

Japanese stiltgrass habit

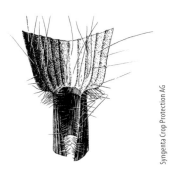

Japanese stiltgrass collar region

Japanese stiltgrass inflorescence

Japanese stiltgrass
young shoot

Japanese stiltgrass seedlings

Basketgrass young shoot

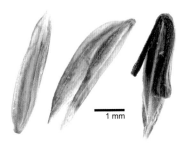

Japanese stiltgrass seeds

1 mm

71

Eulaliagrass or miscanthus (*Miscanthus sinensis* Anderss.)

Synonyms: Chinese silvergrass, Japanese silvergrass

General Description: A **tall**, **tufted perennial grass** that can reach 3 m in height, but typically grows to approximately **2 m tall**, with **floral plumes**. It was first introduced as an ornamental in the late 1800s, and many cultivars are still widely sold in the nursery trade. Native to China, Japan, and Korea.

Propagation / Phenology: Plants spread by **wind-dispersed seeds** and vegetatively through expansion of the clumps. Self-infertile, so isolated plants produce very few viable seeds; however, cross-pollination produces copious viable seeds. Some sterile varieties are available.

Seedling: Seedlings are rarely noticed and are inconspicuous. Leaves are rolled in the bud, ligule is short and membranous, leaves and sheaths are mostly hairless except for some hairs in the collar throat region.

Mature Plant: Plants form large clumps; the bases of the clumps are dense. Plant stems are flexible and often spread or droop, **forming a large, cascading mass of foliage**. The **leaf blades are mostly basal**, **up to 1 m long**, 2–2.5 cm wide, and have a **silvery white midrib**. Tips of the leaves are sharp and re-curving, and the margins are rough.

Roots and Underground Structures: Plants have dense fibrous roots and short, thick rhizomes. Root system is so dense, removal of an established clump is difficult without mechanical aid.

Flowers and Fruit: Plants flower in late summer to early fall on erect stems. The **terminal panicle** is fan-shaped, with **soft-hairy plumes**, 15–25 cm long, **silvery to pink**, with ≥15 erect or ascending branches. Branches of the panicle are clusters of racemes, each 10–20 cm long. Individual spikelets lack hairs, are yellow-brown, and are encircled at the base with white or purple hairs. Fertile lemma is 2–3 mm long with an awn 8–10 mm long, spirally twisted at its base.

Postsenescence Characteristics: Dried, senescenced vegetation is yellowish to tan. Stems and many leaves remain intact with the distinctive inflorescences through winter and into spring.

Habitat: Found along roadsides, forest edges, pastures, old fields, and other disturbed areas. Plants often depend on disturbance to become established, and prefer full sun and moist, rich, well-drained soils.

Distribution: Found throughout the eastern United States and adjacent Canada and is particularly invasive in the southern Appalachians.

Similar Species: Many selected cultivars are in the horticultural trade, and some are sterile. **Amur silvergrass (*Miscanthus sacchariflorus* (Maxim.) Franch.)** is very similar, 2.5 m tall, and rhizomatous. Unlike eulaliagrass, it has longer rhizomes that give it a less tufted appearance, and the hairs at the base of the spikelet are twice as long as eulaliagrass (miscanthus). Its lemmas are awnless, and inflorescences are always white, whereas eulaliagrass can be present in many different colors, depending on the cultivar. It is also native to Asia and is found in Maine, Massachusetts, Connecticut, the Great Lakes states, and adjacent Canadian Provinces. **Giant miscanthus (*Miscanthus × giganteus* J.M. Greef & Deuter)** is a triploid sterile hybrid planted as a biofuel crop. The hybrid is very robust and forms dense stands. Lack of viable seeds limits it spread; however, a fertile selection of this hybrid has been developed.

Miscanthus habit

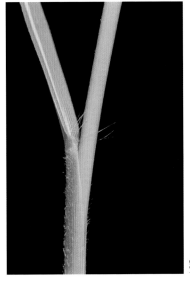

Miscanthus collar and sheath

Miscanthus in winter

Miscanthus inflorescence

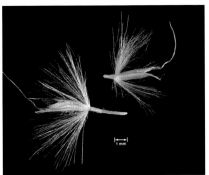

Miscanthus seeds

Wirestem muhly (*Muhlenbergia frondosa* (Poir.) Fern.)

Synonyms: *Muhlenbergia commutata*, *Muhlenbergia mexicana*, mexican drop-seed, satin-grass, wood-grass, knot-root-grass

General Description: A **rhizomatous perennial** that is erect (1 m tall) to sprawling or prostrate. Plants can appear bushy and top-heavy.

Propagation / Phenology: Reproduction is **by creeping rhizomes and by seeds**, which germinate in early to late spring.

Seedling: Seedlings are flat, rough to the touch, and have short blades. **Leaves are rolled in the bud, auricles are absent, and ligules are membranous (0.8–1.5 mm long) and torn or jagged across the top.**

Mature Plant: **Leaves and ligule are similar to those of the seedling. Stems are branched and stiff, with a wiry appearance.** Internodes are smooth and shiny. **Blades are short** (10 cm long by 3–7 mm wide) and **flat**, lack hairs, and have rough margins. **Sheaths** also lack hairs; they are rounded and **shorter than the stem internodes.** The base of the stem bends abruptly and touches the ground, often rooting at the lower nodes.

Roots and Underground Structures: **Fibrous roots** are present at the lower stem nodes and the nodes of **short, thick, scaly rhizomes.**

Flowers and Fruit: Flowers are produced from August to October. **Spikelets are very small** (3 mm) and are produced **in condensed panicles** located at the terminal end of the stems and from the leaf sheaths. Panicles are 3–10 cm long by 0.5–1 cm wide. Terminal panicles are slightly longer than the upper leaf blades; axillary panicles are smaller than the terminal panicles and may be partially covered by the leaf sheath. Spikelets are soft and green or brown to purplish, and, when present, awns are slender (2–7 mm long).

Postsenescence Characteristics: Short, wiry leaves and stems remain intact throughout the winter with the remnants of seedheads still attached within the sheaths.

Habitat: Wirestem muhly is a weed of nursery crops, orchards, vegetables, landscapes, and occasionally agronomic crops. It also grows in waste areas, roadsides, ditches, and streambanks, often on moist, rich soils.

Distribution: Found throughout the northeastern United States, west to North Dakota, and south to Georgia and Texas.

Similar Species: Can resemble **nimblewill (*Muhlenbergia schreberi*)**, although wirestem muhly is more robust, up to 2–3 times as tall. Also, nimblewill lacks scaly rhizomes. **Bermudagrass (*Cynodon dactylon*)** has similar gray-green foliage and spreading habit but has a ciliate ligule; both *Muhlenbergia* species have membranous ligules.

Wirestem muhly emerging from rhizome

Wirestem muhly foliage

R. Uva

W. Curran

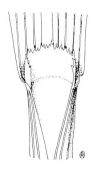

Wirestem muhly
collar region
Bente Starcke King

R. Uva

Wirestem muhly roots and rhizome

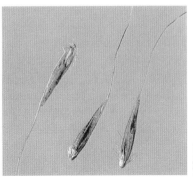

J. DiTomaso

Wirestem muhly seeds, 2.5 mm (not
including awn)

Nimblewill (*Muhlenbergia schreberi* J.F. Gmel.)

SYNONYMS: wire-grass, drop-seed

GENERAL DESCRIPTION: A mat-forming, **stoloniferous, coarse-textured perennial. The foliage is grayish-green.** Stems are erect when young but become branched with age, spreading and bending, and rooting at the nodes. Tips of developed blades strongly arch toward the soil. In unmowed areas, nimblewill grows from 20–60 cm high.

PROPAGATION / PHENOLOGY: Reproduction is from **seeds and stolons**.

SEEDLING: The first leaf blade is linear, tapering gradually to a point, about 5 times longer than wide. It opens parallel to the soil surface and eventually arches downward. **Leaves are rolled in the bud; auricles are absent; and the ligule is membranous, very short (<0.5 mm), and toothed across the top. Blades are 2.5 cm long by 1–2.1 mm wide,** smooth throughout. **Sheaths are smooth, slightly compressed,** and have prominent dark green veins. The collar is white.

MATURE PLANT: **Leaves and ligules are similar to those of the seedling. Blades are short** (2–8 cm long by 2–4 mm wide) **compared with blades of many other grasses** and smooth, except for a few hairs near the ligule. **Sheaths are compressed,** membranous along the margins, and loosely appressed to the stems. The collar is smooth, with long hairs on the edges.

ROOTS AND UNDERGROUND STRUCTURES: Horizontal stems **(stolons) root at the nodes, producing a fine, fibrous root system.** Roots are weakly connected to the stolons and are easily pulled from the ground.

FLOWERS AND FRUIT: Nimblewill flowers from August to October. The **seedheads are spike-like panicles** that are **produced both terminally and at axillary nodes. Panicles are slender,** 5–15 cm long, and flexible. Spikelets are 2 mm long, and the awns (2–5 mm long) are conspicuous. The seed is 1–1.4 mm long.

POSTSENESCENCE CHARACTERISTICS: Nimblewill turns brown in winter; mats of stolons persist and resprout the following spring.

HABITAT: A weed of turf, nurseries, and orchards, nimblewill thrives on moist, rich soil, often in the shade. It is found along shrub borders, fences, and in uncultivated areas. In orchards, nimblewill is abundant where simazine has been used for several years. It rarely grows in conventionally tilled crops because it does not tolerate cultivation well.

DISTRIBUTION: Found from southern Maine, west to Minnesota and Nebraska, and south to Florida and Mexico.

SIMILAR SPECIES: **Bermudagrass (*Cynodon dactylon*)** and **creeping bentgrass (*Agrostis stolonifera* L.)** both resemble nimblewill in growth habit. However, the foliage of creeping bentgrass is finer in texture, the ligule is larger, and no hairs are present around the ligule. Bermudagrass has a ciliate (fringe of hairs) ligule.

Nimblewill habit

J. Neal

Nimblewill
inflorescence

Syngenta Crop Protection AG

Nimblewill collar
region

J. Neal

Nimblewill stolon

Syngenta Crop Protection AG

Creeping
bentgrass collar
region

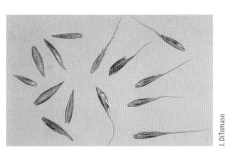

J. DiTomaso

Left, creeping bentgrass seeds (without
awn), 2.5 mm; *right*, wirestem muhly seeds,
2.2 mm (not including awn)

Witchgrass (*Panicum capillare* L.)

SYNONYMS: old witch-grass, tickle-grass, witches-hair, tumble weed-grass, fool-hay

GENERAL DESCRIPTION: A tillering **summer annual**, erect to 80 cm tall, or decumbent, with **characteristically hairy blades and sheaths**.

PROPAGATION / PHENOLOGY: Reproduction is **by seeds**; seeds germinate between late spring and mid-summer.

SEEDLING: The first leaf blade is lanceolate to linear, about 3 times longer than wide and parallel to the soil surface. **Leaves are rolled in the bud, lack auricles, and the ligule is a fringe of hairs** (1–2 mm long). Subsequent leaf blades are 1.5–4 cm long by 4–6 mm wide. **The blade, sheath, and collar are very hairy.** Hairs are relatively stiff and at a 90° angle with the plant surface.

MATURE PLANT: **Leaves, hairs, and ligule are similar to those of seedlings. Blades** (10–25 cm long by 5–15 mm wide) **are hairy on both surfaces**, and the margins are rough. **Sheaths are densely hairy** and may be slightly purplish.

ROOTS AND UNDERGROUND STRUCTURES: **Root system is fibrous.** Tillers root at the base but not at the nodes of elongated shoots.

FLOWERS AND FRUIT: Flowering occurs from July through September. The **seedhead is a large**, **many-branched**, **open panicle** up to half the length of the entire plant (20–40 cm long). Spikelets are 2–4 mm long and produce 1 shiny, smooth, green to dark brown or gray seed (1.5 mm long).

POSTSENESCENCE CHARACTERISTICS: Plants die at first frost, after which the large tillers persist well into the winter. Hairs of the sheaths are distinct well into winter. The panicle may break off and be dispersed by the wind.

HABITAT: Witchgrass is a common weed of agronomic, horticultural, and nursery crops. It is also found in landscapes, gardens, and roadsides, in sandy, dry soil as well as moist, fertile soil.

DISTRIBUTION: Common throughout the United States and southern Canada.

SIMILAR SPECIES: **Fall panicum (*Panicum dichotomiflorum*)** seedlings have densely hairy sheaths, but blades are hairy only on the lower surface. Mature fall panicum blades and sheaths are smooth on both surfaces. Young **large crabgrass (*Digitaria sanguinalis*)** seedlings have hairy sheaths and leaf blades, but crabgrass has a membranous ligule whereas both *Panicum* species have ciliate ligules.

Witchgrass, 5-tiller plant

J. Neal

J. Neal

Witchgrass leaf and sheath hairs

J. DiTomaso

Witchgrass inflorescence

Witchgrass
collar region
Syngenta Crop
Protection AG

J. Neal

Witchgrass seedling

J. DiTomaso

Witchgrass seeds, 2.2 mm with
glumes, 1.4 mm without glumes

Fall panicum (*Panicum dichotomiflorum* Michx.)

SYNONYMS: smooth witchgrass, western witchgrass, sprouting crab-grass

GENERAL DESCRIPTION: A **summer annual** with an erect to sprawling or kneeling habit. It can form large loose tufts and usually grows from 50 cm to 1 m in height.

PROPAGATION / PHENOLOGY: Reproduction is **by seeds**. Seedlings emerge in late spring to mid-summer.

SEEDLING: The first leaf blade is lanceolate to linear, about 5 times longer than wide and opens parallel to the ground. **Leaves are rolled in the bud and lack auricles. The ligule is a fringe of hairs** 1–2 mm long. Blades are 2–3.5 cm long by 5 mm wide. **The first few leaf blades are densely hairy only on the lower surface.** Also, **on the first few leaves, sheaths have dense 1 mm long hairs** and rough margins. **Collars are also densely hairy. Seedlings become less hairy with age and completely lack hairs at maturity.** Plants often have a purplish coloration.

MATURE PLANT: **Leaves are similar to those of seedlings**, and the **ligule is a fringe of hairs** 1–3 mm long. **Stems often have a waxy appearance**, and the swollen and irregular lower nodes give the stem a zigzag appearance. **Blades are smooth on both sides**, dull above and glossy beneath, 10–50 cm long by 5–20 mm wide; **the midvein is conspicuously light green to white. Sheaths are smooth** (rarely hairy), purplish, and slightly compressed. Collars are continuous and broad.

ROOTS AND UNDERGROUND STRUCTURES: **Fibrous root system.** Stems root at the lower nodes.

FLOWERS AND FRUIT: Flowers are produced from July to October. The **seedhead is a large, freely branched, spreading panicle**, 10–40 cm long, which may appear purplish at maturity. Spikelets are 2.5–3 mm long, 2 mm wide, and straw-colored to purple-tinged. Spikelets produce 1 smooth, dull yellow to brown seed (1.5–2 mm long).

POSTSENESCENCE CHARACTERISTICS: Plants die with frost. Stems remain erect for only a short time into winter but persist on the soil surface through the winter and into spring. Remnants of the panicle can remain on the stems. In heavily infested areas, a mulch several inches thick can last until the following spring.

HABITAT: Fall panicum is a weed of cultivated agronomic, vegetable, and nursery crops but can also grow in turfgrass, landscapes, and noncrop areas.

DISTRIBUTION: Found throughout much of the United States.

SIMILAR SPECIES: **Witchgrass (*Panicum capillare*)** is closely related to fall panicum but is very hairy throughout, even at the seedling stage. **Foxtails (*Setaria* spp.)** also have a hairy ligule and can resemble fall panicum in the seedling stage; they can be distinguished by the location of hairs, which are on the lower surface of the fall panicum leaf blade but on the upper surface of foxtail leaf blades or absent altogether. Young foxtail seedlings can be distinguished from those of panicum by seed shape and shininess. Foxtail seeds are fat and dull; panicum seeds are slender and shiny. **Johnsongrass (*Sorghum halapense*)** has a distinctive white midvein and a panicle inflorescence similar to that of fall panicum; however, johnsongrass is a rhizomatous perennial with a membranous ligule that is sometimes fringed at the top.

Fall panicum habit

J. Neal

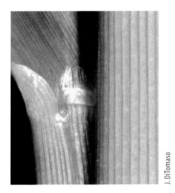

J. DiTomaso

Fall panicum collar and ligule

J. Neal

Fall panicum inflorescence

R. Uva

Fall panicum seedling

J. Neal

Fall panicum leaf

J. K. Clark © 2007 UC Regents

Fall panicum seeds

Wild-proso millet (*Panicum miliaceum* L.)

Synonyms: broomcorn millet, hog millet, panic millet

General Description: A **large, tufted annual grass** (2 m tall) with erect stems branching from the base.

Propagation / Phenology: Reproduction is **by seeds. Seedheads shatter early in the season** and are often spread by harvest equipment.

Seedling: **Leaves are rolled in the bud, and auricles are absent. Ligules are 2–4 mm long, membranous at the base for about half their length, and fringed with hairs (ciliate) at the top. Blades and sheaths are densely covered with stiff hairs.** The **black seed coat persists** under the surface of the soil on very young seedlings.

Mature Plant: **Leaves and ligule are similar to those of the seedling. Blades** are 10–30 cm long by 6–20 mm wide, rounded at the base, and have **long hairs on both surfaces. Sheaths** are open and **densely covered with stiff hairs,** especially on the lower leaves. Sheath margins are hairy, at least near the ligule.

Roots and Underground Structures: Fibrous root system.

Flowers and Fruit: Flowering occurs from July to September. The **seedhead is a pyramidal to cylindrical panicle, rather compact,** nodding or drooping to erect, 10–30 cm long. Spikelets are 4.5–5.3 mm long and produce a single shiny, smooth, yellow or olive-brown to black seed approximately 3 mm long.

Postsenescence Characteristics: Stems, leaves, and inflorescence persist for a considerable time after frost. Inflorescence does not detach from plant. Plants can have a reddish coloration. Seeds remain attached to spikelets.

Habitat: Domesticated forms of proso millet are used as forage in the United States and Europe. Although wild-proso millet is the same species as the domesticated forms, it is a weed of landscapes and of nursery, vegetable, and agronomic crops. It grows rapidly and tolerates sandy, dry soils and high temperatures.

Distribution: Primarily found in the northern, southeastern, south-central, and western United States; also in Canada.

Similar Species: **Seedlings are large and resemble those of volunteer corn (*Zea mays* L.)** but have narrower leaves and are considerably hairier. **Domestic proso millet** has yellow or light brown seeds, whereas those of wild-proso millet are olive-brown to black. Although it also resembles **witchgrass (*Panicum capillare*),** wild-proso millet is considerably larger, especially the inflorescence and spikelets, and its inflorescence does not detach from the plant after senescence as does that of witchgrass.

Wild-proso millet habit

R. R. Hahn

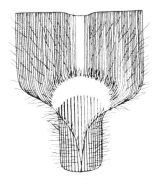

Syngenta Crop Protection AG

Wild-proso millet collar region

J. DiTomaso

Wild-proso millet collar and ligule

R. R. Hahn

Inflorescence: *left*, witchgrass; *right*,
wild-proso millet

J. K. Clark © 2007 UC Regents

Wild proso millet seeds

Dallisgrass (*Paspalum dilatatum* Poir.)

Synonym: caterpillar grass

General Description: A **coarse-textured, clump-forming perennial with short, thick rhizomes.** Center of the clump is often devoid of green leaves. Tolerates frequent mowing but can reach 0.5–1.5 m in height when undisturbed.

Propagation / Phenology: Reproduction is **by seeds**; seedlings emerge in the spring and early summer. Once established, **clumps expand by short rhizomes.**

Seedling: Leaves are **rolled in the bud. Ligule 2–8 mm long and membranous** with a rounded or bluntly pointed tip. Auricles are absent. Blades and sheaths of the first leaves may be softly hairy, but most lack hairs except for long, silky hairs at the collar. Sheaths are flattened with a prominent midrib.

Mature Plant: Robust plants with prostrate or ascending leaves from tillers and short, shallow rhizomes. Mature leaf blades are 10–30 cm long by 6–15 mm wide and **lack hairs,** except for a **few long hairs at the collar. Leaf margins are finely hairy** and rough. **Sheaths lack hairs** (except for the few, older leaves), are **strongly compressed**, with a prominent midvein, and may be tinged red with age. **Collar is broad**, light green, smooth, and often with long hairs at the edges. **Tillers are stout** and do not root at the nodes.

Roots and Underground Structures: Fibrous roots and **short, shallow rhizomes.**

Flowers and Fruit: Plants flower mid-summer to early autumn. **Flowers and seeds are produced on tall** (to 1.5 m), **terminal stalks** (rachis) that bear **3–5** (occasionally more) **spreading or loosely ascending branches** (5–10 cm long). The spikelets are ovate, 3–4 mm long, 2–2.5 mm wide, **covered with silky soft hairs**, and crowded in 4 rows on the racemes. Seeds are oval, shiny, yellow to brown (2.5–3 mm long).

Postsenescence Characteristics: The foliage develops red to maroon pigmentation late in the season. Clumps of straw-colored older leaves and tillers can persist through winter.

Habitat: A major turfgrass weed; also found in pastures, roadsides, and reduced-tillage crops. Well adapted to a variety of soils but most often found in moist sites.

Distribution: Introduced from South America as a forage crop. Widely distributed in the southern and coastal mid-Atlantic states north to New Jersey and west to California.

Similar Species: **Seedlings strongly resemble large crabgrass (*Digitaria sanguinalis*)**, with hairy leaves, rolled leaf buds, and membranous ligules; however, dallisgrass has rhizomes, and the leaves of more mature plants lack hairs, whereas large crabgrass leaves remain hairy. **Knotgrass (*Paspalum distichum* L.)** is a similarly coarse-textured perennial, but with a stoloniferous habit, shorter leaves, long hairy nodes, and fewer (2) racemes, on stalks arising from the leaf axils. **Thin paspalum (*Paspalum setaceum*)** is a clump-forming perennial with broader, glossy green leaves. **Vaseygrass (*Paspalum urvillei* Steud.)** is a warm-season, tufted perennial to 2 m tall, with very short rhizomes. Vaseygrass resembles dallisgrass but is more upright and taller, upper surface of the leaf blades are mostly hairless, inflorescences have many more branches (12–20), and spikelets are 1.5–3 mm long. It occurs primarily in roadsides, hay fields, and pastures in the southeastern states, and extends as far north as Kentucky and Virginia. Native to South America.

J. Neal

Dallisgrass habit

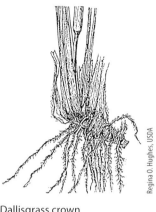
Regina O. Hughes, USDA

Dallisgrass crown

J. Neal

Dallisgrass inflorescence

J. DiTomaso

Inflorescence: *left*, knotgrass; *right*, vaseygrass

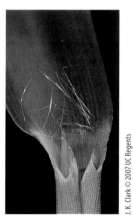
J. K. Clark © 2007 UC Regents

Dallisgrass membranous ligule

J. DiTomaso

Knotgrass collar and hairy node

J. DiTomaso

Left, thin paspalum seeds, 2.4 mm; *right*, dallisgrass seeds, 2.8 mm

Thin paspalum (*Paspalum setaceum* Michx.)

Synonyms: *Paspalum ciliatifolium, Paspalum stramineum,* bull paspalum

General Description: **Clump-forming, perennial** grass, often branching at the base in a radial fashion. The center of plants has dark **maroon pigmentation on the basal leaf sheaths** and stems. Leaves are broader than most other grass weeds in similar habitats and vary from hairy to glabrous and shiny. Seedheads are branched racemes resembling dallisgrass. Species is a complex of varieties varying in leaf pubescence and plant architecture, from spreading to erect.

Propagation / Phenology: Reproduces by seeds. Seeds germinate spring through summer. Plants resprout in spring from persistent crown with very short rhizomes.

Seedling: Leaves **rolled in the bud; auricles absent; ligule membranous and short** (≤0.5 mm long). Leaf blades and sheaths are hairy or glabrous. Leaf sheaths, particularly at plant base, often purple, with hairs on the margins.

Mature Plant: Plants erect or prostrate depending on management and variety. In turf, plants branch radially at the base and form dense clumps. Ligule **short (≤0.5 mm tall) and membranous,** often with **longer hairs** on the blade making the **ligule appear to have a fringe of hairs.** Leaf length and pubescence are quite variable. Leaves up to 30 cm long (more commonly 15 cm) and 1–1.8 cm wide. Blades occasionally crinkled near the base. Leaf margins with regularly spaced hairs, sometimes several millimeters long or very short. Margins straight or wavy.

Roots and Underground Structures: Fibrous root system with very short rhizomes. Rhizomes contribute to enlarging the clump but do not lead to long distance spread.

Flowers and Fruit: In summer, plants produce long, flowering stems that terminate in a branched inflorescence. Flowering stalks nearly hairless, sparsely leafy, 25–50 cm long (rarely to 1 m), erect to prostrate. The inflorescence has 1–6 (more commonly 2–3) racemose branches; bases of inflorescence branches sometimes held within subtending leaf sheath. **Spikelets** are closely appressed to branch stem and **arranged in pairs,** rounded to elliptic and 1.5–2.5 mm long. The seeds (caryopses) are elliptic and white to light green.

Postsenescence Characteristics: Foliage turns brown but the dense crown persists over winter.

Habitat: Primarily a lawn weed but also in disturbed areas and roadsides.

Distribution: Widely distributed throughout the region from Florida to Ontario and west to Colorado.

Similar Species: Several varieties of *Paspalum setaceum* have been described. **Thin paspalum (*P. s.* var. *setaceum*)** has conspicuously hairy leaf blades; **fringeleaf paspalum (*P. s.* var. *ciliatifolium* (Michx.) Vasey)** has scabrous to ciliate leaf margins; and **hurrahgrass (*P. s.* var. *muhlenbergii* (Nash) D.J.)** leaf margins are evenly hirsute. **Alexandergrass (*Urochloa plantaginea* (Link) R.D. Webster)** is a summer annual lacking the persistent basal crown but is otherwise difficult to differentiate. The ligule is ciliate and spikelets solitary, in contrast to thin paspalum with a short membranous ligule and paired spikelets. **Bahiagrass (*Paspalum notatum* J. Fleugge)** is more robust, with V-shaped inflorescences on unbranched 20–110 cm tall stalks, short (<0.5 mm) membranous ligules, and thick, short rhizomes. Bahiagrass and alexandergrass are common in the Southeast but have been reported north to New Jersey and Pennsylvania, respectively.

Thin paspalum habit

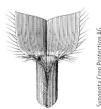

Top, thin paspalum collar region; *bottom*, alexandergrass collar region

Thin paspalum inflorescence

Thin paspalum collar

Bahiagrass inflorescence

Alexandergrass spikelets held singly

Thin paspalum spikelets in pairs

Reed canarygrass (*Phalaris arundinacea* L.)

Synonyms: lady-grass, spires, doggers, sword-grass, ladies'-laces, bride's-laces, London-lace

General Description: A **tall (1.5 m), aggressive, rhizomatous, colony-forming perennial** common in wet areas.

Propagation / Phenology: Although plants produce **seeds**, encroachment is generally by **rhizomes** from ditch banks and other wet areas. Rhizomes can also spread when top-soil or sand is transported from riverbanks.

Seedling: Rarely encountered.

Mature Plant: **Leaves are rolled in the bud; auricles are absent.** The **ligule is membranous** (3–6 mm long) **and rounded to flat-topped. Stems appear bluish-green** (glaucous). **Blades are flat** (10–35 cm long by 5–20 mm wide) and **rough along the margins** but **lack hairs. Sheaths are hairless and rounded. Collars are broad.**

Roots and Underground Structures: Fibrous root system associated with **thick creeping rhizomes.**

Flowers and Fruit: Flowers and seed are produced by August. **The seedhead is a dense, branched panicle** (7–25 cm long by 1–4 cm wide). The **distinctive, pale straw-colored seedheads** extend well beyond the leaves. Although the seedheads are initially compact, the branches spread as they mature. Seeds are shiny, yellow to brown (3 mm long), with a hairy stalk attached to the base.

Postsenescence Characteristics: Straw-colored stems remain erect well into the winter and produce a thick mulch that persists until the following spring.

Habitat: Reed canarygrass is a weed of wet soils, primarily in roadsides and irrigation and drainage ditches. It does not survive under frequent close mowing or cultivation but may encroach from the edges of fields.

Distribution: Found throughout the northern United States and Canada.

Similar Species: **Ribbon-grass (*Phalaris arundinacea* var. *picta*)** is a variety of reed canarygrass that is grown as an ornamental. It has distinctive green-and-white striped leaves. **Other reedgrasses, including common reed (*Phragmites australis*)** and **giant reed (*Arundo donax*)**, can occasionally be confused with reed canarygrass, but both of those grasses are considerably taller (2–6 m tall) and have a larger, more open, inflorescence (15–60 cm long).

Reed canarygrass habit

J. Neal

Juvenile reed canarygrass

R. Uva

Reed canarygrass ligule

J. Neal

Reed canarygrass inflorescence

J. DiTomaso

Reed canarygrass inflorescence and leafy shoot

J. Neal

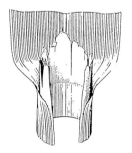

Reed canarygrass collar region

Syngenta Crop Protection AG

Top, giant reed seed, 9.1 mm; *bottom*, reed canarygrass seeds, 3.2 mm

J. DiTomaso

89

Timothy (*Phleum pratense* L.)

Synonym: herd's grass

General Description: A **grayish-green, perennial forage grass** that produces a **swollen bulb-like base** and **forms large clumps as tall as 1 m**. The **distinctive flowering spike** produces a considerable amount of pollen and is **a common allergen**.

Propagation / Phenology: Propagation is generally **by seeds. Clumps enlarge by tillering** and **short rhizomes.**

Seedling: **Leaves are rolled in the bud,** and **auricles are absent. Ligule is membranous** (2–4 mm long) and **toothed at the corners** and at the apex. The **sheath is fused around the stem,** and the foliage lacks hairs.

Mature Plant: **Leaves, sheath, and ligules are similar to those of the seedling. Stems** are whitish and **swollen (bulb-like) at the base** and lack hairs. Leaves are flat and taper to a sharp point. Blades are 5–8 mm wide by 8–23 cm long, hairless, and have rough margins, especially toward the base. Sheaths are rounded.

Roots and Underground Structures: Fibrous root system predominates from **short rhizomes** and **occasionally short stolons.**

Flowers and Fruit: Flowers are produced from June through July in a **terminal, spike-like panicle** (5–10 cm long by 5–8 mm wide). **Panicles are dense, cylindrical, stiff, and somewhat bristly.** Spikelets are flat, overlapping, and fringed with short hairs. Awns are 0.7–1.5 mm long.

Postsenescence Characteristics: Plants persist through the winter. Dead, straw-colored flowering stems may persist, but for only a short time, and are recognized by the distinctive spike-like inflorescence.

Habitat: Timothy is cultivated for hay but can occur as a weed of low-maintenance turfgrass, as well as nursery, orchard, agricultural, and forage crops. It also grows in roadsides and abandoned fields but generally requires nutrient-rich soil.

Distribution: Has become naturalized throughout most of the United States and southern Canada.

Similar Species: The dense, **cylindrical seedheads are similar to the foxtails (*Setaria* spp.)**, but, unlike timothy, foxtails have hairy ligules and bristles subtending the spikelets. In early spring, **emerging shoots can resemble quackgrass (*Elymus repens*) or orchardgrass (*Dactylis glomerata*)**. However, quackgrass has claw-like auricles; timothy does not. Orchardgrass is distinctly folded in the bud, whereas timothy is rolled in the bud.

Timothy habit

J. Neal

J. Neal

Timothy crown with swollen base

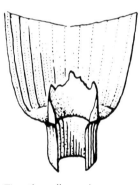

Timothy collar region
The Scotts Company

Timothy
inflorescence

J. DiTomaso

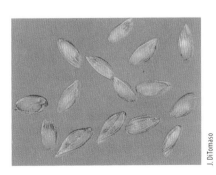

J. DiTomaso

Timothy seeds, 2 mm

Common reed (*Phragmites australis* (Cav.) Trin. ex Steud.)

SYNONYMS: *Phragmites communis*, *Phragmites maximus*, common reedgrass, giant reed

GENERAL DESCRIPTION: A **very large, perennial grass** with erect stems (2–4 m tall). It **spreads by rhizomes** to form large vegetative colonies in wet soils.

PROPAGATION / PHENOLOGY: Viable seeds are rarely produced, thus **reproduction is primarily by vegetative growth**. Populations often spread over long distances by rhizome fragments carried with soil or on equipment.

SEEDLING: Rarely encountered.

MATURE PLANT: **Leaves are rolled in the bud; auricles are absent,** and the **ligule is a ring of silky hairs 1–2 mm long. Stems are hollow, round,** and thickest toward the base (0.5–1.5 cm). **Blades are flat, 20–60 cm long by 1–3 cm wide, conspicuously nerved above,** and hairless or sparsely hairy below. **Margins are rough or sharp.** Sheaths are hairless except on the margins, which overlap.

ROOTS AND UNDERGROUND STRUCTURES: **Long, stout, scaly rhizomes.**

FLOWERS AND FRUIT: The inflorescence is a **conspicuous 15–40 cm long plume-like panicle** that is purple when young and turns light brown with age. Spikelets (1 cm long) are silky-hairy. **Viable seed seldom produced.**

POSTSENESCENCE CHARACTERISTICS: Colonies of rigid stems can persist through the winter and continue to bear the conspicuous plume-like seedheads.

HABITAT: Common reed is found in roadside ditches, marshes, natural wetlands, and other wet areas. It tolerates salt and alkaline conditions and grows in stagnant or flowing water. Although rarely found in crops, it will survive in areas where the subsoil is very damp or where ditch banks are adjacent to agricultural fields.

DISTRIBUTION: Occurs throughout the United States and southern Canada. Common reed is native to North America but weedy infestations are typically attributed to an introduced biotype of the species.

SIMILAR SPECIES: Although **reed canarygrass (*Phalaris arundinacea*)** shares a similar habitat, it is considerably smaller than common reed and has a membranous ligule. **Giant reed (*Arundo donax* L.)** is also commonly associated with wet habitats. Giant reed is a more robust plant than common reed, often growing to 6 m tall, with thick stems resembling corn stalks in the first year of development that branch in the second year. Unlike giant reed, common reed has a blade base (collar) that is gradually narrowed and not rounded or clasping the stem as in giant reed. The inflorescences at the ends of stems are dense, 30–60 cm long; individual flowers have a hairy lemma and hairless spikelet stalk, but produce no viable seed. In contrast, common reed has a hairy spikelet stalk and a hairless lemma. Common reed also has a brown (tawny) to purplish inflorescence, whereas the inflorescence of giant reed is whitish.

Common reed roadside infestation

Common reed collar region

Giant reed collar

Giant reed inflorescence

Common reed inflorescence and foliage

Common reed collar region

Common reed shoot tip from rhizome

Common reed seed, 9 mm (to tip of awn)

Annual bluegrass (*Poa annua* L.)

SYNONYMS: annual meadowgrass, annual spear-grass, dwarf spear-grass, wintergrass

GENERAL DESCRIPTION: The **subspecies *Poa annua* var.** *annua* is an **upright, clump-forming, winter annual.** *Poa annua* var. *reptans* **is a prostrate, clump-forming perennial.** Both may grow to 30 cm in height, and both tolerate close mowing to <4 mm. Both are light green and are prolific seedhead producers.

PROPAGATION / PHENOLOGY: Reproduction is **by seeds**; seeds germinate in late summer, early autumn, and spring. **Clumps enlarge by aggressive tillering.** Tillers of the perennial variety root at the base, forming dense patches. Seeds of the annual variety require a warm after-ripening period before germination; perennial variety seeds have no dormancy and will germinate immediately if weather is conducive.

SEEDLING: The first leaf blade is linear and very narrow, about 30 times longer than wide, and opens perpendicular to the ground. **Leaves are light green, folded in the bud, lack auricles, and have a slightly pointed membranous ligule** (1–2 mm long). **Blades** are 2–5 cm long by 0.7–1.5 mm wide, hairless, **keeled, with a curved prow-shaped tip** and smooth margins. Blades can also be rippled or wrinkled. **Sheaths are compressed and hairless.** The collar is green and smooth.

MATURE PLANT: **Leaves and ligule are similar to those of the seedling. Blades** are 1–14 cm long by 1–3 mm wide, light green, smooth, and keeled, with **curved prow-shaped tips.** **Sheaths** are loose, **smooth, slightly compressed and keeled.** The collar is smooth and narrow.

ROOTS AND UNDERGROUND STRUCTURES: The **root system is fibrous and shallow.** Adventitious roots arise at the base of the tillers.

FLOWERS AND FRUIT: Plants flower from April through October. The **seedhead is an open, greenish-white pyramidal panicle** (2–7 cm long). Spikelets are 4–6 mm long and produce 2–6 flowers.

POSTSENESCENCE CHARACTERISTICS: Hot, dry conditions cause annual bluegrass to become dormant or die. With the return of cool, moist conditions, the perennial variety will resprout from the crown, and the annual variety will germinate from seed.

HABITAT: Annual bluegrass is a weed of turf (particularly golf greens), nursery crops, vegetable crops, landscapes, and other irrigated crops. It grows best in cool, moist conditions and rich soil but tolerates a variety of conditions including compacted soils. In golf greens, the perennial variety will often dominate the annual. Excess irrigation and fertilization will encourage growth.

DISTRIBUTION: Found throughout the United States and Canada.

SIMILAR SPECIES: **Canada bluegrass (*Poa compressa* L.)** and **Kentucky bluegrass (*Poa pratensis* L.)** are both rhizomatous perennials and tend to be darker than annual bluegrass. Annual bluegrass may root at the nodes but is not rhizomatous.

Annual bluegrass habit

R. Uva

Annual bluegrass
collar region
Syngenta Crop Protection AG

Canada
bluegrass collar
region
Syngenta Crop Protection AG

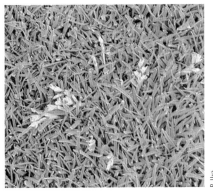

R. Uva

Annual bluegrass flower heads in
bentgrass

J. Neal

Kentucky bluegrass (note
rhizomes)

Kentucky bluegrass
collar region
Syngenta Crop Protection AG

J. K. Clark © 2007 UC Regents

Left to right: Kentucky bluegrass
seeds, 2.0 mm; Canada bluegrass
seeds, 2.4 mm; and annual
bluegrass seeds, 3.0 mm

Roughstalk bluegrass (*Poa trivialis* L.)

Synonym: rough bluegrass

General Description: A **stoloniferous perennial** with erect, bending, or reclining stems (30 cm to 1 m tall). The leaves are often yellow-green, **turning brown to red during periods of drought**.

Propagation / Phenology: Plants spread primarily by **stolons. Seeds** are a common contaminant of uncertified turfgrass seed and may emerge with adequate soil moisture and temperature.

Seedling: Seedlings are small and slow to establish. **Leaves are folded in the bud, with a large, tapering, membranous ligule** (4–6 mm long). **Scabrous hairs are very small and give the plant a rough feel,** accounting for the common name.

Mature Plant: **Leaves and ligule are similar to those of the seedling. Blades are flat, rough,** 3–20 cm long by 2–5 mm wide, with a **prow- or boat-shaped tip. Margins are rough. Sheaths are rough,** keeled, and compressed. The collar is broad and smooth.

Roots and Underground Structures: Fibrous roots and **stolons**.

Flowers and Fruit: Flowers are present mainly in May and June. The **seedhead is an open, pyramidal panicle** 6–15 cm long, composed of whorled branches. Spikelets are flattened (3 mm long), with 2–3 flowers.

Postsenescence Characteristics: Plants may go dormant in summer, but they remain green through the winter, although some winter tip burn is common. Under heat and drought stress, foliage has a maroon coloration.

Habitat: Roughstalk bluegrass is primarily a weed of turfgrass but also grows in orchards, meadows, woods, roadsides, and waste areas. It flourishes in moist, shady locations and is sometimes used in turfgrass mixes for shady areas.

Distribution: Found in the northern and southeastern United States, the Pacific Coast states, and southern Canada.

Similar Species: Roughstalk bluegrass can resemble other bluegrasses, some other turfgrass species, particularly **colonial bentgrass (*Agrostis capillaris* L.** [syn.: *A. tenuis* Sibth.]) and **creeping bentgrass (*Agrostis stolonifera*)**, and **red top (*Agrostis gigantea* Roth)**. However, it is considerably larger than **annual bluegrass (*Poa annua*)** and is lighter in color than **Kentucky bluegrass (*Poa pratensis*)**. In addition, these latter bluegrass species lack stolons. Although the bentgrasses are stoloniferous, leaves are rolled in the bud, whereas leaves of bluegrasses are folded in the bud. In addition, all bentgrasses have a single floret in the spikelets and the bluegrasses have more than one floret. Red top is rhizomatous rather than stoloniferous, and the leaves are rolled in the bud. Additionally, red top panicles are often purplish-red, and those of roughstalk bluegrass are green.

Roughstalk bluegrass habit

Roughstalk bluegrass
inflorescence

Red top differentiated
by having single florets

Colonial bentgrass
collar region
Syngenta Crop Protection AG

Creeping bentgrass
collar region
Syngenta Crop Protection AG

Roughstalk bluegrass
collar region
Syngenta Crop Protection AG

Roughstalk bluegrass stem

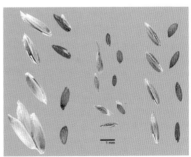

Left to right: Kentucky bluegrass seeds,
creeping bentgrass seeds, and roughstalk
bluegrass seeds

97

Tall fescue (*Schedonorus arundinaceus* (Schreb.) Dumort.)

Synonyms: *Festuca arundinacea, Festuca elatior, Lolium arundinaceum*, alata fescue, reed fescue, coarse fescue

General Description: A dark green, **clump-forming, perennial forage and turfgrass** that has escaped cultivation. **Leaves are broader** and generally grow more rapidly than do leaves of more desirable turfgrasses; blades are at a 45° angle from the soil. In unmowed areas, tall fescue can grow to 1.5 m tall. **Many strains of tall fescue contain endophytes** that can be toxic to livestock.

Propagation / Phenology: Reproduction is **by seeds. Clumps enlarge by tillering.**

Seedling: The first leaf blade is long and narrow. **Leaves are rolled in the bud, auricles are absent,** and the **ligule is membranous and short.** Blades are 9–13 cm long by 1–2 mm wide, glossy on the lower surface, smooth and hairless throughout. **Blades have conspic-uous parallel veins** and taper slowly to the apex. Sheaths are smooth and reddish at the base, round to slightly compressed. **Ligules are short** (1 mm long) and **membranous.** The collar is whitish and divided in the center by the midrib.

Mature Plant: **Leaves are rolled in the bud; auricles are short and blunt with a fringe of marginal hairs.** Ligule is similar to that of seedlings. Blades are 10–60 cm long and much wider (4–12 mm wide) than in the seedling stage. Leaves are dark green with occasional hairs on the basal portion of the upper surface of the leaf. **Margins are rough,** and the **blades are coarse and thick**, with dull surfaces and **prominent veins above** and a **glossy surface beneath**. Sheaths are round and lack hairs. The **collar is broad.**

Roots and Underground Structures: **Root system is fibrous**; rhizomes are not produced.

Flowers and Fruit: Flowers appear in early to mid-summer. Seedheads mature and persist until autumn. The **seedhead is a loose or a compressed panicle**, 10–40 cm in length. Spikelets are 1–1.8 cm long with 3–8 seeds per spikelet. Awns, if present, are 0.3–4 mm long. Seedheads often lay flat in turf and are not injured by mowing.

Postsenescence Characteristics: This perennial grass stays green year-round.

Habitat: Tall fescue is a weed of turf, nurseries, landscapes, orchards, and reduced-tillage crops. It may also be found in fields, dry waste areas, and less commonly in cultivated crops. Cultivars of tall fescue are used as forage and turfgrasses.

Distribution: Found throughout the United States.

Similar Species: **Quackgrass (*Elymus repens*)** and **ryegrasses (*Lolium* spp.)** are similar to tall fescue; however, quackgrass has long, clasping auricles and rhizomes that produce a spreading growth habit. Ryegrasses have claw-like auricles, whereas those of tall fescue, if present, are blunt and short. Tall fescue has dark green, coarse-textured foliage unlike quackgrass and ryegrasses.

Tall fescue habit

J. Neal

Tall fescue collar
region
Syngenta Crop Protection AG

Tall fescue inflorescence

J. Neal

J. Neal

Tall fescue collar region

J. DiTomaso

Tall fescue seeds, 7 mm

Yellow foxtail (*Setaria pumila* (Poir.) Roem. & Schult.)

SYNONYMS: *Setaria glauca*, *Setaria lutescens*, summer-grass, golden foxtail, wild millet

GENERAL DESCRIPTION: A **clump-forming, erect, summer annual** reaching 1 m in height, with characteristic bottle-brush or **"fox tail"–like seedheads**.

PROPAGATION / PHENOLOGY: Reproduction is **by seeds**; seeds germinate from late spring through mid-summer.

SEEDLING: The first leaf blade is linear, about 7 times longer than wide, and opens parallel to the ground. **Leaves are rolled in the bud; auricles are absent, and the ligule is a fringe of hairs approximately 0.5 mm long.** Blades of young seedlings are 4.5–8 cm long by 3–5 mm wide, **smooth on the lower surfaces, with long, wispy hairs on the basal portions of the upper surface. The margins are smooth or slightly rough**, and the blade is keeled in the lower portion. **Sheath is smooth and compressed.** The collar is green and smooth.

MATURE PLANT: **Ligule is a fringe of hairs about 1 mm long. Leaf blades** are 30 cm long by 4–10 mm wide, keeled, and have **long, wispy hairs only on the upper surface at the base. Sheath is smooth, compressed, often reddish at the base**, and has a prominent midvein. The collar is narrow, light green or yellowish, and smooth.

ROOTS AND UNDERGROUND STRUCTURES: Root system is fibrous. Yellow foxtail does not root at the nodes, but tillers will produce roots at the base of the plant.

FLOWERS AND FRUIT: Blooms in mid- to late summer. The **seedhead is a coarse, bristly, spikelike panicle**, 2–15 cm long by 1 cm wide. The mature seedhead is present from late summer through autumn. Spikelets are approximately 3 mm long, and each spikelet is subtended by 5 or more bristles. Bristles are about 10 mm long and yellowish at maturity. Seeds are 2–3 mm long, ridged, and yellow, with small dark markings.

POSTSENESCENCE CHARACTERISTICS: Yellow foxtail can be recognized by the yellowish, bristly inflorescence that persists through early winter. Other foxtails also have persistent bristly inflorescences but turn brown after they senesce.

HABITAT: Yellow foxtail is a weed of most cultivated crops as well as turf, landscapes, and nurseries. It generally grows on nutrient-rich soil.

DISTRIBUTION: Yellow and green foxtail are troublesome weeds worldwide. Giant foxtail is common in the eastern United States, excluding northern New England.

SIMILAR SPECIES: **Giant foxtail (*Setaria faberi* Herrm.)** and **green foxtail (*Setaria viridis* (L.) Beauv.)** closely resemble yellow foxtail in general characteristics—ligule, habitat, growth habit, and reproductive characteristics. **Giant foxtail is the largest of the 3 species, and its seedlings and mature plants have numerous short hairs on the upper surface of the blades and on the margins of the sheaths.** The green to purple, **nodding seedhead is also the largest of the 3. Green foxtail seedlings and mature plants have rough blades that lack hairs, and the sheaths have hairy margins.** The seedhead is larger and greener than that of yellow foxtail, and spikelets are subtended by only 1–3 bristles. Yellow foxtail seedlings can be confused with **fall panicum (*Panicum dichotomiflorum*)** but are easily recognized by the distinctive wispy hairs at the base of the blades. Fall panicum seedlings can be distinguished from foxtails by their hairy sheaths and their blades, which are hairy only on the lower surface.

Yellow foxtail habit

Yellow foxtail seedling

J. Neal

Yellow foxtail collar

L. Sosnoskie

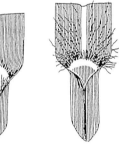  

Green foxtail collar region

Syngenta Crop Protection AG

Yellow foxtail collar region

Syngenta Crop Protection AG

Giant foxtail collar region

Syngenta Crop Protection AG

Yellow foxtail, 5-tiller plant

J. Neal

  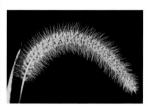 

Green foxtail seedhead

J. DiTomaso

Yellow foxtail seedhead

J. DiTomaso

Giant foxtail seedhead

J. DiTomaso

Left to right: green foxtail seeds, 2.4 mm; giant foxtail seeds, 2.5 mm; and yellow foxtail seeds, 3 mm

J. K. Clark © 2007 UC Regents

Shattercane (*Sorghum bicolor* (L.) Moench ssp. *verticilliflorum* (Steud.) de Wet ex Wiersema & J. Dahlb.)

Synonyms: *Sorghum bicolor* ssp. *arundinaceum*, *Sorghum vulgare*, sorghum, black amber cane, wildcane, milo

General Description: A **summer annual with erect, corn-like stems** that can reach 4 m in height. Stems usually grow individually but may form clumps. Shattercane is a very competitive weed in corn and sorghum and can hybridize with cultivated sorghum or johnsongrass.

Propagation / Phenology: Flowers are produced from July to October. Reproduction is **by seeds**; seeds germinate from mid-spring through early summer. The inflorescences shatter and spread their seeds earlier than do those of cultivated sorghum.

Seedling: **Leaves are rolled in the bud; auricles are absent; and the ligule is membranous at the base and fringed at the top.** The base of the blades is usually hairy on the upper and lower surfaces. **Hairs** can be **present or absent on sheaths.**

Mature Plant: **Ligule is approximately 5 mm long, membranous on the basal two-thirds, and fringed on the top third. Stems are robust and purple-spotted. Blades** are flat, narrowing at each end, and are **30–60 cm long by 3–5 cm wide.** Leaves and sheaths are smooth or hairy, often hairy at the junction between the blade and the sheath (collar). **Tillers are produced at the crown.**

Roots and Underground Structures: **Fibrous root system**, often with adventitious roots arising from the nodes or tillers. Adventitious roots can act as prop roots as in corn.

Flowers and Fruit: The **seedhead is a large open panicle**, 15–50 cm long, and usually hairy along the main axis. Spikelets are in pairs. The lower one is fertile, awned (5–13 mm long), and large (4–6 mm long). The other is infertile, on a stalk (pedicel), and considerably smaller than the fertile spikelet. Seed is egg-shaped, rounded to flattened, shiny, and black to red at maturity.

Postsenescence Characteristics: **Seedheads shatter before grain harvest** and do not persist. After harvest, stubble may remain in the field through the winter.

Habitat: Shattercane grows primarily in cultivated areas and is a weed of agronomic crops, particularly sorghum and corn. It is less common in nursery and vegetable crops.

Distribution: Most common in the northern, southeastern, south-central, and western United States.

Similar Species: **Johnsongrass (*Sorghum halepense*)** is closely related to shattercane and at certain stages of development may be difficult to distinguish; however, it is a perennial with large rhizomes and blades 1–2 cm wide, whereas shattercane does not produce rhizomes and has blades >3 cm wide. In addition, **seeds of shattercane are much larger and more rounded than those of johnsongrass and can be examined by carefully removing young seedlings from the soil.**

Shattercane
in corn

W. Curran

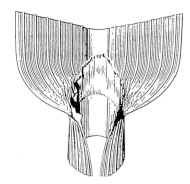

Shattercane collar
region
Syngenta Crop Protection AG

Shattercane inflorescence

W. Curran

W. Curran

hattercane seedling

J. DiTomaso

Left, shattercane seeds, 5 mm; *right*,
cultivated sorghum seeds, 5 mm

Johnsongrass (*Sorghum halepense* (L.) Pers.)

Synonyms: *Holcus halepense*, means-grass, aleppo grass, grass sorghum, Egyptian millet

General Description: A **coarse-textured perennial** with stout, unbranched stems and **thick, aggressive rhizomes**. It can grow to 2 m in height and form large stands.

Propagation / Phenology: Reproduction is **by seeds and rhizomes**. Rhizomes spread to form vegetative stands. When rhizomes are severed by cultivation, equipment can transport small pieces to other areas to form new colonies.

Seedling: The first leaf blade is only 8 times longer than wide and opens parallel to the ground. **Leaves are rolled in the bud; auricles are absent; and the ligule is membranous with shallow teeth across the top.** Blades are 4–18 cm long by 2–5 mm wide, **smooth on both surfaces** and margins, with a **prominent midvein** near the base of the blade. Sheaths are smooth, rounded to slightly compressed, green or with a maroon tinge. The collar is narrow and whitish.

Mature Plant: **Leaves are similar to those of seedlings.** The **ligule** (3–4 mm long) **is membranous** and **may be jagged across the top. Older ligules have a fringe of hairs on the top half but are membranous at the base.** Blades are 15–50 cm long by 10–30 mm wide, smooth below and mostly smooth above, with some hairs present at the base of the blade near the ligule. The margins are rough, and the **blades are flat, with a thick, prominent, white midvein.** Sheath is smooth, pale green, reddish-brown to maroon, compressed, often with hairy margins. The collar is broad, light green or white, and smooth.

Roots and Underground Structures: Fibrous root system is associated with **thick and aggressive rhizomes**. Rhizomes can be purplish and have scales at the nodes.

Flowers and Fruit: Flowers are present from June to July. The **seedhead is a large (15–50 cm long), open, coarse, purplish panicle.** Spikelets are in pairs. The shorter, wider floret (4–5.5 mm long) produces a seed and has a 1–1.5 cm twisted awn that is easily detached. The seed is 3–5 mm long, oval, and dark reddish-brown. The other infertile stalked spikelet is longer but narrower and lacks an awn.

Postsenescence Characteristics: Aboveground portions are killed by frost. The stout stems and seedheads persist well into winter.

Habitat: Johnsongrass is a weed of most cultivated, reduced-tillage, and perennial crops as well as roadsides, meadows, and waste areas. It prefers rich soil but will survive in nearly any soil type. It does not tolerate close mowing.

Distribution: Introduced as a forage crop, johnsongrass has naturalized throughout the southern United States and the West Coast. It is spreading northward into New York, Massachusetts, Michigan, and other regions.

Similar Species: **Shattercane (*Sorghum bicolor* spp. *verticilliflorum*)** is closely related to johnsongrass, but it is an annual and does not have large rhizomes. Shattercane also has leaf blades much wider (>3 cm) than those of johnsongrass (1–3 cm). In addition, **seeds of shattercane are much larger and more rounded than those of johnsongrass** and can be examined by carefully removing young seedlings from the soil. **Fall panicum (*Panicum dichotomiflorum*)** has similar foliage, particularly the white midvein on the leaf blade. However, it is an annual that is usually smaller than johnsongrass and has a hairy ligule that is not membranous at the base.

J. DiTomaso

ohnsongrass habit

J. Neal

Johnsongrass
seedling with
seed coat
attached

Johnsongrass ligule
J. Neal

A. Senesac

Johnsongrass rhizomes

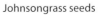

Johnsongrass seeds

J. K. Clark © 2007 UC Regents

R. Uva

Johnsongrass tillers

105

Broadleaf signalgrass (*Urochloa platyphylla* (Munro ex C. Wright) R.D. Webster)

Synonym: *Brachiaria platyphylla*

General Description: A **summer annual** grass. As its common name implies, **leaf blades are wider relative to the length of most other summer annual grasses**. Leaf blades are broader at the base and taper to a pointed tip. **Inflorescence is a branched spike, usually with 1–2 branches.**

Propagation / Phenology: **Reproduces by seeds.** Seeds emerge over an extended period of time in spring through mid-summer, contributing to its avoidance of several management strategies in crops.

Seedling: First leaf is linear to long-elliptic. Subsequent **leaves are wider and shorter** compared to most other weedy grasses, 4–6 cm long by 0.6–1 cm wide, tapering to a point. Leaf **sheaths are hairy; blades are not hairy** except at the margins and collar. **Young leaves are rolled in the bud**; ligule is a short (to 1 mm long) **membrane with a fringe of hairs**; auricles are absent. Leaf sheath is often tinged red.

Mature Plant: Plants form many branches up to 100 cm in length at the base that may root at the nodes near the base. Leaves up to 17 cm long by 1.5 cm wide, margins sometimes tinged red.

Roots and Underground Structures: Fibrous root system.

Flowers and Fruit: Plants flower from July to September (later in southern range). Flowers are in branched spikes, with 2–5 (rarely more) branches. Individual flowers (spikelets) are approximately 4 mm long, 2 mm wide, in 2 rows appressed to the branches and often shiny. Each spikelet contains 1 seed (caryopsis) about 2 mm long.

Postsenescence Characteristics: Dead stems persist only a short time.

Habitat: Common in conventional and reduced tillage cropping systems, disturbed non-crop areas, and occasionally in urban landscapes. Plants generally do not persist in mowed turf.

Distribution: Native to North America. Most common in the southeastern and mid-Atlantic states but present north to Pennsylvania.

Similar Species: **Texas signalgrass, also known as Texas panicum (*Urochloa texana* (Buckley) R. Webster;** syn.: *Brachiaria texana* (Buckley) S.T. Blake), has a similar growth habit and relatively wide leaf blades, vernation is rolled, and the ligule is a very short membrane with a fringe of hairs. However, Texas signalgrass leaves and sheaths are hairy; broadleaf signalgrass is hairless or nearly so. Additionally, the inflorescence of Texas signalgrass is a single, tightly clustered spike, whereas broadleaf signalgrass has a branched spike. Texas signalgrass is also native to North America, distributed throughout the southern United States and north to Illinois. Its range has expanded in recent years. Young seedlings of both species can resemble **large or southern crabgrass (*Digitaria sanguinalis* or *D. ciliaris*)** but are easily distinguished by the ligules. Crabgrasses have tall membranous ligules, whereas both broadleaf signalgrass and Texas signalgrass have short ciliate ligules.

Broadleaf signalgrass

J. Neal

Syngenta Crop Protection AG

Broadleaf signalgrass
collar region

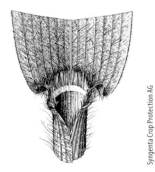

Syngenta Crop Protection AG

Texas signalgrass collar region

J. Neal

Broadleaf signalgrass
collar region

J. Neal

Broadleaf signalgrass
inflorescence

J. Neal

Texas signalgrass
inflorescence

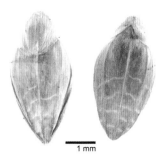

1 mm

M. Bertone

Broadleaf signalgrass seeds

107

Alligatorweed (*Alternanthera philoxeroides* (C. Martius) Griseb)

Synonym: *Achyranthes philoxeroides*

General Description: **Aquatic to terrestrial perennial**, with **opposite leaves** and horizontal to ascending stems to 1 m. The aquatic form has **hollow, floating**, emergent and submerged stems, but the terrestrial form has solid stems. Plants typically root in soil in shallow water and form thick, floating mats extending over the surface of deeper water. Fragments **can break away and colonize new sites.** Serious infestations create anoxic, disease, and mosquito-breeding conditions. Native to South America.

Propagation / Phenology: **Reproduction primarily vegetative from stem fragments.** Each fragment with a node can develop a new plant. Plants seldom inhabit water deeper than 2 m. Seeds rarely develop, and when present are usually not viable.

Seedling: Seedlings seldom encountered.

Mature Plant: Foliage is herbaceous with stems simple or branched, lacking hairs or with 2 opposing lengthwise rows of hairs. **Leaves opposite, narrowly lanceolate** to obovate, 4–11 cm long by 1–3 cm wide. The margins are smooth, **lack hairs**, and are sessile or with narrow, winged, clasping petioles to 1 cm long. **Stems are stolon-like and root at the nodes.** Floating plants have shorter, finer roots than plants rooted in soil.

Roots and Underground Structures: Although stems are generally stolon-like, belowground rhizomes can occur in porous soils.

Flowers and Fruit: **Globe-shaped**, almost clover-like, **white flowers** are fragrant and present June to October. **Spikes head-like**, 1–2 cm diameter, terminal and axillary, on **stalks 4–9 cm long.** Flowers lack petals but have **pearly white, glabrous bracts.** Sepals and fertile stamens (5), with sepals separate, 5–7 mm long, and the fertile stamens opposite the sepals alternating with 5 longer sterile stamens. Fruit is a membranous utricle that does not open to release the seed. Seeds are smooth, disc-shaped to flattened wedge-shaped. Mature fruits seldom encountered.

Postsenescence Characteristics: Dead stems fall over and contribute to formation of the mat. Mild frost kills leaves but not stems. Severe frosts kill emergent stems but not submerged or buried parts.

Habitat: Plants generally found in shallow water, wet soils, ditches, marshes, pond margins, and slow-moving watercourses. They require a warm summer season and can survive saline conditions to 10% salt by volume. Although plants tolerate cold winters, they cannot survive prolonged freezing temperatures.

Distribution: Southeastern states, including Texas. North to Illinois, Kentucky, and Virginia. Biocontrol agents have successfully suppressed alligatorweed in its southernmost range, but cold weather limits survival of the bioagents from the Carolinas north.

Similar Species: The leaf shape of alligatorweed can resemble some **smartweed species** (*Persicaria* **spp.**). However, all *Persicaria* species have an alternate leaf arrangement and alligatorweed has opposite leaves. **Eclipta** (*Eclipta prostrata*) has similar shaped, opposite leaves but is a summer annual with a composite flower. **Winged waterprimrose (*Ludwigia decurrens* Walter)** can look similar but has alternate leaves, winged stems, and yellow flowers. A related aquatic species, **sessile joyweed (*Alternanthera sessilis* (L.) R. Br. ex DC.),** is more restricted in its range. While it is generally a weed of tropical areas including the southeastern US, it was reported from Maryland. Unlike alligatorweed, it has white to pinkish flowers and its rounded inflorescence lacks or has a very short stalk. Sessile joyweed is listed as a federal noxious weed.

Alligatorweed terrestrial habit

Alligatorweed flowering shoot

Alligatorweed stem and adventitious roots

Winged waterprimrose

109

Tumble pigweed (*Amaranthus albus* L.)

Synonyms: tumble weed, tumbling pigweed, white pigweed

General Description: A **bushy-branched, rounded or globular annual**, 20 cm to 1 m in diameter. Senesced plants sever at the soil surface and scatter seeds by tumbling in the wind.

Propagation / Phenology: Reproduction is **by seeds**.

Seedling: Cotyledons are smooth, lanceolate, 3.5–8.5 mm long by 1–1.5 mm wide, green on the upper surface and magenta beneath. **Young leaves are ovate, dark green above, and tinged with magenta on the underside.** The **margins are entire** to wavy, and the **apex is notched**, with a temporary bristle in the notch (mucronate). **Expanding leaves** are sparsely hairy on the margins and veins of the underside. The hairs develop into rough projections as the leaves mature. **Stems are angled**, tinged magenta, with short, rough hairs.

Mature Plant: **Stems are pale green to whitish**, usually smooth, many-branched, erect or prostrate at the base, with an ascending tip. **Leaves are alternate, pale green** on the upper surface and pale green to reddish-tinged on the underside. **Blades are ovate or spatulate** (2.5–8 cm long), with **wavy margins** and conspicuous venation. **Petioles are short** (1.3–3 cm long). **Leaves of the flowering branches are elliptic** to oblong or obovate.

Roots and Underground Structures: Well-developed **taproot**, relatively shallow, **usually not red**.

Flowers and Fruit: **Greenish flowers** are produced from July through August in **short, dense clusters in the leaf axils and not in terminal spikes** characteristic of many other *Amaranthus* species. Male (staminate) and female (pistillate) flowers are separate (monoecious). Petals are absent, but 3 uneven sepals are present in the pistillate flowers. The spiny bracts subtending the flowers are twice as long as the sepals. Fruits are thin-walled, 1-seeded, inflated structures (utricles), 1.3–1.7 mm long, opening around the middle by a cap-like lid. Seeds are glossy, black, round, small (0.7–1.5 mm in diameter), and convex on both sides.

Postsenescence Characteristics: **At maturity, plants abscise just above the ground and are carried with the wind**, scattering seeds. Dead plants accumulate on the leeward side of fields along fences and hedges.

Habitat: Tumble pigweed is a weed of agricultural and horticultural crops, including woody perennial crops such as those in nurseries, orchards, and vineyards. It also grows in ditch banks, waste areas, and roadsides.

Distribution: A native of the arid regions of the Great Plains, now distributed throughout all but the northernmost areas of North America.

Similar Species: **See Table 1 for a comparison with other pigweeds. Livid amaranth (*Amaranthus blitum*)** closely resembles tumble pigweed as a seedling, but its leaves are notched at the tip and at maturity the plants are more prostrate or arching. **Russianthistle (*Salsola tragus* L.)** is also a "tumbleweed," but with much smaller leaves and a distinctly spiny foliage.

J. Neal

Tumble pigweed habit

J. Neal

Tumble pigweed stem, with flowers

J. Neal

Tumble pigweed seedling

J. O'Brien (Russian thistle) and J. K. Clark (tumble pigweed) © 2007 UC Regents

Left to right: Russian thistle seeds, 1.6 mm; and tumble pigweed seeds, 1.4 mm

Livid amaranth (*Amaranthus blitum* L.)

SYNONYMS: *Amaranthus lividus,* purple pigweed, purple amaranth, prostrate pigweed

GENERAL DESCRIPTION: A **prostrate** to ascending **summer annual** (15–40 cm wide, occasionally to 100 cm) with distinctively **notched leaf tips**.

PROPAGATION / PHENOLOGY: Reproduction is by seeds. Seeds germinate in warm soil (≥20 °C) spring through summer. **Freshly shed seeds will germinate** with little or no after-ripening, resulting in multiple generations per year.

SEEDLING: Cotyledons are narrowly elliptic, 6–7 mm long by 3–6 mm wide. Depending on the subspecies, cotyledons have acute or rounded tips. Young leaves are obovate (widest near the apex); leaf blade approximately as wide as long, wedge-shaped at the base (cuneate), and deeply notched (emarginate) at the tip. Stems are smooth and succulent, occasionally maroon at the base.

MATURE PLANT: Stems are fleshy and pliable, light green to reddish-purple, and lack hairs. Leaves are alternate, light green, sometimes with a reddish coloration on the underside. **Leaf blades** are 2-4 cm long, obovate to rhombic, **broader near the tip, tapered at the base**, and distinctively **notched at the tip**. Margins are entire and occasionally wavy. Growth habit may be prostrate or ascending.

ROOTS AND UNDERGROUND STRUCTURES: Taproot with a secondary fibrous root system.

FLOWERS AND FRUIT: Flowers are small, greenish, and are produced from June through August in small, dense clusters in the axils of the leaves; flexuous terminal spikes are also typically present. Fruit (utricles) are approximately 2 mm long; seeds are glossy black, round, and about 1 mm in diameter.

POSTSENESCENCE CHARACTERISTICS: Prostrate stems have a web-like appearance after the leaves senesce, but generally do not persist.

HABITAT: A weed of arable land, particularly vegetables grown on muck soils. Becoming more common in container nursery crops, where it spreads into landscape plantings.

DISTRIBUTION: Introduced from Europe; now widely distributed in the eastern half of the United States with recent reports from the West Coast. Historically the species has been cultivated as a vegetable on several continents.

SIMILAR SPECIES: Variation in leaf size, stem architecture, depth of the leaf notch, presence or absence of terminal inflorescence, and seed size have been used to classify several subspecies and varieties. **Prostrate pigweed (*Amaranthus blitoides* L.)** has a similar growth habit but leaf blades are spatulate and mostly rounded at the tip whereas leaf tips of livid amaranth are notched. **See Table 1 for a comparison with other pigweeds. Common purslane (*Portulaca oleracea*)** and several species of **spurge (*Euphorbia* spp.)** may superficially resemble livid amaranth with prostrate growth habits, but these species lack the notched leaf tips.

Livid amaranth plant

Livid amaranth seedling

Livid amaranth, young plant

Livid amaranth stem

Livid amaranth inflorescence

Prostrate pigweed seedling

Livid amaranth seeds

Pigweeds

Smooth pigweed (*Amaranthus hybridus* L.)
Powell amaranth (*Amaranthus powellii* S. Wats.)
Redroot pigweed (*Amaranthus retroflexus* L.)

SYNONYMS: rough pigweed, amaranth pigweed, green amaranth, careless weed

GENERAL DESCRIPTION: **Redroot pigweed** is an erect, freely branching **summer annual** (10 cm to as much as 2 m in height). Small flowers are enclosed by spiny bracts that give the terminal and axillary spikes a bristly appearance. Two very similar species—**Powell amaranth** or **green pigweed** and **smooth pigweed**—often grow together with redroot pigweed in mixed populations in the Northeast (see Table 1 for comparison). Herbicide-resistant biotypes have been identified.

PROPAGATION / PHENOLOGY: Reproduction of all is **by seeds**. Germination of all 3 species begins in mid-spring, with peak flushes occurring in late spring and summer. Flowering usually begins with decreasing day length in late June. Seeds are produced from late summer to fall, until severe frost.

SEEDLING:

Smooth pigweed: Very **similar to redroot pigweed** as a seedling. **Stems are more densely pubescent** and the **leaves are usually darker green and less wavy.**

Powell amaranth: Leaves are shiny, entire (not undulate), and nearly or completely lack hairs. Blades are smaller and more pointed than are those of the other 2 species. **Lower stem is tinged red and nearly hairless.**

Redroot pigweed: Cotyledons are narrow and pointed (lanceolate), 10–12 mm long (4–5 times as long as wide), dull green to reddish on the upper surface and bright red beneath. **Stems are light green, hairy,** and often red at the base. **Young leaves are alternate, egg-shaped,** and sparsely hairy on the margin and veins. Hairs develop into tiny, rough projections. The blade is green on the upper surface. The lower surface is red- or magenta-tinged, especially on the veins. **Margins are wavy** (undulate), and the apex is slightly notched, with a bristle in the notch. Petioles are purplish, with short, stiff hairs.

MATURE PLANT:

Smooth pigweed: Stems are erect and slender. **Upper stem region is densely hairy,** and the hairs are short. **Leaves** are simple, alternate, **oval to egg-shaped,** green above, light green or magenta below. Occasionally plants have a white (or nearly white) chevron near the center of the leaf blade.

Powell amaranth: Stems are usually erect and stout and **lack or nearly lack hairs throughout. Leaves** are simple, alternate, **diamond-shaped, and more pointed than those of redroot or smooth pigweed.** Blades are shiny green above, with whitish veins on the lower surface.

Redroot pigweed: Stems are erect, stout; the lower part is thick and smooth, **the upper often branched and very hairy. Leaves** are simple, alternate, ovate or rhombic-ovate with **wavy margins. Blades are dull green above, hairy beneath** or at least along the veins. The veins on the lower surface are prominently white.

ROOTS AND UNDERGROUND STRUCTURES: All have a shallow taproot, often pinkish or reddish.

J. Neal

Smooth pigweed habit

R. Uva

Redroot pigweed seedling

R. Uva

Powell amaranth seedling

J. Neal

Redroot pigweed seedling (note hairy stem, reddish at base)

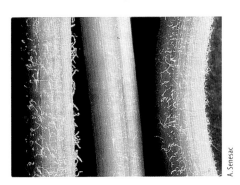

A. Senesac

Left to right: stems of smooth pigweed, Powell amaranth, and redroot pigweed

FLOWERS AND FRUIT:

Smooth pigweed: Plants have 5 styles and tepals. Tepals are erect and pointed. Bracts are often equal to or only slightly exceed the flowers in length. The **utricle cap drops (dehisces)** as the seed matures. **The narrower, often lax, terminal spike, which is smaller and less bristly** than that of the other 2 species, accounts for the common name smooth pigweed.

Powell amaranth: Plants have 3–5 styles on the pistillate flowers and 3–5 tepals (petals and sepals), which look alike. Tepals are erect, tapering to an extended point (acuminate). The **utricle is indehiscent** and persists with the seed as it disperses.

Redroot pigweed: Small, greenish flowers are produced in **dense, stiff, spike-like, terminal panicles** (5–20 cm long and approximately 1.5 cm wide). Smaller inflorescences are in the axils of the lower leaves. Male and female flowers are separate (monoecious). The male flowers abscise soon after the pollen sheds. **Fruits** are thin-walled, 1-seeded utricles, 1.5–2 mm long, that **split open** by a cap-like lid around the middle. Seeds of all 3 species are glossy, black to dark brown, 1–1.2 mm long, ovate to elliptic, somewhat flattened, with a notch at the narrow end.

POSTSENESCENCE CHARACTERISTICS: Erect stems persist, bearing the brown inflorescences of dried bracts, flowers, and seeds. Naturally occurring intraspecifc hybrids are partially sterile and will remain green longer than seed-bearing plants.

HABITAT: All 3 species are weeds of horticultural and agronomic crops, landscapes and nursery crops, and rarely turf. They grow on a wide variety of soil types but thrive under sunny, fertile conditions.

DISTRIBUTION: All are native to North or Central America, or both, but have spread to become weedy throughout the United States and southern Canada. Powell amaranth has infested the northeastern United States and Canada only within the past 50 years.

SIMILAR SPECIES: **See Table 1 for a comparison with other pigweeds. Common lambsquarters (*Chenopodium album*),** at the **cotyledon stage**, is similar in habit and is often found growing with pigweeds. The new growth of lambsquarters seedlings has a granular leaf surface that pigweeds do not have. **Pokeweed (*Phytolacca americana*)** seedlings, with long cotyledons, oval to egg-shaped leaves, and smooth red stems, are sometimes mistaken for pigweeds. By the third to fourth leaf stage, however, pokeweed can be distinguished by the pointed leaf tips.

Left to right: seedheads of smooth pigweed, redroot pigweed, and Powell amaranth

J. Neal

Redroot pigweed foliage

J. Neal

R. Uva

ead pigweed stems in early spring

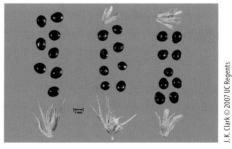

J. K. Clark © 2007 UC Regents

Left to right: smooth pigweed seeds, Powell amaranth seeds, and redroot pigweed seeds

Palmer amaranth (*Amaranthus palmeri* S. Watson)

SYNONYM: Palmer pigweed

GENERAL DESCRIPTION: Troublesome, summer annual weed in southern agricultural crops and spreading into the Northeast. Plants are upright and branched, to more than **2 m in height**, with very rapid seedling growth rates. Stems and leaves lack hairs. **Petioles are equal to or longer than leaf blades**. Otherwise the leaf blades are similar to many other pigweeds. **Herbicide-resistant populations are widespread**, including many that are resistant to multiple modes of action.

PROPAGATION / PHENOLOGY: **Reproduction is by seeds.** Seeds fall near parent plants but are dispersed greater distances with soil movement. Seeds germinate in warm soil from spring through August. Stems can form adventitious roots. Uprooted plants discarded on moist ground can form roots and resume growth.

SEEDLING: Cotyledons are elliptic to nearly linear (10–12 mm long), green to reddish on the upper surface. Young **leaves are broadly egg-shaped**, widest at the blade base, with a small notch at the leaf tip. **Leaves and stems are not hairy.** As seedlings grow, the leaf shape changes with tips becoming more tapered. Leaf blade base varies from obtuse to sharply angled. Leaves alternate but when viewed from above, appear as if whorled, often described as poinsettia-like. Leaf blades often have a V-shaped variegation in the center. Seedling plants may grow more than 5 cm a day under optimum conditions.

MATURE PLANT: Stems branched and often glossy, light green to reddish. At maturity, the stems are thick and woody. Leaves remain hairless, with most petioles similar in length to the blade. Blade varies from egg-shaped, to almost diamond-shaped becoming lanceolate near the top of the stems.

ROOTS AND UNDERGROUND STRUCTURES: A thick taproot with secondary fibrous root system.

FLOWERS AND FRUIT: **Plants are dioecious**; male and female plants are similar until flowering. **Male and female inflorescences are slender**; the female inflorescences are very prickly but the males are soft to the touch. Individual flowers are small, lack conspicuous petals, and are densely arranged in upright, slender, branched terminal spikes 10–50 cm long, often drooping. Some smaller flower clusters form in the leaf axils in the upper third of the plant. **Female flowers have stiff, sharp bracts** up to 6 mm long; male flowers lack the stiff bracts. Plants are prolific seed producers. Fruit (utricles) are nearly spherical, reddish-brown, almost smooth, and approximately 2 mm in diameter. Seeds are glossy, dark reddish-brown, and about 1 mm in diameter.

POSTSENESCENCE CHARACTERISTICS: Upright, woody stems persist well into winter.

HABITAT: A very common weed of cultivated agronomic crops and disturbed areas. Tolerant of a wide variety of soil types.

DISTRIBUTION: Native to the southwestern United States but has spread eastward and continues to expand its range. It is the most economically troublesome broadleaf weed of cultivated agronomic crops in the southeastern United States and Mid-Atlantic states.

SIMILAR SPECIES: Overall growth habit and habitats are similar to other pigweeds. However, the length of the petiole vs. leaf blade differentiates this species from other similar *Amaranthus* species. **See Table 1 for a comparison with other pigweeds.**

Palmer amaranth habit

J. Neal

Palmer amaranth seedling

L. Sosnoskie

Palmer amaranth young foliage with chevron

J. DiTomaso

Palmer amaranth hairless stem

J. Neal

Palmer amaranth male inflorescence

J. DiTomaso

Palmer amaranth spiny female inflorescence

J. Neal

Palmer amaranth petiole equal to or longer than leaf blade

J. Neal

1 mm

Palmer amaranth seeds and bracts

M. Bertone

119

Waterhemp (*Amaranthus tuberculatus* (Moq.) Sauer)

SYNONYMS: *Amaranthus rudis*, roughfruit amaranth, tall waterhemp, common waterhemp

GENERAL DESCRIPTION: One of the most troublesome **summer annual** weeds in mid-West agriculture and spreading into the Northeast. Plants are upright and branched, varying in size from 0.5–2.5 m tall. **Leaves are more slender than other common pigweeds.** Plants are **dioecious**; male and female plants are similar until flowering. Male and female inflorescences are slender and not prickly. **Herbicide-resistant populations** are widespread and common, including many that are resistant to multiple modes of action.

PROPAGATION / PHENOLOGY: Reproduction is by **seeds**. Seeds germinate in warm soil from spring through August. Later season emergence allows the species to "avoid" early season weed control treatments.

SEEDLING: Cotyledons are broadly elliptic to egg-shaped, wider than many other common pigweeds. Young **leaves are slender**, 2.5 to 3x longer than wide with a small notch at the leaf tip, and often with a waxy sheen. **Leaves and stems lack hairs.** As seedlings grow, the leaves remain slender, tapered to a lanceolate leaf tip.

MATURE PLANT: Plants grow vigorously **to 2.5 m in height**. Stems lack hairs, are branched, ribbed, and often glossy. At maturity, the stems are somewhat woody. Leaves on mature plants remain hairless and slender compared to other pigweeds; leaf blades to 15 cm in length. Petioles are ¼ to ½ the length of the leaf blades. Leaf color can vary from green to red and is not associated with sex.

ROOTS AND UNDERGROUND STRUCTURES: Taproot with a secondary fibrous root system.

FLOWERS AND FRUIT: Plants are dioecious, flowering from mid-summer to early autumn. Individual flowers are small and lack conspicuous petals. Flowers are formed in upright, slender, branched, terminal spikes. Unlike Palmer amaranth, the spikes are not prickly to the touch. Plants are prolific seed producers. A single female plant may produce more than 300,000 seeds. Fruit (utricles) are slender, reddish-brown, not ribbed, and approximately 2 mm in diameter; seeds are glossy dark brown, round, about 1 mm in diameter.

POSTSENESCENCE CHARACTERISTICS: Upright, woody stems may persist well into winter.

HABITAT: A very common weed of cultivated agronomic crops. Tolerant of a wide variety of soil types.

DISTRIBUTION: Considered native to the eastern two-thirds of North America. Historically, it was rare in the eastern United States but very common in Midwest agriculture. Its distribution and importance in agriculture is expanding. It is becoming more common in the eastern United States and is expected to become a significant weed in the region.

SIMILAR SPECIES: Overall growth habit and habitats are similar to other pigweeds; however, the wider cotyledon and narrow leaf shape differentiates this species. Other characteristics used to differentiate waterhemp include petiole length, absence of hairs, and lack of flower clusters in the leaf axils. **See Table 1 for a comparison with other pigweeds.**

Waterhemp, late season habit

A. Hager

Waterhemp seedling

J. Neal

Waterhemp young foliage

L. Sosnoskie

Left, male waterhemp inflorescence; *right*, female

L. Sosnoskie

Waterhemp smooth stems

L. Sosnoskie

Left, waterhemp leaf and petiole; *right*, Palmer amaranth leaf and petiole

L. Sosnoskie

Slender amaranth (*Amaranthus viridis* L.)

Synonyms: *Amaranthus gracilis*, green amaranth, green pigweed

General Description: A sprawling to semi-erect, **summer annual** with **terminal and axillary flower** clusters, **smooth stems**, and entire leaves. Generally shorter in height and vigor compared to other weedy amaranths.

Propagation / Phenology: Reproduction is by seeds. Seeds germinate in warm soil spring through mid-summer. Plants die with frost.

Seedling: Cotyledons are linear, 5–8 mm long. **Leaves are alternate, egg-shaped**, broader at the base than at the tip, with entire margins, and often with a tiny "notch" at the tip. **Stems lack hairs (or nearly so)**, often tinted bronze or red at the base. Plants are initially upright but branch near the base, particularly after mowing.

Mature Plant: Plants are **highly branched with a spreading or semi-upright habit** and arching stems. Stems are grooved, and often glabrous; light green, bronze, or tinted maroon. Leaves are egg-shaped to nearly triangular, prominently veined; margins are entire but often wavy (undulate); underside lighter in color with prominent light-colored veins. Leaf blades are up to 7 cm long, as long or longer than the petioles. Petioles and leaves are longer at the base and midsection of the plant, shorter in the upper flowering stems.

Roots and Underground Structures: Taproot with a secondary fibrous root system.

Flowers and Fruit: Individual flowers lack pedicels, are small, greenish, and produced in **axillary and terminal inflorescences** from early summer through autumn. Axillary flowers are in small, rounded clusters. Terminal inflorescences are branched, thin, flexuous spikes, typically 20–30 cm long but may be longer. Fruit (utricles) are indehiscent and approximately 2 mm long; seeds are black, round, and about 1 mm in diameter.

Postsenescence Characteristics: In dry areas, dead stems may persist into winter.

Habitat: A weed of most cultivated cropping systems and disturbed sites. Tolerates some mowing.

Distribution: As a weed, slender amaranth is most common in the southern United States, but the species has been documented north to New England and the Great Lakes.

Similar Species: **Spiny amaranth (*Amaranthus spinosus* L.)** is a summer annual with similarly erect to sprawling growth, leaf shape, flowering habit, and overlapping distribution. Spiny amaranth is easily distinguished by a pair of **sharp spines** (5–10 mm) at the leaf axils. **See Table 1 for a comparison with other pigweeds.**

J. Neal

Slender amaranth plant

J. Neal

Slender amaranth young plant

J. Neal

Left, slender amaranth leaves with wavy margin; *right,* entire margins

J. Neal

Slender amaranth terminal inflorescence

J. Neal

Slender amaranth stem and axillary flower cluster

J. Neal

Spiny amaranth spines at the leaf axil

J. Neal

Left, slender amaranth seeds; *right,* spiny pigweed seeds

123

Bishop's goutweed (*Aegopodium podagraria* L.)

SYNONYMS: ground elder, herb Gerard

GENERAL DESCRIPTION: An erect, **herbaceous, colony-forming, shade-tolerant perennial** (0.1–1 m in height). Occurs with both variegated (white and green) and solid green leaves. The variegated variety is sometimes cultivated as an ornamental, whereas plants found in natural areas are generally green.

PROPAGATION / PHENOLOGY: Reproduces primarily by vegetative expansion from **rhizomes.** Can reproduce from small root fragments. Seed production generally occurs only in sunny habitats, and seedlings are uncommon. Germination occurs in early to mid-spring.

SEEDLING: Cotyledons are lanceolate, petiolate (10–15 mm long), and have no venation. First true leaves are compound (3 lobed) with serrate margins.

MATURE PLANT: Stems of adult plants are light green, hollow, grooved, and hairless. Upper portions of the stem are branched. Leaves are alternate. **Lower and basal leaves** occur on petioles (12–30 cm long), are **bipinnate,** and 5–7 cm long by 3–5 cm wide. Each leaf has a terminal group of 2–3 leaflets and 2 lateral groups of 1–3 leaflets. Leaflets are ovate and hairless with serrate or double-serrate margins; lateral leaflets are occasionally deeply lobed. **Upper leaves are pinnate (1 terminal and 2 lateral leaflets),** with 3 lanceolate leaflets, and occur on petioles to 10 cm in length. Lateral leaflets are sessile or nearly so, while the terminal leaflet has a short stalk (2.5 cm).

ROOTS AND UNDERGROUND STRUCTURES: A fibrous and shallow root system with spreading lateral rhizomes. Rhizomes are thin (2 mm in diameter), branching, and can reach up to 3 m in length.

FLOWERS AND FRUIT: Flowers are produced from late spring to mid-summer. Flowers are terminal, **flat, compound umbels** (3.8–12 cm in diameter). Umbels are composed of 10–20 umbellets of 10–25 flowers each. Peduncles of umbels are 7.5–15 cm long, while umbellet pedicels are up to 0.6 cm long; neither stalk has bracts. Flowers are **white**, small (3 mm in diameter), and have 5 petals that bend inward. Each flower has 5 stamens and an ovary with 2 curved styles. Fruits are oblong (3–4 mm long), flattened, and grooved, and turn from bright green to brown as they ripen. In autumn, each fruit splits into 2 angular, oblong seeds.

POSTSENESCENCE CHARACTERISTICS: Leaves begin to turn yellow in late summer but remain on the plant until the first frost of the season, at which point all upper parts of the plant die back.

HABITAT: A weed of forest edges, open woodlands, waste areas, gardens, and roadsides. May escape cultivation in urban areas. Prefers well-drained soil and partial shade, and can tolerate a range of acidity.

DISTRIBUTION: Occurs throughout the eastern and northern United States and across Canada.

SIMILAR SPECIES: Several other species have similar flowers, but the low growing habit and broader leaflets differentiate bishop's goutweed from most other weeds in the carrot family. **Wild carrot (*Daucus carota*), poison-hemlock (*Conium maculatum*),** and **wild chervil (*Anthriscus sylvestris*)** have similar flowers to bishop's goutweed. These species have fern-like leaves; whereas the leaflets of bishop's goutweed are not dissected. **Spotted waterhemlock (*Cicuta maculata*)** has similar bractless flowers and non-dissected leaflets like bishop's goutweed, but it is larger than bishop's goutweed (0.9–2.1 m tall), with more numerous, narrower (0.5–3 cm wide) leaflets.

N. Doolittle

Bishop's goutweed habit

N. Doolittle

Bishop's goutweed inflorescence

S. Morris

Bishop's goutweed rhizomatous growth

S. Morris

Bishop's goutweed, cultivated forms will revert to green "wild type"

A. DiTommaso

Bishop's goutweed seeds, 3–4 mm long

Wild chervil (*Anthriscus sylvestris* Hoffm.)

SYNONYMS: Cow parsley, mother-die

GENERAL DESCRIPTION: An herbaceous **biennial or short-lived monocarpic perennial** that produces a spreading **basal rosette of divided, fern-like leaves** during the first year and an erect flowering stem (0.3–1.5 m tall) the second to fourth year. **White, lacy flower heads** resemble those of wild carrot.

PROPAGATION / PHENOLOGY: Reproduction is by **seeds and lateral root crown** buds. Plants from seed or root crown buds first produce a rosette of leaves, then flower when the rosette is large enough (after 1 or more years) and after a cold vernalization (size-dependent vernalization).

SEEDLING: Cotyledons are linear, tapered, and without petioles.

MATURE PLANT: Leaves of the first-year (and later) rosettes are triangular, alternate, almost fern-like, 2–3 times pinnately compound, and up to 0.3 m long. Leaflets are lobed, 1.5–3 cm in length, lobed, with toothed margins. Leaves are deeply grooved and shiny above and pubescent to sparsely pubescent beneath. Petioles and leaf branches deeply furrowed, clasping, and often densely hairy. Second-year flowering **stems are hollow,** 0.3–1.5 m tall, **deeply grooved,** and apically **pubescent**. Stems are swollen at the nodes. All parts are aromatic when crushed.

ROOTS AND UNDERGROUND STRUCTURES: A long (to 2 m), thick taproot. Roots develop buds at the crown that grow into new plants with taproot and leaves (daughter roots and shoots). When the mother plant has flowered and set seed, the mother taproot dies and the daughter plants become independent.

FLOWERS AND FRUIT: Flower production occurs from late May through mid-June. Flowers are produced on axillary and terminal compound umbels up to 20 cm in diameter. Each umbel is made up of 10–15 umbellets. Peduncles are sparsely hairy with 4–6 bracts at base. Pedicels are smooth to sparsely hairy and without bracts. Individual flowers are small (3–6 mm in diameter), white to cream-colored with lanceolate to ovate, notched petals. Fruit production occurs from late June through July. Fruits are hairless, dry, and indehiscent schizocarps that comprise 2 mericarps (seeds), with a tiny fringe of hairs at the base. Seeds are lanceolate, 6–10 mm long, and turn from green to brown or shiny black as they ripen.

POSTSENESCENCE CHARACTERISTICS: First-year growth remains green throughout the winter. Flowering stems begin to die in August, and dead flowering stalks may persist throughout autumn and into the winter.

HABITAT: Wild chervil prefers moist soil and partial shade but can persist in dry and sunny habitats. It is a weed of pastures, hayfields, disturbed and edge habitats, streambanks, hedgerows, and roadsides.

DISTRIBUTION: Found in the northeastern United States and adjacent Canada, and south to North Carolina.

SIMILAR SPECIES: The **hedgeparsleys (*Torilis* spp.)** have similar foliage to wild chervil; however, the fruits are hairy and burr-like rather than smooth. **Wild carrot (*Daucus carota*)** flowers later in the season and has a single umbel subtended by long, divided bracts. The leaves of **poison-hemlock (*Conium maculatum*)** are similar in shape to those of wild chervil but are hairless, somewhat waxy in appearance, and have a foul odor. Poison-hemlock is generally taller than wild chervil (1.5–2.5 m tall) and has purple spots throughout the stem. **See Table 2 for a comparison with other weedy members of the carrot family.**

J. Neal

ild chervil habit

K. Torreson

Wild chervil seedling

Wild chervil first-year rosette

J. Neal

S. Morris

Wild chervil mature rosette

J. Neal

ild chervil stem

J. Neal

Wild chervil inflorescence

J. Neal

Wild chervil young seedhead

Poison-hemlock (*Conium maculatum* L.)

Synonyms: deadly hemlock, snake-weed, poison parsley, wode whistle, poison stinkweed

General Description: A **biennial** with a **basal rosette of leaves the first year** and an **erect branched stem (60 cm–2 m in height) the second year.** **Flowers and foliage resemble carrot and parsley.** Plant parts have a disagreeable odor when crushed. All parts of the plant contain toxic alkaloids, including coniine, that cause **respiratory failure** in humans and other animals **when ingested.**

Propagation / Phenology: Reproduction is **by seeds.**

Seedling: Seedlings have a **parsnip-like odor** when crushed. Cotyledons are narrow, elongated-elliptic (30 cm long), with a long petiole (15 mm). The surface of the cotyledons is light green with prominent netted veins on the underside. The **first leaf is smooth** and **2 or 3 times deeply dissected; later leaves are 2 to 3 times pinnatifid.**

Mature Plant: A **basal rosette** is formed in the first year. **In the second year, plants produce erect stems** that are **hairless, purple-spotted, ridged,** and hollow between the nodes. **Leaves** are alternate, dark glossy green, **fern-like,** triangular, **20–40 cm long,** and 3–4 times pinnately compound. The **bases of the lower leaves form a sheath that encircles the stem.**

Roots and Underground Structures: Thick, white, often branched **taproot,** 20–25 cm long, with a well-developed secondary fibrous root system.

Flowers and Fruit: Flowers are produced from June through August in flat to slightly convex umbrella-like clusters (compound umbels) 4–6 cm wide. The 2 seeds are enclosed within the fruit (schizocarp). When the fruit is mature, the 2 halves separate. Each section is oval, 2–3.5 mm long, flattened on one side, with conspicuous pale brown wavy ribs.

Postsenescence Characteristics: Dead flowering stem may persist well into winter. Fruit often remain attached for a considerable period of time after senescence.

Habitat: Primarily a weed of pastures and landscapes, poison-hemlock is also found on borders of fields and in roadsides, ditch banks, and meadows. It thrives on rich, gravelly or loamy soils.

Distribution: Distributed throughout the United States, including the western, northeastern, north-central states and adjacent areas of southern Canada. Poison-hemlock is not as common in parts of the northern Great Plains.

Similar Species: **Spotted waterhemlock (*Cicuta maculata* L.)** is a **very poisonous perennial** found primarily in wet areas. It resembles poison-hemlock but has smooth and purple-spotted stems and leaves that are 2–3 times pinnately compound with considerably **larger leaflets,** and a cluster of fleshy taproots at the base. **Wild chervil (*Anthriscus sylvestris*)** has similar growth, flowers, and leaves, but stems lack purple spots and are swollen at the nodes. **Giant hogweed (*Heracleum mantegazzianum*)** is much larger than the other similar species (2–5 m tall), has purple-blotched stems, and leaves up to a meter long. **See Table 2 for a comparison with other weedy members of the carrot family.**

J. DiTomaso

Poison-hemlock stem

J. DiTomaso

Poison-hemlock mature foliage

J. DiTomaso

Poison-hemlock in flower

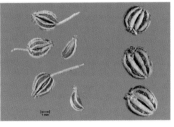

J. O'Brien © 2007 UC Regents

Left, poison-hemlock seeds;
right, spotted waterhemlock seeds

J. DiTomaso

Spotted waterhemlock
chambered fleshy
taproots

Regina O. Hughes, USD

Spotted waterhemlock

Wild celery or marsh parsley (*Cyclospermum leptophyllum* (Pers.) Sprague ex Britt. & E. Wilson)

Synonyms: *Apium leptophyllum, Apium tenuifolium, Cyclospermum ammi*

General Description: Erect to decumbent, branched winter or summer annual to 0.6 m tall, with **finely dissected leaves and small, white flowers in compound and simple umbels**. In warmer climates, plants behave as winter annuals; in cooler climates as summer annuals. The plants have a **distinctive aroma when crushed**.

Propagation / Phenology: Reproduction is only by **seeds**, and seeds fall primarily near parent plants. Seeds germinate in cool, moist soils from mid-spring through mid-autumn. Freshly shed seeds will germinate; thus, plants can produce multiple generations per year. Plants usually do not persist in hot summer weather.

Seedling: Young seedlings strongly resemble wild carrot seedlings. Cotyledons linear, mostly 4–10 mm long, 1 mm wide, and lack hairs. First leaf is deeply 3-lobed, and long-stalked. Leaves initially form a basal rosette. Petioles are long, with a groove on the upper surface, clasping the base.

Mature Plant: **Leaves** are alternate, **dissected 1–3 times, and 3–10 cm long**. Upper leaves are sessile and reduced to thread-like segments, but lower leaves are on stalks 2–12 cm long. **Leaf segments are linear to thread-like**, 0.3–1.5 cm long. Stems lack hairs, and may be erect with few branches, or many-branched forming rounded mounds.

Roots and Underground Structures: Taprooted, with fibrous laterals.

Flowers and Fruit: Plants flower from spring to summer. Umbels are compound and sometimes simple, fairly open compared to similar species. Flowers have 5 small, white petals (sometimes pink-tinted when in bud), and an inferior ovary. Primary umbel rays are 1–3, less than 2 cm long. Fruit (schizocarps) are 2-chambered, oblong to ovoid, 5-ribbed, green turning tan to brown with age, slightly compressed laterally (perpendicular to the central wall), 1–3 mm long and wide, and lack hairs. Fruits have 1 oil tube between each rib.

Postsenescence Characteristics: Flowering stems can persist into winter.

Habitat: Plants prefer persistently moist areas. Found in disturbed places, fields, roadsides, railroad tracks, gardens, orchards, turf, landscaped areas, container nurseries, field and vegetable crops, and associated ditches and margins.

Distribution: Found throughout the southern and mid-Atlantic states, north to New York.

Similar Species: Wild celery resembles **wild carrot (*Daucus carota*)** but wild carrot is hairy throughout, rosettes are fuller and more developed, flowering stems erect, and flower heads are larger and showier. In addition, the seeds of wild carrot have bristly fruit. Seedlings may also resemble young **poison-hemlock (*Conium maculatum*),** but poison-hemlock leaves are more fern-like with broader leaflet segments, and stems are stout, up to 3 m tall, and purple-spotted or -streaked.

J. Neal

Wild celery habit

J. DiTomaso

Wild celery seedling

J. Neal

Wild celery dissected leaf

J. Neal

Wild celery young plant

J. DiTomaso

Wild celery inflorescence

J. O'Brien © 2007 UC Regents

Wild celery seeds

Wild carrot (*Daucus carota* L.)

S<small>YNONYMS</small>: Queen Anne's lace, birds-nest, devils plague

G<small>ENERAL</small> D<small>ESCRIPTION</small>: A **biennial** forming a **basal rosette of leaves the first year** and **an erect flowering stalk** (1 m in height) **the following year**. The **foliage is fern-like** with a carrot-like odor.

P<small>ROPAGATION</small> / P<small>HENOLOGY</small>: Reproduction is **by seeds**. Germination occurs in the spring.

S<small>EEDLING</small>: Hypocotyls are pinkish-brown. **Cotyledons are linear**, approximately 20 mm long by 1 mm wide, lack petioles, and taper at both the base and tip. **Young leaves form a basal rosette** (technically, are alternate), are smooth on the upper surface, grayish-green, with short hairs on the veins of the lower surface and along the margins. **Leaves are 3-lobed; each lobe is deeply pinnately dissected**, with petioles longer than the blade. Seedlings resemble parsley and develop into basal rosettes.

M<small>ATURE</small> P<small>LANT</small>: **In the second year, hollow and vertically ribbed hairy stems are produced from the rosette. Leaves are primarily basal**, with only a few sessile, alternate, reduced leaves on the stem. Leaves are triangular or oblong (up to 15 cm long), **twice pinnately compound** with narrow or lobed segments. Leaf margins are hairy.

R<small>OOTS AND</small> U<small>NDERGROUND</small> S<small>TRUCTURES</small>: A stout, **yellowish-white taproot** with fibrous secondary roots.

F<small>LOWERS AND</small> F<small>RUIT</small>: Flowers are produced from July to September in the second year. Inflorescence is composed of numerous **white, lace-like flowers in a flat-topped compound umbel** (twice-branched). The lower branches of the umbel are subtended by deeply lobed leaf-like bracts. At maturity, flower clusters may close, resembling a bird's nest. Individual flowers are white, sometimes pinkish, with a single deep-purple flower in the center of the cluster. The 2 seeds are enclosed within the fruit (schizocarp). When the fruit matures, the 2 halves separate. Each section is 2–3 mm long, yellow to light grayish-brown, flattened on one side, and ridged with barbed prickles that aid in dispersal. One plant can produce up to 4000 seeds.

P<small>OSTSENESCENCE</small> C<small>HARACTERISTICS</small>: First-year basal rosettes remain green through the winter. After the second year, plants die, but stems persist, with remnants of the flower clusters and finely divided leaves remaining.

H<small>ABITAT</small>: Wild carrot is a weed of low-maintenance turfgrass, pastures, landscapes, nursery crops, and other perennial crops. It is less common in cultivated agricultural crops, except under reduced-tillage practices. Wild carrot most commonly grows on well-drained to dry soils, particularly in old meadows and fallow fields.

D<small>ISTRIBUTION</small>: Found throughout North America.

S<small>IMILAR</small> S<small>PECIES</small>: **Compared to other weedy members of the carrot family, wild carrot stems are more slender and are lacking purplish pigmentation or swollen nodes commonly present on other species. See Table 2 for a comparison with related species.** The **leaves and seedlings of chamomiles (*Anthemis* spp.)** are similar to those of wild carrot, but chamomile plants produce many erect, leafy, flowering stems. **Seedlings of common yarrow (*Achillea millefolium*)** are easily confused with wild carrot, but the leaves of common yarrow are not as wide and are more finely dissected, and the cotyledons are rounded, not linear. As a mature plant, common yarrow is a rhizomatous perennial with flowers typical of the Asteraceae (aster family).

J. Neal

Wild carrot habit

J. DiTomaso

Wild carrot seedlings

J. DiTomaso

Wild carrot flower and
bird's-nest-like seedhead

R. Prostak

Wild carrot rosette

J. K. Clark © 2007 UC Regents

Wild carrot seeds, 2.5 mm

Giant hogweed (*Heracleum mantegazzianum* Sommier & Levier)

SYNONYMS: *Heracleum laciniatum*, *H. persicum*, *H. pubescens*, hogweed

GENERAL DESCRIPTION: Robust **biennial or perennial to 5 m tall** with **large 3-part compound leaves**. It has escaped garden cultivation, often growing in riparian areas, where it can develop a dense canopy. Unlike other emergent aquatic plants, giant hogweed cannot tolerate prolonged root submergence in water. Skin contact with the sap can cause **severe photosensitizing dermatitis (and severe blisters)** on most people and some animals. Cattle and pigs consume giant hogweed without any apparent problem. Native to the Caucasus Mountains of southwestern Asia. Giant hogweed is listed as a **federal noxious weed**.

PROPAGATION / PHENOLOGY: **Reproduction is by seeds** and **vegetatively by forming new crowns from the tuberous rootstocks.** Plants produce many seeds that primarily disperse with water. Seeds can survive 7 years or more under field conditions. Individual plants appear to flower once and die.

SEEDLING: Cotyledons are approximately 3 cm long. The first leaves are palmate, but not deeply cut. Subsequent leaves become larger, more deeply divided, with toothed margins.

MATURE PLANT: The stems and leaf stalks are typically **purple-blotched** and covered with coarse, pustule-based white hairs. Leaves are alternate, pinnate-compound, and **3 m long by 2.6 m wide** with 3 leaflets. Leaflets are deeply bipinnate-lobed and toothed with leaf stalks that are inflated and sheath the stem.

ROOTS AND UNDERGROUND STRUCTURES: Plants have a stout taproot and often develop additional crowns with overwintering buds.

FLOWERS AND FRUIT: The showy inflorescence is a **compound umbel** that grows to more than **0.5 m diameter. Main umbel rays are usually 50–150** and unequal in length. **Petals are white**, 1 cm long. The fruits are elliptic to obovate schizocarps, 8–12 mm long, strongly flattened, laterally winged, and covered with short hairs.

POSTSENESCENCE CHARACTERISTICS: The tall, hollow stalks can remain attached for at least a year after senescence with obvious compound umbel inflorescence. Contact with the dead stems can cause dermatitis.

HABITAT: Plants occur in riparian areas, disturbed sites, roadsides, and waste places, but most often in wet places. Sale is prohibited, but it is sometimes grown by unsuspecting gardeners. This practice is discouraged because of its invasive and toxic nature.

DISTRIBUTION: Isolated occurrences in most northeastern and Great Lake states, North Carolina, Virginia, and also in the Pacific Northwest.

SIMILAR SPECIES: **See Table 2 for a comparison of related species. Wild parsnip (*Pastinaca sativa*)** is a glabrous to minutely hairy biennial, to approximately 2 m tall. Unlike giant hogweed, wild parsnip has yellowish flowers and much smaller 1-pinnate compound leaves. **Purplestem angelica (*Angelica atropurpurea* L.)** is a perennial that also has white flowers on a compound umbel. It grows to 1–2.5 m in height and can be found in shaded woody areas and along streambanks, swamps, and wet meadows. However, its stems are dark purple and, unlike giant hogweed, its leaves are ternately divided (divided three times) with much smaller leaflets. Native to the northeastern United States. **Cowparsnip (*Heracleum maximum* Bartr.** [syn.: *H. sphondylium* L. and *H. lanatum* Michx.]) is a native and very similar to giant hogweed, but much smaller (1–3 m tall) with smaller but similarly lobed leaves (<1 m long).

K. Howard

Giant hogweed habit

Giant hogweed seedling

K. Howard

J. DiTomaso

Giant hogweed inflorescence

M. Bravo

Cow-parsnip habit

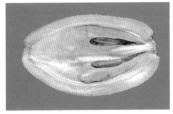

Giant hogweed seed, 8 by 14 mm

S. Hurst, hosted by USDA-NRCS PLANTS Database

Wild parsnip (*Pastinaca sativa* L.)

SYNONYMS: parsnip, common parsnip

GENERAL DESCRIPTION: Generally a **biennial** or monocarpic perennial up to 2 m tall. Plants typically **lack hairs** or are minutely hairy and have a **pungent smell when crushed**. Plants produce many clusters of **yellow flowers arranged in compound umbels**. Wild parsnip is the weedy form of the cultivated parsnip and has an edible root. Native to Eurasia. Plants produce furanocoumarins, exposure to which can cause photosensitive dermatitis in some people.

PROPAGATION / PHENOLOGY: Reproduction is only **by seeds**, and most seeds fall close to the parent plant. The wings on seeds can facilitate movement by wind for a few meters. Seeds falling into water can also move longer distances.

SEEDLING: Seedlings have strap-like cotyledons up to 3 cm long by 4 mm wide that taper to a long petiole. The first leaves have long petioles, are ovate to broadly cordate, and are approximately 1 cm long and coarsely toothed but not lobed.

MATURE PLANT: Non-flowering rosettes, which take a year or longer to mature, have **alternate pinnately compound leaves up to 15 cm long**. Flowering stems develop in the second year and are erect and hollow except at the nodes, and often branched at the upper nodes. The leaves are alternate, once- or twice-pinnate with 5–15 broad, ovate, 40 cm long, sometimes lobed leaflets with toothed margins. Leaves are reduced higher on the flowering stem. Petioles are grooved, broad at the base, and clasp the stem.

ROOTS AND UNDERGROUND STRUCTURES: A **fleshy, thick taproot** that is white to yellowish-brown and can grow up to 1.5 m deep. The root has a distinct parsnip odor.

FLOWERS AND FRUIT: Flowering occurs from late May until October. The yellow flowers are in a loose, flat-topped, 10–20 cm wide compound umbel with 6–25 straight, 2–5 cm long pedicels (rays). Flowers consist of 5 yellow petals, 3.5 mm long, that are curled inward. The sepals are very small or absent. Seeds mature in mid-summer, but generally remain on the stems until late summer or fall. Fruits (schizocarps) are oval and flat, with narrow wings and short, spreading styles. They split into 2 seeds (mericarps), 4–8 mm long, that are pale brown, flat, and winged. The mericarps have 4 conspicuous dark oil tubes on the outer surface and 2–4 on the inner surface.

POSTSENESCENCE CHARACTERISTICS: Dried stems remain intact for up to a year, often with some seed present. The compound umbel is easily recognizable for some time after the plants die.

HABITAT: Primarily found in disturbed sites, rights-of-ways, pastures, perennial crops, and reduced-tillage fields.

DISTRIBUTION: Found throughout the northeastern and mid-Atlantic states.

SIMILAR SPECIES: **See Table 2 for comparisons with other weedy members of the Apiaceae.** Wild parsnip can resemble **poison-hemlock (*Conium maculatum*)** but can be distinguished by its yellow flowers and pinnately compound lower leaves with much larger leaflets. In addition, its crushed foliage has a parsnip-like scent, and the stems lack purple spots. Wild parsnip can also resemble many other species in the carrot family, including **spotted waterhemlock (*Cicuta maculata*), giant hogweed (*Heracleum mantegazzianum*), cow-parsnip (*Heracleum maximum*), and purplestem angelica (*Angelica atropurpurea*)**, but all these species have white flowers and lack a parsnip odor.

J. DiTomaso

Wild parsnip plant

A. DiTomaso

Wild parsnip seedling

J. DiTomaso

Wild parsnip rosette

Wild parsnip flowers

J. DiTomaso

A. DiTomaso

Wild parsnip mature plant in seed

J. O'Brien © 2007 UC Regents

Wild parsnip fruit

137

Japanese hedgeparsley (*Torilis japonica* Houtt.)

SYNONYMS: *Torilis africana*, *Torilis anthriscus*, bur parsley, erect hedge-parsley, upright hedge-parsley

GENERAL DESCRIPTION: A **biennial or winter annual** forming a spreading **rosette** the first year and an erect, 0.6–1 m flowering stalk the second. The stem is branching, with pinnately compound **fern-like leaves**, and **white flowers in a loose, open umbel**.

PROPAGATION / PHENOLOGY: Reproduction is **by seeds**. Germination occurs in spring or during late summer and autumn.

SEEDLING: Little information is available. Cotyledons are **short-stalked**, **linear**, 10–20 mm long by 1–2 mm wide. Hypocotyl darker than cotyledons.

MATURE PLANT: The first-year rosette is low and spreading, with **pinnately divided compound leaves** that are **sparsely hairy on both sides**. The second-year **stem is erect, vertically ribbed, and densely pubescent** with short, stiff, appressed hairs. Stems are branching, and multiple stems may grow from a single rosette. **Leaves are alternate**, petiolate, and similarly shaped to those of the rosette. **Basal leaves are fern-like**, pinnately lobed, up to 13 cm long, and sheathed at petiole base. Apical leaves are smaller, less divided, and have linear lobes. **Leaf margins are toothed.**

ROOTS AND UNDERGROUND STRUCTURES: Thick taproot.

FLOWERS AND FRUIT: Flowers are produced from July to August on terminal and axillary stems in loose, flat, compound umbels (2.5–5 cm in diameter), **resembling an open, less dense wild carrot (*Daucus carota*)** inflorescence. Peduncles are up to 10 cm long and densely hairy. At the base of each umbel are 2 or more narrow, linear bracts, and each umbellet is subtended by up to 8 short bracts. Umbellets have 10–20 small (to 3 mm) white or pink-white flowers with 5–7 deeply cleft, unequally sized petals. The **oval fruit (schizocarp)** is 3–5 mm long, ribbed longitudinally, and **densely covered in hooked bristles**. Each fruit contains 2 seeds and splits into halves (mericarps) when ripe.

POSTSENESCENCE CHARACTERISTICS: First-year rosettes remain green throughout the winter. Seeds remain on dead second-year stems through autumn.

HABITAT: Japanese hedgeparsley is a weed of roadsides, railways, and similar edge habitats. Populations in disturbed sites can spread to grasslands, forests, and forest edges. The bur-like seeds cling readily to clothing and fur and hasten dispersal in areas with human and animal foot traffic.

DISTRIBUTION: Most common in states surrounding the Great Lakes and into the Mississippi and Ohio River basins, with sparse populations throughout the eastern United States, south and west to Texas and along the Pacific Coast.

SIMILAR SPECIES: **See Table 2 for a comparison** with similar white-flowered, weedy members of the carrot family. **Spreading hedgeparsley (*Torilis arvensis* (Huds.) Link)** is very similar in habit and appearance to Japanese hedgeparsley; however, it has few or no bracts at the base of the umbels, and the hairs on the seeds are straight rather than hooked. **Wild carrot** has erect hairs on the stem, and the umbels are subtended by long, pinnately divided involucral bracts. The fruits of **wild chervil (*Anthriscus sylvestris*)** are hairless, and the umbellets have no subtending bracts.

Japanese hedgeparsley habit

Japanese hedgeparsley flowers

Japanese hedgeparsley seedlings

Japanese hedgeparsley rosette

Japanese hedgeparsley stem leaf

Japanese hedgeparsley fruit

Hemp dogbane (*Apocynum cannabinum* L.)

SYNONYMS: dogbane, Indian-hemp, rheumatism weed

GENERAL DESCRIPTION: An erect (0.8–1.8 m tall), herbaceous **perennial** with branching stems on the upper portion of the plant. Plants form colonies by **spreading roots** that give rise to new shoots. All parts of the plant **exude a milky sap** when broken. Hemp dogbane is poisonous to cattle and horses.

PROPAGATION / PHENOLOGY: Reproduction is **by wind-dispersed seeds and by creeping roots**. In the early growing season, new shoots will emerge from crown buds or from buds that form on the lateral roots. Seeds are dispersed by wind in the late summer and throughout the fall. Root fragments are spread by soil movement and infrequent cultivation.

SEEDLING: Seedlings are erect, with a smooth, green hypocotyl. Cotyledons are ovate and pale green (6 mm long) with a white midvein. Seedlings can resprout if cut at ground level.

MATURE PLANT: Stems are green during the spring, turning reddish during the late season, hairless and branched on the top third to top half of the plant. **Leaves are oval to lanceolate**, with a petiole (up to 1 cm long) or sessile, with **smooth margins** and a **prominent white midvein**. Leaves are generally opposite but occasionally alternate and whorled.

ROOTS AND UNDERGROUND STRUCTURES: Expansive spreading system of fleshy roots that can produce new shoots. Roots can extend up to 4 m below the soil surface and up to 6 m laterally.

FLOWERS AND FRUIT: Hemp dogbane flowers from late June through early August. The small (0.3–0.6 cm), bell-shaped, **greenish-white flowers have 5 petals** and occur in terminal clusters (cymes) on the main stems and branches. Seedpods are slightly curved, slender (3 mm diameter), **paired follicles 10–20 cm in length**. Pods turn reddish-brown and open in late summer and early autumn; each pod contains many brown, flat, and thin (3–4 mm long) seeds, with long tufts of silky hairs (coma).

POSTSENESCENCE CHARACTERISTICS: Dried pods and stems persist throughout the winter.

HABITAT: A weed of agricultural and in particular reduced-tillage systems. Hemp dogbane is a common pest in corn, soybeans, wheat, sorghum, and forage crops. It can be found in old fields, roadsides, waste spaces, meadows, and forest edges. It grows best in fertile and medium to heavy textured, moist soils in full sun or partial shade, but it can also tolerate dry, upland habitats.

DISTRIBUTION: Found throughout the United States and Canada. It is most abundant in the Mississippi River Valley and eastward to the Atlantic Coast, although it is becoming more common west of the Mississippi River Valley.

SIMILAR SPECIES: **Spreading dogbane (*Apocynum androsaemifolium* L.)** is closely related to hemp dogbane. It is also a perennial that excretes milky sap when broken, and it has larger, drooping, egg-shaped leaves. The flowers of spreading dogbane are pale pink and larger and less densely clustered than those of hemp dogbane. **Common milkweed (*Asclepias syriaca*)** has larger leaves, an unbranched slightly hairy stem, and larger, purple-pink to white flowers. The **swallowworts (*Cynanchum* spp.)** can resemble hemp dogbane, particularly during the spring, but they do not have milky sap, are vine-like, have waxy dark green leaves, and pink to dark purple flowers.

Hemp dogbane
habit
J. Neal

A. DiTommaso

Hemp dogbane young shoots

Hemp dogbane seedling
. DiTommaso

Hemp dogbane leafy
shoots with seedpods
J. DiTomaso

S. Morris

Hemp dogbane flowers

J. DiTomaso

preading dogbane
owering stem

A. DiTommaso

Hemp dogbane fruit and
seeds

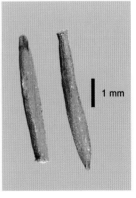

1 mm

K. Chamberlain

Hemp dogbane
seeds, 6 mm

Common milkweed (*Asclepias syriaca* L.)

SYNONYMS: wild cotton, Virginia silk, silkweed, cotton-weed

GENERAL DESCRIPTION: A **perennial with stout, erect** stems (0.6–1.5 m in height). All parts of the plant exude **a milky white sap** when broken.

PROPAGATION / PHENOLOGY: Reproduction is **by seeds and lateral roots that form new shoots.** In the spring, plants develop from buds either on the stem base or roots. Shoots emerge from April through May. **Cultivation can fragment and spread roots.** Seeds are wind dispersed in late summer and autumn.

SEEDLING: Most milkweed plants emerge from overwintering root buds. These are more robust than seedlings and lack cotyledons. Hypocotyls of seedlings are light green and smooth. Cotyledons are dull green, oval, rounded at the tips (1.2 cm long). **Young leaves are opposite**, dark green, waxy, **oblong, and pointed at the apex** with a **prominent white midvein** on the surface of the leaf. Seedlings do not flower during the first year of growth.

MATURE PLANT: Stems are usually unbranched, hollow, erect, covered with downy hairs, **and exude a milky sap.** Stems are green, becoming red later in the season. Leaves are **oblong-elliptic to oval**, 7–20 cm long, opposite, occasionally whorled, on short petioles (approximately 8 mm). Blades are green and smooth on the upper surface, lighter in color, and have downy hairy beneath. Margins are entire, pinnate veins do not reach the leaf margin.

ROOTS AND UNDERGROUND STRUCTURES: An extensive system of **thick, fleshy, white roots.**

FLOWERS AND FRUIT: Flowers are present from late June to early August. **Globe-like flower clusters (umbels)** develop at the end of stems and in the upper leaf axils. Individual flowers are **purplish-pink to white**, fragrant, with 5 hooded petals above, 5 sepals below, and styles united into a disk. Each flower is on a long and slender stalk. **Fruits are large (8-13 cm long), teardrop-shaped pods, grayish-green, and hairy with soft spines.** Each pod opens in early autumn and can contain more than 200 seeds. Seeds are 6–10 mm long, brown, flattened, oval, with a winged margin and a **terminal tuft of long, silky, white hairs facilitating wind dispersal.**

POSTSENESCENCE CHARACTERISTICS: The **characteristic pods** turn grayish-brown and persist on dead stems throughout the winter. Pods are shiny yellow on the inside. Some seeds may remain within the pods for an extended period.

HABITAT: Common milkweed is frequently found in meadows and along roadsides and is a weed of nursery and agricultural crops. It is a significant problem under no-till and reduced-tillage agricultural systems and prefers well-drained soil. It does not tolerate frequent mowing or cultivation.

DISTRIBUTION: Throughout the northeastern United States, south to Virginia and northern Georgia, and west to the Rocky Mountains.

SIMILAR SPECIES: **Hemp dogbane (*Apocynum cannabinum*)** is closely related to common milkweed. It is a large perennial with opposite leaves and milky white sap, but its leaves are smaller than common milkweed and its stem is many-branched in the upper third to half of the plant. In addition, the flowers are smaller, bell-shaped, and greenish-white. The fruit is long, narrow, and curved (8–12 cm long by less than 4 mm wide).

Common milkweed
habit

Common milkweed seedling

Common milkweed young plant

Common milkweed exudes
white sap when broken

Common milkweed fruit
and seeds

Juvenile common milkweed

Common milkweed
seeds, 9 mm

Black swallowwort (*Cynanchum louiseae* Kartesz & Ghandi) and pale swallowwort (*Cynanchum rossicum* (Kleopow) Borhidi)

SYNONYMS: *Cynanchum nigrum*, *Vincetoxicum nigrum*, climbing milkweed; *Vincetoxicum rossicum*, dog-strangling vine

GENERAL DESCRIPTION: **Twining, vine-like perennials** with **stems 1–2 m long.** Plants may form dense ground cover, or climbing stems can envelop small trees and other desirable vegetation in natural areas.

PROPAGATION / PHENOLOGY: Reproduction is **by wind-dispersed seeds** and by perennating **buds from the root crown**. A single seed contains 1–4 embryos and may produce multiple seedlings (polyembryonic).

SEEDLING: Cotyledons remain within the seed coat after germination. The first true **leaves are opposite** and lanceolate with **entire margins**, much like the mature foliage but leaf tips are not sharply tapered.

MATURE PLANT: Stems are mostly unbranched, **climbing or spreading, twining**, and smooth to pubescent. **Leaves are simple, opposite, dark green**, petiolate, oblong to ovate (5–10 cm long), hairless or with scattered hairs along the leaf edges, with **entire margins**. The **leaf tip gradually tapers to a point**, and the base of the leaf blade is rounded.

ROOTS AND UNDERGROUND STRUCTURES: A **large root crown**, which becomes woody as the plants age. Roots are thick, somewhat fleshy, and white to yellowish.

FLOWERS AND FRUIT: Flowers are produced from June through September. Clusters (cymose) of 5–20 **flowers are located in the leaf axils**, on peduncles of variable lengths. Flowers are 5-lobed, from 5–8 mm wide; petals are fleshy. The **fruits are follicles** produced singly or in pairs from each flower. Follicles are smooth (occasionally with numerous small bumps), elliptic, green turning yellow to dark brown, 4–7 cm long, and **at maturity split longitudinally to release seeds**. Seeds are brown, egg-shaped, flattened, with a winged-margin and a tuft of silky hairs at one end, resembling common milkweed seeds. The 2 species can be differentiated by floral characteristics. **Black swallowwort flowers** are **purple-black,** petals fleshy, triangular, 1.5–3 mm long and nearly as wide as long, with tiny (0.1–0.2 mm) hairs on the upper surface. Peduncles are 0.5–1.5 cm long. Seeds are 6–8 mm long by 3–4.7 mm wide. **Pale swallowwort flowers are light pink to red** (rarely white); peduncles are 1.5–4.5 cm long. Petals are lanceolate, 2.5–4.5 mm long, and half as wide as long. Seeds are 4–6.5 mm long by 2.4–3.1 mm wide.

POSTSENESCENCE CHARACTERISTICS: Twining vine-like stems persist after death bearing the papery pods. Pods are gray on the outside and yellow on the inside. Some seeds may remain inside.

HABITAT: Primarily a woodland species but has become an invasive weed in recently cleared areas, conservation habitats, Christmas trees, and other perennial crops, such as alfalfa and nurseries. It is also found in woods, fields and pastures, fencerows, and waste places, often in sunny areas and calcareous soils.

DISTRIBUTION: Found throughout the northeastern United States and Canada and the Great Lakes region.

SIMILAR SPECIES: **White swallowwort (*Cynanchum vincetoxicum* (L.) Pers.)** is similar vegetatively but has white flowers. White swallowwort currently has a more limited distribution around the Great Lakes states and adjacent Canadian provinces. **Honeyvine (*Cynanchum laeve* (Michx.) Pers.)** is a related North American native vine with a similar habit and foliage to black and pale swallowwort. Honeyvine leaves, however, are triangular to heart-shaped, while black and pale swallowwort leaves are oblong or ovate. Vines and foliage also resemble **periwinkle (*Vinca* spp.)**, but periwinkle stems do not twine and the leaf tips are not tapered to a sharp point as are the swallowworts.

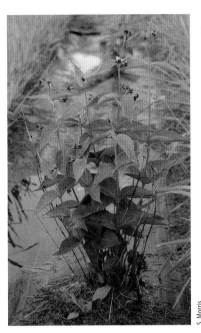

Pale swallowwort habit

S. Morris

S. Morris

Black swallowwort flower

Pale swallow-
wort flowers

A. DiTommaso

L. Smith

Pale swallowwort fruit and seeds

Pale
swallow-
wort
flowering
vine

R. Uva

R. Uva

Pale swallowwort fruit

Honeyvine
foliage

A. DiTommaso

S. Morris

Left, black swallowwort seeds,
6–8 mm; *right*, pale swallowwort seeds, 4–6.5 mm>

145

Water pennywort or dollarweed (*Hydrocotyle umbellata* L.)

SYNONYMS: pennywort, manyflower marshpennywort

GENERAL DESCRIPTION: **Creeping perennial** with **round, shiny leaf blade** with the **petiole attached near the center** (peltate). Plants have stolons or rhizomes and globe-shaped inflorescences. Native species are common in persistently wet areas of the southeastern coastal plain.

PROPAGATION / PHENOLOGY: Reproduction is primarily vegetatively from stems that creep on the surface (**stolons**) or as shallow rhizomes. Stems fragment easily. Reproduction can also be by **seeds**, but seedlings are rarely observed.

SEEDLING: No information available.

MATURE PLANT: Stems are round, hairless, and are either **stoloniferous rooting at most nodes or white, shallow rhizomes**. Leaves are somewhat fleshy, alternate, lack hairs, nearly round, palmate-veined, with peltate leaves. Leaves mostly 1–4 cm wide with entire or shallowly lobed margins. Petioles are thick, mostly 5–35 cm long. Length of the petiole is affected by the growing conditions; petioles will be short in mowed turf but when plants are growing within other vegetation, petioles can be more than 30 cm long.

ROOTS AND UNDERGROUND STRUCTURES: Roots grow from most stolon or rhizome nodes and are shallow in wet soils.

FLOWERS AND FRUIT: Plants flower from spring to summer. **Umbels** are simple, **almost globe-shaped**, often dense with 10–60 flowers. The umbel stalks (peduncles) are longer than that of the leaves. Petals are 5, cream-colored or yellowish-white. Flowers have inferior ovaries and fruits are 2-chambered, with 2 separate styles at the apex. Fruits (schizocarps) are on 1–3 cm long stalks. The schizocarps are 1–3 mm long, elliptic to round with obtuse ribs, flattened laterally (perpendicular to the central wall), and separate into halves (mericarps) at maturity. Each mericarp contains 1 seed.

POSTSENESCENCE CHARACTERISTICS: In warmer climates, foliage can persist overwinter but in mid-Atlantic states and northward, foliage is not persistent.

HABITAT: Most common in persistently moist areas such as ponds, lake margins, marshes, and irrigation and drainage ditches. A common weed of turfgrass and landscape plantings in coastal southeastern and mid-Atlantic states. Fairly salt-tolerant.

DISTRIBUTION: Found throughout the mid-Atlantic states and as far north as New York.

SIMILAR SPECIES: **Coastal plain pennywort (*Hydrocotyle bonariensis* Comm. ex Lam.)** is native to Africa and is quite similar vegetatively but flower heads start as an umbel and elongate (verticillate). **Lawn pennywort (*Hydrocotyle sibthorpioides* Lam.)** is native to Asia and is a low-growing terrestrial perennial of moist, shady sites and is often a weed of turf. The leaves are much smaller than other weedy *Hydrocotyle* species, only 1–2 cm wide with 5–7 shallow lobes. The umbel inflorescences have 3–10 sessile flowers, and the umbel stalk is only 0.5–1.5 cm long. It is found in all the mid-Atlantic states as far north as Pennsylvania. **Floating pennywort (*Hydrocotyle ranunculoides* L.f.)** is an aquatic native perennial with palmate lobed leaves and branched creeping stems that root at the nodes. Plants typically form dense, low-growing mats in shallow water or on wet soil near water. **Carolina dichondra (*Dichondra carolinensis*)** is a creeping perennial weed of turfgrass often mistaken for *Hydrocotyle*, but the leaves are kidney-shaped and not peltate.

J. Neal

Dollarweed foliage

J. Neal

Dollarweed petiole attachment

J. Neal

Dollarweed rhizome / stolon

J. Neal

Dollarweed inflorescence

J. Neal

Lawn pennywort habit

J. Neal

Lawn pennywort leaf

Common yarrow (*Achillea millefolium* L.)

SYNONYMS: yarrow, milfoil, thousand-leaf, bloodwort

GENERAL DESCRIPTION: **Rhizomatous perennial** with pungent foliage, **finely cut leaves**, and heads of white flowers aggregated into flat-topped clusters at the ends of the stems. Although it can grow to 1 m in height, in mowed turf it forms dense patches.

PROPAGATION / PHENOLOGY: Reproduction is **by seeds and rhizomes**. Germination occurs in late April or early May. **Most infestations are created by creeping rhizomes**, which may be introduced with soil or plant material.

SEEDLING: Cotyledons are egg-shaped to oblong and approximately 3.5 mm long by 2 mm wide. **Seedlings initially form a basal rosette. Young leaves are finely dissected** (mostly twice) with sharply pointed lateral lobes or teeth. Surfaces have whitish appressed hairs and are aromatic when the foliage is crushed.

MATURE PLANT: Stems are mostly unbranched (sometimes forking above), with fine white hairs or nearly smooth surfaces. Plants usually grow together in clusters from a common rhizome. **Leaves are lanceolate and finely divided** (2–4 times pinnate), 3–15 cm long by 2.5 cm wide, with soft short hairs. Lower and basal leaves have petioles. Upper leaves are alternate and sessile, generally shorter than leaves on the lower stem.

ROOTS AND UNDERGROUND STRUCTURES: A **deep and extensive system of rhizomes** with fibrous roots enables common yarrow to survive long periods without water.

FLOWERS AND FRUIT: Flowers are produced beginning in June and extending throughout the summer. **Numerous white to sometimes pinkish composite flower heads are in flat-topped or occasionally rounded clusters** (compound corymbose) at the end of branches. Individual flower heads are 3–5 mm in diameter and are composed of 5, 3-toothed, mostly white or sometimes pinkish ray flowers (2–4 mm long) and 10–30 whitish cream to yellowish central disk flowers. Seeds are enclosed within the 1.5–3 mm long fruit (achene). Achenes are oblong and compressed, with fine longitudinal ribs and a winged margin.

POSTSENESCENCE CHARACTERISTICS: In the autumn and winter, the dead stems persist, bearing the flat-topped, many-branched flower clusters. Vegetative portions of the plant remain green through the winter.

HABITAT: Common yarrow is a weed of turfgrass, landscapes, nursery crops, and other perennial crops. It tolerates many soil types but is usually found on poor, dry, sandy soils, often where other plants grow poorly. It is also found in lawns, roadsides, and disturbed areas but is not common in cultivated fields.

DISTRIBUTION: Distributed throughout North America; common in the eastern states.

SIMILAR SPECIES: **Chamomiles (*Anthemis* spp.), pineapple-weed (*Matricaria discoidea*), and wild carrot (*Daucus carota*)** have dissected leaves that may resemble those of common yarrow, but they are not as finely dissected as mature common yarrow leaves. In addition, those species do not have rhizomatous root systems. The youngest seedling leaves and cotyledons of common yarrow are relatively thick and can resemble **common groundsel (*Senecio vulgaris*)**, but common groundsel is not as finely dissected. Some species and cultivars of *Achillea* are used as ornamentals.

Common yarrow
habit

J. Neal

Common yarrow
vegetative habit

J. Neal

ommon yarrow flowers

J. Neal

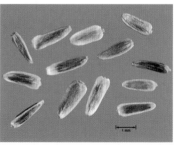

Common yarrow seeds

J. K. Clark © 2007 UC Regents

Common ragweed (*Ambrosia artemisiifolia* L.)

SYNONYMS: *Ambrosia elatior, Ambrosia media*, wild tansy, hog-weed, bitterweed, may-weed, hay-fever weed, blackweed, Roman wormweed, annual ragweed

GENERAL DESCRIPTION: An **erect**, **branching**, **summer annual** (30 cm to 2 m in height). Pollen from common ragweed is a primary cause of **hay fever**.

PROPAGATION / PHENOLOGY: Reproduction is **by seeds**. Common ragweed emerges early in the spring compared with other summer annual broadleaf weeds. Most germination occurs from May through June or when the soil is 10–27°C (50–80°F).

SEEDLING: Hypocotyls are spotted or entirely purple. **Cotyledons** are thick, **dark green, rounded above and narrowed to the base** (spatulate), 6–10 mm long, sometimes with purple spots along the margin. **Youngest leaves are opposite, becoming alternate** by the fourth node. The blades are hairy on the upper surface and margin and densely hairy on the underside. **Leaves are deeply cleft** on the margins, forming **rounded or slightly pointed lobes**.

MATURE PLANT: Stems are erect, branched, and have long (3 mm) rough hairs. **Leaves** are hairy to nearly smooth. **Blades** (4–10 cm long) are narrowly to broadly egg-shaped in outline and **once or generally twice compound (pinnatifid)**. Most **leaves are alternate; sometimes lower leaves are opposite.** Petioles are conspicuous on lower leaves but reduced on the upper leaves.

ROOTS AND UNDERGROUND STRUCTURES: Shallow, fibrous root system.

FLOWERS AND FRUIT: Flowers are typically present from late summer to autumn (August–October). **Flowers produce large amounts of wind-dispersed pollen. Flower heads are small** (2–3 mm long), **green, and inconspicuous** in clusters on terminal branches. Male and female flowers are in separate heads (monoecious). The male flowers are in racemes at the top of the plant, and the female flowers are in the axils of the upper leaves and branches. A single seed is enclosed within each fruit (3–4 mm long). The fruits have several longitudinal ridges ending in short spines (resembling a crown) and can survive for up to 80 years in field soil.

POSTSENESCENCE CHARACTERISTICS: Stems persist throughout the winter with remnants of the inflorescence and finely dissected leaves still attached. Plant has a reddish to purplish coloration.

HABITAT: Common ragweed is a weed of most cultivated crops, landscapes, roadsides, waste areas, and meadows. It grows in clay or sandy soil but prefers heavy, moist soils. It will persist with infrequent mowing.

DISTRIBUTION: Found throughout North America; most common in the eastern and north-central states.

SIMILAR SPECIES: **Spanishneedles (*Bidens bipinnata* L.)** has similar branched, upright habit and deeply lobed to divided leaves. But Spanish needles' leaves are oppositely arranged and lack hairs, whereas mature ragweed plants have alternate leaves that are often hairy. **Ragweed parthenium (*Parthenium hysterophorus* L.)** mid-stem foliage is similar, but parthenium forms a basal rosette and has white button-like composite flowers. Ragweed parthenium causes severe dermatitis to people and is poisonous to livestock, but is currently not widespread in the region.

Common ragweed habit

J. Neal

Common ragweed mature foliage

J. Neal

Common ragweed flowering stem

J. DiTomaso

ɔmmon ragweed seedlings

J. DiTomaso

Common ragweed seeds, 4 mm

J. O'Brien © 2007 UC Regents

1 mm

Giant ragweed (*Ambrosia trifida* L.)

Synonyms: great ragweed, kinghead, crown-weed, wild hemp, horse-weed, bitterweed, tall ambrosia

General Description: An **erect, summer annual** 1.5 m tall, but in fertile, moist soils can reach 4–6 m in height. Stems are unbranched to frequently branched and have **large, distinctive, 3-lobed (occasionally 5-lobed) leaves**. Pollen from giant ragweed can cause **hay fever**.

Propagation / Phenology: Reproduction is **by seeds**, with seedlings emerging mid- to late spring. Seeds mature in mid-August.

Seedling: Cotyledons are round to oblong and thick, 1–1.5 cm wide by 2–4 cm long (3–4 times larger than common ragweed). **Young leaves are opposite** and have rough hairs. The **first pair of leaves is unlobed**, ovate to lanceolate, with large teeth to small lobes on the margin. **Subsequent leaves usually have 3 large lobes.**

Mature Plant: **Stems and leaves are rough and hairy. Leaves are opposite** (15 cm long by 10–20 cm wide) and **palmately lobed** (3-lobed, sometimes 5-lobed or simple). Lobes are ovate to lanceolate, and the margins are toothed. **Petioles are winged** on the margins. **Lower leaves are more deeply lobed; upper leaves** (subtending the inflorescence) **are often simple.**

Roots and Underground Structures: Roots are primarily fibrous, but a short taproot is also present.

Flowers and Fruit: Flowers are present from July through September. **Individual flowers are small, greenish, and inconspicuous.** Male flowers are in long (to 30 cm), narrow racemes at the ends of branches; female flowers are clustered at the base of the racemes and in the axils of the upper leaves. A single seed is enclosed within the large (6–12 mm long) fruit (achene). The brown or gray **achene is crown-shaped** with a long, pointed central beak surrounded by 5 shorter points.

Postsenescence Characteristics: Erect woody stems persist well into winter. Persistent crown-shaped woody fruit indicate the presence of this species.

Habitat: Giant ragweed is a weed of cultivated agronomic and horticultural crops. It is most commonly found in cultivated alluvial, fertile soils, as well as in drainage ditches, roadsides, and other disturbed sites.

Distribution: Giant ragweed is less common than common ragweed. Nevertheless, it is found throughout much of the United States, particularly in the mid-Atlantic states, and the Ohio and Mississippi River Valleys. It is not generally found in northern Maine, southern Florida, and is uncommon on the West Coast.

Similar Species: Giant ragweed can be distinguished by the distinctive 3-lobed leaves. When a large number of leaves are unlobed, giant ragweed can appear similar to **common cocklebur (*Xanthium strumarium*)** and **common sunflower (*Helianthus annuus*)**. However, the leaves of sunflowers and cocklebur are mostly alternate, whereas those of giant ragweed are opposite. The flowering heads and fruit of **common ragweed (*Ambrosia artemisiifolia*)** are similar but smaller than those of giant ragweed. The leaves of common ragweed are usually twice divided and not 3–5 times lobed.

Giant ragweed
habit

J. Derr

A. DiTommaso

Giant ragweed seedling

W. Curran

Giant ragweed inflorescence

J. Neal

Giant ragweed flowering
plant

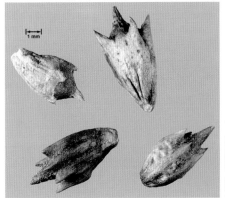

J. O'Brien © 2007 UC Regents

Giant ragweed seeds

Mayweed chamomile (*Anthemis cotula* L.)

SYNONYMS: dogfennel, stink-weed, dogs chamomile, dill-weed, stinking daisy, hogs fennel, fetid chamomile

GENERAL DESCRIPTION: A decumbent to erect, freely branching, **winter or summer annual** growing in large clumps from 10–60 cm tall. It has **finely divided foliage** that produces a **strong unpleasant odor** when crushed. The sap of this plant can cause **dermatitis** in humans.

PROPAGATION / PHENOLOGY: Reproduction is **by seeds**. Germination is in late summer, early autumn, or early spring.

SEEDLING: The hypocotyl is green to maroon. Cotyledons are 7–8 mm long, united at the base to form a transverse ridge across the shoot axis. Cotyledons do not have obvious petioles, and veins are not visible on the smooth surface. **The first true leaves are opposite**; the **subsequent leaves are alternate** but may be closely spaced, producing a **basal rosette**. **Blades** of the first leaves are **finely dissected** and thick. Leaf surfaces have short, somewhat glandular, hairs.

MATURE PLANT: **Elongating stems are highly branched**, erect to decumbent, and nearly smooth. Leaves are yellowish-green, 1.5–6 cm long by 0.5–3 cm wide, alternate, and lack a petiole. **Leaves** are slightly pubescent and **finely, 2–3 times pinnately divided.**

ROOTS AND UNDERGROUND STRUCTURES: Short, thick **taproot** with secondary fibrous root system.

FLOWERS AND FRUIT: **Flower heads are white with yellow centers** and produced in terminal solitary heads on the ends of branches from June to October. Heads are 1.2–2.6 cm in diameter, on short flower stalks. Bracts (phyllaries) taper to the apex. Flowers are of 2 types: **ray florets are white, 3-toothed**, 10–20 per head, each 1 cm long; **disk flowers are yellow** and numerous, **forming a cone in the center** of the flower head. The seed is enclosed within the fruit (achene), which is 1.2–1.8 mm long, rough with rounded bumps, light brown, roundish to nearly quadrangular with approximately 10 ribs. Achenes lack a pappus.

POSTSENESCENCE CHARACTERISTICS: Stems and remnants of leaves and flower heads can persist into the winter.

HABITAT: A weed of landscapes and nursery and agricultural crops, mayweed chamomile is generally found on rich, gravelly soil. It also grows in roadsides and meadows.

DISTRIBUTION: Widespread throughout North America.

SIMILAR SPECIES: **See Table 3 for a comparison with other finely dissected weeds in the aster family. Corn chamomile (*Anthemis arvensis* L.)** is very similar to mayweed chamomile but has smooth achenes **and lacks the offensive odor** and acrid properties. **Scentless chamomile (*Tripleurospermum inodorum* (L.) Sch. Bip.)** also lacks the unpleasant odor of mayweed chamomile but has more (10 to 30⁺) white petals per flower and the receptacle lacks the scales present on corn and mayweed chamomile. **Pineapple-weed (*Matricaria discoidea*)** is a summer or winter annual with similar foliage but emits the pleasant odor of pineapple when crushed. In addition, the flower head is composed of only greenish-yellow disk flowers.

J. DiTomaso

Mayweed chamomile flowers

Corn chamomile seedling

J. Neal

R. Uva

Corn chamomile basal rosette

J. O'Brien © 2007 UC Regents

Left, corn chamomile seeds, 1.8 mm; *right*, mayweed chamomile seeds, 1.6 mm (largest)

Common burdock (*Arctium minus* (Hill) Bernh.)

Synonyms: *Lappa minor*, smaller burdock, clotbur, cockoo-button, cockle-button, lesser burdock

General Description: A **biennial**, producing a **large-leaved rosette in the first year** and a **tall (1.5 m) erect, many-branched stem in the second year.** Plants produce **spiny persistent burs**, from which the common name is derived.

Propagation / Phenology: Reproduction is **by seeds**.

Seedling: Cotyledons are obovate, with a waxy surface, approximately 2.5 cm long, on short stalks. **Young leaves are egg-shaped, truncated across the base,** coarse-veined, and downy on the undersurface. **Petioles** are flared and clasping at base to **form a tubular sheath**.

Mature Plant: Common burdock is a large **basal rosette the first year,** and a many-branched, **erect plant the second year.** Stems are hollow, hairy, and grooved or angular. **Leaves are large** (50 cm by 40 cm), alternate, narrowly to broadly egg-shaped. The larger **basal leaves are heart-shaped** and broadest at the base, with toothed or wavy margins and hollow petioles. The **undersurface is light green and woolly**; the upper surface is darker green and smoother.

Roots and Underground Structures: **Large, thick, fleshy taproot,** as deep as 30 cm below the soil surface.

Flowers and Fruit: Flowers occur from July to October. Flower heads are 1.5–3 cm in diameter and develop from the leaf axils or raceme-like clusters at the end of branches. Bracts (phyllaries) are often covered with short cobweb-like hairs and are shorter than the **purple flowers**. The **outer bracts terminate in Velcro-like hooks** and are successively shorter from the flowers outward. The inner bracts are without hooks. All flowers are of the disk type. The seed is enclosed within the fruit (achene). Achenes are 4–7 mm long with a pappus of short chaffy bristles. The flower head dries to a **bur**, and the **hooked bracts** attach to animal fur or clothing to disperse the entire head.

Postsenescence Characteristics: Dead erect stems are easily distinguished by the distinctive branching pattern and the persistent hooked burs, which remain on the stems through the winter and into the following spring.

Habitat: Common burdock is a weed of landscapes, and nursery and agricultural crops. It is also found on rich soil along fencerows and in roadsides, uncultivated areas, and waste areas.

Distribution: Occurs throughout most of the United States.

Similar Species: The **flower head may resemble some thistles (*Cirsium* and *Carduus* species),** but thistles do not have the large leaves and hooked bracts of burdock. Young seedlings may superficially resemble **broadleaf dock** or **curly dock (*Rumex* spp.),** but the docks lack the downy coating on the undersurface of the leaves.

J. Neal

ommon burdock habit

J. DiTomaso

Common burdock seedling

Common burdock mature foliage

R. Uva

J. Neal

Common burdock flower and hooks

J. DiTomaso

Common burdock seeds, 6 mm

157

Mugwort (*Artemisia vulgaris* L.)

Synonyms: chrysanthemum weed, wormwood, felon herb

General Description: A **colony-forming, rhizomatous perennial** with erect, flowering stems (50 cm–1.5 m tall). Tolerates mowing to 3.5 cm. **Foliage is aromatic.**

Propagation / Phenology: Reproduction is usually vegetative **by rhizomes, rarely by seeds**. Rhizome fragments can be transported by cultivation or with infested balled-and-burlaped nursery stock, topsoil, or composted organic matter.

Seedling: **Seedlings are rarely encountered** because few viable seeds are produced in temperate North America. Cotyledons are egg-shaped (5 mm long) and lack petioles. Young leaves are opposite, bristly-hairy, with white, woolly hairs beneath. Leaves are egg-shaped to rounded, on long petioles. **Initial leaves are generally undivided with inconspicuous teeth,** whereas **older leaves are deeply lobed** and pointed.

Mature Plant: Unmowed stems are erect and branched in the upper ⅓ (flowering portion) and become woody with age. Stems are often red, brown, or purplish, almost hairless, and ridged or angular, but round in cross section. **Leaves** are simple, **alternate,** 5–10 cm long by 3–7 cm wide, with **large pinnatifid lobes.** Surfaces are green and smooth to slightly hairy above; the undersides are covered with white to gray woolly hairs. **Leaves emerging from rhizomes have shallower and broader lobes. Leaves on the mid and upper portion** of the plant have lobes that are **more linear** and more deeply pinnatifid than the lower leaves, and may lack petioles.

Roots and Underground Structures: Plants spread by **long, stout rhizomes.**

Flowers and Fruit: **Flowers** are produced July to October in **inconspicuous composite heads** in leafy spike-like **clusters at the terminal ¼–⅓ of the stems.** Individual heads are **numerous,** 2.5–3 mm wide, on short flower stalks. Flowers are greenish-yellow and of the disk type. The seed is enclosed within the fruit (achene). Achenes are ridged, brown, oblong with a narrow base (1–2 mm long), and have minute bristles at the apex. Viable seeds are rarely produced, except in greenhouses.

Postsenescence Characteristics: Dead, brown, woody stems persist well into winter, but seedheads will persist for only a short time.

Habitat: A weed of turfgrass, nurseries, and landscapes. It is rarely encountered in field, grain, or vegetable crops but grows in waste places and roadsides. Its **persistent rhizomes make mugwort difficult to control in perennial crops.** It is also well adapted to mowing and cultivation and is relatively tolerant of most herbicides.

Distribution: Found throughout the eastern United States. Most infestations have resulted from vegetative introduction in nursery stock, topsoil, or farm equipment.

Similar Species: The leaf shape and aroma of mugwort often lead to confusion with **garden chrysanthemums (*Chrysanthemum* spp.).** Mugwort leaves are white-woolly on the underside; garden chrysanthemum leaves may be only somewhat hairy. Young mugwort plants, 5–20 cm tall, are easily confused with **common ragweed (*Ambrosia artemisiifolia*),** but leaf blades of common ragweed are more deeply dissected. Late autumn mugwort seedheads resemble the dense inflorescence of **horseweed (*Conyza canadensis*),** but the species can easily be separated by differences in leaf shape.

Mugwort habit

J. Neal

Mugwort sprouts from rhizomes

J. Neal

Mugwort
Regina O. Hughes, USDA

Mugwort rhizome

J. Neal

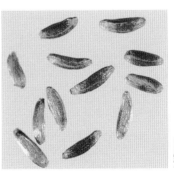
Mugwort seeds, 1.6 mm

J. DiTomaso

159

English daisy (*Bellis perennis* L.)

SYNONYMS: lawn daisy, European daisy

GENERAL DESCRIPTION: A **prostrate**, spreading, herbaceous **perennial** that **forms mats** of **basal rosettes** and **attractive daisy-like white flowers** on short scapes (5–15 cm long). Although English daisy was imported as a cultivated ornamental, it has since become a common weed of low-maintenance lawns.

PROPAGATION / PHENOLOGY: Plants spread from **wind-blown seeds** and vegetatively by **short, thick rhizomes**.

SEEDLING: Cotyledons are round and almost sessile. **Young basal leaves** are rounded to **ovate, narrowing to the petiole**, with short hairs.

MATURE PLANT: **Stems do not elongate.** The only stem-like structures present are the leafless flower-bearing scapes. Foliage may be nearly smooth to hairy. Elliptic, oval, or round **leaf blades** are 1–6 cm long by 0.4–2.5 cm wide and **abruptly narrow to the petiole.** **Margins** are usually **short-toothed** but may be entire.

ROOTS AND UNDERGROUND STRUCTURES: Fibrous roots are associated with **short rhizomes**. The root system is coarse and shallow.

FLOWERS AND FRUIT: Flowers are produced from early spring to mid-June and sometimes to November. **Flower heads are daisy-like** (2–3 cm in diameter), with **white or pinkish petals** (ray flowers) **and yellow central disk flowers. Solitary flower heads are on leafless stalks** (scapes) arising from the basal rosette. The seed is enclosed within a 1–2 mm long oblong achene, which is yellow-brown and marked with fine parallel lines.

POSTSENESCENCE CHARACTERISTICS: Plant is a perennial. Foliage persists well into winter but may decay by spring. New leaves emerge early in the spring.

HABITAT: English daisy is a weed of meadows, pastures, and low-maintenance turfgrass. It is usually found on heavy, moist, fertile soil.

DISTRIBUTION: Found throughout the northern United States and the Pacific Coast states.

SIMILAR SPECIES: **Rosettes resemble many asters (*Symphyotrichum* spp.)**, but unlike aster, English daisy remains as a basal rosette or mat. Habit and leaf shape are similar to **cudweeds (*Gamochaeta* spp. and others)**; however, English daisy leaves lack the whitish underside typical of cudweeds.

English daisy in turf

English daisy habit

English daisy seedling

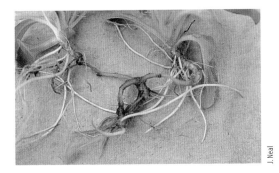

English daisy rhizomes and roots

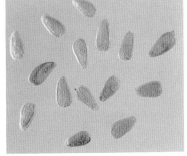

English daisy seeds, 1.2 mm

Devils beggarticks (*Bidens frondosa* L.)

SYNONYMS: beggar ticks, stick-tights, devil's boot jack, bur-marigold, pitchforkweed, tick-seed sunflower

GENERAL DESCRIPTION: **Summer annual** with **erect** stems 20 cm to 1.5 m in height. Stem branches spread toward the top. Plants produce **dark brown, prickly fruits** that stick to skin, clothing, and animal fur, from which the common name is in part derived.

PROPAGATION / PHENOLOGY: Reproduction is **by seeds**. Seeds germinate over an extended period of time, from mid-spring through late summer.

SEEDLING: **Cotyledons** (9–25 mm long by 3–5.5 mm wide) are **petiolated, spatulate-oblong** to ovate, smooth, and have prominent midveins. **Young leaves are opposite**, thin, deep-green above, paler beneath, with **3 leaflets**, the central one larger than the other two; **margins are wavy** with irregular teeth and a few fine soft hairs.

MATURE PLANT: **Stems are smooth** to slightly hairy, somewhat 4-sided. **Leaves are opposite and compound**, with **3–5 leaflets** that are sparsely covered with short hairs. Petioles are 1–6 cm long. **Leaflets are lanceolate with toothed margins** (serrate); the terminal leaflets (and sometimes the others) are on slender stalks.

ROOTS AND UNDERGROUND STRUCTURES: Shallow, many-branched **taproot** with a secondary fibrous root system.

FLOWERS AND FRUIT: Flowers (2.5 cm wide) are produced in heads from July to October. **Flowering heads are surrounded by 5–10 green bracts** (phyllaries), **which are longer than the orange-yellow ray flowers** (petals). Disk flowers in the center of the flower are brownish-yellow. **Some heads may have only disk flowers.** The seed is enclosed within the fruit (achene), which is 6–12 mm long, dark brown to black, flat, and wedge-shaped. **Achenes have 2 barbed spines** that aid in dispersal on animal fur and clothing.

POSTSENESCENCE CHARACTERISTICS: Erect, smooth stems persist into early winter. Some seed will remain attached to the stems.

HABITAT: Devils beggarticks is primarily a weed of landscapes and nurseries but also grows in roadsides, pastures, and waste areas. It usually grows on moist to wet soil but is not limited to those areas.

DISTRIBUTION: Found throughout the United States and southern Canada but most common in the eastern and north-central states.

SIMILAR SPECIES: **Hairy beggarticks (*Bidens pilosa* L.)** has similar foliage but a more open, branched habit, and showy white petals with yellow disk flowers in the center. Hairy beggarticks is more common in the Southeast, but present north to Massachusetts. **Spanish-needles (*Bidens bipinnata* L.)** is similar but has leaves 2–3 times pinnately dissected and strongly resembles **ragweed (*Ambrosia artemisiifolia*)**. However, mature ragweed plants have alternate leaves that are often hairy, whereas *Bidens* spp. have opposite nearly hair-less leaves. **Nodding beggarticks (*Bidens cernua* L.)** has simple and sessile leaves, nodding flowering heads, and yellow ray flowers (petals) either absent or 1.5 cm long.

J. Neal

evils beggarticks habit

J. Neal

Devils beggarticks stem and flowers

J. Neal

ature devils beggarticks

J. Neal

Juvenile devils beggarticks

J. Neal

anishneedles young plant

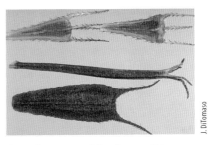

J. DiTomaso

Top to bottom: nodding beggarticks seeds, 8.5 mm (to end of tip); spanish-needles seed, 13.5 mm (to end of tip); and devils beggarticks seed, 11.5 mm (to end of tip)

Musk thistle (*Carduus nutans* L.)

SYNONYMS: plumeless thistle, nodding thistle

GENERAL DESCRIPTION: A **biennial** or occasionally a winter annual with erect stems (to 1.5 m in height) branching near the top of the plant. **Both leaves and stems are spiny**, the stems with spiny wings.

PROPAGATION / PHENOLOGY: Reproduction is **by seeds**. After rosettes form, a period of cold temperature is required before they elongate.

SEEDLING: Seedlings develop into a **basal rosette**. Cotyledons are nearly sessile, oblong (7.5–15 mm long by 2.5–6 mm wide). Cotyledon veins are white and broad, and the tips of the blades are often square. The first 2 true leaves appear to be opposite; subsequent leaves are alternate but **form a rosette**. Leaves are oval to elliptic; a few hairs may be present on the upper surface and on the main veins beneath. Leaves are waxy and pale green. **Leaf margins** are **shallowly lobed** and are **irregularly prickly-toothed**.

MATURE PLANT: **Basal rosettes elongate in the second season. Stems are erect**, and leaves are alternate. **Leaves are deeply pinnately lobed** (25 cm long by 10 cm wide), elliptic to lanceolate, and **the margins are spine-tipped**. Long hairs are only along the main veins. **Leaf bases extend down the stem, creating spiny wings.** Leaves become gradually smaller up the stem.

ROOTS AND UNDERGROUND STRUCTURES: A **long, thick, fleshy taproot**, sometimes branched, can penetrate to 40 cm or more below the soil surface.

FLOWERS AND FRUIT: Flowering occurs from June through October. Flower heads often nod and are produced singly at the end of the branches. **Heads are 3–5 cm wide, with pink to purple or rarely white disk flowers.** The head consists of **many spine-tipped bracts** (phyllaries), the middle and outer bracts are wide (2–8 mm), long (9–27 mm), and flat. The seed is enclosed within the fruit, which is a 3.5–4 mm long achene. **Achenes** are oblong, straw-colored to brown at maturity, with a **hair-like, white pappus** that aids in wind dispersal.

POSTSENESCENCE CHARACTERISTICS: Aboveground portions die with a hard frost. Plants remain intact for an extended period during the winter. They are easily distinguished by the persistent spiny nature.

HABITAT: Musk thistle is a weed of nursery crops, pastures, waste areas, roadsides, and ditch banks. It is often found on dry or gravelly soils.

DISTRIBUTION: Widely established throughout the United States and Canada.

SIMILAR SPECIES: **Bull thistle (*Cirsium vulgare*)** has rough hairs on the upper surface of the leaf blade and thick whitish softer hairs below, whereas musk thistle leaves mostly lack hairs. The flower heads of bull thistle lack the colorful bracts characteristic of musk thistle. **Canada thistle (*Cirsium arvense*)** is smaller, is a colony-forming perennial, and its leaves are not as deeply lobed. **Plumeless thistle (*Carduus acanthoides* L.)** is a biennial to 1.5 m tall with similar spiny leaves, winged stems, and spiny floral bracts. It is native to Europe and can hybridize with other *Carduus* species. It has purple to lavender-colored flowers from May to August. The flower heads are generally smaller (1–3 cm), and the spiny bracts are much smaller than those on musk thistle. In addition, its flower head usually does not nod, as do the flower heads of musk thistle. Plumeless thistle is found throughout the western, north-central and northeastern states.

Musk thistle habit

Musk thistle flower head

Musk thistle seedling

Musk thistle rosette

Plumeless thistle flowering shoot

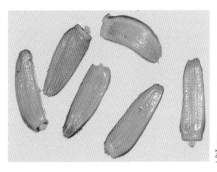

Musk thistle seeds, 4 mm

Cornflower (*Centaurea cyanus* L.)

SYNONYMS: *Leucacantha cyanus*, bachelor's buttons, garden cornflower

GENERAL DESCRIPTION: An erect, summer or **winter annual** to 1 m tall, with **showy blue, purple, or white flower heads**. It is widely planted as a garden ornamental but has escaped cultivation in most regions of the country. Native to southern Europe and is the national flower of Estonia.

PROPAGATION / PHENOLOGY: Reproduction is only **by seeds**. In warmer climates the plants exhibit a winter annual life cycle. In cooler climates they may grow as summer annuals.

SEEDLING: The fairly large, oblanceolate to spatulate cotyledons (1.5–3 cm) are much longer than the initial leaves. Leaves are entire, (ob)lanceolate, and have a grayish appearance caused by the presence of long, appressed hairs.

MATURE PLANT: Leaves are **lanceolate, entire,** or with a few lobes, 1–4 cm long. **Foliage is covered with short, gray, and generally woolly hairs.** Stem leaves are reduced upward. Plants may have a single, upright flowering stem or be highly branched from the base.

ROOTS AND UNDERGROUND STRUCTURES: Plants have a **deep taproot.**

FLOWERS AND FRUIT: Flowers are present from May to October. The bracts below the flowers (phyllaries) are 12–16 mm long, bell-shaped, green, with **appendages fringed with white to black teeth**. Between 25 and 35 disk flowers occur in each flower head. Flowers are typically **blue, but purple, red, pink, and white** forms are also grown and have escaped. Flower heads, 1.5–3 cm diameter, are solitary and terminal on main stems and branches. The sterile outer corollas are 20–25 mm long, funnel-shaped, wider and lobed at the tip, and the fertile inner corollas are slender and mostly 10–15 mm long. Fruits are an achene, 4–5 mm, straw-colored to blue and finely hairy. The pappus is bristly and rigid, 2–3 mm long.

POSTSENESCENCE CHARACTERISTICS: Senesced plants remain for a short time with dried flower heads attached. Dried flower heads have tan-colored spreading phyllaries with long, soft, chaff still attached in the center receptacle.

HABITAT: Plants are often found in urban waste areas but also in disturbed grasslands, grain crops, hay fields, roadsides, and open woods. Plants typically require full light and do not survive under shaded conditions.

DISTRIBUTION: Cornflower is grown as a garden plant in all contiguous states and Hawaii. It has escaped cultivation in every state it is grown.

SIMILAR SPECIES: Cornflower can resemble some of the other knapweed species, particularly **spotted knapweed (*Centaurea stoebe* ssp. *micranthos*)** and **black knapweed (*Centaurea nigra* L.)**. However, both knapweeds can be distinguished from cornflower by a well-branched, mounded growth habit, perennial life cycle, and thinner petals in the flowers. Additionally, spotted knapweed has deeply lobed leaves. Black knapweed phyllaries at the base of the flower head are brown throughout and not just dark at the tips.

Cornflower habit

Cornflower seedling

Cornflower stem leaves

Cornflower flower head

Cornflower flowering heads

Cornflower seeds, 4.8 mm (without papus)

167

Spotted knapweed (*Centaurea stoebe* ssp. *micranthos* (S. G. Gmelin ex Gugler) Hayek)

SYNONYMS: *Centaurea biebersteinii, Centaurea maculosa, Centaurea stoebe,* star thistle

GENERAL DESCRIPTION: A **biennial or short-lived perennial** forming a basal rosette in the first year and growing to 1.5 m in height the following year.

PROPAGATION / PHENOLOGY: Reproduction is **by seeds**.

SEEDLING: Cotyledons are approximately 25 mm long, narrow at the base, and rounded at the tip. **First leaves** are **rounded at the tip** and **taper to a short petiole. Subsequent leaves** become more slender and **lanceolate**, have **downy hairs**, and form a **basal rosette.**

MATURE PLANT: **In the first year, leaves are deeply lobed** (15 cm long) **and in a basal rosette. Stems elongate in the second year. Stems are erect** or ascending, **slender and wiry**, with several branches. **Stem surfaces are rough to slightly woolly-hairy. Leaves are gray-green**, alternate and **pinnately dissected** with many lobes. Surfaces may be rough with minute hairs; leaf margins have rough bristles. **Leaves near the flowers are smaller, narrow, and less lobed to unlobed.**

ROOTS AND UNDERGROUND STRUCTURES: **Stout taproot.**

FLOWERS AND FRUIT: Flowering occurs in mid- to late summer. **Flower heads** (up to 200 per plant) are **solitary at the ends of main and axillary branches** and are 9–15 mm long by 8–15 mm wide. All **flowers are the disk type.** The marginal fertile flowers are enlarged and **pink to purple (rarely white).** Bracts (phyllaries) are 10–13 mm long, with brown margins, **fringed black tips**, and a whitish fringe on each side. The seed is enclosed in the fruit (achene). Achenes are olive-green to blackish-brown, 2.5–4 mm long by 1.1–1.5 mm wide, and notched on one side of the base. Apex of the **achene** has a **short, bristly pappus** that aids in dispersal by animal fur, wool, hairs, or feathers.

POSTSENESCENCE CHARACTERISTICS: Dead stems and heads persist over the winter. Dried bracts of flower heads form a cup, often containing a few fruit.

HABITAT: Spotted knapweed is an increasingly important weed of rangeland and pastures, generally on low-fertility, dry soils. It is also a weed of low-maintenance turfgrass, roadsides, and, less commonly, landscapes, nurseries, and agricultural crops.

DISTRIBUTION: Spotted knapweed continues to spread and is now found throughout the northeastern and north-central states but is most common in the Rocky Mountain states and the Pacific Northwest.

SIMILAR SPECIES: **Cornflower (*Centaurea cyanus*)** is an annual. Its leaves are usually entire, sometimes toothed but rarely lobed; when lobes are present, only the larger leaves are lobed. **Black knapweed (*Centaurea nigra* L.)** is a perennial to 1 m tall that is similar to spotted knapweed but the basal leaves are entire or shallowly lobed and upper leaves are linear to lanceolate. In addition, the phyllaries at the base of the flower head are brown throughout and not just dark at the tips, as in spotted knapweed. Black knapweed is also distinguished by having all flowers fertile and producing fruits. Black knapweed inhabits disturbed places in most northeastern states and adjacent central states. Native to Europe. **Brown knapweed (*Centaurea jacea* L.)** is nearly identical to black knapweed. Differences are based on minor floral characteristics. Interspecific hybrids with *Centaurea nigra* (sometimes referred to as meadow knapweed, *Centaurea* x *moncktonii* C.E. Britton) appear to be more common and more invasive. Some floras consider all 3 species to be subspecies of *Centaurea jacea.*

Spotted knapweed habit

Spotted knapweed rosette

Spotted knapweed foliage and stem

Spotted knapweed flower

Black knapweed flower head

Spotted knapweed seeds, 3.7 mm (not including the pappus)

Chicory (*Cichorium intybus* L.)

SYNONYMS: succory, blue sailors, blue daisy, coffee-weed, bunk

GENERAL DESCRIPTION: A **perennial** from a **basal rosette**. It has **dandelion-like leaves** but produces sparsely leaved, wiry, branching stems (30 cm to 1.7 m tall). Stems and leaves exude a **milky sap** when cut. The plant is sometimes grown as a vegetable crop, and the root has long been used as a substitute for coffee. Chicory occasionally causes **allergenic dermatitis** in humans.

PROPAGATION / PHENOLOGY: Reproduction is **by seeds**.

SEEDLING: Cotyledons are oblong to egg-shaped, widest above the middle, with the apex abruptly indented and the base tapering into the petiole. **Young leaves are oblong** to egg-shaped, also **widest above the middle; margins are wavy or toothed**, with indentations or teeth widely spaced.

MATURE PLANT: Early in the season, chicory forms a **basal rosette very similar to that of dandelion**. The basal leaves may be absent later in the season during flowering. **Flowering stems are erect, round, hollow,** and smooth or with a few bristly hairs. Stems are usually many-branched near the top of the plant but are branched from the base in mowed areas. **Leaves are lanceolate, alternate,** and rough on the upper surface and on the lower surface of the lower leaves. **Leaf margins are coarsely toothed or pinnatifid.** Basal leaves, 8–25 cm long by 1–7 cm wide, are widest above the middle and strongly resemble the leaves of dandelion. The upper leaves are smaller, lanceolate, 3–7 cm long, with clasping leaf bases. Margins may be entire or have small irregular teeth.

ROOTS AND UNDERGROUND STRUCTURES: Dark brown, long, large, fleshy taproot.

FLOWERS AND FRUIT: **Bright blue (occasionally pink, purple, or white) flowers** are produced from late June into October and open primarily in the morning. Flower heads (4 cm in diameter) are produced in clusters of 1–3 on the upper flowering stems (racemes), either sessile or short-stalked in the axils of the much-reduced leaves. The bracts of the head (phyllaries) are in 2 series: an inner one of 8–10 longer bracts and an outer one of 5 shorter bracts. All flowers are ligulate (ray). The seed is enclosed in the fruit (achene), which is 2–3 mm long, wedge-shaped, widest at the apex, tapering to the base, and 4- or 5-angled, with a truncated apex. Minute bristle-like scaly pappus is present on the fruit.

POSTSENESCENCE CHARACTERISTICS: Dead stems persist through winter as branching, brown stalks bearing the remains of the flower heads. The bracts of the flower heads remain attached to the stem and occasionally contain achenes.

HABITAT: A weed of low-maintenance turfgrass, roadsides, meadows, pastures, and other uncultivated agricultural crops. It is most troublesome on calcareous soils but tolerates a wide range of conditions. It does not tolerate cultivation.

DISTRIBUTION: Found throughout the United States; most common in the northern and western states.

SIMILAR SPECIES: Chicory rosettes **strongly resemble dandelion (*Taraxacum officinale*)**. But the toothed lobes of dandelion leaves are generally opposite each other and point back toward the rosette, whereas those of chicory are not always opposite and may point forward, perpendicular, or backward. Also, the basal leaves of chicory are rougher to the touch and have more-prominent coarse hairs. Mature dandelions are easily distinguished by the yellow flowers and solitary, leafless flower stalks.

Chicory habit

J. Neal

R. Uva

Chicory rosette

Chicory seedlings

R. Uva

J. DiTomaso

Chicory flower

Chicory seeds, 2.2 mm (largest)

J. DiTomaso

171

Canada thistle (*Cirsium arvense* (L.) Scop.)

SYNONYMS: *Carduus arvensis*, creeping thistle, small-flowered thistle, perennial thistle, green thistle

GENERAL DESCRIPTION: A spreading, **colony-forming perennial** (0.3–1.2 m in height). Leaves are conspicuously lobed with **spiny** margins.

PROPAGATION / PHENOLOGY: Reproduction is by **wind-blown seed and creeping roots that form new shoots**. Creeping roots allow Canada thistle to develop large colonies from a single plant, but following 1 to 2 growing seasons the root system becomes highly fragmented. Seeds germinate primarily in late spring or early autumn.

SEEDLING: Cotyledons are dull green, relatively thick, rounded-oval to oblong (1 cm long). **Young leaves are thick, egg-shaped** to lanceolate, and covered with **short bristly hairs. Margins are wavy-lobed with sharp spines**; the lobes develop into triangular indentations with age. Shoots emerging from creeping roots lack cotyledons. Newly emerging seedlings develop as a basal rosette but elongate later in the season.

MATURE PLANT: **Stems** are grooved, **erect**, smooth to slightly hairy, and branch at the apex. Upper surface of leaves is dark green and hairless, and lower surface is light green, with or without hairs. **Leaves are alternate, sessile**, oblong to lanceolate, irregularly lobed, with **spiny margins. The base of each leaf surrounds the stem.**

ROOTS AND UNDERGROUND STRUCTURES: An extensive creeping, fleshy root system is present. Fleshy roots can extend more than a meter below the soil surface.

FLOWERS AND FRUIT: Flowers are present from June through August. Flower heads are numerous, arranged in clusters (corymbs) at the ends of the stems and from the upper leaf axils. Canada thistle is dioecious; fertile male and female flowers are produced on separate plants. Female flowers have a pappus of bristly hairs longer than the petals, whereas the pappus of male flowers is shorter than the petals. **Flower heads** (2–2.5 cm in diameter) **are composed of pink to purple, or rarely white disk flowers surrounded by spineless bracts.** The seed (achene) is 2.5–4 mm long, flattened, and brownish. Achenes are curved or straight, the apex abruptly cut off with a rounded bump in the center. The **pappus** is easily detached from the achene, but aids in wind dispersal when present.

POSTSENESCENCE CHARACTERISTICS: Aboveground portions die with a hard frost. The upright stem turns brown and may persist through the winter with prickly leaves and seedheads still attached.

HABITAT: Canada thistle is a weed of many crops but is most troublesome in perennial crops, rangeland, and areas of reduced tillage.

DISTRIBUTION: Found throughout the northern half of the United States and southern Canada.

SIMILAR SPECIES: Canada thistle is a colony-forming perennial, whereas most **other thistle and thistle-like plants** are biennials or annuals. In addition, the flower heads of Canada thistle are generally spineless, but most other thistles and thistle-like weeds have spiny bracts (phyllaries). **Bull thistle (*Cirsium vulgare*)** is often confused with Canada thistle but can be distinguished by its spiny winged stems and rough hairs on the upper leaf surface. Canada thistle has smooth stems and upper leaf surfaces.

J. Neal

Canada thistle habit

J. Neal

Canada thistle flowering stem

A. DiTommaso

Canada thistle tillers

J. Neal

Canada thistle seedheads

J. DiTomaso

Canada thistle seeds (without pappus),
3 mm

173

Bull thistle (*Cirsium vulgare* (Savi) Tenore)

Synonyms: *Carduus vulgare, Cirsium lanceolatum*, spear thistle

General Description: A **biennial** with **prominent spines**. The foliage is covered with coarse to **cobweb-like hairs**. A basal rosette is produced in the first year; erect and branching stems (50 cm to 1.5 m in height) develop in the second year.

Propagation / Phenology: Reproduction is by wind-dispersed **seeds only**.

Seedling: **Cotyledons** are 12–15 mm long, **egg-shaped**, and broadest at the apex. **Young leaves are oval** to oblong **with a fringe of spines**. The second true leaf is dull dark green with dense vertical whitish hairs on the upper surface. **Subsequent leaves are longer, more lanceolate, and have spine-tipped lobes. Young plants form a rosette.**

Mature Plant: In the spring and early summer, the overwintering rosettes of spiny leaves are present, but **by mid-summer of the second year stems elongate. Stems are erect**, often branched, and **winged by the spiny bases of the leaves**. Leaves are alternate and have **stiff spines on the lobes** of the blade with coarse hairs on the upper surface and softer whitish hairs below. Leaves are lanceolate, with deep cuts or toothed margins. **Leaf bases continue** down the stem, **producing the winged-stem** appearance.

Roots and Underground Structures: Fleshy **taproot** formed in the first year, with a secondary fibrous root system.

Flowers and Fruit: Flowers are present from June to October and are produced in heads usually solitary at the end of branches. Heads are 3–4 cm long by 2–4 cm in diameter with **spine-tipped bracts (phyllaries) and numerous rose to reddish-purple (rarely whitish) disk flowers**. The seed is enclosed within the fruit, which is a 3–4 mm long achene with a feathery pappus (20–30 mm long) that facilitates wind dispersal.

Postsenescence Characteristics: Heads with spiny bracts and spiny leaf remnants persist on the dead stem during winter. The basal rosette of leaves in the first year remains green through the winter.

Habitat: A weed of pastures, turfgrass, landscapes, nurseries, orchards, and reduced-tillage agronomic crops, bull thistle prefers a relatively rich, moist soil and is common in old fields and disturbed waste places.

Distribution: Widespread throughout the United States and southern Canada.

Similar Species: Several similar winter annual or biennial thistles are common in the region. In particular, **plumeless thistle (*Carduus acanthoides* L.)** has very similar growth habit and purple to lavender, spiny flowers. However, plumeless thistle flower heads are generally smaller (1–3 cm), and the leaves are not hairy. **Canada thistle (*Cirsium arvense*)** is a colony-forming perennial; its leaves are smooth above and smooth or hairy below. Bull thistle leaves are prickly hairy above and woolly below. Canada thistle lacks the basal rosette of leaves and usually occurs in clumps. Senesced bull thistle plants can be confused with **common burdock (*Arctium minus*)**, but the bracts of burdock are hooked not spiny-tipped.

ull thistle habit

J. Neal

R. Uva

Bull thistle seedlings

J. Neal

Bull thistle rosette

J. DiTomaso

ull thistle flower

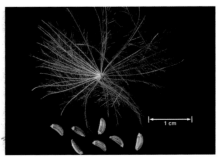

J. O'Brien © 2007 UC Regents

Bull thistle seeds, 3.5 mm (not including pappus)

Horseweed (*Conyza canadensis* (L.) Cronq.)

SYNONYMS: *Erigeron canadensis, Leption canadense*, marestail, fleabane, colt's-tail

GENERAL DESCRIPTION: A **winter or summer annual**. Seedlings develop into a **basal rosette**. Mature plants produce an **erect, central stem** (30 cm to 2 m tall) with a terminal panicle of inconspicuous flowers.

PROPAGATION / PHENOLOGY: Reproduction is **by seeds**; seeds germinate in late summer or spring. Late-summer germination results in overwintering rosettes.

SEEDLING: **Cotyledons are oval**, 2–3 mm long. **Young leaves are egg-shaped**, with **toothed margins**. The lower leaves are on prominent petioles; the upper ones are narrower and taper to the stalk. Seedling leaves form a **basal rosette** and are covered with spreading to ascending short hairs.

MATURE PLANT: **Stems** are erect, bristly **hairy**, with many small, flowering branches in the upper portions. **Leaves** (10 cm long by 10 mm wide) **are hairy, alternate**, numerous, and **crowded along the stem. Blades are sessile, linear to elliptic**, broadest at the apex and tapering at the base. **Leaf margins** can be entire but are usually **toothed**. When growing as a winter annual, the basal rosette is produced in late summer. **After the stem elongates, the basal leaves deteriorate. Stem leaves** are lanceolate to linear, with **nearly entire margins**. Leaves become gradually smaller up the stem.

ROOTS AND UNDERGROUND STRUCTURES: **Short taproot** with secondary fibrous roots.

FLOWERS AND FRUIT: Flowers are present from July through October. Branches from the main stem produce **dense panicles consisting of numerous small (5 mm in diameter) flower heads**. Heads are subtended by 1–2 series of bracts (phyllaries). Ray flowers (25–50) are white or somewhat pinkish; disk flowers (7–12) are yellow. Seeds are enclosed within a 1 mm long achene. Achenes are broadest at the apex and taper to the base. **Pappus** consists of whitish bristles that facilitate **wind dispersal**.

POSTSENESCENCE CHARACTERISTICS: Plants often turn brown before fruit dispersal. Dried, woody stems persist through winter. The main stem often breaks from the weight of the inflorescence. Many seedlings can be found close to the parent plant.

HABITAT: A common weed of most agronomic crops, nursery crops, orchards, and other perennial crops; also common in waste areas and fallow fields and along fencerows. Reduced-tillage practices tend to increase its occurrence.

DISTRIBUTION: Common throughout North America.

SIMILAR SPECIES: **Annual fleabane (*Erigeron annuus* (L.) Pers.)** is a summer annual or rarely a biennial with more prominent toothing on the leaves than horseweed. In addition, the flower heads are larger (approximately 1.3 cm in diameter), with showy white to rarely pinkish ray flowers. **Rough fleabane (*Erigeron strigosus* Muhl. ex Willd.)** has flowers similar to those of annual fleabane, but the lower leaves are more spatulate than are horseweed leaves, and the leaf hairs are shorter and appressed. In the seedling rosette stage, horseweed can be distinguished from **shepherd's-purse (*Capsella bursa-pastoris*)** by the absence of branched (star-shaped) hairs characteristic of shepherd's-purse. **Virginia pepperweed (*Lepidium virginicum*) seedling rosettes** have a strong odor when crushed, and leaf margins are more prominently toothed or lobed than those of horseweed.

Horseweed habit

J. Neal

J. K. Clark © 2007 UC Regents

Horseweed seedling

J. Neal

Horseweed rosette

R. Uva

Annual fleabane flowers

J. Neal

Bolting horseweed

J. O'Brien © 2007 UC Regents

Horseweed seeds, 1.2 mm (not including pappus)

177

Smooth hawksbeard (*Crepis capillaris* (L.) Wallr.)

SYNONYMS: *Crepis cooperi, Lapsana capillaris*

GENERAL DESCRIPTION: Erect winter annual, sometimes summer annual or biennial, to approximately 1 m tall, with **milky sap and small, yellow, dandelion-like flower heads.** Plants exist as **dandelion-like rosettes** until flower stems develop at maturity. Native to Europe.

PROPAGATION / PHENOLOGY: Reproduction is only **by seeds**. Seeds disperse primarily with wind. Newly dispersed seeds can germinate immediately if conditions are favorable.

SEEDLING: Cotyledons are ovate 3 mm long by 2–3 mm wide, and lack hairs. Leaves are alternate. The first leaf is elliptic, 8–15 mm long by 4–5 mm wide, with margins sparsely toothed. The lower leaf surface is often purplish, with short hairs especially on the lower midvein. Leaf stalks are often glandular-hairy. Young plants form a **basal rosette**.

MATURE PLANT: Rosette and lower leaves are oblong, 3–30 cm long, with margins sparsely toothed to pinnate-lobed. Foliage with no hairs to minutely hairy, especially on lower leaf veins. Stems are branched in the upper portion with alternate leaves and **10 or more flower heads on each main stem.** Petioles of stem leaves clasp the stem. Upper leaves are few and bract-like.

ROOTS AND UNDERGROUND STRUCTURES: Taproot short.

FLOWERS AND FRUIT: Flowers from June to September. **Flowering stalks are many-branched.** Each flower head consists of 20–60 yellow, ligulate flowers. Involucre (phyllaries as a unit) cylindrical, mostly 5–8 mm long, and minutely glandular-hairy. Outer phyllaries 8, linear, and much shorter than the inner phyllaries. Inner phyllaries 8–16, lanceolate. All phyllary margins are membranous. Receptacles lack chaffy bracts. Achenes are cylindrical, 1.5–2.5 mm long, taper at both ends, brown, and lack a distinct beak, with 10 longitudinal ribs. Pappus bristles are fine, soft, 3–4 mm long, and white.

POSTSENESCENCE CHARACTERISTICS: Old flower stems with reflexed phyllaries and empty receptacles can persist into the winter.

HABITAT: Primarily found on open dry disturbed sites, fields, pastures, roadsides, waste places.

DISTRIBUTION: Found throughout the Northeast and mid-Atlantic states.

SIMILAR SPECIES: **Common catsear (*Hypochaeris radicata*), smooth catsear (*Hypochaeris glabra*),** and **Carolina false-dandelion (*Pyrrhopappus carolinianus*)** can resemble smooth hawksbeard. All three form a rosette of deeply lobed leaves, branched inflorescences, yellow dandelion-like flowers, and a globe-shaped seedhead. However, common catsear leaves are hairy, and smooth catsear has long scale-like bracts between the flower and leaves that are more rounded at both the tips and lobes compared to smooth hawksbeard. Carolina false-dandelion lobes are rounded and slender, generally pointing forward; flowering stalks are less branched with 1–5 flower heads per main stem.

J. Neal

Smooth hawksbeard flowering stem

J. DiTomaso

Smooth hawksbeard seedling

J. DiTomaso

Smooth hawksbeard leaves

J. DiTomaso

Smooth hawksbeard flowers

J. Neal

Smooth hawksbeard achenes on seedhead

Eclipta (*Eclipta prostrata* (L.) L.)

SYNONYMS: *Eclipta alba*, yerba-de-tago, false daisy

GENERAL DESCRIPTION: A prostrate, ascending or erect, **summer annual**. Plants commonly remain low, produce a mound, or grow to approximately 60 cm in height. **Stems are thick and succulent,** many-branched, and root at the lower nodes. Foliage has stiff hairs appressed to the surface.

PROPAGATION / PHENOLOGY: Propagation is **by seeds**; seeds germinate in late spring or early summer when soil temperatures are warm.

SEEDLING: Cotyledons (<1 cm long by 1.5–2 times as long as wide) are smooth, slightly thickened, and oval, tapering to a short petiole. **Young leaves are opposite**; the first 3–4 are hairy at the base of the upper surface and the underside. Subsequent leaves have short appressed hairs on both surfaces. **Leaves of young plants are ovate** to oblong, **becoming lanceolate** or elliptic **with age. Leaves have short teeth on the margins** that point toward the leaf apex. Blades are green; midveins are yellow-green on the upper surface and light green on the lower surface. Petioles are about ⅕ the length of the leaf. Stems branch at the base and become reddish with age.

MATURE PLANT: **Stems are freely branched**, 20–60 cm tall, green to reddish-brown or purplish. **Lower nodes of stems often produce roots.** Stiff appressed hairs give leaves and stems a rough feel. **Leaves are sessile** (or with a short petiole), **opposite**, narrow to the base, **lanceolate** or lance-elliptic to lance-linear. **Margins have conspicuous, widely spaced teeth.**

ROOTS AND UNDERGROUND STRUCTURES: Fibrous roots are associated with a **shallow taproot** or stem nodes.

FLOWERS AND FRUIT: **Flowers**, produced from July to October, are arranged in **small, composite heads**, alone or in clusters of 2–3 on 0.5–4 cm long stalks at the end of stems or in leaf axils. Heads are 1.5–10 mm in diameter and composed of small, whitish ray flowers (1–2 mm long) surrounding greenish to dusky white disk flowers. **Heads of ripening fruit are green and button-like.** The seed is enclosed within a 1.8–2.5 mm long **achene** that is 3- to 4-angled, **roughly triangular**, tapered to the base, and truncated at the apex. Some flower heads produce straw-colored seeds with a wrinkled or warty surface; others are dark gray to black, flattened, and smooth.

POSTSENESCENCE CHARACTERISTICS: None of significance.

HABITAT: Eclipta is a weed of cultivated agronomic and horticultural crops as well as irrigation and drainage ditches, banks, and riversides. It is often found in moist to wet places that dry out later in the season.

DISTRIBUTION: Found from New York and Massachusetts south to Florida and west to California; most common in the southern states.

SIMILAR SPECIES: Leaves are simple and opposite, resembling leaves of **nodding beggarticks** (***Bidens cernua***). However, leaf bases of the 2 opposite leaves in nodding beggarticks are often fused, whereas those of eclipta are separate. In addition, eclipta flowers are white, and nodding beggarticks has yellow flowers.

Eclipta habit

J. Neal

Eclipta seedlings

J. Neal

J. Neal

Eclipta flower and foliage

1 mm

M. Bertone

Eclipta seeds, 2.3 mm

American burnweed (*Erechtites hieraciifolius* (L.) Raf. ex DC.)

SYNONYMS: *Erechtites hieracifolia, Senecio hieracifolius*, eastern fireweed, pilewort

GENERAL DESCRIPTION: Erect, native, summer annual 1–1.5 (rarely to 3) m tall, with alternate, irregularly toothed leaves. Plants have few branches, except near the top. The foliage has an unpleasant odor and the **flowers are small, pale yellow, in cyclindrical flower heads**.

PROPAGATION / PHENOLOGY: Reproduction is **by seeds**. Seeds germinate from spring to early autumn. Seeds disperse primarily with wind. Soil disturbance, including fire, generally enhances germination.

SEEDLING: Cotyledons are round to oval, to 1 cm in length. First leaves appear opposite but are alternately arranged. **Young plants form rosettes** to 25 cm in diameter. Leaves are ovate to elliptic with finely toothed margins; midveins are often tinged red near the base. With age, the leaves become more irregularly toothed.

MATURE PLANT: Plants are **upright and mostly unbranched** except near inflorescence branches. However, when broken, stems will branch. Mature plants lose basal leaves but retain stem leaves. **Leaves are alternate, lanceolate**, ovate, or oblanceolate, sometimes with pinnate lobes, to 20 cm long by 7–8 cm wide, with a prominent midvein. Upper leaf surface lacks hairs or has scattered white hairs, while **margins are coarsely toothed**. The lower leaves have short petioles, but smaller upper leaves are sessile or even clasping the stem.

ROOTS AND UNDERGROUND STRUCTURES: Root system is shallow and fibrous.

FLOWERS AND FRUIT: Plants flower from late summer to early fall. Flower heads are in branched, open clusters that lack conspicuous petals and consist of **whitish to pale yellow, tubular disk flowers in cylindrical heads 4-8 mm wide at the base. Phyllaries are mostly 10-18 mm long**, usually green but sometimes purplish. The achenes are cylindrical, mostly 2–5 mm long and <0.5 mm diameter, excluding the pappus bristles, and longitudinally ribbed with a few short, coarse, appressed hairs between ribs. Pappus is a tuft of bright white, silky hairs.

POSTSENESCENCE CHARACTERISTICS: Dead flower stems may persist into late autumn with head remnants that consist of a small, bare, nearly flat receptacle with the main phyllaries reflexed downward.

HABITAT: An early colonizing species following disturbance such as fire or cultivation. Plants prefer some shade and moist conditions but are adapted to a wide range of habitats. Found in disturbed places, burned sites, roadsides, railroad tracks, fields, prairies, rocky open woodlands, edges of marshes and bogs, nursery crops and urban landscapes. Not common in agronomic cropping systems.

DISTRIBUTION: Native of eastern North America, the species is distributed throughout the eastern two-thirds of North America and the West Coast.

SIMILAR SPECIES: American burnweed can somewhat resemble **horseweed (*Conyza canadensis*)** but has larger leaves and flowers and generally lacks hairs. **Thickhead or redflower ragleaf (*Crassocephalum crepidioides* (Benth.) S. Moore)** is a recently introduced species very similar in appearance. Seedling leaves are generally thicker and broader than American burnweed. Stem leaves often have a pair of deep lobes near the base. Plants are typically shorter, to approximately 1 m in height. Easily distinguished in flower by the dark to light salmon-red flowers and drooping flower heads. Thickhead is primarily found in the southern United States but is spreading in contaminated nursery crops.

American burnweed habit

American burnweed rosette

American burnweed seedling

American burnweed leaves

American burnweed flowering
and mature seedheads

Thickhead drooping
inflorescence

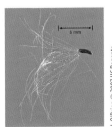

American burnweed
seed

Dogfennel (*Eupatorium capillifolium* (Lam.) Small)

SYNONYMS: summer cedar, hogweed

GENERAL DESCRIPTION: A **short-lived perennial**, 50 cm to 2 m in height, with 1 to several stems from a thick, woody base. Numerous, small flower heads are produced from the upper stem branches. **Leaves are pinnately dissected into fine, linear segments.** Leaves and particularly flowers emit a **strong, foul odor** when crushed.

PROPAGATION / PHENOLOGY: Reproduction is **by seeds**.

SEEDLING: Cotyledons are petiolated, egg-shaped, and hairless. **Young leaves** are opposite; the first and sometimes the second pair of leaves **have 1–3 coarse teeth**, but **subsequent leaves are dissected. Blades and stems are hairy.**

MATURE PLANT: **Stems are erect**, arising from the **woody base**, many-branched in the upper flowering portion, hairy, or sometimes smooth below, reddish-purple at the base. Most leaves are alternate; some lower leaves may be opposite. **Leaves are once or twice pinnately dissected into fine linear segments** (2–10 cm long).

ROOTS AND UNDERGROUND STRUCTURES: Fibrous roots. Woody stem at ground level may resemble a taproot.

FLOWERS AND FRUIT: Flowers are produced in September and October. Flower heads are numerous, in many-branched panicles on the upper ⅓–¼ of the upright stems. **Individual heads are small**, 2–3 mm long, with 3–6 greenish-white disk flowers on each head. The seed is enclosed within the fruit (achene), which is smooth, angled in cross section, gray to black, 1–1.6 mm long, and widest at the apex. The pappus consists of whitish bristles.

POSTSENESCENCE CHARACTERISTICS: Upright, flowering stems persist through the winter and often into spring. In warmer climates, young plants may die back to the crown and resprout in the spring.

HABITAT: Dogfennel is a weed of nurseries, orchards, reduced-tillage crops, and landscapes. It also grows in roadsides and abandoned fields.

DISTRIBUTION: Found along the coastal plain from Massachusetts south, throughout the Southeast to Texas; most common from New Jersey southward.

SIMILAR SPECIES: Both **horseweed (*Conyza canadensis*)** and **mugwort (*Artemisia vulgaris*)** resemble dogfennel in habit and flowering characteristics. Horseweed leaves are lanceolate, not divided, as are mugwort and dogfennel leaves. The mature leaves of mugwort are pinnatifid and may resemble dogfennel, but the leaf segments are not as narrow. Unlike dogfennel leaves, the leaves of mugwort are white-woolly beneath. Young seedlings may resemble **chamomiles (*Anthemis* spp.)**, but dogfennel seedlings have hairy stems, whereas chamomile seedlings form a rosette and lack conspicuous hairs.

J. Neal

Dogfennel habit

J. Neal

Young dogfennel shoot

J. Neal

Dogfennel seedling

Steve Hurst, USDA-NRCS PLANTS Database

Dogfennel seeds

Trampweed (*Facelis retusa* (Lam.) Sch. Bip.)

Synonyms: *Facelis apiculata, Gnaphalium retusum*

General Description: A **low-growing, winter annual** weed of low-maintenance turfgrass, roadsides, and similar habitats. Plants are **very hairy**, making the foliage appear gray. In spring, plants flower and produce copious amounts of seeds with **fluffy, white pappus**. In dense infestations the ground can be covered by the white fluff.

Propagation / Phenology: Germinates in the fall (less commonly in early spring). Plants grow vegetatively in early spring, then flower and fruit in late spring through early summer. Plants die in early summer.

Seedling: Newly emerged seedlings are very small and rarely noticed. Cotyledons are oval, 3–5 mm in length. The first 2 leaves appear opposite, lack petioles, are slightly longer than the cotyledons, about as broad at the base as at the tip. By the fourth or fifth leaf, a more typical leaf shape develops. Young **leaves are alternate, lack petioles**, 15–20 mm long by 2–5 mm wide, rounded near the end with a **tiny, sharp point at the tip** (apiculate). When viewed from above the leaves are **symmetrically arranged** around the stem in a pinwheel fashion. The stem and underside of the leaves are **densely hairy**, but the upper leaf surface may or may not have hairs. Plants branch from the base.

Mature Plant: Leaf shape is similar to seedlings. Unmowed plants are rarely more than 30 cm tall (typically less than 20 cm). Plants are many-branched from the base. Stems are close to the ground at the base but curve upward at the tips (decumbent) and are covered in soft hairs. Leaves are alternate and closely spaced on the stem (almost overlapping on some specimens). Internodes become longer as plants initiate flowering.

Roots and Underground Structures: Fibrous root system.

Flowers and Fruit: Flowers are in leaf axils, clustered at the ends of branches in late spring to early summer. Flowers, subtended by bract-like leaves, lack conspicuous petals and are individually inconspicuous. The most distinctive feature of trampweed is the **cottony mass of seeds that often cover the ground**, similar to cottonwood (*Populus deltoides*). Fruits are approximately 1 mm long, hairy, with many 10–11 mm long, white filaments (pappus) attached directly to the seed (achene).

Postsenescence Characteristics: Plants are not persistent after they die in early to mid-summer.

Habitat: Common in low-maintenance turfgrass, roadsides, pastures, and landscape plantings. Colonizes low-fertility, drought-prone sites where other vegetation does not thrive. From those infestations, seeds can spread to other sites.

Distribution: Introduced from South America. Trampweed is common in the southeastern United States and mid-Atlantic states, north to Virginia.

Similar Species: Before plants flower, several **cudweeds (*Gamochaeta* spp.)** have a similar growth habit and leaf shape. They also have hairs on the stems and backs of leaves giving the plants a gray appearance. However, cudweed foliage is typically larger (longer and broader) and lacks the sharp point at the tip. The pappus on cudweed seeds is much shorter than those of trampweed.

J. Neal

Trampweed habit

J. Neal

Trampweed fruiting stem

J. Neal

Trampweed leafy shoot

J. Neal

Trampweed white-hairy stem and underside of leaves

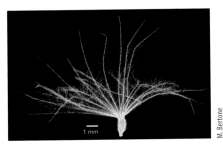

1 mm

M. Bertone

Trampweed achene

Hairy galinsoga (*Galinsoga quadriradiata* Ruiz & Pavón)

Synonyms: *Galinsoga ciliata*, common quickweed, shaggy soldier

General Description: **Summer annual** with erect, freely branching stems, 10–70 cm in height. **Leaves** are broadly **egg-shaped to triangular**, pointed at the apex, and **coarsely toothed on the margins**.

Propagation / Phenology: Reproduction is **by seeds**; seeds germinate from early spring through mid-summer. Peak emergence is in late spring or early summer, but seedlings can emerge between May and September, particularly in disturbed soils. Seeds apparently have **no dormancy** and can germinate soon after shedding, so often several generations occur per season.

Seedling: Hypocotyls are short, green, and turn maroon with age. **Cotyledons** (1 cm long) are rounded to square, **abruptly tapered at the base, slightly indented at the apex**, and smooth on the margin and both surfaces. **Young leaves are opposite, egg-shaped to triangular**, pointed at the apex. **Blades have 3 prominent veins** and are lighter green on the lower surface. **Dense hairs cover the upper leaf surface, stems, and petioles.** Most hairs on the lower leaf surface are near the veins. **Margins are slightly toothed**, with hairs pointing toward the leaf apex.

Mature Plant: **Stems** are erect or spreading, many-branched, and **covered with somewhat coarse hairs**. **Leaves** (2.5–7 cm long by 1.5–5 cm wide) **are opposite**, petiolated, **broadly ovate to triangular**, and pointed at the apex. **Leaf margins are coarsely toothed and hairy.**

Roots and Underground Structures: Shallow fibrous root system.

Flowers and Fruit: Flowers are present from June to October. **Heads are numerous, <1 cm wide**, from terminal stems (in cymes) and leaf axils. **Heads are composed of 4–5 white, sometimes pink, 3-toothed, small (2–3 mm long) ray flowers and several yellow disk flowers.** The seed is enclosed in the fruit (achene). **Achenes** are 1.5 mm long, hairy, black, **4-sided**, widest at the apex, **tapered at the base**, with a **crown of chaffy scales (pappus)**. A single plant can produce up to 7500 seeds. Seeds remain viable for only a few years under field conditions.

Postsenescence Characteristics: Plants turn black at first frost; stems rot and do not persist through the winter.

Habitat: Hairy galinsoga is **one of the most difficult-to-control weeds of vegetable crops**. It is also a weed of landscapes, gardens, ornamental beds, and nurseries. It is usually found on fertile soils.

Distribution: Occurs throughout the world; most common in the eastern United States.

Similar Species: **Smallflower galinsoga (*Galinsoga parviflora* Cav.)** is similar, but the stems are smooth or only sparsely hairy, unlike the densely hairy stem of hairy galinsoga. The ray flowers of hairy galinsoga have a crown of chaffy scales (pappus), whereas a pappus is present only on the disk flowers of smallflower galinsoga. The achenes of the 2 species are nearly identical. **Perilla mint (*Perilla frutescens*)** seedlings may resemble galinsoga in growth habit and leaf shape, but perilla mint stems are square whereas galinsoga stems are round.

Hairy galinsoga habit

Hairy galinsoga flowers

Hairy galinsoga seedling

Hairy galinsoga seeds, 1.3 mm (not including pappus)

Purple cudweed (*Gamochaeta purpurea* (L.) Cabrera)

SYNONYMS: *Gnaphalium purpureum*, cudweed, chafe-weed, catfoot, rabbit tobacco, everlasting

GENERAL DESCRIPTION: A low-growing, **summer or winter annual,** but in warmer climates may be perennial. Plants form a **rosette** (occasionally small clumps) of distinctly **white-woolly foliage. Erect, woolly stems** may reach 40 cm in height. Several related species are common.

PROPAGATION / PHENOLOGY: Reproduction is **by seeds;** seeds germinate very soon after they are shed.

SEEDLING: Cotyledons are smooth, grayish-green, sessile, rounded to oval, 1.5–2.5 mm long by 0.75–1 mm wide. Plants develop as **rosettes;** stems do not elongate in the seedling stage. **Young leaves are widest near the tip** and **taper to a broad petiole** (spatulate or oblanceolate) with a rounded or notched (mucronate) leaf tip. **Leaves** developing **in the bud are covered with a web of long silky hairs.** More mature leaf blades are mostly smooth above with woolly hairs beneath.

MATURE PLANT: **Rosette leaves** are as described above, up to 10 cm long by 2 cm wide. **Elongating stems,** arising from the rosette, do not usually branch and are generally **white-woolly. Leaves on the elongating stems** are alternate, **white-woolly,** sessile, and gradually reduced in size and width, becoming linear. Margins are wavy or entire.

ROOTS AND UNDERGROUND STRUCTURES: Taproot with a secondary fibrous root system. Purple cudweed may form short stolons.

FLOWERS AND FRUIT: Flowers bloom either from mid-spring to early summer or from August to September. **Flower clusters are formed at the ends of the erect stems.** Individual flowers are small, tannish-white, and borne in the axils of reduced leaves. **Bracts are light brown, often pink or purple.** Each seed is enclosed in the **fruit (achene),** attached to which is a **bristly pappus.** Achenes do not persist, as they shed soon after they ripen. The pappus bristles are united at the base and fall off in a ring.

POSTSENESCENCE CHARACTERISTICS: Dead stems do not persist, but plants may overwinter as a rosette.

HABITAT: Often found on sandy, dry soil, purple cudweed is a common weed of low-maintenance turf, including lawns, parks, and roadsides. Its presence is often an indicator of low fertility. It is less common in cultivated fields.

DISTRIBUTION: Found throughout the continental United States but most common in the South.

SIMILAR SPECIES: **Low cudweed (*Gnaphalium uliginosum* L.)** is shorter (5–30 cm), many-branched, with smaller flower heads (2 mm long). **Clammy cudweed (*Pseudognaphalium viscosum* (Kunth) Anderb.)** is distinguished from purple cudweed by its decurrent leaf base, which clasps the stem at and below the node. **Fragrant cudweed (*Pseudognaphalium obtusifolium* (L.) Hilliard & B.L. Burtt)** has similarly white-woolly foliage but is generally taller and more erect, with elliptic leaves and a strong tobacco-like fragrance. **Pussytoes (*Antennaria* spp.)** also have similar white-woolly foliage but are stoloniferous perennials with leafless stems arising from basal rosettes. They are also distinguished by their soft, white flower heads that are aggregated into conspicuous tight clusters, giving the impression of a cat's toes.

Low cudweed habit

Purple cudweed seedling

Pussytoes habit

Purple cudweed flowering spike

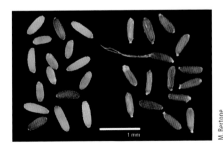

Left to right: purple cudweed seeds and low cudweed seeds

Bitter sneezeweed (*Helenium amarum* (Raf.) H. Rock)

Synonyms: *Helenium tenuifolium*, yellow sneezeweed, fiveleaf sneezeweed, yellowdicks

General Description: A **branching, upright** (15–75 cm tall), herbaceous **summer annual** with showy, **yellow, daisy-like flowers and fine-textured foliage**. Both the leaves and stem exude a bitter, **unpleasant odor when damaged. All parts are toxic** and can cause vomiting and milk bittering in livestock.

Propagation / Phenology: Reproduction is by **seeds**.

Seedling: Young seedlings are fairly inconspicuous. Cotyledons are linear, but broader than mature leaves. Seedlings are upright with closely spaced linear leaves similar to those on mature plants. Plants branch, branches arch upward. A waxy coating makes the **leaves and stem look blue-green** in color.

Mature Plant: Stem is upright, light to blue-green, and generally hairless with numerous branches. **Leaves are alternate, sessile**, and densely arranged on the stem, giving a shrub-like appearance. Individual **leaves are linear to filiform** (1–4 mm wide), **glabrous**, and 1–7.5 cm long. Surfaces of leaves dotted with tiny (visible under hand lens), pitted glands. Lower leaves often become brown and dehisce before flowering.

Roots and Underground Structures: A short, branching **taproot**.

Flowers and Fruit: Flowering begins in early summer and can extend into the fall. **Flower heads are 2 cm in diameter** and occur singly on 2.5–12 cm long peduncles. Each head has 5–10 ray florets and 75 to more than 250 disk florets. The petal-like ray florets are pistillate and have a 3-notched tip. Disk florets are perfect (have stamens and pistil) and tubular with 5 small teeth along the edge. Both ray and disk florets are fertile. By mid-autumn each floret produces a **reddish-brown fruit (achene)**. Each achene is 1–1.25 mm long, oblong, and hairy with bristly scales along the apex.

Postsenescence Characteristics: Plants are not persistent.

Habitat: Prefers full sun and dry, well-drained soil. Bitter sneezeweed grows along roadsides, railroad tracks, and in other disturbed areas; in open areas with sandy or rocky soils; and in pastures and dry, sunny, upland sites. Somewhat shade-tolerant.

Distribution: Bitter sneezeweed grows throughout the southeastern United States and west to Texas. Its northern range extends to Pennsylvania and Massachusetts, and west to Nebraska. Bitter sneezeweed is native to North America.

Similar species: The flowers of other native sneezeweeds, such as **common sneezeweed (*Helenium autumnale* L.)** or **purple sneezeweed (*Helenium flexuosum* Raf.)** may look very similar to those of bitter sneezeweed. These other sneezeweed species do not have the narrow, threadlike leaves of yellow sneezeweed. Flowers are also similar to **lanceleaf coreopsis (*Coreopsis lanceolata* L.)**, a native to North America that is widely cultivated. Coreopsis flowers have prominent sepals, and the leaves are much wider than bitter sneezeweed.

J. Neal

Bitter sneezeweed habit

J. DiTomaso

Bitter sneezeweed flower heads

J. Neal

Bitter sneezeweed young plant

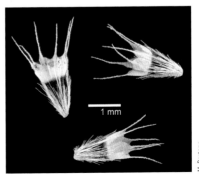

1 mm

M. Bertone

Bitter sneezeweed achenes

Jerusalem artichoke (*Helianthus tuberosus* L.)

SYNONYMS: girasole, earth-apple

GENERAL DESCRIPTION: A **tall (1–3 m), rhizomatous, and tuberous perennial.** It is some-times cultivated for its **edible tubers,** but once established is aggressive and difficult to control.

PROPAGATION / PHENOLOGY: Reproduction is **mainly by tubers** but also by seeds. Tubers produced in the previous year begin to sprout in late spring. Tuber reserves are at their lowest in late June (60–70 days after initial shoot emergence). **Rhizome** production begins just before flowering. Tuber production begins in mid-summer and reaches its peak in late summer to early autumn. The plant tubers can be spread by cultivation. **Dormant tubers are short-lived;** they do not survive for more than 1 or 2 seasons. Consequently, long-term control may be obtained by preventing new tuber formation for 2 years.

SEEDLING: **Cotyledons are oval,** twice as long as wide, and **united at the base,** forming a short tube. The **first leaves are opposite and elliptic.** Blades are dull green on the upper surface, pale on the underside, and covered with **short, stiff hairs.**

MATURE PLANT: **Stems are coarse and stout** with rough hairs. **Leaves are simple,** ovate or **almost heart-shaped** to oblong-lanceolate, tapering to a narrow tip, 10–25 cm long by 4–12 cm wide. Leaf blades are **thick, rough on the upper surface,** with short, **grayish hairs on the lower surface. Margins are coarsely toothed,** and **petioles are winged. Lower leaves are opposite,** but leaves on the **upper half** to 2/3 of the stem **are alternate.**

ROOTS AND UNDERGROUND STRUCTURES: **Short rhizomes bear tubers at their tips.** Tubers are irregularly oval, reddish on the outside, white inside, with knobs or bumps on the surface. Jerusalem artichoke is sometimes cultivated for the edible tubers. A single plant can produce more than 200 tubers in a growing season.

FLOWERS AND FRUIT: **One to 5 flower heads** are produced at the terminal end of stems from August through October. Heads are approximately 5 cm in diameter with 10–20 **yellow ray flowers** (2–4 cm long) **surrounding the darker yellow disk flowers.** Each seed is en-closed within the fruit (achene), which is 4–8 mm long, oblong to wedge-shaped, and flattened.

POSTSENESCENCE CHARACTERISTICS: Aboveground plant parts die back after frost and do not persist. **Plant overwinters as a tuber.**

HABITAT: Jerusalem artichoke is a weed of nurseries, landscapes, orchards, and reduced-tillage agronomic crops, as well as roadsides and waste places. It is often found on rich, moist soil.

DISTRIBUTION: Jerusalem artichoke is continuing to spread in the eastern half of the United States and is increasing in many areas of the midwestern states and states adjacent to Canada. It is also found near the Pacific Coast.

SIMILAR SPECIES: **Common sunflower (*Helianthus annuus* L.)** is an annual with a fibrous root system. Unlike Jerusalem artichoke, it does not produce tubers.

Jerusalem artichoke habit

Left, Jerusalem artichoke; *right*, common burdock

R. Uva

Jerusalem artichoke flowers

J. DiTomaso

Common sunflower seedling

J. DiTomaso

W. Sanok

Common sunflower habit

J. DiTomaso

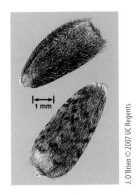

Common sunflower seeds

J. O'Brien © 2007 UC Regents

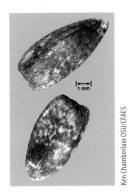

Jerusalem artichoke seeds

Ken Chamberlain OSU/CFAES

195

Yellow hawkweed (*Hieracium caespitosum* Dumort)

SYNONYMS: *Hieracium pratense*, field hawkweed, meadow hawkweed, yellow king-devil

GENERAL DESCRIPTION: A **prostrate, stoloniferous, and rhizomatous perennial** growing in patches or alone as a basal rosette. Leaves, stems, stolons, and flower stalks are **conspicuously hairy. Bright yellow flowers** are on nearly leafless flower stalks that reach 25–90 cm in height. Plants exude a **white sap** when broken.

PROPAGATION / PHENOLOGY: Reproduction is **by seeds, rhizomes, and stolons**. Seeds are dispersed by wind and have no specific dormancy requirements; they germinate soon after they are shed.

SEEDLING: Cotyledons are ovate to rounded (0.5–1 cm long), with short petioles and a small notch at the apex. **Young leaves are hairy**, egg-shaped to elliptic, tapering to very short petioles. Margins are entire and hairy. Leaves in the bud are folded from the base and conspicuously hairy on the inside surface.

MATURE PLANT: Mature plants produce a **rosette of conspicuously hairy leaves. Hairy stolons** root at the nodes and lead to the development of new rosettes. **Leaves are oblanceolate** or narrowly elliptic and **almost sessile. Blades** (5–25 cm long by 1–3 cm wide) are **covered with long hairs** above and below. The midvein is generally white and broadest toward the base. Margins are unlobed but may have a few inconspicuous teeth. Flower stalks (scapes) have only 1–3 well-developed leaves near the base and are **covered with stiff, dark hairs**. Some hairs are tipped with glands; others are branched.

ROOTS AND UNDERGROUND STRUCTURES: Fibrous from rhizomes and stolons.

FLOWERS AND FRUIT: Flowers are produced 3–4 weeks after dandelion, primarily in June and early July, and sporadically throughout the summer. **Flower heads** (5–30) **resemble dandelion (*Taraxacum officinale*) but are smaller** and are **produced in clusters of 2 or more** at the top of nearly leafless, 25–90 cm long, hairy, flower stalks. **Unopened flower heads** are covered with **dense rows of black hairs**. Opened flower heads (2 cm in diameter) are made up entirely of **bright yellow ray flowers** with 5 teeth at the tip. The seed is enclosed in the fruit (achene). Achenes are 1.5–2 mm long, cyclindrical, vertically ridged, dark brown or black, with a single row of small, delicate bristles (pappus) 2–4 mm long.

POSTSENESCENCE CHARACTERISTICS: Foliage can persist throughout the winter.

HABITAT: Common in low-maintenance turfgrass, roadsides, abandoned fields, and meadows, yellow hawkweed does not generally persist in cultivated crops. It is often found on poor, dry, or gravelly soils that usually are low in fertility and acidic.

DISTRIBUTION: Found throughout the northeastern United States and southeastern Canada, west to Michigan, south to North Carolina, northern Georgia, and Tennessee.

SIMILAR SPECIES: **Orange hawkweed (*Hieracium aurantiacum* L.)** has similar vegetative characteristics and is almost identical to yellow hawkweed, but the flowers are bright orange rather than yellow. **Common catsear (*Hypochaeris radicata*)**, also known as false dandelion, has similar yellow flowers on tall, mostly leafless stems. The leaves of common catsear have irregular to rounded lobes on the margins, whereas those of the hawkweeds are not lobed. **All 3 species, as well as dandelion, exude a milky sap when injured.**

R. Uva

Yellow hawkweed (*foreground*), orange hawkweed (*background*)

R. Uva

Yellow hawkweed seedlings

A. Senesac

Yellow hawkweed rosette

J. DiTomaso

Orange hawkweed flowering stem

J. DiTomaso

Yellow hawkweed flowering stem

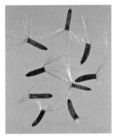
J. DiTomaso

Yellow hawkweed seeds, 1.8 mm (not including pappus)

197

Common catsear (*Hypochaeris radicata* L.)

SYNONYMS: coast dandelion, false dandelion, flatweed, frogbit, gosmore, hairy catsear, long-rooted catsear, rough catsear, spotted catsear

GENERAL DESCRIPTION: A **perennial** forming a **basal rosette** of leaves with **leafless, branched flower stems** to 0.8 m tall. Plants have **milky juice** and **yellow, dandelion-like flower heads.** Native to Europe.

PROPAGATION / PHENOLOGY: Reproduction is by seeds and the **seeds disperse primarily by wind.** Plants can also **reproduce vegetatively** by offsets from the crown in heavily grazed areas or mowed turf, and diffuse clonal patches can develop. Root fragments do not regenerate when detached from the crown.

SEEDLING: Cotyledons are oblanceolate, 8–12 mm long, and lack hairs. Leaves are alternate and form a rosette. The first few leaves are usually hairy, oblanceolate, and 8–15 mm long. The margins are smooth or with a few small teeth.

MATURE PLANT: Leaves are oblanceolate to lyrate and 6–14 cm long. Rosettes form early in the season and are usually prostrate on open ground. The foliage is covered with **coarse hairs that are rough to the touch.** **The leaf margins are variably lobed**; margins may be wavy, shallowly or deeply lobed with rounded lobes to coarsely sharp-toothed.

ROOTS AND UNDERGROUND STRUCTURES: Roots are fibrous, but plants often have several deep, thick, fleshy roots and appear taprooted.

FLOWERS AND FRUIT: Plants flower from May to November. The flowering stems are mostly branched, occasionally simple, leafless, and typically have a few **small bracts**. Yellow flower heads consist only of ligulate flowers conspicuously longer than the phyllaries. Plants form dandelion-like seedheads. **Achenes are of one type**, 3–4 mm long, brown, narrowly oblong or ellipsoid, longitudinally 10-ribbed, and with minute sharp projections in the upper part, often with a slender beak at the apex. The outer pappus bristles are stiff, but the inner pappus is **feather-like** (plumose), 8–10 mm long, dull white to tan.

POSTSENESCENCE CHARACTERISTICS: Plants are perennial, and rosettes will persist over winter in its southern range but lose most of the leaves over winter in colder climates before re-growing from the crown the following spring.

HABITAT: Plants grow in disturbed places, fields, grassland, pastures, turf, roadsides, orchards, vineyards, landscaped areas, and gardens. Tolerates mowing but does not persist in cultivated fields. It is often considered an indicator species for disturbed or low-fertility site conditions.

DISTRIBUTION: The species is commonly found throughout the eastern, mid-Atlantic, and southern states.

SIMILAR SPECIES: **Dandelion (*Taraxacum officinale*)** is also a perennial rosette similar to common catsear but has unbranched flower stems. **Smooth catsear (*Hypochaeris glabra* L.)** is an annual, native to Europe, which is very similar to common catsear but not as common. It also has a milky sap, basal rosette of leaves, and similar flowers, but lacks hairs on the foliage. **Smooth hawksbeard (*Crepis capillaris*)** is an annual, or sometimes a biennial, to approximately 1 m tall, with milky sap and yellow flower heads similar to catsears. Unlike catsears, it lacks chaff scales on the receptacle, and the foliage is nearly glabrous to minutely hairy. Several winter annual **mustards (such as *Sisymbrium* spp.)** form rosettes with deeply lobed and toothed leaves, but flowering stems are leafy, and flowers and seedpods are distinctly different from the composite heads of catsear.

Common catsear habit

Common catsear flower head

Common catsear rosette, with hairs on leaves

Left, common catsear seedhead; *right*, dandelion seedhead

Smooth catsear rosette

Common catsear seeds, 5 mm (shortest)

199

British yellowhead (*Inula britannica* L.)

SYNONYMS: meadow fleabane, yellow starwort, British elecampane

GENERAL DESCRIPTION: A **spreading perennial or biennial** forming a **mat of basal rosettes**, which then bolt in spring or early summer. Stems are erect (15–75 cm in height), sparsely to densely pubescent, and apically branching with **showy, yellow flowers**. Primarily a weed of nursery crops where root fragments are introduced in contaminated transplants, commonly in hosta or daylily divisions. Infested crop plants should be destroyed.

PROPAGATION / PHENOLOGY: Reproduction is by seeds, **creeping roots**, and **root fragments**. Seeds are wind-dispersed; however, the primary means of reproduction in North America are from spreading roots and root fragments.

SEEDLING: To date, seedlings have not been documented in North America. Infestations more commonly arise from root fragments in contaminated nursery crops. Plants arising from root fragments have long, **narrow leaves** 2–4 cm in length, with **no distinct petiole**. Subsequent leaves have broader blades becoming deltoid in shape. Leaves lack obvious hairs. Overwintering plants form a basal rosette.

MATURE PLANT: **Stems are erect, nearly hairless to densely pubescent** with appressed hairs. Mostly unbranched or branching toward the apex. **Leaves are alternate**, with smooth to **finely dentate margins**, and are **densely pubescent on the underside** and sparsely pubescent above. Basal leaves petiolate, elliptical or ovate elliptical, and 4–15 cm long. The **upper leaves** are lanceolate and **sessile or clasping**.

ROOTS AND UNDERGROUND STRUCTURES: Dense, fibrous roots with thickened roots giving rise to shoots. Roots are smooth and pale white.

FLOWERS AND FRUIT: **Yellow, sunflower-like flowers** (2–3 cm wide) are produced singly or in clusters of 2–3 from July through August at the ends of stems and branches. The ray flowers are up to twice as long as the surrounding bracts. Involucral bracts are linear, sometimes recurved, and pubescent. Seeds are contained in 1–2 mm long **fruits (achenes)**, which are oblong, light brown, and longitudinally ridged. The fruits have **pale white, yellow to red-brown pappus**.

POSTSENESCENCE CHARACTERISTICS: Plants are cold-hardy, maintaining green foliage through the winter months. After fruiting, erect stems are brown and nondescript.

HABITAT: Found in moist meadows, ditches, and on stream and riverbanks. Grows best in sites with moist soil and full sun or partial shade. British yellowhead was introduced to the United States in imported hosta rootstocks from the Netherlands and can be especially problematic in nurseries.

DISTRIBUTION: Currently not widely distributed. Introductions in nursery stock have occurred in many states including New York, Michigan, Minnesota, and North Carolina. Naturalized populations have been documented in Michigan and eastern Canada.

SIMILAR SPECIES: Several other species within this genus are sold in the gardening trade, including **elecampane (*Inula helenium* L.)** for which naturalized populations have been reported in most states in the Northeast and Great Lakes areas. Most garden species lack the creeping roots that contribute to the invasiveness of *I. britannica*. The moderate to large, yellow flowers distinguish British yellowhead from most other weedy asters. **Fleabanes (*Erigeron* spp.)** have similar vegetative characteristics but have white or pinkish ray flowers and coarsely serrated or more prominently toothed leaves. Young sprouts may resemble **buckhorn plantain (*Plantago lanceolata*)** seedlings, but plantain leaves will have 5 distinct main veins whereas *Inula* leaves will have netted veins.

British yellowhead plant

British yellowhead flower head

British yellowhead flower

British yellowhead rosettes

British yellowhead creeping root and shoot

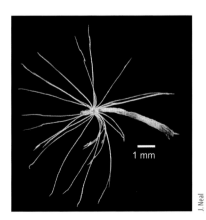

1 mm

British yellowhead achene

Prickly lettuce (*Lactuca serriola* L.)

Synonyms: *Lactuca scariola*, compass plant

General Description: A **summer or winter annual, or a biennial**, that produces erect stems (30 cm to 1.5 m in height) from a **basal rosette of leaves**. The leaf margin has fine prickles, and the midrib (lower leaf surface) is lined with **conspicuous prickles**. Leaves, roots, and stems exude a **milky juice** when injured.

Propagation / Phenology: Reproduction is **by seeds**.

Seedling: Cotyledons are rounded, tapering to the base, 7–8 mm long. Pale green leaves develop into a **basal rosette**. **Young leaves** are broadly club-shaped to egg-shaped, widest at the apex with **distinctly toothed or spiny**, wavy or slightly lobed margins. **Stiff prickles are present on prominent midrib of lower leaf surface.**

Mature Plant: **Flowering stems** are stiff, erect, prickly on the lower portions, and covered with a fine waxy coat. Stems are hollow, pale green to whitish, sometimes with reddish flecks. Usually 1 central stem arises from a basal rosette, branching only in the flowering portions. **Leaves are alternate** (5–25 cm long), oblong to lanceolate, stiff and coarse, unlobed or more often **lobed with rounded sinuses**. The **leaf bases clasp the stem with ear-like lobes.** The upper leaf surface is smooth; **prickles are present on the leaf margin and on the midrib of the lower surface**. Leaves often turn on edge and orient vertically toward the sun. Basal leaves are larger than upper leaves.

Roots and Underground Structures: Large taproot.

Flowers and Fruit: Flowers occur from July to September. Heads are 8–10 mm wide and grouped (13–27) in a pyramidal panicle. The heads are made up of **yellow ray flowers** (7–15), which fade to blue after senescence. The seed is enclosed in the fruit (achene), which is 3–4 mm long, 5–7 ribbed, and grayish-yellow to brown. **A feathery pappus** is attached to a long stalk (4–5 mm).

Postsenescence Characteristics: Plants may overwinter as rosettes in mild climates.

Habitat: A weed of orchards, container-grown ornamentals, horticultural and agronomic crops, as well as roadsides and disturbed sites, prickly lettuce is most common in irrigated crops and on nutrient-rich soils.

Distribution: Naturalized throughout much of the United States.

Similar Species: Several related species are encountered in the region. **Tall lettuce (*Lactuca canadensis* L.)** is common on roadsides, disturbed areas, fencerows, and urban landscapes. Tall lettuce tends to be taller than prickly lettuce, often >2 m; the leaves lack prickles on the back of the midvein. In addition, tall lettuce seeds are oval to elliptic, wider in the middle, whereas prickly lettuce seeds are oblanceolate, wider at the base and tapering to the tip. The **sowthistles (*Sonchus* spp.)** are similar to prickly lettuce but lack the prickles on the midrib of the lower leaves. **See Table 4 for a comparison** with sowthistles.

Prickly lettuce habit

J. DiTomaso

Prickly lettuce seedlings

R. Uva

Prickly lettuce mature leaves
(note spines)

J. DiTomaso

Prickly lettuce flowers

R. Uva

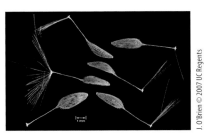

Prickly lettuce seeds, 3 mm (not
including pappus)

J. O'Brien © 2007 UC Regents

Oxeye daisy (*Leucanthemum vulgare* Lam.)

SYNONYMS: *Chrysanthemum leucanthemum, Leucanthemum leucanthemum*, white daisy, whiteweed, field daisy, marguerite, poorland flower

GENERAL DESCRIPTION: A **rhizomatous, clump-forming perennial.** Erect stems (30–90 cm in height) emerge from a rosette of leaves and terminate in **attractive daisy-like flowers. Leaf shape varies with age and location on the plant.**

PROPAGATION / PHENOLOGY: Reproduction is **by seeds and rhizomes.**

SEEDLING: Cotyledons are oval, narrowing into a short petiole. The bases of the petioles are united by a cup-shaped ridge across the axis of the stem. **Young leaves are smooth and mostly hairless** except in the unfolding bud leaves. The first 2 leaves are opposite, untoothed, and spatulate, with prominent petioles. **Subsequent leaves** are alternate but produce a **basal rosette** and have **distinctly rounded wavy lobes or teeth on the margin.**

MATURE PLANT: **Flowering stems develop from the rosettes. Stems are smooth**, hairless, **mostly unbranched** or only somewhat branched near the top. **All leaves are hairless**, smooth, alternate, and have **teeth or rounded lobes on the margins.** Lower and basal leaves are widest and rounded at the apex and taper to the base. They have shallow to deep rounded teeth or lobes. Petiolated leaves are 4–15 cm long. **Upper leaves are narrower than the basal leaves**, lanceolate, sessile, with less conspicuous rounded teeth than the basal leaves. **Leaves become gradually smaller up the stem.** In turfgrass, rosettes consist of mostly thick, leathery, basal-type leaves.

ROOTS AND UNDERGROUND STRUCTURES: Shallow fibrous roots and **short rhizomes.**

FLOWERS AND FRUIT: Flowers are present mainly from June through July and are produced in composite heads 3–5 cm in diameter, arranged singly at the ends of stems. The receptacle is flat and has many bracts (phyllaries) with brown margins. **Individual flowers of the head consist of 20–30 white ray flowers (10–15 mm long) surrounding numerous yellow disk flowers in the center.** The seed is enclosed within the fruit, which is a 1–2 mm long, narrow, **dark brown to black achene**, with white, longitudinal ribs.

POSTSENESCENCE CHARACTERISTICS: In late fall, plants die back to the crown, although in milder climates some basal leaves may persist through winter.

HABITAT: Oxeye daisy is not generally a problem on cultivated soil. It is found in turfgrass and nursery crops, primarily on low-fertility sites, but will tolerate a wide range of soil types. It is also found in meadows, roadsides, and waste areas.

DISTRIBUTION: Occurs throughout much of the United States.

SIMILAR SPECIES: **English daisy (*Bellis perennis*)** is also found in turfgrass, often growing in dense mats. It has flower heads similar to those of oxeye daisy, with white to pink marginal ray flowers and yellow central disk flowers. It can be distinguished by its leaves, which have smooth to only slightly toothed margins and usually reach no more than 10 cm in height. Flowers of English daisy are typically produced in early spring, whereas oxeye daisy flowers in June. **Chamomiles (*Anthemis* spp.)** have similar flowers and growth habit but have finely divided foliage.

Oxeye daisy habit and flower head

Oxeye daisy leaf shapes, *left to right:* basal to upper stem

J. Neal

xeye daisy rosette

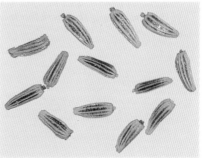

J. DiTomaso

Oxeye daisy seeds, 2 mm

Pineapple-weed (*Matricaria discoidea* DC.)

SYNONYMS: *Chamomilla suaveolens, Matricaria matricarioides, Matricaria suaveolens*, rayless chamomile

GENERAL DESCRIPTION: A low-growing, bushy, branching **summer or winter annual**, reaching 5–40 cm in height with **finely divided, pinnately compound leaves**. Crushed leaves have a **sweet odor** similar to pineapple.

PROPAGATION / PHENOLOGY: Reproduction is **by seeds**. Seedlings emerge in late summer to early fall and again from early spring to early summer.

SEEDLING: **Cotyledons are bright green**, oblong, and **narrow**, 3–12.5 mm long by 1 mm wide, slightly pointed to rounded at the apex and fused at the base. **Young leaves are fragrant, hairless**, shiny **bright green, thick, and succulent.** The first pairs of leaves are opposite, linear, with the margins entire or with a few lobes. **Subsequent leaves** are alternate and **pinnately divided with linear lobes. Young plants form a dense rosette** (approximately 10 cm in diameter) of finely divided leaves.

MATURE PLANT: **Elongated stems** are smooth, hairless, erect or spreading, and branched. **Foliage has a sweet odor** similar to that of pineapple. **Leaves are hairless**, fleshy, **alternate**, 1–5 cm long, **1–3 times pinnately divided with short, linear segments**.

ROOTS AND UNDERGROUND STRUCTURES: **Shallow taproot** with a secondary fibrous root system.

FLOWERS AND FRUIT: Flowers are produced from May through September. One to several flower heads are produced at the end of stems on short peduncles. **Heads are 0.5–1 cm in diameter, rounded to conical. All flowers are tubular (disk)** and **greenish-yellow.** The seed is enclosed within the fruit (achene). Achenes (1–1.5 mm long) are oblong to obovate, 3–5 ribbed, warty at the apex, and yellow, light brown, or gray, often with 2 red stripes. **Pappus is absent** or an indistinct crown.

POSTSENESCENCE CHARACTERISTICS: Senesced plants do not persist, but rosettes remain green over the winter.

HABITAT: Pineapple-weed is a weed of low-maintenance turfgrass, landscapes, and nursery crops, as well as other perennial crops. It is frequently found in roadsides and waste areas but is not a significant problem in cultivated fields. It tolerates compacted soils and mowing, but a combination of frequent mowing and adequate fertilization and water will gradually eliminate pineapple-weed in turf.

DISTRIBUTION: Although native to the Pacific Coast, pineapple-weed is now distributed throughout the United States.

SIMILAR SPECIES: Vegetatively, plants are very similar to **mayweed chamomile (*Anthemis cotula*), corn chamomile (*Anthemis arvensis*)**, and **scentless chamomile (*Tripleurospermum inodorum*)**, but when in flower the chamomiles have showy flowers with petals; pineapple-weed does not. **See Table 3 for a comparison with other weedy members of the aster family that have finely dissected leaves.**

Pineapple-weed habit

J. Neal

Pineapple-weed rosette

J. Neal

J. DiTomaso

Pineapple-weed flowers

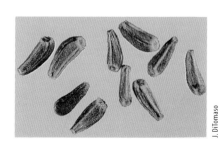

J. DiTomaso

Pineapple-weed seeds, 1.5 mm

Hawkweed oxtongue (*Picris hieracioides* L.)

Synonym: hawkweed ox-tongue

General Description: A biennial or short-lived, monocarpic **perennial** with a **basal rosette** and **branching, upright, flowering stems** reaching 0.3–1.5 m in height. Leaves and stems have **dense, bristly hairs with hooked tips.**

Propagation / Phenology: Reproduction is by wind-dispersed **seeds.**

Seedling: Cotyledons are ovate to spatulate. Young leaves are bristly-hairy, spatulate, with **irregularly toothed margins.**

Mature Plant: Leaves of mature plants form a dense, **basal rosette.** Rosette and lower stem leaves are oblong-lanceolate (5–30 cm long), tapering toward short, winged petioles. **Margins are wavy and coarsely dentate to entire.** Stems are angular, grooved, and branching. Upper stem leaves are lanceolate, sessile, and reduced toward the apex. Margins of upper leaves are wavy and entire to irregularly dentate. **Both stems and leaves are covered with short, bristly hairs** with branching, **hooked tips.** All parts exude a **milky sap** when damaged.

Roots and Underground Structures: A thick taproot.

Flowers and Fruit: Flowering occurs from June through October. Flower heads, composed of **yellow ray-florets resembling** those of **common catsear (*Hypochaeris radicata*)**, are up to 2 cm in diameter and arranged in clusters at the ends of stems and branches (corymbiform). Tips of ray-florets are 5-toothed. Seeds are enclosed in the **fruits (achenes)**, which are 3–5 mm long, **reddish-brown**, with transverse ridges. Each achene has a fringe of 5–7 mm long, white filaments (pappus) to aid in dispersal by wind and water.

Postsenescence Characteristics: Dead stems may persist into the winter. Non-flowering plants overwinter as rosettes.

Habitat: A weed of meadows, old fields, roadsides, railways, and waste areas. Hawkweed oxtongue is not tolerant of heavy grazing but can become abundant in lightly grazed pastures.

Distribution: Found in the eastern United States and Canada, as far south as North Carolina and west to Missouri, and in the Pacific Northwest. Likely more common and widespread in the northeastern United States but is often confused for other similar species.

Similar Species: The rosettes of several other asters, such as **hawkweeds (*Hieracium* spp.)**, **sowthistles (*Sonchus* spp.)**, **dandelion (*Taraxacum officinale*)**, **common chicory (*Cichorium intybus*)**, and **common catsear (*Hypochaeris radicata*)**, may appear similar to those of hawkweed oxtongue, but all lack bristly, hooked hairs on the leaves.

S. Morris

Hawkweed oxtongue rosette

S. Morris

Hawkweed oxtongue seedlings

S. Morris

Hawkweed oxtongue flowering stem

S. Morris

Hawkweed oxtongue seedhead

Tansy ragwort (*Senecio jacobaea* L.)

SYNONYMS: *Jacobae vulgaris*, stinking willie

GENERAL DESCRIPTION: An erect, **biennial or perennial to 1.2 m tall**, with **alternate, pinnate-lobed leaves** with a ruffled appearance, and **yellow flower heads**. Plants have an unpleasant odor when bruised. Many *Senecio* species, including tansy ragwort, contain pyrrolizidine alkaloids and are **toxic to humans and livestock** but are usually avoided by cows and horses. Native to Eurasia.

PROPAGATION / PHENOLOGY: Reproduction is by **seeds and vegetatively from the fleshy roots**. Achenes that disperse with wind usually travel only a few meters. Seeds typically remain viable for at least 6 years under field conditions. Crowns and fleshy roots can develop new root and shoot buds, especially in response to disturbance or injury. Fragments of the fleshy roots can generate new shoots.

SEEDLING: Cotyledons are oval, 3 mm long, tip truncate or slightly indented, and the base rounded-wedge-shaped. First **leaves alternate**, oval with wavy margins. On subsequent leaves the margins are toothed to deeply pinnate-lobed, 6–8 mm long, sometimes with a few glandular hairs. Seedlings first form a basal rosette or basal mound of leaves.

MATURE PLANT: Stems are erect, single or branched from the crown, branched near the top, and often purplish in color near the base. Leaves lack hairs or are lightly covered with long, wavy to cottony hairs, especially on the midveins, lower leaf surfaces, and new growth. Leaves are 5–20 cm long and deeply pinnate-dissected 1–2 times on a 3-dimensional plane so the leaves do not appear flat. Lower leaves taper into indistinct petioles and upper leaves are reduced, sessile, and clasp the stem. Basal leaves are often absent on flowering plants.

ROOTS AND UNDERGROUND STRUCTURES: Crown or short taproot usually develops many spreading, fleshy, lateral roots approximately 15 cm long, with numerous, deeper secondary fibrous roots. New shoots can arise from the fleshy roots especially in response to disturbance such as mowing.

FLOWERS AND FRUIT: Plants flower in the summer. Flower heads **bright yellow**, in dense, flat-topped to slightly rounded **clusters of 20–60 heads**, each flower head in the cluster is up to 2.5 cm in diameter. Phyllaries, or bracts subtending the flower, are often black-tipped and woolly-hairy at the base. Heads consist of numerous **disk flowers surrounded by 12-15 well-spaced ray flowers**. Ray corollas 8–12 mm long, 2 mm wide. Achenes are cylindrical, 1.5–3 mm long, shallow-ribbed, light brown, often pubescent except for ray achenes, which lack hairs. Pappus bristles are numerous, soft, white, and about twice the length of the achene.

POSTSENESCENCE CHARACTERISTICS: Dead brown stems can persist for several months.

HABITAT: Found in disturbed sites, waste places, roadsides, pastures, fields, rangeland, near riparian areas, and in forested areas.

DISTRIBUTION: Most common in Illinois, Michigan, Indiana, New York, Pennsylvania, New Jersey, Massachusetts, and Maine.

SIMILAR SPECIES: Tansy ragwort can somewhat resemble **common groundsel (*Senecio vulgaris*)**, but common groundsel is a much smaller annual that lacks showy ray flowers. Other species in the genus *Senecio* are present in the region but most do not have pinnate-compound leaves characteristic of tansy ragwort. The flowers resemble those of **British yellowhead (*Inula brittanica*)** but is easily distinguished by its entire leaf margins compared to the pinnately lobed leaves of tansy ragwort.

J. Neal

Tansy ragwort habit

A. DiTommaso

Tansy ragwort seedling

A. DiTommaso

Tansy ragwort rosette

A. DiTommaso

Tansy ragwort flower head

J. Neal

Tansy ragwort variation in stem leaves

5 mm

J. O'Brien © 2007 UC Regents

Tansy ragwort seeds

Common groundsel (*Senecio vulgaris* L.)

Synonyms: groundsel, grimsel, simson, bird-seed, ragwort

General Description: A **branched, erect, winter or summer annual** (10–50 cm in height). Leaves are deeply lobed to dissected, irregularly toothed, and somewhat fleshy. Although **not as toxic as tansy ragwort (*Senecio jacobaea*)**, common **groundsel also contains pyrrolizidine alkaloids that cause liver damage in horses and cattle**. Small herbivores, such as sheep, rabbits, and goats are resistant to the toxic effect of *Senecio* spp.

Propagation / Phenology: Reproduction is **by seeds**. Germination begins in early spring and continues to late autumn. Three to 4 generations can be produced in one season.

Seedling: **Cotyledons are slender and club-shaped**, on elongated stalks 10 mm long. Stalks of the cotyledons and young leaves are grooved. **Young leaves** are dark green, egg-shaped to lanceolate, **shallowly toothed to pinnatifid**, sometimes deeply lobed (15–25 mm long). Leaf blades are smooth or softly hairy only on the midrib, with a narrow or winged petiole. Cotyledons and young leaves are often purplish on the lower leaf surface.

Mature Plant: **Erect stems** are usually **many-branched** and smooth, frequently rooting at the lower nodes. **Leaves are alternate**, sparsely hairy to smooth, with coarse and **irregular toothed to pinnatifid (deeply lobed) margins**. Lower leaf blades taper to the petiole; upper leaves are sessile.

Roots and Underground Structures: Root system is a small taproot with secondary fibrous roots. The taproot is not always evident.

Flowers and Fruit: Flowers can be present from April to October. **Flower heads** (1 cm in diameter) **are composed of several yellow disk flowers.** Bracts (phyllaries) subtending flower heads are often black-tipped. Each seed is enclosed in the fruit (achene). Achenes are reddish-brown to gray-brown, 2–4 mm long, vertically ridged, with short hairs along the margins. A pappus consisting of soft bristles that can easily become detached from the fruit aids in wind dispersal. **Opened flowers can develop fully mature seeds after plants have been killed by cultivation or herbicides.**

Postsenescence Characteristics: Plants die during extended hot, dry periods. Erect stems turn brown and persist for several months.

Habitat: Common groundsel is a weed of container-grown and field nursery crops, vineyards, greenhouses, landscapes, and less often of agronomic crops. It is most commonly found on moist, nutrient-rich soil and is most troublesome in spring and autumn, when conditions are cool and wet. Common groundsel has biotypes resistant to triazine herbicides and is also somewhat tolerant of the dinitroaniline herbicides.

Distribution: Found in the northern United States and Canada, south to Texas and west to California.

Similar Species: **Mugwort (*Artemisia vulgaris*) seedlings** are similar, but young leaves are bristly-hairy and have white, woolly hairs beneath. The lobes of the leaves of **seedling common ragweed (*Ambrosia artemisiifolia*)** are much more deeply dissected than common groundsel or mugwort. **Tansy ragwort (*Senecio jacobaea*)** has similar divided leaves but is more robust and has showy, yellow ray flowers that are absent on common groundsel.

Common groundsel habit

Common groundsel seedling

Common groundsel flowers and seedhead

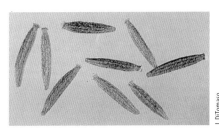

Common groundsel seeds, 2.4 mm

Canada goldenrod (*Solidago canadensis* L.)

SYNONYM: common goldenrod

GENERAL DESCRIPTION: **Tall, erect, leafy, rhizomatous perennial** (50 cm–1.5 m in height). A single rhizome can produce clusters of genetically identical plants.

PROPAGATION / PHENOLOGY: Reproduction is by **wind-dispersed seeds and creeping rhizomes**, which form large patches or colonies. Shoots emerge from rhizomes in mid-April. Seedlings emerge in June or early July but do not produce flowers in their first year of growth. Rhizome production begins after the first year of seedling growth.

SEEDLING: Cotyledons are very small (approximately 5 mm), club-shaped, and elliptic. Young leaves are spatulate-rounded; the bases narrow into a short stalk. **Young leaves form a rosette.** Leaf margins are toothed.

MATURE PLANT: **Rosettes soon produce erect, slender, leafy, mostly unbranched stems.** The stems are generally smooth but have small, soft hairs at least above the middle. **Leaves** are alternate, sessile, **lanceolate** to lanceolate-elliptic (3–15 cm long by 0.5–2.2 cm wide), **tapering to the base and apex**, with mostly toothed margins. Blades are smooth above and hairy beneath, at least on the 3 main veins. Leaves become gradually smaller up the stem.

ROOTS AND UNDERGROUND STRUCTURES: Extensive fibrous root system is associated with long creeping **rhizomes**. Rhizomes are produced primarily from the base of aerial stems and are usually 5–12 cm long, frequently with a **reddish pigmentation**.

FLOWERS AND FRUIT: **Yellow flowers** are produced from August through October in composite heads arranged in backward-curving, **panicle-like clusters**. The branches of the inflorescence form a central axis with the flower heads arranged on only one side of the axis. Bracts are thin, pointed, yellowish with a green tip, 2–4 mm long, and overlapping (imbricate). Individual flowers consist of 13 (10–17) **yellow ray flowers (1–1.5 mm long) surrounding 2–8 yellow disk flowers.** The seed is enclosed in the fruit (achene). A pappus of white hairs is attached to the achenes (1 mm long) to facilitate dispersal by wind.

POSTSENESCENCE CHARACTERISTICS: Erect stems remain somewhat rigid throughout the winter and are often in large clumps or patches. The remains of the branching flower head persist at the apex.

HABITAT: A weed of nursery crops, orchards, and other perennial crops; also found in roadsides, meadows, and ditches. Particularly troublesome in Christmas tree plantations. Canada goldenrod grows under a wide range of conditions but is typically found on moist, medium-textured or muck soils; it is less common on very wet or dry sites.

DISTRIBUTION: Found along the East Coast, west through the north-central states, and south to California, New Mexico, Texas, and Florida.

SIMILAR SPECIES: **Tall goldenrod (*Solidago altissima* L.)** is nearly identical but the mid-stem leaves are not toothed whereas Canada goldenrod mid-stem leaves have serrate margins. **Narrowleaf goldenrod (*Euthamia caroliniana* Green ex Porter & Britton** [syn.: *Solidago lanceolata* var. *minor* Michaux]) leaves are linear with entire margins whereas Canada goldenrod leaves are broader with toothed margins. Narrowleaf goldenrod flowers are arranged in flat-topped clusters, while those of Canada and tall goldenrod occur in a large panicle. **Many other goldenrod species are weedy.** They all produce yellow flowers in summer to early fall, are alternate, simple-leaved, rhizomatous perennials.

Canada goldenrod in flower

Young Canada goldenrod shoots

Canada goldenrod rhizomes

Young shoots (from rhizomes) of 2 *Solidago* species

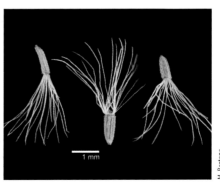

Goldenrod seeds

Lawn burweed (*Soliva sessilis* Ruiz Lopez & Pavon)

Synonyms: carpet burweed, common soliva, field burweed, soliva, spurweed

General Description: Low-growing, **winter annual** to approximately 25 cm diameter and up to 7 cm tall, with **dissected**, **compound leaves** and inconspicuous flower heads. The **bur-like fruits** can puncture the skin of humans and other animals, causing injury to humans when it is a weed in turf. Native to South America.

Propagation / Phenology: **Reproduction is only by seeds**. Seeds germinate in the fall or early spring, produce seeds (burs) in late spring to early summer, and then die.

Seedling: Cotyledons are oblong to narrowly ovate and fused at the base. The first leaf pair is lanceolate, with long-tapered bases that are often sparsely hairy. Subsequent leaves are pinnate-dissected into 4–5 elliptic-lanceolate segments, often sparsely hairy. Seedlings initially form a basal rosette.

Mature Plant: Stems are **prostrate to ascending**, often branched at the base and dark or purple-spotted. A few stems may root at the lower nodes, but plants are not stoloniferous. Foliage is covered with soft, short hairs. Stems often have thickened nodes where several leaves and branches arise. This makes it difficult to discern leaf arrangement on the stems. **Leaves are alternate**, **pinnate-compound**, 1–3 cm long, usually with **palmate-dissected leaflets**. Leaflet lobes are usually 2–8, narrowly elliptic-lanceolate.

Roots and Underground Structures: Roots fibrous.

Flowers and Fruit: Flowers are inconspicuous, generally present from April to June. **Flowering heads are sessile, axillary, mostly 5–10 mm diameter**, 2.5–3 mm long, greenish, and consist of inconspicuous male disk flowers with yellow corollas surrounded by fertile, disk-like, female flowers that lack corollas. Disk flowers are 7–9 per head, with a long, thick style at the apex. Peripheral female flowers are 9–12 per head. Receptacles are flat and lack chaffy bracts. The achenes are ovate, flattened, back slightly convex, body minutely hairy, with a **thick**, **spine-like style at the apex**, 3.5–5.5 mm long including style. Achene body margin is **winged, with a horn-like**, **slightly incurved tooth on each side of the style**.

Postsenescence Characteristics: Dead plants do not persist, but the dried burs will persist on the soil surface through summer.

Habitat: Plants generally grow in turf, compacted paths, roadsides, pastures, waste places, and other disturbed places.

Distribution: Mostly in the southern states, but as far north as Virginia.

Similar Species: **Parsley-piert (*Aphanes arvensis*)** has a similar growth habit, life cycle, and habitats. Vegetatively, parsley-piert can be differentiated by palmately divided leaves. Parsley-piert seeds do not have a sharp spine. **Pineapple-weed (*Matricaria discoidea*)** has dissected leaves that can be confused with those of lawn burweed; however, lawn burweed has achenes with a spine-like style at the apex. In addition, pineapple-weed has a more erect habit and conspicuous greenish-yellow, egg-shaped flower heads on stalks.

Lawn burweed habit

Lawn burweed seedling

Lawn burweed fruiting head

Lawn burweed hairs on stem

Lawn burweed seeds

Perennial sowthistle (*Sonchus arvensis* L.)

SYNONYMS: field sow thistle, creeping sow thistle, gutweed, milk thistle, field milk thistle, corn sow-thistle, swine-thistle, tree sow-thistle, dindle

GENERAL DESCRIPTION: Perennial sowthistle **resembles annual sowthistle** with **prickly-toothed leaves** and erect stems (60–150 cm in height) but is a **perennial** that spreads by creeping, fleshy roots that form new plants. Flowers are similar to those of **dandelion (*Taraxacum officinale*)**, although smaller, and the **sap is milky-white**.

PROPAGATION / PHENOLOGY: Plants reproduce **by seeds** and **spread by horizontal fleshy roots that form new shoots**. In established stands, shoots emerge in late April. Seeds are mature by 10 days after flowering and germinate in mid- to late May, after the soil has warmed. Most seedlings do not flower in the first year.

SEEDLING: Cotyledons are obovate (4–8 mm long by 1–4.5 mm wide) and sessile or on short stalks. **Young leaves** are alternate but form a **basal rosette**. **Blades are bluish-green with a dull surface**; the lower leaf surface often has a powdery white or purplish bloom. Young, expanding leaves may be pubescent but are smooth when fully expanded. **Margins are wavy and lobed** with backward-pointing **spiny teeth**.

MATURE PLANT: **Stems are bluish-green** (glaucous), hollow, ridged, and **smooth**, branching only near the inflorescence. **Leaves** (5–30 cm long by 2–10 cm wide) are alternate and have **prickly-toothed margins**. The **margins** are often **deeply triangular-lobed** (occasionally entire). **Upper leaves** may be **smaller than lower leaves** and are often **unlobed** and **sessile**. The **lower leaves** have a **winged petiole**, and are **clasping at the base**, with rounded lobes (auricles).

ROOTS AND UNDERGROUND STRUCTURES: Thickened, horizontal roots forming adventitious shoots, and a secondary fibrous root system.

FLOWERS AND FRUIT: Flowering begins in early July and extends through late summer. Flowers can resemble dandelion but are not solitary on leafless stalks. Flower heads (3–5 cm wide) consist entirely of ray flowers clustered at the end of branched stems. Flowers are **bright yellow to yellow-orange**. Each seed is enclosed within the fruit (achene). Achenes are 2.5–3.5 mm long, narrowly oval, with a wrinkled surface and 5 or more prominent ribs on each side. The **feathery**, white **pappus** aids in wind and water dispersal.

POSTSENESCENCE CHARACTERISTICS: Plants die back to the ground after first frost.

HABITAT: Perennial sowthistle is common in roadsides and waste areas but less common in landscapes. It prefers slightly alkaline or neutral, fine-textured, rich soils. It does not thrive on coarse sand.

DISTRIBUTION: Found throughout the northern United States and southern Canada, as far west as California.

SIMILAR SPECIES: **See Table 4 for a comparison with other sowthistles and wild lettuces (*Lactuca* spp.).**

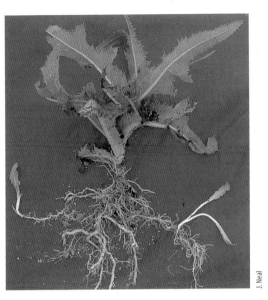

J. Neal

Perennial sowthistle plant with spreading roots

R. Uva

Perennial sowthistle sprouts from root buds

R. Uva

Perennial sowthistle leaves and inflorescence

R. Uva

Perennial sowthistle mature stem and foliage

J. DiTomaso

Perennial sowthistle seeds, 2.5 mm (not including pappus)

Annual sowthistle (*Sonchus oleraceus* L.)

SYNONYMS: common sow-thistle, hares lettuce, colewort, milk thistle

GENERAL DESCRIPTION: An **unbranched annual** with smooth, erect stems (30 cm to 2 m in height). Leaves, stems, and roots exude a **white sap** when cut. Stems and foliage appear succulent and waxy whitish or bluish (glaucous). **Leaf margins are weakly prickly,** but **no other spines are present.**

PROPAGATION / PHENOLOGY: Reproduction is by wind-blown **seeds**. Seeds germinate in mid- to late spring but continue to emerge throughout the season in moist, cool sites.

SEEDLING: Cotyledons are smooth, circular to egg-shaped, 3–8 mm long by 1.5–4 mm wide, and petiolated. Cotyledons and young leaves have a **whitish, powdery coating. The first few leaves** are alternate in a **basal rosette**, rounded to egg-shaped, with irregularly toothed margins. The blades taper abruptly to a winged petiole. **Subsequent young leaves are spatulate,** tapering more gradually to the base. **Leaves in the bud are surrounded by a tangled mesh of hairs,** but hairs are lacking in fully expanded leaves.

MATURE PLANT: **Leaves on elongated stems are alternate,** smooth, 6–30 cm long by 1–15 cm wide. **Blades vary in shape,** but are usually **pinnatifid, with a large, triangular, terminal lobe** and **approximately 3 pairs of lower lobes** that gradually become smaller toward the petiole. **Margins** are irregularly toothed and **only weakly prickly.** Lobes at the base of the petiole clasp the stem. Upper leaves are less divided and smaller than lower leaves.

ROOTS AND UNDERGROUND STRUCTURES: Short taproot.

FLOWERS AND FRUIT: Flowers are produced from July to October. Flower heads (1.2–2.5 cm in diameter), in clusters (corymbiform) at the end of the stems, are composed of **pale yellow ray flowers.** The seed is enclosed in the fruit (achene) and is 2–4 mm long, wrinkled, brown to olive, with 3–5 ribs on each surface. A long **white feathery pappus** aids in seed dispersal by wind.

POSTSENESCENCE CHARACTERISTICS: After frost, plants turn dark brown to black and persist for only a short time.

HABITAT: Annual sowthistle is a common weed of landscapes, nursery crops, orchards, grain fields, cultivated crops, and waste areas.

DISTRIBUTION: Found throughout the United States.

SIMILAR SPECIES: **For a comparison with spiny sowthistle (*Sonchus asper* (L.) Hill), perennial sowthistle (*Sonchus arvensis*), and wild lettuces (*Lactuca* spp.), see Table 4.**

J. Neal

Annual sowthistle rosette

J. K. Clark © 2007 UC Regents

Annual sowthistle flower and seedhead

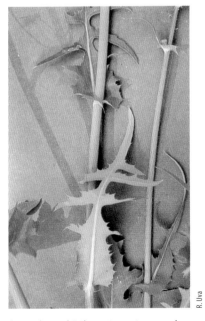

R. Uva

Annual sowthistle mature stems and foliage

R. Uva

Annual sowthistle seedling

J. DiTomaso

Spiny sowthistle habit

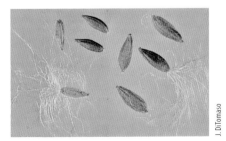

J. DiTomaso

Left, spiny sowthistle seeds, 3.0 mm (largest); *right*, annual sowthistle seeds, 3.2 mm (not including pappus)

White heath aster (*Symphyotrichum pilosum* (Willd.) G. L. Nesom)

SYNONYMS: *Aster pilosus*, awl-aster, subulate-bracted aster

GENERAL DESCRIPTION: **A semi-woody, clump-forming perennial** with several branching erect stems (to 1.5 m high).

PROPAGATION / PHENOLOGY: Reproduction is **by seeds**.

SEEDLING: Hypocotyls are short, green or purple. Cotyledons are green, smooth, lack evident veins, and are egg-shaped (0.5 cm long), with petioles almost as wide as the blade. Young leaves are alternate; both surfaces are smooth, the upper green, the lower grayish-green. Margins are hairy throughout. The **first leaf is rounded** and <1 cm long, **subsequent leaves are more lanceolate**. Margins of young leaf blades and petioles are hairy.

MATURE PLANT: **Clumped, erect stems are often woody at the base and branched in the upper portions**; they are usually hairy or sometimes smooth. Leaves are hairy. **Basal and lower leaves are lanceolate** to broadest above the middle (oblanceolate). Lower stem leaves and basal leaves **often do not persist** through the growing season. **Leaves on the mid-stem are linear** to lanceolate, lack distinct petioles, and are approximately 10 cm long by 1 cm wide, whereas the **uppermost leaves** on the branches near the flowers **are much reduced**, awl-shaped, bract-like, and numerous.

ROOTS AND UNDERGROUND STRUCTURES: White heath aster overwinters as a **woody crown of stems at or just below the soil surface**. Fibrous roots originate at the base of the stems.

FLOWERS AND FRUIT: **Small, white flowers** are produced from late summer to autumn in numerous heads arranged **in a broadly branching panicle at the terminal end of stems**. Panicles can account for more than half the total height of the plant. Individual heads are approximately 1.5 cm in diameter, with **white (rarely pink or purplish) ray flowers** (16–35 per plant) and **yellow disk flowers**. Seeds are enclosed within the fruit (achene), which is 1 mm long, conical, light to dark brown, with bristles at the apex (4–5 mm long).

POSTSENESCENCE CHARACTERISTICS: Erect, leafless stems bearing the dried remains of the flower head and fruit persist through the winter.

HABITAT: White heath aster is a weed of pastures, open fields, roadsides, nursery crops, orchards, and less commonly of low-maintenance turfgrass and reduced-tillage crops. It grows on open sites in rather dry, often sandy soil.

DISTRIBUTION: Found from New England south to northwestern Florida and west to southeastern Minnesota, Nebraska, Kansas, and Louisiana.

SIMILAR SPECIES: **Many other species of asters** are similar in appearance and can also be weedy. **New England aster (*Symphyotrichum novae-angliae* (L.) G. L. Nesom** [syn.: *Aster novae-angliae* L.]) has reddish-purple ray flowers and larger clasping leaves. **Fleabanes (*Erigeron* spp.)** are closely related to the asters, with white (occasionally pinkish) ray flowers and central, yellow disk flowers. However, they have more numerous (50+) and narrower ray flowers than the asters. In addition, fleabanes are annuals (occasionally biennials) that bloom in early summer (June) but may be found into September, whereas asters are perennials that bloom from late August through October. **Horseweed (*Conyza canadensis*)** is similar in habit but has much smaller flower heads (5 mm in diameter).

White heath aster habit

White heath aster, early spring growth from perennial crown

White heath aster flowering shoot

New England aster flowers

New England aster leafy shoot

New England aster seeds, 1.7 mm (not including pappus)

Common tansy (*Tanacetum vulgare* L.)

SYNONYMS: bitter buttons, garden tansy, hindhead, parsley fern, tansy

GENERAL DESCRIPTION: An erect, aromatic **perennial** to 1.5 m tall, with creeping roots, deeply **pinnate-lobed (fern-like) leaves**, and **yellow button-like flower heads**. It is often cultivated as a garden ornamental and is native to Europe. The species is reported to have insect repellent properties, but also to cause dermatitis. Similarly, it has been used as a food additive and as an herbal medicine, but consuming large amounts is reported to be toxic to humans and to cause abortions in cattle.

PROPAGATION / PHENOLOGY: Reproduction is by seeds and also vegetatively from **creeping roots**.

SEEDLING: Cotyledons are ovate to elliptic, 3 mm long by 2 mm wide, and lack hairs. First leaves are alternate, elliptic, mostly 6–12 mm long, 5 mm wide, with lobed or toothed margins.

MATURE PLANT: Plants are erect, mostly unbranched except for flowering branches near the top. Stem bases are sometimes weakly woody. The leaves are alternate, typically 4–10 cm long, deeply pinnately divided with toothed margins, sessile or short-stalked, and evenly dotted with flat or sunken glands. The primary leaf divisions are narrow, mostly with 4–10 pairs, and margins are dentate. The foliage is glandular, and either lacks hairs or is sparsely hairy. Lower leaves are larger than upper stem leaves. Basal leaves do not persist to flowering.

ROOTS AND UNDERGROUND STRUCTURES: Creeping roots are thick, extensive, with numerous lateral roots.

FLOWERS AND FRUIT: Plants produce **clusters of bright yellow, button-like flowers** from late summer through autumn. Flower clusters are dense, flat-topped or slightly rounded (resembling an umbel), that appear to consist of only disk flowers, but actually consist of disk flowers surrounded by a ring of ray flowers that lack corollas. The achenes are cylindrical, 5-angled, minutely glandular, 1–3 mm long, with a minute, crown-like pappus of toothed scales to 0.5 mm long.

HABITAT: Generally found in disturbed places, especially in urban areas, gardens, yards, fields, roadsides, and ditch banks. Plants can form dense colonies from the creeping roots, especially in riparian areas along rivers.

DISTRIBUTION: Present throughout the United States and Canada. Although not as common as a weed, it can be found throughout the northeastern and mid-Atlantic states.

SIMILAR SPECIES: The leaves of common tansy can resemble several other members of the aster family, but plants are much larger and the yellow inflorescences more striking compared to the smaller annual members of the family, such as **mayweed or corn chamomile (*Anthemis* spp.)**, **tansy ragwort (*Senecio jacobaea*)**, and **pineapple-weed (*Matricaria discoidea*)**.

Common tansy habit

Common tansy leaf

Common tansy seedling

Common tansy flower heads

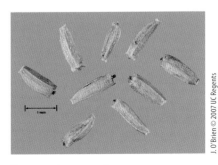

Common tansy seeds

Dandelion (*Taraxacum officinale* Weber in Wiggers)

Synonyms: *Leontodon taraxacum*, lions-tooth, blow-ball, cankerwort

General Description: A **tap-rooted perennial** from a **basal rosette of leaves**. Yellow flowers are produced on leafless stalks.

Propagation / Phenology: Reproduction is by **wind-blown seeds** and by new shoots that develop from broken segments of the taproot. Seeds germinate in the top 2 cm of soil. Seedlings emerge from late spring to early autumn.

Seedling: Cotyledons are smooth, and circular to oval to spatulate, with smooth margins. **Young leaves** are **spatulate or oval with a long petiole**, lack hairs, and **form a basal rosette. By the third true leaf, margins are wavy** with irregular widely spaced teeth. **Older leaves** have some appressed crinkled hairs on upper and lower surfaces and widely spaced **teeth pointing toward the leaf base**.

Mature Plant: Leaves, flower stalks, and the taproot exude a **milky sap** when cut. Plants form a **basal rosette of leaves** and the only noticeable stems are those bearing flower heads. Leaves generally lack hairs but are sometimes sparsely hairy, especially on the midrib and undersurface. Leaves are oblong to spatulate (7.5–25 cm long). **Margins are deeply lobed to pinnatifid**; the **lobes point toward the base**. The terminal lobe is usually the largest, with segments becoming smaller and more deeply divided toward the base. Margins may be variably cleft or entire (primarily on seedlings).

Roots and Underground Structures: A thick, long, **fleshy taproot** that may branch.

Flowers and Fruit: Flowers are produced from May to June, with sporadic flowering thereafter. Flowers do not require pollination to develop viable seed (apomixis). **Bright yellow flower heads**, consisting entirely of ray flowers, are 3–5 cm in diameter, solitary, at the ends of **leafless, hollow flower stalks** (5–50 cm long). Bracts are in 2 rows; the outer row is bent backward, and the inner row is erect and linear. Achenes are yellow-brown (3–5 mm long), with a **feathery pappus attached to a long stalk** (8–10 mm). Collectively, the fruits form a conspicuous, **globe-like, grayish-white seedhead**.

Postsenescence Characteristics: Rosettes remain green throughout the year.

Habitat: Dandelion is a weed of turfgrass, orchards, nursery crops, alfalfa, and other perennial crops. It tolerates many soil types and cultural practices but does not tolerate cultivation.

Distribution: Widespread throughout North America.

Similar Species: Rosettes of **chicory (*Cichorium intybus*), common catsear (*Hypochaeris radicata*), smooth hawksbeard (*Crepis capillaris*)**, and **Carolina falsedandelion (*Pyrrhopappus carolinianus* (Walter) DC.)** all resemble dandelion. The toothed lobes of dandelion leaves are generally opposite each other and point toward the rosette. Those of chicory are not always opposite and point forward or backward. Smooth hawksbeard leaves have more sharply pointed lobes and the flowering stems are branched. Carolina falsedandelion lobes are rounded and slender, generally pointing forward. Lobes on common catsear are rounded and leaves are noticeably hairy. The flowering stalk on dandelion is leafless and unbranched. The flowering stalks of each of the other 3 species are branched with a few leaves. Flowers and seedheads of **coltsfoot (*Tussilago farfara* L.)** are very similar to dandelion, but the foliage which emerges after flowering is quite different. Leaf blades are up to 20 cm long and nearly as wide, with irregularly dentate margins. Coltsfoot is a rhizomatous, colony-forming perennial found especially along roadsides in the Northeast.

Dandelion seedlings

R. Uva

Dandelion habit

J. Neal

Dandelion seedhead

J. Neal

Dandelion achenes

J. DiTomaso

Carolina falsedandelion plant

J. Neal

Coltsfoot flowers and fruit are similar to dandelion, but foliage is different

A. DiTommaso

227

Western salsify (*Tragopogon dubius* Scop.)

SYNONYMS: yellow goat's beard, yellow salsify, western goat's-beard

GENERAL DESCRIPTION: An unbranched (or, rarely, branched), erect **biennial** or occasionally an annual (30 cm to 1 m in height). The **foliage is grass-like**, and the **seedhead resembles that of a very large dandelion (*Taraxacum officinale*)**. Leaves, stems, and taproot exude a **milky sap** when damaged.

PROPAGATION / PHENOLOGY: Reproduction is by **wind-dispersed seeds**; seeds germinate in early summer or autumn. **Seeds remain viable in soil for only 2 years or less.**

SEEDLING: **Cotyledons** are linear and **grass-like** (13 cm long by 2 mm wide). **Young leaves** form a **basal rosette** and are **long and narrow**, usually with a few long, soft, fine, **cobwebby hairs**. **Blades** are keeled, with **parallel veins**.

MATURE PLANT: The **basal rosette** formed in the first year **produces an erect stem the following year**. **Stems are smooth, round, somewhat fleshy**, and thickest at the base. Leaves are also fleshy and smooth, sometimes with a few hairs in the leaf axils. **Leaves are long, linear, and grass-like** (30 cm long by 2 cm wide), tapering uniformly from the base to the apex. The **leaf base is clasping**, enclosing the stem.

ROOTS AND UNDERGROUND STRUCTURES: **Branched, fleshy taproot with milky sap.**

FLOWERS AND FRUIT: **Yellow flowers** are produced in early summer, June or July. Flower heads (2–4 cm in diameter) are produced singly at the end of stems. Flowers open from morning to midday and are oriented toward the sun. The **bracts** (phyllaries, 2.5–4 cm long) **surpass the flowers in length** and continue to elongate (4–7 cm long) as fruit matures. All flowers are yellow and ligulate (ray). The **stalk below the flower head (peduncle) is enlarged and hollow**. The seed is enclosed in the 12–17 mm long fruit (achene). The **spherical fruiting head** is similar to dandelion but is considerably larger (7–10 cm in diameter). The pappus aids in wind dispersal, which can scatter the fruit more than 250 m.

POSTSENESCENCE CHARACTERISTICS: After seed dispersal, a dead central stalk can persist for a short time. Biennial plants persist as a basal rosette through the winter.

HABITAT: Primarily a weed of nursery crops and other perennial horticultural crops, western salsify is found on relatively dry open sites, along roads and railroad tracks, and in disturbed soils. It is less commonly found in cultivated row crops.

DISTRIBUTION: Occurs throughout most of the United States but most common in the West and sporadic in the East; increasing in importance as a weed in the Northeast.

SIMILAR SPECIES: **Meadow salsify (*Tragopogon pratensis* L.)** has recurved, abruptly tapering, slender leaves, often with curled or wrinkled margins and leaf tips. The western salsify stem is hollow and gradually tapered from flower to stem; the meadow salsify stalk (peduncle) below the flower head is abruptly narrowed and not hollow. Both species exude a milky sap when damaged. Seedlings of western salsify and meadow salsify are often mistaken for grasses, but they lack ligules and distinct sheaths.

A. Senesac

Western salsify habit

R. Uva

Western salsify seedling

R. Uva

Western salsify rosette

J. Neal

Western salsify seedhead

A. Senesac

Western salsify taproots

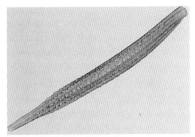

J. DiTomaso

Meadow salsify seed, 14 mm

229

Common cocklebur (*Xanthium strumarium* L.)

SYNONYM: clotbur

GENERAL DESCRIPTION: An erect (20 cm to 1.7 m), branched, **summer annual** with **distinctive prickly burs** in late summer and fall. Stems are brown- to purple-spotted and leaves are triangular with a sandpaper texture. *Xanthium* spp. cause **liver damage in pigs**, and probably in dogs, when ingested at 0.75 to 3% of body weight. The toxin, carboxyatractyloside, is limited to the seedlings and seeds. The spiny coats of mature burs can also cause mechanical injury or obstruction of the intestine in livestock.

PROPAGATION / PHENOLOGY: Reproduction is **by seeds**; seeds germinate from early spring through summer. **Seeds can germinate as deep as 15 cm below the soil surface.**

SEEDLING: Hypocotyls are stout and purple toward the base. Spiny burs remain underground at the base of the hypocotyl. **Cotyledons** are thick, fleshy, lanceolate, tapered at both ends, and **very large** (5 cm long by 1 cm wide). The upper surface of the cotyledons is dark green, the lower light green. The **first pair of leaves are opposite, subsequent leaves are alternate.** Leaf surfaces are rough with short, stiff hairs. **Young leaves are triangular,** with 3 prominent main veins. Leaf **margins have sharp teeth. Stems are green, with purple to brown spots,** and are covered with stiff ascending hairs.

MATURE PLANT: **Stems** are branched, rough, and **hairy with dark spots** and longitudinal ridges. **Leaves are alternate, long-petiolated,** and **similar to those of seedlings but much larger, up to 15 cm long.** Leaf blades occasionally have 3–5 shallow lobes and are often heart-shaped at the base.

ROOTS AND UNDERGROUND STRUCTURES: **Stout taproot,** somewhat woody in texture.

FLOWERS AND FRUIT: Blooms from July to September. Male and female flowers, produced in the axils of the upper leaves, occur on separate heads of the same plant. The male flowers are rounded, abscising soon after pollen is shed; female flowers are enclosed within the bur. At maturity, the **burs are elliptic to egg-shaped,** 1–3.5 cm long, **hard, woody, and covered with hooked prickles. Two long beaks project from the tip of the bur.** The prickles help facilitate dispersal, and burs are buoyant in water. **Each bur contains 2 fruit (achenes),** each with 1 seed. The lower seed can germinate soon after dehiscence, but the upper seed remains dormant for 1 to several years.

POSTSENESCENCE CHARACTERISTICS: Stems, bearing burs, persist into winter.

HABITAT: Primarily a weed of cultivated and reduced-tillage crops; also found in uncultivated fields, nursery crops, waste areas, and sandy beaches.

DISTRIBUTION: Found throughout the United States and other temperate areas of the world. Particularly troublesome in the southern states and in Mexico.

SIMILAR SPECIES: **Spiny cocklebur (*Xanthium spinosum* L.)** has narrower leaves and 3-parted, yellow spines at the leaf bases. Its burs lack the 2 beaks present on common cocklebur. **Common burdock (*Arctium minus*)** has similar foliage and hooked spines on bur-like fruit, but its leaves and overall size are much larger. Also, unlike cocklebur, it has numerous seeds in each fruit and the hooked spines are easily separated from the flowering head. **Jimsonweed (*Datura stramonium*)** seedlings may resemble common cocklebur, but the stems and leaves are smooth, unlike the rough hairy leaves of common cocklebur. Jimsonweed also has a single midvein, entire or lobed margins, and a foul odor.

R. Hahn

common cocklebur habit

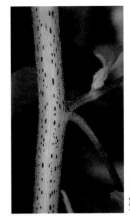

J. DiTomaso

Spots on stems of
common cocklebur

J. Derr

common cocklebur seedling

J. DiTomaso

Spiny cocklebur foliage, spines,
and fruit

J. DiTomaso

fruiting shoot of common cocklebur

J. DiTomaso

Common cocklebur bur, 30 mm long

Asiatic hawksbeard (*Youngia japonica* (L.) DC.)

SYNONYMS: *Crepis japonica*, oriental hawksbeard, false oriental hawksbeard

GENERAL DESCRIPTION: An annual herb, forming a **basal rosette** of leaves **resembling dandelion** but with varying **pubescence**. Flowering stalks are nearly leafless, branched at the top with **small, yellow flower heads** leading to globe-shaped, **fluffy, wind-dispersed seedheads** approximately 1 cm in diameter. Some gardeners with asthma have reported breathing difficulties after hand removal of this weed.

PROPAGATION / PHENOLOGY: Reproduction is **by seeds**. Each seed has a fluffy pappus that aids in wind and water dispersal. Seeds germinate immediately, leading to multiple generations per year. Germination is best in shady, cool, moist soils. Plants persist year-round but grow best in cool, moist conditions.

SEEDLING: Cotyledons are oval on a short petiole. First few leaves are oval, 2–3 cm long by 1.5–2 cm wide, on slender petioles about half the length of the leaf blade. Leaf margins develop small, pointed teeth, becoming more pronounced with age. Leaf blades and petioles are hairy.

MATURE PLANT: Plants form basal rosettes. In sunny sites, mature leaves (blade and petiole) are typically 20–30 cm long, pubescent, wider near the apex and progressively narrower to the base (lyrate), with a prominent midvein. Leaf margins have shallow, irregular, pointed lobes, and deep lobes often to the midvein. Deeper lobes may be absent on seedlings or on plants growing in shade. When deep lobes are present, they are usually opposite, 90° to the midvein or pointing to the base. Overwintering rosettes are often densely hairy in spring, but new leaves emerging in spring or plants in shade are less hairy.

ROOTS AND UNDERGROUND STRUCTURES: Stout taproot with secondary fibrous roots.

FLOWERS AND FRUIT: Plants flower profusely in mid- to late spring and sporadically throughout summer and autumn. In warm climates, flowering occurs through the winter. Flower stems are leafless or with 1 or 2 leaves, commonly 40–50 cm in height but may exceed 1 m under ideal conditions, densely hairy to nearly hairless, branched at the top, and often maroon. A single rosette produces few to many flowering stems. The exposed petals of unopened flower buds are often reddish-orange. Fully opened flowers are bright to pale yellow, approximately 1 cm across; individual petals have toothed tips. The achenes (cypsela) are 1.5–2.5 mm long with long, white, filamentous pappus.

POSTSENESCENCE CHARACTERISTICS: In warm climates, plants persist over winter as young rosettes but mature vegetation does not persist over winter.

HABITAT: Primarily a weed of container nurseries, landscape plantings, and turf but has naturalized in roadsides, forest edges, and noncrop sites.

DISTRIBUTION: Introduced from Asia, now pantropically distributed. Most common in the southeastern and mid-Atlantic states but documented north to New York.

SIMILAR SPECIES: **Tall false hawksbeard (*Youngia thunbergiana* DC.)** is also known in North America; it differs by having 4–10 leaves on the stem, as opposed to 0 or 2 on Asiatic hawksbeard. Growth habit and leaf shape appear similar to **dandelion (*Taraxacum officinale*)**, but dandelion lacks the pubescence common on Asiatic hawksbeard. Easily confused with **hawksbeards (*Crepis* spp.)**, but hawksbeard leaves and stems lack the pubescence common on Asiatic hawksbeard. Flowers of hawksbeard are twice the size and the seeds are larger (>2.5 mm) as compared to Asiatic hawksbeard.

Asiatic hawksbeard growth habit

Asiatic hawksbeard seedling

Left, Asiatic hawksbeard: *right*, dandelion

Asiatic hawksbeard flowering stem

Asiatic hawksbeard seedhead, achenes 1–2 mm (excluding pappus)

Garlic mustard (*Alliaria petiolata* M. Bieb.)

Synonyms: *Alliaria officinalis*, hedge garlic, Jack-by-the-hedge, garlic root

General Description: An herbaceous **biennial** that produces a rosette **of heart-shaped leaves** with **toothed margins** during the first year and an erect, upright-branching stem in the second (30 cm to 1 m tall). Capable of forming dense colonies in forest understories.

Propagation / Phenology: Reproduction is **by seeds**. Seeds germinate in the spring, forming a mounded rosette. Plants overwinter as a rosette; they flower and set seeds in early summer.

Seedling: Hypocotyl is green and up to 2 cm long. Cotyledons are paddle-shaped, ovoid to lanceolate, and up to 6 mm long, with similarly long petioles. The **first true leaves are heart-shaped to triangular** (1–5 mm wide), hairy, and coarsely toothed.

Mature Plant: **First-year rosettes have deeply veined, cordate to rounded leaves** (5 cm wide) with wavy or coarsely toothed margins. Petioles are up to 15 cm long. **Crushed leaves smell similar to garlic.** Second-year stems have short, white hairs on the lower portions and are hairless to sparsely hairy above. Lower stem leaves are similar to those of the rosette; upper leaves are heart-shaped to triangular with toothed margins, and deeply veined. **Leaves are alternate.**

Roots and Underground Structures: A branching, white taproot, which has an odor similar to radish when damaged.

Flowers and Fruit: Second-year stems produce racemes of **white flowers** in mid- to late spring. Racemes are densely arranged initially, becoming more elongated as flowers mature. Flowers have 4 white petals and 4 green, spatulate sepals (6–7 mm long). Six pale yellow anthers (4 long and 2 short) surround the short style. **Fruit capsules (siliques) are upright, hairless, and up to 5 cm long** with short (5 mm) pedicels and a beak at the tip to 1 mm long. Mature siliques split when mature and contain 10–20 seeds arranged in 2 alternate rows along the sinus. Seeds are brownish-black and cylindrical (2.5–3.8 mm long by 1 mm wide).

Postsenescence characteristics: First-year rosettes remain green throughout the winter. Second-year stems die by early summer, and dead stems linger throughout the summer months.

Habitat: Grows best in partial shade and in well-drained fertile, loamy soils. Primarily a weed of deciduous forest understories and edges, garlic mustard can spread to waste areas, roadsides, or other disturbed and shaded habitats including managed landscapes.

Distribution: Found throughout the northeastern and midwestern United States and south to the Carolinas.

Similar Species: Seedlings may resemble some **violets (*Viola* spp.)** but crushed leaves of garlic mustard smell like garlic; leaves of violets do not. Several **bittercresses (*Cardamine* spp.)** share habitats with garlic mustard. These plants are generally smaller than and lack the odor of garlic mustard and have smaller, lobed leaves. Senescent stems of **yellow rocket (*Barbarea vulgaris*)** look similar to those of garlic mustard, but yellow rocket siliques are more numerous and shorter than those of garlic mustard, and the seeds are smaller and square-shaped.

Garlic mustard seedling

Garlic mustard flowers

arlic mustard mature plants

Garlic mustard spring rosettes

arlic mustard stem leaves

1 mm

Garlic mustard seeds

Yellow rocket (*Barbarea vulgaris* R. Br.)

SYNONYMS: winter cress, St. Barbaras cress, bitter cress, rocket cress

GENERAL DESCRIPTION: A **winter annual**, **biennial**, or seldom a perennial, with numerous stems branching from a **basal rosette of deep-green, glossy foliage**. It can grow from 30–90 cm in height and tolerates mowing.

PROPAGATION / PHENOLOGY: Reproduction is **by seeds**, which are produced from May through June and germinate in cool, moist soil in the spring or fall. Seeds may persist in the soil for several years, and each plant may produce 1000 to 10,000 seeds, which germinate to a depth of 1 cm in the soil.

SEEDLING: **Cotyledons are egg-shaped** to round **on long stalks**, and the apex is slightly notched. **Young leaves are rounded**, some with a **heart-shaped base**. **Margins** are entire or wavy and **become distinctly toothed with age**. Seedlings develop into **basal rosettes** of alternate leaves that remain throughout the first year.

MATURE PLANT: **Flowering stems are produced in the second year.** Stems are smooth, angular or ridged, erect, and simple or branching near the top. Leaves are fairly thick and deep-green. Leaves forming the dense basal rosette are smooth and glossy, thick, 5–20 cm long, often persisting through the winter. **Basal and lower stem leaves are lobed,** with 1–5 small, **oppositely arranged lateral lobes and a larger terminal lobe.** The terminal lobe has a distinctive heart-shaped base. Lobes are rounded with wavy, toothed margins. **Stem leaves** are alternate and **become progressively shorter**; the uppermost leaves are approximately 2.5 cm long, with **fewer and smaller lateral lobes** than the lower leaves.

ROOTS AND UNDERGROUND STRUCTURES: Taproot with secondary fibrous roots.

FLOWERS AND FRUIT: **Bright yellow flowers appear in early spring (late April to June)**, and sporadically throughout the summer, on spike-like racemes that form pyramidal clusters at the ends of branches. Flowers have 4 yellow petals, 4 sepals, and 6 stamens (2 stamens are shorter than the other 4). Long fruits (siliques) are produced on 3–6 mm long stalks (pedicels). **Siliques** are approximately 2.5 cm long by 2.4 mm in diameter, beaked at the tip, quadrangular, splitting into 2 valves at maturity. Each valve contains seeds arranged in rows along a central membranous septum. Seeds are 1–1.5 mm long, broadly oval to oblong, notched at one end, light yellow to brown or gray, and somewhat square.

POSTSENESCENCE CHARACTERISTICS: In unmowed areas, the fruiting stalk remains through summer. After the fruit disperse, the central septum of the silique may persist as a thin, silvery membrane with a beak at the tip. Plants survive as perennials in mild summers with adequate moisture but die after fruiting in mid-summer under drier conditions.

HABITAT: A weed of turfgrass, nurseries, and agricultural crops; also found in roadsides and pastures. It is most common on nutrient-rich sandy and loamy soils.

DISTRIBUTION: Found throughout much of the United States but most common in the eastern and central regions.

SIMILAR SPECIES: **The heart-shaped base of the terminal lobe separates yellow rocket from other members of the mustard family.** The **seedling** can be confused with **shepherd's-purse (*Capsella bursa-pastoris*)** and **pepperweeds (*Lepidium* spp.).** The deeper green and glossy foliage and the much rounder terminal lobe distinguish it from those species. Yellow rocket blooms earlier (late April to June) than **wild mustards (*Sinapis* spp.)** and **wild radish (*Raphanus raphanistrum*)**.

Yellow rocket habit

Yellow rocket
flowering stem

A. Senesac

J. DiTomaso

Yellow rocket seedling

J. Neal

Yellow rocket seed stalk

J. DiTomaso

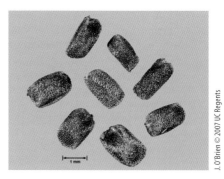

Yellow rocket seeds, 1.2 mm

J. O'Brien © 2007 UC Regents

Hoary alyssum (*Berteroa incana* (L.) DC.)

SYNONYMS: *Alyssum incanum*, hoary false alyssum

GENERAL DESCRIPTION: A **winter annual**, **biennial**, or (rarely) short-lived perennial. Plants are branched at the base, often lacking basal leaves. Stem leaves are **alternate, entire, pubescent**, and lack petioles; the hairs give the plant a gray-green color. In summer, plants produce **white flowers** in terminal racemes, with distinct **oval fruit**. Dried or fresh, the plant is **poisonous to horses**.

PROPAGATION / PHENOLOGY: Reproduces by seeds. Seeds germinate in spring through early autumn. When germination occurs in early spring, plants may flower the same summer; those emerging in late summer or autumn overwinter as rosettes.

SEEDLING: Cotyledons are elliptical, 3–5 mm long, rounded at the tip, glabrous, with a short petiole. First few leaves are oval with rounded tips, on petioles longer than the blade, forming a basal rosette. Later leaves become long and narrow with entire sometimes wavy leaf margins. Petioles become progressively shorter to absent. **Leaves and stems are hairy** giving the entire plant a gray-green color.

MATURE PLANT: Erect or ascending branches may be branched or unbranched above. Stems typically 0.5 m tall, but may reach 1 m. Basal leaves remain in fertile moist sites, but often absent in less fertile conditions. Basal leaves up to 15 cm long, oblong to spatulate with rounded tips and wavy margins. Lower stem leaves oblong, 3–5 cm long by 0.5–1 cm wide, with entire margins. Leaves and stems are hairy and gray-green. When examined under magnification, some hairs are star-shaped. Leaves on flowering stem are much reduced to absent.

ROOTS AND UNDERGROUND STRUCTURES: Taproot and fibrous root system.

FLOWERS AND FRUIT: Flowers are white, in dense racemes at the end of stems; racemes continue to elongate producing more flowers. Individual flowers, approximately 3 mm across, with **4 white petals so deeply divided** they appear as 8 petals. **Seedpods (silicles) are appressed** to stems, pointing upward nearly parallel to the stem, on 5–10 mm long pedicels. Silicles are green, hairy, oval to elliptic, 5–8 mm long, slightly inflated, with a short (~2 mm) beak on the end, each containing up to 6 seeds. The seedpod has 2 chambers separated by a thin, translucent partition (septum) that remains on the stem after seeds are shed. Seeds are brown, oblong or round, flattened (lenticular), and may be narrowly winged.

POSTSENESCENCE CHARACTERISTICS: Stems with remnants of the seedpods can persist into fall. Plants overwinter vegetatively.

HABITAT: Tolerant of poor soils but prefers fertile sites. Found in disturbed areas, hay fields, pastures, fencerows, roadsides, and perennial crops, notably Christmas tree production fields.

DISTRIBUTION: Introduced to North America and now distributed throughout the northern two-thirds of the United States and adjacent Canada.

SIMILAR SPECIES: Spring growth from overwintering crowns can strongly resemble **cudweeds (*Gamochaeta* spp., *Pseudognaphalium* spp.)**, but the hairs on cudweed are not star-shaped. The cudweeds are easily distinguished when in flower, with composite flowers lacking petals. When flowering, hoary alyssum may resemble **field pennycress (*Thlaspi arvense*)**, but field pennycress is not pubescent and flower petals are not divided.

R. Prostak

Hoary alyssum plant

R. Richardson

Hoary alyssum flowers

R. Prostak

Hoary alyssum seedling

R. Prostak

Hoary alyssum young plant

Hoary alyssum fruit

J. DiTomaso

S. Hurst, hosted by USDA-NRCS PLANTS Database

Hoary alyssum seeds,
2 mm

239

Shepherd's-purse (*Capsella bursa-pastoris* (L.) Medicus)

Synonyms: shepherds-bag, pepper plant, case weed, pick-purse

General Description: A **winter annual** producing a **prostrate basal rosette**. The flowering stems are mostly unbranched, reaching 10–60 cm in height, producing **characteristic heart-shaped seedpods**.

Propagation / Phenology: Reproduction is **by seeds**; seeds germinate in late summer, early autumn, or early spring.

Seedling: Hypocotyl is often tinted purple. Cotyledons are egg-shaped to rounded and narrowed to the base. Young leaves are slightly hairy on the upper surface with unbranched and branched (star-shaped) hairs. The **young rosettes have variable leaf margins.** The **first leaves are rounded**, becoming elongated with age, **with untoothed or slightly toothed margins**, but no distinctive lobing. The **older leaves are deeply toothed or lobed** with triangular segments, the largest segment at the apex. Leaves are dark green to silvery gray and occasionally are tinged with purple. **Leaves become more lobed and tapered as seedlings mature.**

Mature Plant: **Flowering stems** are produced in the same year as germination or in the following year. Stems are **erect, slender**, covered with gray hairs, and are usually unbranched or sparsely branched. Leaves are smooth or hairy, variously toothed or lobed, and alternate. The **lower leaves** are 5–10 cm long, oblong, tapering to the base, **deeply toothed** or lobed, and **arranged in a rosette**.

Roots and Underground Structures: Slender, often branched, taproot with secondary fibrous roots.

Flowers and Fruit: **Flowers** are produced in racemes on elongating stems and are present from **spring to early summer and sporadically in late autumn**. Individual flowers are relatively small and inconspicuous. Both white petals (2–4 mm long) and green sepals are in 4's. The **fruit is a triangular to heart-shaped, 2-parted, flattened pod**, 4–8 mm long, and nearly as wide (silicle). Seeds are approximately 1 mm long, oblong, grooved, and yellowish to red or brown. Each plant can produce thousands of long-lived seeds.

Postsenescence Characteristics: Plants die soon after fruiting in late spring or early summer. Dead flower clusters of triangular or heart-shaped pods may persist.

Habitat: A worldwide weed of cultivated crops, including nursery, agronomic, and vegetable crops, shepherd's-purse is also common in disturbed soils and waste areas.

Distribution: Very common throughout North America.

Similar Species: **Pepperweeds (*Lepidium* spp.)** are similar in appearance; however, the fruit of pepperweeds are flat and round, not triangular to heart-shaped. Leaves of pepperweed seedlings are less tapered at the base than are shepherd's-purse leaves. In addition, pepperweed leaves, particularly **Virginia pepperweed (*Lepidium virginicum*)**, have a distinctive tangy, peppery taste.

J. Neal

Shepherd's-purse habit

J. Neal

Shepherd's-purse fruiting stem

R. Uva

Shepherd's-purse seedlings

R. Uva

Shepherd's-purse basal rosette

J. DiTomaso

Shepherd's-purse seeds, 0.8 mm

Hairy bittercress (*Cardamine hirsuta* L.) and flexuous bittercress (*Cardamine flexuosa* With.)

SYNONYMS: hoary bittercress, woodland bittercress

GENERAL DESCRIPTION: **Cool-season annual weeds**, initially forming a basal rosette of variable, pinnately lobed leaves. Fruiting stems ascending (30 cm in height), branching mainly at the base with distinctive, slender seedpods (siliques) that forcefully expel seeds.

PROPAGATION / PHENOLOGY: Reproduces **by seeds**. Hairy bittercress is a winter annual (in North America), typically producing one generation per year. Seeds germinate in autumn or early spring; plants flower and fruit in the spring. Seeds are dormant when shed. In contrast, freshly shed flexuous bittercress seeds are not dormant, can germinate within a few days, and may continue to germinate throughout the growing season in moist, cool soils. Plants can reach reproductive maturity within 4 weeks; thus, flexuous bittercress will produce **several generations in a growing season**.

SEEDLING: Cotyledons are rounded, approximately 3 mm long, on long petioles. First 2 true leaves are heart- to kidney-shaped, subsequent leaves have 2–4 pairs of alternately arranged leaflets, the terminal one the largest. Plants develop as basal rosettes, and leaf surfaces are often hairy.

MATURE PLANT: **Flowering stems are smooth, ascending to erect**, angled, and usually branched at the base with **few leaves**. Basal leaves may or may not be hairy on the upper surface and are more numerous than the smaller stem leaves. Leaves pinnate with 1–3 pairs of alternate, round to kidney-shaped leaflets, becoming more elongate on the flowering stems. Margins are shallowly toothed or with a few lobes.

ROOTS AND UNDERGROUND STRUCTURES: Slender, many-branched taproot.

FLOWERS AND FRUIT: Flowers, 2–3 mm in diameter, are arranged in dense racemes at the ends of stems, with 4 **white petals**, 4 sepals. The **2 species can be differentiated by the number of stamens and silique position**. Hairy bittercress has 4 stamens (occasionally with 6 with 2 reduced in size); flexuous bittercress has 6. Fruit is a **flattened capsule**, 1.5–2.5 cm long and much narrower (silique). Siliques of hairy bittercress are held parallel to a nearly straight rachis; whereas, flexuous bittercress fruit stalks usually flex at the nodes and fruit is held at an angle to the rachis. **Siliques are explosively dehiscent**, propelling seeds more than 3 m from the plant. The 2 valves of the silique coil after dehiscence. Seeds are 0.8–1 mm long, elliptic to square and flattened, yellowish to brown.

HABITAT: Hairy bittercress is a weed of landscapes and turf. Flexuous bittercress is the most common cool-season weed in container nurseries. Also present in landscapes and greenhouses, and occasionally found growing on moist, sandy, or organic soils in waste places as well as cultivated areas, but rarely as a weed in agronomic crops.

DISTRIBUTION: Found throughout the United States and Canada.

SIMILAR SPECIES: The taxonomic classification of flexuous bittercress in North America is unresolved. Some texts place North American specimens in *Cardamine occulta* **Hornem.**; other reports place most specimens in *C. flexuosa*. The 2 species are nearly indistinguishable except *C. flexuosa* retains basal leaves at anthesis whereas *C. occulta* does not. **Little bittercress (*Cardamine oligosperma* Nutt.)**, more common in the western United States, has more rounded leaflets. **New Zealand bittercress (*Cardamine corymbosa* Hook. f.)** has become more common in container nurseries. It is slender, prostrate, with smaller leaves, and siliques are held in a digitate arrangement at the end of the rachis.

Flexuous bittercress siliques

Hairy bittercress siliques

J.Neal

J.Neal

exuous bittercress plant

J.Neal

J.Neal

J.Neal

exuous bittercress seedling

Hairy bittercress rosette

New Zealand bittercress siliques

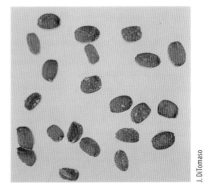

J.Neal

J.DiTomaso

ew Zealand bittercress seedling

Hairy bittercress seeds, 1 mm

243

Damesrocket (*Hesperis matronalis* L.)

SYNONYMS: dame's violet, dame's gilliflower

GENERAL DESCRIPTION: An erect, herbaceous **biennial** or short-lived perennial **to 1.5 m tall with showy flowers** (resembling garden phlox). Plants have been cultivated in many areas of the country and world for their flowers, but the species is now regulated or restricted in several states including Massachusetts. Native to Eurasia.

PROPAGATION / PHENOLOGY: Reproduction is only **by seeds**. Seeds fall primarily close to the parent plant but can be distributed longer distances with human activities.

SEEDLING: Cotyledons are ovate to orbicular and have an indented tip, somewhat kidney-shaped. The first leaves are ovate and very hairy, with a long petiole. Plants form a **basal rosette** of ovate to lanceolate leaves with a prominent midvein and shallowly toothed margins.

MATURE PLANT: First-year growth is only vegetative, producing a basal rosette or a cluster of basal sprouts. Plants flower during the second year and later. Several stems often arise from the crown. Upright stems are hairy and typically unbranched except in the upper flowering stem. The stem leaves are alternate and lanceolate, with very short or no petioles, and usually have shallow serrate or dentate teeth on the margins. Leaves are reduced as they progress up the stems, with the lower leaves to 12 cm long by 4 cm wide. Leaves have short hairs on both surfaces.

ROOTS AND UNDERGROUND STRUCTURES: Plants have a shallow, often-branched taproot.

FLOWERS AND FRUIT: Plants flower from May to August. **Fragrant and showy lavender, purple, or pink (occasionally white) flowers** arise from terminal racemes 30 cm or more long. The flower is 2 cm wide with 4 petals and 6 stamens (4 long and 2 short). Sepals are also 4, similar in color to the petals, and form a tube-like structure around the base of the petals. Fruits are 5–14 cm long siliques, often curving upward, that contain 2 rows of seeds that disperse when the sutures open on either side. A slight constriction can be seen between the seeds. Seeds are oblong, 3–4 mm long by 1–1.5 mm wide.

POSTSENESCENCE CHARACTERISTICS: The stems of dried plants can remain present until the next season with evidence of the inflorescence shape.

HABITAT: Plants have escaped garden cultivation and are now found in forest edges, floodplains, riparian areas including wetlands and meadows, pastures, roadsides and other rights-of-way, and disturbed areas, such as ditches, gardens, and waste areas. Plants grow best in full sun to partial shade in moist to wet woods with good drainage.

DISTRIBUTION: Found throughout the northern three-quarters of the United States and most of Canada.

SIMILAR SPECIES: The distinctive bright showy flowers can resemble native *Phlox* species, which are not weedy, but the 4 petals and alternate leaf arrangement can easily distinguish damesrocket from *Phlox*, which has 5 petals and opposite leaves. May also resemble **bouncingbet (*Saponaria officinalis*)**, but bouncingbet leaves are opposite with swollen nodes.

Damesrocket flowering stem

Damesrocket foliage before flowering

Damesrocket flowers and siliques

Damesrocket flowers

2 mm

Damesrocket seeds

245

Field pepperweed (*Lepidium campestre* (L.) W.T. Aiton)

SYNONYMS: field-cress, field peppercress, field pepperwort, field pepper-grass, downy pepper-grass

GENERAL DESCRIPTION: A **winter annual** forming a **basal rosette of finely toothed leaves**. Rosettes overwinter and produce erect, branched, flowering stems (20–60 cm tall) in early to mid-spring of the following year.

PROPAGATION / PHENOLOGY: Reproduction is **by seeds**; seeds **germinate in late summer or early autumn**, less commonly in early spring, to a depth of 2 cm in the soil. Each plant can produce between 200 and 600 seeds.

SEEDLING: Cotyledons lack hairs, are petiolated, 12–15 mm long, club-shaped to oval. **Young leaves** are alternate (but **form a basal rosette**), rounded to ovate, on long petioles; the blades taper at the base and are rounded at the apex, with **wavy-toothed to deeply cut margins**.

MATURE PLANT: **Lower stem leaves and basal leaves** are oblong, lanceolate, **rounded at the tips and tapering to the base. Margins are lobed, toothed, or entire. Upper stem leaves** are alternate, 2–4 cm long, **sessile, arrowhead-shaped, and clasping at the base**. Margins are entire to partially toothed. Both leaves and stems are densely covered with short hairs.

ROOTS AND UNDERGROUND STRUCTURES: Taproot with secondary fibrous root system.

FLOWERS AND FRUIT: Flowering occurs primarily in May or June and sporadically until September. **Flowers are in dense racemes** to 15 cm long on 4–8 mm stalks (pedicels). **Petals (4) are small**, 2–2.5 mm long, white or greenish. Six stamens are present. **Fruit (silicle)** is broadly ovate, 5–6 mm long by 4 mm wide, oblong to **egg-shaped with wing-like structures** at the apex. Fruit collectively give the flower cluster a **bottle-brush appearance**. Seed is 2–2.5 mm long, oval, and brown.

POSTSENESCENCE CHARACTERISTICS: Dead stems and dried fruit persist throughout the summer.

HABITAT: A weed of orchards, nurseries, and reduced-tillage agricultural crops, field pepperweed is also found on disturbed sites and waste places.

DISTRIBUTION: Distributed throughout North America; particularly abundant in the northeastern and north-central United States.

SIMILAR SPECIES: **Virginia pepperweed (*Lepidium virginicum*)** is similar in appearance; however, the foliage and stem are nearly smooth, and the upper stem leaves taper to the base and do not clasp the stem, as do those of field pepperweed. Fruits of Virginia pepperweed are flat and round; those of field pepperweed are oblong to oval with a wing-like structure at the apex.

Field pepperweed seedlings

Field pepperweed bolting rosette

eld pepperweed habit

Field pepperweed
seedhead

Left, Virginia pepperweed seeds, 2.0 mm;
right, field pepperweed seeds, 2.5 mm

Lesser swinecress (*Lepidium didymum* L.)

SYNONYMS: *Coronopus didymus*, carpet cress, swinecress, swine watercress, wartcress

GENERAL DESCRIPTION: Prostrate or low-growing, winter or summer **annual**, with **deeply pinnate-lobed to dissected leaves** and **small, 2-lobed fruits**. Plants exist as rosettes until flower stems develop at maturity. Stems can be up to 0.5 m long. For many people the foliage has an **unpleasant, skunk-like scent**. Native to Eurasia.

PROPAGATION / PHENOLOGY: Reproduction is only **by seeds**. Fruits fall near the parent plant and can also be dispersed to greater distances with landscape maintenance equipment and agricultural operations. Seeds may germinate in the fall or spring. In warmer climates, plants are winter annuals senescing in hot weather; in cooler climates, they may grow as summer annuals.

SEEDLING: Cotyledons are narrowly oblanceolate to spatulate, 5–12 mm long, tip is rounded, base is long-tapered, glabrous. First and subsequent few **leaves are alternate** and resemble cotyledons, except the margins often have 1 or more rounded coarse teeth. Later leaves have margins toothed to pinnate-lobed.

MATURE PLANT: Foliage lacks hairs or is pubescent with simple hairs. **Stems are prostrate** to decumbent, usually highly **branched, radially from the base**. The lower leaves are stalked and the upper leaves are alternate and nearly sessile. **Leaves are deeply pinnate-lobed** 1–2 times or dissected, 1.5–7 cm long.

ROOTS AND UNDERGROUND STRUCTURES: Taproot is slender, simple or branched, with few fibrous roots.

FLOWERS AND FRUIT: Flowers are present from early spring to October; although in warmer regions plants fruit and die earlier. Racemes are dense, mostly **axillary**, 1–4 cm long. Individual flowers are small and inconspicuous with 4 sepals that are deciduous and 4 very small **(0.5 mm long)** white petals, which are often absent. Stamens are in pairs of 2 or 4. **Pods (silicles) are in a bottle-brush arrangement** on axillary racemes. Each pod is on a short stalk, conspicuously **2-lobed**, each lobe rounded or kidney-shaped, 1.5 mm long, 1–1.25 mm wide. Only 1 seed per chamber. The pod chambers eventually separate at maturity.

POSTSENESCENCE CHARACTERISTICS: Dead plants with fruits can persist for a short period into summer.

HABITAT: Fields, roadsides, gardens, vegetable crops, turf, alfalfa, pastures, orchards, nurseries, ditch banks, other disturbed places. Often found on the edges of cultivated areas.

DISTRIBUTION: Found throughout the northeastern, mid-Atlantic and southern states.

SIMILAR SPECIES: The dissected leaves of lesser swinecress can resemble those of many members of the Asteraceae. However, the fruit and flowers of lesser swinecress are very different from the flower heads of these species, and the skunk-like smell can also help distinguish it from other similar-looking species. In the rosette stage, lesser swinecress resembles **Virginia pepperweed (*Lepidium virginicum*)** or shepherd's-purse (*Capsella bursa-pastoris*), but both of these species have a large terminal lobe on the basal leaves and upright flowering stems. Lesser swinecress rosettes can resemble several **yellow-cresses (*Rorippa* spp.)**, particularly **terete yellowcress (*Rorippa teres*)**, but the yellow-cresses have bright yellow flowers and tubular siliques.

J. Neal

sser swinecress habit

J. Neal

Lesser swinecress fruiting stem

J. Neal

sser swinecress seedling

J. DiTomaso

Lesser swinecress rosette

J. Neal

ft, lesser swinecress; *right*, terete yellowcress

J. O'Brien © 2007 UC Regents

Lesser swinecress seeds

249

Perennial pepperweed (*Lepidium latifolium* L.)

SYNONYMS: *Cardaria latifolia*, tall whitetop

GENERAL DESCRIPTION: Erect, **colony-forming perennial to 2 m tall**, with glabrous foliage, rounded to **pyramidal inflorescences of small**, **white flowers** and an extensive creeping root system. Native to Eurasia. Perennial pepperweed is a regulated species in some states.

PROPAGATION / PHENOLOGY: It reproduces vegetatively from **creeping roots and root fragments, and by seeds**. Root fragments and seeds float and disperse with flooding. Large root fragments can survive extreme desiccation on the soil surface for extended periods. Plants usually produce abundant, often highly viable seeds, but seedlings are seldom detected in the field.

SEEDLING: Cotyledons are obovate to oblong, 3–8 mm long, glabrous, tip rounded, base tapered into a short stalk 2–3 mm long. First leaves are developmentally alternate, but appear opposite, ovate to oblong, 4–12 mm long, lack hairs, with **margins entire to slightly wavy**, on a petiole 5 mm long. Subsequent leaves resemble the first leaves but are increasingly larger. Seedlings initially form a short-lived **basal rosette**.

MATURE PLANT: Crown and lower stems slightly woody. The foliage lacks hairs and is green to gray-green. The **basal leaves** are elliptic or oblong, larger and wider than stem leaves, to 30 cm long by 8 cm wide, **margin serrate**, and on a **petiole 3–15 cm** long. **Stem leaves are alternate**, reduced in size, more **lanceolate in shape**, **sessile** or nearly sessile, base tapered, with margins entire to weakly serrate. Leaf bases do not clasp the stem.

ROOTS AND UNDERGROUND STRUCTURES: Roots are long, **thick, minimally branched**, and vigorously creeping. Most roots occur in the top 60 cm of soil, but some can penetrate to a depth of 3 m or more.

FLOWERS AND FRUIT: Loose clusters of white flowers are produced in the top third of the plant from late spring to late summer. Inflorescences are pyramidal to rounded on top. Petals are 4, white, spoon-shaped, 1.5 mm long. **Pods (silicles)** are 2-chambered, **round to ovate**, **slightly flattened**, lack a notch at the apex, 2 mm long, and usually sparse to moderately covered with long, simple hairs. One seed per chamber, and seeds are ellipsoid, 1 mm long, and reddish-brown.

POSTSENESCENCE CHARACTERISTICS: Aboveground parts typically die in late fall and winter. The pale tan, dead stems can persist for several years.

HABITAT: Typically grows on moist or seasonally wet sites, including saline conditions. The species grows in noncrop areas including wetlands, riparian areas, meadows, salt marshes, floodplains, sand dunes, roadsides, and irrigation ditches, as well as ornamental plantings and agronomic crops, including alfalfa, orchards, vineyards, and irrigated pastures.

DISTRIBUTION: Common in the western United States; its distribution in the East is currently limited to New York, Massachusetts, Connecticut, Indiana, and Wisconsin.

SIMILAR SPECIES: **Hoary cress (*Cardaria draba* (L.) Desv.)** is also a perennial with creeping roots. However, it has inflated pods greater than 2 mm long, leaves that clasp the stem, and is only half the height of perennial pepperweed. **Field pepperweed (*Lepidium campestre*)** is related to perennial pepperweed but is a much smaller annual, growing only to approximately 0.5 m tall. In addition, the foliage is at least sparsely covered with short, simple hairs, and flowers and fruit are in elongated bottle-brush clusters.

J. DiTomaso

J. DiTomaso

Perennial pepperweed
flowering stem

Perennial pepperweed habit

J. DiTomaso

Perennial pepperweed
seedling

Perennial pepperweed young
plant from root

J. DiTomaso

J. DiTomaso

Perennial pepperweed
stem and foliage

J. DiTomaso

Perennial pepperweed rosette

J. O'Brien © 2007 UC Regents

Perennial pepperweed seeds (1 mm)
and capsules

251

Virginia pepperweed (*Lepidium virginicum* L.)

SYNONYMS: poor-man's pepper, pepper-grass, Virginian peppercress

GENERAL DESCRIPTION: A **winter or summer annual**, occasionally a biennial forming a **basal rosette of deeply lobed leaves** and an erect, highly branched stem, 10–50 cm in height. Through much of the growing season the upper portion of the plant produces numerous, small, white flowers and dried seed capsules. Collectively, **the fruit capsules give the ends of stems a bottle-brush appearance**. Young leaves and mature capsules have a **peppery taste**.

PROPAGATION / PHENOLOGY: Reproduction is **by seeds**; seeds germinate **in late summer or early fall**. Some germination can also occur in early spring.

SEEDLING: Cotyledons lack hairs, have a peppery taste, and are unequally oval, 7–10 mm long by 2–3 mm wide with long petioles. The first 2 leaves are opposite; subsequent leaves are alternate in a **basal rosette**. **Young leaves are oval**, **have long petioles and toothed margins**, and are hairy on the upper surface, the veins of the lower surface, and the margins. **Fully expanded leaves are smooth and develop irregular lobes extending to the midrib.** The terminal lobe is large and ovate; the lateral lobes become smaller toward the petiole.

MATURE PLANT: **Erect, branched stems** develop in early spring after overwintering. Stems are covered with tiny hairs. **Basal and lower leaves lack hairs** and are obovate to oblanceolate, pinnately lobed with toothed margins. **Basal leaves do not persist on mature plants. Leaves in upper portions are lanceolate to linear, sessile,** and smaller than the basal leaves. Upper stem leaves are pointed at the apex and narrowed to the base, with toothed or entire margins.

ROOTS AND UNDERGROUND STRUCTURES: Slender taproot with secondary fibrous roots.

FLOWERS AND FRUIT: **Flowers** are produced from April through early summer and sporadically until autumn on numerous, **dense, terminal racemes** at the top of the plant. Flower arrangement gives the plant a bushy appearance. Individual flowers are small (0.7–1 mm long), with 4 white or greenish petals and 2 (rarely 4) stamens. **Fruit (silicle)** is rounded, 2.5–4 mm wide, flattened, **slightly winged and shallowly notched at the apex**, with a short style that does not exceed the notch. Seeds are light brown, oval (1.5 mm long), with one side straight and the other rounded and winged. Seedpods have a peppery taste.

POSTSENESCENCE CHARACTERISTICS: Dead, light brown or tan stems persist through summer. Mature seeds are retained on dead stalks throughout the summer and can be dispersed from broken stems blown in the wind. Plants overwinter as rosettes.

HABITAT: A weed of agronomic, vegetable, orchard, nursery, and other perennial horticultural crops; also found in landscapes, roadsides, and waste areas, often on dry soil in full sun.

DISTRIBUTION: Occurs throughout much of the United States.

SIMILAR SPECIES: **Field pepperweed (*Lepidium campestre*)** is densely covered with short hairs, and the leaves on the stem are sessile with clasping bases. The seedlings tend to be somewhat larger than those of Virginia pepperweed, and the fruit are ovate, 5–6 mm long by 4 mm wide, with a more prominent wing at the apex. **Rosettes of horseweed (*Conyza canadensis*)** are very similar from fall through spring but lack the peppery taste and are not as deeply dissected as pepperweed.

J. Neal

Virginia pepperweed habit

J. Neal

Virginia pepperweed
inflorescence

J. Neal

Virginia pepperweed flowering
shoot

Virginia pepperweed rosette

J. Neal

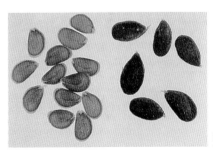

J. DiTomaso

Left, Virginia pepperweed seeds, 2.0 mm;
right, field pepperweed seeds, 2.5 mm

Wild radish (*Raphanus raphanistrum* L.)

SYNONYMS: jointed charlock, white charlock, jointed radish, wild kale, wild turnip, cadlock; sometimes incorrectly called wild mustard

GENERAL DESCRIPTION: A **winter or summer annual**, or rarely a biennial. **Erect, branched, flowering stems**, 30–80 cm tall, develop from a **basal rosette**. Leaves taper toward the base and are elliptic and pinnatifid with a large terminal lobe. Leaf surfaces are covered with bent, coarse, bristly hairs.

PROPAGATION / PHENOLOGY: Reproduction is **by seeds**; seeds germinate in late summer, autumn, or early spring.

SEEDLING: Hypocotyls are purple. **Cotyledons are petiolated, heart- or kidney-shaped**, with a **deeply indented apex** and an abruptly tapered base. Young leaves have appressed hairs and are rough to the touch. The **margins are irregular, wavy, and pinnatifid**, with the rounded and slightly pointed terminal lobe the largest. **Leaf bases are deeply cut**, producing 1 or 2 independent lobes. Petioles are relatively long.

MATURE PLANT: **Erect, branching, flowering stems develop from overwintering basal rosettes. Stems have stiff hairs**, especially on the lower parts, that are parallel to angled lines on the surface. **Leaves are alternate, with toothed margins and coarse hairs. Lower leaves** are long-petioled, elliptic, 20 cm long by 5 cm wide, **tapered toward the base, and pinnately lobed with a large terminal lobe. Upper leaves** are lanceolate, entire to toothed, sessile, and smaller than the lower leaves.

ROOTS AND UNDERGROUND STRUCTURES: Stout **taproot** with a **radish taste and odor**.

FLOWERS AND FRUIT: Flowers are 1–1.5 cm in diameter in long terminal racemes that bloom from April to September. **Petals (4) are light to pale yellow, fading to white with age**, and have purple veins. Sepals have stiff, erect hairs. Flower stalks (pedicels) are ascending, 5–20 mm long. **Pod-like fruit (siliques) are constricted between the seeds**, resembling beads on a string. Each fruit (2–4 cm long) has prominent ribs with a 1–3 cm long beak at the tip. Fruit lower on the flowering stem may be smaller and seedless. At maturity, **the segments break into fragments**, each containing 1–2 seeds. The seeds do not generally become detached from the fruit. Seeds are 2–3 mm long by 1.5–2 mm wide, egg-shaped, grooved in a net-like pattern, and have light brown to black flecks. Each plant produces approximately 160 seeds.

POSTSENESCENCE CHARACTERISTICS: Fruit pods persist on erect stems through the summer and into autumn. Plants may overwinter as rosettes.

HABITAT: A weed of cultivated nursery, horticultural, and agricultural crops, wild radish is also commonly found in fall-seeded forage crops, waste places, and disturbed sites. It thrives on nutrient-rich sandy and loamy soils.

DISTRIBUTION: Found throughout the United States, especially in the Pacific Northwest and the northeastern and north-central states.

SIMILAR SPECIES: **Wild mustard (*Sinapis arvensis*)** has smoother leaves in contrast to the rough hairs on the leaves of wild radish. The leaves of wild radish contain more lobed divisions than those of wild mustard. Hypocotyls and roots of wild radish have a distinctive hot mustard taste. At maturity, the fruit of wild radish break into fragments containing 1–2 seeds each; the fruit of wild mustard open lengthwise along a suture. Wild radish is found predominantly on the coastal plains of the Northeast, whereas wild mustard is mainly distributed on upland soils.

Wild radish seedling

A. Senesac

Wild radish habit (white-flowered form)

J. Neal

Wild radish fruit

J. DiTomaso

Wild radish rosette

J. Neal

Wild radish flower with purple veins

J. Neal

Wild radish seed, 2.5 mm, and seed pod

J. DiTomaso

255

Marsh yellowcress (*Rorippa palustris* (L.) Bess)

Synonyms: *Nasturtium palustre, Radicula palustris, Rorippa islandica*, marsh cress, yellow water cress, common yellow-cress

General Description: An **annual, biennial, or rarely a short-lived perennial**, initially forming a **basal rosette of deeply lobed leaves**, then producing ascending to **erect flowering stems** (30–80 cm tall). Larger plants are commonly many-branched.

Propagation / Phenology: Reproduction is **by seeds, produced 2 or 3 times per year**, and by new **adventitious shoots initiated from the crown or the roots.**

Seedling: Cotyledons are petiolated, elliptic to round, 1–2 cm long. **Young leaves are petiolated, egg-shaped** to elliptic or heart-shaped, **with wavy margins.** More **mature leaves are deeply lobed, pinnatifid.** Plants form a **basal rosette.**

Mature Plant: **Elongating stems are erect, rarely ascending or prostrate**, unbranched or branched, angular, smooth or somewhat hairy below and smoother above. **Leaves** are **alternate**, petiolated (occasionally sessile above), and **pinnatifid with 3–7 irregularly toothed lateral lobes and a larger terminal lobe**. The bases of the petioles of stem leaves are sometimes auriculate (with lobe-like appendages). Upper leaves may be pinnatifid to deeply toothed to entire.

Roots and Underground Structures: Slender, pale yellow taproot with secondary fibrous roots.

Flowers and Fruit: Flowers are produced from May to September in unbranched racemes on the terminal end of stems or in the upper leaf axils. The flowers are 2–3 mm in diameter. **Petals (4) are pale yellow**, 1–2.5 mm long, with 6 stamens. The fruit (silique) is cylindrical to spherical, slightly curved upward, 4–14 mm long by 1–3 mm wide, and consists of 2 valves containing several seeds each. Seeds are egg-shaped, yellow-brown, slightly flattened and notched, and approximately 0.6 mm long.

Postsenescence Characteristics: Overwinters as a rosette of finely lobed leaves.

Habitat: Marsh yellowcress has become an increasingly important weed of small fruit, vegetable, and nursery crops. It is commonly found on heavy, wet, nutrient-rich soil in poorly drained fields, meadows, pastures, and wet ditch banks but tolerates a range of soil types and conditions. Infestations usually start in wet areas and spread outward.

Distribution: Found throughout the United States; most common in the eastern and north-central states.

Similar Species: **Terete yellowcress (*Rorippa teres* (Michaux) Stuckey**; syn.: *Rorippa walteri* (Michaux) Torrey & A. Gray) is very similar to marsh yellowcress but the silique lengths are more than 3 times the width. In contrast, marsh yellowcress siliques are less than 3 times longer than wide. Terete yellowcress is more common in the southeastern United States, but the distribution overlaps with marsh yellowcress in the mid-Atlantic states. Young rosettes of **yellow fieldcress (*Rorippa sylvestris*)** are similar, but yellow fieldcress is a perennial that spreads by creeping roots. Mature plants have more finely divided leaves and siliques are longer and narrower.

A. Senesac

Juvenile marsh yellowcress

J. Neal

Marsh yellowcress habit

J. Neal

Marsh yellowcress
siliques and flowers

J. Neal

Marsh yellowcress rosette

J. Neal

Terete yellowcress siliques

J. DiTomaso

Marsh yellowcress seeds,
0.4 mm

257

Yellow fieldcress (*Rorippa sylvestris* (L.) Besser)

SYNONYMS: *Nasturtium sylvestre*, creeping yellowcress

GENERAL DESCRIPTION: Yellow fieldcress is a **perennial** mustard, **spreading by creeping, fleshy roots** that produce new shoots. Leaves are deeply lobed, with toothed margins. Flowers are pale yellow; siliques are shorter and slimmer compared with many other mustards.

PROPAGATION / PHENOLOGY: Plants reproduce **by seeds**, but the primary means of spread is **by creeping roots**. Root fragments less than 1 cm in length can produce new plants.

SEEDLING: Seedlings are rarely observed. More commonly, sprouts emerge from root buds. The first leaves are roughly egg-shaped, approximately 2 cm long, with entire leaf margins, and a petiole about as long as the leaf blade or longer. By the third or fourth leaf, leaf blades are deeply lobed, beginning with lobes near the base. Subsequent **leaves are deeply divided** throughout. **Seedlings form a rosette.**

MATURE PLANT: Plants form many rosettes from the spreading roots. At maturity the rosettes are typically 20–30 cm in diameter and leaves are deeply lobed (pinnatifid), with toothed margins. In the spring or early summer, plants form upright flowering stems, 15–30 cm tall (occasionally to 60 cm when supported). **Leaves on the flowering stems are alternate, petiolate.** Leaf blades are so deeply divided they appear compound (nearly **fern-like**), with 3–6 opposite lobes and toothed margins. Petioles and leaves become smaller closer to the flowers.

ROOTS AND UNDERGROUND STRUCTURES: Creeping, white, fleshy roots produce new shoots.

FLOWERS AND FRUIT: Flowers from spring through summer. **Pale yellow flowers** are elongated racemes on upright, branched stems. Depending on growing conditions, there may be many stems arising from the base, or a few. Petals are 3–6 mm long, half as wide. **Siliques** are straight, **linear** (rarely oblong), 10–20 mm long, and glabrous. Seeds are rarely produced.

POSTSENESCENCE CHARACTERISTICS: Foliage will persist through winter in warmer climates and persist through summer in cooler climates. In colder climates the foliage may senesce leaving a few remnants over winter.

HABITAT: Primarily a weed of nursery crops and landscape plantings but has escaped these managed habitats to infest streambanks, where it can be invasive. It is frequently introduced as a contaminant in divisions of herbaceous flowering perennials produced in field beds (such as daylily, hosta, and astilbe).

DISTRIBUTION: Introduced to the Hudson Valley of New York from Europe. Despite being a regulated invasive species in several states, it is now distributed throughout the United States and adjacent Canada.

SIMILAR SPECIES: In the rosette stage it is very similar to other *Rorippa* species; however, it is easily distinguished by the creeping, fleshy roots. The siliques are more linear compared to other common *Rorippa* species.

A. DiTommaso

Yellow fieldcress mature growth habit

J. Neal

Yellow fieldcress inflorescence

J. Neal

Yellow fieldcress young plant from root bud

J. Neal

Yellow fieldcress creeping root and root buds

J. Neal

Yellow fieldcress rosette and creeping root with shoots

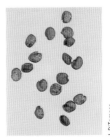

J. DiTommaso

Yellow fieldcress seeds, 0.7 mm

Wild mustard (*Sinapis arvensis* L.)

SYNONYMS: *Brassica arvensis*, *Brassica kaber*, charlock, field mustard, field kale, kedlock, common mustard

GENERAL DESCRIPTION: A **winter or sometimes summer annual.** Flowering stems are erect (20–80 cm tall). At least 2 distinctly **different forms exist: one with prickly, hairy stems, the other with smooth stems.** Otherwise the characteristics are similar.

PROPAGATION / PHENOLOGY: Reproduction is **by seeds**; seeds germinate in late summer, early fall, or spring. **Seeds persist in the soil for many years** and germinate to a depth of 2 cm in the soil. Approximately 1200 seeds can be produced by each plant.

SEEDLING: **Cotyledons are kidney-shaped** or heart-shaped (5–10 mm long by 8–12 mm wide) with a **distinct indentation at the cotyledon tip** and a prominent petiole. **Young leaves** are elliptically **oblong with wavy-toothed margins** and occasionally wrinkled surfaces. Hairs are present on the leaves and stems. Plants initially develop into a **basal rosette.**

MATURE PLANT: **Flowering stems are erect**, usually branched toward the top with **stiff hairs on the lower portions. Leaves are alternate, roughly hairy**, egg-shaped, broadest at the apex and tapering to the base, 5–20 cm long by 2.5–10 cm wide. **Lower leaves** have relatively long petioles and **deep, jagged, irregularly lobed blades. Upper leaves become progressively smaller**; they are lanceolate, not pinnately lobed, and slightly toothed; petioles are absent or short.

ROOTS AND UNDERGROUND STRUCTURES: Slender taproot with fibrous secondary root system.

FLOWERS AND FRUIT: Flowers are produced from May to August at the ends of branches in dense clusters of racemes that elongate with fruit maturation. Flowers are approximately 1.5 cm wide. The 4 **yellow petals** are 8–12 mm long and clawed. **Fruit capsules (siliques)** are 2.5–4.5 cm long by 2–3 mm wide on 5–7 mm long flower stalks (pedicels). Siliques are rounded in cross section, with a **flattened quadrangular conical beak** about half as long as the pod. Seeds are smooth, round, about 1.5 mm in diameter, and black or dark purplish-brown.

POSTSENESCENCE CHARACTERISTICS: Upright, fruiting stems persist for several months bearing remnants of the siliques.

HABITAT: Wild mustard is a common weed of nursery, horticultural, and agricultural crops, particularly small grains and fall-seeded forage crops. It is also frequently found in fields, pastures, waste areas, and disturbed sites.

DISTRIBUTION: Widespread throughout the United States.

SIMILAR SPECIES: **Wild radish (*Raphanus raphanistrum*)** has stiffer hairs on the leaves than wild mustard. In addition, the leaves of wild radish have more and deeper lobes. The hypocotyl and root of wild radish have a distinctive hot radish flavor when chewed. Wild radish is found predominantly on the coastal plains of the Northeast; wild mustard is found mainly on upland soils. Other similar species of mustard occur less commonly as weeds throughout the Northeast: **birdsrape mustard (*Brassica rapa* L.), black mustard (*Brassica nigra* (L.) W.J.D. Koch), Indian mustard (*Brassica juncea* (L.) Czern. & Coss.), and white mustard (*Sinapis alba* L.;** syn.: *Brassica hirta* Moench).

Wild mustard habit, in alfalfa

Wild mustard flowers and siliques

J. DiTomaso

J. Neal

R. Uva

Wild mustard seedling

J. Neal

Wild mustard rosette

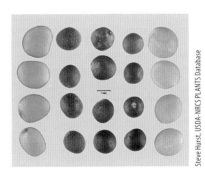

Steve Hurst, USDA-NRCS PLANTS Database

Left to right: Indian mustard seeds, black mustard seeds, birdsrape mustard seeds, wild mustard seeds, and white mustard seeds

Hedge mustard (*Sisymbrium officinale* (L.) Scop.)

SYNONYMS: *Chamaeplium officinale, Erysimum officinale,* hedge weed

GENERAL DESCRIPTION: A **winter or summer annual**, or rarely a biennial, that produces a rosette in the first season. Flowering stems are erect (30 cm to 1 m tall) with spreading branches.

PROPAGATION / PHENOLOGY: Reproduction is **by seeds**; seeds germinate in late summer to early spring.

SEEDLING: Cotyledons are petiolated, elliptic-oblong to club-shaped. **Young leaves** are circular to egg-shaped, with **wavy, toothed margins and petioles. Leaves become deeply lobed to narrowly pinnatifid with age. Surfaces are bristly.**

MATURE PLANT: **Flowering stems are erect, bristly-hairy,** rounded, with spreading branches. **Leaves are alternate, pinnately lobed or divided, with wide, irregular, wavy-toothed segments.** Both leaf surfaces are **bristly-hairy.** The leaf apex is the largest, most distinctly toothed segment. **Lower rosette leaves are deeply pinnatifid,** with oblong to egg-shaped segments and a rounded terminal segment. **Upper leaves are mostly sessile, oblong to lanceolate;** the terminal lobe is narrow, and the margins are toothed or entire.

ROOTS AND UNDERGROUND STRUCTURES: Slender, branched taproot.

FLOWERS AND FRUIT: Flowers are produced from June through September in clusters at the ends of elongated stems. Flowers are 3–6 mm in diameter, have 4 sepals, 4 **yellow petals** (3–4 mm long), and 6 stamens. Flower cluster expands as flowers mature. The **fruit** is an elongated, **awl-shaped,** 1–2 cm long by 1–1.5 mm wide **capsule (silique)** that is **tightly appressed to the stem.** Siliques separate into 2 valves containing 10–20 seeds each. Seeds are egg-shaped to triangular (1–1.5 mm long), light or dark brown to reddish-yellow. Each plant can produce approximately 2700 seeds.

POSTSENESCENCE CHARACTERISTICS: Tightly appressed fruit or remnants of the fruit remain attached to the dead stems.

HABITAT: Hedge mustard is a weed of nursery, horticultural, and agricultural crops. It grows on dry, nutrient-rich, loamy, sandy to stony soils, primarily in cultivated areas and disturbed sites.

DISTRIBUTION: Found throughout most of the United States.

SIMILAR SPECIES: **Tumble mustard (*Sisymbrium altissimum* L.)** is a less hairy, winter or summer annual with more deeply and finely dissected skeleton-like foliage. Its fruit are longer and narrower (6–9 cm long × 1–2 mm wide), almost thread-like, and are not usually appressed to the stem as are those of hedge mustard. Tumble mustard plants are brittle late in the season; they become detached from the roots and distribute seeds by tumbling in the wind. **Wallflower mustard (*Erysimum cheiranthoides* L.),** synonym: treacle mustard) is an erect annual with yellow flowers resembling hedge mustard. The leaves of wallflower mustard are not pinnately lobed as they are in hedge mustard or tumble mustard. Wallflower mustard also has longer (1.5–2.5 cm) fruits (siliques) that are 4-angled with a constriction between the seeds. Fruit are held away from the stem. By comparison, the fruit of hedge mustard are awl-shaped and tightly appressed to the stem on short pedicels. The siliques are shorter and thicker than tumble mustard siliques. Wallflower mustard and tumble mustard are found throughout the Northeast and mid-Atlantic states and are native to Eurasia.

J. DiTomaso

Hedge mustard habit

J. Neal

Hedge mustard flower

Hedge mustard rosette

J. DiTomaso

Hedge mustard rosette

J. Neal

Hedge mustard
erect siliques

J. Neal

Tumble mustard siliques
and flowers

Wallflower mustard stem

J. DiTomaso

J. O'Brien © 2007 UC Regents

Left, tumble mustard seeds;
right, hedge mustard seeds

Field pennycress (*Thlaspi arvense* L.)

SYNONYMS: fan-weed, penny-cress, French-weed, stink-weed, bastard-cress

GENERAL DESCRIPTION: A **winter or summer annual** that initially produces a **rosette** of leaves and then an **erect, flowering stem** (10–60 cm tall). Stems and foliage are smooth and emit an unpleasant odor when bruised. **Fruit are distinctively round to elliptic, winged pods.**

PROPAGATION / PHENOLOGY: Reproduction is **by seeds**; seeds germinate in late summer, autumn, or early spring from as deep as 1 cm in cool, moist soil.

SEEDLING: Cotyledons are bluish-green, oval to elliptic-oblong, 6–8 mm long by 5–6 mm wide, on 5–7 mm long petioles. Tips of the cotyledons curve downward. **Young leaves** are smooth, **round to oval, with distinct petioles. Subsequent leaves** are also petiolated and are **ovate-lanceolate**, with a **wavy, slightly toothed margin**. Young plants produce a **basal rosette** of leaves. Fall-germinating plants will overwinter in this stage.

MATURE PLANT: Basal leaves are light green, hairless, narrowly egg-shaped, with entire or toothed margins and 1.3–5 cm long petioles. **Basal leaves do not persist at maturity. Flower-producing stems are erect, unbranched** or branched above, and smooth. Upper leaves are oblong to lanceolate, with smooth surfaces and toothed or entire margins. **Stem leaves are sessile, with projecting lobes (auricles) where the leaf clasps the stem.**

ROOTS AND UNDERGROUND STRUCTURES: Slender taproot with secondary fibrous roots.

FLOWERS AND FRUIT: Flowers bloom from April through June and are 4–6 mm in diameter, in dense racemes at the end of the stems. **Petals (4) are white**, 3–4 mm long, and about twice as long as the 4 sepals. Six stamens are present. **Racemes elongate with age.** The **distinctive fruit (silicles)** are flat, circular to elliptic, about 1.3 cm in diameter, and distinctly **winged around the margins, with a 2–3 mm notch at the apex.** Silicles separate into 2 valves, each containing 2–8 seeds. Seeds are dark brown, 1.5–2.3 mm long and flattened, with 10–14 concentric granular ridges on each side. A single plant produces about 900 seeds.

POSTSENESCENCE CHARACTERISTICS: The upright stems and fruit clusters may persist. In late summer, the capsules remain as silvery membranes with flat wings and a notch at the apex.

HABITAT: A weed of nursery, horticultural, and agricultural crops, field pennycress is usually found on nutrient-rich soil in cultivated areas.

DISTRIBUTION: Occurs throughout the United States; most common in the northwestern states.

SIMILAR SPECIES: **Claspleaf pennycress (*Microthlaspi perfoliatum* (L.) F.K. Mey.)** is similar, but the lobes (auricles) at the base of the stem leaves are rounded; those of field pennycress are pointed. Claspleaf pennycress has shorter fruit (4–7 mm long), with notches that are mostly wider than deep, whereas field pennycress has notches that are deeper than wide.

Field pennycress seedlings

Field pennycress habit

Field pennycress flowering shoot

Field pennycress flowers and fruit

Thoroughwort
pennycress seeds

Field pennycress
seeds

265

Common venuslookingglass (*Triodanis perfoliata* (L.) Nieuwl.)

SYNONYMS: *Specularia perfoliata*, *Triodanis perfoliata* var. *biflora*, round-leaved triodanis, clasping bellwort

GENERAL DESCRIPTION: A **winter or summer annual**, or occasionally a perennial. The main stem is **erect** (≤0.5 m in height). Unbranched side shoots arise from the base of the plant and may run perpendicular to the primary shoot. Plants can appear prostrate if the main stem dies. Cut stems exude a milky sap.

PROPAGATION / PHENOLOGY: Reproduction is **by seeds**; seeds germinate primarily in the spring.

SEEDLING: **First leaves are opposite**, ovate, with a petiole approximately as long as the leaf blade. **Subsequent leaves become alternate and sessile** (or nearly so) with age.

MATURE PLANT: **Stems are erect**, **sparsely branched**, and hairy or rough on the lower portions. **Leaves** are alternate, 0.5–3 cm long by 6–25 mm wide, rounded to egg-shaped, palmately veined, with **heart-shaped bases that clasp the stem**. Margins are usually toothed.

ROOTS AND UNDERGROUND STRUCTURES: Fibrous root system.

FLOWERS AND FRUIT: Sessile **flowers** (2 cm wide), present in May and June, are produced in **clusters of 1–3 in the leaf axils**. Flowers in the lower leaf axils are self-pollinating and remain closed (cleistogamous), producing seed without opening. The sepals (4–5) are fused. Base of the **petals** (5) are fused into a 2–4 mm long, **deep-purple to pale lavender tube**. Five stamens surround a 3-parted pistil. The **fruit is a vase-like oblong capsule**, opening by 3 small, elongated pores at or slightly below the middle. Seeds are 0.4–0.6 mm long, egg-shaped, dark reddish-brown, smooth, and glossy.

POSTSENESCENCE CHARACTERISTICS: Upright stems with the characteristic seedpods persist only a short time in late summer.

HABITAT: Common venuslookingglass is a weed of low-maintenance turfgrass and landscapes. It is often found on nutrient-poor, dry, sandy or gravelly soil and on disturbed sites with plants that offer little competition.

DISTRIBUTION: Distributed throughout most of the continental United States.

SIMILAR SPECIES: **Small venuslookingglass (*Triodanis biflora* (R. & P.) Green**; syn.: *T. perfoliata* (L.) Nieuwl. var. *perfoliata*) has narrower leaves with less pronounced venation, and only one open flower at the apex. The capsule is more slender compared to common venuslookingglass. Otherwise, small and common venuslookingglass are similar. The alternate, sessile stem leaves of **corn speedwell (*Veronica arvensis*)** resemble those of common venuslookingglass, but the leaves on the base of corn speedwell (non-flowering parts) are opposite and distinctly hairy, with short (1–3 mm) petioles.

Common venuslookingglass habit

Common venuslookingglass
seedling

Common venuslookingglass flowers

Common venuslooking-
glass ribbed stems and fruit

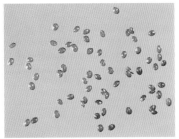

Common venuslookingglass seeds,
0.4 mm

Japanese hops (*Humulus japonicus* Siebold & Zucc.)

SYNONYMS: *Humulus scandens*

GENERAL DESCRIPTION: A robust, **herbaceous, summer annual, climbing or trailing vine** that can reach greater than **3 m in height**. Climbs taller plants and can form dense mats that smother lower vegetation. **Stems and leaves** have short, stiff, and **prickly hairs** that may cause dermatitis. The fruit clusters of Japanese hops **resemble cultivated hops** but are not useful in brewing.

PROPAGATION / PHENOLOGY: Reproduction is **by seeds**. Germination occurs in early spring. In the southernmost regions of its distribution, plants may persist year-round.

SEEDLING: Cotyledons are green, narrow, and linear. **First true leaves are hairy, toothed, and simple.**

MATURE PLANT: **Stems** of mature plants are **pale green to red**, twining, and branched with **longitudinal ridges**, with short, **downward-facing, prickly hairs** along the stem ridges. **Stems twine counterclockwise. Leaves** (5–13 cm long) are **opposite**, coarsely textured, and **palmately lobed** with 5–9 serrated lobes (generally 5). Upper leaves often have fewer lobes than the lower leaves. Lower surfaces of the leaves have prickly hairs; hairs on the upper surfaces are stiff. **Petioles are as long as, or longer, than the leaves.**

ROOTS AND UNDERGROUND STRUCTURES: A shallow and fibrous root system.

FLOWERS AND FRUIT: Flowering begins in mid-summer. Flowers occur in the leaf axils, and **male and female flowers are borne on separate vines (dioecious). Male flowers** occur in an **upright panicle** (25 cm tall by 12.5 cm wide) with spreading, lateral green to (typically) red branches. At the base of each branch is a pair of linear bracts. Individual male flowers (3 mm in diameter) have 5 anthers, 5 green sepals, and no petals. **Female flowers** are nodding, **cone-like spikes** (3.8 cm wide) composed of several overlapping flowers with **conspicuous bracts**. These bracts are triangular (becoming **recurved with age**), hairy, and have ciliate, smooth margins. Each bract has a pair of flowers at the base. Individual female flowers have no petals and fused green to pale red sepals (calyx) surrounding a divided style and a small ovary. By late summer each female flower produces a single, 3–5 mm long, ovoid and **flattened, yellow-brown fruit (achene).**

POSTSENESCENCE CHARACTERISTICS: Dies at first frost. Dead stems linger on other vegetation into the following spring or longer.

HABITAT: A weed of disturbed areas, forest edges, river and stream edges, hedgerows, and roadsides. Prefers full sun but can grow in partial shade.

DISTRIBUTION: Occurs in scattered populations throughout the eastern United States and the Midwest.

SIMILAR SPECIES: **Common hops (*Humulus lupulus* L.)** has foliage and flowers similar to Japanese hops. The leaves of common hops typically have 3 (or no) lobes, whereas the leaves of Japanese hops have 5 or more. Male flower panicles of common hops are yellow in appearance, and those of Japanese hops typically have red branches. Female flowers of common hops have straight, oval bracts, while those of Japanese hops are triangular and recurved. Common hops has yellow glands on the leaves and female flowers that produce the fragrant compound lupulin; Japanese hops does not. The weedy vine **burcucumber (*Sicyos angulatus*)** has 5-lobed leaves and prickly stems, but it has tendrils and Japanese hops does not.

J. Neal

Japanese hops habit

J. Neal

Japanese hops leaf

J. Neal

Japanese hops inflorescence

J. Neal

Downward pointed
hairs of Japanese hops

J. Neal

Japanese hops "cone"

Carole Ritchie, hosted by USDA-NRCS PLANTS Database

5 mm

Japanese hops seeds

Corn cockle (*Agrostemma githago* L.)

SYNONYMS: *Lychnis githago*, purple cockle, corn rose, corn campion, crown-of-the-field, corn mullein, old maids pink

GENERAL DESCRIPTION: A **winter annual** with **erect stems** (30–60 cm tall, sometimes to 1 m), branching mostly in the upper half. Leaves are opposite, long and narrow, with gray hairs. Seeds contain the glucoside githagin, which is a saponin that causes gastrointestinal irritation when ingested. **Grain contaminated with corn cockle seed may be detrimental to livestock and poultry.**

PROPAGATION / PHENOLOGY: Reproduction is **by seeds; seeds germinate in autumn.**

SEEDLING: Cotyledons are relatively large (15–30 mm long by 5–10 mm wide), often unequal in size, dull green, and somewhat waxy. Cotyledon blades are thick; the apex is rounded, and the base gradually narrows into a short petiole. Petioles of the 2 cotyledons are joined by a ridge across the hypocotyl. **Young leaves are opposite**; surfaces are dull green and **densely covered with long, soft, appressed hairs. Blades are lanceolate** and taper to the petiole and to a sharp point at the apex.

MATURE PLANT: **Stems are swollen at the nodes**, branching in the upper parts, and covered with silky hairs. **Leaves** are opposite, **linear to lanceolate**, 8–12 cm long by 5–10 mm wide, with entire margins and appressed **gray hairs. Petioles are joined by a ridge across the node.**

ROOTS AND UNDERGROUND STRUCTURES: Shallow taproot.

FLOWERS AND FRUIT: **Red to purplish-red flowers** are most abundant from May to July but are also present later in the summer. Flowers (2–4 cm in diameter) are solitary on long stalks at the end of branches. The 5 sepals are longer than the petals and are fused into a 12–18 mm long tube with 10 prominent ribs. There are 10 stamens and 5 petals (not fused); each petal is 2–3 cm long. Fruit is an oval, 10-ribbed capsule, 14–22 mm long by 10–15 mm wide. Seeds are 2–4 mm in diameter, triangular, kidney-shaped to round, black or brown with pointed projections (tubercles) on the surface. **Seeds are poisonous** and have a **short viability in the soil.**

POSTSENESCENCE CHARACTERISTICS: Dead stems can persist, with the distinct, long, fused sepal attached. Young plants overwinter as sparsely leafed basal rosettes.

HABITAT: A common weed of winter grain crops, other agricultural crops, and nurseries, corn cockle prefers slightly acid to neutral, nutrient-rich soils.

DISTRIBUTION: Widely distributed throughout the United States but most common in the southeastern states.

SIMILAR SPECIES: **White campion (*Silene latifolia*)** (also commonly known as white cockle) is a biennial or short-lived perennial that vegetatively resembles corn cockle but has white flowers and shorter, broader leaves. White campion can produce new plants from fragmented segments of the root.

R. Uva

A. Senesac

Corn cockle flower and buds

orn cockle flowering habit

A. Senesac

orn cockle stem and foliage

J. DiTomaso

Corn cockle seeds, 3.1 mm

Mouseear chickweed (*Cerastium fontanum* Baumg. ssp. *vulgare* (Hartm.) Greuter & Burdet)

SYNONYMS: *Cerastium vulgatum*, large mouseear chickweed, mouse-ear

GENERAL DESCRIPTION: A **perennial with prominently hairy, prostrate stems** (15–50 cm long) **and leaves.** Stems root at the nodes to form dense mats, especially in turfgrass. In unmowed areas, plants form mounds with ascending branches to 30 cm tall.

PROPAGATION / PHENOLOGY: Reproduction is **by seeds.** Seedlings emerge in late summer, fall, or early spring. In cool moist or irrigated areas, emergence can continue throughout the summer.

SEEDLING: **Cotyledons are rounded** to ovate, 2–7 mm long by 0.5–2 mm wide, generally lacking hairs on the blade but with a few prominent hairs at the base of the stalk. **Young leaves are opposite, spatulate,** dull green, **with prominent hairs** (0.5–1 mm long) on the upper surface and on the veins below. **Stems have 2 rows of dense hairs** and **root at the nodes** when in contact with the soil.

MATURE PLANT: **Stems are similar to those of the seedling. Distinctly hairy leaves** are opposite, sessile, dark green above, elliptic or spatulate to oval or oblanceolate, 3–12 mm wide by 1–3 cm long. **Margins are entire.**

ROOTS AND UNDERGROUND STRUCTURES: Fibrous root system.

FLOWERS AND FRUIT: Flowers are produced from May through October in clusters at the end of stems. **Petals (5) are white,** approximately 6 mm long, and **deeply lobed or notched at the tip (possibly giving the appearance of 10 petals).** Fruit are cylindrical capsules, 8–10 mm long by 2–3 mm wide, and produce many seeds. Seeds are triangular or angular (up to 1 mm long), flattened, notched on the margin, reddish to chestnut-brown with rounded bumps.

POSTSENESCENCE CHARACTERISTICS: Plant may die during hot, dry conditions but generally remains green through the winter.

HABITAT: Mouseear chickweed is primarily a weed of turfgrass and other mowed areas, but it is also found in many crops, as well as in landscapes and nurseries. It can survive in shaded areas.

DISTRIBUTION: Found throughout most of the United States and southern Canada.

SIMILAR SPECIES: **Common chickweed (*Stellaria media*)** is a winter annual resembling mouseear chickweed in growth habit; however, it does not have hairy leaf blades and does not root at the nodes. **Thymeleaf speedwell (*Veronica serpyllifolia* L.)** has a similar leaf shape and growth habit but also lacks hairs on the leaves and stem. Two other members of the genus *Cerastium* are also weedy. **Sticky chickweed (*Cerastium glomeratum* Thuill.)** is an annual with glandular sticky hairs. **Field chickweed (*Cerastium arvense* L.)** has petals 2–3 times longer than the sepals, whereas the petals of mouseear chickweed are nearly the same length as the sepals. In addition, the leaves of field chickweed are more linear, and the hairs are shorter than those on mouseear chickweed. **Umbrella spurry or jagged chickweed (*Holosteum umbellatum* L.)** is a short-lived, winter annual, similar to the chickweeds, with opposite entire leaves that may be pubescent or not. However, the flowers are in an **umbel** on an erect stalk, the ends of the petals are jagged not lobed, and the **pedicels of the flowers reflex downward** with maturity. It has recently become more common in grain crops in the mid-Atlantic states but occurs as far north as Vermont and is native to Europe.

J. Neal

Mouseear chickweed vegetative habit

J. DiTomaso

Mouseear chickweed flower and bud

J. Neal

Young mouseear chickweed seedlings

J. DiTomaso

Ragged chickweed inflorescence and leaves

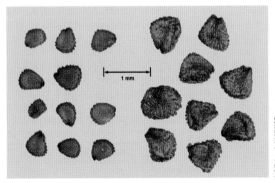

J. O'Brien © 2007 UC Regents

Left to right: sticky chickweed and mouseear chickweed seeds

Birdseye pearlwort (*Sagina procumbens* L.)

SYNONYMS: procumbent pearlwort, birdseye

GENERAL DESCRIPTION: A **small, stoloniferous perennial forming dense turf-like mats** with erect stems. Under close mowing, such as golf course greens, birdseye pearlwort will have few leaves and resembles moss or mowed grass.

PROPAGATION / PHENOLOGY: Propagates **primarily by seeds**, but also **spreads by stolons** or can be transported by stolon fragments, which root at the nodes. **Tiny seeds are dispersed when capsules are shaken by wind or rain.** A short after-ripening period (2–4 weeks) is necessary for germination. Seedlings emerge in cool, moist soil in early spring to fall.

SEEDLING: Seedlings develop as **small, tufted rosettes. Cotyledons are awl- or needle-shaped**, circular in cross section, <1 mm wide and only a few millimeters long. **Young leaves are similar** in shape but somewhat longer (up to 1 cm).

MATURE PLANT: Stems are smooth and slender. They root at the nodes. **Leaves are opposite,** simple, smooth, mostly hairless, **linear to awl-shaped** (1.5 cm long by 1 mm wide), and sharply pointed at the apex. **Leaves may appear whorled when short shoot clusters are congested** in the leaf axils.

ROOTS AND UNDERGROUND STRUCTURES: Shallow, fibrous root system associated with stolons.

FLOWERS AND FRUIT: Flowers appear from May through frost and are produced singly on relatively long and erect pedicels (0.3–2 cm). The pedicels extend beyond the foliage arising from the ends of the stems and the leaf axils. Flowers nod with age, but pedicels become erect again in fruit. **Flowers are inconspicuous**, with 4 green sepals (2–2.5 mm long) and 4 white, unlobed petals (occasionally absent) slightly shorter than the sepals. The **fruit** is a **many-seeded**, 2–3.5 mm long, persistent **capsule. Seeds are tiny** (0.2–0.3 mm long) and dark brown.

POSTSENESCENCE CHARACTERISTICS: In mild winters, plants persist but will become discolored by hard frost.

HABITAT: Sometimes cultivated as an ornamental in rock gardens or between paving stones, birdseye pearlwort has escaped to become an aggressive weed of turfgrass, particularly golf course greens and tees, and container nurseries. It is commonly found in rocky areas and paved footpaths, especially in the crevices of brick walks. It prefers moist soil and cool climates.

DISTRIBUTION: Found throughout the United States and southern Canada but most common in cooler regions.

SIMILAR SPECIES: The small, erect capsules and the mat-forming growth habit are sometimes mistaken for the spore capsules and low habit of many mosses. **Trailing pearlwort (*Sagina decumbens* (Elliott) Torr. & A. Gray)** closely resembles birdseye pearlwort, but the leaves are a bit thicker and longer, and the flowers have 5 sepals and 5 white petals. In contrast, birdseye pearlwort has 4 sepals and typically lacks petals. **Knawel (*Scleranthus annuus*)** can be distinguished by its flowers, which lack petals and are sessile in the leaf axils. **Corn spurry (*Spergula arvensis* L.)** is an annual with longer (1–3 cm) linear leaves in whorls at the nodes. Its flowers are on terminal branches and have 5 conspicuous white petals. **Red sandspurry (*Spergularia rubra* (L.) J.&C. Presl.)** is an annual or short-lived perennial with narrow, awl-shaped leaves up to 2.5 cm long, conspicuous chaffy stipules, and pinkish-red, 5-parted flowers in loose terminal cymes.

Birdseye pearlwort habit

J. DiTomaso

Birdseye pearlwort seedlings

R. Uva

Birdseye pearlwort flowers

R. Uva

Red sandspurry habit

J. DiTomaso

Corn spurry flowering stem

J. DiTomaso

Left: Birdseye pearlwort seeds, 0.2 mm;
right: Red sandspurry seeds, 0.5 mm

M. Bertone; J. O'Brien © 2007 UC Regents

Bouncingbet (*Saponaria officinalis* L.)

SYNONYMS: *Lychnis saponaria*, soapwort

GENERAL DESCRIPTION: An erect **perennial to 1 m tall**, with vigorous rhizomes and **showy pink to white flowers**. Colonies often develop from the rhizomes. Bouncingbet is cultivated as an ornamental and grown to make soap in many areas of the world but has escaped cultivation to become weedy throughout the United States. Native to southern Europe.

PROPAGATION / PHENOLOGY: Reproduction is by seeds **and vegetatively from rhizomes**. Seeds generally disperse only short distances from the parent plant but can be moved long distances with human activities.

SEEDLING: Cotyledons are narrowly elliptic-lanceolate, 9–12 mm long by 1–3 mm wide, lack hairs, with fused bases that are weakly sheathing. First and subsequent **leaves are opposite and decussate** (opposite leaves at right angles to previous pair), **lack hairs**, and are elliptic to oblong, 7–12 mm long by 2–5 mm wide, with their bases tapered to a short stalk 2–4 mm long. **Petioles are fused at base** and sheath the stem.

MATURE PLANT: Stems are leafy with **swollen nodes**. The leaves lack hairs and are opposite and decussate, ovate to elliptic-lanceolate, mostly 3–10 cm long, with **3 main veins** from the base and parallel to leaf margins (androdromous).

ROOTS AND UNDERGROUND STRUCTURES: Rhizomes are short, thick, and white.

FLOWERS AND FRUIT: Plants flower in summer. Flowers are showy, densely clustered at stem tips, nearly sessile, 8–12 mm wide. The fused sepals form a **cylindrical calyx tube**, 15–22 mm long by 4–8 mm wide, with 5 lanceolate lobes 2–5 mm long. There are 5 petals (sometimes doubled), pink to white, and are 3.5–4 cm long including the claw within the calyx tube. Petals are spreading to reflexed, with tip sometimes indented, and with 2 appendages at the junction of the petal blade and claw. There are 10 stamens, fused with petals to the ovary. Capsules are oblong-cylindrical, 15–22 mm long, and surrounded by a persistent calyx tube. The capsules open at the apex by 4 short valves, and the numerous seeds are kidney-shaped, flattened, 1.5–2 mm long, and dark brown to black.

POSTSENESCENCE CHARACTERISTICS: Stems typically die in winter and regenerate from the rhizomes in spring. Dead stems are oppositely branched, often 4-angled, and have conspicuously swollen nodes. Sometimes a few capsules remain intact.

HABITAT: Found in riparian areas, oak woodlands, grasslands, roadsides, waste areas, and other disturbed places.

DISTRIBUTION: Has escaped cultivation and become weedy throughout the United States and parts of Canada.

SIMILAR SPECIES: Bouncingbet can somewhat resemble the **catchfly or campion species (*Silene* spp.)**, but the calyx tube of bouncingbet is more cylindrical and less inflated compared to *Silene*. Furthermore, many species of *Silene* have pubescent leaves and stems. When in flower, bouncingbet plants may resemble **garden phlox (*Phlox paniculata* L.)**, but garden phlox has leaves with herringbone-pattern (camptodromous) veins and is native. **Damesrocket (*Hesperis matronalis*)** has similar showy flower clusters on upright stems, but leaves are alternate.

Bouncingbet habit

J. DiTomaso

Bouncingbet flowering stem

J. DiTomaso

Bouncingbet seedling

J. DiTomaso

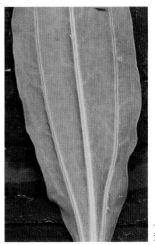

Bouncingbet leaf with parallel veins

J. Neal

Bouncingbet young plants from perennial roots

A. DiTommaso

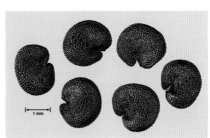

Bouncingbet seeds

J. O'Brien © 2007 UC Regents

277

Knawel (*Scleranthus annuus* L.)

SYNONYMS: German knot-grass, annual knawel

GENERAL DESCRIPTION: A **winter or summer annual**, low-growing to prostrate (reaching only 10 cm in height), and branching. Its **grass-like appearance** enables it to become established in turfgrass without notice. In dry, open areas it forms **low mats or sprawling clumps**.

PROPAGATION / PHENOLOGY: Reproduction is **by seeds**; seeds germinate primarily in early spring but also in late summer or autumn.

SEEDLING: Hypocotyls are light green and smooth. **Cotyledons** are smooth, **sessile**, **linear**, <1 cm long by approximately 1 mm wide. **Young leaves are sessile, opposite**, linear, bristle-tipped at the apex, and have short hairs along the basal portion of the margin. **Opposite leaves are connected at the base by a translucent membrane** surrounding the node. Lateral branches do not develop until late in the seedling stage.

MATURE PLANT: **Stems are branched and spreading. Leaves are linear**, 5–25 mm long, <1 mm wide, and **sharply pointed at the tip**. Leaves are opposite and joined at the node by a translucent membrane, although leaves may appear to be whorled when new shoots are expanding from leaf axils.

ROOTS AND UNDERGROUND STRUCTURES: Small taproot with a secondary fibrous root system.

FLOWERS AND FRUIT: Flowers appear from May to October on sessile or short stalks (pedicels) in clusters from the leaf axils. Flowers are small, green, and spiny to the touch. The fruit—a small, thin-walled, 1-seeded inflated utricle—is enclosed by the 5-toothed, persistent sepal tube (3–4 mm long). Sepal tube and fruit become light brown at maturity.

POSTSENESCENCE CHARACTERISTICS: On dry sites, dead plants can remain throughout the summer, but they do not persist in moist areas.

HABITAT: Knawel is primarily a weed of low-maintenance turfgrass and nursery crops. It is most commonly found on dry, sandy soils.

DISTRIBUTION: Occurs throughout the eastern half of the United States.

SIMILAR SPECIES: Knawel can be distinguished from other similar members of the pink family by its flowers, which lack petals and are sessile in the leaf axils. **Corn spurry (*Spergula arvensis* L.)** is also an annual with similar but slightly longer (1–3 cm) linear awl-shaped leaves. Its flowers have 5 white petals and are on terminal branches. **Red sandspurry (*Spergularia rubra* (L.) J. & C. Presl.)** is an annual or short-lived perennial with very similar leaves; however, it grows prostrate to ascending and produces pinkish-red flowers in loose terminal cymes. **Birdseye pearlwort (*Sagina procumbens*)** is a summer or winter annual that grows as a moss-like mat with awl-shaped leaves approximately 1.5 cm in length. Its flower stalks are erect and bear small, white flowers and persistent seed capsules.

J. Neal

Knawel habit

R. Uva

Knawel seedling

R. Uva

Knawel stems and foliage

R. Uva

Knawel flowering shoot

J. Neal

Corn spurry seedlings

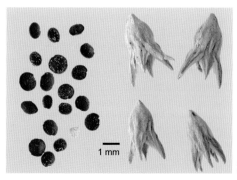

M. Bertone

Left, corn spurry seeds, 1.3 mm; *right*,
knawel seeds, 3.5 mm (including calyx)

White campion (*Silene latifolia* Poir.)

Synonyms: *Lychnis alba*, *Melandrium album*, *Silene alba*, white cockle

General Description: A **winter or summer annual, biennial, or short-lived perennial** initially forming a **basal rosette, subsequently producing a thick, erect** (30 cm to 1 m tall), **branched, leafy stem** with hairy or downy foliage and **white, inflated (balloon-like) flowers**. Stems may become almost woody with age. Seedlings and mature flowering plants are commonly found together in spring and early summer.

Propagation / Phenology: Reproduction is primarily **by seeds** but cultivation can fragment plants and spread **adventitious buds on root and stem segments**. Seedlings emerge in mid- to late spring and again in late summer.

Seedling: Cotyledons are sessile, narrowly oval to egg-shaped (1.5 cm long by 5–7 mm wide), pointed at the apex, and tapering to the base. The surface is slightly granular. **Young leaves are opposite**, lanceolate to ovate, **dull green, soft-hairy**, with some gland-tipped hairs. Leaf blades gradually taper down the long petiole margin. Margins are fringed with hairs. **Young plants produce a rosette.**

Mature Plant: **Winter annual and biennial plants overwinter as basal rosettes. Basal leaves wither when erect stems reach maturity** in summer. **Stems are covered with short hairs**, some glandular on the upper stem. Nodes are swollen. **Leaves are hairy, opposite**, entire, lanceolate to ovate to broadly elliptic (3–10 cm long by 1–4 cm wide). Lower leaves taper into long petioles; upper leaves are sessile. Margins are softly hairy.

Roots and Underground Structures: Taproot and **thick lateral roots**.

Flowers and Fruit: Flowers are produced from May to fall in clusters (or solitary) on long stalks. Plants are dioecious (male and female flowers on separate plants). Male and female flowers have **white (occasionally pink) petals** (2–4 cm long) notched at the tip. The **female flowers have fused, inflated sepals** (calyx), 2–3 cm long, with 20 veins. Sepals of the male flowers are also fused, but they are more slender and have only 10 veins. Flowers open in the evening and have a sweet scent. **Fruits are cone-shaped capsules** opening at the top **with 10 teeth**. As each fruit forms, the surrounding calyx continues to inflate. Seeds are brown to gray, rounded to kidney-shaped (1–1.4 mm in diameter), and flattened on one side, with blunt bumps.

Postsenescence Characteristics: The **calyx disintegrates, leaving the shiny, smooth, light brown capsule.** Winter annuals and biennials survive as basal rosettes.

Habitat: A weed of grains and legume forage crops, other field and vegetable crops, nurseries, waste places, and roadsides. Common in full sun and on rich, well-drained soils.

Distribution: Found throughout much of North America, particularly in the eastern and north-central United States and southern Canada.

Similar Species: **Nightflowering catchfly (*Silene noctiflora* L.)**, a summer annual, has dense, coarse hairs below, sticky hairs above, pink to yellowish flowers, and seed capsules with 6 teeth at the top. **Sleepy catchfly (*Silene antirrhina* L.)** has few hairs, except for glandular hairs near the stem nodes, and does not have an inflated calyx. **Bladder campion (*Silene vulgaris* (Moench) Garcke)** lacks hairs and is a robust perennial with creeping rhizomes. Young rosettes of white campion **may resemble some asters**, but aster stem leaves are alternate, not opposite.

White campion habit and seedpods

White campion seedling

White campion perennial root and shoot

te campion flowers

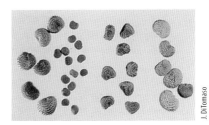

Left to right: bladder campion seeds, 1.3 mm; sleepy catchfly seeds, 0.6 mm; nightflowering catchfly seeds, 1.0 mm; and white campion seeds, 1.3 mm

Little starwort (*Stellaria graminea* L.)

SYNONYMS: grass-leaved stichwort, grassy starwort

GENERAL DESCRIPTION: A slender **perennial**, nearly prostrate or ascending (10–50 cm tall), with **angular or square stems** and small, white flowers.

PROPAGATION / PHENOLOGY: Reproduction is **by seeds**, but plants are **not prolific seed producers** and **seedlings are rarely encountered**. Once established, plants can spread vegetatively when fragmented **stems root at the nodes**. Seeds germinate in the fall or spring in cool, moist soils.

SEEDLING: Cotyledons are slender, egg-shaped, petiolated, and pointed at the apex. Young leaves are similar to cotyledons, narrowly egg-shaped and pointed at the apex.

MATURE PLANT: **Stems** are smooth and hairless, **angular to square**, branched, and light green. They **root at the nodes. Leaves are opposite, sessile**, simple, somewhat succulent, linear or **narrowly lanceolate** (1.5–2.5 cm long by 4–7 mm wide). Plants lack hairs, except for a few marginal hairs near the leaf base.

ROOTS AND UNDERGROUND STRUCTURES: Shallow fibrous root system.

FLOWERS AND FRUIT: **Small, white flowers** are produced for only a short time between May and July. Numerous flowers are produced in spreading clusters (cymes) at the ends of stems and in the leaf axils. Each flower is on a long, slender stalk (pedicel). There are **usually 5 (sometimes 4) petals (5 mm long), which are cleft almost to the base, appearing to be 10 (or 8) petals**. Fruit are egg-shaped capsules (5 mm long). Seeds are 0.8–1.2 mm long, brownish, circular to broadly egg-shaped, with small, rough, irregular ridges on the surface.

POSTSENESCENCE CHARACTERISTICS: None of significance.

HABITAT: Primarily a weed of turfgrass, meadows, and roadsides, little starwort is commonly found in moist to damp areas, often on sandy soils. It is rarely encountered in cultivated crops.

DISTRIBUTION: Common in the northeastern United States and southeastern Canada, especially the Maritime Provinces.

SIMILAR SPECIES: **Common chickweed (*Stellaria media*)** is a winter annual with similar leaves and **nearly identical flowers**, but the leaves are petiolated and broadly elliptic to egg-shaped. Those of little starwort are linear to lanceolate and sessile. In addition, stems of common chickweed are round with 1 or 2 rows of hairs, whereas little starwort stems are angled or square and lack hairs. **Corn spurry (*Spergula arvensis* L.)** is similar in habit but has needle-like leaves in whorls around the stem.

Mature little starwort plant and flower

Little starwort stem

Little starwort flowers

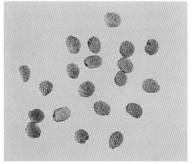

Little starwort seeds, 0.9 mm

Common chickweed (*Stellaria media* (L.) Vill.)

SYNONYMS: *Alsine media*, starwort, starweed, bindweed, winterweed, satin flower, tongue-grass

GENERAL DESCRIPTION: A **winter annual** that **can become perennialized in cool, moist areas.** Common chickweed forms prostrate, dense patches in turfgrass, but it can reach 40 cm in height in other areas.

PROPAGATION / PHENOLOGY: Reproduction is **by seeds**; seeds usually germinate in early spring and late summer. In shady, moist areas, germination can occur throughout the summer. **One or two generations can be produced each year.**

SEEDLING: Cotyledons are slender (1 cm long by 3 mm wide), ovate, with a hairy stalk as long as the blade. **Young leaves are opposite**, rounded to **egg-shaped, pointed at the apex**, with petioles about half the length of the blade. Young plants are erect and begin to branch at the base after 5 leaf pairs have developed.

MATURE PLANT: Stems are prostrate, branching, and smooth, except for 1 or 2 rows of hairs; the upper portions are erect or ascending. Stems and leaves are **light green. Leaves are opposite, broadly elliptic to egg-shaped**, 1–3 cm long, and **pointed at the apex.** Hairy petioles are present on most leaves, but petioles are lacking on some upper leaves.

ROOTS AND UNDERGROUND STRUCTURES: The **root system is fibrous and shallow**; the foliage is easily detached from the roots when pulled.

FLOWERS AND FRUIT: Flowering occurs from early spring to autumn, particularly on protected sites and in mild climates. The flowers are small (3–6 mm wide) and consist of 5 sepals (5 mm long) and **5 white petals**. The petals are shorter than the sepals and are **deeply lobed, giving the appearance of 10 petals.** The fruit is a 1-celled, oval capsule containing numerous seeds. Seeds are flattened, circular with a marginal notch, 1–1.3 mm in diameter, light brown to reddish-brown, with minute bumps on the surface.

POSTSENESCENCE CHARACTERISTICS: Usually senescing in lawns and other sunny areas by mid-summer. Dead plant parts do not persist.

HABITAT: A common weed of turfgrass, landscapes, golf course greens, nursery crops, and irrigated horticultural and agronomic crops, common chickweed tolerates close and frequent mowing. It thrives on moist, shady sites with nutrient-rich soils but is not limited to those areas.

DISTRIBUTION: Widely distributed throughout the world and common in all regions of the United States.

SIMILAR SPECIES: **Mouseear chickweed (*Cerastium fontanum* ssp. *vulgare*)** is a perennial that resembles common chickweed in growth habit; however, its leaves are oblong and densely covered with hairs. **Thymeleaf speedwell (*Veronica serpyllifolia* L.)** is found in similar habitats and has a similar growth habit, color, leaf shape, and arrangement (opposite leaves). It is distinguished by the **leaf tips**, which are rounded to notched, compared with the pointed leaf tips of common chickweed. The appearance and habit of **thymeleaf sandwort (*Arenaria serpyllifolia* L.)** are similar to common chickweed. However, the leaves of thymeleaf sandwort are somewhat smaller, the foliage is sparsely hairy, the hairs are stiff, and the flower petals are entire (appearing as 5), not deeply lobed (appearing as 10) as are common chickweed and mouseear chickweed petals.

Common chickweed
seedling

J. Neal

J. DiTomaso

Common chickweed plants

J. DiTomaso

Common chickweed hairs along
one side of stem

J. Neal

Juvenile common chickweed

J. Neal

Thymeleaf speedwell habit

J. O'Brien © 2007 UC Regents

Common chickweed seeds

Red orach (*Atriplex rosea* L.)

SYNONYMS: red orache, redscale, tumbling orach or oracle, tumbling saltbush

GENERAL DESCRIPTION: Erect summer **annual** to 1.5 m tall, with scurfy, gray-green to reddish, **triangular-ovate leaves,** and small, dense clusters of **firm**, **triangular fruits with toothed margins**. Native to Eurasia.

PROPAGATION / PHENOLOGY: Reproduction is exclusively **by seeds**. In winter, the skeletons of dead plants can break off at the ground and are moved by wind, depositing seeds as the plants tumble.

SEEDLING: Cotyledons are linear-lanceolate, 7–11 mm long by 2 mm wide, and lack hairs. The upper surface is dull green, and the lower surface and stalk below are tinged magenta. First few leaves ovate, opposite, mostly 5–12 mm long, 2–5 mm wide, with margins weakly wavy-toothed, and **surfaces evenly covered with minute salt-excreting glands** that resemble glistening balls.

MATURE PLANT: Plants are many-branched forming a mound. Stems are pale, scurfy (covered, small, scale-like particles), and lacking hairs. **Leaves are alternate,** triangular-ovate, mostly 1–6 cm long, 0.5–3 cm wide, firm, with the base abruptly tapered to a stalk. The leaf margin is coarsely wavy-toothed, **surfaces densely scurfy** giving the leaves a **whitish or gray** appearance, **especially the lower surface; upper surface pale greenish-gray to reddish**.

ROOTS AND UNDERGROUND STRUCTURES: Taproot with fibrous lateral roots.

FLOWERS AND FRUIT: Plants flower from July to October. Separate male and female flowers develop on the same plant (monoecious) in mixed clusters in the leaf axils and on terminal spikes. Flowers lack showy petals. Male flowers consist of a 3- to 5-lobed calyx and 3–5 stamens. Female flowers have 2 bracts that enclose the ovary and 2 stigmas. Only 1 seed per fruit protected by triangular bracts, 4–8 mm long, fused to the middle. The bract margins are acute-toothed (dentate), surface with a few tooth-like projections, and densely white-scurfy. Two types of seeds are produced: 2–2.5 mm wide brown seeds and smaller black seeds.

POSTSENESCENCE CHARACTERISTICS: Senesced plants with persistent fruits can persist into winter. Skeletons of dead plants can be found on fencerows blown by the wind.

HABITAT: Inhabits disturbed places, roadsides, waste places, and fields on many types of soil, but often grows under alkaline or saline conditions. Can also be found as a weed in orchards, vineyards, and crop fields.

DISTRIBUTION: More common in the western and midwestern United States but present in the mid-Atlantic states from Virginia to New York.

SIMILAR SPECIES: Several species of *Atriplex* are present in the region. **Triangle orach (*Atriplex prostrata* Boucher ex DC.;** syn.: *Atriplex triangularis* Willd.) is an ascending to erect, native, summer annual to approximately 1 m tall, with lanceolate to triangular-hastate leaves that are green and glabrous to sparsely scurfy on both sides. Triangle orach often inhabits disturbed, moist, saline and alkaline places, such as salt marshes. **Halberdleaf orach (*Atriplex patula* L.)** resembles red orach except that the leaves are not gray or whitish-green. The leaves lack hairs and are green to sparsely powdery. The gray-green appearance of *Atriplex* species is similar to **common lambsquarters (*Chenopodium album*)**, particularly as young seedlings, but lambsquarters lacks the scurfy texture of *Atriplex* foliage.

Red orach habit

Red orach flowering stem

Red orach fruit

Triangle orach leaves

Red orach seedling

Red orach seeds and bracts

Common lambsquarters (*Chenopodium album* L.)

SYNONYMS: white goosefoot, fat-hen, mealweed, frost-blite, bacon-weed

GENERAL DESCRIPTION: An **erect summer annual** (to 1 m in height) with a **gray-mealy coating**, particularly on the surfaces of younger leaves.

PROPAGATION / PHENOLOGY: Reproduces **by seeds**; seedlings emerge in spring or early summer, from a depth of 0.5–3 cm.

SEEDLING: Hypocotyls are green or tinged with maroon. **Cotyledons are narrowly elliptic**, 12–15 mm long, dull green on the upper surface with maroon on the underside. **Young stems and leaves have a gray-mealy coating, especially on leaf undersides and emerging leaves. The first pair of leaves are opposite; all other leaves are alternate.** Margins on very young leaves are entire or have a few teeth.

MATURE PLANT: **Stems are erect, branching**, hairless, vertically ridged, often with maroon stripes. **Leaves** are petiolate, rhombic, egg-shaped to lanceolate, **alternate**, 3–10 cm long, and **irregularly toothed**. The younger leaves have a white-mealy coating. Lower leaves are 2.5–7.5 cm long, almost always irregularly toothed. Upper leaves are sometimes linear, lack petioles, and may have entire margins.

ROOTS AND UNDERGROUND STRUCTURES: Short and branched taproot.

FLOWERS AND FRUIT: Flowers are produced from June to September on spikes grouped into **panicles arising from the ends of stems and the leaf axils. Individual flowers are inconspicuous**, sessile, small, green, and aggregated into dense, small clusters. Fruit is an utricle with a thin papery covering over a single seed. **The numerous seeds are of 2 types**; the most common **can persist for years in the soil** and are round, black, and 1–2 mm in diameter. A less common type is brown, slightly larger, oval, and more flattened. It does not undergo an extended dormancy.

POSTSENESCENCE CHARACTERISTICS: Erect woody stems and seedheads persist through the winter.

HABITAT: A common weed of most agricultural and horticultural crops, particularly cultivated crops and gardens, but also grows in landscapes, waste places, and disturbed sites, on acidic and alkaline soils.

DISTRIBUTION: Common throughout the United States.

SIMILAR SPECIES: **Mexican tea (*Dysphania ambrosioides* (L.) Mosyakin & Clemant**; formerly *Chenopodium ambrosioides* L.) leaves are longer, more lanceolate, lack the whitish, waxy coating, and have a strong scent. **Nettleleaf goosefoot (*Chenopodium murale* L.)** is also a summer annual introduced from Europe. However, the leaves are shiny dark green above and the lower leaf surface is sparsely covered with a fine, white, powdery scurf. The inflorescence is more openly branched. Although not as common as common lambsquarters, it is widely distributed throughout the northeastern and mid-Atlantic states. ***Atriplex*** species have similar gray-green foliage but the leaf surfaces are rough to the touch. **Clammy goosefoot (*Dysphania pumilio* (R. Br.) Mosyakin & Clemants)** has a similar gray-green appearance but the plants are more prostrate, leaves are smaller and more evenly lobed, and plants have a sticky resin. Clammy goosefoot is not common in the region but has the potential to spread rapidly. **Oakleaf goosefoot (*Chenopodium glaucum* L.)** strongly resembles clammy goosefoot and Mexican tea but lacks the sticky glands and aromatic smell. It is more branched and prostrate compared to common lambsquarters.

J. Neal

Common lambsquarters habit

A. DiTommaso

Common lambsquarters
seedling

R. Uva

Common lambsquarters mature foliage

J. Neal

Common
lambsquarters
inflorescence

J. O'Brien © 2007 UC Regents

Common lambsquarters seeds, 1 mm

Mexican tea habit

Mexican tea flowering stem

Mexican tea seedling

Nettleleaf goosefoot habit

Nettleleaf goosefoot
flowering stem

Nettleleaf goosefoot seedling

J. DiTomaso

Clammy goosefoot habit

J. Neal

Clammy goosefoot flowering stem

Oakleaf goosefoot leaves
and flowers

A. DiTommaso

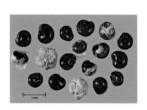

J. O'Brien © 2007 UC Regents

Left to right: Mexican tea, nettleleaf goosefoot, and clammy goosefoot seeds

Kochia (*Kochia scoparia* (L.) Schrad.)

SYNONYMS: *Bassia scoparia*, belevedere, mock cypress, summer-cypress, Mexican fire-weed, red belevedere, belevedere-cypress

GENERAL DESCRIPTION: An **erect, profusely bushy, branched annual** with **fine-textured foliage** (30 cm to 1.5 m tall). Plants are **blue-green to gray-green** but take on a reddish or **purplish coloration later in the season**.

PROPAGATION / PHENOLOGY: Reproduction is **by seeds**; seedlings emerge in the spring.

SEEDLING: Cotyledons are narrow (4.5 mm long by 1.25 mm wide), elliptic to oblong, sessile, thick, dull green above, often magenta on the underside, narrow, and covered with soft, fine hairs. **Young leaves are grayish** with **dense, soft hairs**, linear to narrowly elliptic or oblanceolate and pointed at the apex. Blades are sometimes magenta-tinged beneath; leaves lack defined petioles. Young plants initially develop into a **basal rosette**. Elongated stems are hairy and may be reddish.

MATURE PLANT: **Stems are erect**, many-branched, round, **often red-tinged**, usually with soft hairs above. **Leaves** are simple, **sessile, alternate, linear** to lanceolate (2.5–5 cm long), and hairy to almost smooth, with entire, hairy margins.

ROOTS AND UNDERGROUND STRUCTURES: Taproot with branched fibrous root system.

FLOWERS AND FRUIT: **Small, green, inconspicuous flowers** are produced from July to September in small spikes (5–10 mm long) in the upper leaf axils and in terminal panicles. Spikes are subtended by leafy hairy bracts (3–10 mm long). **Fruits** are small, **bladder-like utricles**. Seeds are approximately 1.8 mm long, irregularly shaped, brown with yellow markings, and grooved on each side.

POSTSENESCENCE CHARACTERISTICS: Dried plant material persists into the winter. Bracts subtending flowers are generally evident.

HABITAT: Kochia is a drought-tolerant weed of dry-land grain crops, rangeland, pastures, and waste areas.

DISTRIBUTION: Introduced as an ornamental for its bright red autumn color but has escaped to become naturalized throughout most of the northern half of the United States and western and southwestern rangelands. Significance as a weed is increasing in the Northeast, as far south as Maryland.

SIMILAR SPECIES: Seedlings may resemble **mouseear chickweed (*Cerastium fontanum* ssp. *vulgare*)** with oval to elliptic, hairy leaves, but mouseear chickweed leaves are opposite whereas kochia leaves are in a rosette or alternate. The inflorescence is similar to that of the closely related **common lambsquarters (*Chenopodium album*) and Mexican tea (*Dysphania ambrosioides*)**. It can also resemble **mugwort (*Artemisia vulgaris*)** in appearance and habitat. However, the leaves of kochia are narrow and not lobed, whereas those of common lambsquarters, Mexican tea, and mugwort are toothed or lobed and considerably wider than kochia leaves.

Kochia habit

Kochia cotyledons and first leaves

Kochia seedling

Kochia vegetative and flowering stems

Kochia stem and flowering branch

Kochia seeds, 1.8 mm

293

Hedge bindweed (*Calystegia sepium* (L.) R. Br.)

SYNONYMS: *Convolvulus sepium*, wild morningglory, devil's-vine, great bindweed

GENERAL DESCRIPTION: A **spreading perennial** with long (3 m) climbing or trailing **viny stems, distinctive triangular leaves,** and **white morningglory-like flowers.**

PROPAGATION / PHENOLOGY: Reproduction is **by seeds and spreading fleshy roots.** Root pieces are spread by cultivation, on farm implements, and in the topsoil. Shoots from root buds emerge in early spring. Seedlings emerge in spring and early summer.

SEEDLING: Cotyledons are smooth, long-petiolated, almost square, with prominent indentations at the apex, heart-shaped bases, and entire margins. **Young leaves are triangular, heart-shaped, or sharply lobed at the base** (hastate) and on relatively long petioles. No cotyledons are present when plants emerge from rhizomes.

MATURE PLANT: **Stems** are smooth or hairy and **trail along the ground or climb on vegetation and other objects. Leaves** are alternate, **triangular-oblong,** 5–10 cm long, smooth, **with a pointed tip and prominent, angular, heart-shaped bases. Lobes point away from the petiole at the base.**

ROOTS AND UNDERGROUND STRUCTURES: Extensive but relatively shallow (to 30 cm) root system with an extensive, deep system of branched, fleshy **rhizomes.**

FLOWERS AND FRUIT: **Flowers,** from June through August, are **solitary in leaf axils** on prominently long flower stalks (5–15 cm). **Two, large (1–2 cm), leafy bracts** conceal the 5 overlapping sepals at the base of the flower. **Petals are usually white, sometimes pink, and are fused into a funnel-shaped tube,** 3–6 cm long. The fruit is an egg-shaped to rounded capsule (8 mm in diameter) containing 2–4 seeds. Capsules are usually covered by the 2 subtending bracts. Seeds are large (4–5 mm long), dull gray to brown or black, with 1 rounded side and 2 flattened sides.

POSTSENESCENCE CHARACTERISTICS: Smooth, round, capsules persist, surrounded with dried bracts. Dead stems remain twined around vegetation or other objects.

HABITAT: A weed of landscapes, nurseries, and row crops; also common on fences and hedges. It thrives in rich, moist, lowland areas.

DISTRIBUTION: Native to the eastern United States, hedge bindweed has spread throughout the United States.

SIMILAR SPECIES: **Field bindweed (*Convolvulus arvensis*)** leaves are smaller than hedge bindweed leaves and have a rounded, rather than a pointed, apex. The leaf bases of field bindweed are pointed or rounded with outwardly divergent lobes. Hedge bindweed leaf bases are cut squarely (truncate). Flowers of field bindweed are smaller (1.2–2.5 cm long) than those of hedge bindweed. Hedge bindweed may also be distinguished from field bindweed by large bracts beneath and concealing the sepals. **Wild buckwheat (*Fallopia convolvulus*)** is a vining annual that has small, inconspicuous flowers in axillary or terminal clusters and a sheath around the stem just above the base of the leaf (ocrea). Wild buckwheat has similar leaves, but it can be distinguished from the other 2 species because the lobes at the base of the leaf point in toward the petiole. **For a detailed comparison with field bindweed and wild buckwheat, see Table 5.** Both bindweeds are sometimes mistaken for **morningglories (*Ipomoea* spp.),** but the morningglories encountered in the northeastern United States are seed-propagated annuals that have broader, heart-shaped leaves and rounded basal lobes. Bindweed leaves have angular basal lobes.

R. Prostak

Hedge bindweed foliage and flower

J. Neal

Hedge bindweed sprouts from roots

J. DiTomaso

Hedge bindweed flowers (note leafy bracts)

J. DiTomaso

Left, field bindweed seeds, 3.8 mm; right, hedge bindweed seeds, 5.0 mm

Field bindweed (*Convolvulus arvensis* L.)

SYNONYMS: small bindweed, bindweed, morningglory, creeping jenny

GENERAL DESCRIPTION: A **spreading perennial** with slender, climbing or trailing, **viny stems** (to 2 m long), **arrowhead-shaped leaves**, and white to pink **morningglory-like flowers**.

PROPAGATION / PHENOLOGY: Reproduction is **by seeds and spreading fleshy roots**. Root pieces are spread by cultivation, on farm implements, and in the topsoil. Shoots from root buds emerge in early spring. Seedlings emerge in spring and early summer.

SEEDLING: Cotyledons are smooth, dark green, relatively large, long-petioled, square to kidney-shaped, usually with a slight indentation at the apex. The margins of the cotyledon are entire, and the venation is whitish. **Young leaves are bell-shaped** (1.5–3.5 cm long), **lobed at the base (hastate)**, and on petioles. No cotyledons are present when young plants emerge from established rhizomes.

MATURE PLANT: **Stems** are smooth to slightly hairy and **trail along the ground or climb on vegetation and other objects**. Leaves are alternate, very **similar to seedling** leaves, 4–6 cm long. **Lobes point away from the petiole at the base.**

ROOTS AND UNDERGROUND STRUCTURES: **Extensive and deep** (6 m or more) **spreading fleshy root system.**

FLOWERS AND FRUIT: Flowers, from June through September, are solitary or 2-flowered (occasionally to 5) in the leaf axils. The flower stalks are shorter than the leaves. **Two small (3 mm long), leafy bracts are at the base of the flower. Petals are usually white, sometimes pink, and fused into a funnel-shaped tube**, 1.2–2.5 cm long. The fruit is an egg-shaped to rounded capsule with 4 seeds. Seeds are large (3–4 mm long), rough, dull gray to brown or black with 1 rounded side and 2 flattened sides.

POSTSENESCENCE CHARACTERISTICS: Dead stems remain twined around vegetation or other objects.

HABITAT: Field bindweed is a weed of most agronomic and horticultural crops, as well as landscapes and turf. It is also commonly found growing on fences, hedges, and in fencerow thickets.

DISTRIBUTION: One of the most troublesome weeds throughout North America.

SIMILAR SPECIES: **Hedge bindweed (*Calystegia sepium*)** has larger leaves than field bindweed, and they have a pointed, rather than rounded, apex. The **leaf bases** of field bindweed are pointed or rounded with outwardly divergent lobes (hastate). Hedge bindweed leaf bases are cut squarely (truncate). Flowers of hedge bindweed are larger (3–6 cm long) than those of field bindweed. Hedge bindweed may also be distinguished from field bindweed by large bracts beneath and concealing the sepals. **Wild buckwheat (*Fallopia convolvulus*)** is a vining annual with similar leaves, but it can be distinguished from the other 2 species because the lobes at the base of the leaf point toward the petiole. It also has small, inconspicuous flowers in axillary and terminal clusters and a sheath around the stem just above the base of the leaf (ocrea). **For a detailed comparison of the bindweeds and wild buckwheat, see Table 5.** Both bindweeds are sometimes mistaken for **morningglories (*Ipomoea* spp.)**, but the morningglories encountered in the northeastern United States are seed-propagated annuals that have broader, heart-shaped leaves and rounded basal lobes. Bindweed leaves have angular basal lobes.

R. Uva

Field bindweed foliage and flower

J. DiTomaso

Field bindweed seedlings

J. DiTomaso

Field bindweed flowers

J. Neal

Field bindweed from rhizome

J. O'Brien © 2007 UC Regents

Field bindweed seeds

Dodder (*Cuscuta* spp.)

GENERAL DESCRIPTION: A **parasitic, annual vine** lacking chlorophyll and distinct leaves. **Thread-like stems twine on other plants** and **are yellow, orange, or red.**

PROPAGATION / PHENOLOGY: Reproduction is **by seeds**. Seeds are **long-lived in the soil**, germinating in the spring and early summer.

SEEDLING: Seedlings develop a small, temporary root system to support 4–10 cm long, thread-like stalks that attach to the host plant. After attachment, the root system no longer functions.

MATURE PLANT: **Stems are yellowish or reddish to orange-brown**, twining counterclockwise and **enveloping other vegetation** to form dense, branching masses. **Leaves are reduced to inconspicuous scales.**

ROOTS AND UNDERGROUND STRUCTURES: **Roots are modified to penetrate the host plant** and extract nutrients and carbohydrates.

FLOWERS AND FRUIT: **Flowers are small, white** or sometimes pink, and numerous **in compact clusters**. The fruit is a small (approximately 3 mm), rounded capsule usually with 4 tiny, orange seeds (1–1.5 mm in diameter).

POSTSENESCENCE CHARACTERISTICS: Plants die at first frost. Dead, matted stems do not persist through the winter.

HABITAT: A weed of landscapes, nursery crops, and agricultural crops, dodder survives only if the appropriate host is present. Common hosts include alfalfa, clover, and other legumes, as well as many bedding plants, chrysanthemums, azaleas, and cranberries.

DISTRIBUTION: **Many different species of dodder** are found throughout the United States.

SIMILAR SPECIES: The orange-red stems easily distinguish this genus.

J. Derr

Dodder in cantaloupe

J. Neal

Dodder flowering stem

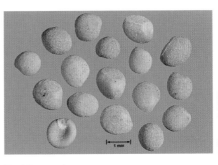

J. O'Brien © 2007 UC Regents

Dodder seeds

Carolina dichondra (*Dichondra carolinensis* Michx.)

SYNONYMS: *Dichondra repens* var. *carolinensis*, Carolina ponyfoot

GENERAL DESCRIPTION: A **low growing, mat-forming, stoloniferous perennial**, occasionally utilized as a non-grass alternative in lawns. Leaves are small, less than or equal to 2 cm wide, **kidney-shaped on slender stolons** that root at the nodes. Primarily a weed of lawns and gardens.

PROPAGATION / PHENOLOGY: Although the species does reproduce by seeds, most spread and reproduction appears to be vegetative. Slender stolons root at the nodes. Small fragments of stolons will produce new plants. Plants are deciduous, losing leaves in the fall. New growth resumes in early spring from stolons.

SEEDLING: Cotyledons are oblong, 1–1.5 cm long. Leaves are kidney-shaped. Seedlings initially form small rosettes but soon form stolons.

MATURE PLANT: The most distinguishing feature is the leaf shape. Leaves are alternate, kidney-shaped, or rounded but cordate at the base, 1–2 cm wide, with entire margins and palmate veins. Leaves wider in shady, moist, fertile soils; narrower in sunny, low-fertility sites. Leaves are on slender petioles 2–10 cm in length, the length affected by site conditions and mowing practices. Leaves lack hairs on the upper surface but may have some on the lower.

ROOTS AND UNDERGROUND STRUCTURES: Fibrous root system. In loose, organic soils some stolons will grow below the surface to be rhizomatous.

FLOWERS AND FRUIT: Flowers and fruit are very small and inconspicuous. When present, the small flowers are white to cream in color with 1.5–3 mm long petals; sepals are hairy on the back, 1.5–3 mm long, and twice as long as wide. Each flower produces 2 small, dehiscent fruits (urticles) 2–3 mm in length. Seeds within the urticles are pear-shaped, slightly shorter than the urticles.

POSTSENESCENCE CHARACTERISTICS: Little of note. Stolons are persistent over winter.

HABITAT: Primarily a weed of turfgrass, landscape plantings, and other managed sites.

DISTRIBUTION: Most common in the southern United States and mid-Atlantic states but documented north to Pennsylvania and Ohio.

SIMILAR SPECIES: **Kidney-weed dichondra or small flowered ponyfoot (*Dichondra micrantha* Urb.)** is nearly indistinguishable from Carolina dichondra. Kidney-weed dichondra is native to Australia and New Zealand. Calyx lobes are <2 times as long as wide; whereas calyx lobes on Carolina dichondra are >2 times as long as wide. Several varieties are sold in the garden trade, often misidentified and inaccurately labeled as *D. repens*. Dichondra is sometimes confused with **lawn pennywort (*Hydrocotyle sibthorpioides* Lam.)**, but leaf margins on lawn pennywort are lobed.

J. Neal

Carolina dichondra habit

J. Neal

Kidney-shaped leaf of Carolina dichondra

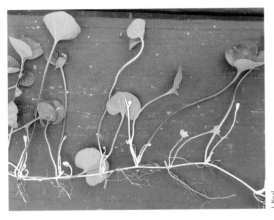

J. Neal

Carolina dichondra stolon with flowers

J. Neal

Carolina dichondra flower

J. DiTomaso

Kidney-weed dichondra

J. Neal

Lawn pennywort with lobed leaf margins

Morningglories

Ivyleaf morningglory (*Ipomoea hederacea* Jacq.)
Pitted morningglory (*Ipomoea lacunosa* L.)
Tall morningglory (*Ipomoea purpurea* (L.) Roth)
Red (or scarlet) morningglory (*Ipomoea coccinea* L.)
Cypressvine morningglory (*Ipomoea quamoclit* L.)

SYNONYMS: **ivyleaf morningglory:** *Ipomoea barbigera, Ipomoea hirsutula, Pharbitis barbigera, Pharbitis hederacea*; **pitted morningglory:** whitestar; **tall morningglory:** *Ipomoea hirsutula*; **red morningglory:** redstar

GENERAL DESCRIPTION: **Summer annual** weeds with long, climbing or trailing, **viny** stems, **heart-shaped to 3-lobed leaves**, and **attractive funnel-shaped flowers**. Morningglories are very competitive and generally difficult to control in most crops.

PROPAGATION / PHENOLOGY: Reproduction is **by seeds**; seeds germinate in early summer.

SEEDLING: Seedlings of all are similar in many aspects but can be identified by the shape of the cotyledons and first few leaves. Hypocotyls of all are maroon at the base, green near the apex, and grooved with the extension of the cotyledon stalk margin.

Ivyleaf morningglory: Cotyledons are butterfly-shaped, deeply notched at the apex, notched at the base, but rather squarish in outline compared with some other morningglories. The upper surfaces of the cotyledons are green, with translucent glands. The **first leaf is unlobed. Subsequent leaves are ivy-shaped** (3 main lobes), with both surfaces covered with **erect hairs** swollen at the base. Petioles and stems are densely hairy.

Pitted morningglory: Cotyledons are similar to those of the other species but **more deeply notched at the tip**; the angle of the notch is greater, and the lobes are more slender and pointed. First and subsequent **leaves are heart-shaped, taper to a more pointed tip** than those of the other species, and **lack hairs** (or are nearly hairless).

Tall morningglory: Cotyledons and first leaf are nearly identical to those of ivyleaf morningglory. Subsequent **leaves are heart-shaped and hairy. Hairs are appressed** (lie flat).

Red morningglory: Cotyledons are nearly identical to ivyleaf morningglory cotyledons, but the first leaf is heart-shaped with a long, tapered tip resembling pitted morningglory.

Cypressvine morningglory: Cotyledons distinct from the other species. Two widely spaced, thin lobes, looking almost like a cut-out of a cartoon mustache. Leaves are pinnately compound, the lobes are long and slender.

MATURE PLANT: **Vining stems** are branched, twining around other plants or spreading on the ground.

Ivyleaf morningglory: Leaves are alternate, **deeply 3-lobed** (rarely 5-lobed or entire), ivy-like, with rounded sinuses and a heart-shaped base (5–12 cm long). Erect hairs are on stems, petioles, and leaves.

Pitted morningglory: Younger leaves are heart-shaped with a slender pointed tip, hairless or nearly so. With age, the foliage develops 3 lobes with pointed tips, not unlike ivyleaf morningglory, but the leaves are smaller and the central lobe is narrower. The depth of the lobes is variable.

Tall morningglory: Leaves are alternate, **heart-shaped**, and densely covered with **appressed hairs** (lying on the surface).

Red morningglory: Vining growth habit but glabrous or nearly so. Leaves are heart-shaped with a long, tapered tip. Margins have a few shallow, pointed lobes. These pointed lobes are variable and may be conspicuous or very small.

A. Senesac

Ivyleaf morningglory habit

J. Derr

Ivyleaf morningglory seedling

J. Neal

Pitted morningglory seedling

J. Neal

Tall morningglory seedling

J. Neal

Pitted morningglory mature, lobed leaf form

J. Neal

Cypressvine morningglory seedling

303

Cypressvine morningglory: Stems are glabrous. Leaves retain a similar shape as seedlings but are larger, approximately 7 cm in length, pinnately compound each lobe 3–4 cm long and about 1 mm wide.

ROOTS AND UNDERGROUND STRUCTURES: Coarsely branched root system.

FLOWERS AND FRUIT: Flowers are present from July to September and are produced on stalks shorter than or equaling the petioles (1–3 flowers at the leaf axil).

Ivyleaf morningglory: Sepals are long (15–25 mm), abruptly tapering to a long, linear recurved tip. The basal portions of the flower are densely hairy. **Petals are purple to pale blue or white** (2.5–4.5 cm long) and **fused into a funnel**. Fruit are spherical capsules containing 4–6 seeds separating into 2–4 portions at maturity. Bristly sepals remain around the capsule. Seeds are 5–6 mm long, minutely hairy, dark brown to black, wedge-shaped with 1 rounded and 2 flattened sides.

Pitted morningglory: Flowers are smaller (1.5–2 cm long) than those of the other morningglories and **white**; sepals are 9–11 mm long with hairs on the margins; seeds are smooth, but otherwise similar.

Tall morningglory: Flowers are similar in color and shape to those of ivyleaf morningglory, but they are larger (4.5–7 cm long) with **shorter sepals** (10–15 mm long). Seeds are similar.

Red morningglory: Flowers are slender, funnel-shaped, red to yellowish-red in color, 2–3 cm long, opening abruptly at the end. Sepals are oblong, to 4–7 mm long, and lack hairs. Fruit is a rounded capsule; seeds are similar.

Cypressvine morningglory: Flowers are slender, funnel-shaped, crimson red, similar to red morningglory but with a more slender tube. Sepals are oblong, to 5–7 mm long. Fruit is a rounded capsule; seeds are similar.

POSTSENESCENCE CHARACTERISTICS: Plants die with the first frost. Vines and fruit will persist into winter.

HABITAT: Weeds of most agronomic, horticultural, and nursery crops, as well as landscapes, fencerows, and noncrop areas; morningglories prefer rich, moist soil but are adapted to a wide range of conditions.

DISTRIBUTION: Common in the southern and central United States; less common in the cooler regions of the Northeast but found as far north as New York and Pennsylvania.

SIMILAR SPECIES: **Several species of *Ipomoea*** can extend into the southern region of the northeastern United States. **Bigroot morningglory (*Ipomoea pandurata* (L.) G.F.W. Meyer)** is a tuber-producing perennial with unlobed or slightly 3-lobed leaves, funnel-shaped white flowers (5–8 cm long) with red centers, and seeds fringed with soft hairs. **A variety of ivyleaf morningglory with unlobed leaves** is sometimes distinguished as ***Ipomoea hederacea* var. *integriuscula* Gray**. Both this variety and bigroot morningglory are more abundant in the southern United States than in the northern states.

Tall morningglory habit

Cypressvine morningglory flower and foliage

Red morningglory flower and leaf

Tall morningglory flowers and foliage

Top left, seeds of pitted morningglory, 4.0 mm; *top right*, red morningglory, 3.5 mm; *bottom left*, tall morningglory, 4.0 mm; and *bottom right*, ivyleaf morningglory, 5.0 mm

Guadeloupe cucumber (*Melothria pendula* L.)

SYNONYMS: creeping cucumber, trailing cucumber

GENERAL DESCRIPTION: Guadeloupe cucumber is an annual or **perennial vine** with alternate leaves; **small, yellow flowers**; and small, **edible fruit** that resembles tiny, green watermelons. Stems readily form roots and climb over other vegetation with the aid of tendrils.

PROPAGATION / PHENOLOGY: Plants reproduce by **overwintering roots and by seeds**. Shoots from overwintering roots emerge in early spring. Seeds germinate in late spring and will continue to emerge throughout the summer.

SEEDLING: Young shoots have alternate leaves on thin, vine-like stems. Stems have minute, **prickly hairs and tendrils** at the nodes that facilitate climbing on and over other vegetation. Leaves of young plants are simple, wider than long, with shallow toothed margins, hairs on upper and lower surfaces (resembling tiny sycamore leaves), with petioles that are longer than the leaf blades.

MATURE PLANT: Vining stems continue to elongate. Leaf shapes are variable within plants, some developing deeper, palmate lobes, with pointed tips and toothed margins. Mature plants will often have small, green to black fruit hanging from stems.

ROOTS AND UNDERGROUND STRUCTURES: Plants produce fibrous roots and thickened, white roots that overwinter in much of its range.

FLOWERS AND FRUIT: Flowers are yellow, single, 0.5–1 cm diameter, 5 petals fused at the base. Individual **fruit resemble tiny watermelons**, green and often striped turning black at maturity, on 15–45 mm pedicels. Fruit is edible and is likely consumed and spread by vertebrates. Seeds are flattened, roughly pear-shaped, 2–4 mm in length.

POSTSENESCENCE CHARACTERISTICS: Foliage is not persistent after frost. Vines may persist if weather allows for desiccation.

HABITAT: Commonly found in managed landscapes, in diverse soil types and sites. Less common in agronomic cropping systems.

DISTRIBUTION: Native to North America. Most common in the southeastern United States but distributed north to Pennsylvania and west to the Mississippi River. Prevalence and distribution as a weed has increased.

SIMILAR SPECIES: Three recognized taxonomic sub-classifications vary in fruit size and leaf width. Variety **'*pendula*'** appears to be the most widespread. **Wild cucumber (*Echinocystis lobata* (Michx.) T. & G.)** has larger leaves, palmately lobed but lacking teeth on margins; flowers are whitish, fruit are in clusters and have bristles or hairs. Guadeloupe cucumber flowers are yellow and are borne singly; fruit is smooth and fleshy. **Yellow passionflower (*Passiflora lutea* L.)**, a native vine, has a similar growth habit and fleshy fruit, but leaves have rounded lobes with smooth margins. See **Table 6 for a comparison of wild cucumbers.**

Guadeloupe cucumber vines and foliage

Guadeloupe cucumber seedling

Guadeloupe cucumber vine with mature fruit

Guadeloupe cucumber flower

Yellow passionflower with rounded lobes and small, black fruit

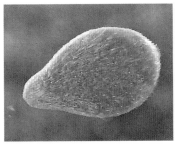

Guadeloupe cucumber seed, 4 mm

Burcucumber (*Sicyos angulatus* L.)

SYNONYMS: one-seeded bur cucumber, star cucumber, nimble kate

GENERAL DESCRIPTION: A **summer annual vine** with branching **stems (>3 m long) that climb by tendrils. Fruit resemble small cucumbers** but are covered with burs.

PROPAGATION / PHENOLOGY: Reproduction is **by seeds**; seeds germinate in mid-spring through early summer.

SEEDLING: Hypocotyls are covered with short, downward-pointing hairs. **Cotyledon** blades are **thick, rounded** to elliptic, often with dense, short, spreading hairs on both surfaces. The stalks of the cotyledons are flat on the upper surface. **Young leaves** are alternate, **hairy**, usually with **5 angles or pointed lobes** and a **toothed margin**. Petioles are short and rounded, with downward-pointing hairs.

MATURE PLANT: **Stems are sticky-hairy**, especially at the nodes, longitudinally ridged, and **climb by branched tendrils. Leaves** are alternate, 6–20 cm long by 6–20 cm wide, **sticky-hairy**, rounded to heart-shaped, with **3–5 shallow, angled lobes**, a sharp apex, and toothed margins.

ROOTS AND UNDERGROUND STRUCTURES: Roots are fibrous.

FLOWERS AND FRUIT: Flowers are produced from July to September. Male and female flowers are separate (monoecious) in the leaf axils. Flowers are greenish-white, with 5 petals and 5 inconspicuous sepals. **Fruit are oval or elliptic,** 1–2 cm long, nearly as wide, **pointed at the apex,** in clusters of 3–20. The **surface of the fruit is covered with long, stiff bristles** and shorter hairs. Each fruit produces 1 seed. Seeds are 1–1.5 cm long, oval, flattened, bumpy, light brown to black, with 2 whitish swellings at the base.

POSTSENESCENCE CHARACTERISTICS: Plants die at first frost. Stems and fruit persist for only a short time.

HABITAT: Burcucumber is a weed of cultivated row crops and vegetables. It is also found in fencerows, thickets, and waste places, generally on damp, rich soils. Burcucumber is a major problem in mechanically harvested vegetables, because the viny stems interfere with harvesting procedures.

DISTRIBUTION: Found throughout the eastern United States, as far south as Florida, and west to Minnesota and Arizona.

SIMILAR SPECIES: Although less commonly encountered, **wild cucumber (*Echinocystis lobata* (Michx.) T. & G.)** is similar in leaf shape and vining habit and the fruit has weak prickles. **See Table 6 for a comparison of weedy cucumbers and similar species.**

Burcucumber habit

Burcucumber immature spiny fruits

Burcucumber seedling

Burcucumber male flower

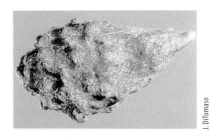

Burcucumber seed, 15 mm

Wild cucumber foliage and flowers

Wild cucumber seed, 17 mm

Chinese yam (*Dioscorea polystachya* Turcz.)

SYNONYMS: *Dioscorea batatas*, cinnamon vine. Note: The name *Dioscorea oppositifolia* L. has been misapplied to this species and, according to the *Flora of North America*, is a different species not currently in North America.

GENERAL DESCRIPTION: A fast-growing, climbing or creeping, **herbaceous**, **perennial vine** capable of growing up to **greater than 5 m in height**. Colonies of vines quickly smother shrubs and other vegetation. **Small bulbils resembling tiny potatoes** are **produced on the stems.**

PROPAGATION / PHENOLOGY: Reproduction is primarily by **potato-like, aerial bulbils** produced in the **leaf axils** or by vegetative expansion via **tuberous roots**. Bulbils are spherical, covered in bumpy adventitious buds, and up to 3 cm long by 2 cm in diameter. Bulbil production can occur on vines as young as 3 months, and a single vine can produce 20 or more. They are readily dislodged and may be spread by water or animals. Damaged or partially eaten bulbils may produce new plants. In warmer climates, bulbils may sprout immediately, though they can remain dormant throughout the winter or longer.

SEEDLING: Seedlings are rarely found. Plants sprouting from tubers are vigorous vines with heart-shaped leaves. As plants age, the leaves become more elongated.

MATURE PLANT: Stems of mature vines are hairless, branching, round in cross section, and twine clockwise. Leaves are alternate on the basal portions becoming opposite higher on the vines, hairless, heart- or arrow-shaped, 3–9 cm long by 3–11 cm wide, with angled or rounded basal lobes. Veins are parallel and radiate from the base of the leaf; leaf margins entire. Petioles may be as long as the leaf blade. Stems, leaves, and petioles often have reddish-purple color, particularly when young.

ROOTS AND UNDERGROUND STRUCTURES: Every season plants produce 1 or more starchy **tubers**. These tubers develop thick, unbranched roots early in the season, which become thinner, branching, and fibrous as vines mature.

FLOWERS AND FRUIT: Flowering occurs from May through August. **Male and female flowers are produced on separate plants (dioecious)**; staminate plants flower annually, pistillate flowers may not. Male flowers are on axillary fascicles with up to 5 branches (spikes), each spike <5 cm long. Individual **flowers are green to white** and occur in a zigzag pattern on spikes. Female flowers occur 1 per leaf axil. Fruits are broadly ovate, membranous **capsules** (12–20 mm wide). **Seeds are winged**, flattened. It is unclear if viable seeds are produced in North America.

POSTSENESCENCE CHARACTERISTICS: Leaves turn bright yellow in autumn before falling. Dead vines persist through winter.

HABITAT: A weed of disturbed riparian areas, stream and river edges, forests and forest edges, and ditches and roadsides. Prefers partial shade, though is tolerant of full sun and shade. Grows best in well-drained, deep, loamy soil.

DISTRIBUTION: Found in central, midwestern, and eastern United States, west to Oklahoma and Nebraska and north to Vermont.

SIMILAR SPECIES: Often misidentified as **air potato (*Dioscorea bulbifera* L.)**, which has a more southern distribution, and leaves are cordate. The native **wild yam (*Dioscorea villosa* L.)** is similar to Chinese yam. Wild yam vines twine from right to left, have hair on the upper surfaces of leaves, lack reddish-purple coloration, and do not produce aerial bulbils. **Morningglories (*Ipomoea* spp.)** and **bindweeds (*Convolvulus* spp.)** may have similar leaves, but do not produce aerial bulbils or tubers, and have showy, trumpet-shaped flowers.

Chinese yam vine emerging in spring from tubers

J. Neal

Chinese yam vine with aerial bulbils

J. Neal

J. Neal

Early season and later-season leaf shapes of Chinese yam

Common teasel (*Dipsacus fullonum* L.)

SYNONYMS: *Dipsacus sylvestris*, wild teasel, card teasel, venus-cup, card thistle, gypsycombs

GENERAL DESCRIPTION: A **large biennial** (0.5–2 m in height), easily recognized by its **prominent, spiny flower heads that persist throughout the year**. Dried flower heads are often used in dried plant arrangements.

PROPAGATION / PHENOLOGY: Reproduction is **by seeds**; seeds germinate in late summer and fall and **overwinter as basal rosettes**.

SEEDLING: Plants develop as **basal rosettes**. Cotyledons are smooth and oval to round, with short stalks. **Young leaves** are oval to egg-shaped, with toothed margins; **surfaces have a wrinkled appearance**.

MATURE PLANT: Basal leaves are widest above the middle, tapering to the base, with rounded teeth along the margin. **Basal leaves generally die early in the second season when the erect stem and flowers are produced. Stems** are angled, marked with fine, parallel lines, and **covered with many short, downward-turning prickles**, especially toward the top of the plant. **Leaves are opposite**, 20–60 cm long, and **prickly on the underside** on the midrib. **Upper leaves are lanceolate and sessile**, with their bases fused around the stem. Margins on the upper leaves are mostly untoothed.

ROOTS AND UNDERGROUND STRUCTURES: Shallow taproot with fibrous secondary root system.

FLOWERS AND FRUIT: Flowers are present from July to September in the second year of growth. **Flower heads are cylindrical to egg-shaped**, 3–10 cm long, **with large, spinelike bristly bracts** curving up around the head, the longer ones surpassing the head in length. Heads are **covered with straight spines**. Individual flowers are 10–15 mm long and bloom in a spiral arrangement around the head. The white petals are tubular, with short (1 mm) **pale purple lobes, giving the head a purple, thistle-like appearance.** Flower clusters are on long, prickly stalks (peduncles). Each seed is enclosed within the fruit (achene). Achenes are 3–4 mm long, 4-angled, and grayish-brown with parallel ridges.

POSTSENESCENCE CHARACTERISTICS: The woody, erect stems and **characteristic dead flower heads persist** throughout the winter. Dead flower heads are spiny, egg-shaped, and have bracts that curve up and around the head from underneath. Dead stems are spiny.

HABITAT: A common weed of roadsides and low-maintenance turfgrass, meadows, and waste areas, common teasel is rarely a problem in cultivated crops. Often found on damp, rich soils.

DISTRIBUTION: Found throughout most of the United States except for the northern Great Plains. Most common in the Northeast, including New York, Pennsylvania, and New Jersey; less common in New England. Also common in the Pacific Coast states.

SIMILAR SPECIES: **Cutleaf teasel (*Dipsacus laciniatus* L.)** can be distinguished by its pinnatifid upper leaves. Common teasel can be mistaken for other **thistles (*Cirsium* spp. or *Carduus* spp.)** owing to the similar shape and color of the flower head and the presence of prickles on the stem. Unlike thistle leaves, however, common teasel leaves are wrinkled and have spineless margins.

Common teasel seedling

A. DiTommaso

Common teasel habit

J. Neal

R. Uva

Common teasel rosettes

R. Uva

Common teasel inflorescence

A. DiTommaso

Common teasel
overwintering inflorescences

J. O'Brien © 2007 UC Regents

Common teasel seeds, 3.5 mm

Virginia copperleaf (*Acalypha virginica* L.)

SYNONYMS: three-seeded mercury, wax balls, copper-leaf, mercury-weed

GENERAL DESCRIPTION: A **summer annual** with **erect, branched stems** (10–60 cm tall). **Foliage develops a distinct copper pigmentation**, particularly when growing in sunny locations.

PROPAGATION / PHENOLOGY: Reproduction is **by seeds**; seeds germinate in late spring.

SEEDLING: **Cotyledons are round, notched** at the apex, smooth, and on short petioles. **First leaves are opposite; subsequent leaves are alternate.** Leaves are narrow to widely ovate, glossy, and sparsely hairy, with rounded teeth on the margin.

MATURE PLANT: Stems are hairy to sparsely hairy. **Leaves are similar to those of the seedling**, but are narrowly to **broadly lanceolate** (2–8 cm long) and petiolated (1–4 cm long). Lower leaves are opposite and glossy green, upper leaves are alternate. **Younger leaves have a copper coloration.** In many areas, leaves soon become damaged by insect feeding.

ROOTS AND UNDERGROUND STRUCTURES: Shallow taproot with a secondary fibrous root system.

FLOWERS AND FRUIT: **Flowers** are produced from June through October. Male and female flowers are produced separately on the same plant (monoecious). Both flower types are **greenish, inconspicuous**, and produced **in clusters in the leaf axils** on the upper portions of the stem. Female flowers are surrounded by **9–15 conspicuous, deeply lobed bracts**. Bract persists, sheathing the **3-chambered seedpod** (1 seed per chamber). Seeds are egg-shaped, 1.4–1.8 mm long, dull reddish-brown or gray with reddish-brown spots.

POSTSENESCENCE CHARACTERISTICS: After frost, upright woody stems persist for a short time. Otherwise, no distinctive winter characteristics.

HABITAT: Virginia copperleaf is a weed of nursery crops, landscapes, roadsides, fields, streambanks, and waste areas. It can also be found in cultivated, agronomic, and horticultural crops under a wide variety of soil types and moisture conditions, ranging from dry to wet.

DISTRIBUTION: Occurs throughout much of the eastern two-thirds of the United States from Maine south to Florida, west to South Dakota and Texas.

SIMILAR SPECIES: Several related species of *Acalypha* have overlapping distributions. The leaves of **rhombic copperleaf (*Acalypha rhomboidea* Raf.)** are lanceolate to ovate or rhombic (diamond-shaped), and the petioles are usually more than half as long as the blades. The female flowers of rhombic copperleaf are surrounded by bracts, which are 5–9 lobed, those of Virginia copperleaf are 9–15 lobed. The leaves of **narrowleaf copperleaf (*Acalypha gracilens* A. Gray)** are linear-lanceolate to linear-oblong with petioles up to 5 mm long; Virginia copperleaf petioles are 1–4 cm in length. The floral bracts of female flowers of narrowleaf copperleaf are 3–5 lobed, whereas those of Virginia copperleaf are 9–15 lobed. **Hophornbeam copperleaf (*Acalypha ostryifolia* Riddell)** has heart-shaped leaves with serrated margins. Additionally, male flowers of hophornbeam copperleaf occur in axillary clusters and female flowers are in spikes. Female flowers for the other *Acalypha* species described herein are axillary. **Brittlestem hempnettle (*Galeopsis tetrahit* L.)** is vegetatively similar but it is in the Lamiaceae (mint family) and has square stems, and small pink to white flowers in the upper leaf axils. It is a summer annual, introduced from Eurasia, now widely distributed in the upper half of North America.

J. Neal

Virginia copperleaf habit

J. Neal

Virginia copperleaf flowers and leafy bracts

J. Neal

Virginia copperleaf seedling

J. Neal

Virginia copperleaf mature foliage

A. DiTommaso

Brittlestem hempnettle seedling

J. DiTommaso

Virginia copperleaf seeds, 1.5 mm

Tropic croton (*Croton glandulosus* L.)

SYNONYMS: northern croton, tooth-leaved croton, sand croton, Vente conmigo

GENERAL DESCRIPTION: A **summer annual herb** with erect, apically branching, hairy stems that reach 30 cm at maturity.

PROPAGATION / PHENOLOGY: Reproduction is **by seeds**.

SEEDLING: Cotyledons are oval, nearly as long as the first leaf. The first **true leaves** are **ovoid with toothed margins**, on short petioles.

MATURE PLANT: Mature plants are upright and branched. **Stems densely pubescent** with short, stellate (star-shaped), white hairs. **Leaves are sharply toothed**, **alternate**, up to 5 cm long by 2.5 cm wide, and ovate below and lanceolate above. Petioles reach 2 cm in length and have similar hairs to the stem. Most leaves have 2 abaxial, glandular stipules at the base.

ROOTS AND UNDERGROUND STRUCTURES: A thick taproot with an unpleasant, pungent odor.

FLOWERS AND FRUIT: From July to October small, **white flowers** are produced in short (1.5 cm), **terminal or axillary racemes**. Each raceme has 1–4 pistillate (female) flowers at the base and 10–20 staminate (male) flowers toward the apex (monoecious). Male flowers occur on short (0.8–2 mm) pedicels and have 7–13 stamens and ciliate petals 0.8–1.5 mm long. Female flowers have green lanceolate sepals, are without petals, and are sessile or have pedicels up to 5 mm long. Beginning in August flowers are replaced by globular, 3-lobed **capsules**, 3.5–6 mm in length, which **turn brown when ripe**. Each capsule produces 3 gray, oblong (to 1.2 mm long) seeds that become shiny and speckled with black as they mature.

POSTSENESCENCE CHARACTERISTICS: Dead, upright stems may persist a short time in early winter.

HABITAT: Tropic croton grows in disturbed areas with dry or well-drained sandy soils. A weed of waste areas, agricultural fields, pastures, roadsides, and railways.

DISTRIBUTION: Common throughout its native range in the southeastern United States, tropic croton has spread to the Great Plains and the Midwest, and as far as Pennsylvania and New Jersey in the Northeast.

SIMILAR SPECIES: Several varieties of *Croton glandulosus* have been described, differing mainly in pubescence and leaf size. The foliage of **eclipta (*Eclipta prostrata*)** and **prickly sida (*Sida spinosa*)** are similar to that of tropic croton. Unlike tropic croton, eclipta has opposite leaves, and stems are not conspicuously hairy. Compared to tropic croton, prickly sida is less hairy, with 2 spine-like tubercules at the base of the petiole, and has yellow flowers.

J. Neal

Tropic croton habit

J. Neal

Tropic croton stem with bristly hairs

R. Uva

Tropic croton seedlings

J. Neal

Tropic croton flowering stem

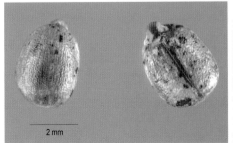

S. Hurst, hosted by USDA-NRCS PLANTS Database

2 mm

Tropic croton seeds

Leafy spurge (*Euphorbia esula* L.)

Synonyms: *Tithymalus esula*, Faitour's grass

General Description: A **colony-forming perennial** with **erect, tough, woody stems** (30–70 cm tall). All parts of the plant exude a **milky sap** when injured. Although palatable to sheep and goats, leafy spurge is **mildly toxic to cattle**, who will avoid foraging in areas contaminated with only 10% of the weed.

Propagation / Phenology: Reproduction is **by seeds, buds of lateral roots**, and **buds that develop on root segments** fragmented by cultivation. Shoots emerge from crowns and root buds in early spring. Seeds germinate in early spring.

Seedling: **Cotyledons** are smooth (13–19 mm long by 2–4 mm wide), linear to oblong, often with a **powdery, grayish or whitish coating** (glaucous). The first few leaves are opposite; subsequent leaves are alternate. **Young leaves are thin, narrowly elliptic**, entire, **bluish-green**, smooth, and hairless.

Mature Plant: **Stems are smooth, yellowish-green, unbranched** or branched above. **Leaves are sessile**, alternate, **linear to lanceolate** (3–8 cm long by 4–8 mm wide), usually wider above the middle (oblanceolate), and **spirally arranged on the stem**, making them appear whorled. The margins are entire but slightly wavy. Leaves associated with the inflorescence are much shorter, broader, and heart- to kidney-shaped.

Roots and Underground Structures: New shoot buds are produced from **vertical and horizontal fleshy roots**. Developing **crowns** remain attached to the parent plant by lateral roots. Many **pinkish, scaly buds** form on the crowns and roots just below the soil surface. Extensive root and crown systems contain large nutrient reserves that enable the plant to survive mechanical weed control efforts.

Flowers and Fruit: Both male and female flowers are clustered into a cup-like structure (cyathium). The cyathium is small and inconspicuous but surrounded by **conspicuous greenish-yellow bracts** (1–1.3 cm long). Flower clusters are produced from June through August on axillary shoots and on **flat-topped umbellate inflorescences** at the end of branched stems (7–15 branches). The **fruit** is a 3–3.5 mm long, 3-celled capsule (1 seed per cell) that can **explode at maturity, projecting seeds 5 m**. Seeds are 2–3 mm long, oval to elliptic, grayish, with red markings and a dark line on one side.

Postsenescence Characteristics: Neither leaves nor fruit persist on unbranched stems. However, stiff, erect stems persist throughout the winter and often into the following spring. Pink buds (1 cm long) are evident on the root crown just below the soil surface throughout the year.

Habitat: A weed of rangeland, pastures, roadsides, uncultivated perennial crops, and reduced-tillage crops, leafy spurge is less common in traditionally cultivated crops.

Distribution: Found throughout much of the northern United States; less common in the Northeast than in other northern states. A major rangeland weed from Idaho to Minnesota, south to Colorado and Nebraska.

Similar Species: **Cypress spurge (*Euphorbia cyparissias* L.)** is similar in both appearance and habit but is shorter (15–30 cm tall) and has narrower leaves (1–3 cm long by 1–3 mm wide) congested on side branches. **Sun spurge (*Euphorbia helioscopia* L.)** is an annual to 0.5 m tall, with similar flower heads but broadly obovate leaves that have finely toothed margins. It is found in all northeastern and mid-Atlantic states, except Kentucky and is native to Europe. In the spring, emerging shoots may resemble **yellow toadflax (*Linaria vulgaris*)**; however, yellow toadflax does not exude milky white latex when cut.

J. DiTomaso

Leafy spurge habit

J. DiTomaso

Leafy spurge flowers

Cypress spurge habit

J. Neal

J. Neal

Sun spurge habit

J. DiTomaso

Left, cypress spurge seeds, 2.0 mm; *right*, leafy spurge seeds, 2.4 mm

Hyssop spurge (*Euphorbia hyssopifolia* L.)

Synonyms: *Chamaesyce hyssopifolia*, hyssopleafed sandmat

General Description: Native **summer annual**, with opposite leaves, asymmetrically oblique leaf base, and **milky sap**. Unlike the prostrate stems of spotted and prostrate spurge, hyssop spurge has **ascending to erect stems** to approximately 0.5 m tall.

Propagation / Phenology: Reproduction is by seeds. Most seeds fall near the parent plant, but some are **forcefully ejected up to 2 m** from the parent plant. Some seeds lack dormancy and germinate soon after dispersal. As such, plants will have multiple generations per year. Seeds germinate in warm, moist soils from mid-spring through late summer.

Seedling: Cotyledons are oval to oblong, 3–5 mm long by 2–3 mm wide, and lack hairs. The first leaf pair is wider at the tip and tapers to the base, nearly wedge-shaped. The first few leaf pairs are opposite and oblanceolate to obovate, 5–7 mm long by 4 mm wide.

Mature Plant: Stems are branched and ascending to erect, slightly drooping or nodding near the tip, glabrous (or nearly so), often red. In areas mowed or trampled, plants can be prostrate with ascending tips. **Leaves are opposite**, **oblong**, 8–35 mm long, with bases **obliquely asymmetric** and on a short stalk. Leaf blades are palmately veined at the base and glabrous; margins are finely toothed, occasionally with a few hairs.

Roots and Underground Structures: Taproots slender, fibrous.

Flowers: Plants mature rapidly, flowering within 5 weeks of emergence and continuing to flower from early summer through fall. The greenish-white, occasionally light pink flowering units (cyathia) are densely clustered (rarely solitary) in the axils at the stem tips. The glands are yellow-green to red and oblong with an appendage width greater than gland width. Capsules lack hairs and are 3-lobed, 3-chambered, 1.7–1.8 mm long, ovoid, with 1 seed per chamber. Seeds are brown to gray, 4-sided, 1–1.4 mm long by 1 mm wide, with 2–3 transverse ridges.

Postsenescence Characteristics: Dead plants generally do not persist.

Habitat: Found in landscaped areas, walkways, roadsides, gardens, turf, waste places, orchards, vineyards, agronomic and vegetable crops, nursery crops, and other disturbed places. Increasing and spreading as a weed in container nurseries.

Distribution: Common in the southeastern United States and mid-Atlantic states, with potential to spread farther northward.

Similar Species: Hyssop spurge is often confused with **nodding spurge (*Euphorbia nutans* Lagasca** [syn.: *Chamaesyce nutans* (Lag.) Small]). They are similar in growth habit, life cycle, branching structure, leaf shape, and flowers. The new growth, both stems and foliage, of nodding spurge is usually hairy whereas the new growth of hyssop spurge is glabrous or nearly so. Nodding spurge is more widely distributed through the northeastern states in roadsides and cultivated fields; but where introduced hyssop spurge appears to be a more aggressive invader. **Garden spurge (*Euphorbia hirta* L.)** has asymmetric leaves with shallowly toothed margins, but in contrast to hyssop spurge it maintains the asymmetry with age. Garden spurge is smaller in stature but spreads rapidly following introduction. It is more common in warmer climates but present to New York and the Great Lakes.

Young nodding spurge habit

Hyssop spurge seedling

Hyssop spurge flowering stem

Nodding spurge flowering stem

Garden spurge large and small leaf forms

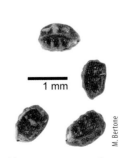

1 mm

Hyssop spurge seeds

Spotted spurge (*Euphorbia maculata* L.)

Synonyms: *Chamaesyce maculata*, *Euphorbia supina*, prostrate spurge

General Description: A **prostrate** to ascending, branching, **mat-forming summer annual** (40 cm in diameter). Stems and foliage exude a **milky sap** when injured.

Propagation / Phenology: Reproduction is **by seeds**; seeds germinate from spring to late summer. Spotted spurge **does not root at the nodes. Seeds are produced when emerging plants are only a four weeks old.**

Seedling: Hypocotyls are short, pink, and smooth. Cotyledons are oval, green on the upper surface, maroon below, and have short, purple petioles. **Young leaves are opposite**, hairy, **green, often with a maroon blotch** on the upper surface. The lower surface is maroon with a powdery coating. Leaf bases are unequal, and the petioles are reddish. Stems are pinkish and densely hairy.

Mature Plant: **Stems and leaves are similar to those of the seedling. Leaves are opposite**, **oblong** or somewhat egg-shaped or linear (5–15 mm long and less than half as wide, widest below the middle), on short petioles subtended by lanceolate stipules. Leaf margins may be toothed toward the apex.

Roots and Underground Structures: Shallow taproot with secondary fibrous roots.

Flowers and Fruit: **Flowers** are present from May to September **in the axils of the upper leaves.** Flowers appear to be single but are composed of several male and 1 female flower aggregated into a small cluster (cyathium) and surrounded by a cup-like structure (involucre). The **fruit is a 3-lobed,** 3-seeded **capsule,** 1.5 mm long, with stiff hairs on the surface. Seeds (1 per cell) are approximately 1 mm long, 4-angled, oblong or egg-shaped, grayish-brown to reddish-brown, with transverse ridges. Seeds are forcefully expelled up to 0.5 m from the fruit and become mucilaginous and sticky when wet, facilitating dispersal.

Postsenescence Characteristics: Stems persist for only a short time after frost.

Habitat: A common summer weed of landscapes, turfgrass, and nursery crops, spotted spurge is also found in cultivated fields, gardens, brick walks, and waste areas. It survives on dry or sandy, low-nutrient soil and on compacted or disturbed sites and thrives in container-grown nursery crops.

Distribution: Throughout the East and the Midwest, and on the Pacific Coast.

Similar species: **Creeping spurge (*Euphorbia serpens* Kunth.)** is widely distributed throughout eastern North America but has recently become more common as a weed in nursery crops and landscape plantings. It differs from spotted spurge by having more rounded leaves, and the stems root at the nodes. **Ground spurge (*Euphorbia humistrata* Engelm.),** often incorrectly called prostrate spurge, is quite similar and roots at the nodes; however, ground spurge is rare in the region. **Prostrate spurge (*Euphorbia prostrata* Ait.),** also called **prostrate sandmat,** is very similar to spotted spurge except the leaves generally lack the dark spot, are rounded to oval (not oblong), and more tightly arranged on stems. Leaves resemble creeping spurge, but the stems do not root at the nodes. These species may also resemble **hyssop spurge (*Euphorbia hyssopifolia*)** and **nodding spurge (*Euphorbia nutans* Lagasca),** but seedlings of those species grow erect rather than prostrate.

R. Uva

Spotted spurge seedlings

J. Derr

Spotted spurge

A. Senesac

J. Neal

J. Neal

Spotted spurge flowers   Prostrate spurge   Creeping spurge

J. O'Brien © 2007 UC Regents

J. O'Brien © 2007 UC Regents

J. O'Brien © 2007 UC Regents

Left, spotted spurge with hairs throughout pod; *center*, prostrate spurge with hairs on lobes of pod; *right*, creeping spurge lacking hairs

Goatsrue (*Galega officinalis* L.)

SYNONYMS: goat's rue, professor weed, galega, French lilac, Italian fitch

GENERAL DESCRIPTION: An **herbaceous**, clump-forming **perennial** that reaches 0.6–1.5 m in height, with clusters of attractive **white to purple flowers**. A single plant can produce up to 20 stems. Goatsrue is listed as a **federal noxious weed**. All parts contain the **toxic** alkaloid galegine, which can be hazardous to **ruminants**. Plants are generally unpalatable to cattle, but poisonings of sheep have been reported. Goatsrue has been used in herbal medicine; however, it can inhibit platelet aggregation, which results in excessive bleeding and interacts with several classes of prescription medicines.

PROPAGATION / PHENOLOGY: Reproduction is by seeds and vegetative growth from the **dense root crown**. Mature plants can produce as many as 15,000 seeds, which can survive in the soil for more than 15 years.

SEEDLING: Cotyledons are oblong and dark green.

MATURE PLANT: **Mature stems are smooth to sparsely hairy**, upright, **hollow**, and branched. **Leaves are alternate**, hairless, and **odd-pinnate compound** (a single terminal leaflet) with an arrow-shaped appendage at the base (**stipule**) and 6–10 pairs of leaflets. Leaflets are opposite, 1–5 cm long, lanceolate with entire margins, and tipped with a short, hair-like structure. Leaves resemble **vetch (*Vicia* spp.)** but larger. Mature plants may have a foul odor.

ROOTS AND UNDERGROUND STRUCTURES: A dense, **fibrous root system with a long taproot**. Like other legumes, roots have small, nitrogen-fixing nodules.

FLOWERS AND FRUIT: **White or blue to purple flowers** are produced from June until frost in **terminal or axillary racemes**, ≥25 cm long, with 30–50 flowers each. Pedicels are 3–5 mm long. Individual flowers are irregular, 7–10 mm long, and tubular at the base with a 2–3 mm long, 5-lobed calyx. Each flower is subtended by a linear bract (3–5 mm long). **Fruits** are linear, cylindrical, semi-erect, torulose (pinched along its length) **pods** (0.2–0.5 cm long). Pods are dehiscent and contain up to 10 oblong (3–4.5 mm long) and somewhat irregular yellow to reddish-brown seeds.

POSTSENESCENCE CHARACTERISTICS: None of note.

HABITAT: Goatsrue thrives in many soil types and tolerates a wide range of acidity. A weed of disturbed areas, wet meadows, fields, and stream and riversides. Prefers full sun but is shade-tolerant and can spread along forest edges and into open woodlands.

DISTRIBUTION: Occurs in the northeastern United States and New England and south to Maryland. Also found in the western United States and the Pacific Northwest. Occurrences of this species should be reported to appropriate state agencies.

SIMILAR SPECIES: True **vetches (*Vicia* spp.)** have smaller leaves and vine-like stems, whereas goatsrue is generally upright. The tips of vetch leaves have tendrils while goatsrue does not. **Trailing crownvetch (*Securigera varia*)** has similar leaves but a vine-like habit and flowers in umbels. Goatsrue is very similar to native legumes, **American or northern wild senna (*Senna hebecarpa* (Fernald) Irwin & Barneby)** and **wild licorice (*Glycyrrhiza lepidota* Pursh)**. Goatsrue has white to purple flowers and hollow stems; wild senna has yellow flowers and wild licorice stems are not hollow.

Goatsrue seedling

Goatsrue foliage and flowers

Juvenile goatsrue

Goatsrue vegetative habit

Goatsrue white flowered form

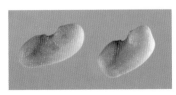

Goatsrue seeds, 4 mm

Annual lespedeza (*Kummerowia striata* (Thunb.) Schindl.)

Synonyms: *Lespedeza striata*, common lespedeza, Japanese clover, Korean clover

General Description: **Prostrate to ascending summer annual** with palmately **trifoliolate** compound leaves having **parallel veins**. Introduced from Asia as a forage.

Propagation / Phenology: Reproduction is **by seeds**. Seeds germinate spring through summer.

Seedling: Cotyledons are oval, less than 1 cm long and not persistent. The first true leaf may be simple, resembling mature leaflets, but subsequent leaves are similar to mature plants. Seedlings are initially upright but soon branch from the base.

Mature Plant: Mature plants have mostly prostrate, branched, tough, **wiry stems**, with **appressed hairs** that point toward the base (retrorsely appressed). Stems do not root at the nodes. Older stems become woody and hairless with age. Compound leaves are **alternate, trifoliolate**, on short (1–2 mm) petioles and subtended by a **persistent leafy stipule** 4–6 mm long. Leaflets are oblong to elliptic, 1–2 cm long and about 1/3 as wide, with entire margins and parallel veins; tips are rounded to obtuse (not emarginate), bases are tapered. The 3 leaflets arise from the same point, sessile or on short petiolules. Leaflets appear glabrous but have short hairs.

Roots and Underground Structures: A coarse, branched root system.

Flowers and Fruit: Plants flower from early summer through autumn. Flowers are pea-like, purple, pink, and white, small (2–7 mm long), borne 1–3 in the leaf axils. Petals (5) and sepals (5-toothed and hairy) are fused at the base to form a cup. Plants with 2 types of flowers, one with colored petals and the other with no petals. Flowers may be sessile in the leaf axils or on short (to 4 mm long) stalks. The fruits are 1-seeded, 3–4 mm long legumes. Seeds are roughly kidney-shaped, approximately 2 mm long, brown often mottled with lighter colors, and remain in the pods.

Postsenescence Characteristics: Stems die after frost. Woody stems often persist through winter.

Habitat: A common weed of low maintenance turf, roadsides, pastures, and disturbed areas. The species tolerates dry conditions that other common plants do not. Prefers full sun but will grow in partial shade.

Distribution: Found throughout the eastern half of the United States, north to New York.

Similar Species: **Korean clover (*Kummerowia stipulacea* (Maxim.) Makino)**, also introduced from Asia, is very similar but can be distinguished by petioles on the mid-stem leaves (4–10 mm long), leaflets with emarginate tips, and appressed stem hairs that point toward the tip. In comparison, annual lespedeza mid-stem leaves have shorter petioles, leaflets tips are not emarginate, and stem hairs point toward the base. The 2 species have overlapping distributions and may hybridize. Before flowering, annual lespedeza may be confused with **black medic (*Medicago lupulina*)**, but black medic has yellow flowers and more rounded leaflets. **See Table 7 for a comparison of weedy, trifoliolate legumes and woodsorrels.**

J. Neal

Annual lespedeza habit

J. Neal

Annual lespedeza with 3
leaflets and parallel veins

J. Neal

Annual lespedeza flowering stem

J. Neal

Annual lespedeza seedling

K. Hurst, hosted by USDA-NRCS Plants Database

Annual lespedeza seeds

327

Sericea lespedeza (*Lespedeza cuneata* (Dum.-Cours.) G. Don.)

SYNONYMS: Chinese bushclover, silky bushclover

GENERAL DESCRIPTION: An **herbaceous** (to semi-woody), erect, branching, and **shrub-like perennial** (0.5–2 m in height) with a thick, **woody taproot**. Sericea lespedeza was introduced in the early and mid-20th century for erosion control and as wildlife forage.

PROPAGATION / PHENOLOGY: Reproduction is **by seeds**. Each stem can produce up to 1000 or more seeds, which may remain viable for up to 20 years. Seeds are dispersed by gravity but can be spread in hay, as a seed contaminant, or through manure.

SEEDLING: Cotyledons are not persistent. **First leaves are opposite, simple, and oval. Subsequent leaves** are **alternate, palmately compound** with leaflets much longer than wide, rounded at the tip and tapering at the base. With age, leaflets become more elongated.

MATURE PLANT: Mature plants have up to 30 branching stems giving them a bushy appearance. **Stems are light green to gray-green, ridged**, and lined with several vertical rows of appressed white hairs. Lower portions of the stems become woody and hairless with age. **Compound leaves** are held ascending or erect on short petioles and are **alternate, trifoliolate with lanceolate leaflets** (1–3 cm long by 2–7 mm wide), and densely arranged on the stem. Upper surfaces of the leaves are hairless, while the **undersides are densely pubescent** with appressed white hairs. **Margins are entire** and leaflets often have a fine point at the tip. Upper leaves may appear to be sessile.

ROOTS AND UNDERGROUND STRUCTURES: A robust, **branching taproot** (up to 1 m long) with a **woody root-crown** (caudex) 2.5–8 cm below the soil surface.

FLOWERS AND FRUIT: Flowers are produced from July into September from the leaf axils on short, terminal stalks. Each stalk bears 2–4 **pea-like flowers** (to 8 mm long). Flowers are **white to cream-colored with a purple throat**. Some flowers remain closed and self-pollinate (cleistogamous). By late fall each flower is replaced with a **hairy, indehiscent, oval seedpod** (2.5–3.5 mm long) containing a single seed. Seeds are 1.5–2.5 mm long.

POSTSENESCENCE CHARACTERISTICS: Stems die after frost. Woody portions often persist through winter.

HABITAT: A weed of old fields, prairies, thickets, open woodlands, waste areas, and roadsides. Prefers full sun but can grow in partial shade. Sericea lespedeza is drought- and flood-tolerant, can tolerate low pH soils, and is most competitive in low-fertility soils. Thus, the species is often planted for soil stabilization in eroded sites.

DISTRIBUTION: Found throughout the eastern and midwestern United States.

SIMILAR SPECIES: **Native bushclovers (*Lespedeza* spp.)** may be confused with sericea lespedeza. **Round-headed lespedeza (*Lespedeza capitata* Michx.)** and **hairy lespedeza (*Lespedeza hirta* (L.) Hornem.)** have similar flowers, but *L. capitata* has wider leaflets and *L. hirta* has egg-shaped leaflets and fewer stem branches. **Slender lespedeza (*Lespedeza virginica* (L.) Britton)** has similar foliage but has purple or pink flowers and longer leaflets (to 3.8 cm long).

Sericea lespedeza habit

Sericea lespedeza seedling

Sericea lespedeza flowering stem

Sericea lespedeza sprout from perennial root

Sericea lespedeza hairy stem

Sericea lespedeza seeds, 1.8–2 mm

329

Birdsfoot trefoil (*Lotus corniculatus* L.)

Synonyms: bloom-fell, cat's-clover, crow-toes, ground honeysuckle, sheep-foot, hop o'my thumb, devil's-claw

General Description: A **low to prostrate, mat-forming perennial** resembling **clover**, but with 2 leaf-like stipules at the base of the petiole. Stems are approximately 60 cm long and can become woody with age.

Propagation / Phenology: Reproduction is **by seeds** and also by **stolons and rhizomes** that spread to form large colonies. Most aboveground growth occurs in early spring. Rhizome growth and new shoot development occur in the fall. Seed germination is primarily in the spring, occasionally in the fall.

Seedling: Minute cotyledons emerge in mid-spring, but seedlings are rarely seen.

Mature Plant: Stems are square at the top, round at the base, with or without hairs. **Leaves** are alternate, nearly sessile, **compound with 3 terminal leaflets** (trifoliolate) and 2 leaf-like stipules at the base of the petiole. **Leaflets** are oval to **oblanceolate**, pointed at the apex, 5–20 mm long by 2–9 mm wide. Margins are usually entire but can be minutely serrate.

Roots and Underground Structures: Well-developed **rhizomes and stolons** and a coarse, secondary root system.

Flowers and Fruit: **Flowers** are produced in late June through the fall in **branched clusters** (umbels with 2–6 flowers) at the end of a 3–10 cm long stalk arising from the upper leaf axils. Flowers **resemble those of pea** and are 1.3 cm long, **bright yellow** (sometimes coppery or brick red), often with fine red lines. **Fruits are 2.5 cm long pods arranged in the form of a bird's foot**, accounting for its common name. Seeds are irregularly rounded to somewhat flattened (1–1.3 mm long), shiny, brownish to black and frequently speckled.

Postsenescence Characteristics: Plants die back to the ground at first frost. Dead stems become brittle and do not persist long into winter.

Habitat: Birdsfoot trefoil is **often seeded for soil stabilization or as a forage crop** but can easily escape into roadsides and waste areas. It can become a persistent weed in turfgrass and meadows and tolerates a wide variety of soil types (e.g., gravelly areas) and moisture regimes, including drought. Its presence is often indicative of low-fertility, drought-prone soils.

Distribution: Found throughout the United States; common in the Northeast and southern Canada.

Similar Species: **See Table 7 for a comparison of weedy, trifoliolate legumes and wood-sorrels.** Birdsfoot trefoil resembles **black medic (*Medicago lupulina*)** and **some clovers (*Trifolium* spp.)**; however, birdsfoot trefoil has entire or very nearly entire leaflets, whereas black medic and clovers have more conspicuously toothed leaflets. The center leaflet of black medic is on a short stalk (petiolate); the clovers and birdsfoot trefoil have a sessile terminal leaflet. Black medic also has yellow flowers, but they are smaller and more numerous than birdsfoot trefoil flowers. Among the weedy clovers, **hop clover (*Trifolium aureum* Pollich)**, **large hop clover (*Trifolium campestre*)**, and **small hop clover (*Trifolium dubium* Sibth.)** have yellow flowers, and the flowers are numerous in rounded heads.

J. Neal

Birdsfoot trefoil habit

J. Neal

Birdsfoot trefoil flower cluster

R. Uva

Birdsfoot trefoil mature leaf

J. Neal

Birdsfoot trefoil flowers and fruit

J. DiTomaso

Birdsfoot trefoil
seeds, 1.2 mm

Black medic (*Medicago lupulina* L.)

Synonyms: trefoil, black clover, none-such, hop medic, hop clover

General Description: A low-growing to **prostrate summer annual**, or less commonly a winter annual or biennial, with stems 10–60 cm long.

Propagation / Phenology: Reproduction is **by seeds**; seeds germinate in early autumn or spring.

Seedling: **Cotyledons** are dull green above, pale on the underside, and oblong (4–9 mm long). Young leaves have a few short hairs. **The first leaf is simple; subsequent leaves are palmately compound with 3 leaflets.** Petioles are long and hairy, with stipules at the base. In early stages of growth, numerous leaves arise from the base, but stems elongate and begin to trail with age.

Mature Plant: Stems are hairy, somewhat square, and many-branched at the base; they do not root at the nodes. **Leaves** are alternate, **compound with 3 wedge- to egg-shaped leaflets**, widest near the apex, with a small projecting tip (mucronate). **Leaflet margins are toothed.** The **center leaflet has a longer stalk (2–4 mm long petiolule) than the lateral leaflets.** Toothed stipules are present at the base of the petiole. The lower leaves have longer petioles than the upper leaves.

Roots and Underground Structures: Shallow **taproot** with secondary coarsely branched roots. Small nodules are attached to the roots.

Flowers and Fruit: Flowers are present from May to September. The inflorescence is composed of **10–50 flowers in a spherical to short-cylindrical, clover-like cluster**. Individual flowers are 4–5 mm long, with 5-cleft sepals that persist during fruit formation and 5 **yellow** irregularly shaped petals resembling those of a tiny pea flower. Flowers have 10 stamens, 9 fused and 1 separate. The **fruit** is a recurved, kidney-shaped, **black**, hairy, **1-seeded pod**, 2–3 mm long. Seeds are 1.5–2 mm long, oval to kidney-shaped, and yellow-green to brown.

Postsenescence Characteristics: Prostrate stems turn dark brown to black and persist for several months, with black seedpods remaining attached.

Habitat: Primarily a weed of turfgrass, particularly in nutrient-poor and drought-prone soils, black medic is also found on disturbed soils and waste areas.

Distribution: Occurs throughout the United States.

Similar Species: **See Table 7 for a comparison of weedy, trifoliolate legumes and wood-sorrels. Hop clover (*Trifolium aureum* Pollich), small hop clover (*Trifolium dubium* Sibth.**), and **large hop clover (*Trifolium campestre*)** have similar habits, foliage, and yellow flowers, but the leaves and flowers are larger than those of black medic. Also, the flower petals of hop clovers turn tan or brown and remain attached, whereas the petals of black medic drop off, revealing a cluster of pods that turn black at maturity. The **woodsorrels (*Oxalis* spp.)** also have 3 leaflets on each leaf; however, the individual leaflets are prominently indented at the apex and appear heart-shaped. **Birdsfoot trefoil (*Lotus corniculatus*)** also has trifoliolate leaves with entire (not toothed) or nearly entire margins; black medic leaflet margins are toothed.

J. Neal

Black medic habit

R. Uva

Black medic seedling

A. DiTommaso

Black medic immature fruit

R. Uva

Black medic leaves, flowers, and fruit

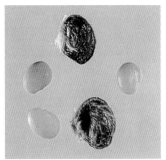

J. DiTomaso

Black medic seedpods, 2.3 mm, and seeds, 1.5 mm

333

Yellow sweetclover (*Melilotus officinalis* (L.) Lam.) and white sweetclover (*Melilotus albus* Medik.)

Synonyms: field melilot, yellow melilot, sweetclover. Note: some floras consider both species to be *Melilotus officinalis*.

General Description: Erect **biennials**, **sometimes annuals** or even short-lived perennials, to 2 m tall or more. The 2 species are nearly indistinguishable except by floral characteristics. Stems are upright; leaves are compound with 3 leaflets. Yellow sweetclover has yellow flowers; white sweetclover has white flowers arranged in a raceme. Both are native to Eurasia; introduced to the United States as forage crops and for re-vegetation of disturbed sites such as roadsides.

Propagation / Phenology: Reproduction is only **by seeds**. Seeds primarily fall near the parent plant. Most mature seeds are hard-coated and can remain viable for up to 20 years or more under field conditions. Some references suggest that white sweetclover is an obligate biennial, germinating in the spring, growing vegetatively to approximately 30 cm in height, setting basal buds in an overwintering crown, then growing to mature height and flowering the second summer.

Seedling: Cotyledons are oblong, 5–8 mm long, 3–4 mm wide, and lack hairs. The first leaf is simple, obovate, 2–5 mm long and wide, with a squared tip and a minute, nipple-like point (cuspidate). Subsequent leaves are pinnate-compound with **3 leaflets, the terminal leaflet is short-stalked**.

Mature Plant: Plants are erect and branched. Foliage lacks hairs or is sparsely minute-hairy. Leaves are alternate, pinnate-compound with 3 leaflets, terminal leaflet short-stalked. Leaflets are ovate to oblong, mostly 1–2.5 cm long, tip rounded or weakly squared, with the margins smooth to weakly toothed. The stipules are narrowly triangular, mostly 0.5–1 cm long.

Roots and Underground Structures: Roots are tough or woody, slender to thick, typically **deep taproots** that are associated with nitrogen-fixing bacteria.

Flowers and Fruit: Plants flower from late spring to summer. The **flowering racemes** are 3–12 cm long, slender, **axillary and terminal**, and elongate as flowers mature. **Flowers are pea-like**, 4–7 mm long, slender, sweetly fragrant, and on short stalks. Pods are ovoid, lack hairs, 3–5 mm long, light brown, on stalks that bend downward (reflexed). The pods contain 1 seed, rarely 2, and do not open to release seeds. The 2 species are separated by flower color, **bright yellow or white**, and other subtle floral differences. White sweetclover flowers are 3.5–5 mm long and the wing petals are about as long as the keel. Yellow sweetclover flowers are 5–7 mm long and the wing petals are generally longer than the keel.

Habitat: Grows along roadsides, and in open fields, pastures, agronomic crops, and other open disturbed places. White sweetclover is often found along waterways, while yellow sweetclover is rarely in wetland environments.

Distribution: Found throughout the United States and Canada.

Similar Species: The upright growth habit of sweetclovers differentiate them from most other **clovers (*Trifolium* spp.)**. Before flowering, sweetclovers can be mistaken for **sericea lespedeza (*Lespedeza cuneata*)**, which is found in similar habitats and also has 3-parted leaves with long leaflets. However, lespedeza leaves are held more erect, leaflets are more lanceolate, and the stems and undersides of leaves are hairy.

White sweetclover habit

White sweetclover seedling

Yellow sweetclover leaf

Inflorescences: *left,* white sweetclover; *right,* yellow sweetclover

Both by J. DiTomaso

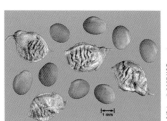

Yellow sweetclover seeds and pods

Kudzu (*Pueraria montana* (Lour.) Merr. var. *lobata* (Willd.) Maesen & S.M. Almeida ex Sanjappa & Predeep)

Synonyms: *Pueraria lobata, Pueraria thunbergiana*

General Description: An **aggressive, climbing or trailing, herbaceous to semi-woody perennial vine** with **large, trifoliolate leaves** (3 leaflets). **Vines can grow 10–30 m in a growing season** (up to 30 cm a day) but die back to the ground in fall. If not managed, kudzu can rapidly overgrow all other vegetation, including trees.

Propagation / Phenology: Reproduction is **by seeds** and **spreading roots** that **develop adventitious shoots**. Seedlings and adventitious shoots emerge in spring.

Seedling: Little information is available on seedling characteristics. **Young vines are covered with tan to bronze hairs.** Leaves are alternate and compound, with **3 leaflets**. The lateral leaflets are on short (≤1 cm) stalks; the center leaflet is on a longer stalk (1.5–2 cm). Leaflets are broadly ovate and hairy, with 1–3 lobes. The 2 lateral leaflets are often lobed on one side, whereas the center leaflet has lobes on both sides (much like an ivy leaf).

Mature Plant: Vegetative characteristics are **similar to juvenile growth, except larger** (leaflets up to 18 cm long by 12 cm wide). **Hairs deteriorate on mature vines, and stems become woody with age.**

Roots and Underground Structures: **Extensive fleshy root system** with **large, mealy, tuberous roots**. Adventitious shoots are produced from the roots and tuberous roots.

Flowers and Fruit: Plants flower in late July through early September. Plants may not flower in more northern limits of its range. **Reddish-purple flowers** are produced in **axillary, 10–20 cm long racemes** (resembling a small wisteria flower cluster). Legume-like flowers are **fragrant**; each is 2–2.5 cm long. Flattened, hairy **fruiting pods** mature in late summer or early fall. Pods (4–5 cm long) produce numerous kidney-shaped seeds, 3–4 mm long. Seeds are retained within the pod.

Postsenescence Characteristics: Very susceptible to frost. Aboveground portions die back to the ground in the fall, leaving tan or straw-colored vines.

Habitat: Kudzu is a weed of forests, rights-of-way, roadsides, abandoned fields, fencerows, and noncrop areas. It thrives on many soil types, including nutrient-deficient, sandy, clayey, or loamy soils. It does not tolerate cultivation or repeated mowing but may encroach into managed areas from adjacent infestations.

Distribution: Introduced as a forage and soil conservation plant from Japan. Escaped cultivation and is now common throughout the southeastern United States, west to Texas, and in the mid-Atlantic states. Can occasionally be found as far north as the southern portions of New York.

Similar Species: None of note for mature vines. Seedlings are similar to the native **prostrate ticktrefoil (*Desmodium rotundifolium* DC.)**, but prostrate ticktrefoil leaflets are rounded at the tip, whereas leaflets on kudzu seedlings have pointed tips.

Kudzu habit, on hillside

Kudzu flowers and fruit

Kudzu leaf (3 leaflets per leaf)

Kudzu seeds, 3.5 mm

Sicklepod (*Senna obtusifolia* (L.) H. S. Irwin & Barneby)

SYNONYMS: *Cassia obtusifolia*, Java-bean, arsenic weed, coffee-pod

GENERAL DESCRIPTION: A vigorous, native, semi-woody summer annual to approximately 2.5 m tall, with evenly **pinnate-compound leaves**, **oval leaflets**, and slightly asymmetrical, **yellow flowers** that develop distinctive **sickle-shaped seedpods**. The lower stems can sprawl along the ground in open areas but are usually erect. Foliage can have a slightly foul smell. Native to tropical and some warm-temperate regions of North America, including Mexico and the southern and eastern United States.

PROPAGATION / PHENOLOGY: Reproduction is **by seeds** that germinate over an extended time from spring through summer. Seeds can emerge from 10 cm depth in sandy loam soils and can remain viable for several years. Some seeds survive ingestion by livestock.

SEEDLING: Cotyledons are rounded, 15–20 mm broad, green above and light green below, with 3–5 distinct veins in the upper surface joining the midvein. The stems appear smooth but are covered with short, downward-pointed hairs. First true leaf is even-pinnately lobed; leaflets are oval and sessile with entire margins, subsequent leaves are similar but larger with more leaflets.

MATURE PLANT: **Stems** are **usually hairless and smooth**. In open spaces, plants branch from the base but are more upright when growing within a crop. **Leaves are alternate, even-pinnate-compound** with 2–3 pairs of obovate leaflets, 2–3 cm long by 1.5–2 cm wide, and a single elongated gland, 2 mm long, on the main leaf stalk between the lowest pair of leaves. Terminal pair of leaflets often larger than lower pairs of leaflets. Leaflet margins are entire with short, appressed hairs. The stipules at the base of the leaf are hairy, linear, and 1–2 cm long.

ROOTS AND UNDERGROUND STRUCTURES: Root system consists of long, curved taproot and secondary fibrous roots.

FLOWERS AND FRUIT: Plants flower mid-summer through early autumn. Bright yellow, showy flowers occur in the upper leaf axils and are solitary or in pairs, with petals 8–17 mm long. Sepals are unequal, 5–10 mm long by 2–5 mm wide, usually fringed with hairs. The flower stalks (pedicels) are 7–28 mm long and often nod slightly downward. The fruit is a slender, downward-curving pod (hence the name sicklepod) to 18 cm long, 5 mm wide, and 4-angled. The pods turn brownish-green as they mature. Seeds are 4–6 mm long, angular, light to dark brown.

POSTSENESCENCE CHARACTERISTICS: Dead, brown, semi-woody stems retain seedpod remnants for several months.

HABITAT: Primarily in agronomic fields, particularly cotton, peanut, and soybean, and waste areas, roadsides, and along railroads. Found in forests, open woodlands, and moist meadows along rivers in its native range.

DISTRIBUTION: Found throughout the southern and mid-Atlantic states but specimens reported as far north as New York and Massachusetts.

SIMILAR SPECIES: The distinct leaves; large, showy, yellow flowers; and sickle-shaped fruit are easy to identify. **Hemp sesbania (*Sesbania herbacea*)** resembles sicklepod but has many smaller leaflets, is taller, and has mottled yellow flowers. Hemp sesbania has a similar range but is more commonly found in persistently wet habitats. **Coffeeweed (*Senna occidentalis* (L.) Link)** leaflets are pointed and pods are straight or curved upward, unlike sicklepod. Coffeeweed is common in the southern United States, but uncommon in the Northeast.

Sicklepod habit

Sicklepod 2-leaf seedling with cotyledons

Sicklepod flowering and fruiting stem

Sicklepod 5-leaf seedling

Sicklepod flower

Sicklepod flower

Sicklepod seeds

Hemp sesbania (*Sesbania herbacea* (Mill.) McVaugh)

SYNONYMS: *Sesbania exaltata*, bigpod sesbania, coffeeweed, indigoweed

GENERAL DESCRIPTION: An erect, native, **summer annual** nitrogen-fixer **to 3 m tall**, with many pairs of oblong leaflets, a showy, yellowish flower, and distinctive seedpods.

PROPAGATION / PHENOLOGY: Reproduction is only **by seed**s. Seeds are not dispersed far from the parent plant except by water. Like other members of the pea family, the seeds can survive for many years in the soil. Most seedlings emerge in the spring, but some will continue to emerge through summer.

SEEDLING: Cotyledons lack hairs, are thick, oblong, 10–25 mm long by 4–10 mm wide, and are green on the upper surface, gray-green on the lower surface. The first true leaf is simple, but the subsequent leaves are pinnate-compound with 6–8 pairs of leaflets, 5–10 mm long, that occur opposite each other along the leaf axis. Seedlings are upright, unbranched, with alternate leaves.

MATURE PLANT: Stems lack hairs and become semi-woody with age. At maturity, plants can be 3 m tall and the lower stem is stout and woody. **Leaves are alternate, evenly pinnately compound**, with 20–70 **oblong to linear elliptic leaflets**, each 1–3 cm long by 2–6 mm wide, arranged opposite to each other. Leaflets have entire margins and the tips have a small abrupt point (mucro). The stipules at the base of the leaves are narrowly triangular, 1 cm long.

ROOTS AND UNDERGROUND STRUCTURES: Root system consists of deep taproot and branched fibrous roots.

FLOWERS AND FRUIT: Plants flower from summer to fall. Inflorescence is a small raceme of **pea-like** flowers in clusters of 2–6 arising from the leaf axils. Flowers are **yellow to pale orange**, 1–1.5 cm long, often with maroon speckled on the upper petal (banner). Flowers typically open in the evening. **Pods** are 4-sided, straight or drooping, curved, **linear, 15–20 cm long**, 3–5 mm wide, with straight margins. Each pod contains 30–40 seeds. Seeds are cylindrical, rounded to slightly truncate at the ends, 3–5 mm long, glossy dark brown to tan with dark spots.

POSTSENESCENCE CHARACTERISTICS: Dead, brown, woody stems with remnants of the seedpods can persist through winter and sometimes in the following spring.

HABITAT: Prefers moist to wet areas. Generally found weedy in disturbed sites, including moist agronomic fields, waste areas, roadsides, railroads, and ditches. In its native range it is not considered a weed in natural riparian areas or along streambanks.

DISTRIBUTION: Found throughout the southern and mid-Atlantic states and as far north as New York and Massachusetts.

SIMILAR SPECIES: The erect growth, many leaflets, and yellow flowers with maroon speckling make this species easy to distinguish from **sicklepod (*Senna obtusifolia*)** or **coffeeweed (*Senna occidentalis* (L.) Link)**.

Hemp sesbania habit

Hemp sesbania flower and leaf

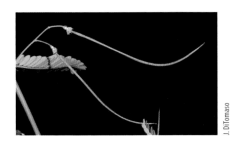

Hemp sesbania fruit

Hemp sesbania seedling

Hemp sesbania 2-leaf seedling with cotyledons

Hemp sesbania seeds

1 mm

Rabbitfoot clover (*Trifolium arvense* L.)

Synonyms: stone clover, old-field clover, hare's-foot clover

General Description: A **winter or summer annual** with erect (10–40 cm tall), freely branching, **densely hairy stems and leaves.** Rabbitfoot clover can tolerate mowing. The **grayish, hairy flower heads** resemble a rabbit's foot.

Propagation / Phenology: Reproduction is **by seeds.**

Seedling: Cotyledons are round to oval, on short stalks. **First leaves are simple** (lacking leaflets), semicircular to kidney-shaped, and petiolated. **Subsequent leaves are trifoliolate** (3 leaflets), **densely hairy,** on 1–3 cm long petioles. As seedlings, leaves form a **basal rosette** or mound.

Mature Plant: **Stems are erect,** many-branched, **soft-hairy,** often reddish. **Leaves** are alternate, trifoliolate, with **3 narrow, oblong (strap-like) leaflets** (1–2.5 cm long). **Leaflets have soft hairs** on the upper and lower surfaces and smooth margins, except for small teeth at the apex. Petioles are usually shorter than the leaflets, and stipules are longer than the petioles.

Roots and Underground Structures: Taproot (5–20 cm long) with a secondary fibrous root system.

Flowers and Fruit: **Flowers** are produced from July to September **in dense, grayish, hairy, egg-shaped to cylindrical (1–3 cm long) clusters.** Flower heads are attached to a relatively short (1.5–2.5 cm) stalk (peduncle). Individual flowers are pale pink to whitish and are enveloped by 5 bristly sepals (3–5 mm long) covered with silky hairs. Flowers are hidden within the hairy sepals. Fruit is a 1-seeded pod. Seeds are 1 mm long, yellow to brown and oval.

Postsenescence Characteristics: Dried stems and leaves are hairy, and seedheads persist on plant.

Habitat: Rabbitfoot clover is a weed of low-maintenance turfgrass and is most often found on low-nutrient, dry, sandy or rocky soil.

Distribution: Occurs throughout much of the United States; most common on the eastern coastal plain. Restricted to dry, sandy locations inland.

Similar Species: **See Table 7 for a comparison of weedy, trifoliolate legumes and woodsorrels.** Rabbitfoot clover can superficially resemble **spotted spurge (*Euphorbia maculata*)** but does not exude a milky latex when cut. Other weedy clovers (*Trifolium* spp.) have rounded rather than cylindrical flower heads. **White clover (*Trifolium repens*), strawberry clover (*Trifolium fragiferum* L.),** and **alsike clover (*Trifolium hybridum* L.)** are perennials with petioles much longer than the leaflets; petioles of rabbitfoot clover are shorter than the leaflets. **Hop clovers (*Trifolium aureum* Pollich, *Trifolium campestre*, and *Trifolium dubium* Sibth.)** have yellow flowers, and **red clover (*Trifolium pratense* L.)** is a perennial with red flowers.

Rabbitfoot clover habit

Rabbitfoot clover flowering stem

Rabbitfoot clover foliage

Left to right: alsike clover seeds, 1.1 mm; red clover seeds, 1.9 mm; and rabbitfoot clover seeds, 0.8 mm

Large hop clover (*Trifolium campestre* Schreb.)

Synonyms: field clover, low hop clover

General Description: A **winter annual** or occasionally a biennial to 10–30 cm tall, with distinctive **bright yellow, cylindrical flower heads** in the spring, and typical 3-parted clover leaves.

Propagation and Phenology: Plants reproduce only by seeds, which can be distributed long distances by humans. Seeds germinate in fall or early spring. **Plants flower in late spring to early summer.**

Seedling: Cotyledons are oval-oblong, glabrous, stalked, and 2–5 mm long. First leaf is simple and nearly round with a slightly indented tip, 2–6 mm long, and lacks hairs. Subsequent few leaves resemble mature leaves but are smaller.

Mature Plant: The stems are green or reddish-green and hairy with a tendency to sprawl. Stems do not root at the nodes. **Leaves are alternate and trifoliolate** (3 leaflets per leaf) with long petioles. Leafy bracts (stipules) at the base of the petiole are ovate, pointed, and often with hairy margins. Leaflets are oblong, ovate or elliptical, and 4–10 mm long. **The petiole of the middle leaflet is conspicuously longer** than the petioles of the lateral leaflets, which are generally lacking.

Roots and Underground Structures: Taproots are slender, branched, with fibrous lateral roots. Roots are associated with nitrogen-fixing bacteria.

Flowers and Fruit: Plants flower during late spring to early summer. Flower head is a cylindrical or spherical collection of 20–40 individual flowers, approximately 1.2 cm across, on stalks about 2 cm long. The petals of the flowers are striated with translucent veins and curl downward at the tips. They are persistent, turning light brown or nearly white on the flower heads. Each flower produces a single seedpod that is shorter than the persistent keel.

Postsenescence Characteristics: Dead foliage generally decomposes rapidly, but some remnants of the dried flower heads can remain for a few months after senescence.

Habitat: Plants thrive in moist sites, and other disturbed grassy places, as well as in savannas, abandoned fields, pastures, degraded meadows, woodland margins, paths and roadsides, turf, wastelands and occasionally in cultivated land. A very common winter annual weed in warm-season turfgrasses.

Distribution: Found throughout the United States and Canada. Native to Europe and western Asia.

Similar Species: **Hop clover (*Trifolium aureum* Pollich) and small (or low) hop clover (*Trifolium dubium* Sibth.)** have similar foliage, flowers, and habitats. Unlike large hop clover, the middle leaflet of small hop clover and hop clover have petioles that are no longer (generally sessile) than the lateral leaflets. Small hop clover has a globose inflorescence with 5–10 flowers per head; hop clover and large hop clover have more than 20 flowers per head. **Black medic (*Medicago lupulina*)** has similar flowers and foliage, most resembling small hop clover, although its coiled, black seedpods are quite different from the clover species. Also, black medic is a summer annual, flowering in mid- to late summer, whereas the hop clovers typically flower in the spring. **See Table 7 for a comparison of weedy, trifoliolate legumes and woodsorrels.**

J. Neal

Large hop clover habit

J. Neal

Small hop clover seedling

J. Neal

Small hop clover leaf

J. Neal

Flowers: *left*, large hop clover; *right*, small hop clover

J. Neal

Large hop clover flowering shoot

J. Neal

Small hop clover flowering shoot

J. O'Brien © 2007 UC Regents

Large hop clover seeds (indistinguishable from low hop clover seeds)

White clover (*Trifolium repens* L.)

Synonyms: Dutch clover, honeysuckle clover, white trefoil, purplewort

General Description: A mat-forming **perennial** with **low, creeping, branched stems** that root at the nodes, trifoliolate leaves, and white flowers.

Propagation / Phenology: Reproduction is **by seeds** and **stolons. Seed coats are very hard, ensuring extended dormancy.** Seeds germinate under cool, moist conditions in spring, early summer, or early fall. Stolons can spread at a rate of 18 cm per year. Clones can persist indefinitely even though few plant parts survive more than a year.

Seedling: Cotyledons are smooth and spatulate (6–7 mm long), with blades tapering into the petiole. The **first leaf is simple** (no leaflets), rounded to broadly oval, truncated at the base. **Subsequent leaves are trifoliolate** (3 leaflets), alternate, smooth, grayish-green on the lower surface, green on the upper surface, usually with a light green splotch near the base of each leaflet. Leaflet margins have small teeth; apexes are very slightly indented. Petioles have 2 small, membrane-like stipules at the base.

Mature Plant: **Stems are prostrate and rooting at the nodes**, smooth or only sparsely hairy. **Leaflets resemble those of the seedling**, broadly elliptic to egg-shaped (1–3.5 cm long) and widest at the apex. The apex is rounded, with an indentation at the tip. **Petioles are long** (3–8 cm) and perpendicularly upright from the prostrate stems. Two stipules are appressed to the petiole to form a pale, tubular, clasping sheath.

Roots and Underground Structures: Plants spread by creeping aboveground stems (stolons) that root at the nodes.

Flowers and Fruit: **Flowers** are produced throughout the summer in **rounded heads** (1.5–2 cm wide) at the end of long (to 7 cm) flower stalks (peduncles) that arise from the leaf axils. **Heads are an aggregate** of 20–40 individual flowers, each 8–10 mm long, **white or sometimes pinkish,** with minute, greenish veins. Individual flowers are on 6-mm stalks (pedicels). Flowers turn brown and persist while the fruiting pods (legumes) develop. Fruits are 4–5 mm long, 3–6 seeded. Seeds are approximately 1 mm long, yellow to brown, kidney-shaped, or irregularly rounded, somewhat flattened.

Postsenescence Characteristics: Foliage may discolor and decompose over the winter, but stolons persist and produce new shoots in early spring.

Habitat: White clover is a weed of turfgrass, landscapes, orchards, and nursery crops. Because it tolerates close mowing, it is a common weed of high-maintenance turfgrass. It grows on many soil types, especially clays, and tolerates a wide range of soil acidity.

Distribution: Found throughout most of North America.

Similar Species: **See Table 7 for a comparison of weedy, trifoliolate legumes and woodsorrels. Strawberry clover (*Trifolium fragiferum* L.)** is less frequently a turfgrass weed but is almost identical to white clover. It can be distinguished by its rosy flowers, which appear swollen when mature, and by the lack of a whitish band typically present on the leaflets of white clover. **Alsike clover (*Trifolium hybridum* L.)** and **red clover (*Trifolium pratense* L.)** are similar but have more upright, clump-forming growth habits and generally larger, more elongated leaflets than white clover. Alsike clover has similar flower color, white to tinged pink, but red clover flowers are distinctly pink to red. Unlike white clover, **black medic (*Medicago lupulina*)** and **hop clovers (*Trifolium* spp.)** have a stalked central leaflet and yellow flowers. The **woodsorrels (*Oxalis* spp.)** are also trifoliolate, but a prominent indentation at the apex of the individual leaflets produces heart-shaped leaflets.

White clover habit (J. Neal); *inset*, white clover leaf (J. DiTomaso)

Cotyledons and first leaves of white clover

Red clover inflorescence

Left to right: strawberry clover, white clover, alsike clover, and red clover

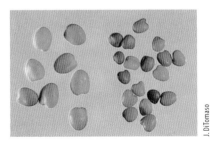

Left, strawberry clover seeds, 1.5 mm; *right*, white clover seeds, 1.0 mm (red clover seeds are shown on p. 343)

Vetches (*Vicia* spp.)

GENERAL DESCRIPTION: The weedy vetches are trailing, **vine-like, herbaceous annuals** or perennials that form sprawling mats or envelop other plants. **Leaves are alternate, pinnately compound**, with a terminal leaflet modified into a **twining tendril**.

PROPAGATION / PHENOLOGY: Life cycles and season of emergence vary with species. All propagate by seeds.

SEEDLING: Cotyledons remain within the seed coat below the soil surface. **First leaves lack tendrils** and have **1–2 (sometimes more) pairs of elliptic or linear leaflets.**

MATURE PLANT: **Older leaves develop tendrils and have many leaflet pairs.** Stem bases can become somewhat woody with age.

ROOTS AND UNDERGROUND STRUCTURES: Branched, fibrous root system.

FLOWERS AND FRUIT: Flowers and fruiting pods differ in number per cluster and in color.

SPECIES DESCRIPTIONS:

Bird vetch (*Vicia cracca* L.): Perennial with **spreading rhizomes** and **trailing or climbing stems** (1–2 m long). **Leaflets are linear** to narrowly oblong, pointed at the tip (1–3 cm long), **5–11 pairs per leaf. Flowers** (July to August) are **bluish-purple** (occasionally white), 8–13 mm long, **20–50 flowered** on 1-sided long-stalked racemes. **Pods are light brown** at maturity, **flat,** 2–3 cm long. Found throughout the northern United States and southern Canada.

Narrowleaf vetch (*Vicia sativa* L. ssp. *nigra* (L.) Ehrh.) (also known as *Vicia angustifolia* L.): A **summer or winter annual** with erect to ascending or climbing stems (1 m long). **Leaflets are linear** to narrowly elliptic, 1.5–3 cm long, **3–5 pairs per leaf. Flowers** (July to August) are **blue or violet** (occasionally white), 1–1.8 cm long, in pairs arising from the upper leaf axils. **Pods** are 4 cm long, **dark brown** to blackish at maturity. Found throughout the United States and southern Canada. **Common vetch (*Vicia sativa* L.) is similar** to narrowleaf vetch but has larger flowers (1.8–3 cm long) and light brown pods at maturity.

Sparrow vetch (*Vicia tetrasperma* (L.) Schreb.) (also known as four-seed vetch): A **fine-textured, climbing annual** with long stems (30–60 cm), prostrate at the base and ascending at the tip. **Leaflets are linear-oblong** to narrowly elliptic (1–2 cm long), **2–5 pairs per leaf**. Seedlings emerge mostly in early spring and fall, some in summer. **Flowers** (June to September) are **light purple** to white, 3–7 mm long, 1–6 flowers (usually in pairs) on 1–3 cm stalks (peduncles) from the upper leaf axils. **Pods are smooth** and 4-seeded. Found throughout the eastern and southeastern United States; also in northern California.

Hairy vetch (*Vicia villosa* Roth): A **summer or winter annual, or biennial,** with **hairy stems** (1 m long). **Leaflets are narrowly oblong** to linear-lanceolate, 1–2.5 cm long, **5–10 pairs per leaf. Flowers** (June to August) are **reddish-purple** to violet, 1.5–1.8 cm long, **10–14(–30) flowers** on a long-stalked, 1-sided raceme. Fruits are 2–3 cm long pods. Found throughout the northern United States and southern Canada, as far west as California.

POSTSENESCENCE CHARACTERISTICS: Mat of dead, dark brown stems and occasionally leaves remains entangled around other plants.

HABITAT: All species are weeds of waste places, roadsides, meadows, pastures, and perennial horticultural crops, including landscapes. Hairy vetch and narrowleaf vetch are common weeds in fall-sown winter annual cereals. Vetches are often found on, but are not limited to, sandy or gravelly soils. Some species are used as cover crops.

DISTRIBUTION: Varies with species.

SIMILAR SPECIES: **Trailing crownvetch (*Securigera varia* (L.) Lassen;** syn.: *Coronilla varia* L.) is a perennial similar in appearance; however, its leaves lack the terminal tendril, and its flowers are arranged in an umbel. Trailing crownvetch is often planted as a cover along highways and on embankments.

Bird vetch flowering shoot

R. Uva

Narrowleaf vetch foliage and flower

J. Neal

Immature sparrow vetch habit

J. Neal

349

J. Neal

Sparrow vetch seedling

J. Neal

Seedling narrowleaf vetch with immature
and mature leaves

J. DiTomaso

Hairy vetch seedling

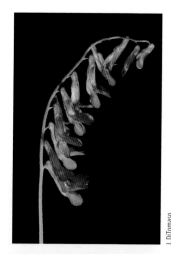

J. DiTomaso

Hairy vetch flowers

J. Neal

Narrowleaf vetch flower

A. DiTommaso

Trailing crownvetch flower

J. Neal

Narrowleaf vetch seedpods

J. DiTomaso

Hairy vetch seedpods

J. Neal

Sparrow vetch foliage, flowers, and fruit

Left, hairy vetch seed, 4.0 mm; *center top*, sparrow vetch seeds, 1.8 mm; *center bottom*, common vetch seed, 4.0 mm; *right*, bird vetch seeds, 2.1 mm

J. DiTomaso

Redstem filaree (*Erodium cicutarium* (L.) L'Hér. ex Ait.)

SYNONYMS: filaree, common storksbill, heronsbill, alfilaria, pin-weed, pin-grass

GENERAL DESCRIPTION: A **winter annual** that overwinters as a **prostrate basal rosette of fern-like leaves**. Stems elongate the following spring and can reach 10–50 cm in height. **Leaves and stems are often reddish.**

PROPAGATION / PHENOLOGY: Reproduction is **by seeds**; seeds germinate in late summer, early autumn, or spring.

SEEDLING: **Cotyledons are deeply 3–4 lobed**, the center lobe the largest. **Young leaves** are alternate or opposite and also **deeply lobed or cut**. Stems and leaves are bristly hairy. **Young plants develop into rosettes the first year.**

MATURE PLANT: **Stems** are low, hairy, sparsely leaved, and **develop from a prostrate basal rosette. Basal leaves** are petioled, **hairy, compound (3–9 leaflets)**, 3–20 cm long by 0.5–5 cm wide, dark green (with some red coloration), and lanceolate. **Leaflets are deeply cut**, nearly to the midvein. **Stem leaves are reduced** but also **compound and deeply cut**, sessile, 1–2.5 cm long. Stipules are present.

ROOTS AND UNDERGROUND STRUCTURES: Coarsely branched, shallow taproot with secondary fibrous root system.

FLOWERS AND FRUIT: Flowers are produced primarily from April to June but occasionally throughout the summer. **Flowers are in umbel-like clusters of 2–8**, each on a 1–2 cm stalk (pedicel). The flower clusters are attached to a long, leafless stalk (peduncle) arising from the stem leaf axils. The sepals (5) are 5–7 mm long and bristle-tipped. The **petals (5) are pink to purple**, 5–8 mm long. Each flower (1–1.3 cm wide) produces a **beak-like fruit** that separates into 5 sections (mericarps) when mature. Each section consists of a **seed and a spirally twisted, hairy tail** (style) that coils under dry conditions and uncoils when moist. Seeds are cylindrical, approximately 5 mm long, hairy, light brown to orangish. Each plant can produce up to 600 seeds.

POSTSENESCENCE CHARACTERISTICS: Leafless stems with characteristic fruit persist for only a short time.

HABITAT: Redstem filaree is a weed of many perennial crops including nursery crops, orchards, and Christmas trees. It can also be a problem in turfgrass and landscapes. It is usually found on dry, sandy soil.

DISTRIBUTION: Established throughout the United States.

SIMILAR SPECIES: **Whitestem filaree (*Erodium moschatum* (L.) L'Hér. ex Ait.)** has much broader, longer compound leaves (up to 30 cm) and leaflets much less deeply cut than redstem filaree. Whitestem filaree stems are whitish and larger (60 cm tall). Flowers and seedheads of **Carolina geranium (*Geranium carolinianum*)** resemble redstem filaree, but its leaves are rounded and palmately veined. In addition, the fruit beaks of Carolina geranium are outwardly coiled at maturity, whereas redstem filaree beaks are tightly twisted.

Redstem filaree habit

J. DiTomaso

Redstem filaree flowers and fruit

J. DiTomaso

Redstem filaree seedlings

R. Uva

Whitestem filaree leaf and fruit

J. DiTomaso

Redstem filaree stem with foliage, flowers, and fruit

R. Uva

Top, redstem filaree seeds, 5.5 mm (seed without stalk); *bottom*, whitestem filaree seeds, 5.9 mm (not including stalk)

J. DiTomaso

Carolina geranium (*Geranium carolinianum* L.)

SYNONYMS: wild geranium, Carolina crane's-bill, crane's-bill

GENERAL DESCRIPTION: A winter annual, occasionally summer annual or biennial. Leaves initially form a branching **basal rosette**, the stems subsequently elongate, freely branch, and reach a height of 10–80 cm.

PROPAGATION / PHENOLOGY: Reproduction is **by seeds**; seeds germinate in late summer, early autumn, or spring.

SEEDLING: Seedlings develop into a **basal rosette** of leaves. Hypocotyls are brownish-pink, with short, downward-pointing hairs. Cotyledons are broadly kidney-shaped to square-oval; the apex is indented (emarginate) and has a small point (mucronate). Cotyledons are heart-shaped at the base, green above, and pink below with short hairs on both surfaces. **Young leaves** are alternate, **palmately veined**, with brownish-pink petioles that are covered with downward-pointing hairs. **Two stipules** are present **at the base of the petiole.** The leaf blades are green on the upper surface, often tinged pink below, and have short hairs on both surfaces. The **margins of the blade are deeply toothed or lobed.**

MATURE PLANT: **Elongated stems are erect**, branching near the base. Stems are densely hairy and greenish-pink to red. **Leaves** are hairy on both surfaces, rounded to kidney-shaped, and **deeply palmately divided into usually 5 segments. Each segment is also lobed or coarsely toothed.** Leaves are 2.5–7 cm wide, on long petioles subtended by stipules. Leaves are usually alternate near the base and opposite above. Leaves and stems are reddish in sunny, low-fertility, or dry sites.

ROOTS AND UNDERGROUND STRUCTURES: Fibrous roots with a shallow taproot.

FLOWERS AND FRUIT: Flowers are present from May to August. Two or more flowers are clustered at the tip of stems and branches arising from the upper leaf axils. Sepals (5) are awl-shaped and awn-tipped, about equal in length to the 5 (1 cm long) **whitish-pink to purple petals. Fruits are produced at the base of long styles, giving the entire structure the appearance of a crane's bill.** At maturity, the fruit splits into 5 curled sections (mericarps), each bearing 1 seed. Seeds are 1.5–2 mm long, oval to oblong, light to dark brown, with a conspicuous network of veins.

POSTSENESCENCE CHARACTERISTICS: Plants overwinter as rosettes. Plant parts do not persist after fruiting.

HABITAT: Carolina geranium is a weed of turfgrass, landscapes, orchards, and nursery crops. Also found in wooded areas, fields, and roadsides, it generally grows on dry, sandy, and nutrient-poor soils.

DISTRIBUTION: Found throughout the United States; most troublesome in the southern and western states.

SIMILAR SPECIES: **Cutleaf geranium (*Geranium dissectum* L.)** is very similar and distributed throughout the eastern United States, but has violet-pink flowers, 1–2 per cluster. **Dovefoot geranium or cranesbill (*Geranium molle* L.)** and **smallflower geranium (*Geranium pusillum* L.)** are also winter annuals or biennials with rounded leaves, not as deeply divided as those of Carolina geranium or cutleaf geranium. They can also be distinguished from Carolina geranium because their sepals are not awn-tipped, flowers are red-violet, and seeds are smooth. The mature foliage of Carolina geranium may resemble that of **tall buttercup (*Ranunculus acris*)**, but tall buttercup has showy, yellow flowers.

J. Neal

Carolina geranium habit

J. DiTomaso

Cutleaf geranium flowering
and fruiting stem

R. Uva

Smallflower geranium rosette

J. Neal and J. DiTomaso (inset)

Carolina geranium foliage, flowers,
and fruit (inset)

J. DiTomaso

Dovefoot geranium leaves and flower

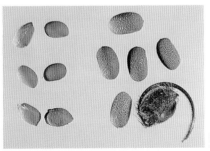

J. DiTomaso

Left, dovefoot geranium seeds, 1.3 mm;
right, Carolina geranium seeds, 2.0 mm

Common St. Johnswort (*Hypericum perforatum* L.)

Synonyms: *Hypericum marylandicum*, goatweed, klamathweed, St. John's-wort, tipton weed

General Description: Erect perennial to 1.2 m tall, with rhizomes and **showy, bright yellow flowers that have numerous stamens**. Leaves are dotted with tiny translucent and black oil glands that contain hypericin, a red pigment that is toxic to livestock when consumed in quantity, especially to animals with light-colored skin. In herbal medicine, hypericin is the antidepressant ingredient in St. Johnswort remedies and is sometimes cultivated as a crop.

Propagation / Phenology: **Reproduces by seeds and vegetatively from rhizomes.** Seed and capsules typically disperse short distances or longer distances by water. Germination occurs autumn through spring. Brief exposure to fire often stimulates germination.

Seedling: Cotyledons lanceolate to ovate, 1.5–3 mm long by 1–2 mm wide. Subsequent leaves opposite, oval to elliptic, increasingly larger. As in mature leaves, the underside of leaf margins dotted with a few elevated, black glands.

Mature Plant: Stems highly branched near the top, glabrous, often reddish, with black glands along 2 longitudinal ridges. The main stem or stems usually have numerous sterile shoots 2–10 cm long in the lower leaf axils. When young, these axillary shoots (or fascicles) make the leaves appear whorled. **Leaves opposite, sessile**, elliptic-oblong to linear, 1–3 cm long, tip rounded, glabrous, 3–5 veined from the base, **dotted with numerous, tiny, translucent glands** that are visible when a leaf is held up to the light; margins rolled under (revolute).

Roots and Underground Structures: Taproot stout, with many-branched, lateral roots, to approximately 1.5 m deep. Rhizomes develop just below the soil surface from the crown and can extend outward to about 0.5 m. New shoots grow from the crown and rhizomes in early spring. Fragmented rhizomes can develop into new plants.

Flowers and Fruit: Flowers throughout the summer. Flowers are bright yellow, approximately 2 cm in diameter, clustered at the stem tips. Petals 5, separate, 8–12 mm long, typically **dotted with black glands along the margins** (visible under 10x magnification). Sepals 5, linear-lanceolate, 4–5 mm long, much shorter than petals. **Stamens yellow, numerous.** Plants typically do not flower the first year. Capsules ovoid, 3-chambered, sticky-glandular, 5–10 mm long, with 3 persistent styles 3–10 mm long, open longitudinally to release seed. Seed shiny black to brown, nearly cylindrical, 1 mm long, densely pitted, often coated with gelatinous material from the capsule that aids with dispersal.

Postsenescence Characteristics: Dried stems often have a reddish appearance well into the winter.

Habitat: Not a significant or common weed of most agronomic crops but often found on poorly maintained pastures. Typically associated with waste areas, field edges, roadsides, and forest clearings or burned areas.

Distribution: Native to Europe, and now has worldwide distribution. Found throughout the Northeast and mid-Atlantic states.

Similar Species: **Garden or yellow loosestrife (*Lysimachia vulgaris* L.)** is an erect, showy, yellow-flowered rhizomatous perennial to 1 m tall. Native of Eurasia and is particularly invasive in riparian and wetland sites. Unlike common St. Johnswort, it has pubescent foliage, has much larger leaves (7–12 cm long), and the base of the petals are fused.

Common St. Johnswort habit

Common St. Johnswort
seedling

Common St. Johnswort leaf with dotted glands

Common St. Johnswort flower

Garden loosestrife flowers

Common St. Johnswort seeds

357

Ground ivy (*Glechoma hederacea* L.)

SYNONYMS: *Nepeta hederacea*, gill-over-the-ground, creeping Charlie, cats-foot, field balm

GENERAL DESCRIPTION: A **perennial** with long (20–75 cm), **creeping, square stems that root at the nodes** and form dense prostrate patches. The foliage emits a strong **mint-like odor** when bruised, uprooted, or mowed.

PROPAGATION / PHENOLOGY: Reproduction is primarily by **creeping stems** that root at the node and **less commonly by seeds**. Infestations occur primarily by encroachment of vegetative fragments from adjacent areas.

SEEDLING: Cotyledons are short-oblong to broadly spatulate, curving abruptly into a long stalk. **Young leaves are opposite**, shiny on the upper surface, smooth to minutely hairy, **kidney-shaped to rounded** or heart-shaped (1–4 cm in diameter), with **broad, rounded teeth** on the margin. Seedlings are rarely encountered.

MATURE PLANT: **Stems are lax, square**, mostly smooth or with backwardly directed, short, stiff hairs. **Stems trail along the ground, rooting at the nodes. Leaves are similar to those of the seeding** and are on long, horizontal, petioles (3–5 cm). Blades are prominently palmately veined.

ROOTS AND UNDERGROUND STRUCTURES: Fibrous roots are produced at the base of the plant and from nodes on trailing stems. **Rhizomes are also present.**

FLOWERS AND FRUIT: **Flowers** are produced as early as April to June on stems that are shorter and more ascending than the long and trailing vegetative stems. Flowers are 1–2 cm long on short flower stalks arranged **in clusters of 2–3 in the upper leaf axils**. Sepals are fused into a hairy, **5-lobed tube. Petals are tubular, purplish-blue, and 2-lipped,** the upper lip 2-cleft, the lower lip 3-lobed. Fruit are egg-shaped nutlets (<1 mm long), smooth, elliptic, brown, flat on 2 sides and round on the third side.

POSTSENESCENCE CHARACTERISTICS: Plants remain green throughout the winter.

HABITAT: Ground ivy is a common weed of turfgrass and landscapes as well as perennial fruit crops. It is most commonly found in damp, shady areas but can tolerate full sunlight.

DISTRIBUTION: Most common throughout the northeastern and north-central United States but also found in the southern states.

SIMILAR SPECIES: Ground ivy can look similar to **slender speedwell (*Veronica filiformis*)** when leaf size is reduced by stress or close mowing, but it has square stems, unlike the round stems of slender speedwell. Although **henbit (*Lamium amplexicaule*)** can sometimes resemble ground ivy, its stems do not creep along the ground or root at the nodes. The leaf shape of ground ivy leads to confusion with **bristly mallow (*Modiola caroliniana*)** and **common mallow (*Malva neglecta*)**, but the mallows have alternate leaves with pointed teeth and rounded stems. **Catnip (*Nepeta cataria* L.)** is also a perennial in the mint family but is more erect and often has larger lanceolate to ovate leaves (to 7.5 cm long). Ground ivy is prostrate with leaves that are round or kidney-shaped. In addition, the inflorescence of catnip is a dense, terminal spike of white flowers with purple spotting. Catnip was widely cultivated as an ornamental but has escaped to become weedy in streambanks, pastures, fencerows, rights-of-way, and disturbed areas. Found throughout the region.

Ground ivy leaves and stems

Ground ivy flowering stem

Catnip flowering stem

Ground ivy seedling

Ground ivy seeds (1.5 mm long) and pod

Henbit (*Lamium amplexicaule* L.)

S<small>YNONYMS</small>: dead nettle, blind nettle, bee nettle

G<small>ENERAL</small> D<small>ESCRIPTION</small>: A **winter annual** branching at the base (10–40 cm tall).

P<small>ROPAGATION</small> / P<small>HENOLOGY</small>: Reproduction is **by seeds**; seedlings emerge from moist, cool soil in early spring and fall. Self-pollinated flowers may produce seeds without opening (cleistogamy).

S<small>EEDLING</small>: Hypocotyls initially are green but become purple with age. Cotyledons are round to oblong on hairy petioles. The base of the cotyledon blade is notched where it meets the petiole. **Young leaves** have petioles and are **opposite**, with **soft hairs** on the dark green upper surface and along the veins of the lower surface. The **upper surface is prominently veined and crinkled.** Leaf blades have **2–4 large, rounded teeth on each side. Stems are square**, green to purple, with basally pointing hairs.

M<small>ATURE</small> P<small>LANT</small>: **Mature stems** are square, green to purple, nearly hairless, prostrate or curved at the base, with an **erect or ascending tip. Leaves** (1.5–2 cm long) are **palmately veined. Lower leaves are petiolated**, rounded to heart-shaped, with rounded teeth. **Upper leaves are sessile, deeply lobed, encircling the stem at the base.** In the flowering portions, stem internodes are shorter and leaves can look whorled.

R<small>OOTS AND</small> U<small>NDERGROUND</small> S<small>TRUCTURES</small>: Fibrous root system. Stems root where the lower nodes contact the soil surface.

F<small>LOWERS AND</small> F<small>RUIT</small>: **Showy pink to purple flowers** are produced in early spring but may appear sporadically from March to November. **Flowers are in whorls in the axils of the sessile upper leaves.** Sepals are united into a tube with 5 teeth; petals are pink to purple, united into a 2-lipped tube, 1–1.5 cm long. Fruit (nutlets) are egg-shaped to oblong, 3-angled, brown with white spots, and 1.5–2 mm long. Four nutlets, each with 1 seed, are enclosed within the persistent sepals. Each plant can produce 200 seeds.

P<small>OSTSENESCENCE</small> C<small>HARACTERISTICS</small>: Henbit and other members of the mint family have persistent square stems and fused, persistent sepals (in whorls at the nodes) that often contain the seeds. Henbit may overwinter as a seedling.

H<small>ABITAT</small>: More common in warm-season than cool-season turf; also found in landscapes, orchards, gardens, nurseries, winter grain crops, and other winter annual crops. Thrives in early spring and fall on cool, rich, fertile soils.

D<small>ISTRIBUTION</small>: Found throughout the United States; most common in eastern North America and on the West Coast.

S<small>IMILAR</small> S<small>PECIES</small>: **Purple deadnettle**, also known as red deadnettle (***Lamium purpureum*** **L.**), is a winter annual that flowers in early spring. The upper leaves and square stems are conspicuously red. The leaves are more triangular and less deeply lobed than those of henbit and differ also in that the upper leaves are petiolated and crowded at the end of the branches. Purple deadnettle flowers are also lighter purple than henbit flowers. **Spotted deadnettle (*Lamium maculatum* L.)** is a perennial ground cover with white markings on its leaves and square stems. It has escaped cultivation to become a weed in some areas. **Persian speedwell (*Veronica persica* Poir.)** can resemble henbit, especially as a young seedling or in dense stands. Leaves of Persian speedwell seedlings are similar to henbit leaves but are more triangular, and the stems are round.

J. Neal

Henbit habit

J. DiTomaso

Henbit seedling

R. Uva

Purple deadnettle habit

J. Neal

eft, henbit; *right*, purple deadnettle

M. Bertone

Left, purple deadnettle seeds, 1.9 mm; *right*, henbit seeds, 1.8 mm

Perilla mint (*Perilla frutescens* (L.) Britton)

Synonyms: beefsteak plant, perilla, purple mint, shiso, and others

General Description: An upright, branched, **summer annual**, to 1 m in height, with **square stems**, broad **opposite leaves** with **prominent veins** and **toothed leaf margins**. Stems and leaf veins are often purple tinted; leaves may be green to purple. Several selections are grown as culinary herbs, for seed-oil extraction, or for their ornamental foliage. Plants have a distinct aroma different from other culinary mints. All parts of the plant produce perilla ketone, which is **toxic to cattle**, horses, and other farm animals, causing emphysema when sufficient quantities are ingested. Though generally not palatable, cattle will feed on perilla mint when forage is limited or when present in hay.

Propagation / Phenology: Reproduces **by seeds**. Seedlings emerge in the early spring and begin flowering in early to mid-summer. Plants continue to produce flowers and seeds until frost.

Seedling: Cotyledons are nearly semi-circular to kidney-shaped. First leaves are opposite, sessile, or on very short petioles. Leaf blades are broadly ovate, with shallowly toothed margins, prominent veins, fine hairs, and the midvein is often purple.

Mature Plant: Mature plants have a strongly **upright growth** habit with **ascending branches**. Stems are pubescent, less so at the base, often purple, square and ribbed, and may be woody at the base. Leaves opposite with pubescent petioles about half the length of the leaf blades. Leaf blades are **broadly ovate**, 5–10 cm long, ½ to ¾ as wide as long, with **prominent veins and toothed leaf margins**. Variety 'crispum' has pointed and curled lobes. Leaves may be green, slightly tinted purple, or deep maroon.

Roots and Underground Structures: Coarsely branched, fibrous root system.

Flowers and Fruit: Flowers on axillary racemes, to 10 cm long. Petals tubular, white to lavender, 2-lipped, to 1 cm long. The persistent pubescent sepals form a distinctly 2-lipped tube. Inflorescence and fruit are persistent. Seeds are brown to reddish, round to oval, and 1.2–2 mm in diameter.

Postsenescence Characteristics: Stems, inflorescence, and sepals (calyx) are persistent through winter.

Habitat: Occurs in pastures, roadsides, and woodland edges. Reported to be invasive in riparian habitats and is becoming more common in urban landscapes where it has escaped cultivation. Toxic to cattle, making it a concern in pastures and hay crops.

Distribution: A native of East Asia, perilla mint is now distributed throughout the eastern half of the United States and southern Canada.

Similar Species: Resembles **stinging nettle (*Urtica dioica*)** but lacks the stinging hairs on the stems. Additionally, when in flower, stinging nettle flowers lack the distinct tubular, 2-lipped fruit. Young seedlings may resemble **galinsogas (*Galinsoga* spp.)**, but galinsoga stems are not square. Plants also resemble **garden coleus (*Plectranthus scutellarioides* (L.) R. Br.)**, but coleus does not persist as a weed.

Perilla mint plant

Perilla mint inflorescence

Perilla mint cotyledons

Perilla mint seedlings

Perilla mint stem

Perilla mint seeds

Healall (*Prunella vulgaris* L.)

SYNONYMS: *Brunella vulgaris*, self-heal, carpenters-weed

GENERAL DESCRIPTION: A branched, **prostrate, stoloniferous perennial** that spreads to form dense patches but can grow erect to 5–60 cm tall in unmowed areas.

PROPAGATION / PHENOLOGY: Reproduction is **by seeds** and **creeping stems that root** at the nodes.

SEEDLING: Cotyledons are ovate, widest toward the base, notched at the apex, with lobed margins pointing toward the hypocotyl. **Young leaves are egg-shaped**, **pointed** at the apex, with entire or round-toothed (crenate) margins. Young plants branch at the base; adventitious roots are produced at the nodes.

MATURE PLANT: **Stems are square**, hairy when young, becoming smooth with age. **Leaves are opposite**, ovate (2–9 cm long by 0.7–4 cm wide), and have petioles. Leaf blades are sparsely hairy to smooth, broadest at the base, and taper to a rounded tip. Margins are obscurely round-toothed or untoothed. **Lower leaves are wider** and more rounded at the base than the upper leaves. **Upper leaves may be sessile.** Drought, low fertility, and mowing reduce leaf size and internode length. Shade and infrequent mowing result in larger leaves, longer petioles, and larger internodes.

ROOTS AND UNDERGROUND STRUCTURES: **Creeping stems root freely at the nodes**, producing a shallow but aggressive fibrous root system.

FLOWERS AND FRUIT: **Flowers** are present from June to September **in dense spikes at the end of ascending stems**. Sepals are green or purple, 7–10 mm long, and fused into a toothed tube. **Petals** are also **fused into a tube**, **pale violet to deep-purple** (rarely pink or white), 1–2 cm long, and 2-lipped. Flowers are sessile and subtended by large, hairy, green to purple bracts. Fruits are slightly flattened nutlets (4 per flower) approximately 1.5 mm long. Each pear-shaped, brown nutlet encloses 1 seed.

POSTSENESCENCE CHARACTERISTICS: Plants remain green and persist year-round. Flower spikes, bracts, sepals, and nutlets remain for an extended period.

HABITAT: Primarily a weed of turfgrass, healall is found on shady, moist, or sandy, drought-prone areas. It frequently grows in recently cleared woodland areas, where it prefers shady, moist sites. It is rarely a problem in crops because it does not tolerate cultivation or intense crop management.

DISTRIBUTION: Found throughout the United States; common in the northeastern United States and southern Canada.

SIMILAR SPECIES: **Creeping thyme (*Thymus praecox* Opiz. ssp. *arcticus* (Dur.) Jalas)** is similar in habit but has more-slender stems and smaller, oblong to oval leaves. Additionally, creeping thyme flowers are 4–6 mm long, about half the length of healall flowers. **Purple deadnettle (*Lamium purpureum* L.)** (also called red deadnettle) is a winter annual that flowers in early spring. Upper leaves and stems are conspicuously red, and leaves are triangular and crowded at the end of the branches. The upper leaves of **henbit (*Lamium amplexicaule*)** encircle the stem, whereas those of healall are petiolated.

Healall habit in turfgrass

J. Neal

Healall flowering stem

J. DiTomaso

Healall seedling

A. DiTommaso

Healall seeds, 1.7 mm

J. DiTomaso

Florida betony (*Stachys floridana* Shuttlw. ex Benth.)

Synonyms: Florida hedgenettle, rattlesnake weed, wild artichoke

General Description: Florida betony is an aggressive, **rhizomatous, and tuberous perennial** with erect, **square stems**; opposite leaves, triangular in outline with toothed margins. It has slender underground stems (rhizomes) with segmented white tubers that resemble the tip of a rattlesnake tail. The tubers are edible. It is considered native to Florida but is **a regulated species** in some other states.

Propagation / Phenology: Reproduces primarily vegetatively by rhizomes and tubers, but viable seeds are produced. Considered a **winter perennial**, tubers sprout in early autumn, grow vigorously until early spring, flowers in mid- to late spring, and dies back during the summer. From tubers planted in early summer, new sprouts emerged in the fall over 2 m from the tuber placement. Long-distance spread is presumed to occur with contaminated nursery plants.

Seedling: None have been observed, but they are assumed to occur. Young plants typically are from rhizomes or tubers and resemble mature plants.

Mature Plant: Stems erect, square, and branched, often hairy. Plant height is variable, and when grown in isolation plants are shorter in height, but when growing within other vegetation, stems can reach 1 m. Plants also tolerate mowing. Plants remain vegetative until mid- to late spring when flowering is initiated. Leaves are opposite; petioles 1–3 cm long; leaf blades elongated triangular up to 5 cm long by 2.5 cm wide; margins are shallowly lobed. The leaf base may be heart-shaped or blunt; leaf tips taper to a blunt point.

Roots and Underground Structures: Plants produce long, **white rhizomes and tubers** throughout the growing season. In well-drained soils, rhizomes reach more than 30 cm deep. The distinctive **tubers are segmented** and resemble a white rattlesnake's rattle, usually 3–10 cm long (rarely up to 3 m) by 1–1.5 cm in diameter.

Flowers and Fruit: In mid- to late spring, lavender to purple flowers occur in clusters of 3–6 in the upper leaf axils. The flowers are similar to that of many mints. Sepals are fused, forming a tube up to 5 mm long, with 5 lobes. Petals are fused, 2-lipped, and approximately 1 cm long. The dry fruit (schizocarp) splits into 2 halves, each about 1 cm long, containing 1 mm long seeds.

Postsenescence Characteristics: Plants do not persist through summer.

Habitat: Most commonly found in turf or landscape plantings and nearby roadsides or disturbed areas, where they are considered difficult to control. Rarely found in agronomic crops.

Distribution: Considered native to Florida but has spread throughout the southeastern United States north to Virginia.

Similar Species: Flowers are very similar to other members of the mint family, but the presence of rhizomes and unique tubers distinguish this species. **Catnip (*Nepeta cataria* L.)** is a rhizomatous perennial in the mint family, with square stems, and lanceolate leaves with shallowly lobed margins, but it lacks the distinct tubers formed by Florida betony. Also, catnip emerges in the spring and senesces in the fall; in contrast, Florida betony emerges in the fall and senesces in early summer.

Florida betony plants in spring

Florida betony square stem

Florida betony flowers

Florida betony rhizome and tubers

Catnip leaves

Purple loosestrife (*Lythrum salicaria* L.)

Synonyms: purple lythrum, bouquet-violet

General Description: A many-branched (as many as 30–50 branches), **erect** (1–2 m tall), **perennial** that forms a **large, tough root crown** with age. **Large colonies develop near moist or marshy sites** and are particularly conspicuous when **showy, purple-magenta flowers** bloom from July through September.

Propagation / Phenology: Reproduction is **by seeds and thick, fleshy roots that produce adventitious shoots**. Plants can produce seed in their first growing season. Seeds germinate in late spring or early summer. After mowing, **stem fragments can root** to produce new plants.

Seedling: Seedlings are very small and resemble the adult plants. Young plants also develop from root buds or the root crown. Leaves are lanceolate and opposite. Shoots emerging from the roots or crown lack cotyledons.

Mature Plant: **Stems are square, sometimes 6-sided.** Stems and leaves either lack hairs or, more often, have short, upward-pointing hairs. **Leaves are sessile,** lanceolate to linear, 3–10 cm long, **opposite or in whorls of 3.** Larger leaves are heart-shaped at the base.

Roots and Underground Structures: **Thick, fleshy roots** and a fibrous root system are produced. Forms a **large, woody crown** with age.

Flowers and Fruit: **Purple-magenta flowers** are produced from July to September in **conspicuous 10–40 cm long terminal spikes.** Fused sepals form a tube surrounding the ovary. Petals (5–7) and stamens (10–14) are attached to the top of the fused sepals. Numerous, small, reddish-brown seeds (1 mm long) are contained within the capsules. A single plant can produce more than 2 million seeds a year.

Postsenescence Characteristics: Foliage turns red at the end of the season. Dead, brown stalks persist through winter, with capsules arranged in spire-shaped spikes.

Habitat: Purple loosestrife was introduced from Europe and has become widely distributed in wet or marshy sites. It is **a major weed of wetlands and natural areas,** where it displaces native vegetation and wildlife. It is also a weed of roadsides, canals, ditches, spring-flooded pastures, and cranberry bogs. Although purple loosestrife is **classified as a noxious weed in many states,** it continues to be sold in the nursery and landscape trade.

Distribution: Common in the temperate regions of North America, including southern Canada and the northern and northeastern United States to Virginia and Missouri; also in scattered areas along the Pacific Coast.

Similar Species: **Early in the season, fringed willowherb (*Epilobium ciliatum*) and hairy willowherb (*Epilobium hirsutum*)** may resemble purple loosestrife seedlings or root sprouts, but both are annuals and much smaller than purple loosestrife. Fringed willowherb has round stems and smaller, fewer, pink flowers, with 4 petals. Hairy willowherb is similar to northern willowherb but has long spreading hairs. **Garden or yellow loosestrife (*Lysimachia vulgaris* L.)** is also a riparian invasive plant that looks similar to purple loosestrife vegetatively; however, it has yellow flowers and does not have square stems.

Purple loosestrife habit in cranberries

Purple loosestrife vegetative stems

Purple loosestrife with whorled leaves

Garden loosestrife flowers

Purple loosestrife flowering stem

Garden loosestrife young plant

Purple loosestrife seeds, 0.9 mm

369

Velvetleaf (*Abutilon theophrasti* Medicus)

Synonyms: pie marker, buttonweed, Indian mallow, butter print, velvet weed, butter-weed, Indian hemp, cotton-weed, wild cotton

General Description: An **erect** (1–1.5 m tall), **summer annual**, usually with unbranched stems. Heart-shaped **leaves and stems are covered with soft hairs, velvety to the touch.**

Propagation / Phenology: Reproduction is **by seeds,** which can germinate from more than 5 cm below the soil surface. Seedlings emerge in mid- to late May.

Seedling: Hypocotyls are stout, green or maroon at the base, and covered with short hairs. **Cotyledons are heart-shaped,** sometimes tinted with maroon. The cotyledon margins and both surfaces are **covered with short hairs. Young leaves are heart-shaped, densely hairy on both surfaces (velvety),** and **bluntly toothed along the margin.** Leaves are alternate, angled downward over the seedling, with the apexes pointing to the ground. **Stems are hairy.** Leaves and stems emit an **unpleasant odor** when crushed.

Mature Plant: **Stems are erect,** mostly **unbranched,** and covered with short, **velvety,** branched **hairs. Leaves are heart-shaped,** gradually and concavely tapering to a sharp point (acuminate), 10–15 cm long and nearly as wide, **soft-hairy,** with toothed margins. Petioles are about equal in length to the blades. Leaves are alternate and palmately veined.

Roots and Underground Structures: Fibrous root system with a shallow **taproot.**

Flowers and Fruit: Plants flower from July or August into the autumn. Flowers (1.5–2.5 cm wide) are produced on short stalks (pedicels) in the upper leaf axils and consist of 5 fused sepals, **5 yellow petals,** and numerous stamens fused into a tube. The **fruit is a circular cup-shaped disk of 9–15 carpels** (schizocarp), **each with a beak on the margin** of the disk. Each carpel contains 3–9 seeds and splits along a central suture. Seeds are approximately 3 mm long, grayish-brown to black, flattened, and notched. **Seeds** have small, star-shaped hairs on the surface and **can remain viable in the soil for up to 50 years.**

Postsenescence Characteristics: The **stems persist** throughout the winter, **bearing the characteristic disk of beaked fruit.** Fruit turns black, and each section falls off individually throughout the autumn and winter.

Habitat: Velvetleaf is considered one of the most important weeds of corn production in the United States. It is common in nursery, horticultural, and agronomic crops, particularly in areas of continuous corn production or in other crops where triazine herbicides are commonly used. Is also grows in roadsides and gardens. Velvetleaf thrives on nutrient-rich cultivated soils.

Distribution: Common throughout the United States.

Similar Species: **Common mallow (*Malva neglecta*) seedlings** have cotyledons that are also heart-shaped, but they lack hairs. At maturity, the leaves of common mallow are roundish rather than heart-shaped.

J. Neal

Velvetleaf habit

A. DiTommaso

Velvetleaf mature fruit

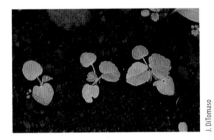

J. DiTommaso

Velvetleaf seedlings

J. Neal

Velvetleaf flower and fruit

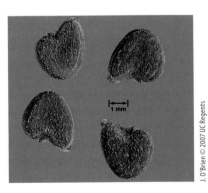

J. O'Brien © 2007 UC Regents

Velvetleaf seeds, 3 mm

371

Venice mallow (*Hibiscus trionum* L.)

SYNONYMS: flower-of-an-hour, bladder ketmia, modesty, shoo-fly

GENERAL DESCRIPTION: A **summer annual** with **3- or sometimes 5-lobed or deeply cut leaves,** each with rounded teeth or lobes on the margins. Stems are usually branched at the base, spreading to erect (20–50 cm tall).

PROPAGATION / PHENOLOGY: Reproduction is **by seeds**; seedlings may emerge throughout the summer, particularly after cultivation. **Seeds persist in the soil,** remaining dormant for long periods.

SEEDLING: Hypocotyls are stout and hairy. **Cotyledon blades** are yellow-green, thick, **rounded or heart-shaped.** Cotyledon petioles are hairy and longer than the blades. **Young leaves are alternate. The first 2 leaves are toothed and irregular in shape; subsequent leaves are deeply 3-lobed.** Leaf blades are densely hairy below and sparsely hairy above.

MATURE PLANT: Stems are hairy, branching near the base to form a tuft. **Leaves are alternate,** approximately 7.5 cm long and wide, and **deeply 3-lobed or sometimes 5-lobed; each lobe has coarse, rounded teeth or small lobes.** Leaves are oblong to egg-shaped, larger toward the apex, on long petioles subtended by 2 stipules. Leaves are reduced near the top of the plant.

ROOTS AND UNDERGROUND STRUCTURES: Fibrous root system with a **shallow taproot**.

FLOWERS AND FRUIT: **Flowers** are present from July to September, **opening only for a few hours a day in the morning.** Flowers are subtended by several linear bracts and are produced singly or in groups of 2 or 3 in the upper leaf axils. Sepals (5) are pale green with dark green veins and are fused into an inflated membranous bladder. **Petals (5) are 1.5–4 cm long, pale yellow to white with purple bases.** Stamens are united into a column; the filaments are dark purple, and the anthers are yellow-orange. The fruit (capsule) contains 30 seeds and is enclosed within the expanded bladder. Seeds are approximately 2 mm long, kidney-shaped to triangular, rough, and grayish-black. Seeds have small, star-shaped hairs on the surface.

POSTSENESCENCE CHARACTERISTICS: Plant parts do not persist after frost. The distinctive seedheads remain attached for only a short time.

HABITAT: Venice mallow is a weed of nursery, horticultural, and agronomic crops. Most common in cultivated areas, it tolerates drought and gravelly, sometimes alkaline, soils.

DISTRIBUTION: Initially introduced from southern Europe as an ornamental but has escaped to become a common weed in the eastern half of the United States, particularly in the southeastern and midwestern states.

SIMILAR SPECIES: **Musk mallow (*Malva moschata* L.)** has similar foliage, but its leaves are 5–7 parted, whereas those of Venice mallow are usually 3-parted. In addition, the basal leaves of musk mallow are rounded and lobed; those of Venice mallow are dissected. Musk mallow flowers are rose-colored or white with pink veins.

Venice mallow habit

J. Neal

Venice mallow seedling

J. Neal

Venice mallow mature fruit

J. DiTomaso

Venice mallow flower, fruit, and mature leaves

J. Neal and S. Morris (inset)

Venice mallow seeds, 2.1 mm

J. O'Brien © 2007 UC Regents

373

Common mallow (*Malva neglecta* Wallr.)

SYNONYMS: cheese-weed, cheeses, cheese mallow, dwarf mallow, running mallow, malice, round dock, button weed, round-leaved mallow, low mallow

GENERAL DESCRIPTION: A **winter or summer annual or biennial**, growing erect (10–30 cm tall) or, more often, **prostrate to decumbent**.

PROPAGATION / PHENOLOGY: Reproduction is **by seeds**, which may emerge continuously between spring and early autumn. **Fragmented stems can produce adventitious roots** from the nodes under moist conditions.

SEEDLING: Hypocotyls are green to white, with short soft hairs. **Cotyledons are smooth, heart-shaped, with 3 main veins**, 5–7 mm long by 3–4 mm wide, on relatively long and grooved stalks that are hairy on the ridges. Plants initially develop as **basal rosettes. Young leaves** are alternate, somewhat crinkled, and hairy on both surfaces. **Blades are circular, shallowly lobed, and toothed.** Petioles are grooved, hairy, 2–3 times longer than the width of the blade.

MATURE PLANT: Stems branch and elongate at the soil surface. The **base of each stem lies close to the soil surface**, with the **tip turned upward** (decumbent). **Leaves are alternate**, on narrow petioles (5–20 cm long), **palmately veined, circular to kidney-shaped** (2–6 cm wide), with **toothed margins** and 5–9 lobes. Short hairs are present on both leaf surfaces and on the margins and stem.

ROOTS AND UNDERGROUND STRUCTURES: Short to deep, straight taproot with coarsely branched secondary root system.

FLOWERS AND FRUIT: **Flowers** are present from May throughout the summer and into October, either singly or in clusters arising from the leaf axils. Petals (5) are 0.6–1.3 cm long, 2 times as long as the sepals, **white or whitish-lavender, often tinged with purple**. Flowers are on long stalks (1–4 cm) and produce **fruit that resemble a button or a wheel of cheese**. Fruit consists of 12–15 wedge-shaped, 1-seeded segments arranged in a flattened round disk (schizocarp). Seeds are reddish-brown to black, flattened, circular with a marginal notch (1.5 mm in diameter).

POSTSENESCENCE CHARACTERISTICS: Green stems persist well into winter. Plants can occasionally sprout from the crown the following spring.

HABITAT: Common mallow is a weed of low-maintenance turfgrass, landscapes, and nursery crops. It is less common in agronomic crops.

DISTRIBUTION: Widespread throughout North America.

SIMILAR SPECIES: Few species are confused with common mallow. The **leaves of ground ivy (*Glechoma hederacea*)** are similar but opposite, with rounded teeth. Ground ivy also emits a mint-like odor and has square stems. **Bristly mallow (*Modiola caroliniana*)** is similar but the stems and leaves are bristly hairy, is generally more prostrate, and flowers are red to orange.

Common mallow habit

A. Senesac

Common mallow seedlings

R. Uva

Common mallow flower

J. DiTomaso

Common mallow fruit

J. DiTomaso

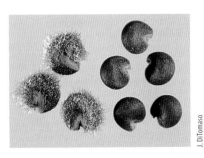

Left, musk mallow seeds, 2.0 mm; *right*, common mallow seeds, 1.6 mm

J. DiTomaso

Bristly mallow (*Modiola caroliniana* (L.) Don.)

SYNONYMS: *Modiola multifida*, Carolina bristlemallow

GENERAL DESCRIPTION: Bristly mallow is a **summer or winter annual** (persisting as a perennial in warmer regions), with **prostrate or spreading stems** to approximately 0.5 m long but usually shorter. Leaves are alternate. **Orange to dull orange-red flowers** develop singly in the leaf axils. Native to the southern United States and/or South America.

PROPAGATION / PHENOLOGY: Reproduction is **by seeds**, but plants can also spread by **rooting at the stem nodes**. Seeds germinate from spring through early autumn. In the northeastern states, bristly mallow is a summer annual. Farther south, the plants may have a winter annual or even perennial life cycle.

SEEDLING: Cotyledons are deltoid, with petioles as long as the blades. Midveins are obvious. **First leaves** are developmentally alternate (but emerge **from the base in a radial fashion**), **ovate**, sparsely hairy, with serrate or crenate toothed margins, and long petioles. The major veins on leaves are palmate. Branches form at the base, growing prostrate in a radial pattern.

MATURE PLANT: **Leaves are highly variable**, ranging from **round or ovate to deeply palmate lobed** (3–7 lobes) or dissected, with coarsely toothed margins. Leaves are 3–4 cm long by 2–3 cm wide with petioles about twice the length of blades. Stems and leaves from **bristly hairs** to nearly glabrous. Lower stems contacting ground often root at the nodes. Stems spread to 15–45 cm long.

ROOTS AND UNDERGROUND STRUCTURES: A course, thick root system.

FLOWERS AND FRUIT: Flowers present spring to early autumn and **are red or orange-red**, round, and less than 13 mm wide. Flowers are borne solitarily or rarely in pairs in the leaf axils, on pedicels 2–4 cm in length. Flower subtended by 3 leafy bracts, linear to lanceolate, approximately 5 mm long and hairy. Sepals are 5–6 mm long and hairy. Petals (5) are slightly longer than the sepals. The staminal column is shorter than the petals, yellowish in color. The **hairy sepals and bracts are persistent** around the fruit. Fruit is a schizocarp with 14–22 black, kidney-shaped, hairy mericarps in a wheel 7–9 mm in diameter. Each mericarp is 2-chambered, 1 seed per chamber, 4 mm long, with 2 horn-like beaks on the back. Seeds lack hairs or are minutely pubescent, 1.5 mm long, and flat with a notch on one side.

POSTSENESCENCE CHARACTERISTICS: Aboveground portions of the plants do not persist long after senescence. The diagnostic fruits remain attached to stems for a short while after foliage senesces.

HABITAT: Bristly mallow inhabits turf, edges of paths, alfalfa fields, and other disturbed places.

DISTRIBUTION: Plants are most common in the southeastern states but have been reported as north as Pennsylvania, Delaware, and Massachusetts.

SIMILAR SPECIES: Bristly mallow resembles other members of the mallow family, particularly **common mallow (*Malva neglecta*)**; however, it is usually much hairier and more prostrate in form. In addition, the flowers are red-orange and not white to lavender as in common mallow. In turf and landscapes, bristly mallow is often mistaken for **ground ivy (*Glechoma hederacea*)**, but ground ivy has opposite leaves whereas bristly mallow has alternate leaves.

stly mallow habit

stly mallow 3-leaf seedling

Young bristly mallow with basal branching

stly mallow leaf variation on one plant

Bristly mallow seeds and fruit

Prickly sida (*Sida spinosa* L.)

SYNONYMS: false mallow, Indian mallow, spiny sida, thistle mallow

GENERAL DESCRIPTION: An **erect, branched, summer annual** (20–50 cm tall). **Spiny projections on the stem nodes** account for the common and scientific names.

PROPAGATION / PHENOLOGY: Reproduction is **by seeds**; seeds may germinate over an extended period from spring through mid-summer.

SEEDLING: Cotyledons are rounded to heart-shaped (6.5–14 mm long by 5–8 mm wide), with a shallow indentation or notch at the apex. The hypocotyl and the margins of the leaves and cotyledons are densely covered with short, gland-tipped hairs. Young leaves are alternate. **Initial leaves are rounded to egg-shaped; subsequent leaves develop a pointed tip.** Blades are thin, soft, hairy, with prominent veins beneath. Petioles of young leaves are rounded, at least one-third as long as the blade, and bear short, gland-tipped hairs. Stipules are present at the base of the third and subsequent leaves.

MATURE PLANT: **Stems are many-branched** and **softly hairy, with small spines** at the leaf nodes. Hairs are branched (star-shaped). **Leaves are alternate**, **softly hairy**, 2–5 cm long, and oval or oblong to lanceolate. Margins are round- to sharp-toothed. Petioles are 1–3 cm long, with **linear stipules** (5–8 mm long) at the base.

ROOTS AND UNDERGROUND STRUCTURES: Slender, branching **taproot**.

FLOWERS AND FRUIT: **Flowers** are produced from June to September **alone or in clusters** on 2–12 mm flower stalks arising **from the leaf axils**. Flowers are **pale yellow**, with 5 petals, 4–6 mm long. Stamens are united over half their length to form a column. **Fruit** (schizocarp) is a ring of five 1-seeded segments (mericarps), 1.8–3 mm long, with 2 sharp spines at the apex. **Seed** usually **remains enclosed within the mericarp**, but is flattened on 2 sides and rounded on the other (2–2.5 mm long).

POSTSENESCENCE CHARACTERISTICS: Woody, erect stems with spines in the axils may persist into early winter.

HABITAT: A weed of most cultivated, agronomic, and horticultural crops, prickly sida is also found in landscapes, fields, pastures, gardens, and waste places.

DISTRIBUTION: Found throughout the eastern United States extending north to Massachusetts and Michigan, and west to Nebraska; most common in the southeastern states.

SIMILAR SPECIES: **Arrowleaf sida (*Sida rhombifolia* L.)** is an erect, summer annual with rhombic or diamond-shaped leaves tapered at the base. Stems lack the small spines at the leaf nodes present on prickly sida. Arrowleaf sida is native to the southern United States but extends as far north as New Jersey and Pennsylvania. Seedlings of **tropic croton (*Croton glandulosus*)** strongly resemble prickly sida, but tropic croton has hairy stems and lacks the spurs at the nodes. Seedlings of **spurred anoda (*Anoda cristata* (L.) Schltdl.)** are similar, but the leaves are broader, triangular-shaped, and have less coarsely toothed margins than prickly sida. At maturity, spurred anoda plants are larger, to 1 m tall and wide, with long (≥1 mm) hairs on most plant parts, broad triangular leaves, with light blue to lavender flowers arising from leaf axils, and a distinctive *Malva*-like fruit. Both tropic croton and spurred anoda are more common in warmer climates. Foliage of prickly sida is also similar to **Virginia copperleaf (*Acalypha virginica*)** but can be distinguished by the coloration and spines at the stem nodes.

Prickly sida habit

Prickly sida spine (at leaf node)

Prickly sida flower and leaf

Prickly sida seedlings

Arrowleaf sida flower

Spurred anoda flowers

Prickly sida seeds, 2.2 mm, and mericarps

379

Carpetweed (*Mollugo verticillata* L.)

SYNONYMS: Indian chickweed, whorled chickweed, devils-grip

GENERAL DESCRIPTION: A small, many-branched **prostrate annual forming circular mats** to 40 cm in diameter. Leaves are rounded, widest above the middle and narrowing to the base.

PROPAGATION / PHENOLOGY: Reproduction is **by seeds**. Germination is generally later in the season than that of many other summer annuals, but growth is rapid.

SEEDLING: **Seedlings develop as small, flattened basal rosettes.** Cotyledons are oblong, thick, smooth, 1.5–3.5 mm long, and lack noticeable veins. Young **leaves are alternate, thickened, rounded above** and **narrowed to the base.** Petioles may have a few marginal hairs. Leaf surfaces are dull green, smooth, pale beneath, and pinkish-brown toward the base.

MATURE PLANT: Stems are smooth and many-branched, forming **prostrate mats** along the soil surface. **Leaves are in whorls of 3–8 at each stem node.** Leaves are sessile, smooth, 1–3 cm long and <1 cm wide, rounded above and narrowed to the base (spatulate) or widest above the middle and tapering to the base (oblanceolate).

ROOTS AND UNDERGROUND STRUCTURES: Sparsely branched taproot.

FLOWERS AND FRUIT: Although they are occasionally present in June, flowers commonly bloom from July through September. Flowers, in clusters of 2–5 in the leaf axils, are small, 4–5 mm across, white or greenish-white, with slender, 5–15 mm long stalks (pedicels). Fruits are small, thin-walled, 3-valved, egg-shaped capsules, 1.5–4 mm long. Seeds are small, 0.5 mm long, flattened, kidney-shaped, orange-red to orange-brown.

POSTSENESCENCE CHARACTERISTICS: None of note.

HABITAT: Carpetweed is a weed of most cultivated agronomic and horticultural crops and newly seeded or thin turfgrass. Abundant on damp, rich soil in tilled crops, it is also commonly found on dry, gravelly or sandy soils in waste areas.

DISTRIBUTION: Found throughout temperate North America. Common in the eastern United States, less common in the northern Great Plains.

SIMILAR SPECIES: Whorls of 3–8 leaves at the stem nodes and the profuse branching pattern easily distinguish carpetweed from other species. Most other prostrate weeds have alternate or opposite leaves. The **bedstraws (*Galium* spp.)** and **field madder (*Sherardia arvensis*)** also have whorled leaves but can be distinguished by their square or winged stems.

Carpetweed habit

Carpetweed flowering shoot

Young carpetweed plant

Carpetweed flower

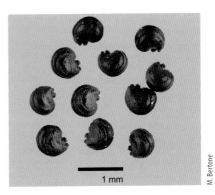

Carpetweed seeds

Mulberryweed (*Fatoua villosa* (Thunb.) Nakai)

Synonym: hairy crabweed

General Description: Mulberryweed is an erect, branching, **summer annual** that resembles mulberry (*Morus* spp.) seedlings but with **hairy stems**. **Leaves are alternate**, roughly triangular, with prominently toothed margins.

Propagation / Phenology: Reproduction is only **by seeds**. Seeds germinate in early spring and continue to emerge throughout the summer and early autumn. **Plants flower when very young** and may produce viable seed within 14 days after reaching the 2-leaf stage of growth. **Seeds are forcefully expelled** over 1 m from the parent plant. Individual plants produce several thousand seeds that have little or no dormancy. These traits result in **multiple generations per year** and **rapid spread**.

Seedling: Cotyledons are oval to round. The first leaves are roughly triangular in shape with shallow, pointed lobes. **Stems and leaves are hairy.** The first 2–4 true leaves may appear opposite but as the plant grows, leaves are alternate. Small flower clusters may form in the axils of the leaves when plants have only 2–4 true leaves.

Mature Plant: Plants are upright with densely hairy stems. In shady areas they are often unbranched, up to 1 m in height, but in full sun plants are branched and typically less than 50 cm tall. Leaves are alternate, roughly triangular in outline, with shallowly toothed margins. Leaf surface is pubescent and prominently veined, but may lose its hairs and appear glossy. Leaf blades are typically 3–5 cm in length (occasionally longer). Petioles are about ½ to 1 time as long as the leaf blade.

Roots and Underground Structures: Fibrous root system with a thin taproot.

Flowers and Fruit: Flowers are in **globe-shaped clusters (cyme) in the leaf axils**. Clusters may be 10–15 mm in diameter; purple when young, fading to dark brown with age. Individual flowers are inconspicuous, white to cream, and petals are not persistent. Seeds are creamy white in color, approximately 1 mm long, flattened on 2 sides, with a rough surface. Seeds are forcefully expelled more than 1 m from the fruit.

Postsenescence Characteristics: Plants not persistent after first frost.

Habitat: Almost exclusively a weed of container nursery crops, landscape plantings, and greenhouses. However, some populations have naturalized in shady, moist woodland areas and roadsides.

Distribution: Mulberryweed was recently introduced (~1964) from eastern Asia. It is distributed throughout most of the eastern United States from New York to Florida and west to Texas and Oklahoma, with some established populations on the West Coast. Long-distance spread has likely been via contaminated nursery crops.

Similar Species: Strongly resembles **mulberry tree (*Morus* spp.)** seedlings but easily distinguished by the densely hairy stem; stems of mulberry seedlings are hairless (or nearly so). Very young seedlings may resemble **galinsoga (*Galinsoga* spp.)**, with hairy stems and similar leaf shapes, but galinsoga has opposite leaves whereas mulberryweed leaves are alternate.

Mulberryweed habit

Mulberryweed 2-leaf seedling

Mulberryweed leaves

Mulberryweed seedling with flowers

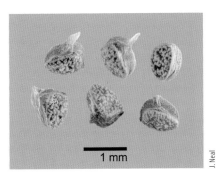

Mulberryweed seeds, 1 mm long

Mulberryweed inflorescence
with seed visible

Fringed willowherb (*Epilobium ciliatum* Raf. ssp. *ciliatum* and ssp. *glandulosum* (Lehm.) P. Hoch & Raven)
Hairy willowherb (*Epilobium hirsutum* L.)

Synonyms: **fringed willowherb:** American willowherb or willowweed, northern willowherb; **hairy willowherb:** codlins and cream, great willowherb, hairy willowweed

General Description: Willowherbs are perennials in wildlands or their native habitats but act as **cool-season annuals** in cropping systems. Plants are upright, 0.5–1 m tall (rarely to 2 m), with ascending branches, **opposite leaves, and long, slender flowers**. Hairy willowherb is densely hairy; the leaves and stems of fringed willowherb are sparsely hairy. Both species form **distinctive, long, slender fruit** that splits from the tip. Fringed willowherb is native to North America but hairy willowherb is native to North Africa and Eurasia.

Propagation / Phenology: Reproduction is primarily by **wind-dispersed seeds**. Fringed willowherb can also reproduce vegetatively by leafy rosette offsets at the base.

Seedling: Cotyledons ovate, tip rounded to slightly truncate. Leaves are opposite, sometimes tinged red, sessile, broadly lanceolate with a prominent midvein. Early leaves may have entire margins but subsequent leaves will have shallowly lobed or toothed margins. Seedlings of hairy willowherb are densely pubescent. Fringed willowherb seedlings are typically glabrous.

Mature Plant: Leaves are nearly sessile, 1–15 cm long, broadly lanceolate, opposite near the base but alternate when subtending flower stalks, with prominent veins and toothed or shallowly lobed margins. Leaves are persistent on stems. **Fringed willowherb:** Plants are loosely clumped, often with leafy rosette offsets at the base. Upper foliage sparsely to densely hairy. Lower foliage lacks hairs or is sparsely hairy. Lower stems often reddish, weakly woody, but green above. **Hairy willowherb** has woolly, hairy leaves and stems.

Roots and Underground Structures: **Fringed willowherb:** Main root and crown weakly woody, with numerous fibrous lateral roots. Subspecies *glandulosum* develops offshoots with fleshy, scale-like leaves. **Hairy willowherb** can form a thick rhizome.

Flowers and Fruit: Plants flower from early to late summer. Fringed willowherb racemes are sparsely to densely hairy, sometimes glandular. Hairy willowherb racemes are densely hairy. Both species form distinctive, 4–8 cm long, slender tube-like flowers with 4 notched petals at the tip. Fringed willowherb has pale pink to rose-pink petals, 3.5–5 mm long; hairy willowherb flowers are bright pink or violet-pink, 10–16 mm long. Capsules are hairy, 5–7 cm long, slender, cylindrical, 4-chambered, and open at the apex by 4 back-curved valves. Seeds are obovoid, flattened, 0.8–2 mm long with a tuft of long, soft, white hairs at the apex. Fringed willowherb seeds are longitudinally ridged; hairy willowherb seeds are not.

Postsenescence Characteristics: Dead stems with open capsules can persist into winter.

Habitat: Both species common in moist sites such as streambanks, riparian areas, ditches, and irrigated crops but can grow in upland sites such as roadsides, nursery crops, orchards, and vineyards.

Distribution: Fringed willowherb, the more common of the 2 species, is present in most contiguous states, but both are present in all northeastern states.

Similar Species: Seedling willowherbs are similar to **eclipta (*Eclipta prostrata*)**, with sessile, broadly lanceolate, opposite leaves, but eclipta has a composite flower heads and is a summer annual germinating in warm, moist soils. Willowherbs are more common in cool-moist sites.

J. Neal

Fringed willowherb habit

J. Neal

Fringed willowherb flowers and developing fruit

J. DiTomaso

Fringed willowherb seed capsule

J. DiTomaso

Fringed willowherb seedlings

J. Neal

Hairy willowherb flowering stem

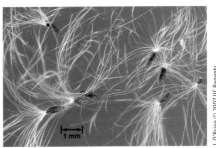

J. O'Brien © 2007 UC Regents

Fringed willowherb seeds

Cutleaf evening-primrose (*Oenothera laciniata* Hill)

Synonyms: *Oenothera sinuata, Raimannia laciniata*

General Description: A **biennial, winter, or rarely a summer annual, branching from a basal rosette.** Elongating stems can sprawl close to the ground or grow erect to 10–80 cm in height.

Propagation / Phenology: Reproduction is **by seeds**; seeds germinate in warm, moist soil from early summer through early fall.

Seedling: Cotyledon blades are oval, gradually tapering to a stalk, or occasionally kidney-shaped on a flattened petiole. **Leaves form a basal rosette.** The upper surface of young leaves is covered by short hairs; the lower surface is smooth. **Blades are oblong with distinct white midveins** on the upper surface. **Subsequent leaves develop deeply cut teeth** or regular lobes. Purple to reddish coloration may be present on and around the petiole. Seedling overwinters as a basal rosette.

Mature Plant: **Stems** are hairy, often reddish, **prostrate to ascending** from the base with an erect tip. Leaves are green, sparsely hairy to smooth above. Blades are long (3–8 cm) and narrow, oblanceolate, oblong, or lanceolate. **Margins are wavy, coarsely toothed, irregularly lobed, or pinnatifid.** Leaves are alternate and petiolated. Upper stem leaves are sessile and smaller than lower leaves.

Roots and Underground Structures: Taproot.

Flowers and Fruit: **Flowers** bloom from May through October and are **sessile in the upper leaf axils.** Flowers are **usually yellow** but **occasionally reddish-brown.** Petals are 5–25 mm long, attached at the base of the fused sepals. Sepals form a 1.5–3.5 cm long narrow tube. The tips of the sepals (6–12 mm long) are reflexed downward. **Fruit** is a 2–4 cm long by 3–4 mm wide, 4-lobed, **cylindrical and often curved capsule.** Seeds are angular (1 mm long), pale brown, conspicuously pitted, and arranged in rows within the capsule.

Postsenescence Characteristics: Stems and hairy capsules persist for a short time into late fall.

Habitat: Cutleaf evening-primrose is a weed of nurseries, Christmas tree plantations, orchards, landscapes, and low-maintenance turfgrass; it is less common in agronomic row crops. It is also found in pastures, waste areas, and roadsides, frequently growing on dry, usually sandy soil.

Distribution: Native to the southern and eastern United States. Exists as a weed from Maine, throughout the Southeast, and west to New Mexico and California.

Similar Species: **Common evening-primrose (*Oenothera biennis* L.)** is similar while **in the rosette stage** but has an **erect growth habit** and **entire (unlobed) leaf margins.** Common evening-primrose stems and seed capsules are woody and often persist through the winter. Capsules of common evening-primrose are thickest near the bottom, whereas capsules of cutleaf evening-primrose are linear throughout.

Cutleaf evening-primrose habit

J. Neal

J. Neal

Cutleaf evening-primrose flower and fruit

J. Neal

Cutleaf evening-primrose seedling

R. Uva

Common evening-primrose rosette

Common evening-primrose flowering shoot

J. Neal

J. DiTomaso

Left, common evening-primrose seeds, 1.4 mm; *right*, cutleaf evening-primrose seeds, 1.1 mm

Yellow woodsorrel (*Oxalis stricta* L.)

SYNONYMS: *Oxalis dillenii, Oxalis europaea, Xanthoxalis cymosa, Xanthoxalis stricta*, sour-grass

GENERAL DESCRIPTION: A **clover-like perennial** that **can act as a summer annual** in cooler climates. Plants grow from as low as 3 cm to as high as 50 cm.

PROPAGATION / PHENOLOGY: Reproduction is **primarily by seeds**, but plants can also **spread by rhizomes**. Seeds germinate shortly after dispersal, when conditions allow.

SEEDLING: **Cotyledons** are smooth, **rounded** to oblong, <0.5 cm long, often tinged pink on the underside, on short stalks. **Young leaves are trifoliolate** (3 leaflets) and alternate, **with heart-shaped leaflets.** The upper surface of leaflets is smooth; margins and veins of the lower surface are sparsely hairy. Petioles are hairy, long, and pinkish-brown toward the base.

MATURE PLANT: **Stems** are green to purple, hairy, **usually erect**, and mostly unbranched or with several **branches from the base. Leaves** are alternate and **long-petioled**; they consist of **3 heart-shaped leaflets**, 1–2 cm wide, which often fold up at midday and night. Leaf surfaces are smooth, and the margins are fringed with hairs.

ROOTS AND UNDERGROUND STRUCTURES: **Long, slender, succulent, white to pink rhizomes** with a secondary fibrous root system.

FLOWERS AND FRUIT: **Flowers** are produced from May to September, year-round in greenhouses, **in clusters that arise from long stalks at the leaf axils.** Flowers are 7–11 mm wide with 5 sepals and 5 **yellow petals**, 4–9 mm long. Stamens are in 2 groups of 5, one group short and the other long. **Fruits** are 5-ridged, **cylindrical, pointed, erect, hairy capsules**, 1–1.5 cm long. **Seeds** are brown to maroon, oval, 1–1.5 mm long, and flattened with a transversely ridged surface and a **sticky coating. Seeds disperse from capsules by explosively ejecting as far as 4 m.**

POSTSENESCENCE CHARACTERISTICS: Plants die back to the ground in cold climates, often leaving branched yellow stems.

HABITAT: A weed of turfgrass, container-nursery stock, and greenhouse crops, as well as landscapes. Yellow woodsorrel is also found on disturbed sites, in roadsides, and on the edge of woodlands. It tolerates a wide range of soil types and site conditions, from moist and shady to sunny and drought-prone.

DISTRIBUTION: Distributed throughout the world.

SIMILAR SPECIES: **Slender yellow woodsorrel (*Oxalis dillenii* Jacq.)** is nearly identical to yellow woodsorrel with overlapping distributions. *Oxalis dillenii* has appressed, strigose, non-septate hairs on stems, whereas O. *stricta* stems are glabrous or with villous, often septate hairs that are not appressed to the stem. **Creeping woodsorrel (*Oxalis corniculata* L.)** is more prostrate, frequently roots at the nodes, and often has more purplish leaves. However, **leaf color is variable in both species and cannot be used as a diagnostic characteristic.** Creeping woodsorrel lacks the underground rhizomes of yellow woodsorrel but **spreads by aboveground stolons.** It is common in and around greenhouses and container crops. Woodsorrels can be distinguished from trifoliolate legumes, such as **clovers and black medic**, by the heart-shaped leaflets and the absence of stipules at the base of the petiole. **See Table 7 for a comparison with weedy, trifoliolate legumes and woodsorrels.**

Yellow woodsorrel habit

Mature yellow woodsorrel with rhizome

Yellow woodsorrel seedling

Creeping woodsorrel flowers and fruit (leaf color not diagnostic)

Left, creeping woodsorrel seeds, 1.2 mm; *right*, yellow woodsorrel seeds, 1.2 mm

Greater celandine (*Chelidonium majus* L.)

SYNONYMS: celandine, rock poppy, swallow wort

GENERAL DESCRIPTION: Initially a **rosette of deeply divided leaves** resembling a winter annual mustard; later an upright, **short-lived herbaceous perennial** with branching stems (30–80 cm tall) and **bright yellow flowers**. When damaged, all parts exude a **bright orange sap** that reddens after exposure to air.

PROPAGATION / PHENOLOGY: Reproduction is by ant-dispersed **seed**. Germination occurs during spring.

SEEDLING: Cotyledons are ovate to nearly triangular, on short petioles. First leaf is kidney-shaped with scalloped edges. The second or third leaves are deeply lobed. Seedlings form a rosette of deeply, pinnately divided leaves. The divisions (appearing as leaflets) are oblong to rounded, the terminal division broader; margins have shallow, rounded lobes. Bases of the petioles are hairy. The rosette and leaves resemble some mustards.

MATURE PLANT: Plants form upright stems with alternate leaves. Stems are glaucous, ribbed, and sparsely pubescent with short, white hairs. The leaves are pinnately compound (generally 5 leaflets) and up to 35 cm long by 7.5 cm wide. Leaflets lobed and roughly oval with irregularly dentate, wavy margins. Leaf surfaces are green above, pale green on the undersides and usually hairless except along the veins.

ROOTS AND UNDERGROUND STRUCTURES: A shallow and brittle taproot.

FLOWERS AND FRUIT: Flowering begins in late spring and continues throughout the summer. The flowers are bright yellow and occur on axillary stalks (2–10 cm long) in umbellate clusters of 3–8. Pedicels 1–2.5 cm long with scattered hairs. Each flower has 4 egg-shaped petals and 2 sepals, **resembling wild mustard flowers**. Seeds are produced in 2–5 cm long, upright, **cylindrical capsules** that become torulose (pinched along its length) as they mature. Seeds are oval, shiny, and flattened with a pitted surface. Each seed has a small, white nutrient packet (elaisome), which attracts ants.

POSTSENESCENCE CHARACTERISTICS: Aboveground parts senesce in autumn at first frost.

HABITAT: Full sun to partial shade. Grows along forest edges, in waste areas, along roadsides, and in gardens and urban areas.

DISTRIBUTION: Widespread throughout New England and mid-Atlantic states and west to Iowa. Populations have also been reported in the Pacific Northwest and Montana.

SIMILAR SPECIES: The flowers and silique-like seed capsules of greater celandine may look similar to members of the Brassicaceae (mustard family), and rosettes are similar to **ragweed parthenium (*Parthenium hysterophorus* L.)**. But the bright orange sap easily distinguishes greater celandine from other weeds. The native wildflower **celandine poppy (*Stylophorum diphyllum* (Michx.) Nuttall)** has similar foliage, but it has larger flowers (up to 5.5 cm in diameter) and ovoid, densely hairy seed capsules.

Greater celandine habit

Greater celandine seedling

Greater celandine rosette

Greater celandine flower and fruit

Front and back of ragweed parthenium leaves

Chamberbitter (*Phyllanthus urinaria* L.) and long-stalked phyllanthus (*Phyllanthus tenellus* Roxb.)

SYNONYMS: **chamberbitter:** leaf flower, gripeweed; **long-stalked phyllanthus:** tipsywood

GENERAL DESCRIPTION: Erect, branched, late-germinating, **summer annuals. Lateral branches have alternate, oblong to obovate leaves** giving the appearance of a pinnately compound leaf. Flowers and fruit are borne in leaf axils on lateral branches.

PROPAGATION / PHENOLOGY: Reproduction is **by seeds.** Seeds germinate in warm soil spring through summer. **Seeds are forcefully expelled** from the seed capsules up to 1 m. Plants produce multiple generations per year. Under optimum conditions, seeds can germinate within 6 days, and plants flower in less than 25 days of emergence.

SEEDLING: Cotyledons are oval. Young **leaves alternate**, with entire margins, and lack hairs. The first few true leaves on chamberbitter are wider at the tip, tapering at the base. Long-stalked phyllanthus leaves are oval, tapering at the base. Petioles are short, <1 mm. Stems lack hairs and may be maroon. Seedlings start to branch when very young. Lateral branches resemble pinnately compound leaves, but the branches are short with alternate leaves (phyllathoid branches). Chamberbitter leaf blades are oval with roughly parallel margins, 1–1.5 cm long and half as wide, with a rounded tip often minutely pointed. **Long-stalked phyllanthus leaves are oval to elliptic and taper at the base, whereas chamberbitter leaves do not.**

MATURE PLANT: Chamberbitter branches close to the ground with ascending stems; tolerates mowing but may grow taller than 40 cm. Long-stalked phyllanthus has an upright, growth habit and may grow taller than 60 cm. Leaves and stems are similar to seedlings.

ROOTS AND UNDERGROUND STRUCTURES: Plants have coarsely branched fibrous root systems.

FLOWERS AND FRUIT: Flowers are produced in the leaf axils on lateral branches from early summer to the first frost. They are inconspicuous, creamy-white to greenish, with 5 lobes and persistent sepals. Plants are monoecious with male flowers on the distal ends of the branches and female flowers closer to the main stems. Fruit capsules are green to yellow (sometimes red), roughly round, 2–3 mm diameter with 3–5 distinct lobes. **Chamberbitter fruit are sessile** (stalks <0.5 mm) whereas **long-stalked phyllanthus fruit stalks are 6–12 mm long.** Seeds are wedge-shaped, 0.8–1.2 mm in length, light brown. Chamberbitter seeds have lateral ridges whereas long-stalked phyllanthus seeds are bumpy and lack ridges.

POSTSENESCENCE CHARACTERISTICS: Plants die at first hard frost and are not persistent.

HABITAT: Both species are common in container nurseries and mulched landscape beds. Chamberbitter tolerates mowing and is a common weed of turf. Long-stalked phyllanthus is occasionally on roadsides and woodland edges, and perhaps pine forests. Neither is common in agronomic cropping systems.

DISTRIBUTION: Introduced from Asia (chamberbitter) and the Mascarene Islands (long-stalked phyllanthus). Both are now distributed throughout the southeastern United States, north to New Jersey and Illinois, and west to Texas. Long-distance transport appears to be primarily in contaminated nursery stock.

SIMILAR SPECIES: Seedlings may be mistaken for upright species of spurge, such as **hyssop spurge (*Euphorbia hyssopifolia*)**, but spurges produce a milky sap when stems are broken. The leaf arrangement on the lateral branches is similar to some legumes, leading to the plant being mistakenly referred to as "mimosa-weed."

J. Neal

Chamberbitter habit

J. Neal

Chamberbitter seedling

J. Neal

Long-stalked phyllanthus fruiting stems

J. Neal

Long-stalked phyllanthus seedling

J. Neal

Chamberbitter fruit (above); long-stalked phyllanthus fruit and flowers (below)

J. Neal

J. Neal

Chamberbitter (*top* 4, 1 mm) and long-stalked phyllanthus (*bottom* 4) seeds

Common pokeweed (*Phytolacca americana* L.)

Synonyms: *Phytolacca decandra*, pokeberry, Virginia poke, scoke, pigeonberry, garget, ink-berry, red ink plant, coakum, American cancer, cancer jalap

General Description: **A large**, branched, **herbaceous perennial** (0.9–3 m tall) **resembling a small tree. Fresh leaves and roots** are particularly **toxic**, and leaves must be cooked properly to avoid poisoning. The primary toxicant is the triterpene saponin phytolaccin, which causes gastrointestinal irritation. **Berries can also be poisonous.** Poisoning rarely results in fatalities in humans; however, deaths have been reported in pigs and cattle.

Propagation / Phenology: Reproduction is **by seeds**. Seedlings may emerge from mid-spring through early summer.

Seedling: Hypocotyls are tender, succulent, and swollen at the base, often tinged with purple. Cotyledons are egg-shaped (25 mm long by 12 mm wide) and pointed at the apex. Cotyledons and young **leaves are pale green, often tinted reddish on the underside and the petioles**. Young leaves are alternate, smooth, egg-shaped to rounded, and pointed at the apex. The reddish coloration of the petioles continues down the stem. **Shoots emerging from established plants** in spring **are similar to seedlings, but are more robust**, lack cotyledons, **and are in compact clusters**.

Mature Plant: **Mature plants are tree-like. Stems are smooth, erect**, and branched above, **usually reddish. Leaves are alternate**, petiolated, **egg-shaped** to lanceolate-oblong (9–30 cm long by 3–11 cm wide), and decrease in size toward the top of the plant. Margins are entire or slightly wavy.

Roots and Underground Structures: **Large, fleshy taproot**, 30 cm long by 10 cm thick in older plants. Taproot is white inside.

Flowers and Fruit: **Flowers** are present from July to the autumn on long (10–20 cm), narrow, **nodding to erect, reddish-stemmed racemes** at the end of the upper branches. Individual flowers are small, 6 mm wide, and have 5 white (or greenish white to pink), rounded, petal-like sepals. **Fruit are conspicuous berries, green when immature, turning purple to dark purple-black at maturity.** Berries produce a profuse amount of red juice. Fruits are rounded, slightly flattened, approximately 1 cm in diameter, and contain 10 seeds each. Seeds are small, glossy black, round, and flattened, 3 mm in diameter.

Postsenescence Characteristics: Dead, brown to black stems persist throughout the winter. Stems turn pale tan and decay early the following spring.

Habitat: Common pokeweed is a weed of landscapes and nursery crops, but it also is found where seeds are dropped by birds: around fields and in roadsides and fencerows. It thrives in deep, rich, gravelly soils.

Distribution: Most common in the eastern, southern, and southeastern United States but also occurs as far west as California.

Similar Species: Shoots from the taproot may resemble **Japanese knotweed (*Fallopia japonica*)** or **some hardwood seedlings such as common cottonwood (*Populus deltoides*)**; however, the leaves of Japanese knotweed are subtended by a membranous sheath (ocrea), and the stems of hardwood species are woody.

J. DiTomaso

Common pokeweed habit

J. Neal

Common pokeweed seedling

A. Senesac

Common pokeweed shoots from
perennial rootstock

J. Neal

Common pokeweed foliage and fruit

J. DiTomaso

Common pokeweed seeds, 3 mm

Yellow toadflax (*Linaria vulgaris* Mill.)

Synonyms: *Antirrhinum linaria*, butter-and-eggs, ramsted, flaxweed, wild snapdragon, eggs-and-bacon, Jacobs-ladder

General Description: A **colony-forming perennial with creeping roots**. Stems are mostly **unbranched** (30–90 cm tall), with many long, **narrow, gray-green leaves**, and terminate in a cluster of **attractive yellow flowers**.

Propagation / Phenology: Reproduction is **by seeds** and **creeping roots** that produce adventitious shoots, forming clumps or colonies of plants. Creeping roots are spread by cultivation, in topsoil, and with infested nursery stock.

Seedling: Cotyledons are diamond-shaped to lanceolate; the apex is rounded at the tip. **First true leaves are smooth, egg-shaped, but subsequent leaves** are longer and **lanceolate to linear**. Margins of young leaves are rolled inward. Leaves are covered with white spots.

Mature Plant: **Stems are erect, smooth, mostly unbranched, pale green**, and very leafy. **Leaves are alternate**, pale green to **gray-green**, sessile, **linear** (2–6 cm long by 2–4 mm wide), and narrowed at the base, with entire margins. Leaves are numerous, often so closely spaced on the stem they appear to be whorled. Some of the lowermost leaves may be opposite or whorled, but these do not persist.

Roots and Underground Structures: **Creeping roots** (resembling rhizomes) and a secondary fibrous root system.

Flowers and Fruit: **Yellow, snapdragon-like flowers** are produced from June through early autumn **in compact clusters (racemes) at the end of stems**. Flowers are 2–3.5 cm long and consist of 5 sepals and 5 petals fused to form 2 yellow lips with an orange throat on the lower lip and an elongated spur at the base. Fruits are round to egg-shaped, 2-celled capsules containing many seeds. Capsules open by 2–3 pores located below the apex. Seeds are 1.5–2 mm in diameter, dark brown or black, circular, flattened, and winged.

Postsenescence Characteristics: Dead plants bearing the 2-celled, toothed capsules persist for a considerable time. Dead branches, when present, twist and curve around each other.

Habitat: Yellow toadflax is a weed of low-maintenance turfgrass, landscapes, orchards, nursery crops, and other perennial crops, but it is not common in cultivated crops. It often grows in areas with dry, gravelly or sandy soils, such as roadsides and waste areas.

Distribution: Found throughout much of North America; most common in the eastern states and on the Pacific Coast.

Similar Species: **Oldfield toadflax (*Nuttallanthus canadensis* (L.) D. A. Sutton;** syn.: *Linaria canadensis* L. Dumont) is a biennial or winter or summer annual with very slender, smooth, erect stems (10–75 cm tall) and short, trailing, prostrate stems produced in rosette-like clusters at the base of the plant. Leaves are linear; flowers are blue to purple, rarely white. Spring shoots may resemble some **narrow-leaved goldenrods (*Solidago* spp.)**.

Yellow toadflax habit

Yellow toadflax rhizomes

Yellow toadflax flowering shoot

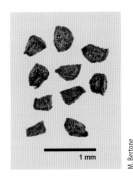

Oldfield toadflax seeds, 0.4 mm

Yellow toadflax seeds, 1.6 mm

R. Prostak

R. Uva

J. O'Brien © 2007 UC Regents

M. Bertone

J. DiTomaso

397

Buckhorn plantain (*Plantago lanceolata* L.)

SYNONYMS: English plantain, narrow-leaved plantain, rib-grass, ribwort, black-jacks

GENERAL DESCRIPTION: A **narrow-leaved**, **parallel-veined perennial** forming **a basal rosette** or a clump of several rosettes.

PROPAGATION / PHENOLOGY: Reproduction is **by seeds** and by new shoots produced at the base of the plant. Buckhorn plantain often flowers in the first year of growth and is a prolific seed producer. Most seedlings emerge in spring or early autumn. Seeds may germinate in darkness and can become established even in tall, dense vegetation.

SEEDLING: **Cotyledons are grass-like** (linear), smooth, narrow (>5 times as long as wide), with a furrow on the upper surface. The first leaves are hairy only on the margins; subsequent leaves are sparsely hairy and have cobwebby hairs near the base. **Leaves are lanceolate** (>5 times as long as wide), **parallel-veined**, and widened at the base, where they clasp the short stem forming the **basal rosette**.

MATURE PLANT: **Leaves remain in a basal rosette.** Well-established plants may produce a clump of several rosettes from the same crown. **Leaves are lanceolate** to elliptic, widest above the middle, often twisting or curled, 5–25 cm long by 1–2.5 cm wide, with 3–5 **prominent parallel veins on the blade.** Margins can be entire or slightly toothed. Blades are usually smooth but **can have long, silky hairs at the base.** Leaves are somewhat erect, except in turfgrass, where they tend to be more prostrate. **Overwintering leaves are wider than those produced in the summer.**

ROOTS AND UNDERGROUND STRUCTURES: Fibrous roots are produced from a **thick,** tough, short, **taproot-like woody underground stem** (caudex).

FLOWERS AND FRUIT: **Flowers and seedheads** are present from June through September **on the ends of leafless, unbranched, ridged stalks in dense, cylindrical, cone-like spikes or heads**. Individual flowers of the heads are inconspicuous. Fruits are 2-seeded, 3–4 mm long, and capsules open transversely by a lid. Seeds are 1.5–3.5 mm long, brownish, shiny, with an indentation on one side. Seeds become sticky when wet, aiding in animal dispersal.

POSTSENESCENCE CHARACTERISTICS: Plants overwinter as basal rosettes. Flower stalks and cylindrical, cone-like spikes can persist for an extended period.

HABITAT: Buckhorn plantain is a weed of turfgrass, landscapes, orchards, nursery crops, and other perennial crops. It is common on drier sites and on neutral to basic soils. Although buckhorn plantain often grows on compacted soils, it does not survive in areas that are routinely trampled. It tolerates close mowing.

DISTRIBUTION: Widespread throughout the United States and Canada.

SIMILAR SPECIES: **Bracted plantain (*Plantago aristata* Michx.)** is vegetatively similar, but has narrower, hairier leaves that lack the deep ribs common to buckhorn plantain. In addition, **the flower spikes have conspicuous hairy bracts** up to 2 cm in length. Bracted plantain is most commonly found on sandy, drought-prone sites.

Buckhorn plantain habit

J. DiTomaso

A. Senesac

Bracted plantain (note bracts on inflorescence)

R. Uva

Buckhorn plantain seedlings

J. DiTomaso

Bracted plantain seeds, 2.3 mm

J. Neal

Buckhorn plantain rosette

J. DiTomaso

Buckhorn plantain seeds, 2.8 mm (largest)

Broadleaf plantain (*Plantago major* L.)

SYNONYMS: *Plantago asiatica*, dooryard plantain, common plantain

GENERAL DESCRIPTION: **Broadleaf plantain** and the closely related species **blackseed plantain (*Plantago rugelii* Dcne.)** are **rosette-forming, perennial weeds** of high- or low-maintenance turf. Both have **broad, oval leaves** with somewhat **parallel venation**. For a short period in summer, plants produce **leafless, unbranched, flowering stems** (scapes) (5–30 cm long) with small, inconspicuous flowers.

PROPAGATION / PHENOLOGY: Reproduction is **by seeds**, which germinate in late spring through mid-summer and sporadically in the early fall.

SEEDLING: Seedlings develop as **basal rosettes. Cotyledons are 3-veined, spatulate,** 0.7–1.75 cm long by 0.5–1 mm wide, united at the base, and temporarily covered with a powdery coating. **Young leaves** are pale green, with **3–5 prominent veins.** Leaves are **oval to elliptic,** abruptly narrowing to a well-defined petiole that encircles the rosette and curves upward. The leaf surface often has scattered hairs on short, rounded, blunt projections. Blade margins become wavy on older leaves.

MATURE PLANT: **Leaves** are smooth or inconspicuously hairy, **elliptic to oval,** 4–18 cm long by 1.5–11 cm wide, **abruptly narrowing to a well-defined petiole.** Prominent veins run parallel with the margins, which are entire, often wavy, rarely toothed. Leaf surfaces are often waxy and blue-green. Petioles are sometimes reddish at the base.

ROOTS AND UNDERGROUND STRUCTURES: **Short taproot** with fibrous roots.

FLOWERS AND FRUIT: Small, inconspicuous **flowers** are produced from June through September on 5–30 cm **long, leafless flower stalks** (scapes) arising from the rosette. Petals are whitish, approximately 1 mm long. **Bracts** surrounding the flowers are **broad, ovate, blunt,** 2–4 mm long, with a sharp-pointed keel. **Seeds** are produced in an **oval, 2-celled, 3–5 mm long capsule, opening by a lid around the middle.** Each capsule contains 6–30 light to dark brown, glossy seeds, 1–1.5 mm long.

POSTSENESCENCE CHARACTERISTICS: Overwintering rosettes remain green where winters are mild, but die back to the crown in colder climates. Fruiting stalks turn dark brown or black and persist for an extended period.

HABITAT: Broadleaf and blackseed plantain are primarily turfgrass weeds; they are also weedy in nurseries, landscapes, orchards, and reduced-tillage crops. Although they grow in roadsides and waste areas, they prefer nutrient-rich, moist soils. Both tolerate close mowing, heavily compacted soils, wet soils, and dry sites.

DISTRIBUTION: Broadleaf plantain is found throughout the United States and southern Canada. Blackseed plantain is generally restricted to the eastern United States.

SIMILAR SPECIES: **Blackseed plantain, very similar** to broadleaf plantain, can be distinguished by its **cylindrical, 4–6 mm long, 4–10 seeded capsules that split below the middle,** and its **lanceolate,** gradually tapering, **slender-tipped bracts.** Blackseed plantain **leaves tend to be lighter green, less waxy,** more tapered at the tip, and are **more red to purple at the base of the petiole.** Petioles also tend to be narrower. **Bracted (*Plantago aristata*)** and **buckhorn plantain (*Plantago lanceolata*)** have narrower leaves than do blackseed or broadleaf plantain.

Broadleaf plantain
habit

J. Neal

R. Uva

Left, broadleaf plantain; *right*, blackseed plantain

J. Neal

Broadleaf plantain with flower heads and seedheads

J. Neal

Broadleaf plantain seedling

J. DiTomaso

Left, blackseed plantain seed capsule, 6.0 mm, and seeds, 2.0 mm; *right*, broadleaf plantain seed capsule, 4.9 mm, and seeds, 1.0 mm

Corn speedwell (*Veronica arvensis* L.)

Synonyms: rock speedwell, wall speedwell

General Description: A **winter annual** with **ascending branched stems** (5–15 cm, occasionally to 35 cm, in height) **radiating from the base** of the plant.

Propagation / Phenology: Reproduction is **by seeds**; seeds germinate in late summer, fall, or early spring, sometimes throughout the growing season in cool, moist areas.

Seedling: Seedlings branch at the base, forming a **dense mat**. Cotyledons are approximately 2 mm wide, triangular to 4-angled, with rounded apexes. **Leaves** are **opposite**, sparsely **hairy, egg-shaped**, on short petioles. Margins have **rounded teeth**.

Mature Plant: **Stems branch and radiate from the base** of the plant. **Lower leaves** on non-flowering parts of the plant are **opposite, petiolated** (1–3 mm long), hairy, egg-shaped or (less commonly) round (6–15 mm long), with 5–12 broad to narrow **rounded teeth on the margin**. Upper leaves on flowering stems are **alternate, sessile**, and narrow or oblong. They are much **smaller than lower leaves** and have **fewer teeth**, which occur only near the leaf base.

Roots and Underground Structures: Fibrous, shallow root system.

Flowers and Fruit: Flowering peaks in late spring but may continue through August. **Flowers** are borne **solitary in the leaf axils, crowded on the upper ⅔ of the flowering stem**, which becomes elongated with age. **Flowers are small**, 2–4 mm in diameter, **pale blue to white**, and borne on stalks (pedicels) <1 mm long. The **fruit is a heart-shaped**, hairy pod, deeply notched at the apex, with a minute, <1 mm long style at the apex. Each pod contains 14–20 tiny, yellow seeds (0.7 mm long).

Postsenescence Characteristics: Erect stems turn dark brown to dark gray and can persist through summer, but brittle stems do not persist in heavily trampled areas.

Habitat: A weed of lawns, landscapes, nursery crops, and winter grains; also found in gardens and open waste areas. Not as common in cultivated fields, where fall or spring cultivation provides effective control. Although adapted to a wide range of conditions, it usually grows in dry, sandy or rocky soils and shaded lawns and woods.

Distribution: Abundant throughout much of North America; a common lawn and landscape weed in the northeastern and upper midwestern states.

Similar Species: **See Table 9 for a comparison of *Veronica* species. Persian speedwell (*Veronica persica* Poir.)** is a winter annual with a similar leaf shape but long, slender flower stalks. The stalks of corn speedwell flowers are <1 mm long. The leaves of Persian speedwell are generally larger, less hairy, and more deeply lobed than those of corn speedwell. Also, Persian speedwell leaves retain their basic shape and size on vegetative and flowering stems, whereas leaves on the flowering stem of corn speedwell become reduced upward. **Ivyleaf speedwell (*Veronica hederifolia* L.)** is also a winter annual with a similar habit but has distinctive **3-lobed, ivy-like leaves**. **Field speedwell (*Veronica agrestis* L.)** and **wayside speedwell (*Veronica polita* Fries)** are similar but are summer annuals and are less common than corn speedwell. Their larger leaves are petiolated, even on the flowering stem. **Purslane speedwell (*Veronica peregrina* L.)** has a growth habit similar to corn speedwell's, but its **leaves are hairless**.

Corn speedwell seedling

Corn speedwell heart-shaped seedpods

Persian speedwell foliage and flower

Ivyleaf speedwell leaves and fruit

Purslane speedwell seedling

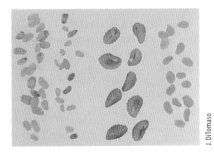

Left to right: Persian speedwell seeds, 0.7 mm; purslane speedwell seeds, 0.5 mm; field speedwell seeds, 1.5 mm; and corn speedwell seeds, 0.7 mm

Slender speedwell (*Veronica filiformis* Sm.)

SYNONYMS: creeping speedwell, creeping veronica, Whetzel weed

GENERAL DESCRIPTION: A **prostrate, creeping perennial** with **slender stolons, small, round leaves with scalloped leaf margins,** and **attractive light blue flowers in the spring.** Slender speedwell may form dense mats, particularly in turfgrass. The stems grow up to 50 cm long and root at the nodes.

PROPAGATION / PHENOLOGY: Reproduction is **predominantly vegetative in North America.** Creeping and fragmented stems can root at the nodes. Even 1 cm long stem fragments with a single node can produce adventitious roots and continue to grow. Plants are generally spread by mowers, in lawn clippings, yard compost, or landscape plant material.

SEEDLING: **In North America, this species apparently does not produce viable seed.**

MATURE PLANT: **Stems** are relatively **slender and delicate, rooting at the nodes** and becoming densely intertwined. **Leaves** are small, 8–12 mm wide, **rounded to kidney-shaped,** and sparsely hairy. Lower leaves are **opposite; those on the flowering stems are alternate.** Petioles are short (2 mm long). Leaf **margins** have **rounded teeth.**

ROOTS AND UNDERGROUND STRUCTURES: Creeping stems root at the nodes, forming a shallow, fibrous root system.

FLOWERS AND FRUIT: **Attractive light blue flowers** (8 mm in diameter) are produced from May to early summer singly in the leaf axils on long (up to 2.5 cm), slender flower stalks. Flowering among a population is usually synchronized over a 2-week period, producing an attractive floral display. The fused (4-lobed) petals are light blue with darker blue stripes. Only 2 stamens are present, and the style is 2–3 mm long. In North America, this species does not produce seed, but **in Europe the seeds are produced in heart-shaped pods.** All plants in North America are suspected to have originated from a single self-incompatible parent. When present, empty pods are heart-shaped, 3 mm long and about as wide, hairy, and broadly notched.

POSTSENESCENCE CHARACTERISTICS: Plants remain green through winter, although many leaves senesce. Stems become defoliated in hot, dry weather, but stolons survive and reestablish when weather permits.

HABITAT: A weed of turfgrass and adjoining landscapes, slender speedwell is found only in lawns, gardens, parks, and golf courses. It does not tolerate cultivation and, thus, is rarely found in cultivated fields. It tolerates a wide variety of soil types and conditions but thrives in cool, moist, shaded turf, on nutrient-rich soils.

DISTRIBUTION: Introduced into the northeastern United States as an ornamental in the 1920s; has spread via introductions to the north-central states and the Pacific Northwest.

SIMILAR SPECIES: **See Table 9 for a comparison with other *Veronica* species.** Slender speedwell is most similar to **Persian speedwell (*Veronica persica* Poir.), field speedwell (*Veronica agrestis* L.), or germander speedwell (*Veronica chamaedrys* L.),** except that slender speedwell leaves are more rounded and have rounded teeth. The other species have leaves that are longer than wide and have pointed teeth or lobes on the margins. **Ground ivy (*Glechoma hederacea*)** may look similar to slender speedwell when closely mowed or when growing under stressful conditions that markedly reduce the leaf size, but its square stems easily distinguish it from slender speedwell, which has round stems. **Lawn pennywort (*Hydrocotyle sibthorpioides* Lam.)** has similar stoloniferous growth, and small rounded leaves with shallowly lobed margins, but has alternate leaf arrangement.

Slender speedwell habit

NY State Turfgrass Association

D. Loparco

Slender speedwell vegetative and flowering stems, with opposite and alternate leaves, respectively

R. Uva

Germander speedwell habit in turfgrass

D. Loparco

Germander speedwell flowering and vegetative stems

J. DiTomaso

Left to right: common speedwell seeds, 1.0 mm; thymeleaf speedwell seeds, 0.8 mm; and germander speedwell seeds, 1.3 mm

Wild buckwheat (*Fallopia convolvulus* (L.) Á. Löve)

SYNONYMS: *Polygonum convolvulus*, black bindweed, knot bindweed, bear-bind, ivy bind-weed, climbing bindweed, climbing buckwheat, corn-bind

GENERAL DESCRIPTION: A fast-growing, **annual vine** that can trail along the ground or twine around other plants, shading and strangling them or interfering with mechanical harvest-ing. **Heart-shaped leaves** and growth habit strongly resemble field or hedge bindweed.

PROPAGATION / PHENOLOGY: Reproduction is **by seeds**. Most germination occurs from mid-May through June.

SEEDLING: **Cotyledons are oblong-oval**, approximately 20 mm long by 3 mm wide, and rounded at the apex, with a **granular waxy surface. Young leaves are alternate, bluish-green** on the upper surface, and reddish on the lower surface and stem. **Leaf blades are heart-shaped, pointed at the apex**, with entire to minutely toothed margins. Petioles on older leaves have discrete rough projections on the upper surface at the base of the midrib. A **membranous, cylindrical sheath (ocrea)** surrounds the stem at the base of each leaf. On emerging leaves, margins are rolled under the blade.

MATURE PLANT: Stems and leaves lack hairs. Vining stems are branched at the base, and in-ternodes are long. **Leaves are alternate, triangular to heart-shaped** (2–6 cm long), with the **basal lobes pointing inward toward the petiole. Upper leaves are more lanceolate.** The blade tapers toward the apex, and the margins are entire. An **ocrea** encircles the stem at the base of the petiole.

ROOTS AND UNDERGROUND STRUCTURES: Fibrous root system.

FLOWERS AND FRUIT: **Flowers** are produced from July through October. Individual flowers are inconspicuous, greenish-white, approximately 4 mm long, and **clustered** in **irregu-larly spaced groups (3–6) on 2–6 cm long elongated racemes originating from the leaf axils.** The seed is enclosed in the fruit (achene). **Achenes are 3-angled,** dull black (3–4 mm long), and enclosed in the remains of the green, **flattened, and winged sepals.**

POSTSENESCENCE CHARACTERISTICS: Dead, woody vines can persist through the winter, par-ticularly where they cover other plants.

HABITAT: Wild buckwheat is a weed of landscapes, orchards, and nursery, vegetable, and agronomic crops, especially grain crops. It usually grows in cultivated areas but is also found in roadsides and waste areas. It is well adapted to a wide range of climates and soil types.

DISTRIBUTION: Found throughout the United States and southern Canada.

SIMILAR SPECIES: **For a detailed comparison with field and hedge bindweed (*Convolvulus arvensis* and *Calystegia sepium*), see Table 5.**

Wild buckwheat habit

Wild buckwheat flowers and leaf

Wild buckwheat cotyledons

Wild buckwheat seedhead

Wild buckwheat seeds, 3 mm

Japanese knotweed (*Fallopia japonica* (Houtt.) Ronse Decr.)

SYNONYMS: *Pleuropterus zuccarinii, Polygonum cuspidatum, Reynoutria japonica,* Japanese bamboo

GENERAL DESCRIPTION: A **fast-growing, aggressive, rhizomatous perennial** reaching **2 m in height**, often appearing to be a woody shrub. Often **forms dense clumps** in which little or no other vegetation survives. Both manual and chemical control are difficult. Young, newly emerged shoots are edible.

PROPAGATION / PHENOLOGY: Spreads **primarily by rhizomes** but **produces viable seeds**. The shoots are stout and easily emerge through heavy mulch or, on occasion, asphalt.

SEEDLING: Seedlings rarely encountered. Young reddish shoots emerge from rhizomes in early spring.

MATURE PLANT: **Stems** are hollow and jointed, **bamboo-like**, and stout. Leaf base and branching points are sheathed with elongated stipules forming an **ocrea**. The **leaves** are alternate, **broadly egg-shaped**, 7.5–15 cm long.

ROOTS AND UNDERGROUND STRUCTURES: **Thick rhizomes.**

FLOWERS AND FRUIT: **Small, white flowers** are produced **in elongated** (10–13 cm long), **erect clusters (panicles)** arising from the leaf axils. Flowers bloom in **late summer**. A single seed is enclosed within the 3-winged calyx. Seeds are triangular (3 mm) and dark brown.

POSTSENESCENCE CHARACTERISTICS: Plants are very susceptible to frost. Dead, hollow, bronze-colored stems persist through the winter. The fruit remain on the stems for only a short time after senescence.

HABITAT: Introduced to North America from Japan as an ornamental, Japanese knotweed has escaped cultivation and become a weed of landscapes, sodded storm drains, and riverbanks. It also grows in roadsides, waste areas, and untended gardens. It thrives on moist, well-drained, nutrient-rich soil, particularly on shaded banks.

DISTRIBUTION: Found throughout the Northeast, west to California, and south to Georgia.

SIMILAR SPECIES: Stems can resemble **bamboo (*Phyllostachys* spp.)**, but leaves are clearly not grass-like. **Giant knotweed (*Fallopia sachalinensis* (F. Schmidt ex Maxim.) Ronse Decr.** (synonyms: *Polygonum sachalinense, Reynoutria sachalinensis*) is also a large, rhizomatous perennial that closely resembles Japanese knotweed. It can grow to 4 m tall and hybridizes with Japanese knotweed. Viable seeds are rarely produced and reproduction is primarily through vegetative means. It can be distinguished from Japanese knotweed by its much larger, more broadly lanceolate leaves (15–35 cm long compared to 10–15 cm long in Japanese knotweed) and by the heart-shaped leaf base. It was introduced from the mountains of Japan and Sakhalin Islands, and like Japanese knotweed, is generally found on disturbed, moist sites, roadsides, riparian and wetland areas throughout the northeastern and mid-Atlantic states.

J. Neal

Japanese knotweed habit

J. Neal

Japanese knotweed flowering shoot

J. Neal

Giant knotweed foliage and flowers

R. Uva

Japanese knotweed shoots from rhizomes

J. DiTomaso

Japanese knotweed seeds, 3 mm, and seed capsule

Pennsylvania smartweed (*Persicaria pensylvanica* (L.) Gómez)

Synonyms: *Polygonum pensylvanicum*, swamp persicary, glandular persicary, purple head, pinkweed, hearts-ease

General Description: An erect or **ascending, many-branched summer annual** (30 cm to 1.2 m in height).

Propagation / Phenology: Reproduction is **by seeds**; seeds germinate in the spring or early summer.

Seedling: Hypocotyls are smooth, pink at the base. Cotyledons are elliptic-oblong to lanceolate, smooth on the upper and lower surfaces, with gland-tipped hairs on the margins. **Young leaves are alternate, lanceolate to elliptic**, tinged purple on both surfaces, hairy on the upper surface and margins, smooth on the lower surface. A **conspicuous, membranous sheath (ocrea)** surrounds the stem at the base of the leaves. **Stems are smooth, reddish-purple**, with swollen and angled nodes.

Mature Plant: **Stems** are branched, green or reddish, **swollen and jointed at the nodes**, smooth or often with appressed stiff hairs. Upper parts of the stems have stalked glands. An **ocrea** is present at the base of the petiole. **Leaves** are alternate, lanceolate to elliptic or egg-shaped (5–15 cm long and up to 3 cm wide), smooth or with sparse hairs. The center of both surfaces of the leaf is **sometimes marked with a purple blotch**. The blotch is more prevalent in other, closely related species.

Roots and Underground Structures: Fibrous roots from a shallow taproot.

Flowers and Fruit: **Bright pink to white flowers** bloom from July to October. **Individual flowers are small and organized into dense, spike-like clusters** on glandular, hairy stalks. The seed is enclosed in the fruit (achene). Achenes are glossy black, smooth, circular to oval (2.5–3.5 mm wide), flattened, and pointed at the apex.

Postsenescence Characteristics: Foliage turns brown to reddish with first frost. Stems are angled at the swollen nodes. Ocrea remains, but plants do not persist through the winter.

Habitat: A weed of horticultural, agronomic, and nursery crops, as well as landscapes, Pennsylvania smartweed is rarely a problem in turfgrass. It tolerates a range of soil types and conditions, including sandy and nutrient-rich soils and particularly moist areas.

Distribution: Distributed throughout the United States.

Similar Species: **Ladysthumb (*Persicaria maculosa* Gray**; formerly *Polygonum persicaria* L.) and **tufted knotweed or bristly ladysthumb (*Persicaria longiseta* (Bruijn) Kitagawa**; formerly *Polygonum caespitosum* Blume) each have a distinctly fringed ocrea, whereas that of Pennsylvania smartweed can be torn or ragged but is never fringed. The fringes of tufted knotweed ocrea are long, as long as the membranous ocrea, whereas those on ladysthumb are short, less than half the length of the membranous ocrea. Ladysthumb and tufted knotweed generally have a darkly pigmented mark on the leaf blade that is usually lacking on Pennsylvania smartweed. **Pale smartweed (*Persicaria lapathifolia* S.F. Gray**; formerly *Polygonum lapathifolium* L.) also lacks a dark pigment mark on the leaf blade, but unlike the other 3 species, has nodding inflorescences. Like Pennsylvania smartweed, it typically lacks a fringe on the ocrea (or if present <1 mm), but only has 4 perianth parts, whereas Pennsylvania smartweed has 5.

Ladysthumb habit

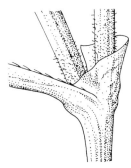

Pennsylvania smartweed
ocrea

Syngenta Crop Protection AG

J. DiTomaso

J. DiTomaso

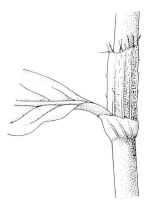

Ladysthumb ocrea

Syngenta Crop Protection AG

Pennsylvania smartweed
leafy shoot (note ocrea)

Pennsylvania
smartweed
inflorescence

R. Uva

Tufted knotweed seedlings

J. DiTomaso

Left, ladysthumb seeds, 2.3 mm; *right*,
Pennsylvania smartweed seeds,
3.0 mm

411

Mile-a-minute or clasping-leaf smartweed (*Persicaria perfoliata* (L.) H. Gross)

Synonyms: *Polygonum perfoliatum*, *Tracaulon perfoliatum*, devil's tear-thumb, minute weed, mile-a-minute vine, giant climbing tear-thumb

General Description: A **spiny, summer annual vine** growing to 7 m in length. Stems can become woody with age. It can climb over shrubs, small trees, and structures, forming dense mats. Its **stems, petioles, and major leaf-veins have 1–2 mm long reflexed prickles.**

Propagation / Phenology: Reproduction is **by seeds**. Seedlings are established by late April and grow rapidly between May and August.

Seedling: No information available.

Mature Plant: **Stems** are branched, green vines, red-brown toward the base, with **reflexed prickles (1–2 mm long). Leaves are alternate**, smooth, **waxy**, light green or often reddish when young, **triangular to somewhat heart-shaped at the base, pointed at the apex** (3–8 cm long and as wide at the base). Leaf margins are rough. **Petioles have recurved spines** and are slightly longer than the blade. **A prominent leaf-like sheath (ocrea)** encircles the stem at the base of the petiole. The upper branches may have ocreae without developed leaves.

Roots and Underground Structures: Shallow, fibrous root system.

Flowers and Fruit: **Flowers** are produced as early as June, but typically from late July through August, at the end of branches or in the leaf axils **in spike-like racemes**, 1–2 cm long. **Individual flowers are inconspicuous**, greenish-white to yellow, rarely pink, 3–5 mm long. The **fruit** (achene) is enclosed within a **berry-like (4–6 mm in diameter) structure consisting of swollen, metallic-blue floral parts (perianth).** The outer coating dries and wrinkles with age. Achenes are round, black, and shiny (3 mm long), ripening late in the season (mid-September into November).

Postsenescence Characteristics: Fruit and prickles may remain after the vine is dead.

Habitat: Mile-a-minute is a weed of landscapes, nursery crops, and orchards, as well as clear-cut timberlands, roadsides, drainage ditches, and rights-of-way. It grows on moist, well-drained soil, and although it tolerates shady areas, it thrives in full sunlight.

Distribution: This invasive species is spreading in the region. Currently populations are known to occur from North Carolina to New York and west to Ohio. It is a regulated species in several states. Report new occurrences to appropriate state agencies.

Similar Species: **Wild buckwheat (*Fallopia convolvulus*)** is a summer annual vine lacking reflexed prickles. In addition, it has heart-shaped, not triangular, leaves. **Most other similar vines also lack the prickles.**

Mile-a-minute habit

Mile-a-minute downward pointing barbs

Mile-a-minute leafy shoot

Mile-a-minute saucer-like ocrea

Mile-a-minute distinctive blue fruit in clusters

Mile-a-minute seeds, 3 mm

413

Prostrate knotweed (*Polygonum aviculare* L.)

SYNONYMS: knot-grass, door-weed, mat-grass, pink-weed, bird-grass, stone-grass, way-grass, goose-grass

GENERAL DESCRIPTION: A **summer annual** with **prostrate** to ascending, branching stems, 10–60 cm long, rarely taller than 10–20 cm.

PROPAGATION / PHENOLOGY: Reproduction is **by seeds**. Prostrate knotweed is **one of the first summer annual weeds to emerge in the spring** (up to a month before crabgrass) but can also emerge throughout the spring and summer. Seedlings develop slowly, becoming more noticeable in mid-summer.

SEEDLING: Hypocotyls are brownish-red and smooth. Both cotyledons and young leaves have a waxy whitish coating. **Cotyledons are very narrow** (10–15 mm long by 1–2 mm wide), almost grass-like. **Young leaves** are alternate, elliptic to lanceolate, and **dull blue-green**. Emerging leaves are rolled, with the upper sides facing outward. **A whitish-brown, membranous sheath (ocrea) surrounds the stem at the base of the leaf.**

MATURE PLANT: Plants form a tough, prostrate, wiry mat. Stems are slender, branched, longitudinally ridged, and swollen at the nodes. **Leaves are alternate**, lanceolate or **elliptic** to oblong (1–3 cm long by 1–8 mm wide), narrowed at the base and pointed at the apex. Petioles are very short, with a **conspicuous ocrea sheathing the stem at the leaf base.**

ROOTS AND UNDERGROUND STRUCTURES: **Thin taproot.**

FLOWERS AND FRUIT: **Flowers** are produced from June through November in groups of **1–5 in axillary clusters** on short flower stalks slightly longer than the membranous, tubular sheaths. **Flowers are small and inconspicuous**; the sepals (2–3 mm long) are white to green with pinkish margins. Petals are absent. The seed is enclosed in the fruit (achene). Achenes are 2–3 mm long, 3-angled, teardrop-shaped, and dark reddish-brown to black. **Fruits mature before the sepals fall off** but have a complex dormancy.

POSTSENESCENCE CHARACTERISTICS: **Clusters or mats of dead, wire-like stems, often reddish**, remain through the winter around walkways and in lawns. Remnants of the cylindrical membranous sheath (ocrea) may persist at the nodes.

HABITAT: Prostrate knotweed is a weed of turfgrass, nursery crops, landscapes, and occasionally agricultural crops. In turfgrass, it is most often found on **hard, compacted soil or areas damaged** in spring or summer by traffic or trampling, including paths and walkways, areas where road salt accumulates, and athletic fields. Prostrate knotweed is not particularly competitive; it usually survives in stressed areas where other species do not grow well or are damaged.

DISTRIBUTION: Found throughout the United States and southern Canada.

SIMILAR SPECIES: **Several very similar subspecies** of *Polygonum aviculare* are recognized and widely distributed in the northeastern United States and southern Canada. The *Flora of North America* differentiates subspecies *aviculare*, *buxiforme*, *depressum*, and *neglectum* based on a combination of traits including tepal margin color, persistence of the ocrea, aggregation of leaves, and leaf blade length to width ratios. Several **spurges (*Euphorbia* spp.)** with prostrate habits resemble prostrate knotweed, but spurges exude a milky sap when injured and knotweed does not.

J. Neal

Prostrate knotweed habit

A. DiTommaso

Prostrate knotweed flower

J. DiTommaso

Prostrate knotweed mature shoot
(note ocreae at nodes)

J. Neal

Prostrate knotweed seedlings in early spring

Prostrate knotweed seeds, 2 mm

J. DiTommaso

Red sorrel (*Rumex acetosella* L.)

SYNONYMS: sheep sorrel, sour-grass, Indian cane, field sorrel, horse sorrel, sour weed, red-top sorrel, cow sorrel, red-weed, mountain sorrel

GENERAL DESCRIPTION: A **rhizomatous perennial** (to 45 cm tall) **with primarily basal, arrowhead-shaped leaves** and a sparsely leaved flowering stem. Plants accumulate high concentrations of soluble oxalates, which give them a **sour taste** and **occasionally cause fatalities in livestock, particularly sheep.**

PROPAGATION / PHENOLOGY: Reproduction is **by seeds and rhizomes**. Rhizome buds sprout in early spring and produce basal rosettes.

SEEDLING: Cotyledons are dull green, smooth, slightly thickened, and oblong (10 mm long). Stalks of the cotyledon are flattened on the upper surface and united basally to form a short membranous tube **(ocrea)**. **Seedlings produce a rosette of foliage** in which **leaf shapes change with age. Young leaves are egg-shaped**, smooth, and slightly thickened; the margins are entire, and the bases taper into the petiole. Both **surfaces of the leaves are covered with waxy granules. The characteristic basal lobes develop on the third, fourth, or fifth leaf.** Petioles are grooved on the upper surface and expand basally into a white membranous **ocrea. Shoots emerging from rhizomes are more robust** than seedlings.

MATURE PLANT: **Leaves** are thick, petiolated, smooth, 2.5–7.5 cm long, dull green, and **arrowhead-shaped with 2 narrow and spreading basal lobes.** A papery or membranous sheath **(ocrea)** surrounds the stem just above the point of leaf attachment. Most leaves develop from the **basal rosette; stem leaves are fewer and alternate**. Upper leaves on the stem are linear, sometimes without basal lobes. **Flowering stems** (1 to several) are **slender, erect**, branched toward the top, 4-sided, **vertically ridged**, and usually maroon, especially toward the base. In spring, leaves are narrow and thin; in autumn, leaves are broader and fleshy.

ROOTS AND UNDERGROUND STRUCTURES: Extensive but shallow root system consists of a **yellow taproot** and numerous **slender rhizomes**.

FLOWERS AND FRUIT: **Flowers** are produced from May to September in **branched, terminal clusters (panicles)**. Male and female flowers are produced on separate plants (dioecious). **Male flowers are yellowish-green; female flowers are reddish-brown.** The panicles appear reddish when mature. **S**eed is enclosed within a **triangular achene**, 1–1.5 mm long, reddish-brown, and usually surrounded by rough persistent flower parts.

POSTSENESCENCE CHARACTERISTICS: Foliage often turns yellowish in late autumn, but plants typically are green throughout the year.

HABITAT: Red sorrel is a weed of turfgrass, landscapes, and nursery crops. It is often found on, but not limited to, acid soils and areas with poor drainage, low nitrogen, and little competition from other species.

DISTRIBUTION: Distributed throughout the United States and southern Canada.

SIMILAR SPECIES: The unique leaf shape and sour taste can distinguish it from other weed species.

Red sorrel habit

R. Uva

Red sorrel seedlings

J. DiTomaso

Red sorrel rosette from rhizome

J. Neal

Red sorrel mature leaves

J. DiTomaso

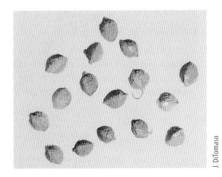

Red sorrel seeds, 1.2 mm

J. DiTomaso

Curly dock (*Rumex crispus* L.)

Synonyms: *Rumex elongatus*, sour dock, yellow dock, narrow-leaved dock

General Description: A **taprooted perennial** developing a **basal rosette of wavy-margined leaves** and a sparsely leaved flowering stem reaching 1 m in height. **At maturity, fruit and flowering stems are conspicuously reddish-brown.**

Propagation / Phenology: Reproduction is **by seeds**; seeds germinate in cool, moist soil from late spring through early fall as conditions permit. Perennial plants emerge from the taproot in mid-spring, producing a robust rosette.

Seedling: Hypocotyls are green, tinged maroon at the base. Cotyledons are hairless, dull green, granular-coated, and spatulate to long-oval, with petioles that are connected by a ridge across the shoot axis. **Young leaves** are in a **basal rosette**, smooth, **egg-shaped**, with **red spots** on the upper surface. **Older leaves** have slightly **wavy margins**. A papery membranous sheath (ocrea) surrounds the stem at the base of the petiole (difficult to see in rosettes). Emerging leaf margins are rolled underneath the blade.

Mature Plant: Emerging perennials produce a robust **basal rosette of 15–30 cm long leaves with wavy margins.** Leaves are shiny, progressively becoming more reddish-purple through the season. **Lower leaves are longer** and **more rounded** than the stem leaves. **Elongating flowering stems** are smooth, **ridged**, often reddish, branched toward the top with enlarged nodes. **Stem leaves are alternate**, **subtended by an ocrea**, and **reduced** in both number and size compared with basal leaves.

Roots and Underground Structures: Large, thick, somewhat branched **taproot.**

Flowers and Fruit: Flowers primarily in June but also throughout the summer. **Flowers are in clusters** (15–60 cm long) on narrowly spaced branches **on the upper portions of the elongating stem.** Flowers consist of greenish sepals that become **reddish-brown at maturity.** The seed is enclosed within the fruit (achene). The calyx develops into a **papery or corky, 3-winged, triangular structure that surrounds the achene.** Achenes (approximately 2 mm long) are **triangular, glossy,** and reddish-brown at maturity. Corky structures (tubercles) on the outside of the calyx allow the fruit to float on water, thus facilitating dispersal.

Postsenescence Characteristics: Erect, brown, ridged **flower stalks persist** through winter, bearing the **distinctive reddish-brown**, 3-winged fruit.

Habitat: Curly dock is a weed of low-maintenance turfgrass, orchards, nursery crops, landscapes, roadsides, meadows, pastures, and forage crops, but usually not cultivated row crops. It also grows along drainage ditches and in waste areas. Curly dock thrives on nutrient-rich, heavy, damp soils but does not tolerate cultivation.

Distribution: Found throughout the United States and southern Canada.

Similar Species: The leaves of **broadleaf dock (*Rumex obtusifolius* L.)** have **heart-shaped lobes at the base** and are **wider and less wavy than those of curly dock**. The calyx lobes that develop into the wings of the fruit have toothed margins in broadleaf dock but are entire in curly dock. Both species have ocreae.

R. Uva

J. Neal

Left, broadleaf dock rosettes; *right*, curly dock rosettes

Curly dock flowering shoot

J. DiTomaso

Broadleaf dock seedlings

A. DiTommaso

Curly dock
mature seedhead

J. Neal

Broadleaf dock leaf shapes, *right to left:* basal to
flower stalk

J. DiTomaso

Left, curly dock seeds (achenes), 1.8 mm (without
papery bracts); *right*, broadleaf dock seeds (achenes),
2.0 mm (without papery bracts)

Common purslane (*Portulaca oleracea* L.)

Synonyms: pusley, pursley, wild portulaca

General Description: A **summer annual** with a **prostrate, mat-forming habit** (30 cm or more in diameter) and **thick, succulent stems and leaves**.

Propagation / Phenology: Reproduction is **by seeds** and by fragmented stem segments that root at the nodes. Seeds germinate from late May or early June through August, when soil-surface temperatures are high, 30°C (86°F).

Seedling: Young seedlings are erect but soon become prostrate. Hypocotyls are maroon, succulent, erect to ascending (approximately 16 mm long). **Cotyledons** are oblong (10 mm long), somewhat **club-shaped and succulent**, green or maroon on the top surface and maroon on the lower surface. **Young leaves are opposite** or nearly opposite; **blades** are smooth, green on the upper surface, maroon-tinged or maroon on the lower surface, **oblong, broadest and rounded at the apex**, tapering toward the base (7 mm long by 4 mm wide). Petioles are short (<2 mm) or absent. **Stems are succulent**, green in the younger portions, maroon in the older portions.

Mature Plant: **Stems are many-branched, purplish-red** or green, smooth, completely **prostrate** or turned up at the ends. **Leaves are opposite or alternate**, 1–3 cm long, **thick and fleshy**, with smooth, untoothed margins. **Blades are wedge-shaped, rounded at the apex, and narrowed to the base** (spatulate). **Petioles are absent**; stipules may be present, but if so, are reduced to soft bristles.

Roots and Underground Structures: A thick taproot with many fibrous secondary roots.

Flowers and Fruit: **Flowers appear** from July through September, **only 4–6 weeks after seedlings emerge**. Flowers are 5–10 mm wide, alone in the leaf axils or **clustered at the end of stems**. The **yellow petals** (5) are slightly shorter than the sepals and open only when it is sunny. The fruit is an oval, 4–8 mm long, many-seeded capsule that opens by splitting transversely around the middle. Seeds are black, flattened, rounded to kidney-shaped, 1 mm or less in diameter, with rounded bumps on the surface.

Postsenescence Characteristics: Leaves decay quickly after frost, leaving the prostrate, branched stems. Stems persist for only a short time and are generally decomposed by spring.

Habitat: A weed of landscapes, thin or newly seeded turfgrass, and nursery, vegetable, fruit, and agronomic crops. Common purslane is found in most cultivated crops, home gardens, and annual flower beds. It is also a weed of crevices between bricks and in cracked cement. Common purslane thrives on nutrient-rich, sandy soils but tolerates poor, compacted soils and drought. It prefers areas of high light and warm growing conditions.

Distribution: Widespread throughout the world.

Similar Species: **Paraguayan or pink purslane (*Portulaca amilis* Speg.)** is very similar but has pointed leaves, wispy hairs at the leaf bases, and bright pink flowers. Prostrate habit may lead to confusion with the **spurges (*Euphorbia* spp.)** or with **prostrate knotweed (*Polygonum aviculare*)**. Spurges, however, exude milky latex when stems and leaves are injured. Prostrate knotweed is not succulent and has small papery sheaths (ocrea) around the leaf bases. Seedlings of prostrate knotweed generally emerge earlier in the spring than those of common purslane or spurge. **Water purslane or marsh seedbox (*Ludwigia palustris* (L.) Elliott)** (Onagraceae) also has prostrate, hairless, succulent stems with red pigmentation and opposite leaves. But its leaves have pointed tips, flowers are inconspicuous, and angled fruit capsules with 4 spreading sepals are in the leaf axils. Water purslane is more common in persistently wet sites.

Common purslane habit

J. Neal

J. DiTomaso

Common purslane seedlings

J. DiTomaso

Common purslane flower

A. Senesac

Common purslane seedpods

J. DiTomaso

Common purslane seeds, 1 mm

J. Neal

Paraguayan or pink purslane flower and leaves

421

Scarlet pimpernel (*Anagallis arvensis* L.)

SYNONYMS: poor man's weather-glass, red chickweed, poison chickweed, shepherds clock, eye-bright

GENERAL DESCRIPTION: A **prostrate or ascending** to erect, **low-growing**, branching, **annual** with a delicate appearance. Scarlet pimpernel tolerates mowing and is usually <15 cm tall (occasionally to 30 cm).

PROPAGATION / PHENOLOGY: Reproduction is **by seeds**. Seedlings may emerge over an extended period of time.

SEEDLING: Seedlings are dark green and shiny. **Cotyledons** are smooth, **triangular to diamond-shaped** (0.75–3 mm wide by 1–6 mm long), broadest at the base, with a dull point at the apex, with tiny glandular hairs. **Young leaves are opposite, triangular** to almost rounded or heart-shaped. **Petioles are very short or absent. Leaf surfaces are smooth** or have glandular hairs; the **lower surfaces have small, purple spots**.

MATURE PLANT: **Stems are 4-angled or square**, smooth, and branched from the base, ascending upward. **Leaves are similar to seedling leaves**, although more egg-shaped to elliptic (2 cm long) and **occasionally in whorls of 3**.

ROOTS AND UNDERGROUND STRUCTURES: Shallow, fibrous root system.

FLOWERS AND FRUIT: Flowers are present mainly from June to August. **Small, bell-shaped flowers** are produced singly in the leaf axils on relatively long, nodding stalks. Petals (5) are **salmon to brick-red** (rarely white, pink, or blue), ovate with a fringe of tiny glandular hairs on the margin. Sepals (5) are green and awl-shaped. The fruit is a smooth, rounded, 1-celled, many-seeded capsule; the top half comes off like a lid at maturity. Seeds are approximately 1.3 mm long, 3-angled, elliptic, dull brown or black.

POSTSENESCENCE CHARACTERISTICS: None of note.

HABITAT: Primarily a weed of turfgrass and landscapes, scarlet pimpernel is also found in roadsides and waste areas. It is less common in cultivated crops.

DISTRIBUTION: Introduced from Europe; now distributed throughout the United States, particularly in sandy soils. Most troublesome in the mid-Atlantic states and on the Pacific Coast.

SIMILAR SPECIES: **Common chickweed (*Stellaria media*)** is similar in leaf shape and habit; however, chickweed has round stems, whereas scarlet pimpernel stems are 4-angled or square. The 2 species also differ in flower and leaf color. The flowers of chickweed are white with 5 deeply lobed petals (giving the appearance of 10), and leaves do not have purplish dots on the underside, as do scarlet pimpernel leaves.

Scarlet pimpernel habit

J. Neal

Scarlet pimpernel seedling

J. Neal

Scarlet pimpernel flowering stem

A. DiTommaso

Scarlet pimpernel stem and leaves (note square stem and spots on underside of leaves)

R. Uva

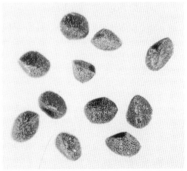

Scarlet pimpernel seeds, 1 mm

J. DiTommaso

423

Moneywort (*Lysimachia nummularia* L.)

Synonyms: creeping loosestrife, yellow myrtle, creeping Jenny, creeping Charlie, herb two-pence, two-penny grass

General Description: An introduced ornamental; still sold in the nursery industry as a **creeping, perennial ground cover**. Forms mats of prostrate, branched stems (15–50 cm long).

Propagation / Phenology: Reproduction is **primarily by creeping and rooting stems**. Although **viable seeds are produced**, they are not considered to be a major means of plant dispersal.

Seedling: No information available.

Mature Plant: Foliage lacks hairs but has smooth glandular dots on the surface. **Leaves are opposite, square to round**, 1–3 cm long, with a **pointed tip**. Petioles are short.

Roots and Underground Structures: **Stems root at the nodes**, producing a shallow, fibrous root system.

Flowers and Fruit: **Bright yellow flowers** (2–3 cm in diameter) are produced **individually on stalks (pedicels) in the leaf axils**. Petals (5) are 10–15 mm long and lobed. The fruit is a 1-celled spherical capsule that splits vertically when mature. Seeds are approximately 1 mm long, elliptic, 3-angled, dark brown to black, with a rough surface produced by scaly ridges.

Postsenescence Characteristics: Plants are not conspicuous during the winter.

Habitat: Although primarily a weed of turfgrass and landscapes, moneywort is also found in gardens, ditches, and low fields. It prefers moist, shady sites and seldom survives under excessively dry conditions.

Distribution: Escaped cultivation and has become naturalized throughout the northeastern United States, north to Newfoundland and Ontario, south to Georgia, and west to Missouri and Kansas.

Similar Species: Moneywort can be distinguished from **thymeleaf speedwell (*Veronica serpyllifolia* L.)** by its leaves. Thymeleaf speedwell leaves are generally smaller and often slightly notched at the tip, whereas those of moneywort are rounded to pointed. Moneywort may also resemble a robust specimen of **common chickweed (*Stellaria media*)**; however, common chickweed is a winter annual with white flowers, and moneywort is a perennial with yellow flowers. Also, the leaves of common chickweed taper to a point; moneywort leaf tips are rounded or squarish with a pointed end.

J. Neal

Moneywort habit

R. Uva

Moneywort flowers and foliage

R. Uva

Moneywort flower buds

Tall buttercup (*Ranunculus acris* L.)

Synonyms: giant buttercup, showy buttercup

General Description: **Tufted perennial** with short rhizomes, palmately 3-parted to deeply palmately dissected leaves on long petioles, and bright yellow "buttercup" flowers on erect stems 20–60 cm tall. Can be poisonous to livestock but is avoided by cattle, reducing pastures' grazing quality.

Propagation / Phenology: Plants reproduce **by seeds**. **Short rhizomes** enlarge the clumps. Small pieces of the rhizome can regenerate plants, facilitating spread by cultivation. Seeds germinate from spring through autumn in response to soil disturbance.

Seedling: Cotyledons are oval, rounded at the apex, with petioles almost as long as the blade. **First true leaves are hairy, with 3-lobes**. Initially, all leaves are basal, wide leaf bases overlapping at the base, 3-parted; each lobe is lobed or toothed. The terminal leaflet is not stalked.

Mature Plant: Basal leaves with long, hairy petioles, 10–50 cm long. Leaf blades are pentagonal or **round in outline**, the width equal to or greater than the length, and deeply 3–5 lobed, each lobe further divided (**dissected**) with the ultimate segments thin lanceolate. **The middle lobe is not stalked**; all lobes are sessile on the petiole. In spring, plants produce leafy, erect, branched flowering stems. The stems, petioles, and leaves are usually hairy but some lack hairs. Stem leaves are alternate and similar to mature basal leaves. **Upper leaves subtending flowers are sessile**, less divided becoming entirely linear, and smaller than the lower leaves.

Roots and Underground Structures: Plants form **short, thick rhizomes** that enlarge the clump.

Flowers and Fruit: Plants flower in late spring and continue sporadically through autumn. Flower heads bright yellow, 1.5–2.5 cm wide, on long, branched, unfurrowed stalks. **Bright, shiny, yellow petals** (5) are broadly rounded at the apex with wedge-shaped bases, and 8–11 mm long. Sepals (5) are green turning yellow with age, spreading (not reflexed), and hairy. Fruit heads are globe-shaped, 5–7 mm wide with 30–50 flattened achenes, 2–3.5 mm long, glabrous, with a short (0.5 mm), curved beak; green turning brown to black at maturity.

Postsenescence Characteristics: In milder climates, the plants can remain green.

Habitat: An important weed of pastures. Also found in roadsides, hay crops, and disturbed areas.

Distribution: Present throughout most of the United States and Canada. Introduced from Europe.

Similar Species: **See Table 8 for a comparison with other *Ranunculus* species.** Similar to **bulbous buttercup (*Ranunculus bulbosus*)**, but tall buttercup does not produce a bulbous base and the sepals are not reflexed. **Creeping buttercup (*Ranunculus repens* L.)** has similar foliage and flowers but is a stoloniferous perennial; stems root at the nodes and are covered with stiff hairs. Creeping buttercup leaves are 3-lobed, the **middle lobe has a long stalk**, and each lobe is often further divided with toothed margins; and on long, hairy petioles. Flowers are large and showy, with 5 bright yellow petals; sepals are spreading (rarely reflexed), with stiff hairs. Fruits are in a rounded head up to 8 mm in diameter, individual achenes are flattened, approximately 3 mm in length with a persistent, curved beak 0.8–1.2 mm long. Several subspecies and varieties have been described.

Tall buttercup habit

Tall buttercup 2-leaf seedling

Tall buttercup flower with hairy sepals

Tall buttercup leaf shapes

Creeping buttercup leaf shapes

Creeping buttercup stolon

Tall buttercup achenes

Bulbous buttercup (*Ranunculus bulbosus* L.)

SYNONYMS: bulbous crowfoot, yellow weed, blister flower, gowan

GENERAL DESCRIPTION: **Tufted perennial** forming a **basal rosette of 3-parted leaves** arising from a thickened **bulb-like (corm) base**. Flowering stems are usually erect (20–60 cm tall), but low to prostrate in turfgrass. Buttercups can be poisonous to livestock but are usually not palatable. Dried plants in hay are not toxic as the toxic compounds volatilize during drying.

PROPAGATION / PHENOLOGY: Plants **overwinter as corms** but **reproduction is by seeds**.

SEEDLING: Cotyledons are elliptic, rounded at the apex, with relatively long petioles that sheath the stem at the base. **Young leaves** are hairy, with **3-lobed** on relatively **long petioles**. Young **plants form a tuft**.

MATURE PLANT: The basal and lower stem leaves are on long, hairy petioles, are 3-parted with rounded to ovate, deeply cleft and lobed divisions. **The middle lobe is stalked, the 2 lateral lobes are sessile.** In late spring, plants produce sparsely leaved, erect, flowering stems. Stems are hairy at the base and sometimes hairy above. Stem leaves are alternate and similar to basal leaves. Upper leaves are sessile, less divided, and smaller than lower leaves.

ROOTS AND UNDERGROUND STRUCTURES: The stem is thickened at, and just below, the soil surface into a bulb-like base (corm) with fibrous roots below.

FLOWERS AND FRUIT: Flowers (1.5–3 cm wide) appear from April to July and are solitary at the ends of long, furrowed stalks. **Bright, shiny, yellow petals** (5–7) are broadly rounded at the apex with wedge-shaped bases, and 8–16 mm long. Sepals (5) are green and **curve back toward the stem (reflexed)**. Both stamen and pistils are numerous. Each seed is enclosed within the fruit (achene), and numerous achenes are produced in rounded heads. Individual fruits are flattened (2.5–3.5 mm long), with short, curved beaks and distinct margins.

POSTSENESCENCE CHARACTERISTICS: Foliage dies back to the corm. No distinctive winter characteristics.

HABITAT: A common weed of turfgrass, landscapes, and pastures. Rarely weedy in conventionally, traditionally, cultivated crops.

DISTRIBUTION: Common in the northeastern, southeastern, and western United States and Canada.

SIMILAR SPECIES: **See Table 8 for a comparison with other *Ranunculus* species. Hairy buttercup (*Ranunculus sardous* Crantz)** is a winter annual, forming a rosette and then a multi-stemmed clump to 40 cm tall. Most leaves are basal on long, hairy petioles; deeply 3–5 lobed, terminal segment is stalked, lobes are divided or have lobed margins; blades are hairy. Flowering stems are hairy, branched with few stem leaves. Stem leaves are much smaller than basal leaves; lobes are fewer and thinner. Flowers are bright yellow, approximately 2.5 cm in diameter, with showy petals 5–8 mm long (shorter than bulbous buttercup petals), and reflexed, hairy sepals. The fruit cluster is rounded to oval with 15–30 achenes; each 2–3 mm long with a 0.4–0.7 mm long curved beak. Hairy buttercup is an annual lacking the perennial, swollen base of bulbous buttercup. As seedlings, these 2 species are nearly identical. **Tall buttercup (*Ranunculus acris*)** is similar, but the leaves are more rounded in outline and the central lobe is not on a long stalk, the sepals are not reflexed, and it does not have a bulb-like base.

Bulbous buttercup habit

Bulbous buttercup seedling with cotyledons

Hairy buttercup unopened flower with reflexed sepals

Bulbous buttercup leaf

Hairy buttercup stem leaf

Bulbous buttercup seeds, 3.5 mm

429

Lesser celandine (*Ranunculus ficaria* L.)

Synonyms: *Ficaria verna*, fig buttercup

General Description: A **prostrate, herbaceous, perennial ground cover** with **heart-shaped leaves** on long petioles, and **showy, yellow flowers** in the spring. Introduced from Europe as a garden plant.

Propagation / Phenology: **Reproduction is by seeds, rhizomes, tuberous roots, creeping stems, and bulbils.** Seedlings and bulbil sprouts emerge in early spring. Plants are ephemeral, present for a relatively short time in the spring, flowering, and then senescing in summer under warmer conditions.

Seedling: Little information is available. Many infestations are from vegetative reproduction.

Mature Plant: Plants may form dense mounds or thick ground cover. Leaves are dark green, fleshy, glabrous, and cordate to oblong, with entire or shallowly wavy/crenate margins and long (10–30 cm), succulent petioles. Stems are prostrate, succulent, lack hairs, and root at the nodes producing a leafy crown. Leaves emerge in a tight cluster from the crowns but are alternate on creeping stems. Stem leaves are similar to the basal leaves. **Two subspecies form bulbils** (tuber-like structures) in the leaf axils; other subspecies lack aerial bulbils.

Roots and Underground Structures: Clusters of thickened, tuberous roots and fibrous roots are present. Tubers are formed on spreading roots. Plants oversummer as perennial crowns, tuberous roots, and tubers.

Flowers and Fruit: Bright, yellow flower heads 2.5–6 cm in diameter are held at or above the foliage on long, fleshy stalks. **Flowers have 3 glabrous sepals and 8–12 (rarely up to 26) bright, shiny, yellow petals**, fading to pale yellow with age. Fruit heads are globe-shaped, with 30–60 oval, flattened achenes, often remaining green. Achenes lack the beak present on most other species of *Ranunculus*.

Postsenescence Characteristics: Aboveground plant parts do not persist after senescence.

Habitat: Most infestations are in close proximity to water sources in shady, persistently moist habitats such as streambanks, moist floodplains, and irrigated turf and landscapes. However, plants are well adapted to a variety of habitats including relatively dry upland soils, lawns, gardens, and woodlands. Rarely occurrs in cultivated crops.

Distribution: Distributed throughout the northeastern United States and eastern Canada; south to the Carolinas and west to the Mississippi Valley.

Similar Species: **See Table 8 for a comparison with other *Ranunculus* species.** New growth in the spring can resemble perennial **violets (*Viola* spp.)**, with petiolate, cordate leaves. However, leaf tips of violets are more acute compared to lesser celandine leaves. *Viola* and *Ranunculus* are easily differentiated when in flower. The bright, yellow flowers are similar to other *Ranunculus* species but have more numerous petals. There are 5 distinct subspecies of *Ranunculus ficaria* documented in North America with similar growth, flowers, and distributions. The subspecies can be differentiated by the presence of bulbils, leaf patterns, length and width of leaf blades, and petiole length. All subspecies appear to have similar invasive potential.

Lesser celandine habit

Lesser celandine sprouting
from a tuber

Lesser celandine flower and foliage

Lesser celandine green fruits

Lesser celandine tuberous roots

Lesser celandine aerial bulbils

431

Smallflower (hairy) buttercup (*Ranunculus parviflorus* L.)

Synonym: stickseed crowfoot

General Description: A **prostrate** or ascending winter annual, with **hairy stems, leaves**, and petioles, and palmately **lobed leaves with toothed margins**. Flowers are not showy, with petals absent or much reduced.

Propagation / Phenology: Reproduction is **by seeds.** Seedlings emerge in autumn or early spring.

Seedling: Cotyledons are oval, rounded at the apex. Young leaves are hairy, with 3-lobes on petioles that are longer than the leaf blades. Young plants initially form a rosette but soon lateral branches form at the base, often growing in a radial pattern from the crown.

Mature Plant: Stems are prostrate or ascending (occasionally erect when growing within dense vegetation), hairy with alternate leaves, forming mats or mounds. Prostrate stems usually do not root. Leaves are hairy, palmately lobed, the center lobe is not stalked; margins irregularly toothed.

Roots and Underground Structures: A shallow, fibrous root system.

Flowers and Fruit: Flowers are on long stalks from the leaf axils. **Petals are typically absent**; occasionally 1–2 short petals, approximately 5 mm long, are present. The 5 sepals are densely hairy and reflexed, curving back toward the stalk. Each seed is enclosed within the fruit (achene), with 10–20 achenes in each rounded, 5 mm diameter head. Individual fruits are flattened, about 2 mm long, with a short, deltate beak and slender recurved tip, 0.4–0.6 mm.

Postsenescence Characteristics: Dead stems may persist a short time into summer.

Habitat: A common weed of turfgrass, landscapes, pastures, roadsides, and disturbed sites. Rarely weedy in cultivated crops.

Distribution: Distributed throughout the eastern United States, north to New York, and west to the Mississippi Valley. Introduced from Europe.

Similar Species: **See Table 8 for a comparison with other *Ranunculus* species.** The creeping habit is similar to **creeping buttercup (*Ranunculus repens* L.)**, but creeping buttercup stems root at the nodes, the middle lobe on the leaves is stalked, and it has showy, yellow flowers. Palmately lobed leaves with sharply pointed leaf margins and pubescence distinguish smallflower buttercup from most other weeds in similar habitats.

Smallflower buttercup habit

Smallflower buttercup seedling

Smallflower buttercup mature foliage

Smallflower buttercup flower and fruit

Both photos by J. Neal

Smallflower buttercup seeds

Crowfoot buttercup (*Ranunculus sceleratus* L.)

SYNONYMS: celery-leaf buttercup, cursed buttercup

GENERAL DESCRIPTION: A winter annual (rarely short-lived perennial), forming a rosette and then multi-stemmed clump. Leaves are mostly basal, deeply divided, 3–5 lobes, and lack hairs; the lobes connected by leaf tissue and terminal lobe is not stalked. Flowers are not showy, with short, yellow petals and a cylindrical seedhead. Origin is unclear; possibly native to North America.

PROPAGATION / PHENOLOGY: Reproduction is **by seeds**.

SEEDLING: Little information is available about the seedlings. Plants initially form a rosette of palmately divided leaves on petioles longer than leaf blades.

MATURE PLANT: Forms a dense clump with multiple upright, branched stems, rooting at the base. **Stems, leaves, and petioles are glabrous** (or nearly so), thick and almost succulent. Most leaves are basal, on long petioles; blades are rounded to kidney-shaped in outline; 3-parted, the middle lobe not stalked. Margins are shallowly lobed or wavy. Stem leaves are alternate and similar to the basal leaves but gradually reduced in size; sessile and linear when subtending flower branches.

ROOTS AND UNDERGROUND STRUCTURES: Large, multi-stemmed crown with coarse roots.

FLOWERS AND FRUIT: **Flowers are not showy**; present in spring, and sporadically into summer. Erect stems are many-branched with >30 flowers per stem. Petals (5) are pale yellow and 3–4 mm long. Sepals (5) are hairy, curve back toward the stem **(reflexed)**, and are about as long as the petals. The seedhead elongates to be cylindrical with many (>100) achenes. Individual achenes are not strongly flattened; oval and approximately 1 mm long.

POSTSENESCENCE CHARACTERISTICS: No distinctive winter characteristics.

HABITAT: Plants are more commonly found in persistently wet areas, such as streambanks and drainage ditches. Rarely weedy in conventionally cultivated crops.

DISTRIBUTION: Present throughout the eastern two-thirds of North America.

SIMILAR SPECIES: **See Table 8 for a comparison with other *Ranunculus* species. Small-flower buttercup or kidney-leaf buttercup (*Ranunculus abortivus* L.)** is also a winter annual (or biennial) forming a rosette and then multi-stemmed clump, with **glabrous** stems and leaves. It can be distinguished by **basal leaves that are mostly heart- or kidney-shaped** (much like *Ranunculus ficaria* or *Viola* spp.), with wavy entire margins, on long petioles. Leaves on the flowering stems are sessile, deeply divided to trifoliolate, with long, narrow lobes. Flowers are present but not showy. The 5 petals are pale greenish-yellow and shorter than the sepals. Sepals are spreading (not reflexed), 3–4 mm long, and lack hairs. Fruit is a rounded to oval head of achenes, each approximately 1.5 mm long, flattened, with a curved beak 0.1–0.2 mm long. Plants occur in woodlands, pastures, turfgrass, and disturbed sites. Native throughout North America except the desert Southwest. There are 3 subspecies that differ in stem thickness, depth of the lobes on the stem and basal leaves, and distribution.

Crowfoot buttercup habit

Crowfoot buttercup basal leaf

Crowfoot buttercup flower and fruit

Smallflower buttercup plant and flower

Crowfoot buttercup seeds

S. Hurst, hosted by USDA-NRCS
PLANTS Database

Parsley-piert (*Aphanes arvensis* L.)

SYNONYMS: *Alchemilla arvensis*, field parsley-piert

GENERAL DESCRIPTION: A **prostrate**, mat-forming, **winter annual** rarely reaching more than 10 cm in height. Leaves are distinctively deep **palmately lobed**, on short petioles with stipules at the base. **Stems and leaves are hairy.** Flowers and fruit are small and inconspicuous.

PROPAGATION / PHENOLOGY: Reproduces **by seeds**. Seeds germinate early autumn through mid-spring. In cool, moist sites, germination may continue through early summer. Plants flower and fruit in late spring and early summer.

SEEDLING: Cotyledons are oval, 3–5 mm in length. First leaf is typically 3-lobed. **Leaves** of second and third leaf are **deeply lobed to palmately compound**. As plant matures, leaflets develop deep lobes. Stems and leaves are hairy. Plants branch at the base forming dense mounds or mats.

MATURE PLANT: Similar to the seedlings but internodes will often elongate revealing the alternate leaf arrangement. Leaf blades 4–10 mm long, at least as wide as long, hairy and divided into 3 (sometimes 4) leaflets, each leaflet deeply lobed. **Petiole is short**, up to 5 mm long, with **leafy stipules at the base.**

ROOTS AND UNDERGROUND STRUCTURES: Fibrous root system is not persistent.

FLOWERS AND FRUIT: Flowers are borne in small clusters, opposite the leaves, sessile (or nearly so). The flowers are inconspicuous and enveloped and almost completely obscured by the leafy stipules. Fruits are 1.7–2.5 mm long, vase-shaped, hairy, and each containing a single seed.

POSTSENESCENCE CHARACTERISTICS: Plants persist through winter, flower and fruit, and then die in early summer and do not persist.

HABITAT: A very common weed of turfgrass and urban landscapes, usually associated with thin or disturbed turf.

DISTRIBUTION: Native to North America. Widely distributed throughout the United States and into southern Canada.

SIMILAR SPECIES: **Lawn burweed (*Soliva sessilis*)** has a similar growth habit, life cycle, small, deeply divided leaves, and grows in similar habitats. It is differentiated from parsley-piert by having opposite leaves, mature leaves are pinnately divided (as opposed to palmately), and lawn burweed fruit have a sharp spine. Small seedlings might also superficially resemble **speedwells (*Veronica* spp.)** and inhabit similar sites. But, leaves of speedwells are not deeply lobed like parsley-piert.

Parsley-piert habit

Parsley-piert 2-leaf seedling

Parsley-piert seedling rosette

Parsley-piert leafy stem

Parsley-piert fruit 1.7 mm long

Indian mock-strawberry (*Duchesnea indica* (Andr.) Focke)

SYNONYMS: *Fragaria indica*, *Potentilla indica*, false strawberry, Indian strawberry

GENERAL DESCRIPTION: A prostrate, perennial herb that spreads from **stolons**, has **trifoliolate** (3 leaflets per leaf) leaves on long petioles, **bright yellow flowers**, and bright **red fruit that resemble strawberries**. Native to eastern and southern Asia but has been introduced to many other areas as an ornamental plant.

PROPAGATION / PHENOLOGY: Reproduction is **by seeds** and by **creeping stolons** that root and produce new crowns at each node. Birds probably disperse seeds longer distances by eating the fruit (drupes).

SEEDLING: Cotyledons are slightly thickened, with hairs along the margins only. The first 2 or 3 leaves are simple, but the subsequent leaves are trifoliolate with toothed margins. Stolons develop at about the 5-leaf stage.

MATURE PLANT: Stolons are hairy. **Leaves are alternate**, **trifoliolate**, coarsely veined beneath, dark green, and arise on long petioles from short crowns or from stolons. Leaflets are ovate, obovate to elliptic, 1.5–3 cm long by 1–2.5 cm wide, hairy underneath and mainly lacking hairs above, with **toothed (serrate) or doubly serrate margins**. Each leaflet has a short, 1–6 mm long, petiolule, and the main petiole is long with appressed, white hairs.

ROOTS AND UNDERGROUND STRUCTURES: The root system consists of a crown with secondary roots. Plants also produce and spread primarily by creeping stolons and possibly rhizomes.

FLOWERS AND FRUIT: Plants flower from mid-spring to early summer, and sporadically thereafter. The crowns produce 1 or more, long, flowering stalks, each with a single yellow flower. Flowers consist of 5 yellow petals with large, leafy sepals beneath. Flowers are approximately 2 cm across and have numerous stamens and a central, yellow receptacle with numerous pistils. **Fruits are red drupes**, 1 cm across, and entirely covered with red seed-like achenes. Although the fruit are edible, they have very little flavor. Sepals turn upward around the drupe.

POSTSENESCENCE CHARACTERISTICS: Foliage generally persists through the winter.

HABITAT: Plants are primarily weedy in landscapes and turfgrass and prefer shady locations.

DISTRIBUTION: Found in the eastern two-thirds of the United States, north to New York, the Great Lakes states, and adjacent Canadian provinces.

SIMILAR SPECIES: **Wild strawberry (*Fragaria virginiana*)** is a trailing perennial that is nearly indistinguishable from Indian mock-strawberry vegetatively. However, wild strawberry has white flowers compared to the yellow flowers of Indian mock-strawberry, and the fruits of wild strawberry are flavorful and usually hang downward, whereas Indian mock-strawberry fruit are erect and not flavorful. **Oldfield cinquefoil (*Potentilla simplex*)** has a similar low-trailing habit and yellow flowers, but has 5 leaflets rather than 3. **Rough cinquefoil (*Potentilla norvegica* L.)** also produces yellow flowers and a crown of trifoliolate leaves that are hairy on both surfaces. However, it does not produce stolons and is much hairier than Indian mock-strawberry.

Indian mock-strawberry foliage and flower

Indian mock-strawberry flower

Indian mock-strawberry leaf and fruit

Indian mock-strawberry fruit

Indian mock-strawberry stolon

Indian mock-strawberry seeds, 1.0 mm

Wild strawberry (*Fragaria virginiana* Duchesne.)

SYNONYM: thick-leaved wild strawberry

GENERAL DESCRIPTION: A low-trailing **perennial that spreads by creeping stolons** and forms dense patches. Usually 7.5–15 cm in height; tolerates mowing to <5 cm. Wild strawberry is **similar to cultivated strawberry** but has smaller leaves, much smaller fruit, and a stronger stoloniferous habit.

PROPAGATION / PHENOLOGY: Reproduction is **by seeds and stolons**. Although seedlings are rarely noticed, seed dispersal by animals and birds is an important means of spread. Once established, plants spread by stolons, forming large patches.

SEEDLING: Because seedlings are rarely noticed, little information is available. Seedlings are slow to establish. They produce a rosette of small, trifoliolate (3 leaflets) leaves, which resemble those of mature plants but are smaller.

MATURE PLANT: **Basal leaves arise from a crown or from long, creeping stolons. Leaves are trifoliolate**, nearly smooth to long-silky beneath, and on **long** (up to 15 cm), **hairy petioles**. Leaflets are dark green to blue-green, thick and firm, 2.5–3.8 cm long, with **toothed margins** on the upper ⅔–¾ of the leaf.

ROOTS AND UNDERGROUND STRUCTURES: Shallow, fibrous root system from crowns and stolon nodes.

FLOWERS AND FRUIT: Flowers (2 cm wide) are produced from April to June and have **white petals (5)** with many yellow stamens and pistils. Sepals (5) alternate with bracts. Flowers are oriented **in loose clusters** (corymbiform) on stalks (peduncles); most stalks are shorter than the leaves. The receptacle of the flower enlarges into a **small, red strawberry** (1–1.5 cm thick) with many small, seed-like fruits (achenes) in shallow pits on the surface. Achenes are brown, oval, and curved at the tip (1–1.5 mm long). Fruit mature in early summer.

POSTSENESCENCE CHARACTERISTICS: Plants remain green throughout the winter.

HABITAT: Primarily a weed of low-maintenance turfgrass and landscapes, wild strawberry is also found in meadows, fields, and on the edges and in the clearings of woods. It thrives on gravelly, well-drained soils.

DISTRIBUTION: Found throughout much of the United States and Canada.

SIMILAR SPECIES: **Indian mock-strawberry (*Duchesnea indica*)** is a low-trailing perennial usually found in moist, shady locations. Its leaves are also trifoliolate but have roundish teeth (crenate), whereas wild strawberry leaves have sharp-pointed teeth. The flowers of Indian mock-strawberry are yellow; those of wild strawberry are white. **Oldfield cinquefoil (*Potentilla simplex*)** has a similar low-trailing habit, but it has 5 leaflets rather than 3. **Rough cinquefoil (*Potentilla norvegica* L.)** produces a crown of trifoliolate leaves that are hairy on both surfaces; wild strawberry leaflets are mostly smooth, or hairy only on the underside. Rough cinquefoil produces yellow flowers on erect stems.

Wild strawberry habit

Wild strawberry flowers

Wild strawberry fruit

Wild strawberry stolon and leaves

Wild strawberry
seeds, 1.2 mm

Oldfield cinquefoil (*Potentilla simplex* Michx.)

Synonym: old-field five-fingers

General Description: A low-growing **perennial** with **prostrate, wiry,** tough, **stoloniferous stems** radiating from a **small crown** and **palmately compound leaves** with **3 to (more commonly) 5 leaflets.** Often found on poor soils. Valued for its **attractive yellow flowers.**

Propagation / Phenology: Reproduction is **by stolons and seeds.**

Seedling: Seedlings develop into **small crowns.** Cotyledons are egg-shaped, widest at the apex, 1.5 mm long by 3 mm wide. The **first leaves** are simple, alternate, and egg-shaped, with **a few tooth-like lobes,** petioles that clasp the stem, and a dull surface. **Subsequent leaves have stipules** and are compound with **3 leaflets.** The **lateral leaflets may be cleft nearly to the petiole,** giving the appearance of 5 leaflets.

Mature Plant: Stems and basal leaves grow from a **small rosette.** Early in the season, **stems elongate, but then arch to the ground and root at the tips.** Stems are hairy to almost smooth, slender, tough, and wiry. Hairs on stems and petioles are appressed. Leaves are alternate; the blades are glossy, dark green on the upper surface, and hairy to sometimes white-woolly beneath. **Leaves are palmately compound with 5 leaflets** and have stipules at the base of the petiole. **Leaflets** are narrow, elliptic or egg-shaped, widest at the top, tapering to the base (obovate); **margins are toothed.**

Roots and Underground Structures: **Long stolons** are important in spread. **Short rhizomes** (to 8 cm) are also present. Coarse, fibrous roots are associated with both.

Flowers and Fruit: **Bright yellow flowers** (10–15 mm wide) bloom from May through June and are produced singly on long, slender pedicels in the leaf axils. Petals (5) are bright yellow, and stamen and pistils are numerous. Each seed is enclosed in the fruit (achene). Achenes are smooth, yellowish-brown, 1.2 mm long, on hairy receptacles.

Postsenescence Characteristics: Foliage generally dies back to the crown and stolons in winter but may persist in mild climates.

Habitat: A weed of low-maintenance turfgrass and landscapes. Also found in meadows and dry woods and fields, generally on acidic, nutrient-poor, dry, sandy soils.

Distribution: From Newfoundland to Minnesota, south to Alabama and Texas.

Similar Species: **Indian mock-strawberry (*Duchesnea indica*)** and **wild strawberry (*Fragaria virginiana*)** are similar in habit but have 3 leaflets, and wild strawberry has white flowers. **Dwarf (or common) cinquefoil (*Potentilla canadensis* L.)** is a prostrate rhizome- and stolon-producing perennial **very similar** to oldfield cinquefoil. But the rhizomes are shorter (0.5–2 cm long), hairs on the stem and petiole are spreading, not appressed, and stipules on basal leaves are oblong-lanceolate and flat; those of oldfield cinquefoil are linear-lanceolate and rolled. **The following weedy cinquefoils** have yellow flowers but **are not stoloniferous** and do not root at the nodes. Reproduction in these species is by seeds only. **Silvery cinquefoil (*Potentilla argentea* L.)** has erect to almost prostrate stems, 5–7 leaflets, with a dense mat of **silvery-white hairs** on the undersides, and yellow flowers 7 mm to 1 cm wide. **Rough cinquefoil (*Potentilla norvegica* L.)** has erect branched stems, **3 leaflets,** which are hairy and green on both sides, and small, yellow flowers, 0.7–1 cm wide. **Sulfur cinquefoil (*Potentilla recta* L.)** has erect unbranched stems, **5–9 leaflets,** 1.5–2.5 cm wide yellow flowers, and long hairs on the stems and leaves.

Oldfield cinquefoil habit

Sulfur cinquefoil mature leaf and flowering shoot

Rough cinquefoil habit

Silvery cinquefoil flowering shoot

Rough cinquefoil flowering shoots

Left to right: sulfur cinquefoil seeds, 1.0 mm; rough cinquefoil seeds, 0.9 mm; silvery cinquefoil seeds, 0.6 mm; and oldfield cinquefoil seeds, 1.2 mm

443

Virginia buttonweed (*Diodia virginiana* L.)

SYNONYMS: *Diodia hirsuta, Diodia tetragona,* buttonweed

GENERAL DESCRIPTION: A **prostrate** to ascending, spreading **perennial** that tolerates close mowing but can grow 20–80 cm tall if undisturbed. The light to dark green **foliage is often yellow-mottled by a virus.** Stems are thick and stout, often tinged red.

PROPAGATION / PHENOLOGY: Reproduction is **by seeds and adventitious sprouts from fleshy roots.** Once introduced, plants spread by root sprouts and **prostrate stems** that **root at the nodes.**

SEEDLING: Cotyledons are elliptic, rounded at the apex, thickened, green on the upper surface and light green underneath. **Young leaves are opposite, elliptic,** with **short hairs** on the margin; they **lack petioles** and are **connected across the stem by a membrane with 1–3 bristly, linear stipules** (3–5 mm long). **Stems are covered with gland-tipped hairs.**

MATURE PLANT: **Vegetative characteristics are similar to those of the seedling. Stems** are generally **prostrate, rooting at the lower nodes,** sometimes hairy on the angles, and frequently tinged red. **Leaves are opposite, elliptic** to oblong-lanceolate, 3–6 cm (rarely to 10 cm) long by 1–2 cm wide, with rough margins. Petioles are absent. **The center stipule is often thickened and thorn-like.**

ROOTS AND UNDERGROUND STRUCTURES: A coarse, branched, **fleshy root system** giving rise to **adventitious shoots. Underground flowers** are also produced.

FLOWERS AND FRUIT: **Flowers** are produced from June through August, both aboveground in the leaf axils and belowground. Little is known about the belowground flowers. Aboveground flowers are **white, sometimes tinged pink,** approximately 1 cm wide by 7–11 mm long, and sessile, 1 or (rarely) 2 in the leaf axils. Two sepals are linear to lance-shaped, 4–6 mm long. **Petals (4) are star-shaped,** united into a tube at the base (salverform). **Sepals and petals are hairy.** The **fruit** is an oval to elliptic (5–9 mm long), **8-ribbed,** hairy (occasionally smooth), **leathery capsule** that floats in water. Each capsule contains 2 indehiscent seeds.

POSTSENESCENCE CHARACTERISTICS: Aboveground portions die back to the ground in the winter.

HABITAT: Although Virginia buttonweed is a major weed of turf in the southeastern United States, it does not tolerate cultivation and thus is rarely encountered in conventionally tilled crops. It is difficult to control with currently available technologies. It is found on sandy soils as well as moist areas.

DISTRIBUTION: Primarily a weed in the coastal southeastern United States west to Texas but has been identified as far north as southern New Jersey and southern Illinois.

SIMILAR SPECIES: **Poorjoe (*Diodia teres* Walt.)** is a summer annual with a similar leaf shape, stem, and flower, but leaves are narrower and flowers have 4 sepals. **Florida pusley (*Richardia scabra*)** is also a summer annual vegetatively resembling Virginia buttonweed; however, the leaves and stems are densely hairy and the flowers are 6-parted not 4-parted.

J. Neal

Virginia buttonweed
seedling

J. Neal

Virginia buttonweed habit

J. Neal

Virginia buttonweed thickened roots with new
shoot

J. Neal

Virginia buttonweed flower

J. Neal

Virginia buttonweed seedpods

J. DiTomaso

Virginia buttonweed seed capsules,
6.5 mm (largest)

Catchweed bedstraw (*Galium aparine* L.)

SYNONYMS: cleavers, bedstraw, catchweed, goose-grass, scratch-grass, grip-grass

GENERAL DESCRIPTION: A **semiprostrate or mat-forming summer or winter annual**, often attached to or climbing over other vegetation. **Stems, leaves, and fruit have short, prickly hairs.**

PROPAGATION / PHENOLOGY: Reproduction is **by seeds** that germinate in cool, moist soil, from very early to late spring and late summer to early autumn.

SEEDLING: Hypocotyls are stout, greenish or purple, and smooth. **Cotyledons are egg-shaped** (8–15 mm long by 6–9 mm wide), **on prominent petioles**, notched at the apex, green on the upper surface, and maroon on the lower surface. The upper cotyledon surface and margins have rough, short, ascending hairs. **Young leaves are produced in whorls of 4 or more**; the upper surfaces, margins, petioles, and lower midvein have **short, stiff, sharp hairs.**

MATURE PLANT: **Stems are square** (20 cm to 1.5 m long), **with recurved prickles on the 4 ridges and leaves.** Prickles allow foliage to cling to other plants. Upper leaf surfaces are hairy; lower surfaces have short, spiny hairs along the midrib. **Leaves are sessile, in whorls of 6–8 at the nodes.** Blades are narrow, oval to lanceolate (3–8 cm long by 4–10 mm wide), pointed at the apex, rough on the margins.

ROOTS AND UNDERGROUND STRUCTURES: Branched, shallow, fibrous roots.

FLOWERS AND FRUIT: **Flowers** are produced from late May to mid-June **on stalked clusters in the axils of the leaf whorls.** Flowers are 2 mm in diameter and consist of 4 white petals and 4 stamens. **Fruit (schizocarps)** are composed of **2 rounded segments**, 1 seed per segment, that separate at maturity. Fruit are rounded (2–3 mm in diameter), brownish at maturity, and **generally are covered with curved hooks** but occasionally are smooth. Seeds are dispersed by animals or float on water.

POSTSENESCENCE CHARACTERISTICS: Dead stems turn dark brown or gray and often have remnants of the spiny fruit. Stems become brittle and persist for only a short time.

HABITAT: Primarily a weed of winter grain crops, landscapes, Christmas trees, and high-cut turfgrass. Also found in meadows, fencerows, and disturbed areas. Thrives in shady, moist areas and prefers nutrient-rich, high organic soils.

DISTRIBUTION: Widespread throughout North America.

SIMILAR SPECIES: **Smooth bedstraw (*Galium mollugo* L.)** is a **perennial spreading by rhizomes and stolons.** Unlike catchweed bedstraw, it has **smooth or nearly smooth stems and fruits** and smaller whorled leaves (1–3 cm long by 2–4 mm wide). Leaves are rough only on the margins. Smooth bedstraw is a weed of low-maintenance turfgrass, small grains, Christmas trees, landscapes, and roadsides. **Yellow (or lady's) bedstraw (*Galium verum* L.)** is a rhizomatous and stoloniferous perennial with winged stems and prickly hairs on stems and whorled leaves, but prickly hairs are not on the fruit; flowers are yellow (rarely white). Although less common than catchweed bedstraw, it is present throughout the region. **Field madder (*Sherardia arvensis*)** has whorled and prickly leaves, but leaves are smaller than bedstraw and flowers are pink to lavender and sessile in the leaf axils. **Carpetweed (*Mollugo verticillata*)** also has 3–8 whorled leaves and a prostrate growth habit, but carpetweed has round stems and lacks prickly hairs.

J. Neal

Catchweed bedstraw habit

J. Neal

Catchweed bedstraw
seedling with cotyledons

J. DiTomaso

Catchweed bedstraw flower and fruit

R. Uva

Smooth bedstraw habit

Catchweed
bedstraw mature
stem and foliage

J. DiTomaso

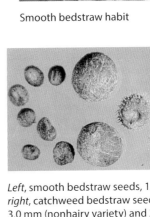

J. DiTomaso

Left, smooth bedstraw seeds, 1.2 mm;
right, catchweed bedstraw seeds,
3.0 mm (nonhairy variety) and 2.0 mm
(hairy variety)

Brazilian pusley (*Richardia brasiliensis* (Moq.) Gomez) and Florida pusley (*Richardia scabra* L.)

SYNONYMS: Florida purslane, tropical Mexican clover

GENERAL DESCRIPTION: Nearly identical species of **prostrate to ascending summer annuals**, with light green and conspicuously hairy stems and leaves. At maturity, plants form 15–30 cm tall mounds topped with small, 6-parted white flowers.

PROPAGATION / PHENOLOGY: Reproduction is **by seeds**. Seeds germinate from spring through summer.

SEEDLING: Cotyledons are elliptical, rounded at the apex, thickened, and lack hairs. **Young leaves are opposite, elliptic**, and **densely hairy** with a prominent midvein. As plants age, veins in the leaves become more conspicuous. Petioles are absent (or nearly so). Leaves are connected across the stem by a membrane with 3–5 bristly, linear stipules (3–5 mm long). **Stems** are stout and **very hairy**.

MATURE PLANT: Vegetative characteristics are similar to those of the seedling. Stems are green, stout, branched, and very hairy. **Leaves are opposite**, elliptic, 3–6 cm (rarely to 10 cm) long by 1–2 cm wide. The **upper leaf surface is prominently veined with conspicuous hairs**. The 2 species are differentiated by the location of hairs on the leaves. **Brazilian pusley is densely hairy on the entire upper leaf surface, whereas Florida pusley lacks hairs in the central third of the leaf blade**. As in seedlings, petioles are absent and **opposite leaves are connected across the stem by a membrane with 3–5 stipules**. When plants start to flower, internodes are reduced and leaves below the flowers are very close together.

ROOTS AND UNDERGROUND STRUCTURES: Plants have a shallow, branched fibrous root system. With age, Brazil pusley develops a thickened, woody root.

FLOWERS AND FRUIT: Flowers are produced from June through the first frost. Flowers are in terminal clusters, **white**, sometimes tinged pink, 5–8 mm long, **funnel-shaped, and 6-parted. Sepals and petals are hairy.** The fruits are hard and leathery, roughly oval, bumpy (tuberculate), separating into 4 parts.

POSTSENESCENCE CHARACTERISTICS: Plant dies at first hard frost. Stems may persist into winter.

HABITAT: Common weeds of conventionally tilled crops, orchards, turf, and landscape plantings. More commonly found in coastal plain sandy soils but adapted to many soil types and microclimates. Somewhat tolerant of the herbicide glyphosate and has, with the adoption of herbicide-tolerant crops, become more common.

DISTRIBUTION: Primarily a weed in the coastal southeastern United States west to Texas but has been collected as far north as New York and southern Illinois.

SIMILAR SPECIES: **Poorjoe (*Diodia teres* Walt.) and Virginia buttonweed (*Diodia virginiana*)** are somewhat alike, with similarly shaped opposite leaves and common habitats, but poorjoe and Virginia buttonweed lack the prominent hairs present on the leaves and stems of both species of pusley.

J. Neal

Brazilian pusley habit

J. DiTomaso

Brazilian pusley flower

J. Neal

Brazilian pusley seedling

J. DiTomaso

Florida pusley leaf with hairs on outer 1/3 of blade

J. DiTomaso

Florida pusley flowering stem

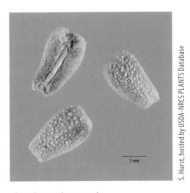

S. Hurst, hosted by USDA-NRCS PLANTS Database

Florida pusley seeds

Field madder (*Sherardia arvensis* L.)

Synonym: blue fieldmadder

General Description: A **matted winter annual** with prostrate to ascending stems, **whorled leaves**, and **square stems**. Leaves and stem have short, **bristly hairs**. The lavender or pink flowers are arranged in small, head-like clusters in leaf axils. Native to the Mediterranean region.

Propagation / Phenology: Reproduction is only **by seeds**. Seeds germinate in the fall or early spring. Plants fruit and die in late spring to early summer. Fruits often disperse with soil movement or human activities, such as mowing and cultivation.

Seedling: Cotyledons are broadly obovate to nearly round, 5–15 mm long, with slightly indented tips. Leaves are whorled and nearly sessile, and the stems above the cotyledons are square in cross section.

Mature Plant: The foliage is covered with short, straight, scabrous hairs. Hairs on the leaves are erect or pointing toward the blade tip. **Stems** are prostrate to ascending, **square with distinct edges**, often forming a dense mat. **Leaves are 4–6 per whorl**, elliptic-lanceolate, 5–10 mm long, tapered to a point at the tip, and minutely bristle-tipped.

Roots and Underground Structures: Taproots slender, simple or branched, with fibrous lateral roots.

Flowers and Fruit: Plants flower from early spring through mid-summer. Flowers are lavender to pink, trumpet-shaped, 4–5 mm long, mostly 4-lobed, and inferior with 2-lobed ovaries and 2 basally fused styles. **Flower clusters are head-like in the leaf axils**, consist of 2–3 sessile **flowers with 6–8 leaf-like bracts** approximately 8 mm long at the base. Fruits are 2–3 mm long by 1.5–2 mm wide, 2-lobed (schizocarp), and eventually separate into 2 nutlets (mericarps).

Postsenescence Characteristics: Generally, dead plants are not persistent. In dry areas, dead stems with a few remaining fruits can persist for a short time in the summer.

Habitat: Primarily found in turf and nearby landscape plantings but also found in pastures, orchards, vineyards, roadsides, riparian areas, oak woodlands, and grasslands.

Distribution: More common in the southeastern and mid-Atlantic states but present throughout most of the United States and eastern Canada.

Similar Species: Field madder is similar, and related to, the **bedstraws (*Galium* spp.)**. While all these species have whorled leaves, field madder has pink to lavender flowers that are sessile in the leaf axils. Bedstraws have white, or sometimes yellow, flowers that have a stalk. **Piedmont bedstraw (*Cruciata pedemontana* (Bellardi) Ehrend.;** syn.: *Galium pedemontanum* (Bellardi) All.) is easily mistaken for field madder. It has square stems, leaves in whorls of 4 (rarely to 6), and occupies similar habitats. It is less common, generally smaller and less robust, and leaves are not sharply pointed. Hairs on the leaves are longer and not stiff. Flowers are small, pale yellow to cream colored on short stalks in leaf axils. Piedmont bedstraw is native to Europe and is also a winter annual weed of turf, pastures, and disturbed sites.

Field madder habit

Field madder flowering stem

Field madder whorled leaves
and fruit

Field madder seedlings

Piedmont bedstraw
leafy stem

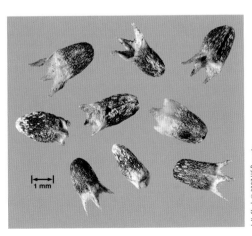

Field madder seeds

Common mullein (*Verbascum thapsus* L.)

SYNONYMS: velvet dock, big taper, candle-wick, flannel-leaf, woolly mullein

GENERAL DESCRIPTION: A **biennial** forming a **large (20–60 cm in diameter) basal rosette** the first year and an erect, usually unbranched, stem (to 1.8 m tall) in the second year. The **entire plant is densely hairy** and has a grayish-green appearance.

PROPAGATION / PHENOLOGY: Reproduction is **by seeds**, which germinate in late summer or early autumn or spring.

SEEDLING: **Fuzzy**, slightly serrated, **oval leaves form a basal rosette** (20–60 cm in diameter).

MATURE PLANT: **Leaves of the basal rosette are densely hairy**, oblong or lanceolate, widest at the apex, approximately 30 cm long, tapering to a short petiole. **Densely hairy, erect**, stout, and usually unbranched **stems** elongate in the second year. **Leaves** on the upright stem are **alternate, woolly-hairy**, with entire or bluntly toothed margins. Upper leaves are sessile, narrower, and more pointed at the apex than the basal leaves. Leaves are reduced in size progressively up the stem.

ROOTS AND UNDERGROUND STRUCTURES: Thick, fleshy **taproot** with shallow, secondary, fibrous root system.

FLOWERS AND FRUIT: **Flowers**, present from June through September, are **sessile on 1 or 2 terminal cylindrical spikes** (20–50 cm long by 3 cm wide). Individual flowers are 2.5 cm in diameter and have **fused yellow petals** (rarely white) with 5 lobes. Sepals are 5-lobed and woolly. There are 5 stamens; the upper 3 are shorter than the lower 2. Fruit is a 2-celled, many-seeded, rounded capsule (6 mm in diameter). Seeds (0.8 mm long) have wavy ridges alternating with deep grooves, resembling corncobs.

POSTSENESCENCE CHARACTERISTICS: Basal rosettes remain light green over winter. After flowering, plants die, leaving the remains of the tall stem and capsules. Dead stems can persist for more than a year.

HABITAT: Common mullein is a weed of landscapes, perennial crops, and roadsides, and less commonly of cultivated nursery and agricultural crops. It is often found where the soil is dry and gravelly or stony.

DISTRIBUTION: Widespread throughout the United States and southern Canada.

SIMILAR SPECIES: Owing to its distinctively hairy leaves, few species could be confused with common mullein. A **related species, moth mullein (*Verbascum blattaria* L.)**, lacks hairs on the leaves and has a toothed margin. The rosette leaves are sessile, whereas common mullein leaves are on short petioles. Flowers of moth mullein are yellow to white with soft purple hairs on the stamens. Although moth mullein may reach 1.5 m in height, it has slender stems, smaller leaves, and lacks the robust appearance of common mullein.

J. Neal

Common mullein habit

J. DiTomaso

Common mullein flowers

A. DiTommaso

Common mullein rosette

J. DiTomaso

Moth mullein flowering and fruiting shoot

R. Uva

Moth mullein rosette

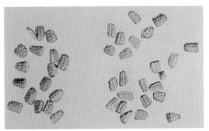

J. DiTomaso

Left, moth mullein seeds, 0.8 mm; *right*, common mullein seeds, 0.7 mm

Jimsonweed (*Datura stramonium* L.)

SYNONYMS: *Datura tatula*, Jamestown-weed, thorn-apple, mad-apple, stinkwort

GENERAL DESCRIPTION: A **large summer annual** with **erect, branching stems** (30–150 cm tall) and distinctive **egg-shaped seed capsules covered with prickles**. The foliage has a strong **unpleasant odor**. Jimsonweed has long been known to be **toxic to all classes of livestock and to humans**. All parts of the plant are poisonous, but toxic effects on humans usually occur after seeds are ingested. Plants contain tropane alkaloids, of which the most notable are atropine, hyoscyamine, and scopolamine.

PROPAGATION / PHENOLOGY: Reproduction is **by seeds**. Seedlings emerge between mid-May and mid-June and throughout the growing season if adequate moisture is available.

SEEDLING: Hypocotyls are maroon and hairy. **Cotyledons** are thick, smooth, lanceolate **(5 cm long by approximately 6 mm wide)**. Petioles of the cotyledons are hairy on the upper surface. The seed coat is attached to the cotyledons long after germination. **Leaves are alternate. First leaves are entire; subsequent leaves have a few irregular teeth.** Seedlings emit a strong unpleasant odor.

MATURE PLANT: Stems are smooth, green or purple, with inconspicuous hairs. **Leaves are alternate, large** (7–20 cm long), on stout petioles, oval to ovate, smooth, dark green above. Leaf **margins** resemble those of oak leaves, **coarsely and unevenly toothed**.

ROOTS AND UNDERGROUND STRUCTURES: Thick, shallow, and extensively branched **taproot**.

FLOWERS AND FRUIT: Flowers are produced from June or mid-July until frost and open in late afternoon and evening. **White to purple flowers are large and conspicuous, funnel-shaped**, 5–12.5 cm long, arising from short stalks (pedicels) solitary in the branch axils. Sepals are strongly 5-ridged, 5-toothed, and enclose the lower part of the floral tube. **Petals are fused into a 5-lobed floral tube. Fruit (capsules) are 3–5 cm long**, green when immature, **egg-shaped**, 4-celled, and **covered with stiff prickles**. Mature capsules are brown and hard, splitting into 4 segments, each containing several kidney-shaped, flattened, pitted and wrinkled, dark brown to black seeds (3 mm long).

POSTSENESCENCE CHARACTERISTICS: **Leafless stems persist after death, bearing the distinctive spiny, 4-parted capsules.** Sepals form a skirt-like structure at the base of the capsule.

HABITAT: A weed of most agronomic, horticultural, and nursery crops, jimsonweed is found on most soil types but prefers nutrient-rich soils.

DISTRIBUTION: Distributed throughout most of the United States except for the Northwest and northern Great Plains; most common in the South.

SIMILAR SPECIES: **Oakleaf datura or large thornapple (*Datura quercifolia* Kunth**; syn.: *Datura ferox* L.) is very similar but spines on the fruit are fewer and much larger, each spine may be up to 2.5 cm long. Oakleaf datura is native to North America but uncommon in the region. **Apple of Peru (*Nicandra physalodes* (L.) Scop.)** has a similar growth habit and tubular white or blue flowers, but fruits are not spiny. Also, cotyledons are oval to deltoid and leaf margins have rounded lobes whereas jimsonweed leaves have pointed lobes. Apple of Peru is native to South America and widely distributed throughout eastern North America but is less common than jimsonweed. Seedlings of **common cocklebur (*Xanthium stumarium*)** have larger cotyledons than jimsonweed. The young leaves are not smooth and have more pronounced teeth on the margins with purple mottling on the stems. Common cocklebur also lacks the distinctive odor of jimsonweed.

J. Neal

Jimsonweed habit

J. K. Clark © 2007 UC Regents

Jimsonweed seedling with cotyledons

J. DiTomaso

Jimsonweed fruit

J. DiTomaso

Jimsonweed flower and young fruit

J. Derr

Jimsonweed seedling

J. Neal

Apple of Peru habit

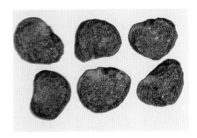

J. DiTomaso

Jimsonweed seeds, 3 mm

Smooth groundcherry (*Physalis longifolia* Nutt. var. *subglabrata* (Mack. & Bush) Cronq.)

SYNONYMS: *Physalis subglabrata*, husk-tomato

GENERAL DESCRIPTION: **Perennial** with deeply buried, **thick, fleshy rhizomes**, branched erect stems (20–90 cm tall), and a **characteristic papery, bladder-like case over the fruit.** Unripe fruit is **suspected of causing poisoning in some animals,** particularly sheep.

PROPAGATION / PHENOLOGY: Reproduction is **by seeds and rhizomes.** Seedlings emerge in warm soil in late spring or early summer.

SEEDLING: Cotyledons are smooth, green, 4–9 mm long by 1–4 mm wide. **Young leaves are alternate**, approximately 1.5 cm long, and have a **characteristic nightshade odor** when bruised. Emerging perennial shoots lack cotyledons and are more robust than seedlings.

MATURE PLANT: Stems are angled, slightly hairy on young growth, smooth on older tissue. **Leaves are alternate**, ovate to lanceolate, 5–7.5 cm long, pointed at the tip, long-petioled (3–5 cm), smooth or slightly hairy. **Margins** are entire or with **a few small teeth.** Stems become woody with age.

ROOTS AND UNDERGROUND STRUCTURES: Deep, penetrating and spreading fibrous roots associated with **rhizomes**.

FLOWERS AND FRUIT: Flowers bloom from June through September on short, recurved pedicels solitary in the axils of the branches and leaves. Sepals are fused (calyx), with 5 triangular lobes. **Petals are yellow or greenish-yellow with purplish centers, fused and bell-shaped, 5-lobed,** 1.5–2.2 cm in diameter. As the fruit matures, the calyx expands to form a **papery, bladder-like casing** (3–4 cm long) **completely enclosing the small, tomato-like berry. Berries are orange to red or purple** when mature and contain many seeds. Seeds are 1.5–2 mm in diameter, flattened, circular, and yellowish.

POSTSENESCENCE CHARACTERISTICS: Erect, woody stems persist well into winter. Dried fruit may also remain attached within the inflated calyx.

HABITAT: Smooth groundcherry is a weed of many cultivated agronomic, vegetable, and nursery crops. It also grows in meadows, pastures, landscapes, waste areas, and roadsides, often on coarse, gravelly soils.

DISTRIBUTION: Found throughout the eastern United States, westward to Washington, and in Utah and Texas.

SIMILAR SPECIES: **Clammy groundcherry (*Physalis heterophylla* Nees)** is similar but **covered with sticky (clammy) hairs**. In addition, the berries of clammy groundcherry are yellow when mature. Clammy groundcherry is primarily a weed in the eastern United States and extends as far west as the Rocky Mountains. **See Table 10 for a comparison with weedy, solanaceous species.**

Smooth groundcherry habit

J. Derr

Smooth groundcherry flower

J. Neal

Juvenile smooth groundcherry

J. Neal

Smooth groundcherry seedling

A. DiTommaso

Clammy groundcherry shoot with flower and fruit

J. Neal

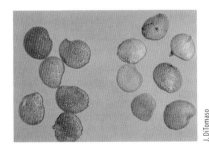

Left, clammy groundcherry seeds, 1.8 mm; *right*, smooth groundcherry seeds, 1.5 mm

J. DiTomaso

457

Horsenettle (*Solanum carolinense* L.)

SYNONYMS: bull nettle, apple-of-Sodom, wild tomato, devil's tomato, devil's potato, sand briar

GENERAL DESCRIPTION: An **erect perennial** (30 cm to 1 m tall), **spreads by seeds and adventitious shoots from roots. Stems and leaves have conspicuous spine-like prickles.** Vegetative parts and fruit of horsenettle can **poison livestock.** All parts of the plant, except the mature fruit, contain the glycoalkaloid solanine, which is not lost upon drying. Symptoms of toxicity include gastrointestinal irritation. Reports of horsenettle poisoning in animals is rare, as the prickly vegetation deters foraging.

PROPAGATION / PHENOLOGY: Reproduction is **by seeds and creeping roots** that can produce new shoots as far as 1 m away from the central plant. Root fragments can also be spread by cultivation. Shoots emerge around mid-May.

SEEDLING: Short, stiff hairs are present on the stem and hypocotyl. Cotyledons are oval to oblong, approximately 1.2 cm long, hairy on the margins, glossy green above, light green below. **Young leaves are alternate**; the first 2 are sparsely hairy on the upper surface, with unbranched and star-shaped (4–8 rayed) hairs. **Subsequent leaves are wavy or lobed, and hairy and prickly on both surfaces.**

MATURE PLANT: **Stems are erect**, angled at the nodes, somewhat branched, with **sharp, stout, yellowish or white prickles** (6–12 mm long), and star-shaped hairs. **Leaves are alternate**, 7–12 cm long and about half as wide, **egg-shaped**, with **wavy or 2–5 shallow lobes** on the margin and star-shaped hairs on both surfaces. **Prominent sharp prickles are present on the veins, midrib, and petioles.**

ROOTS AND UNDERGROUND STRUCTURES: Deep, fleshy, **spreading roots producing adventitious shoots.**

FLOWERS AND FRUIT: Flowers are produced in clusters on **prickly flower stalks** (peduncles) as early as June and continuing through the growing season. **Flowers (2 cm in diameter) resemble those of potato** and consist of 5 fused hairy sepals, **5 fused white to violet petals**, and 5 stamens **with prominent, bright yellow anthers** in a cone surrounding the pistil. **Fruits** are smooth, round (1–1.5 cm diameter), **yellow berries (green when immature)** containing 40–170 seeds. Berries become wrinkled late in the season. Seeds are round and flattened (2–3 mm in diameter), smooth and glossy, orange to dark or light yellow. A single plant can produce up to 5000 seeds.

POSTSENESCENCE CHARACTERISTICS: Dead stems bear persistent yellow, wrinkled berries. Prominent prickles, conspicuous during the growing season, may fall off by winter.

HABITAT: Horsenettle is a weed of orchards, pastures, nursery crops, and other perennial crops. It is also weedy in conventionally tilled and reduced-tillage crops including corn, small grains, and vegetables. It is **particularly difficult to control in solanaceous crops**, such as tomato and potato. Horsenettle grows on a wide range of soil types but thrives on sandy or gravelly soils.

DISTRIBUTION: Native to the southeastern United States but has spread northward to the eastern and north-central states and into southern Canada and west to Texas.

SIMILAR SPECIES: **The groundcherries (*Physalis* spp.)** resemble horsenettle but do not have the conspicuous prickles on the stems and leaves. The berries of groundcherry are enclosed by an inflated papery membrane (calyx). **See Table 10 for a comparison with other weedy, solanaceous species.**

Horsenettle habit

Horsenettle foliage,
prickles, and flowers

Horsenettle fruit

Horsenettle flowering shoot

Horsenettle young plant

Horsenettle seeds, 2.8 mm

459

Eastern black nightshade (*Solanum ptychanthum* Dun.)

Synonyms: *Solanum americanum, Solanum ptycanthum* (misapplied), deadly nightshade, East Indian nightshade, poison berry, garden nightshade

General Description: An **erect, branching, summer annual** or short-lived perennial (15–60 cm tall). Vegetative parts and fruit can **poison all classes of livestock**. All parts of the plant, except the mature fruit, contain the glycoalkaloid solanine, which is not lost upon drying. Symptoms of toxicity include gastrointestinal irritation. The mature fruit have erroneously been noted as being poisonous.

Propagation / Phenology: Reproduction is **by seeds**. Germination occurs in late spring and continues throughout the summer if sufficient moisture is available.

Seedling: Hypocotyls are green, but often tinged maroon, and are covered with short hairs. Cotyledons are smooth on both surfaces, green on the upper surface and tinged maroon on the lower surface. **Young leaves are alternate, wavy,** and **tinged purplish on the underside.** Foliage and stems are generally smooth, or not obviously hairy. **Petioles and stems are purplish.**

Mature Plant: Stems are round and angular, smooth or only partially hairy, and branching. **Leaves are alternate**, slightly hairy, **triangular-ovate** to elliptic (2–8 cm long by 1–5.5 cm wide). **Margins** are entire or have **irregular, blunt teeth**.

Roots and Underground Structures: **Slender taproot** with a branched, fibrous root system.

Flowers and Fruit: Flowers are present from mid-June throughout the summer; the berries mature 4–5 weeks after flowering. **Flowers are star-shaped** (4–10 mm in diameter) **in small, drooping, lateral umbellate clusters of 5–7.** Sepals are 1.5–2 mm long, **the 5 fused petals are white or purple-tinged or with stripes. Five bright yellow anthers** form a cone surrounding the pistil. **Fruit are glossy black, spherical berries**, approximately 10 mm in diameter, each containing 50–110 seeds, which are spread by birds and other animals. Seeds are round, flattened, 1.5–2 mm long, yellow or nearly white.

Postsenescence Characteristics: After frost, stems and fruit can persist until winter.

Habitat: Eastern black nightshade is a weed of nursery crops, landscapes, and horticultural, agronomic, and many vegetable crops, particularly solanaceous species (e.g., potato and tomato). Although found on sandy, nutrient-poor disturbed sites, it thrives on moist, fertile, cultivated soils.

Distribution: Primarily a weed of the eastern United States.

Similar Species: **See Table 10 for a comparison of weedy, solanaceous species.** Several species are known as black nightshade. Eastern black nightshade is most common east of the Rocky Mountains, **black nightshade (*Solanum nigrum* L.)** is more common in the western states, and **American black nightshade (*Solanum americanum* Mill.)** is common in many southern and coastal areas. **Hairy nightshade (*Solanum sarrachoides* Sendtner or *S. physalifolium* Rusby)**, occurs throughout most of North America. Hairy nightshade has prominent hairs on the stems and leaves, and the mature fruit is greenish-yellow or brownish. [Note: *Solanum physalifolium* is reported to be more common in states in the West and *S. sarrachoides* in the East, but resources disagree on the nomenclature and synonymy.] **Horsenettle (*Solanum carolinense*)** is a rhizomatous perennial that is easily distinguished by conspicuous spines on the stems and leaves.

A. DiTommaso

astern black nightshade habit

J. Neal

Hairy nightshade stem with foliage, flowers, and fruit

J. Neal

astern black nightshade seedling

J. K. Clark © 2007 UC Regents

Hairy nightshade seedling

R. Uva

Eastern black nightshade foliage and fruit

J. DiTomaso

Left, black nightshade seeds, 1.4 mm; *right*, eastern black nightshade seeds, 1.9 mm

Buffalobur (*Solanum rostratum* Dunal)

SYNONYMS: *Androcera rostrata*, *Solanum cornutum*, buffalobur nightshade

GENERAL DESCRIPTION: Buffalobur is a native, sparsely branched summer annual with **yellow flowers**, **spiny stems and fruit**, lobed leaves, and star-shaped **hairs on stems and leaves**. It is a common contaminant of bird seed and is often associated with locations where people have bird feeders or where bird seed has been distributed.

PROPAGATION / PHENOLOGY: Reproduction is **by seeds** only. Fruits are generally dispersed with human activities and by animals that have the spiny fruit attached to their fur. Under windy conditions in fall, plants sometimes detach at the base and scatter seeds as they tumble along the ground.

SEEDLING: Cotyledons are large and linear-lanceolate with a prominent midvein. The first true leaves are alternate and shallowly round-lobed. Lobes deepen on subsequent leaves.

MATURE PLANT: The stems are branched above, erect and bushy, 15 to 60 cm long. The entire plant, except for the flower petals, is covered by straight, yellow **spines**, 5–10 mm long. **Leaves are alternate** and 4–12 cm long, including the stalks. Each leaf, somewhat resembling a deeply lobed oak (*Quercus*) leaf, is **irregularly deeply lobed** halfway to all the way to the midrib into 5–7 lobes. The sinuses are rounded and margins of the lobes are wavy to entire. The tips of the lobes are generally rounded or occasionally pointed. Plants have an unpleasant odor when crushed.

ROOTS AND UNDERGROUND STRUCTURES: Fibrous taproot.

FLOWERS AND FRUIT: Plants bloom from May to early August, and the seeds mature from July to October. **Yellow flowers** are 5-lobed, wheel-shaped, 2–3 cm across, in few-flowered clusters on spiny flower stalks. The collective **sepals (calyx) are also covered by spines** and enlarge to form a **spiny bur** that encloses and completely covers the fruit (berry). Seeds are almost circular, 1 cm or slightly more in diameter, brown to reddish-brown, flattened, irregularly angled, with a finely pitted surface.

POSTSENESCENCE CHARACTERISTICS: Plants can be easily identified even after senescence by the opened spiny fruits that can persist until the next season.

HABITAT: Plants typically grow in disturbed areas, fields, overgrazed pastures, yards, agronomic and vegetable crops, waste areas, and along roadsides. It is best adapted to sandy soils but can also grow on dry, hard soils to rich, moist soil, such as those found in agricultural sites.

DISTRIBUTION: Found throughout the northeastern and mid-Atlantic states.

SIMILAR SPECIES: Buffalobur can be similar to **horsenettle (*Solanum carolinense*)**, but buffalobur has yellow flowers; horsenettle flowers are white to lavender. In addition, buffalobur leaves are more deeply lobed, the plant is much spinier, and the berries are completely enclosed in a spiny, bur-like calyx. **See Table 10 for a comparison of weedy, solanaceous species.**

Buffalobur flowering stem

J. DiTomaso

Buffalobur seedling

J. DiTomaso

Buffalobur late-season fruit pods

J. DiTomaso

Buffalobur fruit

J. DiTomaso

Buffalobur seeds

S. Hurst, hosted by
USDA-NRCS PLANTS Database

463

Stinging nettle (*Urtica dioica* L. ssp. *gracilis* (Ait.) Seland.)

Synonyms: *Urtica dioica* var. *procera*, *Urtica gracilis*, *Urtica procera*, tall nettle, slender nettle

General Description: An **erect, rhizomatous perennial** (2 m tall), usually unbranched or slightly branched near the top. Large colonies develop from **rhizomes. Leaf surfaces are bristly hairy** with fewer, but larger **stinging hairs.** Stinging nettle is a mechanical **skin irritant** rather than a contact allergen. The large hairs are tapered, elongated cells, constricted just below the tip with a bulbous base embedded in a sheathing pedestal. When the tip of the hair is broken off on contact with the skin, it acts as a hypodermic needle, injecting the toxins histamine, acetylcholine, and 5-hydroxytryptamine into the wound. Localized pain occurs rapidly, followed by a reddish swelling and prolonged itching and numbness.

Propagation / Phenology: Reproduction is **by seeds and rhizomes.** Rhizomes can spread at a rate of 2.5 m a year. Cultivation can fragment rhizomes, further increasing the rate of spread. Seeds do not require a period of cold temperatures to germinate.

Seedling: Cotyledons are oval (1.5–4 mm long by 1 mm wide), notched at the apex, with a few short hairs on the upper surface. **Young leaves are opposite, oval, with rounded teeth** on the margin. The **upper leaf surface has short hairs and a few stinging hairs**; the underside has short hairs on the veins. Stipules at the base of the leaf senesce early. Stems are hairy.

Mature Plant: **Stems are 4-angled,** with **stinging hairs,** but shorter hairs may be absent. **Leaves are opposite,** 5–15 cm long, broadly egg-shaped to ovate or lanceolate, the base rounded to rarely heart-shaped, the apex sharply pointed. Blades are smooth on both surfaces, to sparingly hairy beneath. **Stinging hairs are on the lower surface of the blade. Margins are deeply toothed** (2–3.5 mm). Petioles are ¼ to 2/3 the length of the blade. Stipules at the base of the petiole are oblong to linear-lanceolate (5–12 mm long).

Roots and Underground Structures: **Extensive rhizome system** with secondary fibrous roots.

Flowers and Fruit: Flowers are produced from late May to October. Male and female flowers are separate but on the same plant (monoecious). **Both flower types are inconspicuous, greenish-yellow,** in branched clusters arising from the leaf axils. The seed is enclosed within the egg-shaped fruit (achene). Achenes are white to brown, 1–1.5 mm long.

Postsenescence Characteristics: Erect stems turn dark brown and persist through the winter.

Habitat: A weed of landscapes, nurseries, orchards, and vegetable crops, stinging nettle is also found in pastures and roadsides, and along streams and drainage ditches, generally in lowland areas. It thrives in damp, nutrient-rich soil and does not grow well on low-fertility soil.

Distribution: Found throughout most of the United States, except southern Florida, and southern Canada.

Similar Species: **The introduced European variety, *Urtica dioica* ssp. *dioica*,** is dioecious and less common in North America than ssp. *gracilis*. Its branched stems are weak and tend to sprawl along the ground. Leaves and stems are commonly more hairy than the native species, and the stinging hairs are located on both the upper and lower leaf surfaces. **Garlic mustard (*Alliaria petiolata*)** plants may appear similar but leaves are alternately arranged, and plants lack stinging hairs.

Stinging
nettle
mature shoot

Stinging nettle flower clusters in leaf axils

Stinging nettle juvenile plant

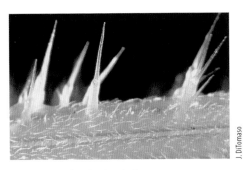

Stinging nettle stinging hairs

Stinging nettle seeds, 1 mm

Garden valerian (*Valeriana officinalis* L.)

SYNONYMS: valerian, garden heliotrope, all-heal

GENERAL DESCRIPTION: A **tall** (0.6 to 1.5 m), **upright, rhizomatous, herbaceous perennial** with numerous **showy white to pale pink**, fragrant flowers and distinctive almost fern-like, opposite leaves. Garden valerian is widely available as a garden perennial but has escaped cultivation and is invasive through a large portion of the northeastern United States.

PROPAGATION / PHENOLOGY: Reproduction is principally **by wind-dispersed seed**, though plants can expand clonally. Germination occurs in mid-to-late spring.

SEEDLING: Cotyledons are **long-stalked**, orbicular, and notched at the tip. Early leaves are simple, orbicular to ovoid, and have wavy or slightly toothed margins.

MATURE PLANT: **Stems of mature plants are pale green to red**, grooved, hollow, and smooth to somewhat hairy, particularly at the nodes. **Leaves are opposite** (occasionally whorled), up to 20 cm long, and **odd-pinnately compound** (terminate with a single leaflet) with 5–10 pairs of lanceolate leaflets. **Leaf undersides are usually hairy**, whereas upper surfaces are smooth to sparsely hairy. **Leaflets are lanceolate with dentate or entire margins**, resembling a horseweed (*Conyza canadensis*) leaf, and **about the same size from the base to the tip** of the leaves. Petioles are longer toward the base of the stem, and upper leaves are sometimes sessile.

ROOTS AND UNDERGROUND STRUCTURES: Roots are shallow, dense, and fibrous with numerous short rhizomes.

FLOWERS AND FRUIT: Flowering occurs from late May through August on erect stems. **Small** (4 mm), **fragrant, white or pale pink flowers** are produced apically in large, **branching panicles** (resembling umbels) 5–12 cm in diameter. Individual flowers are trumpet-shaped, with 5 fused petals and a short, toothed calyx. Each flower has 3 stamens a tripartite pistil. Fruits are 3–5 mm long, lanceolate to ovoid **achenes** with a fringe of short white hairs.

POSTSENESCENCE CHARACTERISTICS: None of note.

HABITAT: Garden valerian grows best in full sun and in moist, loamy soil. Grows in disturbed areas on roadsides, in wet meadows, along ditches and river beds, and in other habitats with moist soil. It can adapt to drier habitats, such as grasslands and open woodlands.

DISTRIBUTION: Garden valerian is native to Europe and Asia. It grows throughout the northeastern United States, south to Virginia and west to Iowa and Minnesota.

SIMILAR SPECIES: The fern-like, opposite leaves of garden valerian distinguish it from most other plants. Native *Valerian* species such as **swamp valerian (*Valeriana uliginosa* (Torr. & A. Gray) Rydb.)** have similar flowers and stem foliage to garden valerian, but the lower leaves of these species are not divided. Members of the Apiaceae (carrot family), such as **wild chervil (*Anthriscus sylvestris*)** or **poison-hemlock (*Conium maculatum*)** have somewhat similar flowers, but these plants have alternate, more finely divided leaves, and the flowers are borne in umbels rather than panicles.

Garden valerian habit

Young garden valerian plant

Garden valerian stem leaves

Garden valerian flowers

Garden valerian fruit

1 mm

Garden valerian seeds

Field violet (*Viola arvensis* Murr.)

Synonyms: wild pansy, field pansy, hearts-ease, European field-pansy

General Description: Usually a **winter annual**, but a summer annual in cool, moist climates. Stems are **erect or ascending**, branching from the base (10–30 cm tall). **Plants resemble cultivated Johnny-jump-ups (*Viola* spp.).**

Propagation / Phenology: Reproduction is **by seeds**; seeds germinate in late summer or early fall.

Seedling: Young plants develop as **basal rosettes.** Elongating stems are angular to cylindrical. Cotyledons are petiolated, oval, 3–5 mm long by 3–4 mm wide, blunt (or sometimes with a small notch) at the tip. **Young leaves are oval, on long petioles.** Blades are truncate at the base, blunt-pointed to rounded at the apex, with rounded teeth on the margins. **Subsequent leaves are hairy at the base and have deeply lobed stipules.**

Mature Plant: Stems may be branched or unbranched, angled or rounded, with short hairs at the branch angles. **Leaves are alternate,** hairy, at least on the veins of the underside, with **rounded teeth on the margin.** Leaves are **spatulate**; the blades of the lower leaves tend to be more rounded or egg-shaped, whereas the upper blades are longer and narrower. **Two large, leaf-like stipules at the base of the petiole are divided into 5–9 narrow segments** with one larger, central, leaf-like segment. Lower leaves are 2–3.5 cm long and have smaller stipules. Upper leaves are 2–8 cm long by 1–1.5 cm wide.

Roots and Underground Structures: Fibrous root system with a wintergreen odor when crushed.

Flowers and Fruit: **Typical violet-like flowers** are produced from March to May and from September to October on long stalks (pedicels) arising from leaf axils. Flowers are 1–1.5 cm long and approximately 1 cm wide, **pale yellow or yellow with purple.** Petals (5) are irregular in shape; the lower is spurred and larger than the others. The fruit is a 5–10 mm long spherical, 1-celled capsule opening into 3 valves. Seeds are oval, 1–2 mm long, yellowish-brown to dark brown, and glossy.

Postsenescence Characteristics: Plants decompose rapidly after senescence or can remain green as winter annuals.

Habitat: Field violet is a weed of nursery crops, landscapes, and small fruits, especially strawberry. It is often found on gravelly or sandy soils. Its importance as a weed is increasing in irrigated horticultural crops.

Distribution: Found in the northern, southeastern, and western United States and in southern Canada. Increasing in importance in the Northeast.

Similar Species: **Pansy or Johnny-jump-up (*Viola tricolor* L.)** and **field pansy (*Viola bicolor* Pursh;** syn.: *V. rafinesquei* Greene) have petals that are 2 and 3 times, respectively, longer than the sepals. Petals of field violet are shorter or equal to the sepal length. Unlike field pansy, the middle lobe of the stipules in pansy is not toothed. Plants and flowers resemble cultivated Johnny-jump-ups (various species of *Viola*) but are more aggressive with less attractive floral displays.

Field violet habit

J. Neal

Field violet flower

J. Neal

Field violet seedling

J. Neal

Pansy habit

J. DiTomaso

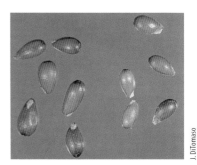

Left, pansy seeds, 2.0 mm; *right*, field violet seeds, 1.6 mm

J. DiTomaso

Common blue violet (*Viola sororia* Willd.)

Synonyms: *Viola papilionacea*, dooryard violet, meadow violet, hooded blue violet

General Description: A **low-growing** (7.5–20 cm), colony-forming **perennial** with smooth, green, **heart-shaped leaves** and **typical violet-like flowers**. Plants spread by short, stout, branching **rhizomes**. Leaves arise basally from a **crown** on relatively long petioles.

Propagation / Phenology: Reproduction is **by seeds and rhizomes**.

Seedling: Not usually noticed.

Mature Plant: Plants are hairless, leaves (8 cm long) arise from a **basal crown**. **Leaf blades are heart-shaped**, pointed at the apex, with rounded teeth on the margin. **Petioles are about twice as long as the leaf blade.**

Roots and Underground Structures: **Stout**, **branching rhizomes** and a coarse root system.

Flowers and Fruit: **Flowers**, produced from April through June, are **usually deep-purple or blue (sometimes gray, light violet, or white)**, 1.3–2 cm wide, with 5 petals. The 2 lateral petals are bearded; the lower 1 is spurred. Flowers are produced **on leafless stalks that are usually no longer than the leaves**. Cleistogamous flowers may also be present. Fruits are 3-valved capsules (10–12 mm long) containing dark brown seeds (2 mm long).

Postsenescence Characteristics: Foliage is not susceptible to frost and persists through the fall but will decay under snow cover during the winter.

Habitat: Primarily a weed of turfgrass and landscapes. Blue violet, for unknown reasons, is common in the turfgrass of cemeteries. It frequently escapes from old flower gardens. It is also found in damp woods, meadows, and roadsides. Although blue violet thrives on cool, moist, shady sites, once established it will tolerate drought-prone soils.

Distribution: Found throughout eastern North America.

Similar Species: **English violet (*Viola odorata* L.)** can be distinguished by its wiry rhizomes and prominent creeping **stoloniferous** habit. Leaves are basal, heart-shaped to ovate, hairy, with 2–6 cm long blades. Flowers are white or purple and **fragrant**. **Field pansy (*Viola bicolor* Pursh) and field violet (*Viola arvensis*)** are 2 common winter annual weeds that can be confused with common blue violet, but they have leafy, branching, ascending to erect stems, unlike the basal leaves of common blue violet. In addition, they have spatulate leaves with long, prominent stipules. Field pansy has purple or bluish-white to cream flower petals longer than the sepals. Field violet has pale yellow to purplish-tinged petals shorter than or equal to the sepal length. **Garlic mustard (*Alliaria petiolata*)** and **lesser celandine (*Ranunculus ficaria*)** have similar heart-shaped leaves in early spring. Crushed leaves of garlic mustard will have a distinct aroma; however, violets do not. Lesser celandine leaves are thick and margins are not toothed.

Common blue violet
habit in turfgrass

J. Neal

A. Senesac

Common blue violet flower

A. Senesac

Common blue violet mature crown, with
seedlings around base

R. Uva

English violet, white-flowered form

471

Puncturevine (*Tribulus terrestris* L.)

Synonyms: bullhead, caltrop, goathead, puncture weed

General Description: A **prostrate summer annual** with stems usually up to 1 m long, **even-pinnately compound leaves**, and small, solitary, **yellow flowers**. Plants produce many **burs with stout spines** that can injure people and animals and puncture bicycle tires. Native to the Mediterranean region. Listed as a regulated **noxious weed** in many states.

Propagation / Phenology: Reproduction is only **by seeds**. Individual spiny nutlets disperse by adhering to vehicle tires (including mowers), the shoes and clothing of people, and the fur, feathers, and feet of animals.

Seedling: Cotyledons are oblong, 4–15 mm long, thick, creased down the center, tip slightly indented. The first few leaves appear to be lateral branches but are pinnately compound, resembling those of mature plants. Plants mature rapidly. Young stems are generally hairy, plants branch from the base.

Mature Plant: Stems are occasionally longer than 1 m, highly branched, and prostrate, radiating out from the crown on open ground to nearly erect when shaded or competing with other plants. Stems do not root at the nodes. Young stems are hairy but lose the hairs with age. **Leaves are opposite**, evenly pinnate compound, mostly 3–5 cm long with 3–7 pairs of leaflets per leaf and a small extension at the tip. The leaflets typically have hairs on the margins. Upper and lower surfaces of the leaflet blades lack hairs or are moderately covered with silky and/or bristly, silver hairs.

Roots and Underground Structures: **Taproot** is slender and deep (to 2.6 m). Roots can associate with nitrogen-fixing bacteria and develop nodules.

Flowers and Fruit: Flowers from early summer through October. Flowers are single in the leaf axils, **bright yellow**, often shiny (like a *Ranunculus* flower), 5–15 mm in diameter, with **5 petals and 5 sepals**, and on a stalk that is shorter than the associated leaf. Burs are woody, 5-lobed and -angled, 5–10 mm diameter, and rounded. They eventually separate into 5(4) wedge-shaped nutlets, each with 2 stout spines 4–7 mm long and several short prickles. The 3–5 seeds per fruit remain enclosed within the nutlet.

Postsenescence Characteristics: After frost, the dead stems remain for some time into winter. In the fall, the stems may have a light orange color. Burs often remain on senesced plants or the soil surface.

Habitat: Generally found in disturbed places, roadsides, railways, waste places, and walkways. It is prevalent in areas with a hot summer and compacted or sandy soils.

Distribution: Although found in most states, except in the states northeast of New York, it is rare in the region (and we are hopeful it will remain so). Occurrences should be reported to the appropriate state agency and controlled.

Similar Species: Puncturevine is unlikely to be confused with any other species. Seedlings may be confused with some species of **vetch (*Vicia* spp.)**, which also have pinnately compound leaves and a trailing growth. However, vetch leaves have a tendril at the tip.

Puncturevine habit

J. DiTomaso

Puncturevine flowers and fruit

J. DiTomaso

J. Neal

Puncturevine flower and leaf

J. Neal

Puncturevine fruit

Puncturevine 3-leaf seedling with cotyledons

J. Neal

Staghorn sumac (*Rhus typhina* L.)

SYNONYMS: *Rhus hirta*, staghorn

GENERAL DESCRIPTION: A **shrub or small tree typically growing in colonies**; older plants are in the middle and smaller, younger plants radiate out on the sides. **Leaves are alternate and pinnately compound**, each with **9–31 serrate leaflets**. Twigs and petioles are densely hairy.

PROPAGATION: **Reproduction is by seeds and rhizomes.** Seeds are dispersed by birds. Once established, colonies enlarge by rhizomes and new seedlings at the margins.

FLOWERS AND FRUIT: **Red, hairy fruits** are on terminal ends of the branches in cone-shaped clusters. Fruit appears in the autumn and persists into spring.

POSTSENESCENCE CHARACTERISTICS: In autumn, the foliage turns bright orange or dark red; after leaves drop the red fruits remain. The characteristically branched stems and red fruit persist through the winter.

HABITAT: Staghorn sumac is often found on poor, dry soil and in areas where other plants find conditions too difficult to survive. It readily produces new sprouts at the base of existing plants. Seedlings can grow in cracks in the pavement. Although it is often planted as an ornamental, staghorn sumac can rapidly encroach into gardens, lawns, and walkways.

DISTRIBUTION: Native to the eastern United States, ranging as far south as Georgia.

SIMILAR SPECIES: **Dwarf (winged) sumac (*Rhus copallinum* L.)** is similar but has raised dots on the stem. The leaflets of dwarf sumac have entire margins, and the main axis (rachis) is winged between the leaflets. **Smooth sumac (*Rhus glabra* L.)** lacks hairs on the stems and petiole. Staghorn sumac can hybridize with smooth sumac, with the hybrids possessing intermediate characteristics. **Poison-sumac (*Toxicodendron vernix* (L.) Kuntze)** is usually found in swampy areas and has white, hairless fruit, hairless stems, and entire leaf margins. Unlike the *Rhus* species, poison-sumac causes dermatitis in sensitive individuals. **Tree-of-heaven (*Ailanthus altissima*)** has a similar habit and pinnately compound leaves but, unlike *Rhus* species, the leaflets have only 1–2 teeth near their base.

Staghorn sumac fall color

J. Neal

Staghorn sumac inflores-
cence and leaf

R. Uva

Dormant staghorn sumac

R. Uva

Staghorn sumac foliage

R. Uva

J. DiTomaso

Left to right: staghorn sumac seeds,
4 mm; smooth sumac seeds, 3 mm;
and dwarf sumac seeds, 3 mm

Eastern poison-ivy (*Toxicodendron radicans* (L.) Kuntze)

Synonyms: *Rhus radicans*, markweed, poison creeper, three-leaved ivy, picry, mercury

General Description: A climbing or trailing, **deciduous woody vine** with **3 leaflets,** each approximately 10 cm long. Leaflet margins are toothed, lobed, or entire; leaflets vary in shape but often are egg-shaped. Leaflet stalks (petiolule) are short except on the middle leaflet. When growing as a climbing vine, eastern poison-ivy attaches to trees or rocks by aerial roots. On older plants, aerial roots give the stems a hairy, fibrous appearance. Eastern poison-ivy is the major cause of **allergenic dermatitis** in the eastern United States. All parts of the plant contain resinous compounds, known as urushiols, that cause inflammation of the skin, blistering, and itching. About 50–60% of Americans are sensitive to urushiols. The toxic compounds can be transmitted in smoke and by direct contact with the plant or with objects or animals exposed to the plant, including tools, pets, and clothing. The dermatitis response can occur year-round, even following contact with overwintering stems and roots. Urushiols can remain active on objects and in dead plants for more than a year.

Propagation: Reproduces **by seeds, creeping rootstocks, and stems that root** where they contact the soil. Seeds are dispersed by birds.

Flowers and Fruit: Plants produce small, yellowish-green flowers on axillary panicles from May to June. Greenish to grayish-**white berries** (5 mm long) lack hairs and are produced in late summer. They can persist on the plant throughout the winter.

Postsenescence Characteristics: In autumn, leaves often turn bright red, then drop by midseason. Woody stems persist.

Habitat: Eastern poison-ivy can invade landscapes, disturbed sites, woodlands, and wetlands by creeping stems or seeds deposited by birds. It thrives under a variety of conditions.

Distribution: Native and widespread throughout the midwestern, northern, and eastern United States and parts of Canada.

Similar Species: **Atlantic poison-oak (*Toxicodendron pubescens* Mill.)** and **western poison-ivy (*Toxicodendron rydbergii* (Small ex Rydberg) Greene)** are similar but grow more erect, shrub-form, and not vine-like. Atlantic poison-oak has blunt-tipped leaf apexes, and hairs on both surfaces of the blade. Atlantic poison-oak is found only from New Jersey southward. Western poison-ivy leaves are glabrous or nearly so, with glabrous petioles. It is present but uncommon in the Northeast, more common in the Midwest and western states. **Virginia-creeper (*Parthenocissus quinquefolia*)** is similar **but has 5 leaflets per leaf** and climbs by tendrils with terminal adhesive disks.

Eastern poison-ivy foliage

R. Uva

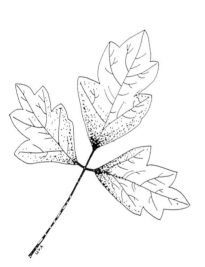

Atlantic poison-oak leaf (with 3 leaflets)
R. Uva

J. Neal

Eastern poison-ivy flowers

J. Neal

Eastern poison-ivy seedling

477

Common periwinkle (*Vinca minor* L.)

SYNONYMS: myrtle, lesser periwinkle, dwarf periwinkle

GENERAL DESCRIPTION: Common periwinkle is an **evergreen, herbaceous, vine-like, trailing perennial** ground cover with milky sap. Flower-bearing stems develop showy **lavender-blue, funnel-shaped flowers**. Common periwinkle is commonly cultivated as an ornamental ground cover but has escaped cultivation in many places. Native to central and southern Europe.

PROPAGATION: Reproduces vegetatively from trailing stems that root at the tips and stem fragments and rarely by seeds. Plants and stem fragments disperse with human activities, such as purposeful landscape planting and careless disposal of yard waste. Under favorable conditions, stem cuttings left on the ground can take root. In riparian areas, water currents can fragment stems and carry them downstream where they may root if lodged in a suitable place. Fruits with viable seeds rarely develop.

SEEDLING: Rarely encountered. Cotyledons narrow elliptic, base long-tapered, glabrous. Leaves resemble those of mature plants but are usually slightly smaller.

MATURE PLANT: Slender, green stems typically arching, rooting at the nodes and tips. Leaves opposite but alternating orientation at each node (**decussate**), mostly glabrous, semi-glossy, oval to lanceolate, 2–4.5 cm long by 1–2.5 cm broad, with an entire margin.

ROOTS AND UNDERGROUND STRUCTURES: Perennial rootstock tough and woody.

FLOWERS AND FRUIT: Flowering occurs in spring and sporadically into early summer. Flowers are solitary in leaf axils, lavender-blue, funnel-shaped, 2.5–3 cm diameter, on slender stalks (pedicels). Corolla 5-lobed, lobes overlapping and pinwheel-like in bud. Fruits and seeds rarely develop. Pods (follicles) 1 or 2 per flower, slender, curved, cylindrical, approximately 2.5 cm long, tip pointed, and open on 1 side to release seeds. Seeds nearly cylindrical, mostly 5–8 mm long, slightly compressed, grooved on 1 side, truncate at both ends.

POSTSENESCENCE CHARACTERISTICS: Plants are evergreen.

HABITAT: Frequently found in well-drained, open, disturbed areas of shaded woods, old homesteads, moist woodlands, edges and roadsides.

DISTRIBUTION: Found in all northeastern and mid-Atlantic states.

SIMILAR SPECIES: **Big (or large) periwinkle (*Vinca major* L.)** is an ornamental evergreen ground cover that closely resembles common periwinkle. Big periwinkle is distinguished by having larger leaves approximately 7 cm long, and larger flowers to 3–5 cm diameter. Big periwinkle leaves are opposite, but typically not decussate. Like common periwinkle, big periwinkle rarely develops fruits. Big periwinkle is not as widespread as common periwinkle in the eastern United States, but the opposite is true in the western states where big periwinkle has become a major invasive plant problem. **Wintercreeper (*Euonymus fortunei* (Turcz.) Hand.-Maz.)** (Celastraceae) is also an evergreen woody vine that forms a dense ground cover or may climb small trees and shrubs. Stems are not winged; leaves are opposite, broadly lanceolate with shallowly toothed margins, and prominent netted veins. The flowers are inconspicuous. Several selections of wintercreeper are widely planted as an ornamental ground cover but have escaped cultivation to invade woodland habitats throughout eastern North America.

Common periwinkle habit

J. Neal

Common periwinkle flower and leaves

J. Neal

Big periwinkle flower and leaves

J. DiTomaso

Left, leafy stems of winter-creeper; *middle*, common periwinkle; and *right*, big periwinkle

J. Neal

English ivy (*Hedera helix* L.)

Synonym: ivy

GENERAL DESCRIPTION: English ivy is a **shade-tolerant, woody evergreen vine or ground cover**. When established, it creates a **dense ground cover** with attractive dark green foliage, long woody stems that spread on the ground or climb other vegetation and structures with the aid of adventitious roots. **Vines can climb mature trees**, eventually smothering and killing the tree. There are **2 distinct growth forms: juvenile and mature**. The juvenile form has prostrate to climbing vines, **dark green, glossy leaves 5–8 cm wide, with 3-5 lobes**, the center lobe typically longer than the lateral lobes, and tips of lobes are pointed, with entire margins and prominent veins. The mature (reproductive) form can be shrub-like or as horizontal branches from climbing vines. The **leaves of mature plants lack lobes**, are broadly or narrowly cordate, and often have wavy margins.

PROPAGATION: Plants reproduce **by seeds** and spread vegetatively **by creeping stems** that root continuously along the stems. Stem pieces left in shady, moist areas can form adventitious roots.

FLOWERS AND FRUIT: Mature plants produce small, greenish-yellow flowers in branched inflorescences beginning in early summer. The inflorescence branches have globe-shaped clusters of flowers. Individual flowers lack distinct pedicels, and the 5 sepals are spreading (star-shaped) or reflexed. Ripened fruits are dark blue (to black), round drupes.

POSTSENESCENCE CHARACTERISTICS: Plants are evergreen.

HABITAT: Introduced to North America as an ornamental ground cover and has escaped cultivation to invade diverse woodlands, riparian areas, streambanks, and parklands. In contrast to many other invasive species, English ivy can invade undisturbed shaded woodlands.

DISTRIBUTION: Throughout the eastern and western regions of the United States.

SIMILAR SPECIES: Many cultivars of English ivy with variable leaf shapes and pigmentation have been planted, which contribute to some diversity in wild populations. Other species of ivy introduced as ornamental ground covers have escaped cultivation including **Atlantic ivy (*Hedera hibernica* (G. Kirchner) Carrière)**. It differs from English ivy by having larger leaves (>8 cm wide) and typically does not climb.

English ivy juvenile foliage

J. Neal

English ivy flowers

J. Neal

English ivy flowers and mature foliage

J. Neal

English ivy fruit

J. DiTomaso

481

Groundsel shrub (*Baccharis halimifolia* L.)

Synonyms: coyote bush, eastern baccharis, saltbush, silverling

General Description: **Woody shrub with distinctively gray-green foliage** to 3 m in height. Plant flowers in autumn and winter. In winter, the female plants can be covered with white flowers and seeds. Sometimes planted in gardens for winter interest, where it often becomes weedy.

Propagation: Plants flower in winter, producing plumes of **wind-dispersed seeds**.

Seedling: Young plants generally lack the waxy coatings that give mature specimens a gray appearance. Seedlings upright with green, often unbranched, stems and alternate leaves. Leaves are oblong with margins variably coarsely toothed or lobed.

Mature Plant: Stems upright and branched with rough bark. Leaves and stems on mature plants covered with wax, giving the plant a gray-green color. Lower leaves are egg-shaped with shallow lobes. Leaves subtending the flowering branches are narrower, shorter, and lack lobes.

Roots and Underground Structures: A tough, fibrous root system. Does not sprout from the roots.

Flowers and Fruit: Plants are dioecious (separate female and male plants), flowering from late autumn through early winter. Fruits are shed in winter to early spring. Both female and male flowers lack visible petals and are in branched clusters at the branch tips. Male flowers are creamy yellow, female flowers are inconspicuous except for the long, white or light cream-colored pappus, approximately 1.5 cm in length. Fruits are small achenes attached to a pappus that aids in wind and water dispersal.

Postsenescence Characteristics: Plants retain most of their leaves through winter but lose lower leaves with age, and stringy bark becomes more visible.

Habitat: Prefers moist sites but once established are tolerant of a wide variety of soils, including saline soils. Commonly found on roadsides, in drainage ditches, and has become common in container nurseries and gardens.

Distribution: Native to eastern North American coastal riparian areas, the plant is now widely distributed throughout the eastern United States, north to New England and west to Texas.

Similar Species: The growth habit of seedlings and waxy gray-green foliage are similar to **common lambsquarters (*Chenopodium album*)**. But, young common lambsquarters seedlings will develop the distinctive waxy foliage, whereas seedling groundsel shrub will have green foliage and stems. As plants age, they are easily differentiated by the overall growth habit and stem structure. Several related species occur in the genus *Baccharis* in the eastern United States, but those species are more restricted to coastal plant communities and generally are not "weedy."

J. Neal

Groundsel shrub habit (female plant)

J. Neal

Groundsel shrub juvenile plant

Groundsel shrub mature foliage

J. Neal

J. Neal

Left, groundsel shrub female flowers; *right*, male flowers

Japanese barberry (*Berberis thunbergii* DC.)

Synonyms: Thunberg's barberry, red barberry

General Description: A compact, multi-stemmed, **deciduous or semi-evergreen shrub** that reaches 0.5–2.5 m tall by 1–2.5 m wide. Plants are densely branched; stems are spreading, deeply grooved with a single **sharp spine at each node**. The tip of each spine is barbed. Where arching stems touch the ground they may produce roots. **Leaves** occur in **alternate** clusters (occasionally solitary) at the nodes and are **spatulate to ovate**, glabrous, 0.5–2.5 cm long, with entire margins and short (to 8 mm) petioles. Foliage may be green to deep maroon in color.

Propagation: Reproduction is primarily **by seeds**. Plants produce **bright red berries** that are eaten by birds, dispersing the seeds. One publication reports reproduction by rhizomes but this appears to be rare. Low hanging stems can root where they contact the soil. This may account for some reports of rhizome spread.

Flowers and Fruit: Flowering begins in mid-spring and continues in early summer. Small, pale yellow flowers (8–15 mm wide) are borne singly or in drooping umbels of 2–5 along the branches. Flowers have 6 spreading sepals and 6 cupped petals. Fruits mature from July to October and are **bright red, oblong berries** (7–11 mm long) with dry flesh. Seeds are 4–5 mm long, elliptical to obovate, with a pitted appearance.

Postsenescence Characteristics: Foliage turns yellow to red during the autumn. **Berries persist on stems into the winter.** Dark brown to reddish-brown, spiny stems persist and resprout in the spring.

Habitat: Japanese barberry can grow in full sun to shade and can form dense thickets in forest understories and along streambanks. It is a weed of post-agricultural woodlands and fields, meadows, and riparian habitats.

Distribution: A common horticultural plant, Japanese barberry has escaped and become naturalized throughout the eastern United States and Canada, and the Midwest.

Similar Species: **Common barberry (*Berberis vulgaris* L.)** and **American barberry (*Berberis canadensis* Mill.)** have a similar habit to Japanese barberry, but these species have leaves with toothed margins, flowers borne on racemes, and often have branching spines at the nodes. In contrast, Japanese barberry leaves are entire, the flowers occur in umbels, and each node has only a single, unbranched spine.

J. Neal

Japanese barberry spring growth

Japanese barberry leafy shoot

J. Neal

Japanese barberry
fruiting stem

R. Prostak

J. Neal

Japanese barberry thorns

485

Trumpetcreeper (*Campsis radicans* (L.) Seem. ex Bureau)

Synonym: cow-itch

GENERAL DESCRIPTION: A fast-growing, **aggressive**, **deciduous**, **woody vine** that either climbs on other vegetation or trails along the ground. Sometimes grown as an ornamental, it can easily escape cultivation. **Leaves** are alternate, **pinnately compound** (30 cm long), with **7–11 coarsely toothed leaflets**. Trumpetcreeper climbs with the aid of aerial roots along its stems and can produce suckers from the roots.

PROPAGATION: Reproduction is **by seeds**, **root sprouts**, **and stems that root** where they touch the ground.

FLOWERS AND FRUIT: **Orange, trumpet-shaped flowers** (6–8 cm long tube-like corolla) are present from July through September and produce pod-like structures containing numerous winged seed.

POSTSENESCENCE CHARACTERISTICS: In autumn, leaves turn yellow-green, then drop. Woody vines persist.

HABITAT: Commonly found in orchards, vineyards, nursery stock, landscapes, along fencerows, and in wooded areas, trumpetcreeper can also emerge in sidewalk cracks and around foundations.

DISTRIBUTION: Native to the eastern half of the United States.

SIMILAR SPECIES: Although the compound leaves of trumpetcreeper are similar to the sumacs (*Rhus* spp.), the sumacs are not viny.

Trumpetcreeper in flower

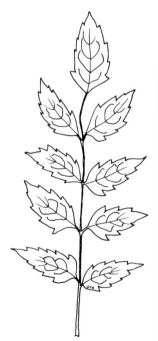

Trumpetcreeper leaf
R. Uva

Trumpetcreeper seedling in late spring

Japanese honeysuckle (*Lonicera japonica* Thunb.)

Synonym: Chinese honeysuckle

GENERAL DESCRIPTION: A twining, **climbing, or trailing vine** that is **deciduous** in **colder climates but semi-evergreen to evergreen in more southerly locations**. Leaves are opposite and simple, ovate to oblong, with entire, or sometimes lobed, margins. Both the **leaves and twigs are hairy**. Stems are woody and have a hollow pith.

PROPAGATION: Plants spread **by seeds and rapidly growing runners that root** at the nodes. Runner growth can exceed 9 m a year.

FLOWERS AND FRUIT: **Fragrant white to yellow flowers** (to 38 mm long) bloom in May. Flowers are produced in pairs attached to a short common stalk (peduncle) arising from the upper leaf axils. Fruit are black berries (6 mm in diameter) that mature in late summer but persist into autumn.

POSTSENESCENCE CHARACTERISTICS: Semi-evergreen vine. Leaves may take on a purplish tinge in autumn and may persist through mild winters. Woody stems persist.

HABITAT: A weed of perennial crops in orchards, Christmas tree plantations, nurseries, and landscapes, Japanese honeysuckle can engulf small plants and saplings. In the southeastern United States, it can displace native vegetation but is less vigorous and more easily contained in the Northeast.

DISTRIBUTION: Japanese honeysuckle is native to eastern Asia and was introduced to the United States as an ornamental in the 1800s. It has become naturalized and has spread over much of eastern, central, and western North America from Massachusetts west to California, south to Florida and Texas. It is a significant problem on the East Coast from New Jersey south.

SIMILAR SPECIES: Other weedy honeysuckles, including **bush honeysuckles (*Lonicera* spp.)**, are shrubby, whereas Japanese honeysuckle is viny. In addition, bush honeysuckles have red berries; the berries of Japanese honeysuckle are black.

Japanese honeysuckle stem
and leaves
R. Uva

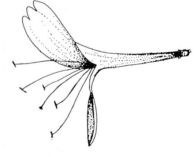

Japanese honeysuckle flower
R. Uva

J. Neal

Japanese honeysuckle flowering vine

R. Uva

Japanese honeysuckle juvenile leaves

Bush honeysuckles

Amur honeysuckle (*Lonicera maackii* (Rupr.) Herder)
Morrow's honeysuckle (*Lonicera morrowii* A. Gray)
Sweet breath of spring (*Lonicera fragrantissima* Lindl. & Paxton)
Tatarian honeysuckle (*Lonicera tatarica* L.)

GENERAL DESCRIPTION: **Branching shrubs** (3–5 m high), in which the upper branches are often arching upward from spreading older branches. **Stems** are scaly between each season's growth and have a hollow pith. Bark is light brown to tan and longitudinally splitting or peeling. Leaves of **seedlings are opposite, egg-shaped**, with entire margins, typically hairy. On **mature plants**, the leaves are opposite, egg-shaped to oblong (3–8 cm long), with entire margins. Leaf size, shape, and pubescence are highly variable.

PROPAGATION: **Berries are round, red, and ingested by birds that disperse the seeds.** Seed germinates over an extended season, from mid-spring to mid-summer.

FLOWERS AND FRUIT: **Pink to white (fading to yellow), fragrant** flowers (1.5–2 cm long) bloom in pairs on a common long stalk (peduncle) arising from the leaf axils. Flowers are produced in spring and attractive red berries (6–8 mm in diameter) develop in pairs in late summer.

POSTSENESCENCE CHARACTERISTICS: No distinctive fall leaf color. Arching woody stems with tan, peeling bark are notable from autumn through spring.

HABITAT: Primarily a weed in woodlands, parks, riparian areas, and landscape plantings.

DISTRIBUTION: Introduced from Eurasia to the United States as ornamental shrubs and have since escaped to become naturalized over much of the eastern states. The species have overlapping distributions.

SIMILAR SPECIES: The 4 species have many overlapping characteristics outlined in Table 11. Amur honeysuckle is distinguished from the other shrub honeysuckles by long, tapered leaf tips and flower stalks (peduncles) that are shorter than the petioles. Sweet breath of spring, Morrow's honeysuckle, and tatarian honeysuckle each have acute or obtuse leaf tips and peduncles longer than the adjacent leaf petioles. Tatarian honeysuckle leaf blades are shorter, 2–5 cm in length; whereas sweet breath of spring and Morrow's honeysuckle leaf blades are up to 8 cm long. Sweet breath of spring flowers are glabrous on the outside but hairy on the inside; the other species are variably hairy or glabrous in and out. **Bell's honeysuckle (*Lonicera* x *bella* Zabel)** is an interspecific hybrid between *L. morrowii* and *L. tatarica* and has intermediate traits.

Tatarian honeysuckle leaves and fruit

Amur honeysuckle flowering branch

Amur honeysuckle peduncle (flower stalk) is shorter than the length of petiole

Sweet breath of spring seedling

Oriental bittersweet (*Celastrus orbiculatus* Thunb.)

SYNONYM: Asiatic bittersweet

GENERAL DESCRIPTION: An invasive, **climbing, deciduous, woody vine**. Young vines are green, often with conspicuous lenticels. Leaves are somewhat rounded to obovate (2–12 cm long), alternate, simple, with bluntly toothed margins. Leaf tips may taper to a sharp point or not. **Foliage turns bright yellow in autumn** revealing brightly colored fruits. Despite being listed as a **noxious weed** in some states, stems bearing the fruit are harvested and used in winter holiday decorations, contributing to the spread of the species.

PROPAGATION: Reproduced by seeds. Cut stems readily resprout from the base, and large stems left on the ground can form roots.

FLOWERS AND FRUIT: Inconspicuous, greenish-white flowers form in the spring, singly or in clusters from the leaf axils. Immature fruit are green turning bright yellow. Fleshy, **red seeds are enclosed in yellow capsules** and are produced during the autumn. The fruit has been sporadically **reported to be poisonous to humans**.

POSTSENESCENCE CHARACTERISTICS: Leaves turn bright yellow in autumn, then drop. Distinctive **yellow fruit with red seeds** persist to late fall and early winter.

HABITAT: Forms **tangles and thickets** when growing alone but **can strangle other shrubs and small trees by girdling their stems**. Oriental bittersweet is often found in landscapes, along roadsides, and other uncultivated areas.

DISTRIBUTION: A native of Eastern Asia. Introduced to the United States as an ornamental in the late 1800s and has since escaped from cultivation and become naturalized over much of the northeastern states, south to the Carolinas.

SIMILAR SPECIES: **American bittersweet (*Celastrus scandens* L.)** is native to the United States. It has been replaced in some areas by the more aggressive Oriental bittersweet. American bittersweet has ovate to oblong-ovate leaves, whereas the leaves of Oriental bittersweet are typically more rounded. American bittersweet fruit clusters are orange and at the ends of branches; whereas oriental bittersweet fruit clusters are yellow and in the leaf axils.

J. Neal

Oriental bittersweet fruit

Oriental bittersweet sprout from a cut stump

J. Neal

Oriental bittersweet leafy shoots
J. Neal

Oriental bittersweet
immature fruit
J. Neal

493

Burning bush (*Euonymus alatus* (Thunb.) Sieb.)

SYNONYMS: winged euonymus, winged spindle tree

GENERAL DESCRIPTION: A **deciduous shrub** (to 3 m tall) or occasionally small tree (up to 6 m tall) that has escaped cultivation and can form dense thickets. Plants often have multiple low-branching trunks with brown to gray fissured bark. Young stems have green to dark green stripes and prominent, **cork-like wings. Leaves are opposite** to sub-opposite, elliptical to obovate (3–5 cm long) with **finely serrated margins, turning bright red in autumn**. Plants typically produce 1 flush of growth per year.

PROPAGATION: Reproduction is **by seeds**. The seeds are eaten by birds and other animals, which facilitates dispersal.

FLOWERS AND FRUIT: Flowering occurs in late spring. The 4-petaled **flowers are greenish-yellow**, small (1.3 cm wide), and **occur in clusters of 3** near the leaves. Fruits begin to form during the summer, ripening to **dark red, dehiscent capsules** (0.75 cm long) by mid-September. The capsules split to reveal a fleshy, orange aril.

POSTSENESCENCE CHARACTERISTICS: Foliage turns bright red to purple during autumn, with less brilliant colors in shaded habitats. Brightly colored fruit can persist into winter. Distinctively winged stems are visible through winter.

HABITAT: Found in hedgerows, along roadsides and fence lines and similar edge habitats. Burning bush has been widely planted as a landscape plant and has spread to woodlands and old fields.

DISTRIBUTION: Found throughout the eastern United States, south to Georgia and west to Iowa, and in Montana.

SIMILAR SPECIES: **Native *Euonymus*** species may resemble burning bush; however, none of these shrubs have the winged, corky bark characteristic of winged burning bush. In winter, the winged stems may resemble a young **winged elm (*Ulmus alata* Michx.)**, but winged elm forms a small tree not a branched shrub and has alternate leaves, whereas burning bush has opposite leaves.

R. Prostak

Burning bush fall color

J. Neal

Burning bush leafy stem

J. Neal

Burning bush flowering stem

A. DiTommaso

Winged stem of burning bush

Autumn-olive (*Elaeagnus umbellata* Thunb.)

SYNONYMS: oleaster, wild olive, silverberry

GENERAL DESCRIPTION: A fast-growing, **deciduous shrub** with **multiple, upright stems** reaching 6 m in height (more commonly 2–3 m tall and wide). Short twigs develop into **sharp thorns** >3 cm long. Lateral branches are lax. **Leaves are alternate**, oval to lanceolate, green to gray-green above, but **undersides are silvery**. Plants have **red fruit**. Establishes rapidly from seeds and fixes nitrogen, adding to its competitiveness in low-fertility sites. Although widely planted for reclamation of depleted soils, it is now recognized as invasive and is prohibited from sale in several states.

PROPAGATION: Reproduction is **by seeds**. Most fruits remain on trees until distributed by animals, especially birds. Seeds survive ingestion by animals. Plants can resprout from base after cutting or injury.

FLOWERS AND FRUIT: Flowers in spring to early summer. **Flowers are silvery white to yellow,** borne singly or in groups of up to 10 from the leaf axils. Flowers are highly **fragrant**, bisexual, mostly 5–10 mm long and wide, lack petals, and consist of a narrow, bell-shaped calyx (sepals as a unit) with 4 acute lobes. Fruits are bright red, drupe-like with a single seed, ovoid, approximately 10 mm long, and dotted with silvery scales. Fruits ripen in mid-summer and are persistent until removed by birds.

POSTSENESCENCE CHARACTERISTICS: Dormant plants without leaves usually retain a few fruits. Stems with thorns are recognizable in winter.

HABITAT: Grows in intact woodlands, riparian areas, floodplains, grasslands, roadsides, fencerows, seasonally moist pastures, ditches, and other disturbed sites.

DISTRIBUTION: Found throughout the eastern half of the United States and Canada, with populations also in the Pacific Northwest.

SIMILAR SPECIES: Both **thorny-olive (*Elaeagnus pungens* Thunb.) and Russian-olive (*Elaeagnus angustifolia* L.)** are similar to autumn-olive. All 3 are native to Asia. The 3 species can be distinguished by leaf characteristics. Russian-olive leaves are narrowly lanceolate or elliptic, with smooth margins, and with upper surface gray-green and moderately covered with silvery star-shaped hairs and scales. Thorny-olive has persistent leaves that are oval with wavy margins. The upper surfaces are shiny green, lack scales, and the lower surfaces are covered with dull white scales and dotted with light brown scales. Autumn-olive has deciduous leaves that are oval or lanceolate, with a smooth or wavy margin. Leaves are dull green above and silvery beneath. Few other species resemble autumn-olive. The **privets (*Ligustrum* spp.)** can resemble Russian-olive and share a similar habitat, but all privets have dark green and shiny leaves, whereas Russian-olive has grayish-green leaves.

Autumn-olive flowering stem

J. Neal

Autumn-olive underside of leaves and fruit

J. Neal

Thorny-olive leaves, bottom and top sides

J. Neal

Russian-olive flowers and leaves

J. DiTomaso

497

Silktree (*Albizia julibrissin* Durazz.)

SYNONYMS: mimosa, Persian silktree

GENERAL DESCRIPTION: A small, **deciduous tree** with spreading branches that form a wide crown. Trees can reach more than 15 m in height but are more commonly 8–10 m; usually wider than tall. **Leaves are distinctively bipinnately compound** and 20–50 cm long. No leaflets occur on the main rachis, but 20–30 pairs of 1–1.5 cm long oblong leaflets are closely spaced on the secondary divisions. At night or in heavy rains, the leaflets fold downward. Plants have rapid growth rates but are relatively short-lived due to weak branches and susceptibility to insect and disease damage. Introduced from Asia in the late 1700s as an ornamental, it has been widely planted, primarily for its floral display that attracts many pollinator species and hummingbirds.

PROPAGATION: Propagation is by seeds. Most seeds are dispersed near the parent plant but some will be moved by water and animals. Seeds remain viable in the soil for many years and can emerge over an extended time from spring through summer. Cutting the tree stimulates **adventitious sprouts from shallow roots** and resprouting from the stumps.

FLOWERS AND FRUIT: In early summer, plants produce **showy pink, fragrant flower clusters** in branched terminal racemes. The inconspicuous petals are 5–8 mm long and fused into short tubes. The most noticeable feature of individual flowers is the cluster of white to pink, silky thread-like stamens. It is the colorful stamens that constitute the attractive floral display. Fruit is a multi-seeded, **flat legume** (bean pod), up to 20 cm long by 2.5 cm wide. Pods are green turning dark brown, then light tan in winter. Seeds are oval, 6–8 mm long, smooth, and tan to dark brown.

POSTSENESCENCE CHARACTERISTICS: The wide branching pattern is fairly distinctive. Seedpods persist into winter and the shed seedpods often persist on the ground near the parent into spring.

HABITAT: Adapted to a wide range of habitats. Plants persist in low-fertility sites where other species are less competitive, but they also thrive in fertile sites. Common in abandoned fields, fencerows, rights of ways, forest edges, and urban landscapes.

DISTRIBUTION: More common in the southern half of the United States but present north to the Ohio River Valley and New York. Plants are damaged by temperatures below –4°C (24° F), limiting its northern distribution.

SIMILAR SPECIES: **Honeylocust (*Gleditsia triacanthos*)** has similar bipinnately compound leaves, but honeylocust stems have spines that silktree lacks.

Silktree habit

J. Neal

Silktree foliage and flower

J. Neal

Silktree seed-pods

J. Neal

5 mm

S. Hurst, hosted by USDA-NRCS PLANTS Database

Silktree seed

Scotch broom (*Cytisus scoparius* (L.) Link)

Synonyms: *Spartium scoparium*, Scot's broom, English broom

General Description: **Deciduous shrub** to 3 m tall, with photosynthetically active **green stems** (older stems and branches brown) and **yellow, pea-like flowers**. Stems are erect, dense, and green. Most **stems are sharply 5-angled** or -ridged, star-shaped in cross section, and often with few leaves. Leaves are alternate, compound with 3 leaflets, sometimes with 1 leaflet on new twigs, and typically drought-deciduous. Leaflets are 5–20 mm long, oblong to obovate, upper surface lacks hairs or sparsely hairy, and lower surface sparse to densely covered with flattened (appressed), short hairs. Native to Europe and northern Africa.

Propagation: Reproduction is **by seeds**. Pods typically burst apart into spiral halves, ejecting seeds a short distance from the parent plant. Several species of ants are attracted to the seed appendages and disperse seeds while foraging. Seeds are hard-coated and can survive 30 years or more under field conditions. Scotch broom can resprout from the crown when cut. Individual shrubs can live 10–15 years.

Flowers and Fruit: Plants flower in spring to early summer. **Flowers are pea-like**, ranging from **bright yellow** to pale yellow or even maroon-red. Flowers mostly 1–2.5 cm long, single or paired in leaf axils. **Pods are dark brown to black** at maturity, flattened, mostly 2–5 cm long by 1 cm wide, with only the margins densely lined with long, silky, golden to silvery hairs. Seeds are 5–9 per pod and ovoid, compressed, 2 mm long, shiny, greenish-brown to black, with an appendage that is attractive to certain species of ants.

Postsenescence Characteristics: Plants tolerate frost, but typically die back after severe cold winter conditions; however, roots or lower stems survive and generate new growth.

Habitat: Grows best in open disturbed sites, such as logged or burned sites, roadsides, and pastures; also relatively undisturbed grasslands, woodlands, riparian corridors, and open forests. Scotch broom plants can fix nitrogen and thus are able to colonize low-fertility sites.

Distribution: More prominent as a weed in the western United States, but it is found throughout most of the northeastern and mid-Atlantic states.

Similar Species: The showy flowers, green stems, and small leaves make Scotch broom easy to recognize.

Scotch broom habit

Scotch broom flowering
stem with immature fruit

Scotch broom seedpods

Scotch broom seedlings

Scotch broom leaf and winged stem

Scotch broom seeds

Chinese wisteria (*Wisteria sinensis* (Sims) Sweet)

SYNONYMS: *Glycine sinensis, Rehsonia sinensis*, wisteria

GENERAL DESCRIPTION: A vigorous, **woody, deciduous vine**, spreading on the ground or **climbing vegetation to 30 m**. Young stems are green and hairy, losing hairs with age, becoming woody and thick. **Leaves are alternate, odd pinnately compound** with 7–13 leaflets. Leaflets are elliptic to ovate, 3–8 cm long, tips tapering to a point, and margins entire. New growth is often bronze, turning green soon after elongation. Climbing vines can kill a tree by excluding light and/or by girdling the stems. Additionally, Chinese wisteria vines will grow between trees connecting them in a web of woody vines. In high winds, the connected vegetation can catch the wind (like a sail) and contribute to increased storm damage from broken tops and even felling trees that otherwise would withstand the storm.

PROPAGATION: Propagation is **by seeds** and **spreading vines** that can root.

FLOWERS AND FRUIT: Plants produce numerous flowers that persist for only a few weeks. Flowers emerge in the spring just before the leaves, in many-flowered, 20–30 cm long, pendulous clusters (racemes). Individual flowers are pea-like, 20–25 mm long, **light blue, lavender to purple (occasionally white), and very fragrant**. Fruits are 10–15 cm long, **flattened pods covered in velvety hairs**. Pods contain few seeds (1–3 are common); seeds are 1.5–1.7 cm long, round to oval, flattened, and hard-coated. When seedpods are mature, they pop open, forcefully dispersing the seeds several meters.

POSTSENESCENCE CHARACTERISTICS: Woody vines persist over winter and may be gray to brown and many-branched.

HABITAT: Tolerant of a wide range of conditions including moist riparian forests to dry, upland sites. Plants grow best in full sun but will tolerate some shade, climbing other plants or structures to reach sunlight. Commonly found in edges of woodlands, urban parks and forests, and forest openings.

DISTRIBUTION: Throughout much of the eastern United States, north to Massachusetts, Vermont, and the Great Lakes states, and west to the Mississippi River Valley.

SIMILAR SPECIES: **Japanese wisteria (*Wisteria floribunda* (Willd.) DC.)** is difficult to distinguish from Chinese wisteria vegetatively but has a longer inflorescence, 30–50 cm long, and 13–19 leaflets. Recent research, however, suggests that **the majority of naturalized populations are hybrids** between *W. sinensis* and *W. floribunda*. These hybrids will have overlapping morphological traits.

Chinese wisteria enveloping trees

Chinese wisteria leaves

Chinese wisteria vine on a pine tree

Chinese wisteria
immature fruit

Chinese wisteria flowers and new growth

Chocolate vine (*Akebia quinata* (Houtt.) Decne.)

SYNONYMS: *Rajania quinata,* five-finger akebia, five-leaf akebia

GENERAL DESCRIPTION: A **deciduous** or semi-evergreen, perennial, **woody vine** with **distinctive palmately compound leaves** on long (2–12 cm) petioles. **Leaflets, typically 5, are oval**, about twice as long as wide, with smooth margins. Plants flower in the spring; **flowers are dark purple**, in clusters, and fragrant. Sold in the nursery trade as an ornamental vine, the species has escaped cultivation and naturalized in woodlands, parks, and riparian areas. Woody vines climb structures and other vegetation to form thickets.

PROPAGATION: Spread **by seeds**. Plants flower in the spring and produce fruit in late summer to autumn. Fruits are eaten by birds and other animals, dispersing the seeds. Stems can root, and some spread has been attributed to stem fragmentation.

FLOWERS AND FRUIT: Plants have separate male and female flowers within each raceme. Both male and female flowers are chocolate-purple, approximately 2.5 cm wide, in clusters of 6–8, with a fragrant vanilla scent. Flowers lack petals; 3 colorful sepals resemble petals. Fruit (follicle) is purple, oblong, 5–15 cm long, and contains many black seeds embedded in whitish pulp. At maturity, the fruit split on one side.

POSTSENESCENCE CHARACTERISTICS: Woody vines are persistent.

HABITAT: An invasive weed in woodlands, parks, riparian areas, and landscape plantings.

DISTRIBUTION: Introduced from East Asia; distributed through the horticultural trade. The species has naturalized throughout the eastern United States, north to New England.

SIMILAR SPECIES: Chocolate vine is easily distinguished from other common vines by the 5-fingered compound leaves with entire leaflet margins. **Three-leaf akebia (*Akebia trifoliata* (Thunberg) Koidzum)** is also available in the nursery trade. It is similar to chocolate vine but its compound leaves have 3 leaflets (occasionally 5).

Chocolate vine habit

J. Neal

Chocolate vine leaves

J. Neal

Chocolate vine flowers

J. Neal

Chinaberry (*Melia azedarach* L.)

Synonyms: *Melia japonica* var. *semperflorens,* chinaberry tree, umbrella tree

General Description: Native to Australasia, chinaberry was introduced as an ornamental tree for its attractive growth habit, dramatic foliage, and attractive and fragrant flowers. Mature trees have a rounded crown 10–12 m in height, nearly that in width. **Leaves are large, up to 50 cm long**, alternate, with a long petiole, triangular in outline, **twice (to 3 times) odd pinnately compound**, with 2–4 pairs of major divisions, each with 2–4 pairs of well-defined leaflets, plus terminal leaflets that may or may not be on short stalks. Leaflets are dark green, oblanceolate, 4–7 cm long, with uneven bases and toothed margins. Foliage turns yellow in the fall. Seeds within the fruit are **poisonous** to livestock and humans, causing diarrhea and other gastric problems, and in high doses is a neurotoxin. Not poisonous to birds.

Propagation: Primarily reproduces **by seeds**. Birds consume the fruit and disperse the seeds.

Flowers and Fruit: **Flowers are in large panicles** from the axils of leaves at the base of the current season's spring growth. Individual flowers are **fragrant**, 1–1.3 cm long, with **purple tube** and 5 slender white petals. Fruits are 1-seeded drupes, globe shaped, 1–1.5 cm in diameter, ripening slowly from green to yellowish-tan. **Fruits persist after the leaves have fallen.**

Postsenescence Characteristics: Trees are deciduous. Clusters of fruit persist well into spring.

Habitat: Adapted to a wide range of conditions and habitats. Often in abandoned fields, roadsides, rights-of-ways, fencerows, riparian areas, and urban parks.

Distribution: A common invasive tree in the southeastern United States, north to Virginia. Occasionally present as far north as New York. Chinaberry seedlings are often in proximity to established plantings. Because seeds are dispersed by birds, plants may emerge in disturbed areas some distance from known chinaberry trees.

Similar Species: Seedlings may be mistaken for the native **devil's walking stick (*Aralia spinosa* L.)**, which has similar large, bipinnately compound leaves. Devil's walking stick stems are armed with sharp spines, whereas chinaberry stems are not. Otherwise, chinaberry's leaves, flowers, and persistent fruits distinguish it from other species.

J. Robbins

Chinaberry tree

J. Neal

Chinaberry leaf

J. Robbins

Chinaberry flowers

Chinaberry leaflet

J. Neal

J. Neal

Chinaberry immature fruit

J. Neal

Chinaberry persistent fruit

Privets

Amur privet (*Ligustrum amurense* Carrière)
Japanese privet (*Ligustrum japonicum* Thunb.)
Glossy privet (*Ligustrum lucidum* Ait. f.)
Border privet (*Ligustrum obtusifolium* Siebold & Zucc.)
California privet (*Ligustrum ovalifolium* Hassk.)
Chinese privet (*Ligustrum sinense* Lour.)
European privet (*Ligustrum vulgare* L.)

GENERAL DESCRIPTION: Ornamental **evergreen or semi- to deciduous shrubs or trees** from 3–10 m tall, with simple opposite leaves. Privets have **leathery, glossy leaves** more than 2.5–10 cm long and that lack hairs. All species are native to Asia, particularly China, Japan, and Korea, except European privet which is native from Europe to southwest Asia. Glossy privet and Japanese privet are larger evergreen shrubs to small trees. When held to the light, glossy privet leaf margins have an opaque, waxy edge that is absent on Japanese privet leaves. Amur, border, California, and European privets are semi-evergreen in their southern range but deciduous in their northern range. All species are sold in the horticultural trade.

PROPAGATION: Privet seedlings often emerge in landscaped areas near mature plantings, particularly in riparian areas or woodlands, but isolated seedlings can emerge in woodlands when deposited by birds. Cutting plants can lead to resprouting from the base.

FLOWERS AND FRUIT: Large clusters of small, **cream-colored, and strongly scented flowers** are insect-pollinated. Fruits are clusters of small, oblong, 0.5–1 cm long, **purplish-black drupes.** Birds disperse the fruit.

HABITAT: Generally prefer woodlands, riparian areas, forest margins and gaps, old fields, hedgerows, open areas, and disturbed urban forests.

DISTRIBUTION: **Amur privet** naturalized populations have been reported from Alabama to Maine. **Japanese** and **glossy privet** are widespread in the southeast but winter-hardy only as far north as Maryland. **Border privet** is found in nearly all the Northeast and mid-Atlantic states but is most common from northern Virginia to Massachusetts. **California privet** is grown as a landscape shrub from the Carolinas to Maine but reports of weedy infestations are limited to New England. **Chinese privet** is widespread in the southeast to Maryland; present but less common north to Massachusetts. **European privet** is found throughout the Northeast with additional populations in the Ohio and Mississippi River Valleys.

SIMILAR SPECIES: **See Table 12 for a comparison of characteristics to separate the privet species.** The 2 evergreen species can be differentiated based on the foliar characteristics described above. To differentiate among the deciduous and semi-evergreen species requires a combination of traits, the most reliable of which are floral parts, specifically corolla tube length and position and length of the anthers. During the winter months or early spring, the deciduous privets may be mistaken for **autumn-olive (*Elaeagnus umbellata*)**, but autumn olive leaves are gray-green above and white or silvery below.

J. Neal

Left, Chinese privet; *right*, Japanese privet

J. Neal

Chinese privet flowering stem

J. Neal

Chinese privet fruit

J. DiTomaso

Glossy privet flowering stem

J. DiTomaso

Glossy privet in fruit

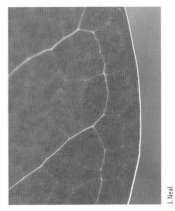

J. Neal

Glossy privet leaf margin with diagnostic translucent margin

Princesstree (*Paulownia tomentosa* (Thunb.) Siebold & Zucc. ex Steud.)

Synonyms: *Bignonia tomentosa*, empress tree, royal paulownia

General Description: A fast-growing, **deciduous tree** with **large, pubescent foliage**. Despite its reputation as a fast-growing tree, seedlings are slow to establish, growing to only 20–30 cm in the second year. Once established, plants grow quickly. When cut, plants sprout from the base and may grow 4–5 m in 1 year. Young stems are green and densely hairy. Older stems have gray bark and prominent leaf scars. **Leaves opposite, heart-shaped, hairy** above and below, and large, but vary in size; the largest on stump sprouts and smallest near the flowers. Stem leaves are 15–30 cm long by 10–25 cm wide, with entire leaf margins. Leaves from cut-stump sprouts are twice as large and have points on the margins at the major veins. Petioles are hairy and about half as long as the blade.

Propagation: Propagation is **by seeds**. Seed capsules open in winter and dispersal by wind and water is facilitated by papery wings on seeds.

Flowers and Fruit: Plants flower in early spring before leaves emerge. Flower buds and persistent sepals are bronze to brown and hairy. **Flowers are lavender** to light purple (occasionally white), in terminal, 18–40 cm long, conical, branched inflorescences (thyrses). Individual flowers are pendant (hanging downward); petals are fused to form a tube 4–6 cm long, flaring at the tip with unequal lobes. **Fruit is a hard, oval capsule**, approximately 5 cm long by 2.5 cm in diameter, **with a curved beak** at the tip. Smaller capsules may resemble a pecan. The numerous seeds are 3–4 mm long with papery wings.

Postsenescence Characteristics: Seedpods are persistent on plants through winter.

Habitat: Adapted to a wide range of soil types and tolerant of poor conditions where other species have difficulty growing. Found in disturbed areas, roadsides, fencerows, clearcuts, urban forests, and riparian areas.

Distribution: Common in the southeastern and mid-Atlantic states, present throughout the eastern United States; west to Missouri and Oklahoma and north to Massachusetts. Princesstree was introduced from Asia as an ornamental and has been planted experimentally for forest wood products.

Similar Species: Very similar to native **catalpa (*Catalpa speciosa* (Warder) Warder ex Engelm.** and *Catalpa bignonioides* **Walter)**. Compared to princesstree, catalpa leaves are generally more slender with fewer hairs above. Additionally, fruits are long, slender, bean-like pods.

Princesstree habit

Juvenile princesstree

Princesstree flowers

Princesstree fruit

Princesstree seedling

Princesstree seed

511

Golden bamboo (*Phyllostachys aurea* Carriere ex Rivière & C. Rivière)

Synonyms: running bamboo, fishing pole bamboo

General Description: A **hardy, perennial grass with erect, woody stems (culms)** to >10 m tall that spread via rhizomes to form dense colonies excluding all other vegetation. Culms emerging in the spring are commonly referred to as "bamboo shoots." These shoots can emerge through dense mulches, even pavement, and elongate rapidly, reaching mature height by mid-summer. Culms are segmented with swollen nodes, very hard and woody with age, 4–10 cm in diameter (occasionally to 15 cm), and may become golden-yellow. Two unequal leaves occur at each node; arranged in a "fan" shape on short, lateral stems; blades are long and narrow (4–15 cm long by 5–23 mm wide). Rhizomes are thick, segmented, and to 30 cm deep. In bamboo plantings, containment barriers must extend deeper than 30 cm and rise above ground to prevent surface rhizomes from overtopping the barrier.

Propagation: Plants reproduce exclusively **by rhizomes**. Rhizome fragmentation from streambank infestations can allow for downstream spread. Long-distance spread is through human activity. Soil removed from infested sites will contain rhizome fragments that can establish new populations where the soil is dumped.

Flowers and Fruit: Flowering and seed production are rare, even in its native range.

Postsenescence Characteristics: Erect canes persist. Foliage is evergreen.

Habitat: Tolerant of a wide variety of soil types and habitats, from streambanks to upland sites.

Distribution: Naturalized infestations can usually be traced to spread from a purposeful planting or disposal of infested soil. Naturalized sites are common in the southeastern and mid-Atlantic states, but plants are hardy north to New England and the Great Lakes. Most plantings of running-type bamboos will eventually spread.

Similar Species: Many species of bamboo have been introduced from Asia. Although a few clump-types have very slow rates of spread, the majority of the species available in the horticultural trade spread aggressively. **Black bamboo (*Phyllostachys nigra* (Lodd. ex Lindl.) Munro)** has smaller diameter culms that turn from green to dark purple, almost black. It is common in gardens, but naturalized populations are not as common as golden bamboo. Planting of **moso or tortoise shell bamboo (*Phyllostachys edulis* (Carrière) J. Houz.)** is promoted as an alternative forest product. It is one of the largest bamboos, with culms ≥15 cm in diameter. Once established, all 3 of these bamboos (and all other running types) can be invasive and difficult to control.

Black bamboo shoot
(culm)

Golden bamboo habit

Black bamboo culm

Golden bamboo rhizome

513

Virgin's bower (*Clematis virginiana* L.)

SYNONYM: clematis

GENERAL DESCRIPTION: A herbaceous to **soft-woody vine that climbs by twining petioles**. **Leaves** are opposite and **palmately compound** with 3 (sometimes 5) toothed leaflets (5 cm long). The sap of stems and leaves causes **irritant dermatitis**. Pollen of introduced *Clematis* has been reported to cause sinus allergies.

PROPAGATION: Reproduction is **by seeds**.

FLOWERS AND FRUIT: **Feathery, white flowers** (2.5 cm in diameter) are produced in loose clusters from July through September. Seed is enclosed within the fruit, which is a **feathery achene**, 4.5 cm long. Each flower produces a large number of achenes.

POSTSENESCENCE CHARACTERISTICS: Woody vines persist. No notable fall leaf color. Distinctive fruits persist for a short time.

HABITAT: Found in open woodlands climbing on trees and shrubs, virgin's bower also grows in woody perennial crops, along fencerows, and in landscapes. It climbs by twisting its petioles over other plants and over structures such as fences.

DISTRIBUTION: Native to the eastern United States, as far west as Kansas.

SIMILAR SPECIES: **Sweet autumn virgin's bower (*Clematis terniflora* DC.)** is a semi-evergreen vine introduced from Asia and now distributed throughout the eastern half of the United States. Most leaflets have entire margins; plants flower in late summer to early fall. **Eastern poison-ivy (*Toxicodendron radicans*)** can be distinguished because its leaves are alternate, it has broader leaflets, and it climbs by aerial roots rather than twining petioles.

J. Neal

Sweet autumn virgin's bower vine and leaves.

Virgin's bower mature foliage and stem

R. Uva

Virgin's bower fruit

J. Neal

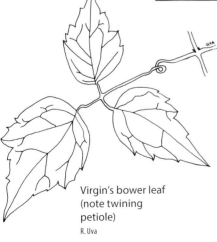

Virgin's bower leaf
(note twining
petiole)
R. Uva

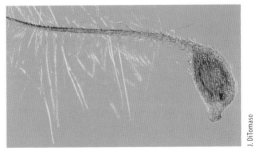

Virgin's bower seed, 3.5 mm (not including
feathery style)

J. DiTomaso

Glossy buckthorn (*Frangula alnus* P. Mill.)

SYNONYMS: *Rhamnus frangula*, glossy false buckthorn, alder buckthorn, breaking buckthorn

GENERAL DESCRIPTION: A **deciduous shrub or small tree** (up to 9 m tall). Young plants are generally multi-stemmed shrubs, which develop into small trees as they mature. Mature trunks are up to 10 cm in diameter, with **dark gray bark**. New growth is reddish-green, with distinct white lenticels and fine hairs. Branches become gray-brown with age. **Leaves are alternate**, ovate to broadly elliptical (5–8 cm long by 1.5–4 cm wide), tapered at the base, coming to a short point at the tip, **dark green and glossy above** and smooth or pubescent along the veins beneath; **veins are prominent. Leaf margins are entire.**

PROPAGATION: Reproduction is by bird-dispersed **seeds**. Glossy buckthorn does not spread vegetatively, but damaged trunks or root crowns of top-killed plants resprout prolifically.

FLOWERS AND FRUIT: Small (0.5 cm wide), yellow-green flowers appear in leaf axils of new growth in late spring, and flowering may continue throughout the summer. Flowers are bell-shaped with 5 petals and occur in clusters of 2–8. **Fruits are small** (0.6 cm diameter) **drupes** and appear as early as July, turning from **red to dark purple** as they ripen by mid-September. Each drupe contains 2–3 seeds.

POSTSENESCENCE CHARACTERISTICS: Leaves senesce late in the season, turning yellow or remaining green until killed by frost. **Fruit may linger on stems into the winter.**

HABITAT: Found along forest edges and in open woodlands, and in old fields, wetlands, and meadows. An early colonizer of disturbed areas. Prefers mesic to moist soils.

DISTRIBUTION: Most common in the Great Lakes states and New England, but populations can be found throughout the northeastern United States and adjacent Canada, and as far west as Idaho.

SIMILAR SPECIES: **European or common buckthorn (*Rhamnus cathartica* L.)** is closely related to and similar in appearance to glossy buckthorn. Leaves of European buckthorn are opposite or sub-opposite with **serrated margins**, whereas leaves of glossy buckthorn are alternate with entire margins. Also, most **branches are tipped with a sharp thorn**. European buckthorn flowers are 4-petaled and imperfect, while flowers of glossy buckthorn have 5 petals and are perfect. Male flowers are in clusters of 2–40 flowers; female flowers are in clusters of 2–30. European buckthorn is also present throughout the northeastern United States and Great Lakes states, and adjacent Canada. These 2 invasive species should not be confused with native **alderleaf buckthorn (*Rhamnus alnifolia* L'Hér.),** which is a smaller shrub that forms colonies through tip-layering.

J. Neal

Glossy buckthorn plant

J. Neal

Glossy buckthorn flowering stem

Glossy buckthorn leafy
branch and flowers

J. Neal

Callery pear (*Pyrus calleryana* Decne.)

SYNONYMS: wild pear, Bradford pear

GENERAL DESCRIPTION: A fast-growing, **deciduous tree** to 30 m in height (more commonly 10–15 m). Young trees have upturned branches forming a narrow, pyramidal canopy; older specimens have broader, more rounded crowns. Young stems are pubescent and brown bark, turning gray with age, often with sharp thorns. **Plants produce a profusion of white, unpleasantly scented flowers in the early spring** before leafing out. Leaves are variable in shape but usually broadly triangular to obovate, 5–8 cm long and about as wide, with shallowly toothed (occasionally entire) and often wavy margins. Variable leaf forms may result from hybridization with other *Pyrus* species. In autumn, the foliage is colorful with variable shades of yellow, orange, and red. Branches have erect branch angles and are frequently broken in ice or snow. Plants are susceptible to fireblight and may be a source of inoculum for nearby susceptible species.

PROPAGATION: Reproduction is **by seeds**. Most fruits remain on trees until distributed by animals, especially birds. Plants resprout from the base after cutting. Selected cultivars are grafted onto seedling rootstocks, but basal sprouts will be "wild type" plants.

FLOWERS AND FRUIT: Flowers occur in spring before leaves emerge. Flowers are in clusters from many short, flowering branches; each flower is 15–25 mm in diameter, with 5 white petals and prominent anthers. Flowers persist for only a few weeks in the spring. In summer, clusters of round, bronze to dark brown fruits (pomes), approximately 1 cm in diameter, are formed. Fruits are often persistent after leaves have dropped.

POSTSENESCENCE CHARACTERISTICS: Dormant plants usually retain a few fruits. Stems with gray bark and **thorns** are recognizable in winter.

HABITAT: Adapted to many soil types and sites. Found in intact woodlands, grasslands, floodplains, fencerows, rights-of-ways, and urban forests.

DISTRIBUTION: Present throughout the eastern half of the United States, north to the Great Lakes states.

SIMILAR SPECIES: 'Bradford' was the first ornamental cultivar widely planted, and the name "Bradford pear" has been incorrectly used generically for the species. Other varieties of cultivated pears will have similar flowers and foliage, but the fruits will be much larger. **Serviceberry (*Amelanchier arborea* (Michx.) Fern.)** is a native tree that produces white flowers about the same time of year as Callery pear, but serviceberry is usually a multi-stemmed, small tree, and flowers do not emit the fetid odor like Callery pear.

Callery pear in flower

Callery pear, young plant

Callery pear foliage

Thorn-like spur on weedy Callery pear

Callery pear flower cluster

Callery pear fruit

Multiflora rose (*Rosa multiflora* Thunb. ex Murr.)

GENERAL DESCRIPTION: A rapid-growing, **prickly-stemmed shrub** (1–3 m tall) that can form thickets or scramble over other plants with its arching stems. The **compound leaves** are alternate, **subtended by large, fringe-like stipules**, and are composed of 7–9 serrate leaflets (2–4 cm long). Once established, multiflora rose is difficult to control.

PROPAGATION: Reproduction is **by seeds and runners (stems), which form adventitious roots. Seeds are spread by birds and other animals** that eat the fruit. Runners from existing plants can quickly transform unmanaged areas into impenetrable thickets.

FLOWERS AND FRUIT: **White flowers** are 2.5 cm in diameter, bloom in May to June, and produce **clusters of red fruit** that persist into the winter.

POSTSENESCENCE CHARACTERISTICS: Woody stems with sharp prickles persist. The red fruits last into winter.

HABITAT: Multiflora rose is a common weed of pastures, rangeland, landscapes, and fencerows. It tolerates most soil conditions and is often found in uncultivated and unmowed areas, such as roadsides, rights-of-way, and fields.

DISTRIBUTION: A native of East Asia, multiflora rose was introduced into the United States in the late 1800s as a rootstock for other roses. It has escaped cultivation and is now naturalized over much of the United States, where it has become a serious weed of rangeland.

SIMILAR SPECIES: Multiflora rose can be distinguished from **other roses** by the presence of fringed stipules on the leaf petiole.

Multiflora rose stem, leaf, and fruit (note
feathery stipules at leaf base)
R. Uva

Multiflora rose habit

Multiflora rose flowering shoot

Feathery stipules at the leaf base of multiflora rose

Multiflora rose flowers

Multiflora rose, mature fruit

Brambles: raspberries and blackberries (*Rubus* spp.)

GENERAL DESCRIPTION: The genus *Rubus* contains many native and introduced species. The weedy members of the genus, sometimes referred to as brambles or caneberries, include raspberries and blackberries. Brambles have **upright and arching to trailing stems** (3–4 m high) arising from root buds. **Leaves are alternate and compound**, composed of 3–7 leaflets with serrate margins. Stems are red or green, with bristles or **prickles**. Plants are **perennial**, but individual stems generally survive for 2 years. Details of some common weedy species are below.

Wine raspberry (*Rubus phoenicolasius* Maxim.) leaves generally have 3 leaflets, whereas raspberries and blackberries have 5–7. Wine raspberry can also be distinguished from other Rubus species by abundant red hairs on the stems.

Blackberries (*Rubus allegheniensis* Porter) produce darker black fruits that do not separate from the receptacle when ripe.

Red raspberries (*Rubus idaeus* L.) produce red fruits that separate from the receptacle, but the fruits do not remain encased by the calyx as in wine raspberry.

PROPAGATION: Brambles spread **by seeds, root sprouts, rhizomes, and tip-layering**. Plants can form prickly, impenetrable thickets.

FLOWERS AND FRUIT: Plants **flower on the second-year canes** (floricanes). **Flowers have 5 white petals and a star-shaped calyx.** On wine raspberry, the calyx is densely covered in red hairs. Plants produce red or black, berry-like fruits (aggregate), actually composed of a cluster of smaller fruits (drupes). Fruit size varies among species and with site fertility. Fleshy portion of fruit dries over seed to form a pitted structure (2 mm long).

HABITAT: Common in perennial crops such as orchards, along fencerows, roadsides, and in other open, sunny locations. Seedlings are common in mulched landscapes.

DISTRIBUTION: Many of the brambles are native to North America, and many species occur throughout the region.

SIMILAR SPECIES: The prickly stems, compound leaves, flowers, and fruits distinguish brambles from most other weedy species.

Raspberry foliage and fruit

R. Uva

Spines on the stem of brambles are
variable in size and density

Wine raspberry fruit

Bramble seedling

Bramble seeds, 2 mm

Tree-of-heaven (*Ailanthus altissima* (Mill.) Swingle)

GENERAL DESCRIPTION: A **large, deciduous tree** (to 18 m in height) but can be **weedy as a sapling** or small tree. Grows rapidly, 1–1.5 m per year. **Leaves are alternate and pinnately compound** (60 cm long), with 11–25 or more leaflets per leaf. Leaflets have 1–2 **(thumb-like) teeth** near their base. Twigs are stout, with a large, brown pith and conspicuous leaf scars. **Foliage has a peanut butter or popcorn-like odor**, although not everyone can smell this aroma. Some people are allergic to the pollen of the male flowers. Contact with this plant has been known to cause **dermatitis**.

PROPAGATION: After being cut down, the plant can spread **by suckers**, sprouting as far as 3.5 m from main stem. Also produces a large number of **seeds**, which can be **dispersed short distances by wind**.

FLOWERS AND FRUIT: Plants are generally dioecious (separate female and male plants), but a few bisexual flowers can also develop. Small, greenish-yellow flowers (June) are produced in long clusters. Fruits of female plants are a single-seeded, winged samara. Clusters of samaras (3–4 cm long) persist on trees long into winter. The male flowers have a popcorn-like odor, similar to that of the foliage.

POSTSENESCENCE CHARACTERISTICS: No notable fall color. Woody stems persist.

HABITAT: At one time planted along city streets, tree-of-heaven has escaped into waste areas, vacant lots, noncultivated fields, and nurseries. It survives under the harshest of urban conditions, growing along foundations, in cracks in cement, and in rubble.

DISTRIBUTION: Native to eastern Asia and introduced into North America in 1751. It has become naturalized across much of the United States.

SIMILAR SPECIES: **Sumacs (*Rhus* spp.)** also have large, compound leaves, but their leaflets have toothed margins and lack the "thumb" at the leaf base common on tree-of-heaven. In winter, **staghorn sumac (*Rhus typhina*)** is easily distinguished by conspicuous red, cone-shaped, hairy fruit clusters at the end of the branches. **Poison-sumac (*Toxicodendron vernix* (L.) Kuntze)** is also a small tree with large compound leaves, but the margins of its leaflets are not toothed. Also, poison-sumac has white, berry-like fruit and causes allergenic dermatitis.

Tree-of-heaven habit

"Thumbs" at base of tree-of-heaven leaflets

Tree-of-heaven foliage and fruit

Tree-of-heaven male inflorescence

Poison-sumac habit

Tree-of-heaven urban habit

Left, poison-sumac seeds, 6 mm; *right*, staghorn sumac seeds (with seed coat), 6 mm

Tree-of-heaven seeds, 40 mm

Roundleaf greenbriar (*Smilax rotundifolia* L.)

Synonyms: common greenbriar, common catbriar, bullbriar, horsebriar

General Description: A **woody vine** that forms thickets or climbs other vegetation by tendrils attached to the petiole. Leaves are alternate, simple, heart-shaped or rounded (5–13 cm long), with entire margins and parallel venation. **Stems are green**, either angled or rounded, and **armed with sharp prickles**. Sharp prickles on vines can entangle ankles, calves, and arms, causing considerable injury.

Propagation: Plants slowly creep into new areas **by rhizomes, or seeds can be deposited in the landscape by birds**. Seedlings emerge from spring through mid-summer. Rhizomes are usually shallow and stout. Plants form a woody crown with multiple growing points. If disturbed by cultivation, the severed sections can sprout.

Flowers and Fruit: Greenish flowers bloom from April through August. The **berry-like fruit are bluish-black**, mature in September, and may persist through the winter. Seeds are round, reddish, and 5–6 mm in diameter.

Postsenescence Characteristics: Green, vining stems with sharp prickles are persistent.

Habitat: Roundleaf greenbriar may form impenetrable patches around clearings, in roadsides, and in open woods. Often found along moist edges of swampy woods and in drier upland areas, it is also a common weed in landscapes, Christmas tree plantations, and orchards.

Distribution: Native to the eastern United States, extending to Illinois, Oklahoma, Florida, and Texas.

Similar Species: **Cat sawbriar (*Smilax glauca* Walt.)** has round stems with weak prickles, and the leaves are whitish on the underside. **Catbriar (*Smilax bona-nox* L.)** has 4-sided stems and bristly edged leaves. Both cat sawbriar and catbriar are found primarily on moist to dry, sandy soil.

Roundleaf greenbriar rhizome

J. Neal

Roundleaf greenbriar foliage

J. Neal

Roundleaf greenbriar stem and thorns

R. Uva

Catbriar leaf and stem

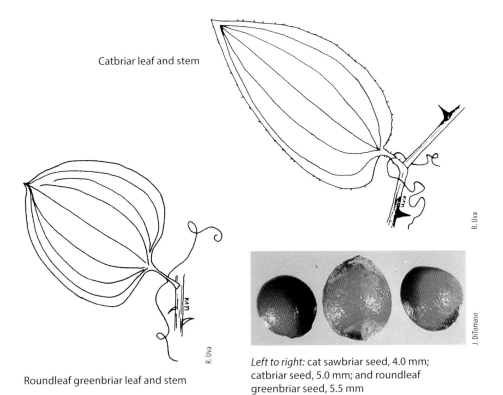

R. Uva

Roundleaf greenbriar leaf and stem

R. Uva

Left to right: cat sawbriar seed, 4.0 mm; catbriar seed, 5.0 mm; and roundleaf greenbriar seed, 5.5 mm

J. DiTomaso

Bittersweet nightshade (*Solanum dulcamara* L.)

SYNONYMS: European bittersweet, bitter nightshade, blue nightshade, woody nightshade, poison berry, climbing nightshade, scarlet berry, blue bindweed, dogwood, fellenwort

GENERAL DESCRIPTION: A **semi-woody to herbaceous perennial vine** growing to 2–3 m tall. The foliage can twine over other plants, trail along the ground, or grow erect with arching, hollow stems. **Leaves** (5–12 cm long) are petiolated, alternate, and of **2 forms**. One has 2 **basal lobes; the other is ovate to oval**. The margins of both leaf types are smooth. Foliage is purple-tinged and has an unpleasant odor. **Vegetative parts and fruit can poison all classes of livestock.** The plant contains the glycoalkaloid solanine, which is not lost upon drying. Symptoms of toxicity include gastrointestinal irritation. The **berries have been reported to poison children.**

PROPAGATION: Spreads **by seeds and creeping prostrate stems**, which root at the nodes.

FLOWERS AND FRUIT: **Flowers** (12–16 mm in diameter) consist of petals that are fused at the base but deeply 5-lobed, **resembling the flowers of potato. Petals are purple** to blue **with a yellow center. Fruit is a thin-skinned, oval, red berry** (8–12 mm long) containing many flat, round, yellowish seeds (2 mm in diameter).

POSTSENESCENCE CHARACTERISTICS: None of note.

HABITAT: Bittersweet nightshade is found in landscapes, nurseries, orchards, along edges of cultivated fields, and in uncultivated or wooded areas, often on moist soils.

DISTRIBUTION: Native to Eurasia, bittersweet nightshade was introduced as a cultivated ornamental. It has become naturalized over much of the United States but is most common in the eastern and north-central states.

SIMILAR SPECIES: **See Table 10 for a comparison with other weedy, *Solanum* species. Eastern black nightshade (*Solanum ptychanthum* Dun.)** is similar to bittersweet nightshade but is an upright, branched annual with wavy leaf margins and black berries. **Oriental bittersweet (*Celastrus orbiculatus*)** is an unrelated (Celastraceae) woody plant with unlobed leaves and reddish-orange seeds in yellow capsules.

Bittersweet nightshade seedling

Krzysztof Ziarnek

Bittersweet nightshade
flowers

S. Morris

J. DiTomaso

Bittersweet nightshade fruiting stem

A. DiTommaso

Bittersweet nightshade mature leaf shape

1 mm

S. Hurst, USDA-NRCS PLANTS Database

Bittersweet nightshade seeds, 2 mm

Porcelainberry (*Ampelopsis glandulosa* (Wall.) Momiy. var. *brevipedunculata* (Maxim.) Momiy.)

SYNONYMS: *Ampelopsis brevipedunculata*, Amur peppervine, porcelain vine

GENERAL DESCRIPTION: A woody, deciduous, tendril-twining **vine, strongly resembling grape vines** but with **brightly colored, shiny fruit**. Vines can form dense ground covers or climb to smother small shrubs, trees, and other vegetation. Mature stems have longitudinally ridged bark with lenticels and **white pith** throughout. **Alternate leaves** (6–12 cm long) have **coarsely toothed margins** and are cordate at the base and unlobed, or with 3–5 slightly to deeply cleft **lobes**. Leaf surfaces are glabrous above and smooth to hairy below. Petioles 1–7 cm long. Branched tendrils grow opposite the leaf bases on new (green) stem growth.

PROPAGATION: Reproduction is primarily **by seeds**, which are often dispersed by birds. Fruits are buoyant and may also spread along waterways.

FLOWERS AND FRUIT: Flowering begins in June and continues through August. Flowers (1–2 mm wide) are greenish-white, with 5 petals, and are borne in clusters (cymes) opposite the leaves on 1–2.5 cm long peduncles. The fruits, which occur from mid-summer though October, are speckled, round berries of varying color including yellow, green, pink, purple, and blue. It is common to have several fruit colors present at the same time because fruit color changes from green to white to bright blue to purple as fruits age. The brightly colored berries are 2–8 mm in diameter and contain 1–4 ovoid, ridged seeds.

POSTSENESCENCE CHARACTERISTICS: Younger stems may die back after frost. Some fruits may linger throughout the winter.

HABITAT: A weed of forest edges, thickets, old fields, roadsides, waste areas, streambanks, and similar disturbed and edge habitats. Porcelainberry is sometimes cultivated as an ornamental and becomes weedy in urban areas. Somewhat shade-tolerant, but prefers full sun.

DISTRIBUTION: Found in the Midwest and southern United States, north to Virginia and southwest to Texas.

SIMILAR SPECIES: **Grapes (*Vitis* spp.)** have similar leaves and vining growth. The bark of grapes appears shredded or peeling, unlike the ridged bark of porcelainberry. The native **peppervine (*Ampelopsis cordata* Michx.)** has a similar habit and berries, but it has unlobed leaves, whereas porcelainberry leaves are lobed. [Note: Some authors describe varieties of porcelainberry based largely on leaf morphology, but there is no consensus on these divisions.]

R. Prostak

Porcelainberry foliage and habit

J. Neal

Porcelainberry 1-leaf seedling

J. Neal

Porcelainberry flowers and immature fruit

J. Neal

Porcelainberry fruit

J. Neal

Porcelainberry variable leaf shapes from a single plant

Virginia-creeper (*Parthenocissus quinquefolia* (L.) Planch.)

SYNONYMS: woodbine, American ivy, five-leaved ivy

GENERAL DESCRIPTION: A **woody vine** that climbs on objects or vegetation or trails along the ground. The **vines climb by tendrils** that have oval, **adhesive disks** at their tips. **Leaves are alternate and palmately compound, with 3–7, but usually 5, leaflets.** Leaflets are 6–12 cm long with **toothed margins**.

PROPAGATION: Plants are often **established from seeds** dropped by birds but **spread by stems**, which root when in contact with the ground.

FLOWERS AND FRUIT: Inconspicuous green-white flowers yield small, blue-black berries in the autumn.

POSTSENESCENCE CHARACTERISTICS: Leaves turn deep red in the fall. Woody stems persist.

HABITAT: Valued for its fall color, Virginia-creeper is often **grown as an ornamental and is often found growing on brick buildings**. It is a common weed of landscapes, orchards, and vineyards, as well as fencerows and other noncultivated areas. It tolerates a wide range of conditions including dry, sandy sites, moist, nutrient-rich soil, shade, sun, and high salinity.

DISTRIBUTION: Native to the eastern United States.

SIMILAR SPECIES: **Eastern poison-ivy (*Toxicodendron radicans*)** has compound leaves with 3 leaflets; the terminal leaflet is attached to a short stalk (petiolule). Eastern poison-ivy climbs by aerial roots not by adhesive disks.

Virginia-creeper habit

Virginia-creeper mature foliage

Virginia-creeper stem and palmately compound leaves

Virginia-creeper spring growth

533

Wild grape (*Vitis* spp.)

GENERAL DESCRIPTION: **Several species of wild grape** invade landscapes as **climbing, woody, deciduous vines**. The vines can form a canopy over large trees and are capable of blocking enough light to kill or significantly reduce the trees' growth. Thickets of wild grape can also grow over low shrubs and along the ground. **Leaves are alternate, simple with toothed margins, palmately veined**, rounded, and often 3-lobed. Wild grapes **climb by forked tendrils** that are opposite the leaves. Stems are brown, and the **bark shreds in strips**.

PROPAGATION: Spread **by seeds**, which may be dispersed by birds or other animals. **Cut stems can readily resprout.**

FLOWERS AND FRUIT: Flowers in late spring to early summer. **Fruit are purplish-black berries, smaller than cultivated grapes.** Berries are produced from August into the autumn.

POSTSENESCENCE CHARACTERISTICS: No notable fall color. Woody stems have brown bark that shreds in strips. Tendrils persist and become dark and brittle.

HABITAT: Wild grapes are common weeds of orchards, vineyards, landscapes, nurseries, Christmas tree plantations, and fencerows. Some species thrive on moist, rich soils; others on sandy, dry sites.

DISTRIBUTION: Many species of wild grape are native and grow throughout eastern and central North America.

SIMILAR SPECIES: The weedy species of wild grape in the northeastern states include **summer grape (*Vitis aestivalis* Michx.), fox grape (*Vitis labrusca* L.), riverbank grape (*Vitis riparia* Michx.), and frost grape (*Vitis vulpina* L.)**. Additionally, in the mid-Atlantic states, **muscadine grape (*Vitis rotundifolia* Michx.)** is common. **Porcelainberry (*Ampelopsis glandulosa*)** has similar vining growth habit and similar leaves, and it is often mistaken for wild grapes. The bark of porcelainberry is ridged, whereas the bark of grapes appears shredded or peeling. When in fruit, porcelainberry is easily distinguished by the showy, multi-colored fruits. **Virginia-creeper (*Parthenocissus quinquefolia*)** has compound leaves, whereas the leaves of all wild grape species are simple. In addition, wild grape has conspicuous tendrils and does not climb by adhesive disks, as does Virginia-creeper.

Muscadine grape young leaves and vine

Wild grape vine

Wild grape stem, leaf, and tendril
R. Uva

Young wild grape vine, with lobed leaf form

535

Hardwood Seedlings

Seedlings and root sprouts of these and other hardwood trees can be troublesome weeds in landscapes, nurseries, Christmas tree plantations, orchards, and no-till crops.

Aceraceae (Maple Family)

Box elder (*Acer negundo* L.): tree to 20 m at maturity; seedlings and saplings weedy; **leaves opposite, 3–5 pinnately compound**; leaflets lanceolate to ovate or oblong, each 6–10 cm long; margins entire to coarsely toothed or lobed; twigs often green or purplish with a whitish, waxy coat; paired, winged fruit (schizocarp), wings of fruit spread apart at <90° angle.

Norway maple (*Acer platanoides* L.): tree to 25 m at maturity; seedlings and saplings weedy; leaves opposite, simple, 7–12 cm long, 5–7 lobed, lower surface green, margins toothed; exudes **milky latex**; paired, winged fruit (schizocarp), wings of fruit spread apart at 180° angle.

Red maple (*Acer rubrum* L.): tree to 35 m at maturity; seedlings weedy; leaves opposite, simple, 5–20 cm long, 3–5 lobed, lower surface gray or white, margins irregularly toothed; paired, winged fruit (schizocarp), wings of fruit spread apart at <90° angle.

Young box elder plant

A. DiTommaso

Box elder leaves and fruit

J. Neal

Red maple seedlings

J. Neal

Norway maple seedling (note milky sap on broken petiole)

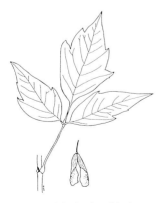

Box elder leaf and fruit
R. Uva

Red maple mature leaves and fruit
R. Uva

Fabaceae (Pea or Bean Family)

Honey locust (*Gleditsia triacanthos* L.): tree commonly to 20–35 m at maturity; seedlings or root sprouts weedy in landscapes; **stems spiny**; leaves alternate (15–20 cm long), **once or twice pinnately compound**; leaflets numerous, lanceolate to oblong, 1–2 cm long, margins faintly toothed, often appearing entire; fruit a many-seeded, twisting pod (legume), 30–45 cm long.

Black locust (*Robinia pseudoacacia* L.): tree to 30 m at maturity; root sprouts or seedlings weedy; **leaves alternate**, **once compound**; leaflets 2.5–5 cm long, ovate, 6–20 per leaf; **stems with sharp spines**; fruit a 2–10 seeded pod (legume).

R. Uva

Young honey locust habit

Black locust flowering stems

J. DiTomaso

Black locust thorns

J. Neal

Black locust sprout

R. Uva

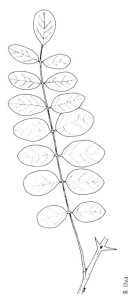

Black locust leaf and stem (with thorns)

R. Uva

539

Moraceae (Mulberry Family)

White mulberry (*Morus alba* L.): tree to 15 m at maturity; saplings weedy; leaves alternate, simple, 7–18 cm long, margins toothed, **leaves both lobed and unlobed; milky sap from young twigs**; male and female flowers on separate plants (dioecious); **fruit berry-like.**

Oleaceae (Olive Family)

White ash (*Fraxinus americana* L.) and **green ash (*Fraxinus pennsylvanica* Marshall):** large tree, 18–25 m at maturity; seedlings or saplings weedy; leaves opposite, once pinnately compound, 5–9 leaflets, usually 7; leaflets oblong to ovate or lanceolate, 11 cm long, margins entire to toothed; fruit a single-seeded samara; buds large and brown. White ash lacks hairs on undersurface of leaf, and the wing of the samara is terminal to the seed. Green ash is hairy below, at least on midrib, and the wing of the fruit is lateral and terminal to the seed.

J. Neal

White ash seedling

White mulberry in ground cover bed

J. Neal

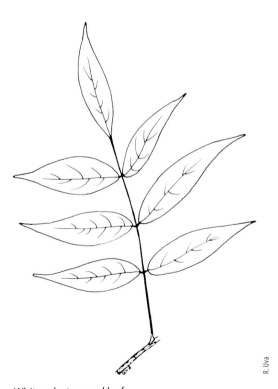

White ash stem and leaf

R. Uva

White mulberry leaves (2 forms)

R. Uva

541

Rosaceae (Rose Family)

Black cherry (*Prunus serotina* Ehrh.): tree to 25 m at maturity; seedlings or saplings weedy; **leaves alternate, simple, lanceolate** to oblong, 6–12 cm long, midrib on underside with white to brown hairs, margins with incurved teeth; **petiole with a pair of glands just below the leaf base;** bark aromatic; fruit a purple to black drupe.

Common chokecherry (*Prunus virginiana* L.): similar to black cherry, but only 10 m tall at maturity; teeth on leaf margin point outward, midrib on underside of blade lacks hairs; fruit a deep red drupe.

Salicaceae (Willow Family)

Common cottonwood (*Populus deltoides* Marshall): also known as poplar, tree to 23 m at maturity; seedlings and root sprouts weedy; **leaves** alternate, simple, 8–13 cm long, **triangular**, serrate margins, flattened petioles; fruit a capsule, with **seeds surrounded by cotton-like hairs** that aid in wind dispersal.

Black willow (*Salix nigra* Marshall): Several species and interspecific hybrids of willow are widely distributed in the eastern United States. One of the most common "weedy" species is black willow, also known as swamp willow. It is native to, and common in, riparian areas throughout the eastern half of the United States and adjacent Canada. Black willow is an upright, branched, woody shrub to tree, often present as a multi-stemmed small tree, but mature specimens grow 20–40 m in height. Leaves are long and narrow, and variable in length (typically 6–12 cm) tapering to a pointed tip. Seedlings have leaves like the parent, long and narrow, but with shallowly toothed margins. Leafy (foliaceous) stipules may be present at the base of the leaves on young stems. Young stems are smooth and sometimes reddish. Plants flower and produce seeds over a short time in late spring to early summer. Mature seeds have fluffy filaments that aid in wind and water dispersal of the seeds. Seeds are viable for only a short time (less than 30 days at room temperature). Seedlings emerge and establish quickly. Willow stem cuttings root readily. Black willow "live stakes" are often planted in riparian area restorations. Willow seedlings are common weeds in ditch banks, nursery crops, and other irrigated crops near streams or riparian corridors containing mature willow trees.

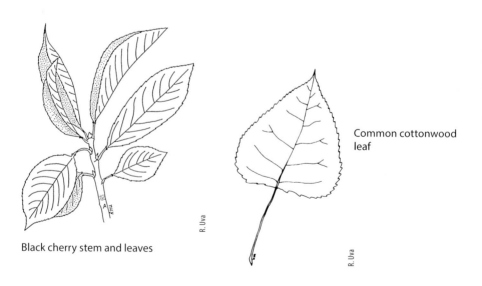

Common cottonwood leaf

Black cherry stem and leaves

R. Uva

R. Uva

Common chokecherry
flowering stem

Common chokecherry
fruiting stem

Black willow seedling

Wild cherry seedling

Leafy stipules on a young willow

Common cottonwood sapling

Common cottonwood seeds

543

COMPARISON TABLES

Table 1. Comparison of pigweeds and amaranths (*Amaranthus* spp.)

Character	Tumble pigweed (*A. album*)	Prostrate pigweed (*A. blitoides*)	Livid amaranth (*A. blitum*)	Smooth pigweed (*A. hybridus*)	Palmer amaranth (*A. palmeri*)	Powell amaranth (*A. powellii*)	Redroot pigweed (*A. retroflexus*)	Spiny amaranth (*A. spinosus*)	Waterhemp (*A. tuberculatus*)	Slender amaranth (*A. viridis*)
Stem	Stems whitish, not hairy	Not hairy	Not hairy	Small hairs or smooth	Few to no hairs	Upper stem mostly smooth	Upper stem hairy	No hairs, sharp spines at leaf axils	Not hairy	Not hairy
Leaf blade	Egg-shaped with wavy margins, blades less than 5 cm long	Obovate to spatulate, most with a rounded tip	Oval or spatulate with distinctive notched tip	Egg-shaped, margin wavy	Egg-shaped, no hairs, often with V-shaped variegation, margin sometimes wavy	Egg-shaped, entire, similar to *A. hybridus* and *A. retroflexus* but tips more tapered	Egg-shaped, younger leaves hairy, leaf margins wavy	Egg-shaped, no hairs, often with V-shaped variegation	Narrow elliptic	Egg-shaped to broadly ovate, almost triangular
Petiole length relative to the leaf blade	Very short to about ½ blade length	Very short to ½ blade length	Very short to ½ blade length	½–⅔ blade length	Equal or longer than blade length	< ¾ blade length	< ¾ blade length	~ ½–¾ blade length	< ½ blade length	Equal or slightly less than blade length
Inflorescence position(s)	Axillary	Axillary	Axillary and terminal	Terminal	Terminal	Terminal	Terminal	Terminal	Terminal	Axillary and terminal

Terminal inflorescence structure	Lacking	Lacking	Not branched	Tight, branched but branches longer than *A. retroflexus*	Long and slender; with a few shorter spikes	Tightly clustered on main stem, branches vertically oriented	Tight, short, upright branches	Long and slender, branched	Long, slender, branched, vertical	Long, slender, and lax, 1 or 2 branches
Monoecious or dioecious	Monoe-cious	Monoecious	Monoe-cious	Monoecious	Dioecious, male soft to the touch, female prickly	Monoecious	Monoecious	Monoecious, male flowers at top, female lower	Dioecious	Monoecious
Growth habit	Mound-forming	Prostrate	Prostrate to mounding	Upright	Upright	Upright	Upright	Upright, with arching branches	Upright	Upright, but if cut will form a low mound

Table 2. Comparison of the erect and tall (generally >0.5 m) weedy species in the carrot family (Apiaceae)

Species	Life cycle	Height	Stems	Leaves	Compound umbel (flower cluster)
Purplestem angelica (*Angelica atropurpurea*)	Perennial	1–2.5 m	Smooth, dark purple or blotched	20–60 cm long, 2–3 times pinnately compound; leaflets 5–10 cm long	To 30 cm wide
Wild chervil (*Anthriscus sylvestris*)	Biennial	0.6–1.5 m	Pubescent, ridged	10–30 cm long, 2–3 times pinnately compound; leaflets 1–3 cm long, pinnatifid	2.5–8 cm wide
Spotted waterhemlock (*Cicuta maculata*)	Perennial	0.5–2 m	Smooth, purple spotted	3–12 cm long, 2 times pinnately compound; leaflets 2–5 cm long	To 12 cm wide
Poison-hemlock (*Conium maculatum*)	Biennial	0.6–2 m	Smooth, purple spotted, ridged	20–40 cm long, 3–4 times pinnately compound; leaflets finely cut	4–6 cm wide
Wild carrot (*Daucus carota*)	Biennial	0.2–1 m (rosette tolerates mowing)	Bristly hairy, vertically ribbed	To 15 cm long, many times pinnately compound, finely dissected	8–16 cm wide
Giant hogweed (*Heracleum mantegazzianum*)	Biennial or monocarpic perennial	2–5 m	Coarse hairy, purple-blotched, thick (4–8 cm)	To 1 m long, 1–2 times pinnately compound	To 50 cm wide (rarely to 70 cm)
Wild parsnip (*Pastinaca sativa*)	Biennial	0.5–2 m	Smooth, vertically angled and grooved	To 30 cm long, once pinnately compound; leaflets 5–10 cm long	To 20 cm wide
Japanese hedgeparsley (*Torilis japonica*)	Winter annual or biennial	0.5–1.2 m	Densely pubescent, appressed hairs, and ribbed	To 13 cm long, multiple pinnately compound	5–7.5 cm wide

Table 3. Comparison of 4 members of the aster family that have finely dissected leaves

Character	Corn chamomile (*Anthemis arvensis*)	Mayweed chamomile (*A. cotula*)	Pineapple-weed (*Matricaria discoidea*)	Scentless chamomile (*Tripleurospermum inodorum*)
Odor	Pleasant chamomile odor when crushed	Unpleasant pungent odor when crushed	Sweet pineapple-like odor when crushed	No distinct odor
Leaves	Similar to *A. cotula* but slightly less finely dissected	2–3 times pinnatifid, 2–6 cm long; segments narrow	1–3 times pinnatifid, 1–5 cm long; segments short, linear or filiform	2–3 times pinnatifid, 6–7 cm long; segments linear to filiform, with acute tips
Ray flowers	10–16 white flowers, 6–12 mm long	10–16 white flowers, 5–11 mm long	Absent	15–35 white flowers, 10–20 mm long
Receptacle	Chaffy scales all over receptacle surface	Chaffy scales on receptacle surface only toward the middle	Receptacle naked	Receptacle naked

Table 4. Comparison of sowthistles (*Sonchus* spp.) and weedy lettuces (*Lactuca* spp.)

Character	Tall lettuce (*Lactuca canadensis*)	Prickly lettuce (*L. serriola*)	Perennial sowthistle (*Sonchus arvensis*)	Spiny sowthistle (*S. asper*)	Annual sowthistle (*S. oleraceus*)
Life cycle	Biennial	Annual	Perennial	Annual	Annual
Root system	Large taproot	Large taproot	Creeping, spreading rhizomes	Taproot	Short taproot
Flower head width	0.5–1 cm	0.8–1 cm	3–5 cm	1.2–2.5 cm	1.2–2.5 cm
Ray flower color	Pale yellow, rarely bluish	Yellow	Yellow to bright yellow-orange	Pale yellow	Pale yellow
Achenes	1–3 longitudinal short spiny ribs on each side, brown to black, often mottled, rough, 2.5–3.5 mm long	5–7 longitudinal ribs on each side, long-beaked, grayish-yellow to brown, 3–4 mm long	5–7 prominent longitudinal ribs on each side, wrinkled, dark brown, 3 mm long	3 (4–5) prominent longitudinal ribs, smooth, light brown, 2–3 mm long	3–5 longitudinal ribs on each side, wrinkled, light brown to olive, 4 mm long
Auricles	Acute (sagittate)	Acute (sagittate)	Small and rounded	Prominent and rounded	Sharply acute
Leaf margin	Entire (upper) to denticulate toothed, not prickly	Fine prickly toothed	Prickly	Very prickly	Weakly or sparsely prickly
Leaf midrib (underside)	Not prickly or sparsely bristly or with fine hairs	Stiff, sharp prickles	Not prickly	Not prickly	Not prickly
Leaf shape	Pinnatifid, linear to oblong, elliptic, lanceolate, or ovate in outline	Pinnatifid, with half-moon lobes	Entire to deeply pinnatifid	Pinnatifid or obovate and lacking lobes	Pinnatifid
Leaves, stems, and roots	Exude milky sap when cut	Exude milky sap when cut	Exude milky sap when cut	Exude milky sap when cut	Exude milky sap when cut

Left to right: spiny sowthistle, perennial sowthistle, and annual sowthistle

Table 5. Comparison of bindweeds and wild buckwheat

Character	Hedge bindweed (*Calystegia sepium*)	Field bindweed (*Convolvulus arvensis*)	Wild buckwheat (*Fallopia convolvulus*)
Life cycle	Perennial	Perennial	Annual
Leaf shape			
Ocrea	Absent	Absent	Present
Flower	Usually white, sometimes pink; petals fused into a funnel-shaped tube 3–6 cm long	Similar to hedge bindweed, but 1.2–2.5 cm long	Greenish-white, inconspicuous, about 4 mm long
Bracts below flower	Very large, concealing the sepals	Small, well below the sepals	Absent

Drawings by R. Uva

Table 6. Comparison of wild Cucurbitaceae and similar species

Species	Hairs on stems	Leaf shape	Hairs on leaves	Flower	Fruit
Wild cucumber (*Echinocystis lobata*)	Rarely hairy	5 lobes, margins toothed	Hairs only on nerves of upper leaf surface	6 petals and sepals, male flowers on long panicle, female at base of panicle; white	Fruit single, weak prickles, not hairy, 3–6 cm, 2-celled and 4-seeded
Burcucumber (*Sicyos angulatus*)	Bristly hairs	3–5 lobes, margins variable toothed or nearly entire	Upper surface nearly hairless, tendrils hairy	5 petals and sepals, male flowers on long panicle, female flowers at base of panicle; white	Fruits in clusters, bristly and hairy, <2 cm long, 1-celled and 1-seeded
Guadeloupe cucumber (*Melothria pendula*)	Small, stiff hairs	0–5 lobes, margins toothed	Hairs on leaves and petioles	5 petals, borne singly; yellow	Single, smooth surface, to 1 cm long, fleshy with many seeds
Yellow passion-flower (*Passiflora lutea*)	Not hairy	3 lobes, margins entire	Not hairy	Distinctive passionflower shape; pale yellow	Single, smooth, green turning black

Notes: All species have vining growth habit, alternate leaves, and tendrils. Plants differ in location and prevalence of hairs, fruit size, and prickles; leaf margins.

Table 7. Comparison of weedy, trifoliolate (3 leaflets) legumes and woodsorrel (*Oxalis* spp.)

Species	Life cycle / growth form	Leaflet shape	Terminal leaflet stalk	Petiole length	Flower color	Flower head
Woodsorrel (*Oxalis* spp.)	Erect to prostrate, annual or perennial	Heart-shaped	Absent	Longer than leaflets	Yellow	Individual flowers, branched inflorescence
Annual lespedeza (*Kummerowia striata*)	Prostrate to ascending, summer annual	Elliptic to oblong	Absent	Shorter than leaflets	Lavender to pink	No heads, 1–3 flowers from leaf axils
Birdsfoot trefoil (*Lotus corniculatus*)	Prostrate to suberect, perennial	Elliptic to oblanceolate	Absent	Shorter than leaflets	Yellow	4–8 flowers, each 1.5 cm long
Black medic (*Medicago lupulina*)	Prostrate to ascending, summer annual	Elliptic to obovate	Present	Shorter than leaflets	Yellow	10–50 flowers, globose
Rabbitfoot clover (*Trifolium arvense*)	Erect, annual	Oblong	Absent	Shorter than leaflets	Pink to white	Numerous flowers, cylindrical
Hop clover (*T. aureum*)	Ascending, annual	Oblong to obovate	Absent	Shorter than leaflets	Yellow	>20 flowers per head, cylindrical
Large hop clover (*T. campestre*)	Low, spreading, winter annual	Obovate	Present	Usually shorter than leaflets	Yellow	>20 flowers per head, globose
Low hop clover (*T. dubium*)	Low, spreading, winter annual	Obovate	Present but short	Shorter than leaflets	Yellow	5–10 flowers per head, globose
Strawberry clover (*T. fragiferum*)	Creeping, perennial	Obovate	Absent	Longer than leaflets	Pink to rose	Numerous flowers, globose to ovoid
Alsike clover (*T. hybridum*)	Ascending, perennial	Oval to elliptic	Absent	Longer than leaflets	White to pink	Numerous flowers, globose
Red clover (*T. pratense*)	Ascending, short-lived perennial	Oval	Absent	Shorter than leaflets	Red or magenta to pink	Numerous flowers, globose
White clover (*T. repens*)	Creeping, perennial	Broadly elliptical to obovate, rounded tip	Absent	Longer than leaflets	White, or tinged with pink	Numerous flowers, globose

Left to right: strawberry clover, white clover, alsike, and red clover

Left to right: white clover, black medic, yellow woodsorrel, and birdsfoot trefoil

Rabbitfoot clover flowering stem

Table 8. Comparison of weedy buttercups (*Ranunculus* spp.)

Species	Life cycle / growth habit	Basal leaves	Cauline leaves	Leaf surface	Leaf margin	Petals	Sepals	Fruit
Smallflower buttercup (*R. abortivus*)	Winter annual or biennial; clumping	Long petioles, kidney-shaped to cordate, many not lobed	Sessile, deeply divided to trifoliolate	Not hairy	Entire or shallow toothed	Not showy, shorter than sepals, 1.5–3.5 mm long	Not reflexed, not hairy	Globose, smooth
Tall buttercup (*R. acris*)	Perennial; clumping with short rhizomes	Long petioles, round in outline, deeply lobed	Petiolate, deeply divided into slender lobes	Hairy or not	Toothed or lobed	Showy, 5 petals, 8–11 mm long, 7–13 mm wide	Not reflexed, hairy	Globose, smooth
Bulbous buttercup (*R. bulbosus*)	Perennial; clumping with bulbous base	Long petioles, palmately lobed, central lobe stalked	Sessile, smaller, less divided	Hairy	Deeply lobed, lobes toothed	Showy, 5 petals, 9–13 mm long, 8–11 mm wide	Reflexed, hairy	Globose, smooth
Lesser celandine (*R. ficaria*)	Perennial; creeping stems, thick tuber-like roots	Long petioles, cordate, not divided	Petiolate, cordate to oval	Not hairy	Entire, or shallowly crenate	Showy, 8–12 petals, 5–10 mm long	Spreading, not hairy	Ovate, smooth
Smallflower (hairy) buttercup (*R. parviflorus*)	Winter annual; prostrate to ascending, hairy stems	Petioles hairy, ~= leaf blades, palmately lobed	Petiolate, similar to basal but lobes more pointed	Hairy	Deeply lobed, lobes may be toothed	Not showy, 0–5 petals, 1.1–1.8 mm long	Reflexed, densely hairy	Globose, papillate, recurved tip
Creeping buttercup (*R. repens*)	Perennial; creeping by stolons	Not present	Long petioles, palmately lobed, central lobe stalked	Hairy (sparse or dense)	Deeply lobed and toothed	Showy, 5 petals, 6–18 mm long, 5–12 mm wide	Not reflexed, hairy	Globose, smooth, recurved tip

Hairy buttercup (*R. sardous*)	Annual; clump-forming	Long hairy petioles, deeply lobed, 3–5 parted, center lobe stalked	Much smaller than basal, 1–3 parted, narrow lobes	Hairy	Variable, shallow to deeply lobed, blunt or toothed	Showy, 5 petals, 7–10 mm long, 4–8 mm wide	Reflexed, hairy	Globose, papillate or smooth
Crowfoot buttercup (*R. sceleratus*)	Winter annual; clump-forming	Long, hairless petioles, deep lobes, 3–5 parted, center lobe not stalked	Deeply lobed, 3–5 parted, sessile	Not hairy	Shallow or deeply lobed	Not showy, 3–5 petals, 2–5 mm long, 1–3 mm wide	Reflexed	Elongated, oval or cylindrical, smooth

Table 9. Comparison of selected speedwell species (*Veronica* spp.)

Species	Life cycle	Leaf shape, margin, and surface	Leaf arrangement		Flower arrangement
			Lower	Upper	
Field speedwell (*V. agrestis*)	Annual		Opposite	Alternate	
Corn speedwell (*V. arvensis*)	Annual		Opposite	Alternate	
Germander speedwell (*V. chamaedrys*)	Perennial		Opposite	Opposite	
Slender speedwell (*V. filiformis*)	Perennial		Opposite	Alternate	
Ivyleaf speedwell (*V. hederifolia*)	Annual		Opposite	Alternate	
Common speedwell (*V. officinalis*)	Perennial		Opposite	Opposite	
Purslane speedwell (*V. peregrina*)	Annual		Opposite	Alternate	
Persian speedwell (*V. persica*)	Annual		Opposite	Alternate	
Thymeleaf speedwell (*V. serpyllifolia*)	Perennial		Opposite	Alternate	

Notes: Drawings by Bente Starcke-King.

Table 10. Comparison of groundcherries, nightshades, and related species (Solanaceae)

Character	Clammy groundcherry (*Physalis heterophylla*)	Smooth groundcherry (*P. longifolia* var. *subglabrata*)	Horsenettle (*Solanum carolinense*)	Bittersweet nightshade (*S. dulcamara*)	Black nightshade (*S. nigrum*)	Eastern black nightshade (*S. ptychanthum*)	Hairy nightshade (*S. sarrachoides*)	Buffalobur (*S. rostratum*)
Life cycle	Rhizomatous perennial, 20–90 cm tall	Rhizomatous perennial, 20–90 cm tall	Rhizomatous perennial, to 60 cm tall	Rhizomatous climbing or trailing perennial	Annual, to 50 cm tall	Annual, rarely a short-lived perennial, to 1 m tall	Annual, to 80 cm tall	Annual, to 60 cm tall
Stem	Very hairy	Young shoots slightly hairy, older smooth	Armed with sharp prickles	Viny, woody at the base, slightly hairy	Round to angular, hairs absent or few	Round to angular, hairs absent or few	Round to slightly angular, many spreading hairs	Armed with many sharp spines
Leaf surfaces	Very hairy	Smooth to slightly hairy	Sharp prickles and sparsely branched hairs	Hairs absent or short and few	Leaves slightly hairy	Nearly lacking hairs	Soft spreading and sticky glandular hairs	Sharp prickles and hairy
Inflorescence	Solitary in leaf axils	Solitary in leaf axils	Racemose	Compound cyme	Racemose	Umbellate	Racemose, or occasionally umbellate	Racemose
Flower	Petals yellow to greenish, with purplish centers	Petals yellow to greenish, with purplish centers	Petals purple, sometimes whitish	Petals blue to purple	Petals white or faintly bluish	Petals white or faintly bluish	Petals white	Petals yellow
Fruit	Yellow, enclosed in a papery bladder	Orange to red or purple, enclosed in a papery bladder	Yellow, approximately 60 seeds per berry	Bright red, 40–60 seeds per berry	Dull black, 15–60 seeds per berry	Glossy dark purple to black, 50–110 seeds per berry	Green, olive green, or yellow berry, 10–35 seeds per berry	Red berry enclosed in spiny bur

Table 11. Comparison of 4 species of bush honeysuckles (*Lonicera* spp.)

Traits	Amur honeysuckle (*L. maackii*)	Sweet breath of spring (*L. fragrantissima*)	Morrow's honeysuckle (*L. morrowii*)	Tatarian honeysuckle (*L. tatarica*)
Leaves				
Leaf shape	Ovate	**Round** to ovate, **about as wide as long**	Ovate	Ovate
Leaf tip	**Long, tapered**	Acute	Acute or obtuse	Acute or obtuse
Blade length	3.5–8.5 cm	To 8 cm	To 8 cm	**2–5 cm**
Leaf hairs	Sparse	Variable	Underside hairy	Variable
Flowers				
Peduncle length	**1–3 mm, <½ length of adjacent petioles**	To 15 mm long; longer than the adjacent petioles	To 13 mm long; longer than the adjacent petioles	**15–25 mm long;** longer than the adjacent petioles
Petals: color	White to yellow	White to pink fading to yellow	Pink to white fading to yellow	Pink or white, **never yellow**
Petals: presence or absence of hairs	Hairy or glabrous	**Outside: glabrous, inside: hairy**	**Hairy**	**Glabrous**
Fruit	Round, red	Round to oblong, red	Round, orange to red	Round, red

Notes: Boldface indicates most important distinguishing characteristics.

Table 12. Comparison of weedy privets (*Ligustrum* spp.)

Species	Height (m)	Leaf length (cm)	Drupe size (mm)	Leaf shape	Hairs on young twigs	Petiole length (mm)	Inflorescence position and length (cm)	Corolla tube length
Evergreen species								
Japanese privet (*L. japonicum*)	<3	5–8	6–8	Elliptic, ovate, obovate	No	5–12	Terminal, 6–15	≥ length of flower lobes
Glossy privet (*L. lucidum*)	<10	6–10	8–10	Ovate	No	10–20	Terminal, 7–16	≤ length of flower lobes
Deciduous or semi-evergreen species								
Amur privet (*L. amurense*)	<5	5–7	5	Elliptic, ovate, oblong	Yes, hairs of uneven lengths	1–2	Terminal and axillary, 4	1.5–2X longer than flower lobes
Border privet (*L. obtusifolium*)	<4	2.5–5	5	Elliptic, oblong, obovate	Yes, hairs of uneven lengths	1–2	Terminal and axillary, 2–2.5	2–3X longer than flower lobes
California privet (*L. ovalifolium*)	<4	4–10	6–8	Elliptic, oval	None, stem glabrous and shiny	3–10	Terminal, 4–7	2–3X longer than flower lobes
Chinese privet (*L. sinense*)	<4	2–7	5–7	Elliptic, oblong	Straight or upcurved hairs	2–8	Numerous terminal and axillary, 4–11	≤ length of flower lobes
European privet (*L. vulgare*)	<5	2–6	4–6	Oval, lanceolate	Glabrous to minute upcurved hairs of even lengths	1–2	Terminal, 3–6	≤ length of flower lobes

GLOSSARY

Definitions are modified from Hitchcock 1950, Jones and Luchsinger 1986, Walters and Keil 1988, and Gleason and Cronquist 1991.

Abscission   The process by which fruit, flowers, or leaves are separated from a plant by the normal development of a thin layer of pithy cells produced at the base of the part to be separated.

Achene   A single-seeded, dry fruit that does not open at maturity (e.g., a sunflower seed).

Acuminate   With a long, tapering point and concave sides.

Adventitious root   A root that originates from stem or leaf tissue rather than from another root.

Alternate   Arranged singly along an axis; 1 leaf per node (Fig. 7). *Contrast* Opposite; Whorled.

Androecium   All of the stamens of the flower collectively (Fig. 2). *Contrast* Gynoecium.

Annual   A plant that completes its life cycle within one year. *See* Summer annual; Winter annual.

Anther   The pollen-bearing portion of the stamen.

Apex   The tip of a leaf blade (Fig. 6), a root, or a stem.

Apomixis   The production of seeds without fertilization.

Appressed   Closely and flatly pressed against.

Auricle   In grasses, a small, projecting lobe or appendage found where the blade meets the sheath (Fig. 1), or at the base of the blade in broadleaf plants.

Awn   A slender bristle of a grass floret.

Axil   The position between the stem and a leaf or other lateral organ.

Basal rosette   A circular cluster of leaves radiating from the stem of a plant at ground level (e.g., the leaf arrangement in dandelion). Basal rosettes result from a series of very short internodes; the leaves are not considered to be whorled. *Contrast* Whorled (Fig. 7).

Biennial   An herbaceous plant that requires 2 years to complete its life cycle. During the first season, the seed germinates and only vegetative growth follows; in the next season, after winter vernalization, flowering, seed set, and death occur (Fig. 12).

Bipinnate   Having 2 rows of lateral branches, appendages, or other parts along an axis, which are themselves again divided into 2 rows along an axis (Fig. 8).

Blade   The part of a leaf above the sheath in grasses, and above the petiole in broadleaf plants (Figs. 1, 6).

Boat-shaped   *See* Prow-shaped.

Bolt   To produce erect, elongate stems from a basal rosette; often associated with winter annual or biennial species that have rapidly elongating, erect, flowering stems.

Bract   A specialized leaf that is usually greatly reduced in size and is associated with flowers (Fig. 4).

Broadleaf plants   Dicots; characterized by having relatively wide leaves of various shapes. Distinguished from grasses, which are monocots and have narrow leaves with parallel veins.

Bud   An undeveloped leafy shoot or flower.

Bulb   A short, thickened, vertical underground shoot composed of modified scale-like leaves in which food is stored.

Bur   A fruiting structure covered with spines or prickles.

Calyx   The sepals of a flower collectively (Fig. 2).

Carpel   The organ that bears the juvenile seed (Fig. 2). *See also* Pistil.

Caudex   A perennial stem, below the ground or at ground level, often resembling a taproot.

Chaff   Small, thin, dry scales on the receptacles of many of the Asteraceae (Fig. 3).

Ciliate   Having a fringe of hairs.

Cleft   Cut halfway to the midrib or base.

Cleistogamous flower   A self-pollinating flower that produces seeds without opening; grows mostly on or under the ground.

Clump-forming (tufted)   Describes a grass that grows in a compact cluster attached at the base.

Collar   The outer side of a grass leaf at the juncture of the blade and sheath (Fig. 1).

Composite   A member of the Asteraceae.

Composite head   The dense inflorescence of the Asteraceae, usually composed of florets, a receptacle, and bracts (Fig. 3).

Compound leaf   A leaf with 2 or more leaflets.

Compressed   Flattened laterally, as are the sheaths and spikelets of some grasses.

Cordate   Heart-shaped (Fig. 10).

Corm   A thickened, short, vertical, underground, perennial stem in which food is stored.

Corolla   The petals of a flower collectively (Fig. 2).

Corymb   A flat-topped or convex flower cluster in which the outer flowers open first (Fig. 4). *Contrast* Cyme.

Cotyledon   A seed leaf (Fig. 5).

Crenate   Having a margin with rounded teeth (Fig. 9).

Crown   The part of a perennial plant, at or just below the ground, where the stem and root join and from which new shoots are produced.

Cyathium   The inflorescence of spurges (*Euphorbia* spp.); consists of cup-like bracts that contain a central female (pistillate) flower and several male (staminate) flowers.

Cyme   A flat-topped or convex flower cluster in which the central flowers open first (Fig. 4). *Contrast* Corymb.

Decumbent   Lying on the ground but with the tips ascending.

Decurrent   With an attached wing or margin extending down the axis (e.g., the margin of a leaf extending down a stem).

Dehiscent   Describes fruit that open at maturity. *Contrast* Indehiscent.

Dentate   With spreading, pointed teeth (Fig. 9).

Denticulate   With very small, spreading, pointed teeth (Fig. 9).

Dicot   *See* Dicotyledon.

Dicotyledon   A plant in the class of angiosperms (Magnoliopsida) that is characterized by embryos (seedlings) with 2 cotyledons, netted leaf veins, flower parts in multiples of 4 or 5, and cambium; broadleaf plants. *Contrast* Monocotyledon.

Dioecious   Producing male and female flowers on different plants. *Contrast* Monoecious.

Disciform head   A composite head composed of filiform florets (pistillated florets with very slender, tubular corollas) and disk florets.

Discoid head   A composite head composed of disk florets only.

Disk flower   A tubular, radially symmetric flower (i.e., floret) of the Asteraceae with male and female organs (Fig. 3). *Contrast* Ligulate flower; Ray flower.

Dissected   Divided into many slender segments (Fig. 10).

Divided   Cut into distinct parts. A divided leaf is cut to the midrib or the base.

Drupe   A fleshy fruit containing one seed enclosed in a hardened ovarian wall.

Elliptic   Widest in the middle, narrowing equally toward both ends (Fig. 10).

Emarginate   With a small notch at the apex.

Entire   With a continuous, untoothed margin (Fig. 9).

Fibrous root   A thin root arising from another root or from stem tissue.

Filament   The stalk of a stamen (Fig. 2).

First leaf   In a seedling, the next leaf that grows after the cotyledons.

Floret   An individual flower of a defined flower cluster, as an individual flower of a grass spikelet or of a composite head.

Folded   Describes grass blades or grass leafbuds that are folded together lengthwise so that the upper surface is inside the fold (Fig. 1). *Contrast* Rolled.

Gemmae   In liverworts, small bud-like outgrowths that become detached and can grow into new plants.

Glabrous   Without hairs. *Contrast* Pubescent.

Glaucous   Covered with a removable, powder-like, waxy coating, as is commonly seen on the fruit of grape and plum.

Glume   One of usually a pair of bracts at the base of a grass spikelet.

Grasses   Monocots; members of the Poaceae. *Contrast* Broadleaf plants.

Gynoecium   The female organs of a flower collectively (Fig. 2). *Contrast* Androecium.

Hastate   Shaped like an arrowhead but with the basal lobes more divergent (Fig. 11).

Hypocotyl   The part of the stem below the cotyledons of a seedling (Fig. 5).

Indehiscent   Describes fruit that remain closed at maturity. *Contrast* Dehiscent.

Inflorescence   A flower cluster.

Internode   The part of a stem between 2 successive nodes.

Involucre   One or more whorls of bracts beneath a flower or inflorescence, often forming a cup-like structure (Fig. 3).

Keel   The sharp fold at the back of a compressed sheath or blade. Figs. 5 and 6 illustrate leaves of broadleaf plants.

Lacerate   Appearing to have been torn or irregularly cut.

Lanceolate   Much longer than wide; widest below the middle and tapering to both ends or rounded at the base (Fig. 10).

Landscape   A section of land whose natural features have been altered with the intention of making it more attractive, usually by the addition of a lawn, trees, and shrubs.

Lateral   On or at the sides.

Leaf   In grasses, the lateral organ of a stem, consisting of a sheath and blade. Figs. 5 and 6 illustrate leaves of broadleaf plants.

Leafbud   A bud on a plant from which a leaf develops. *See* Rolled and folded grass leafbuds (Fig. 1).

Leaflet   One subunit of a compound leaf (Fig. 8).

Legume   A several-seeded, usually dry fruit produced by members of the Fabaceae (bean family) or a closely related family; composed of a single carpel that opens down both sutures at maturity. Also, a plant in the Fabaceae or a closely related family.

Lemma   In grasses, the lower of the 2 bracts enclosing the floret.

Ligulate flower   A flower (i.e., floret) of the Asteraceae with stamens and a pistil that has a strap-shaped, 5-lobed corolla. Ligulate florets occur only in ligulate heads, never with other kinds of florets. *Contrast* Disk flower; Ray flower.

Ligulate head   A composite head composed of ligulate florets only.

Ligule   In grasses, the thin membranous appendage or a ring of hairs on the inside of a leaf at the junction of the sheath and blade (Fig. 1).

Linear   Very long and narrow, with essentially parallel sides (Fig. 10).

Lobe   A projecting segment of a leaf that is larger than a tooth but with the adjoining sinus extending less than halfway to the midrib (Fig. 9).

Lyrate   Pinnatifid, with the terminal lobe the largest and usually more rounded than the smaller lateral lobes (Fig. 10).

Membranous   Thin, transparent, and flexible, membrane-like (Fig. 1).

Mericarp   An individual section of a schizocarp.

Midrib   The central vein of a leaf (Figs. 1, 6).

Midvein   *See* Midrib.

Monocarpic   Living a few years, blooming once, then dying.

Monocot   *See* Monocotyledon.

Monocotyledon A plant in the class of angiosperms (Liliopsida) characterized by embryos (seedlings) with 1 cotyledon, parallel-veined leaves, flower parts in multiples of 3, and no secondary growth; grasses and grass-like plants such as sedges, rushes, and lilies. *Contrast* Dicotyledon.

Monoecious Producing male and female organs in different flowers (imperfect flowers) on the same plant. *Contrast* Dioecious.

Mucronate Describes a leaf or leaflet that terminates in a short, abrupt spur or spiny tip.

Node A place on a stem where a leaf is or has been attached (Fig. 1).

Nutlet A small nut. Also, a 1-seeded segment of the ovary found in members of the mint family.

Ob- In a reverse direction.

Oblanceolate Much longer than wide, like lanceolate, but widest above the middle and tapering to the base.

Oblong Longer than wide, with parallel sides; more or less rectangular (Fig. 10).

Obovate Egg-shaped and widest at the apex (Fig. 10).

Ocrea A papery sheath that encloses the stem at the nodes; made from the fusion of 2 stipules; found in members of the Polygonaceae.

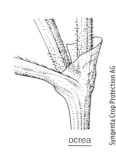

ocrea

Syngenta Crop Protection AG

Opposite Arranged in pairs along an axis; 2 leaves per node (Fig. 7). *Contrast* Alternate; Whorled.

Ovary The expanded basal part of a pistil, containing the ovules.

Ovate Egg-shaped and widest near the base (Fig. 10).

Palea In grasses, the upper of the 2 bracts enclosing the flower.

Palmate With 3 or more lobes, nerves, leaflets, or branches arising from a common point (Fig. 8).

Panicle An inflorescence with a main axis and many subdivided branches; may be compact and spike-like (Fig. 4).

Pappus A modified calyx consisting of dry scales, bristles, or awns that often facilitate wind dispersal of seeds (e.g., the feathery portion of a dandelion "seed"); common in the Asteraceae and other families.

Parted Deeply cut, usually more than halfway to the midvein or base.

Pedicel The stalk of a single flower of a flower cluster (Fig. 4).

Peduncle The stalk of a flower cluster or of a solitary flower (Fig. 4).

Peltate Leaf with the petiole attached near the center of the leaf blade.

Perennial Plants that generally live for more than 2 years (Fig. 12).

Perianth All of the sepals and petals collectively (Fig. 2).

Petal One of the inner floral leaves that make up the corolla; typically white or brightly colored (Fig. 2).

Petiolated With a petiole.

Petiole The stalk between the leaf blade and the stem (Fig. 6).

Petiolule A stalk, similar to a petiole, attaching a leaflet to the rachis of a compound leaf.

Phenology Study of the timing of biological changes with the progression of the season; such as seedling emergence or bloom time.

Phyllary One of the involucre bracts at the base of the head in the Asteraceae (Fig. 3).

Pinnate With 2 rows of lateral branches, appendages, or parts along an axis (Fig. 8).

Pinnatifid More or less deeply cut with 2 rows of lateral appendages (Fig. 10).

Pistil The female organ of a flower, composed of stigma, style, and ovary; the pistil consists of 1 or more carpels (Fig. 2).

Prickle A sharp outgrowth of the outermost layer of cells (epidermis) or bark.

Protonema A thread-like growth, arising from germinating spores, that develops into small moss plants.

Prow-shaped Shaped like the bow of a boat; common shape of *Poa* spp. leaf tips.

Pubescent With hairs. *Contrast* Glabrous.

Raceme An elongated inflorescence in which the stalked flowers arise from an unbranched central axis (Fig. 4).

Rachis The main axis of a compound leaf. Also, an axis bearing flowers.

Radiate head A composite head composed of disk and ray florets.

Ray flower A flower (i.e., floret) of the Asteraceae that has a pistil or is neutral and has a 3-lobed strap-shaped lip (Fig. 3). *Contrast* Disk flower; Ligulate flower.

Receptacle Basal part of the flower, representing the end of the stem (pedicel or peduncle) to which the flower parts are attached (Fig. 2). Often greatly enlarged, as in the Asteraceae (Fig. 3).

Recurved Bent or curved downward or backward.

Reflexed Abruptly bent or curved downward or backward.

Reniform Kidney-shaped (Fig. 10).

Rhizoids Root-like filaments of liverworts and mosses.

Rhizome A creeping underground stem (Fig. 1).

Rhombic Diamond-shaped (Fig. 10).

Rolled Describes a grass leafbud that is positioned as if turned on its axis over and over (Fig. 1).

Root crown *See* Crown.

Rosette *See* Basal rosette.

Runcinate Sharply cleft or pinnatifid, with backward-pointing segments.

Runner *See* Stolon.

Sagittate Arrowhead-shaped, with the basal lobes more or less in line with the body (Fig. 11).

Samara A winged fruit such as that of maple and ash.

Scape A leafless peduncle arising from ground level.

Schizocarp A fruit that splits into separate carpels (mericarps) at maturity.

Seedhead An inflorescence bearing mature fruit (Fig. 1).

Sepal One of the outer floral leaves that make up the calyx; typically green (Fig. 2).

22 silicula

Syngenta Crop Protection AG

Serrate Toothed along the margin with sharp, forward-pointing teeth (Fig. 9).

Sessile Lacking a petiole.

Sheath In grasses, the lower part of a leaf that encloses the stem and younger leaves (Fig. 1).

Silicle A fruit of the Brassicaceae that is similar to a silique but not much (if at all) longer than wide.

Silicula *See* Silicle.

Siliqua *See* Silique.

Silique A fruit of the Brassicaceae that is an elongated capsule in which the 2 valves split open when mature.

Simple leaf A leaf blade that lacks leaflets; may be deeply lobed or divided.

Sinuate With a strongly wavy margin (Fig. 9).

Spatulate Shaped like a spatula; rounded above and narrowed to the base (Fig. 10).

siliqua

Syngenta Crop Protection AG

Spike An unbranched inflorescence in which the spikelets or flowers are sessile on the main axis (Fig. 4).

Spikelet In grasses, an inflorescence consisting of 1 to many florets and minute specialized leaves (Fig. 1).

Spike-like panicle A panicle with compact branches hidden by the spikelets of grasses or the flowers of broadleaf plants.

Spine Sharp-pointed projection originating from the axil. Modified leaf, scale, or stipule.

Stamen The male, or pollen-producing, part of a flower (Fig. 2).

Stigma The part of the pistil that receives the pollen (Fig. 2).

Stipule   One of a pair of basal appendages of a leaf (Fig. 6).

Stolon   A horizontal stem at or just above the surface of the ground that gives rise to a new plant at its tip or from axillary branches (Fig. 1).

Style   The slender stalk that typically connects the stigma(s) to the ovary.

Subulate   Awl-shaped (Fig. 10).

Sucker   A shoot on a plant that arises from below ground level; more precisely, a shoot arising from an adventitious bud on a root. Also, to bear suckers or shoots.

Summer annual   A plant that germinates in the spring or summer, flowers, sets seed, and dies during a single growing season (Fig. 12).

Taproot   An enlarged vertical main root.

Tepal   An undifferentiated sepal or petal.

Thorn   Sharp-pointed structure on the stem. Modified branch.

Tiller   A shoot growing from the base of the stem of a grass plant (Fig. 1).

Tip-layering   A means of plant propagation in which rooting and new shoot growth occurs at stem tips that are in contact with the ground.

Trifoliate   Refers to a plant with 3 leaves; term often misused to describe a plant with trifoliolate leaves.

Trifoliolate   Refers to a compound leaf consisting of 3 leaflets (e.g., poison-ivy and most clovers) (Fig. 8).

Truncate   Appearing as if cut off transversely straight at the end.

Umbel   A cluster of flowers in which the stalks (pedicels) arise from a common point; may be simple or compound (Fig. 4).

Undulate   With a wavy margin.

Urticle   A thin-walled, 1-seeded, more or less inflated fruit.

Vein   One of the bundles of vascular tissue forming the framework of a leaf blade, particularly those that are externally visible (Fig. 6).

Whorled   Arranged in 3 or more along an axis; 3 or more leaves per node (Fig. 7). *Contrast* Alternate; Basal rosette; Opposite.

Winter annual   A plant that germinates in late summer to early spring, flowers, and produces seeds in mid to late spring, after which it dies (Fig. 12). Many winter annual weeds thrive under cool, moist conditions.

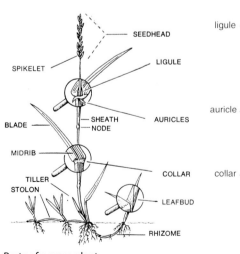

1. Parts of a grass plant
(The Scotts Company)

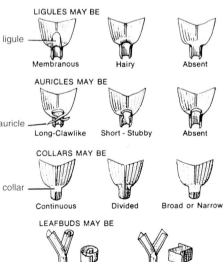

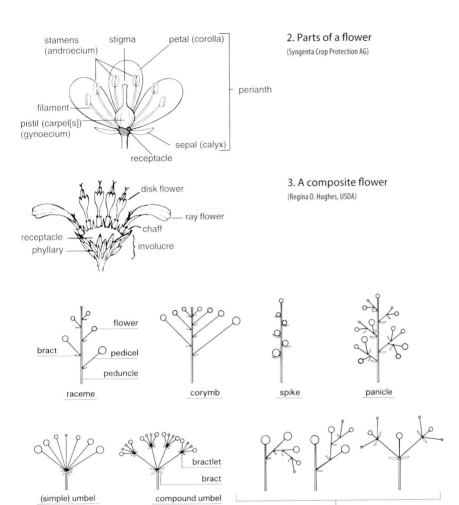

2. Parts of a flower
(Syngenta Crop Protection AG)

stamens (androecium)
stigma
petal (corolla)
perianth
filament
pistil (carpel[s]) (gynoecium)
sepal (calyx)
receptacle

3. A composite flower
(Regina O. Hughes, USDA)

disk flower
ray flower
chaff
receptacle
phyllary
involucre

flower
bract
pedicel
peduncle
raceme
corymb
spike
panicle

(simple) umbel
bractlet
bract
compound umbel
19 cyme

4. Inflorescence types
(Syngenta Crop Protection AG)

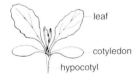

5. A dicot seedling
(Syngenta Crop Protection AG)

leaf
cotyledon
hypocotyl

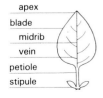

6. A dicot leaf
(Syngenta Crop Protection AG)

apex
blade
midrib
vein
petiole
stipule

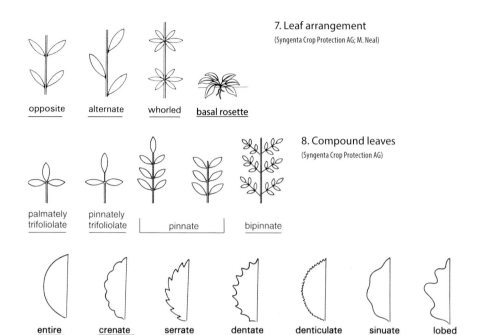

7. Leaf arrangement
(Syngenta Crop Protection AG; M. Neal)

opposite   alternate   whorled   basal rosette

8. Compound leaves
(Syngenta Crop Protection AG)

palmately trifoliolate   pinnately trifoliolate   pinnate   bipinnate

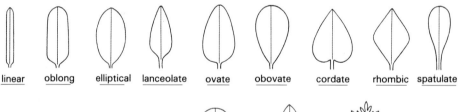

entire   crenate   serrate   dentate   denticulate   sinuate   lobed

9. Leaf margins
(Syngenta Crop Protection AG)

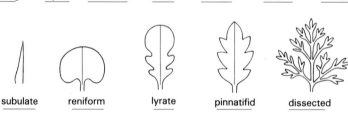

linear   oblong   elliptical   lanceolate   ovate   obovate   cordate   rhombic   spatulate

subulate   reniform   lyrate   pinnatifid   dissected

10. Leaf shapes
(Syngenta Crop Protection AG)

11. Specialized leaf bases
(Syngenta Crop Protection AG)

sagittate   hastate

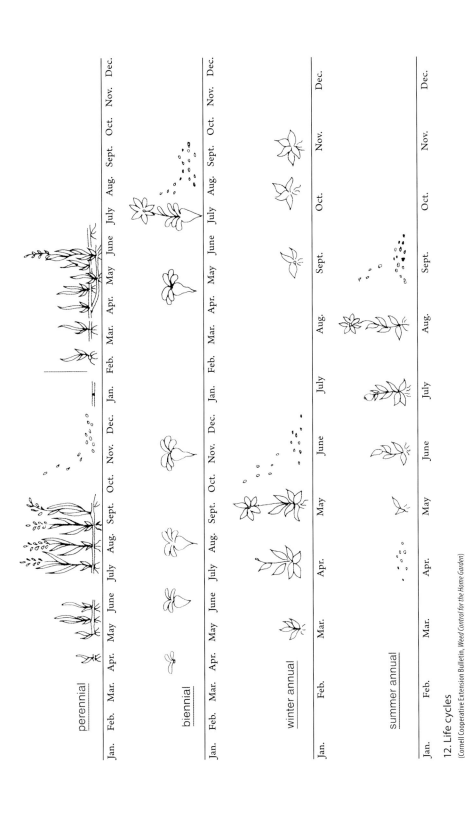

perennial

Jan.	Feb.	Mar.	Apr.	May	June	July	Aug.	Sept.	Oct.	Nov.	Dec.

biennial

Jan.	Feb.	Mar.	Apr.	May	June	July	Aug.	Sept.	Oct.	Nov.	Dec.

winter annual

Jan.	Feb.	Mar.	Apr.	May	June	July	Aug.	Sept.	Oct.	Nov.	Dec.

summer annual

Jan.	Feb.	Mar.	Apr.	May	June	July	Aug.	Sept.	Oct.	Nov.	Dec.

12. Life cycles
(Cornell Cooperative Extension Bulletin, *Weed Control for the Home Garden*)

BIBLIOGRAPHY

Alex, J.F. 1992. Ontario weeds. Ontario Ministry of Agriculture and Food, Toronto.

Axtell, A.E., A. DiTommaso, and A.R. Post. 2010. Lesser celandine (*Ranunculus ficaria*): a threat to woodland habitats in the northern United States and southern Canada. Invasive Plant Sci. Manage. 3: 190–196.

Barkley, T.M. 1983. Field guide to the common weeds of Kansas. Contribution 82-547-B. Kansas Agricultural Experiment Station and Division of Biology, Kansas State University, Manhattan.

Bassett, I.J., and C.W. Crompton. 1978. The biology of Canadian weeds. 32. *Chenopodium album* L. Can. J. Plant Sci. 58: 1061–1072.

Bassett, I.J., and D.B. Munro. 1985. The biology of Canadian weeds. 67. *Solanum ptycanthum* Dun., *S. nigrum* L. and *S. sarrachoides* Sendt. Can. J. Plant Sci. 65: 401–414.

Bassett, I.J., and D.B. Munro. 1986. The biology of Canadian weeds. 78. *Solanum carolinense* L. and *S. rostratum* Dunal. Can. J. Plant Sci. 66: 977–991.

Bayón, N.D. 2015. Revisión Taxonómica de las Especies Monoicas de *Amaranthus* (Amaranthaceae): *Amaranthus* subg. *Amaranthus* y *Amaranthus* subg. *Albersia*. Annals of the Missouri Botanical Garden 101(2): 261–383. https://doi.org/10.3417/2010080.

Bellinder, R.R., R.A. Kline, and D.T. Warholic. 1989. Weed control for the home vegetable garden. Information Bulletin 216. Cornell Cooperative Extension, Ithaca, New York.

Bhowmik, P.C., and J.D. Bandeen. 1976. The biology of Canadian weeds. 19. *Asclepias syriaca* L. Can. J. Plant Sci. 56: 579–589.

Britton, N.L., and H.A. Brown. 1913. An illustrated flora of the northern United States and Canada. Dover, New York.

Brown, L. 1976. Weeds in winter. Norton, New York.

Brown, M.L., and R.G. Brown. 1984. Herbaceous plants of Maryland. Department of Botany, University of Maryland, College Park.

Bryson, C.T., and M.S. DeFelice (eds.). 2009. Weeds of the South. University of Georgia Press, Athens.

Chancellor, R.J. 1966. The identification of weed seedlings of farm and garden. Blackwell Scientific, Oxford.

Cody, W.J., and V. Wagner. 1980. The biology of Canadian weeds. 49. *Equisetum arvense* L. Can. J. Plant Sci. 61: 123–133.

Consortium of Northeastern Herbaria (CNH). http://portal.neherbaria.org/portal/.

Cooperative Extension University of California. 1991. Growers weed identification handbook. Publication 4030. Division of Agriculture and Natural Resources, Davis, California.

Crockett, L.J. 1977. Wildly successful plants. Collier Books, New York.

Dirr, M. 1990. Manual of woody landscape plants: their identification, ornamental characteristics, culture, propagation and uses. Stipes Pub., Champaign, Illinois.

DiTomaso, J.M., and E.A. Healy. 2003. Aquatic and riparian weeds of the West. University of California Agriculture and Natural Resources, Publ. #3421. 442 pp.

DiTomaso, J.M., and E.A. Healy. 2007. Weeds of California and other western states. University of California Agriculture and Natural Resources, Publ. #3488. 1808 pp.

DiTommaso, A., F.M. Lawlor, and S.J. Darbyshire. 2005. The biology of invasive alien plants in Canada. 2. *Cynanchum rossicum* (Kleopow) Borhidi (= *Vincetoxicum rossicum* (Kleopow) Barbar.) and *Cynanchum louiseae* (L.) Kartesz & Gandhi (= *Vincetoxicum nigrum* (L.) Moench). Can. J. Plant Sci. 85: 243–263.

DiTommaso, A., D.R. Clements, S.J. Darbyshire, and J.T. Dauer. 2009. The biology of Canadian weeds. 143. *Apocynum cannabinum*. Can. J. Plant Sci. 89: 977–992.

DiTommaso, A., S.J. Darbyshire, C.A. Marschner, and K.M. Averill. 2014. North-east, north-central, mid-Atlantic United States and southern Canada: Japanese hedgeparsley (*Torilis japonica*)—a new invasive species in the United States? Invasive Plant Sci. Manage. 7: 553–560.

Douglas, B.J., T.A. Gordon, I.N. Morrison, and M.G. Maw. 1985. The biology of Canadian weeds. 70. *Setaria viridis* (L.) Beauv. Can. J. Plant Sci. 65: 669–690.

Doust, L.L., A. MacKinnon, and J.L. Doust. 1985. The biology of Canadian weeds. 71. *Oxalis stricta* L., *O. corniculata* L., *O. dillenii* Jacq. ssp. *dillenii* and *O. dillenii* Jacq. ssp. *filipes* (Small) Eiten. Can. J. Plant Sci. 65: 691–705.

Duncan, W.H., and M.B. Duncan. 1987. The Smithsonian guide to seaside plants of the Gulf and Atlantic Coasts from Louisiana to Massachusetts, exclusive of lower peninsular Florida. Smithsonian Institution Press, Washington, D.C.

Fernald, M.L. 1950. Gray's manual of botany. 8th ed. American Book Co., New York.

Fire Effects Information System (FEIS). USDA and US Forest Service [last modified 2019 Aug 1]. https://www.feis-crs.org/feis/.

Flora of North America (online). http://beta.floranorthamerica.org/Main_Page.

Fogg, J.M., Jr. 1956. Weeds of lawn and garden, a handbook for eastern temperate North America. University of Pennsylvania Press, Philadelphia.

Frankton, C., and G.A. Mulligan. 1970. Weeds of Canada. Publication 948. Canada Department of Agriculture, Ottawa.

Gleason, H.A. 1963. The new Britton and Brown illustrated flora of the northeastern United States and adjacent Canada. The New York Botanical Garden, Bronx, New York.

Gleason, H.A., and A. Cronquist. 1991. Manual of vascular plants of northeastern United States and adjacent Canada. 2nd ed. The New York Botanical Garden, Bronx, New York.

Häfliger, E., and H. Scholz. 1980. Grass weeds 1. Ciba-Geigy, Basel, Switzerland.

Häfliger, E., and H. Scholz. 1981. Grass weeds 2. Ciba-Geigy, Basel, Switzerland.

Häfliger, E., U. Kühn, et al. 1982. Monocot weeds 3. Ciba-Geigy, Basel, Switzerland.

Hanf, M. 1983. The arable weeds of Europe. BASF Aktiengesellschaft, Ludwigshafen.

Hitchcock, A.S. 1950. Manual of the grasses of the United States. 2nd ed. Misc. Publ. No. 200. United States Department of Agriculture, Washington, D.C.

Hulten, E. 1962. The circumpolar plants I: vascular cryptogams, conifers, monocotyledons. Almqvist & Wiksell, Stockholm.

Hume, L., J. Martinez, and K. Best. 1983. The biology of Canadian weeds. 60. *Polygonum convolvulus* L. Can. J. Plant Sci. 63: 959–971.

Invasipedia, hosted by BugwoodWiki. Developed by the Center for Invasive Species and Ecosystem Health, University of Georgia. https://wiki.bugwood.org/Invasipedia.

Jones, S.B., and A.E. Luchsinger. 1986. Plant systematics. McGraw-Hill, New York.

Kummer, A.P. 1951. Weed seedlings. University of Chicago Press, Chicago.

Liberty Hyde Bailey Hortorium. 1976. Hortus third: A concise dictionary of plants cultivated in the United States and Canada. 3rd ed. Macmillan, New York.

Lorenzi, H. 1987. Weeds of the United States and their control. Van Nostrand Reinhold, New York.

Manitoba Agriculture. 1986. Weed seedling identification guide. Manitoba Agriculture and the crop protection section of Saskatchewan Agriculture, Agdex 640.

Maun, M.A., and S.C.H. Barrett. 1986. The biology of Canadian weeds. 77. *Echinochloa crus-galli* (L.) Beauv. Can. J. Plant Sci. 66: 739–759.

Miyanishi, K., and P.B. Cavers. 1980. The biology of Canadian weeds. 40. *Portulaca oleracea* L. Can. J. Plant Sci. 60: 953–963.

Muenscher, W.C. 1987. Weeds, with a new foreword and new appendixes by Peter A. Hyypio. Cornell University Press, Ithaca, New York.

Mulligan, G.A., and B.E. Junkins. 1976. The biology of Canadian weeds. 17. *Cyperus esculentus* L. Can. J. Plant Sci. 56: 339–350.

Murphy, T.R. (ed.). Weeds of southern turfgrass. University of Georgia Cooperative Extension Service, Athens.

Nesom, G.L. 2009. Taxonomic overview of *Ligustrum* (Oleaceae) naturalized in the United States. Phytologia 91: 467–482.

Niering, W.A., and N.C. Olmstead. 1979. The Audubon Society field guide to North American wildflowers. Alfred A. Knopf, New York.

North Central Regional Technical Committee NC-121. 1981. Weeds of the north central states. North Central Regional Res. Publ. No. 281. University of Illinois at Urbana-Champaign, College of Agriculture, Agricultural Experiment Station.

O.M. Scott & Sons. 1985. Scott's guide to the identification of dicot turf weeds. O.M. Scott & Sons, Marysville, Ohio.

O.M. Scott & Sons. 1985. Scott's guide to the identification of grasses. O.M. Scott & Sons, Marysville, Ohio.

Page, N.M., and R.E. Weaver Jr. 1975. Wild plants in the city. New York Times Book Co., New York.

Peterson, L.A. 1977. A field guide to edible wild plants of eastern and central North America. Houghton Mifflin, Boston.

Petrides, G.A. 1977. A field guide to trees and shrubs. Houghton Mifflin, Boston.

Pohl, R.W. 1978. How to know the grasses. 3rd ed. Wm. C. Brown, Dubuque, Iowa.

Puntener, W. (ed.). 1988. Dicot weeds 1. Ciba-Geigy, Basel, Switzerland.

Rice, R.P., Jr. 1992. Nursery and landscape weed control manual. Thomson, Fresno, California.

Schuster, R.M. 1949. The ecology and distribution of Hepaticae in central and western New York. Am. Midl. Naturalist 42(3): 513–710.

Stucky, J.M., T.J. Monaco, and A.D. Worsham. 1981. Identifying seedling and mature weeds common in the southeastern United States. AG-208, Bulletin No. 461. North Carolina Agricultural Research Service and North Carolina Agricultural Extension Service, Raleigh.

Thompson, J.D., and R. Turkington. 1988. The biology of Canadian weeds. 82. *Holcus lanatus* L. Can. J. Plant Sci. 68: 131–147.

Tiner, R.W., Jr. 1988. Field guide to nontidal wetland identification. Maryland Department of Natural Resources, Annapolis.

Tucker, G. 1989. The genera of Commelinaceae in the southeastern United States. Faculty Research and Creative Activity 182. Eastern Illinois University Institutional Repository. http://thekeep.eiu.edu/bio_fac/182.

Turkington R., and J.J. Burdon. 1983. The biology of Canadian weeds. 54. *Trifolium repens* L. Can. J. Plant Sci. 63: 243–266.

Turkington, R., and P.B. Cavers. 1979. The biology of Canadian weeds. 33. *Medicago lupulina* L. Can. J. Plant Sci. 59: 99–110.

Turkington, R., N.C. Kenkel, and G.D. Franko. 1980. The biology of Canadian weeds. 42. *Stellaria media* (L.) Vill. Can J. Plant Sci. 60: 981–992.

United States Department of Agriculture. 1971. Common weeds of the United States. Dover, New York.

Upadhyaya, M.K., R. Turkington, and D. McIlvride. 1986. The biology of Canadian weeds. 75. *Bromus tectorum* L. Can. J. Plant Sci. 66: 689–709.

USDA Natural Resources Conservation Service. 2019. The PLANTS Database. National Plant Data Team, Greensboro, North Carolina. http://plants.usda.gov.

Walters, D.R., and D.J. Keil. 1988. Vascular plant taxonomy. Kendall/Hunt, Dubuque, Iowa.

Warwick, S.I. 1979. The biology of Canadian weeds. 37. *Poa annua* L. Can. J. Plant Sci. 59: 1053–1066.

Warwick, S.I., and L.D. Black. 1983. The biology of Canadian weeds. 61. *Sorghum halepense* (L.) Pers. Can. J. Plant Sci. 63: 997–1014.

Warwick, S.I., and A. Francis. 2006. The biology of invasive alien plants in Canada. 6. *Berteroa incana* (L.) DC. Can. J. Plant. Sci. 86: 1297–1309.

Weakley, A.S. 2015. Flora of the southern and mid-Atlantic states. University of North Carolina at Chapel Hill Herbarium. http://www.herbarium.unc.edu/flora.htm.

Weaver, S.E., and W.R. Riley. 1982. The biology of Canadian weeds. 53. *Convolvulus arvensis*. Can. J. Plant Sci. 62: 461–472.

Weed Science Society of America (WSSA). 2020. Composite list of weeds. http://wssa.net/wssa/weed/composite-list-of-weeds/.

Werner, P.A., and S.D. Judith. 1976. The biology of Canadian weeds. 18. *Potentilla recta* L., *P. norvegica* L. and *P. argentea* L. Can. J. Plant Sci. 56: 591–603.

Werner, P.A., I.K. Bradbury, and R.S. Gross. 1980. The biology of Canadian weeds. 45. *Solidago canadensis* L. Can. J. Plant Sci. 60: 1393–1409.

Whitson, T.D. (ed.). 1991. Weeds of the West. Western Society of Weed Science, in cooperation with the Western U.S. Land Grant Universities Cooperative Extension Service and the University of Wyoming, Laramie.

INDEX

Page numbers in **boldface** indicate the location of the main text descriptions. Page numbers not in boldface are for synonyms or listings of similar species.

ABOUT THE AUTHORS

Joseph C. Neal is professor of weed science at North Carolina State University, Raleigh, and formerly on the faculty of Cornell University. His research and extension programs have focused on weed management in urban landscapes, nursery crops, and turfgrass systems as well as the biological control of weeds. He was the president and is currently a fellow of the Northeastern Weed Science Society. Richard H. Uva is a horticulturist and farmer, and with his family operates Seaberry Farm, LLC, in Federalsburg, Maryland. He earned his master's degree and PhD in horticulture from Cornell University. Much of the information in the first edition, and the way it was presented, was derived from his master's thesis. Joseph M. DiTomaso was a professor of weed science at Cornell University for eight years and

Joseph C. Neal

Richard H. Uva

Joseph M. DiTomaso

Antonio DiTommaso

a professor and extension specialist at the University of California, Davis, for twenty-two years. His research and extension programs focused on weed identification and understanding the ecology and management of invasive plants. He was the president and is currently a fellow of the Weed Science Society of America and the Western Society of Weed Science. Antonio DiTommaso is a professor and weed scientist at Cornell University. His research focuses on the ecology and biology of agronomic weeds and invasive plants of natural areas in the Northeast. He was the president and is currently a fellow of the Northeastern Weed Science Society.